THE
ARMY OF THE CUMBERLAND

THE
ARMY OF THE CUMBERLAND

BY

THOMAS B. VAN HORNE, U.S.A.

SMITHMARK

This edition published in 1996 by SMITHMARK Publishers,
a division of U.S. Media Holdings, Inc., 16 East 32nd Street,
New York, N.Y. 10016.

SMITHMARK books are available for bulk purchase for
sale promotion and premium use. For details write or call the
manager of special sales, SMITHMARK Publishers,
16 East 32nd Street, New York, N.Y. 10016; (212) 532-6600.

ISBN: 0-8317-5621-7

Printed in the United States of America

10 9 8 7 6 5 4 3 2 1

CONTENTS

CONTENTS

CONTENTS

CONTENTS

CONTENTS

HISTORY

OF THE

ARMY OF THE CUMBERLAND.

CHAPTER I.

DEVELOPMENT OF THE STATUS OF KENTUCKY.

At the inception of our gigantic civil war, the leading types of political sentiment prevalent throughout the entire country were represented by large classes in Kentucky. Bold unionists confronted arrant secessionists; timid loyalists and wavering rebels joined hands in an impracticable conservatism. As an expression of the reigning chaos of opinion, and by the consent of multitudes in direct antagonism, Kentucky assumed the position of neutrality. All her citizens not radically and unconditionally for the Union, protested against the march of armies for the suppression of the rebellion upon the soil of the State. It was the great blunder of Southern Union men, that they so early and so fully committed themselves against the coercion of the seceded states, or the maintenance of the Union by force, that when war was actual, they were driven into rebellion in no small degree by their previous false position. The loyal men of Kentucky barely escaped the common fate of the Union men in other Southern States. Several prominent men in Kentucky had, from the time of the election of Mr. Lincoln, been so bold in opposition to the secession of the state, and so open in their declaration of purpose to sustain the general government, that coercive measures were hailed with delight. But very many of those claiming to be Union men, while ostensibly opposing the secession of Kentucky, were reticent with regard to their action in the event of war. They were not in open sympathy with the secession movement, but clamorous in their demand for armed neutrality as the legitimate and only safe position for Kentucky. So prevalent was this opinion, and so bold its expression, that "armed neutrality" was the accredited status of the state before her legislature gave it the more formal pretense of legitimacy.

Governor B. Magoffin, in his message to the legislature convened in extra session January 17, 1861, recommended that the state militia should be put upon a war footing, in readiness for the forcible assumption of such position as the State might choose. He also recommended that a convention should be called, and plainly indicated his desire for the secession of the state.

The legislatures of the more Southern States were mainly composed of men elected upon other issues, but generally pledged to secession. Hence their readiness to call conventions, and even assume the prerogatives of conventions. But fortunately for Kentucky, the Union men in her legislature were too prudent and too patriotic to unite with the secessionists in calling a convention; and thus they prevented the usual initial step in secession. Neither did the legislature meet the governor's expectation in providing for the equipment of the state militia.

The history of Kentucky, during the period beginning with the presidential election and ending with the fall of Sumter, furnishes no facts of great moment beyond the steady resistance of the masses of her people and the majority of her legislature to every movement inclining to secession. There were, however, marked indications of divided sentiment and purpose. One instance may serve as the type of many. It was determined by the loyal citizens of Louisville that the national flag should be raised with suitable pomp upon the court-house on the 22d day of February. Hon. James Speed delivered a patriotic address on the occasion. The address elicited no disloyal demonstration; but when the flag was raised, Simon B.

Buckner, in chief command of the state guard as inspector-general of the state, gave no order to salute, as required by the published programme and patriotic duty. In manifest disloyalty to the flag, Buckner, and a large portion of his command, moved from the court-house yard. Major Woodruff and his battalion, the "Marion Rifles," in emphatic contrast remained and saluted the national colors. The two officers, and those acting with them, represented not only the antagonistic sentiment of the state guard, but also of the citizens of the entire state.

But though political affairs in Kentucky were chaotic during the early months of 1861, the issues of the grand contest, whose sweep and power were soon to solve with inexorable definiteness all the problems engrossing the thought and sentiment of the whole country, were gradually assuming positive shape. Fort Sumter fell on the 14th day of April. On the day following, the President issued the proclamation calling for seventy-five thousand men, and assigning the quotas of all the states. In response, Governor Magoffin addressed the following message to the Secretary of War:

"FRANKFORT, *April* 15, 1861.

"HON. SIMON CAMERON, *Secretary of War:*

"Your dispatch has been received. In answer, I say emphatically that Kentucky will furnish no troops for the wicked purpose of subduing her sister Southern States.

"B. MAGOFFIN,
"*Governor of Kentucky.*"

This bold presumptuous answer, though not prophetic, gave hope to the South that Kentucky would secede. Radical secessionists, as a class, were noisy, madly assertive, and in the realm of hypothesis, amazingly unprophetic; and Governor Magoffin, interpreting public sentiment by his own feelings, and mistaking secession clamor for the revealed purpose of Kentucky, defiantly ignored the constitutional subordination of the state to the general government. As yet Kentucky had taken no steps indicating secession as a probable contingency; neither had she made unequivocal assertion of loyalty; and as in the past, so now in the crisis of the border slaveholding states, the official declaration of her governor was only the expression of individual opinion.

Kentucky, as a state, was not yet ready to furnish troops for the United States service, but there were citizens in great numbers ready to commit themselves to the unconditional support of the general government. And while at this period, as previously, the flag of revolt had been boldly unfurled throughout the state, and men had been openly recruited for the rebel army, there were many eager to take position under the flag of their country.

On the 6th day of May, the legislature of Kentucky convened in extra session, for the third time since the election of Mr. Lincoln. The message of Governor Magoffin evinced the expectation that the state would immediately secede. The legislature affirmed "armed neutrality" as the status of the state, and then by implication censured the governor for the language of his official announcement. Still, the fact was patent that Kentucky, as represented by her legislature, though advancing in loyal expression, was yet far from active loyalty. Neutrality, in such a contest, was itself, proof of a lack of fealty. During this extra session, another advance was made in the right direction. The militia law of the state was so amended as to compel the state guard to take the oath of allegiance, not only to Kentucky, but also to the United States. This act recognized the obligation of the state to the general government, but it did not reach active support.

While the politicians in the seceded states took the lead in all treasonable movements, and were far in advance of the people in intensity of disloyalty, those in Kentucky who were loyal, were in the main far behind the masses in loyal feeling, and were far more timid in open resistance to the formidable organized effort to precipitate the state into alliance with those in rebellion. As soon as the grand issue was fairly made by the bombardment of Fort Sumter, undercurrents against the rebellion, compassing, for the most part, quiet citizens, set in with great power. During the extra legislative session of May, and while the old political leaders, though claiming to be loyal, were timid to the degree of moral cowardice, a few citizens of Louisville, unknown to the political arena, gave existence to an organization that doubtless determined the status of Kentucky. This organization was called the " Union Club."

Previous to the 17th of May, the Union men of Kentucky had no such organization as could determine their numerical strength and consolidate their power. The " Citizens and Working Men's Association " had triumphed in the election of J. M. Delph, as mayor of Louisville. This association claimed to be, par excellence, the Union party of Louisville. It demanded fidelity to the Union at the expense of former party affiliations, and on this simple issue, unaided by a single journal of the city, carried the municipal election. The administration of the city government, conducted under circumstances which demanded great prudence and firmness, demonstrated the wisdom of those whose votes placed Mr. Delph in office. This organization, however, had not sufficient compactness for a revolutionary period. The rebels in Kentucky and throughout the entire South were most thoroughly organized, in anticipation of the necessity of overriding majorities. The notorious Bickley, at the head of the " Knights of the Golden Circle," was at this period drilling squads in the streets of Louisville. Outspoken loyalists were threatened with assassination. Under the pressure of such circumstances, G. A. Hall, C. C. Hull, R. E. Hull, J. P. Hull, R. L. Post, C. Z. Webster, H. G. S. Whipple, Thos. A. Morgan, W. B. Hegan, F. H. Hegan, Robert Ayars, and a few others, on the 17th day of May, 1861, organized this " Union Club." The members were solemnly sworn to unconditional loyalty. The ritual was mainly compiled from the grand declarations of Washington, Webster, and Clay. It especially enforced the patriotic affirmation of the latter : " If Kentucky to-morrow unfurls the banner of resistance, I never will fight under that banner. I owe a paramount allegiance to the whole Union ; a subordinate one to my own state." With such declarations, as expressive of its purpose and patriotism, this organization was meet for the times. Secret associations are the concomitants of modern revolutions, powerful for good or evil, in accordance with the principles they embody and the ends they subserve. This one was potent, if not decisive, in saving Kentucky from secession. It soon diffused itself throughout the state, reaching the legislature with its influence, and on the 1st of July, the day for a special congressional election, it gave a hundred thousand loyal votes. During the months of July and August the development and expression of loyalty was so marked, that the secessionists despaired of the withdrawal of the state, except through an appeal to arms. The election held early in August demonstrated that a large majority of the people of Kentucky were opposed to secession. This fact did not deter John C. Breckinridge and his compeers in treason from efforts to force the state from the Union. Not being ready for the execution of the war measures which they were planning, they called themselves the Peace party. Though they held the doctrine of state-rights, they declined acquiescence in the declared purpose of the state to remain in the Union, and while clamoring for peace, they secretly arranged with the so-called Confederate government to supply them with arms, and extend its military jurisdiction over the state. There was no thought of submission to the overwhelming public sentiment which had been repeatedly expressed through the previous elections. These traitors assumed that the National government was broken up; that the Confederate government had attained lawful existence, and that Kentucky, whether the majority of her people were willing or unwilling, belonged to the Confederate government.

CHAPTER II.

INTERNAL MILITARY AFFAIRS OF KENTUCKY.

THE history of military affairs in Kentucky during the year 1861 can not be complete, even in outline, without adequate mention of the " State Guard" and " Home Guard."

The prominent disunionists in Kentucky doubtless knew, long before it occurred, that the presidential election of 1860 would either give national sway to their radical views of state sovereignty, or furnish the pretext for the dissolution of the Union. Men of the state-rights school in the Gulf States could not entertain strong assurance of their independence without the co-operation of the border slave-holding states. Their alliance in the event of war, and their support in the event of peaceable secession, were regarded as conditions of success. And as the latter states would be the first to suffer the consequences of secession, if secession should result in war, it was a matter of great moment to the secessionists in Kentucky, as well as those farther south, that there should be a military force on the border, ready for war. For this purpose, doubtless, the organization of the militia of Kentucky was effected. This object was so disguised that men the farthest removed from disloyalty co-operated in the passage of a law authorizing an army in Kentucky of compactness and numbers equal to some of the standing armies of Europe.

The act of the legislature which gave existence to the " State Guard," became a law by approval of the governor, March 5, 1860. It was drafted mainly by S. B. Buckner, and gave great power to those who had chief command of the troops organized in conformity to its elaborate provisions. The citizens capable of bearing arms were divided into three classes, designated "The Militia of Reserve," "The Enrolled Militia," and "The Active, or Volunteer Militia."

The militia of reserve consisted of white persons, resident in the state, less than eighteen years of age, and more than forty-five, and of all persons exempt by law from enrollment and military service, and not members of the "Active Militia." In extreme danger the reserve militia could be called to active service.

The enrolled militia consisted of all able-bodied white male persons between the ages of eighteen and forty-five, who were citizens or residents of the state, except persons who had served five years in the army or navy of the United States, persons who were members of the active volunteer militia, and those exempted from military service by the laws of the United States or the State of Kentucky.

The volunteer militia, or state guard, were organized into companies, battalions, brigades, divisions, and army corps, with uniforms and equipments complete. Most of the independent military companies of the state became component parts of the state guard upon its organization. Provision was made for the election of one colonel, one lieutenant-colonel, and as many majors as necessary in each county. General officers were to be multiplied in proportion to the extent of the organization. The inspector-general of the state, under the governor, was commander-in-chief of the volunteer militia, with the rank of major-general, wearing, when on duty, the uniform of a lieutenant-general. This officer had power to disband at will such companies, or larger organizations, as failed to conform to the law or his view of military propriety. Thus, through the rigid subordination of officers, from the highest to the lowest, there was a concentration of power in the commander-in-chief unusual in a free state during actual war.

At first, beyond the election and appointment of officers of high rank, political influence did not palpably rule in the organization of the state guard. S. B. Buckner was appointed inspector-general, and Thomas L. Crittenden elected brigadier-general. In the end, many of the officers joined the Confederate army, while many became commanders in the United States service. The prominent Union men of Kentucky give concurrent testimony to the fact that it was the original design of the authors of the "Act for the better organization of the Kentucky militia," to use the forces authorized by its provisions to precipitate the state from the Union. It is certain that the encampments, discipline, and general conduct of the state guard were adapted to prepare a force for revolutionary surprise. The history of the commander-in-chief warrants the belief that it was his intention, when the foreshadows of war were plainly visible, to use his command to force Kentucky out of the Union, if possible, and in the event of failure in this, to transfer it to the rebel army. When the issue came, the scheme failed in its main purpose, and almost entirely in its contingent one. A prominent cause of failure was the inability of Governor Magoffin and his inspector-general to provide arms for such a military establishment as their purposes demanded. The legislature refused adequate appropriations, and such arms as they desired could not be purchased. Hence, the "armed neutrality" of Kentucky consisted more in assumption than in actual military strength. Strenuous efforts, however, to secure arms were made. Governor Magoffin, soon after the fall of Sumter, accredited Buckner to the North and Dr. Blackburn to the South for their purchase.

Colonel Prentiss, at Cairo, engaged the attention of Buckner in a direction opposite to that of his mission, but Dr. Blackburn brought arms from the extreme South, so nearly worthless as, in his own language, to be "suitable for neutrals." If, however, Dr. Blackburn did not purchase good guns for his rebel friends in Kentucky, he revealed their intentions in a speech in New Orleans. Having been called to the rostrum upon the arrival of a military company from Kentucky, the doctor boldly pledged his state to the rebellion.

For some time after war was threatened, it was deemed desirable that the loyal men in the state guard should remain, but when the time came for loyal organization it was at first found to be difficult for them to withdraw. Later, the requirement by the legislature of a new oath afforded easy means of withdrawal, as discretion was allowed. Thereafter, the state guard was known to be acting in the interests of the rebellion.

Another military organization, though of less imposing

form, exerted more power in the struggle in Kentucky than the state guard. This was the home guard. Improvised, loosely organized military companies called " Home Guards," sprang into existence in the city of Louisville and other places, when first the cloud of war began to gather blackness. Their avowed object was home defense. Those comprising them represented the parties contending for supremacy in the state, with a predominance of the loyal element.

The "Home Guard" proper was originally organized by authority of an ordinance enacted by the general council of the city of Louisville, and was subsequently extended to other portions of the state. The ordinance approved by Mayor Delph, May 25th, was nominally based upon a vague provision of the city charter. The imminence of revolution, rather than the charter, induced the city authorities to provide for the formation of the "Home Guard." The ordinance made provision for a brigade of two regiments, with the necessary field and staff officers. The members were required to take the oath prescribed for other city officers, and were further required to swear that they would obey all orders of officers legally placed over them. The mayor was the commander-in-chief, with power to appoint a brigadier-general and other officers. Lovell H. Rousseau was first appointed as brigadier-general. He soon became an officer in the United States service, and James Speed succeeded him in command. The home guard was soon filled to its maximum strength. The Marion Rifles, already favorably mentioned as a portion of the state guard, found congenial associations in this loyal organization. The opposition to it by the state guard and secessionists generally was open, persistent, and menacing. Buckner, the commander of the state guard, formally called on General Speed and threatened bloodshed. But Speed and his brigade were too much in earnest, too patriotic and brave, to give heed to private or official threats. Arms were obtained from the general government through Lieutenant W. Nelson, of the navy, and ammunition from Governor Morton, of Indiana.

During the winter and spring, Lieutenant Nelson, a native of Kentucky, had repeatedly visited the state. His purpose was to ascertain the undercurrents of sentiment and the probable action of prominent men should the government be forced, in the prosecution of the war, to disregard, directly or indirectly, the neutrality of Kentucky. He reached the conclusion, in mingling with all classes, that the Union sentiment needed the support of bayonets. He learned that such support of the Southern cause was meditated, and believing that prompt action would prevent the secession of Kentucky, he told President Lincoln that he must furnish the loyal men with arms, or, in the end, fight for the restoration of the state to the Union. The President acted upon this suggestion, and made Lieutenant Nelson the agent for the transmission of arms to Kentucky. Ten thousand guns were placed at his disposal, and money furnished to pay for their transportation. Lieutenant Nelson went to Kentucky in advance of his guns, and arranged with Joshua F. Speed, of Louisville, for a secret meeting of prominent Union men at Frankfort. This meeting occurred in the latter part of April, and was attended by J. J. Crittenden, Garret Davis, James Harlan, Joshua F. Speed, James Speed, Charles A. Wickliffe, Thornton F. Marshall, Lieutenant Nelson, and four others. Men were designated who could be safely intrusted with the disposition of arms. Nelson's guns reached Kentucky soon after the formation of the home guard of the city of Louisville. The regiments of the city, and all companies of fifty men, in the northern, central, and eastern portions of the state, were supplied by Lieutenant Nelson, upon the order of Joshua F. Speed, who had been designated by President Lincoln for this duty.

Thus armed, the home guard confronted the state guard, and defeated the schemes of the secessionists in respect to Kentucky. Encampments of the state guard were ordered subsequently, and its companies and battalions were drilled, but all to no purpose. Armed Union men were soon in the ascendant, and "armed neutrality" waned in proportion to the number of guns in their hands. Collisions were threatened, but fortunately for the secessionists, they never occurred, as the parades of the two organizations revealed the superiority of the home guard. The magazine containing the ammunition belonging to the state, was under the control of

Buckner, but Mayor Delph boldly demanded the keys, and overawed by the strength of the mayor's command, Buckner reluctantly surrendered them.   Subsequently, the state guard was despoiled of their arms by the mayor's order, and as fugitives they drifted to the Southern army.

CHAPTER III.

DURING the excitement which immediately succeeded the inauguration of war at Charleston, it was unsafe in Louisville and other parts of the state to utter Union sentiments; much greater danger was incident to an avowal of purpose to enlist troops for the United States service. Still there were men bold enough to do this, despite threats of assassination. Immediately after the President's call for troops, James V. Guthrie, a resident of Covington, Ky., and W. E Woodruff, major commanding the battalion of Marion Rifles of Louisville, offered their services to the President, and asked authority to raise two regiments, as a part of the quota of their state. The authority was given on the 23d of April. Their camp was established on the north bank of the Ohio river, just above Cincinnati, and was designated " Camp Clay." On the 6th day of May, two full regiments of three months' men were mustered into the service of the United States, as the 1st and 2d regiments of Kentucky Volunteer, Infantry—the former under the command of Colonel Guthrie, the latter under Colonel Woodruff. Though thus styled, the majority of the enlisted men were from Ohio.

Colonels Guthrie and Woodruff at once concluded that men enlisted for the short period of three months would be of little value in a war that already promised protraction, and sought and obtained permission to reorganize their regiments for three years' service, or during the war. The length of the proposed term deterred many from re-enlisting. Very many of those who refused to re-enlist were from Ohio, and in the reorganization of the regiments, recruits were drawn from

Kentucky. Colonel Woodruff and his officers, in full uniform, openly recruited in Louisville and other parts of Kentucky, and soon refilled their regiment. Their action induced denunciation and threats. Recruiting for the Southern army in the state had been open and demonstrative. It had not been unusual to see the Confederate flag flying above men on the march for the South, as the enemies of their country, but to enlist for loyal service was regarded as an invasion of rights.

Colonel Woodruff's regiment was remustered into the service of the United States on the 9th of June, Colonel Guthrie's on the day following, each with designation unchanged. As Kentucky had not recognized these regiments, they were armed and equipped by the authorities of Ohio.

On the 9th of July, the First and Second Kentucky Infantry, as a portion of the brigade of Brigadier-General J. D. Cox, embarked on steamers for Western Virginia. Colonel Guthrie went up the Kanawha, and Colonel Woodruff passed up the Ohio to Guyandotte. The river was at a low stage, and it was frequently necessary for the regiment to disembark, that the steamer might pass the bars. Whenever practicable, the landing was made on the Ohio side, but in one instance it was impossible to avoid the Kentucky shore. As a consequence, the neutrality of the state was first formally violated, by her own sons marching under the national flag on her soil. After efficient service in Western Virginia, these regiments were transferred, in January, 1862, to the Army of the Ohio.

Early in June, Lovell H. Rousseau repaired to Washington, to impress the national authorities with the necessity of enlisting troops for the United States army, and to request authority to raise one or more regiments in Kentucky. Rousseau, as senator in the legislature of Kentucky, had been very bold in opposing the plans of his disloyal compeers, and had been remarkably earnest in urging the committal of the state to the support of the general government. He, with General J. T. Boyle and a few others, had opposed the neutrality policy from its first mention. It was fitting then, that he should be amongst the first to propose the organization of troops in Kentucky.

Rousseau was appointed colonel, and invested with authority to raise two regiments; but the location of his camp was to be determined by a few of the most prominent Union men of Kentucky.

Upon Rousseau's return from Washington, General James Speed, in compliance with instructions from President Lincoln, called a meeting at Louisville, to determine the location of Rousseau's camp. Hon. James Guthrie was chairman of the meeting. There were present, in addition, Garret Davis, C. D. Pennabaker, Samuel Gill, James Speed, J. F. Speed, Samuel Lusk, J. T. Boyle, Morgan Vance, T. E. Bramlette, E. Graves, A. B. Hobson, J. H. Ward, James Harlan, Colonels Hawkins, Dudley, and Rousseau. Of these, James Speed, Vance, Ward, and Rousseau were in favor of establishing the camp in Kentucky. The majority, fearing that this step would affect unfavorably the congressional election, appointed for the first of July, urged its location in Indiana. Accordingly, "Camp Joe Holt" was established on the north bank of the Ohio river, between Jeffersonville and New Albany. Influenced by the same consideration, Lieutenant Nelson had previously commenced the enrollment of troops in central Kentucky without an encampment, and his action was regarded as a judicious precedent, in view of the paramount importance of electing Union men to Congress.

His camp having been established, Colonel Rousseau, with the aid of his officers and a few friends of earnest loyalty, but in the face of menacing persistent opposition, soon recruited the "Kentucky Legion" (afterward the Fifth Kentucky Infantry), "Stone's Battery," and several companies of infantry and calvary, which subsequently became the initial elements of the "Sixth Kentucky Infantry" and the Second Kentucky Cavalry.

"Camp Dick Robinson," situated between Danville and Lexington, Ky., was established by Lieutenant Nelson, on the 2d day of July, 1861. The officers of four regiments had previously been appointed, and nearly two thousand men had been very quietly recruited. These went immediately into camp to the amazement of rebels, "constitutional union men," and "neutrals." The rebels threatened in vain; timid Union men expostulated with Nelson and his prominent associate officers, on the ground that the camp was irritating the people, and sent a delegation to Washington to request President Lincoln to remove the camp from the state. Governor Magoffin officially demanded its removal in order to prevent civil war. The President refused compliance on the ground that the troops were Kentuckians, and were not menacing their fellow-citizens. The camp was therefore maintained and fortified. The first four regiments organized at this camp were the Third, Fourth, and Seventh regiments of infantry, and the First Kentucky Cavalry, commanded respectively by Colonels T. E. Bramlette, Speed S. Fry, T. T. Garrard, and Frank Wolford.

CHAPTER IV.

COMMAND OF GENERAL ANDERSON.

THE foregoing topical presentation of affairs, civil and military, in Kentucky, has been made, that explanatory digressions might be avoided, and that the narrative might proceed with events, as far as practicable, in their exact chronological order and logical connection.

On the 28th day of May, 1861, that portion of Kentucky, extending one hundred miles south of the Ohio river, was constituted a military department, designated as the "Department of Kentucky," with Brigadier-General Robert Anderson as commander. As the national authorities, at this period, were dealing very gently with Kentucky, General Anderson's headquarters were established at Cincinnati, Ohio. During the months of June, July, and August, his command of this department was only a nominal one. He did not directly interfere with the movements of loyal men or secessionists. Colonel Prentiss, of another command, as early as the 5th of June, had broken up a Confederate camp five miles inland from Cairo. But otherwise, Kentucky, though claiming neutrality, but unofficially furnishing troops for loyal and disloyal service, was allowed the untrammeled management of her own affairs. Rousseau and Nelson were enrolling troops for the United States army, not strictly according to prescribed forms, but as best they could, improvising what was not supplied by government, and forcing success in the midst of formidable difficulties.

During this period of Kentucky's neutrality, collisions and bloodshed were anticipated by all parties. A conflict was especially imminent at Louisville on the 22d of July, the day following the defeat of General McDowell at Bull Run, as then the secessionists of the city, under the leadership of the notorious Tompkins, local chief of the "Knights of the Golden Circle," plainly indicated their purpose to control the city or hazard a conflict. As, however, in olden time it often occurred that great armies accepted the issues of dualistic contests between leaders or champions, so in Louisville, the killing of Tompkins by G. A. Green, a loyal policeman, seemingly at least, arrested the preparations for a general struggle. The excitement consequent upon this event revealed such a host of loyal men in the city, that secessionists were intimidated in the midst of their exultation over their victory in Virginia.

The month of August was the crisis. The plans of the secessionists were fully matured at a meeting in Scott county, on the 17th of August. The governor's protest against Camp Dick Robinson was one feature of it, and its purpose doubtless was to remove all the national troops from Kentucky, that with the help of Confederate soldiers from Tennessee, the secessionists might commit the state to the rebellion. This having failed, their next efforts were to embarrass the organization of national troops, and secretly organize themselves to co-operate with external forces to compel Kentucky to take her proper place amongst her "sister Southern States."

The soldiers at Camp Dick Robinson were without arms, except ordinary rifles and shot-guns, and it was a difficult and delicate matter to secure a supply. The government, at the request of Lieutenant Nelson, now acting brigadier-general, had sent six thousand muskets, one hundred thousand rounds of ammunition, and a quantity of powder and lead had been shipped to Cincinnati. The secessionists knew of this and were determined to prevent their transmission to Camp Dick Robinson.

The munitions were first put on the cars at Covington, Kentucky, and sent toward Lexington. The train was stopped in Harrison County by a band of armed men and compelled to return to Cincinnati, and the principal stockholder of the road was notified that it would be destroyed if it was used to transport arms into Kentucky. The arms and ammunition were next shipped on a steamboat for the Kentucky river, to be delivered at Hickman's bridge near the camp. The steamer was stopped in Owen county and forced to return. They were then shipped to Louisville, and thence by a special train to Lexington. General Nelson having been advised of their shipment by telegraph, sent Colonel Thomas E. Bramlette to Lexington, with instructions to send them by railroad to Nicholasville, whence they were to be hauled to camp in wagons guarded by a squadron of Colonel Wolford's cavalry, under Lieutenant-Colonel Letcher. When near Lexington, Colonel Bramlette, having learned from Captain Dobyns and Lieutenant Wheat, that great excitement was prevailing in the town in regard to the arms, and that the secessionists were preparing to seize them, and had so alarmed the officials of the road as to prevent their farther transportation by rail, directed the captain and lieutenant to proceed to Nicholasville and order up the transportation and cavalry with all possible speed. On reaching Lexington, he found that Dr. Ethelbert Dudley, afterward colonel in the national army, who had a company of "Home Guards," had made arrangements for the prompt assembling of his men should the secessionists attempt to seize the arms. Upon the arrival of the cavalry, this class became intensely excited and rallied under the leadership of J. C. Breckinridge, who threatened to drive the "Lincoln hirelings" from the town. John H. Morgan assembled at the armory the "State Guards" under his command, to assist Breckinridge in his work of treason. Messengers were sent requesting Colonel Bramlette to withdraw his troops from the town to avoid bloodshed, promising that Breckinridge would then use his influence to have the arms pass unmolested. Colonel Bramlette replied "that he would not depart without the arms and munitions, and that if armed rebels appeared upon the street, blood would be shed, and he would not leave a living secessionist in Lexington." He then loaded the arms and munitions, and took them to Camp Dick Robinson without further molestation.

On the 15th of August, General Anderson's command was extended so as to embrace the States of Kentucky and Tennessee, under the title of the "Department of the Cumberland;" his headquarters, however, were not removed from Cincinnati until the 1st of September, when they were established in Louisville. By this time it was plainly manifest that even the nominal neutrality of Kentucky could be maintained no longer. The leading secessionists had despaired of the secession of the state through the independent action of Kentuckians, and many of them had joined the Confederate forces, encamped on the northern confines of Tennessee. As these men could no longer organize rebellion within the limits of Kentucky, they invited invasion as the only means untried to force her into alliance with the Confederacy, against the expressed decision of the majority of the people—a course which was a burlesque upon their vaunted attachment to the doctrine of state-rights.

At this time there were three Confederate generals with encampments and organized troops near the southern boundary of Kentucky. General Polk was on the Mississippi river, in the northwest corner of Tennessee; Buckner, who had recently exchanged the uniform of a lieutenant-general, which he had worn as inspector-general of the "State Guard," for that of a brigadier-general in the rebel army, was at Camp Boone, situated near the Louisville and Nashville railroad within the limits of Tennessee, and Zollicoffer was in Tennessee, south of Barboursville, Kentucky. These generals were waiting for a pretext to invade the state.

The initial invasion was made by Leonidas Polk, who, having thrown aside his insignia as a minister of the "Gospel of Peace," had grasped the sword.

This quondam bishop occupied Hickman and Chalk Bluffs, Kentucky, with his command, on the 5th of September, under the pretext of military necessity, and on the 7th took possession of Columbus. As a counter movement, on the 6th, Brigadier-General U. S. Grant landed troops at Paducah, with two gunboats in support, and was reinforced on the 7th. A few days later, Zollicoffer occupied Cumberland Gap, and threw a portion of his forces into Kentucky. Thus the armies of the United States and those of the so-called Confederate States were upon the soil of Kentucky, and she was compelled to abandon her neutrality, and choose alliance with one or the other belligerent power, or retain her position by resisting both. Fortunately, a loyal legislature was in session to take action in the crisis—a legislature whose members could not reflect the sentiments of their constituents and attempt the maintenance of neutrality, or withhold positive allegiance to the national government. On the 9th, General Polk, having first obtained an official approval of his act from the Confederate President, informed Governor Magoffin, that under a military necessity he had occupied Columbus. The governor promptly communicated the facts to the legislature, by special message, and the legislature, on the 12th, by a large majority of votes, directed the governor to issue a proclamation ordering the Confederate troops, encamped in the state, to evacuate the soil of Kentucky, and resolutions were adopted asserting the wanton violation of the peace and neutrality of Kentucky, the invasion of her soil, and the infringement of the rights of her citizens by the so-called Confederate forces; empowering the governor to call out the military forces of the state to expel the invaders; invoking the United States to give such assistance to Kentucky as was warranted by the fourth article of the national constitution, and requesting Brigadier-General Robert Anderson to enter upon his duties as commander of the district embracing Kentucky. This action terminated formal neutrality, and committed the state to the positive support of the national government.

This position of Kentucky has historic interest, from the fact that the experiment had such issue that its repetition is not probable. Neutrality considered as a principle, or viewed in relation to the organic subordination of the individual state to the general government and the imperative requirements of patriotism, is wholly without justification. As an expedient even, its assumption by loyal men can not be justified or palliated by the fact that advantages may have resulted from it. That Kentucky's neutrality was not wholly evil is very apparent, and to this day many of the leading loyal men of the state, some of whom opposed the position from first to last, believe that the cause of the "Union" gained more than that of the "Rebellion" by the equivocal status of Kentucky for the first six months of the war. As, however, the results of the early positive loyalty of the Union men of Kentucky can now be only conjectural, the consequences of their neutrality, in comparison, can not be determined. It is not, however, improbable that had the loyal people precipitated action, the proximate results would have been disastrous, as under the pressure of passion and prejudice, secession might have resulted, since the secessionists were organized, and loyal citizens were not. At the beginning of the war, it was evident that a large portion of the people of Kentucky were in hearty sympathy with the rebellion, and the strength of this party was seemingly much greater than it really was, in consequence of their surpassing noisiness. Another large class was entirely undecided. Delay of state action gave time for reflection, for the organization of loyal men, and the development of the true issues of the war, and threw open to the vision of the far-sighted the terrible consequences of secession. The statesmen of Kentucky must have foreseen that neutrality could not be maintained through a protracted war, involving the decided action of all the other states, but in view of the apparent strength of the disloyal and the uncertainty with regard to a loyal majority, it may have been expedient for them to delay final action as long as possible. Neutrality practically was only procrastination in the choice of Northern or Southern alliance. The intelligent of the whole country knew that the bombardment of Fort Sumter rendered futile all further efforts for the conciliation of the two great sections. The purpose of the Northern States was not dubiously revealed, that the "National Flag" which was lowered at Charleston should float there again, no matter how long or how bloody might be the intervening war. And the Southern people knew full well that their independence could only be gained by the sword.

The fame of Kentucky has suffered through her neutrality, but still her fifty-six thousand loyal soldiers, displaying gallantry and patriotism in the great Western battles, give warrant to the historian to say, with emphasis, that though the state was tardy in the expression of loyalty, she made a good record, especially for a slaveholding state, in a war which overthrew the institution which commanded her inveterate attachment. Great honor should be awarded the multitudes in Kentucky, who, though they hesitated at the threshhold of unconditional loyalty, yet at last, true to the traditional patriotism of the state, and despite their community of material interests, and their social and political harmonies with the revolted states, did reach that high type of loyalty, which has its revelation on fields of blood. Some hesitation was natural, if not commendable, at a time when the final action of the state in the event of a general war was problematical to her wisest statesmen. But most emphatic praise is due to those who, in face of what seemed to be the dominant sentiment of the people of the state in April, boldly drew their swords for the maintenance of the Union. And, in striking contrast, the severest condemnation should rest upon those who were alike disloyal to the nation and their own state—supporting the rebellion against the general government and fighting against Kentucky.

August 15th, Brigadier-General George H. Thomas relieved Lieut. William Nelson as commander of Camp Dick Robinson; the latter was soon after raised to the rank of brigadier-general, and assigned to duty at Maysville, Kentucky, to organize a force to operate in the eastern portion of the state. The going of the former to the camp was known to the secessionists, and combinations were formed to prevent it; but from some cause he was not molested in the passage. He found four partly organized Kentucky regiments, in almost total destitution of quartermaster and commissary stores. Directing personally the minutest details, he hurried the completion of what Nelson had begun—the organization and equipment of the primal Kentucky brigades. Beyond his camp he was connected with matters which imposed additional responsibility and labor. The general direction of the "Home Guard" in central Kentucky devolved upon him; his proximity to the capital connected him with the interests there focalized, and what was of greater moment, the enemy was in his front. Zollicoffer's strength and attitude were regarded as extremely threatening. His movement had been made to subserve several purposes: to prevent the escape to the national lines of loyal East Tennesseeans; to oppose an advance to that region to succor Union men, and cut or hold the Tennessee and Virginia railroad; and with the ulterior intention of co-operating with Polk and Buckner in the permanent occupancy of Kentucky. The members of the legislature, and loyal citizens in central Kentucky, fearing invasion and revolutionary surprise, General Thomas was requested by the formal action of the former, to send troops to Lexington for the protection of Union men.

General Thomas soon mustered into the service four Kentucky and two Tennessee regiments, and organized the First Kentucky brigade, the first formed in the state, which was consequently the first brigade of the Army of the Cumberland, and its nucleus. This army had other lines of origin. But as among the initial sources of rivers, one spring, from the force and direction of its living current, has precedence, so has this brigade in the organization of this army. The Third and Fourth Kentucky Infantry and the First Kentucky Cavalry were the first formed in the state, and the two former were at first designated as the First and Second Kentucky Infantry; but when the state became officially loyal, her legislature recognized the two regiments that Colonels Guthrie and Woodruff had organized in Ohio, then Bramlette's and Fry's regiments became the Third and Fourth. Besides, this brigade has claims as the leading source, because the troops composing it were the first to perform duty in Kentucky as soldiers of the United States. Thus from the time of the organization of this brigade, the number of troops embraced, their movements in the state under the national colors before any others, and its subsequent designation as the first brigade, first division of the army, its claims, as *the nucleus*, are unquestionable.

A second invasion was conducted by S. B. Buckner, on the 17th of September. As the commander of the state guard, this Kentuckian and ex-officer of the United States had served the Southern cause to the extent of his power. Just before he entered the Confederate army he visited Washington, and had the freedom of the city and its defenses by virtue of his declared purpose to be a non-combatant during the war. But three weeks from the day he left Washington, having in the meantime gone to Richmond and accepted a commission as brigadier-general from the Confederate President, he moved from his camp in Tennessee to capture Louisville. Rumors of his advance had been current in Louisville for a day or two. Even reliable information had reached General Anderson that he meditated this movement. Dr. J. M. Bailey, late consul to Glasgow, and surgeon of the Twenty-sixth Kentucky during the war, residing at the time in the vicinity of Camp Boone, learned on the 15th that an effort would be immediately made for the capture of Louisville, and the day following communicated the fact to General Anderson. Buckner planned a surprise. He doubtless knew that General Anderson had no organized army, and but few troops of any type. Anticipating assistance in Louisville, he was sanguine of an easy capture. He seized the morning train in passage to the North, cut the telegraph wire, and started toward Louisville. The earliest indications of his coming were the delay of the train due early in the evening, and the interruption of telegraphic communication. These occurrences, however, were not rightly interpreted at first. A train was sent to relieve the one expected, on the supposition that an ordinary accident had detained it. As this train did not return, a locomotive was sent. The locomotive was seized as the train had been; but from the engine a fireman had escaped, who hurried to Louisville on a hand-car and made known what had occurred. Invasions by railroad had not this early in the war been reduced to a science, and Buckner having failed to anticipate the difficulties of such an advance, where all were not friends, was suddenly arrested in his rolling march. The displacement of a rail between Bowling Green and Elizabethtown, by Crutcher, a loyal young man, caused the locomotive to leave the track, and produced a delay fatal to his success.

As soon as General Anderson received positive information of the advance of Buckner, he sent Brigadier-General W. T. Sherman, second to himself in command, to Camp Joe Holt to order Colonel Rousseau to report with all his available troops, as quickly as possible, at the Nashville depot in Louisville. In the meantime, in obedience to the order of Mayor Delph, the home guard, under command of Major A. Y. Johnston, chief engineer of the fire department of the city, in great numbers assembled at the depot. Before midnight their train was ready to move. As it started, the van of Rousseau's command entered the depot. Rousseau soon followed, and overtook the advance train at Shepherdsville at dawn next morning.

General Anderson threw forward at once about three thousand men, nearly all his available force. There were twelve hundred in Rousseau's command, the remainder were of the home guard. He placed General Sherman in command, deeming it his duty to remain in the city that he might hurry forward the troops expected from the adjoining Northern States. General Sherman moved very cautiously during the darkness. He had with him in the front car Mr. Fink, superintendent of the railroad, and Major Johnston, that he might be advised concerning the country, and be ready to make his dispositions with respect to the train and troops in the event of an emergency.

On reaching the Rolling fork of Salt river, General Sherman ascertained that the railroad bridge had been burned by order of Buckner, to prevent the rapid advance of our troops, as he had learned on reaching Elizabethtown that they were in motion toward him. During the day the troops under Rousseau forded the stream, and advanced to guard Muldraugh's hill. The home guard went into camp at Lebanon Junction, using the tents of which the state guard had been despoiled. In the evening, Lieutenant-Colonel R. W. Johnson, of the Third Kentucky Cavalry, bringing with him some additional companies of the home guard, reached the camp and assumed general command, by order of General Anderson.

Buckner having failed in his main purpose, soon withdrew to Bowling Green and intrenched himself. General Sherman established his camp at Muldraugh's hill, and guarding the railroad in his rear, awaited the coming of reinforcements. The waiting was not protracted. The home guard had been ordered to active duty for ten days; but previous to their return to Louisville, several regiments from Ohio, Indiana, and Illinois had reached Sherman. The earlier regiments were the Sixth, Thirty-eighth, and Thirty-ninth Indiana, respectively under Colonels Crittenden, Scribner, and Harrison; the Forty-ninth Ohio, under Colonel Gibson; and the Twenty-fourth Illinois, under Colonel Hecker.

In conjunction with Buckner's movement upon Louisville, Zollicoffer advanced from Tennessee, through Cumberland Gap, to Cumberland Ford, threatening Camp Dick Robinson. Zollicoffer's vanguard reached Barboursville on the 18th, and skirmished with a small body of the home guard. General Thomas threw forward Colonel T. T. Garrard, with the Seventh Kentucky Infantry and the First Kentucky Cavalry, to Rock Castle hills, with instructions to obstruct the road and oppose the advance of the enemy. Captain Brown was advanced to London, as a party of observation, and to intercept any small body of disloyal citizens seeking to join the enemy. These dispositions and Buckner's retreat from Muldraugh's hill, caused Zollicoffer to retire.

Simultaneously with these movements, the secessionists hitherto discomfited in every effort to invite or force Kentucky from the Union, made a final effort to accomplish this end. A call was published in the various newspapers throughout the state in the interests of the rebellion, as also in posters scattered broadcast, urging the "State-Rights" and "Peace Men" to assemble at Lexington on the 20th of September, for the purpose of having a camp drill, to continue for several days, under the supervision of Major J. C. Breckinridge, Colonel Humphrey Marshall, and other distinguished men. Information received by General Thomas indicated that under cover of this call the disloyal element of the state intended to concentrate and organize at Lexington, seize upon all the arms there and in the arsenal at Frankfort, then to unite with Zollicoffer in the expectation that the combined forces could compel the evacuation of Camp Dick Robinson, and subsequently, in conjunction with Buckner, to reach Louisville and secure Kentucky to the rebellion. On the 18th, General Thomas directed Colonel Bramlette to move immediately to Lexington and occupy the "Fair Grounds," with instructions to observe the gathering very closely, and in the event of any demonstrations or movements of hostile nature, to arrest the persons making them; but should there be none, not to arrest those having assembled.

In compliance with these instructions, Colonel Bramlette marched to Nicholasville, seized a train of cars, and moved to Lexington, occupying the fair grounds at 4 P. M. on the 19th. The secessionists had been notified of his approach about midnight, and Major Breckinridge, Colonel William Preston, George C. Hodge, and others fled through the mountains toward Virginia, Colonel Marshall to his camp, and John H. Morgan and his men joined Buckner at Muldraugh's hill just before his retreat. Zollicoffer's advance prevented General Thomas from sending Wolford, with a part of his cavalry, to Lexington, to co-operate with Bramlette as he had intended, otherwise many of these men might have been captured.

The presence of rebel armies in Kentucky had no tendency to make rebels of Kentuckians. The rampant secessionists who had left the state had made their Southern friends believe that the military occupancy of Kentucky would insure her withdrawal from the Union; but the effect was antipodal to the one anticipated. As has been mentioned, the legislature, as early as September 12th, by resolution directed the governor to issue a proclamation ordering the invading forces to leave the state, and had invited General Anderson to enter immediately upon the active discharge of his duties as commander of the department.

In response to this invitation, General Anderson assumed command by proclamation issued September 21st, in which he earnestly invoked the citizens of his native state to arm themselves for self-defense and for the expulsion of the invaders. About the same time, General Thomas L. Crittenden, commander of the "State Guard," with equal earnestness urged the members of his command to repair to places designated for rendezvous, to be mustered into the service of the United States. On the 25th of September, the legislature passed a bill providing for the enlistment of forty thousand volunteers, to serve from one to three years.

This turn of affairs imposed heavy duties upon the department commander, and General Anderson's health failing, he was relieved, at his own request, October 7th. The day following, General Sherman assumed command of the department.

CHAPTER V.

OPERATIONS OF GENERAL THOMAS, IN KENTUCKY, UNDER GENERAL SHERMAN.

As yet, no effort had been made to give an army organization to the troops of the department. Those on the Louisville and Nashville railroad were without even regular brigade organization. There had been too much hurry in their movements to allow this initial step. But now, as regiments in great numbers were coming into the department, and as the establishment of numerous camps of rendezvous and instruction for volunteers promised the speedy formation of a large number of Kentucky regiments, the organization of a grand army became the paramount duty of the hour.

There were, however, unusual embarrassments attending its performance. Many of the regiments were of very recent organization, and all had been hurried to the front to repel invasion, and at the same time to link themselves together in the simple and complex relations of a great army, in the immediate presence of the enemy. With them the school of the soldier involved the experience of war, and as a consequence the facts of organization and the events of actual conflict demand concurrent narration. At first, troops were massed as emergencies required. Subsequently, these improvised commands were transformed into brigades and divisions. And as there was no general movement of the forces in Kentucky until the advance of the "Army of the Ohio," under Brigadier-General D. C. Buell, after the fall of Fort Donelson, it is obviously appropriate to group anterior events, as connected with the troops comprising each division, beginning with the first.

Very soon after the formation of the Kentucky brigade,

composed, as has been stated, of four Kentucky and two Tennessee regiments, several regiments from Ohio and Indiana were added to the command of General Thomas. Such, however, was the necessary diffusion of these troops that regular brigade organization could not at once be effected.

The first movement General Thomas meditated for his command was an advance from Camp Dick Robinson to Cumberland Ford. The threatening attitude of the enemy, and the protection of Union men on the southeastern border of Kentucky, already clamorous for help, rendered it imperative that an advance toward Tennessee should be undertaken as soon as practicable. But an immediate advance was plainly impracticable. It was known that the rebel authorities were transporting troops in large numbers from Virginia and the far South to Barboursville, Kentucky, and that the force under the Confederate general, Zollicoffer, was augmenting more rapidly than the command of General Thomas. Besides, the national troops were raw, and destitute of adequate equipments, artillery, and transportation. Under these circumstances, General Thomas used the "Home Guard" to protect roads and keep the disloyal element in awe, and holding his other troops for emergency and discipline, waited impatiently for reinforcements and munitions.

Immediately after the withdrawal of Zollicoffer, General Thomas suggested to General Anderson the importance of concentrating for an advance to Knoxville, Tennessee, to seize the East Tennessee and Virginia railroad, destroy all the bridges for some distance east and west from Knoxville, and then to turn upon Zollicoffer while in the passes of the Cumberland Mountains, and by getting between him and his supplies, effect the capture or dispersion of his army. The desirableness of this movement was enhanced by the fact that Nashville had recently been made a base of supplies for the Confederate army in Virginia. Its success would sever the most direct railroad connection between the Confederate armies east and west, and relieve from tyranny the loyal people of East Tennessee.

But barely sufficient troops for successful defense were furnished, and in a few days General Thomas was again thrown upon the defensive, by the advance of Zollicoffer to London. In this emergency, he sent forward all the Ohio troops and the Third Kentucky Infantry; ordered the obstruction of the Richmond road, on the north side of Rock Castle hills, from the river to Big Hill, and the one connecting the Richmond and Mount Vernon roads, and urged Brigadier-General O. M. Mitchell, in command at Cincinnati, Ohio, to send reinforcements and artillery. As, however, the enemy made no effort to force the passage of Rock Castle hills, and soon retired to Cumberland Ford, General Thomas was again urgent for such reinforcements as would justify him in the assumption of the offensive. He suggested, in addition, that a column of four regiments should move up the Big Sandy through the counties of Floyd, Letcher, and Harlan, in co-operation with his own advance by Barboursville to East Tennessee. In response, six regiments were sent to him, but they were destitute of such munitions as would warrant an advance to East Tennessee. A few days later he asked for four well-equipped regiments and two field batteries, believing that this addition to his force and requisite transportation would assure the capture of Knoxville. The regiments were furnished, but as in the case of others before them, in destitution of such appointments as were necessary for such a campaign as he proposed. Anxious to assume the offensive, he was nevertheless forced to await the pleasure of the enemy.

To give support to the troops at Rock Castle hills, General Thomas ordered Colonel Connell, in command of the Seventeenth Ohio Infantry, to move from Camp Dick Robinson to Big Hill, to observe the Richmond road. He subsequently directed him to advance to London, but as the force at Rock Castle hills was again threatened by Zollicoffer, Colonel Connel's destination was changed, while en route to the latter place, where he arrived on the 20th of October. General Thomas also sent from Camp Dick Robinson, Brigadier-General Albin Schoepf, who had recently reported to him for duty, with the regiments of Colonels Coburn, Wolford, and Steedman, and Standardt's battery, to Colonel Garrard's support. General Schoepf, with Coburn's and Wolford's regiments, reached Rock Castle hills during the afternoon of the 20th.

On the following morning, Steedman and Standardt arrived with their commands.

The arrival of reinforcements was opportune, as late in the forenoon of the 21st, Zollicoffer, having found his command in close proximity to the positions of Colonels Coburn and Wolford, and under concealment of a dense forest, suddenly appeared in their front. The foremost rank bore their hats on their bayonets and claimed to be friends. Soon throwing off disguise, they opened fire, which being unexpected and vigorous caused decided confusion in the ranks of the national troops. The enemy's advantage, however, was only temporary, as Colonels Coburn and Wolford soon rallied their regiments and gallantly repulsed him. Colonels Connell and Steedman, assisted by Standardt's battery, engaged the enemy with similar result. In the afternoon, Zollicoffer made another assault, pressing most heavily against the position of Colonel Garrard, but he was again repulsed at all points, and during the following night retreated toward London. The enemy fought bravely, coming within fifty yards of the works. Their loss was thirty killed and a large number wounded. General Schoepf's loss was five killed and eighteen wounded.

The issue of this engagement rendered fruitless the movement of three or four thousand rebels, a few days later, from Burksville to Albany, with their advance thrown forward to Monticello, menacing Somerset, held by the Twelfth Kentucky Infantry under Colonel W. A. Hoskins. This force was doubtless intended for co-operation with Zollicoffer in the invasion of central Kentucky, in the event of his success at Rock Castle hills. The union of this force with his command, would have given Zollicoffer an army of ten or eleven thousand men, adequate in the extravagance of Southern arrogance and expectation, for the grandest achievements.

The defeat of Zollicoffer prevented the projected conjunction of these columns, and the one at Monticello, having knowledge of this defeat, and of the reinforcements sent to Somerset by General Thomas, withdrew into Tennessee without inviting an engagement.

Immediately after the battle of Rock Castle Hills, General Thomas resumed preparation for an advance to Cumberland

Gap. He moved the command of General Schoepf, augmented by the Tennessee troops, to the junction of the Richmond and Crab Orchard roads, subsequently posting it at London, and established his headquarters and a depot of supplies at Crab Orchard. But circumstances beyond his control still prevented his long-contemplated campaign. Before leaving Washington for a command in Kentucky, assigned to him at the earnest solicitation of General Anderson, he had tried to impress General Scott with the necessity of full preparation to meet a heavy force of the enemy in the direction of East Tennessee, and upon his assumption of command at Camp Dick Robinson, he had addressed himself to the accomplishment of this object. His oft-repeated requests for troops, had only secured tardy reinforcements of raw troops, destitute of adequate equipments, artillery, and transportation. He now held the line from the Ohio to London, and from Lexington to Frankfort; Cincinnati was his base of supplies, and Camp Dick Robinson his main depot. His communication by rail terminated at Nicholasville. Foreseeing defeat, should he attempt the invasion of East Tennessee without having an army of ample strength and equipment, as he was persistently urged to do by prominent loyalists from that region, he repeated his request for such appointments for his command as the proposed campaign demanded. Hitherto, General Sherman had approved his plans and his efforts for their execution, but now, fearing that the long weak line which connected General Thomas with his base of supplies might be severed by the enemy, he forbade his farther advance.

On the 11th of November, General Sherman informed General Thomas that he had received a telegram from Brigadier-General A. McD. McCook, at Camp Nevin, that the enemy had disappeared from Green river, and that there was a rumor that Buckner was moving in force upon Louisville, between him and General Thomas. Giving partial credence to this rumor, General Sherman ordered General Thomas, if not engaged in front, to withdraw his command back of the Kentucky river, and act as circumstances should demand. General Thomas replied that he did not credit the report, but would give orders at once for the retrograde movement. He accord-

ingly ordered General Schoepf to break up his camp immediately, and join him with all his troops, at Crab Orchard or
Nicholasville. The following day, General Sherman expressed
the conviction that the rebel General Albert Sidney Johnston
who had assumed command of the insurgent army at Bowling
Green, with Hardee and Buckner as his lieutenants, was preparing " to strike a great blow in Kentucky, by moving from
Bowling Green with a force not far short of forty-five thousand
men, with a large portion of artillery," and directed General
Thomas to hold himself in readiness for a prompt withdrawal
to Danville, leaving the Tennessee troops and Colonel Garrard
near Rock Castle river, to watch the enemy in the direction
of Cumberland Gap. General Sherman was not fully assured
that Johnston meditated so bold an assumption of the offensive, but regarded such an event as very probable. On any
other supposition it seemed difficult to account for the activity
of the insurgent forces in Kentucky, or the boastful expect-
ancy of secessionists, that the day of their triumph was near.
Johnston had impressed a large number of wagons in the vicinity of Bowling Green—a fact which pointed to the probable
advance of his army. Zollicoffer had retired into East Tennessee, and had blockaded the roads in his retreat—a step which
might indicate his re-approach by Somerset from a more reliable base of supplies, or his union with Johnston on his northward march. A force of nearly three thousand men were also
reported in motion from Tompkinsville, toward Columbia,
menacing Colonels Grider and Haggard, who were recruiting
regiments at the latter place. As, however, the purpose of
the enemy was in doubt, General Sherman directed General
Thomas to remain at Crab Orchard, ready to move to Somerset
or Danville, as circumstances should require, but to make effort to intercept the force moving from Tompkinsville.

HEADQUARTERS DEPARTMENT OF THE CUMBERLAND,
LOUISVILLE, KY., *October* 25, 1861.
General Geo. H. Thomas, Camp Dick Robinson.
SIR:—Do n't push too far. Your line is already long and weak. I can
not now re-enforce you. Nelson has got into difficulty with the militia,
and I have no person to send there. An interruption of the railroads,

by an incursion from Prestonburg, would cut you off from that source of supply.   Call to your assistance the regiment from-train.   The state board is impressed with the necessity of energy in the organization of volunteers, but we are still embarrassed for want of clothing and arms. Promises are a poor substitute for them, but are all we have.   I will again urge on the department the pressing necessity for more good officers and large re-enforcements of men.

W. T. SHERMAN,
Brigadier-General Commanding.

CHAPTER VI.

OPERATIONS OF GENERAL THOMAS, IN KENTUCKY, UNDER GENERAL BUELL, INCLUDING THE BATTLE OF MILL SPRINGS.

By general orders No. 97, war department, issued November 9th, the Department of the Cumberland was discontinued, and the Department of Ohio constituted, embracing the States of Ohio, Michigan, Indiana, Kentucky (east of the Cumberland river), and Tennessee, and Brigadier-General D. C. Buell was assigned to its command.

General Buell assumed command of the new department on the 15th of November. General Sherman advised General Thomas of the fact, and directed him to await orders from the new commander.

On the 17th, General Buell ordered General Thomas, by verbal message, expressed through Captain T. S. Everts, assistant adjutant-general, to move his command to Columbia, leaving the First and Second Tennessee and Seventh Kentucky regiments, under Lieutenant Carter, U. S. N., acting brigadier-general, at London, to observe any approach of the enemy through Kentucky, from Cumberland Gap. Four days later, General Carter was ordered to break up camp at London, and join General Thomas at Lebanon. This movement was considered so urgent, that he was directed to impress wagons if he could not hire them. Still the order requiring it was revoked before the troops were put in motion, and with the exception of the sick who were sent to Crab Orchard, the command was left temporarily at London. In moving as directed, General Thomas sent General Schoepf, with the Fourteenth Ohio and Fourth Kentucky regiments, and Standardt's and Kinney's batteries, by way of Stanford and Danville, the prescribed route through Liberty being impassable, and followed with the Tenth, Seventeenth and Thirty-eighth Ohio regiments, the Thirty-third Indiana having been left at Crab Orchard, until the sick could be removed and the depot broken up. He had previously sent Colonels Bramlette's and Wolford's regiments from Somerset, to assist Colonels Grider and Haggard at Columbia, in opposing the rebel force approaching from Tompkinsville, which, without making or inviting an attack, fell back into Monroe county.

General Thomas reached Danville, November 22d. At this time, General Schoepf, with a part of his command, was encamped at Broomfield, between Danville and Lebanon. Colonel Steedman and Captain Standardt had taken the wrong road at Stanford, and were moving on Lebanon through Hustonville. On the 26th, General Thomas ordered General Schoepf to move to Lebanon, and directed Colonels Connell and Bradley to march their regiments from Danville to the same place. By his order, Colonel Barnes proceeded from Irvine, through Richmond, Lancaster, and Danville, to the same destination. This movement of troops was both costly and fruitless. The roads were exceedingly bad, the march was a hurried one, and no enemy was found at Lebanon or Columbia, and none even threatening these points, with Louisville and Cincinnati as ultimate objectives, as had been anticipated by the department commanders.

While General Thomas, in obedience to orders, was concentrating his command at Lebanon and Columbia, Zollicoffer having marched from Cumberland Gap through Jacksboro', Huntsville, and Jamestown, Tennessee, made his appearance with a strong force at Monticello, Kentucky, and threw forward a detachment to the Cumberland river, threatening Colonel Hoskins, in position near Somerset. Officers on the outlook at remote points reported the approach of the enemy. General Carter, at London, through a reconnoisance by Lieutenant-Colonel Spears, with six hundred men, in the direction of Cumberland Ford, had learned as early as the 24th that Zollicoffer had moved with nearly all his troops toward Jamestown. A day or two earlier Colonel Hoskins, near Somerset, and Colonel Bramlette, at Columbia, had each ascertained that he had reached Monticello. Each of these officers communicated the fact to General Thomas, who made prompt dispositions to arrest his advance at the Cumberland river. He sent five hundred of Wolford's cavalry from Columbia to reinforce Colonel Hoskins, and ordered General Schoepf, with Standardt's battery from Lebanon, and Colonel Connell and Bradley's regiments, en route thither, to move to the Cumberland river in front of Somerset, and fortify a position commanding the crossing and the river above and below the crossing. Captain Prime, of the engineers, was sent by General Buell to superintend the fortifications. General Schoepf was also specially urged to ascertain the movements of the enemy, and promptly report them, and not only to resist his crossing, but to prevent him from collecting the means of crossing.

For some days the situation of Colonel Hoskins was very critical. He was confronting an army in close proximity, whose cavalry skirmished with his pickets at Mill Springs, a point near his position. Doubtful of his ability to maintain his ground until the arrival of reinforcements from Lebanon, he called upon General Carter, at London, for assistance, who being restrained by his orders from General Buell, refused compliance. Fortunately, the enemy made no effort to cross the river before the arrival of General Schoepf, which occurred December 1st. General Schoepf at once selected a position on the north bank of the Cumberland, six miles from Somerset, and well sheltered from the artillery of the enemy on the opposite side of the river.

On the 29th of November, General Buell placed General Thomas in command of all troops east of New Haven, instructing him to make no important movement except in the event of danger, without his approval, but to prepare for emergencies, while avoiding a threatening attitude. The line of defense assigned to him extended from London to Columbia, and his troops were distributed as follows: The First and Second Tennessee, and Seventh Kentucky regiments, under command of General Carter, held London; the Fourth and Tenth Kentucky, Fourteenth Ohio, and Tenth Indiana regiments, and battery E, First Ohio Artillery, were posted at

Lebanon; the Third Kentucky Infantry, and First Kentucky Cavalry, at Columbia; the Thirty-third Indiana at Crab Orchard; the Thirty-first Ohio regiment, and battery A, First Ohio Artillery, at Camp Dick Robinson; the Seventeenth and Thirty-eighth Ohio, and battery B, First Ohio Artillery, confronted Zollicoffer near Somerset; and the Eighth Kentucky and Thirty-fifth Ohio were in motion toward Lebanon.

On the 2d of December the enemy made a brisk but harmless bombardment of General Schoepf's camp, and then moved toward Mill Springs.   Believing that this movement looked to a lodgment on the north side of the Cumberland, General Schoepf sent Captain Dillion with two companies of cavalry, to guard the ford and prevent his crossing, and ordered Colonel Connell, with his regiment, the Seventeenth Ohio, three pieces of artillery, and one company of cavalry, to march from Somerset to co-operate with Captain Dillion. The latter, in palpable disregard of orders, went into camp two miles from Fishing Creek, and neglecting even to post pickets to watch the ford, allowed Zollicoffer to establish himself on the north bank of the Cumberland, not only without opposition, but without his knowledge. Ignorant of the success of the enemy, Colonel Connell reached the vicinity of the ford to find himself confronted by a strong force on his own side of the river, and with such means of crossing reinforcements as not only to preclude his own attack, but even to imperil his command. Waiting for the aid of darkness, he withdrew his troops in safety back of Fishing creek, in absence of a tenable position in closer proximity to the enemy. As the lodgment of the enemy on the north bank of the river, and his threatening bearing, revealed a purpose beyond mere menace, General Schoepf, on the 5th, requested General Carter, at London, and Colonel Coburn, at Crab Orchard, to move to his support, and discovering that the force of the enemy on the north bank, already superior to his own, was constantly increasing, and that his position, being between roads leading from the different ferries, was susceptible of easy lateral approach, he withdrew to a strong position, three miles beyond Somerset, commanding the Crab Orchard and Stanford roads, and again urged General Carter to come to his assistance. General Thomas, however, had previously made provision for General Schoepf's reinforcement. December 3d he ordered Colonels Walker and Vanderveer's* regiments from Camp Dick Robinson to Somerset, and Captain Hewitt's battery from Broomfields. While these regiments seemed easily available for the emergency at Somerset, and were in motion thither, Colonel Walker was remanded to Camp Dick Robinson by General Buell. It is evident that at this time, and for some weeks subsequently, General Buell did not anticipate any serious trouble from Zollicoffer at Somerset. Acting upon this belief, he turned back troops en route to Somerset, and reversed orders in other cases requiring the movement of reinforcements to that point. He even forbade General Thomas to send other troops to General Schoepf until he had first secured his approval, asserting that the force at Somerset was sufficient. His apprehension of the situation, however, was not entertained by general officers in Southern Kentucky, and General Carter, deeming the danger to the command at Somerset a justification for moving without direct orders, left London with the First and Second Tennessee regiments December 7th, and reached General Schoepf on the 9th. When he started he sent a messenger to recall Colonel Garrard from a reconnoissance which he was conducting toward Barboursville, that he also might follow as quickly as possible; but subsequent orders required Colonel Garrard to remain at London.

On the 2d of December, General Buell issued an order giving brigade and division organization to the troops under his command, styling them collectively the "Army of the Ohio," and assigning brigade and division commanders. By this order the brigades were numbered consecutively throughout the army and not by divisions. On the 6th, in obedience to the general order of the department .commander, General Thomas formally assumed command of the First Division. This division comprised four brigades, and other troops, designated as follows:

---

* Colonel Vanderveer had been ordered to Camp Dick Robinson while en route to Lebanon.

First Brigade.

Brigadier-General Albin Schoepf commanding.

33d Regiment Indiana Volunteers, Colonel John Coburn.
17th Regiment Ohio Volunteers, Colonel J. M. Connell.
12th Regiment Kentucky Volunteers, Colonel W. A. Hoskins.
38th Regiment Ohio Volunteers, Colonel E. D. Bradley.

Second Brigade.

Colonel M. D. Manson commanding.

4th Regiment Kentucky Volunteers, Colonel S. S. Fry.
14th Regiment Ohio Volunteers, Colonel J. B. Steedman.
10th Regiment Indiana Volunteers, Colonel M. D. Manson.
10th Regiment Kentucky Volunteers, Colonel J. M. Harlan.

Third Brigade.

Colonel Robert L. McCook commanding.

18th United States Infantry, Colonel H. B. Carrington.
2d Regiment Minnesota Volunteers, Colonel H. P. Van Cleve.
35th Regiment Ohio Volunteers, Colonel F. Vanderveer.
9th Regiment Ohio Volunteers, Colonel R. L. McCook.

Twelfth Brigade.

Brigadier-General S. P. Carter commanding

1st Regiment East Tennessee Volunteers, Colonel R. R. Byrd.
2d Regiment East Tennessee Volunteers, Colonel J. P. T. Carter.
7th Regiment Kentucky Volunteers, Colonel T. T. Garrard.
31st Regiment Ohio Volunteers, Colonel M. B. Walker

Troops not assigned to Brigades.

1st Regiment Kentucky Cavalry, Colonel F. Wolford.
Squadron Indiana Cavalry, Captain Graham.
Battery B, 1st Kentucky Artillery, Captain J. M. Hewitt.
Battery B, 1st Ohio Artillery, Captain W. E. Standart.
Battery C, 1st Ohio Artillery, Captain D. Kinney.

Major W. E. Lawrence commanding artillery.

As Zollicoffer, having a force greatly superior to General Schoepf, withheld attack, General Buell still feared that, under cover of his offensive attitude at Somerset, he might advance with the greater portion of his command on Columbia, and then unite with Buckner, he ordered General Thomas to place Brigadier-General J. T. Boyle in command at Columbia, with instructions to fortify his position, and observe the enemy very closely toward the Cumberland river. He also directed General Thomas to move Brigadier-General Ward, with his command, from Campbellsville to Green river, in readiness to reinforce General Boyle in case of need. In harmony with these precautions, Colonel Wolford, with a portion of his regiment, was posted for outlook at Williams' farm, six miles from the Columbia and Somerset road, with his pickets well offered toward the enemy, to give timely notice of his approach to Columbia, or of his march into central Kentucky, through Caseyville.

In the meantime, Zollicoffer became more demonstrative in the vicinity of Somerset. His cavalry on the right, provoked a spirited skirmish with the Thirty-fifth Ohio, three miles from Somerset, which resulted in the loss of two or three men on each side. The enemy had previously captured Major Helveti, of the cavalry, and Captain Prime, who had been too venturesome in making observations.

Fearing that General Schoepf might be overpowered by Zollicoffer, General Thomas requested General Buell to permit him to go to his assistance. As has been stated, General Buell had previously directed him to withhold reinforcements, and now, when danger seemed still more imminent, he forbade him to take troops to Somerset, expressing the hope that General Schoepf would be able to drive Zollicoffer across the Cumberland, and asserting that he did not intend to be diverted from more important purposes by the annoying affairs at Somerset. These purposes doubtless had reference to operations in the direction of Columbia, as he ordered General Thomas to be ready for a quick transfer of one or two brigades to that place. As the only help for General Schoepf at command, General Thomas, December 11th, ordered Colonel M. B. Walker from Camp Dick Robinson to Somerset.

At this time, Zollicoffer's cavalry were ravaging the country about Jamestown and Creelsboro, and General Hindman, in command of about seven thousand men, was threatening Columbia from Bear Wallow and More's Hill. The cavalry of the enemy were driven back conjointly, by Colonel Wolford from Williams' farm; Lieutenant-Colonel Letcher, of the First Kentucky Cavalry, from Columbia, and Colonel Haggard, in act of conveying a large party of loyal Tennesseeans, from Burksville. Thus, General Hindman's advance resulted in nothing beyond menace. The Confederate generals in Kentucky, seemed reluctant to assume the offensive with such positiveness as had been anticipated. Two facts may account for their gentleness: Their armies were weaker than our commanders had supposed, and they were doubtless waiting for more active support from Kentucky secessionists. For while it was true that Kentuckians swelled the Confederate armies very considerably, Kentucky secessionists, as a whole, were more noisy than warlike To quicken their zeal for the rebellion and elicit their active support, Zollicoffer issued a proclamation December 16th, in which he presented Southern opinions concerning the causes of the war, and the purposes of the North in prosecuting it, and, appealing to their prejudices and passions, urged Kentuckians to assist him in driving the Northern hordes across the Ohio river. He intimated that if brave Kentuckians would refuse to aid the disheartened forces of the government in their effort to subjugate the South, and heartily join their Southern brethren, the success of the South would be assured. There was, however, no response, even in approximate correspondence, with the boastful tone of the proclamation.

A reconnoissance by General Schoepf, in strong force, with artillery, on the 18th, revealed the fact that Zollicoffer was intrenching on the north side of the Cumberland, in the angle formed by the junction of Fishing creek and that river, with his lines of fortification extended to each stream. General Schoepf moved toward this position in two columns, the heavier under his own command, and the other under General Carter. But not intending an assault, he accomplished nothing beyond pushing back the cavalry of the enemy, and ascertaining his probable purpose, as indicated by his repose behind his fortifications. The same day Colonel Hoskins made a reconnoissance to Waitsboro, but found no enemy.

General Buell, having finally concluded that it was important to dislodge Zollicoffer, directed General Thomas, December 29th, to communicate with General Schoepf, and arrange for a combined attack. General Thomas was to move in force from Lebanon, through Columbia, and strike Zollicoffer's left flank, while General Schoepf should assault in front. Accordingly, on the 31st, General Thomas started from Lebanon, with Colonel Manson's brigade and two regiments of Colonel McCook's, to march by way of Campbellsville, Columbia, and Webb's Cross-roads. Heavy rains had swollen the streams and rendered the roads almost impassable, and the progress of the command was very slow, and at times was almost entirely arrested. But after a toilsome march of eighteen days, portions of Manson's and McCook's brigades and Kinney's battery reached Logan's Cross-roads, a point ten miles from Zollicoffer's intrenched camp. As the Fourth and Tenth Kentucky regiments, the Fourteenth Ohio, and Eighteenth United States Infantry were still in the rear, General Thomas halted to await their arrival and communicate with General Schoepf. He made a careful disposition of the troops in hand, posting the Tenth Indiana, Wolford's cavalry, and Kinney's battery on the direct road to the enemy's position, and placing the Ninth Ohio and Second Minnesota regiments on the Robertsport road, three-fourths of a mile to the right. To prevent surprise, he threw out strong pickets beyond the junction of the Somerset and Mill Springs road with the one leading directly to the enemy, and posted cavalry pickets some distance in advance of those of the infantry. After consultation with General Schoepf, General Thomas directed him to send to his camp the Twelfth Kentucky, First and Second Tennessee regiments, and Standardt's battery, to remain until the troops in the rear should come up. Having heard in the evening of the 17th of January, 1862, that a large train of wagons, with its escort, was encamped on the Robertsport and Danville road, six miles from the camp of the Fourteenth Ohio, he ordered Colonel Steedman to send his wagons forward under strong guard, and then to march with his own and Colonel Harlan's regiment to the place where the train and escort were said to be encamped, and capture or disperse them. The next day, the Fourth Kentucky regiment, the battalion of Michigan engineers, and Wetmore's battery joined General Thomas.

General Crittenden, who had recently assumed command of the Confederate army at Mill Springs, was not ignorant of the approach of General Thomas, and hoping to crush him before he could concentrate his command, moved against him early on the morning of the 19th. At about $5\frac{1}{2}$ o'clock A. M. the national cavalry pickets encountered the enemy, and, slowly retiring, reported to Colonel Manson the approach of the army. Colonel Manson immediately threw forward the Tenth Indiana, ordered the Fourth Kentucky to move in support, and then in person made known to General Thomas the state of affairs at the front. General Thomas sent him back to his command, with instructions to hold the enemy in check until the other troops could be brought into action. In a few minutes all were formed and in motion to the field, except the battalion of Michigan engineers and Captain Greenwood's company of the Thirtieth Ohio, who were left as camp guard.

Upon going to the field soon after, General Thomas found the Tenth Indiana formed in front of their encampment, apparently awaiting orders, and threw them forward to the support of the Fourth Kentucky, which was the only entire regiment then engaged. He then rode forward to observe the enemy, and make such dispositions as successful resistance demanded. When he reached the position held by the Fourth Kentucky, Tenth Indiana, and Wolford's cavalry, he discovered the enemy advancing through a corn-field to gain the left of the Fourth Kentucky, which was resisting the foe in front with persistent bravery. To thwart this flank movement, he ordered up General Carter's brigade, which was yet some distance in the rear, and a section of Kinney's battery, and promptly put Kinney's guns in position at the edge of the field to the left of the Fourth Kentucky, which rendered efficient service in arresting a regiment of Alabamians moving against the left of Colonel Fry's regiment. He also brought up the Second Minnesota and Ninth Ohio, put the former in the room of the Fourth Kentucky and Tenth Indiana, now nearly out of ammunition, and placed the Ninth Ohio in line on the right of the road.

Immediately after these dispositions had been made, the enemy opened fire in such manner as indicated his determination to overwhelm General Thomas before additional troops could be brought into action. For nearly half an hour the contest was most obstinately maintained, on both sides, when the two gallant regiments (Second Minnesota and Tenth Ohio) were supported on the left by the First and Second East Tennessee regiments under General Carter, and the Twelfth Kentucky, under Colonel Hoskins. The fire of these fresh troops soon caused the enemy's right to give ground, and while the Second Minnesota kept up a most galling fire in the center, the Ninth Ohio, with fixed bayonets, made a most determined charge and completely turned his left flank, when the whole line was swept from the field.

As soon as practicable the regiments were reformed, supplied with ammunition, and pressed forward in vigorous pursuit. A show of resistance was made by a small body of cavalry, which was routed by a few shots from Standardt's battery, otherwise the whole force, in disorderly rout, hurried to the protection of their intrenchments. Colonel Steedman, with his own regiment, and Colonel Harlan's, and General Schoepf, with his brigade, joined General Thomas in time to participate in the pursuit.

When near the intrenched camp of the enemy, the troops were deployed, and advanced in line of battle to the summit of the hill at Moulden's. From this hill vigorous cannonading by Standardt's and Wetmore's batteries was maintained until dark. Kinney's battery was placed on the extreme right at Russell's to deter the enemy from crossing at the ferry, and full preparation was made for storming the intrenchments on the following morning. But during the night the enemy abandoned his fortifications, and everything within them, crossed the river quietly and burned his boats. The national troops moved upon the fortifications the next morning, but found no enemy to defend them. The destruction of the boats prevented immediate pursuit, and the dispersion of the enemy in all directions in their utter demoralization and haste to escape, rendered any subsequent general pursuit en·

tirely useless, and General Schoepf's brigade alone followed the enemy to Monticello.

The enemy left in his intrenchments all his badly wounded, twelve pieces of artillery, a heavy amount of ammunition, a large number of small arms, one hundred and fifty wagons, more than a thousand horses and mules, and abundant quartermaster and commissary stores. His flags, left upon the battle-field, gave evidence of his positive defeat, and the wounded left in the intrenchments revealed his absorbing anxiety to reach the south bank of the Cumberland.

General Crittenden moved against General Thomas with ten regiments of infantry, besides independent companies, six pieces of artillery, and two or more battalions of cavalry. He was defeated by six regiments of infantry, one battery, and a portion of Wolford's cavalry. He lost, as far as known, in killed, wounded, and prisoners, three hundred and ninety-two men. Of this aggregate, one hundred and ninety-two were killed, including General Zollicoffer, who was killed by a shot from the pistol of Colonel S. S. Fry. As he fell in the crisis of the engagement, his loss greatly contributed to the discomfiture of the enemy. Lieutenant Bailie Peyton was also among the slain. Both of these were men of prominence and influence in the rebellion.

General Thomas lost thirty-nine killed, including one commissioned officer, and two hundred and seven wounded. Among the latter were Colonel Robert McCook and Lieutenant Andrew Burt, of the Tenth Ohio, acting aid-de-camp to the general commanding.

The victory at Mill Springs was the first decisive one that crowned the national arms, and it gave joy and hope to the loyal everywhere. In its positiveness, it was the type of the grander triumph at Nashville in the last but most decisive field engagement which occurred in the West during the war.

The President issued a congratulatory order, and the general in chief charged General Buell to convey his thanks to General Thomas and his troops for this brilliant victory. These official expressions of thanks were not more emphatic than was the spontaneous utterance of gratitude by the people.

Immediately after the battle of Mill Springs, General Thomas concentrated his command at Somerset, and there awaited the development of general plans for offensive operations. The success of General Grant and Commodore Foote at Fort Henry, on the Cumberland river, February 6, 1862, induced General Buell to concentrate his forces for a co-operative movement in pressing back the enemy's line. He accordingly ordered the first division to Lebanon. At Lebanon (February 15th), General Thomas received orders to move his division as rapidly as possible by way of Bardstown, New Haven, and Munfordsville, to take part in the contemplated operations against Bowling Green. Before this movement could be executed, the order requiring it was revoked, and on the 22d General Thomas was directed to proceed with his division, and the First Ohio Cavalry, then at Bardstown, by forced marches, to Louisville, to embark for the Cumberland river. This order was promptly executed, and on the 26th the division took boats at Louisville and debarked at Nashville during the 2d, 3d, and 4th days of March.

CHAPTER VII.

ORGANIZATION AND OPERATIONS OF THE SECOND, THIRD, FOURTH, FIFTH, AND SIXTH ·DIVISIONS.

WHEN General Sherman assumed command of the department he left Brigadier-General L. H. Rousseau, recently promoted, in command· of all the troops on the Louisville and Nashville road, near Elizabethtown. The latter at once moved his command to Nolin, fifty-three miles distant from Louisville. Here, Camp Nevin was established, in which the Second division was organized.

By General Sherman's order, Brigadier-General A. McD. McCook assumed command, October 14th. He proceeded at once to organize brigades. Hitherto the regiments had been thrown together without definite relations. On the 18th, General McCook announced the organization of the central division, composed of three brigades, designated as the Fourth, Fifth, and Sixth, and commanded respectively by Brigadier-Generals L. H. Rousseau, T. J. Wood, and R. W. Johnson. This division was simply a provisional one, and sustained no special relations to other commands in the department. Such organization was imperatively needed, both for the instruction of new troops and for effective resistance, in the event of attack. As separate regiments arrived, they were added to the brigades already formed. But when the brigade under Brigadier-General J. S. Negley reached Camp Nevin, its organization was maintained, and it was styled the Seventh brigade.

Upon the organization of the "Army of the Ohio," General McCook's command became the Second division. This change of designation was officially announced December 3d. Its permanent organization was as follows:

Fourth Brigade.

Brigadier-General L. H. Rousseau commanding.

1st Regiment Ohio Volunteer Infantry, Colonel B. F. Smith.

5th Regiment Kentucky Volunteer Infantry, Colonel H. M. Buckley.

6th Regiment Indiana Volunteer Infantry, Colonel T. T. Crittenden.

1st Battalion, 15th U. S. Infantry. ⎱ Major John H. King.
1st Battalion, 19th U. S. Infantry. ⎰

Fifth Brigade.

Brigadier-General T. J. Wood commanding.

29th Regiment Indiana Volunteer Infantry, Colonel John F. Miller.

30th Regiment Indiana Volunteer Infantry, Colonel Sion S. Bass.

34th Regiment Illinois Volunteer Infantry, Colonel E. N. Kirk.

77th Regiment Pennsylvania Volunteer Infantry, Colonel F. S. Stambaugh.

Sixth Brigade.

Brigadier-General R. W. Johnson commanding.

15th Regiment Ohio Volunteer Infantry, Colonel M. R. Dickey.

49th Regiment Ohio Volunteer Infantry, Colonel W. H. Gibson.

32d Regiment Indiana Volunteer Infantry, Colonel August Willich.

39th Regiment Indiana Volunteer Infantry, Colonel T. J. Harrison.

Seventh Brigade.

Brigadier-General J. S. Negley commanding.

1st Regiment Wisconsin Volunteer Infantry, Colonel J. C. Starkweather.

38th Regiment Indiana Volunteer Infantry, Colonel B. F. Scribner.

78th Regiment Pennsylvania Volunteer Infantry, Colonel William Sirwell.

79th Regiment Pennsylvania Volunteer Infantry, Colonel H. A. Hambright.

———

1st Regiment Kentucky Cavalry, Colonel Buckner Board.

Battery A, 1st Ohio Artillery, Captain C. S. Cotter.

Battery A, 1st Kentucky Artillery, Captain D. C. Stone.

26th Pennsylvania Artillery, Captain Chas. F. Mueller.

Nearly two months had now been spent in preparing this division for active service. As yet no attempt had been made to press back the enemy, and no fighting had occurred, except a skirmish with the enemy's cavalry by a detachment of the Thirty-ninth Indiana, under Lieutenant-Colonel Jervis, a few miles from Camp Nevin, which resulted in a slight loss to the enemy. But on the 9th of December, pursuant to instructions from General Buell, General McCook issued orders for an advance. The next morning General Johnson moved his brigade toward Munfordsville, a village on the north bank of Green river. He encamped at Bacon creek to await the construction of bridges for the passage of trains and artillery, but threw forward a detachment of the Thirty-second Indiana to Green river, the enemy retiring as our troops advanced. Two days later, the remaining brigades of the division reached Bacon creek, and the Fifth brigade moved upon its vanguard at Green river. Colonel Willich threw two companies of his regiment across the river to prevent surprise during the construction of a temporary bridge. By working day and night, the Thirty-second Indiana completed the bridge on the morning of the 17th. Four companies of this regiment, under Lieutenant-Colonel Von Trebra, at once crossed and advanced to the declivity of a hill near Rowlett's Station, and an equal number were placed at the bridge as a reserve. Early in the afternoon the pickets observed the enemy in the woods to their right and front, and Colonel Von Trebra sent two companies against them. The enemy fell back without resisting, and the national troops in pursuit suddenly received a volley from a squadron of cavalry. They returned the fire, and then fell back in order. This was the commencement of a spirited fight, which was maintained for an hour and a half. With each alternation of advance and retreat, additional troops were brought into action, until the eight companies were hotly engaged with a greatly superior force, including infantry, cavalry, and artillery, The enemy's cavalry made repeated charges, at times with temporary success, but with final defeat, under the lead of Colonel Terry, of the "Texas Rangers," whose fall caused their precipitate flight from the field. At this juncture, Colonel Willich, who had been on duty at brigade headquarters, appeared, and observing that the right of his line was giving way before two regiments of infantry, he drew back and made a new allignment. The enemy then retreated. General Hindman claimed in his official report that he withdrew his command in consequence of the approach of McCook's division. It was true that the division was on the north bank of the river, and that the proximity of reinforcements was announced by Cotter's battery from the south side; but no other help was afforded the Thirty-second Indiana.

The marked feature of this contest was the repeated repulsion of a heavy force of cavalry attacking with great gallantry, by one-half of a full company of infantry, well handled in resistance.

General Hindman's force consisted of two regiments and a battalion of infantry, a regiment and a squadron of cavalry, and a battery. The fighting, however, was done mainly by the cavalry.

The Thirty-second Indiana lost Lieutenant Sachs and eight men killed and ten wounded. The enemy's loss was undoubtedly greater, although General Hindman's report only admitted the loss of Colonel Terry and three others killed and ten wounded.

General Buell commended the conduct of the Thirty-second Indiana in orders, and authorized the name of "Rowlett's Station" to be inscribed on their regimental colors.

The Second division, after marching and countermarching, as the exigencies of the campaign required, followed the

Third division to Nashville, reaching that city on the 3d of March.

During the summer and fall, Brigadier-General O. M. Mitchell was in command at Cincinnati, chiefly engaged in equipping troops, collecting supplies, and forwarding men and munitions for the various campaigns in progress in the West. On the 19th of November he was relieved and assigned by General Buell to the command of Camp Jenkins, near Louisville, Kentucky. He was soon after ordered to Camp John Quincy Adams, at Bacon creek, to give discipline and organization to troops there collecting. December 3d, he was assigned to the command of the Third division, then created, which comprised three brigades.

Eighth Brigade.

Colonel J. B. Turchin commanding.

19th Regiment Illinois Volunteer Infantry, Colonel J. B. Turchin.

37th Regiment Indiana Volunteer Infantry, Major J. S. Hull.

18th Regiment Ohio Volunteer Infantry, Colonel T. R. Stanley.

24th Regiment Illinois Volunteer Infantry, Colonel G. Mihalotzy.

Seventeenth Brigade.

Brigadier-General E. Dumont commanding.

3d Regiment Ohio Volunteer Infantry, Colonel John Beatty.

13th Regiment Ohio Volunteer Infantry, Colonel W. S. Smith.

10th Regiment Ohio Volunteer Infantry, Lieutenant-Colonel J. W. Burke.

15th Regiment Kentucky Volunteer Infantry, Colonel Curran Pope.

Ninth Brigade.

Colonel J. W. Sill commanding.

22d Regiment Ohio Volunteer Infantry, Colonel J. W. Sill.

21st Regiment Ohio Volunteer Infantry, Colonel J. S. Norton.

2d Regiment Ohio Volunteer Infantry, Colonel L. A. Harris.

10th Regiment Wisconsin Volunteer Infantry, Colonel A. R. Chapin.

Artillery.

Captain C. O. Loomis commanding.

Battery E, First Ohio Artillery, Captain W. P. Edgarton.
Battery, Fifth Indiana, Captain P. Simonson.
Battery, Cold Water, Michigan, Captain C. O. Loomis.

A large portion of these troops, recently transferred to the
"Department of the Ohio," had seen service under General
Rosecrans in Western Virginia, and General Nelson in Eastern
Kentucky. Their experience of war gave veteran character
to the division, and warranted its assignment to the van in the
movement upon Bowling Green and Nashville, and its subsequent perilous insulation on the Memphis and Charleston railroad. When, on February 13th, the Second division was
turned back from Munfordsville in the effort to reinforce General Grant at Fort Donelson, the Third division moved with
great celerity toward Bowling Green to deter the enemy from
throwing troops to the beleaguered fort. Its arrival on the
north bank of Barren river, opposite Bowling Green, on the
day following, was announced by the roar of cannon, whose
bombs bursting in the city spread terror among the inhabitants and hurried the retreat of the rear-guard of General
Johnston's army. During the night previous, the enemy
burned both bridges over Barren river, and before leaving the
city had set fire to the public buildings, railroad cars, and other
property. The swollen stream, without bridges, prevented the
immediate advance of the troops to arrest the conflagration.
The night following, however, by means of a small ferry-boat,
found a few miles down the river, Turchin's brigade and a few
troopers effected a passage and occupied the city at 5 o'clock
the next morning, saving from destruction a portion of the
rolling-stock of the railroad.

The continued high water offered such a barrier to the transfer of troops, artillery, and trains to the south bank, that a
week elapsed before General Mitchell could resume his march
toward Nashville. Having, during this time, by great labor,
effected the landing of two brigades and a half on the south
bank, he, on the morning of the 22d, put them in motion without trains, and marching by Franklin, Mitchellsville, and Tyree

Springs, reached Edgefield, opposite Nashville, in the evening of the 24th, simultaneously with General Buell, who, with a thousand men, had used the rolling-stock captured at Bowling Green. General Buell had learned on the 20th, that General Johnston had withdrawn his troops from Clarksville, and had fallen back to Nashville, burning both bridges at the latter place. He had also telegraphed to General Halleck, and sent a courier to Clarksville, giving information of his movements, and requesting that gunboats be sent up the river to Nashville.

Soon after, Lieutenant William Nelson, U. S. N., was superseded by General Thomas, at Camp Dick Robinson, he was promoted to the rank of brigadier-general, and ordered to Maysville, Kentucky, to organize a force to operate in the eastern part of the state. Having driven the rebels from Eastern Kentucky, he was, late in November, ordered with his command to Louisville. On the 3d of December, he was placed in command of the Fourth division, composed of three brigades, designated and organized as follows:

Tenth Brigade.
Colonel Jacob Ammen commanding.

24th Regiment Ohio Volunteer Infantry, Colonel Jacob Ammen.

51st Regiment Ohio Volunteer Infantry, Colonel Stanley Matthews.

36th Regiment Indiana Volunteer Infantry, Colonel William Grose.

6th Regiment Ohio Volunteer Infantry, Lieutenant-Colonel N. L. Anderson.

Nineteenth Brigade.
Colonel W. B. Hazen commanding.

41st Regiment Ohio Volunteer Infantry, Colonel W. B. Hazen.

9th Regiment Indiana Volunteer Infantry, Col. G. C. Moody.

6th Regiment Kentucky Volunteer Infantry, Colonel W. C. Whittaker.

Twenty-second Brigade.

Colonel S. D. Bruce commanding.

20th Regiment Kentucky Volunteer Infantry, Colonel S. D. Bruce.

1st Regiment Kentucky Volunteer Infantry, Colonel D. A. Enyart.

2d Regiment Kentucky Volunteer Infantry, Colonel T. D. Sedgewick.

Cavalry and Artillery.

2d Regiment Indiana Cavalry, Colonel E. M. McCook.

Battery D, 1st Ohio Artillery, Captain A. J. Konkle.

Battery 10, 1st Indiana Artillery, Cap. J. B. Cox.

Battery 7, 1st Indiana Artillery, Captain S. J. Harris.

The division was immediately transferred to Camp Wickliffe, near New Haven. On February 13th, General Nelson, with two brigades, moved from New Haven to the Ohio river, to embark to reinforce General Grant, at Fort Donelson. Not reaching this destination in time to participate in the reduction of the fort, he proceeded by water to Nashville, arriving there on the 25th. Here he was soon after joined by Colonel Bruce with his brigade, who had marched thither by the direct route through Bowling Green.

Early in October, General Sherman placed Brigadier-General T. L. Crittenden, in command of the troops organizing at Owensboro and in the vicinity of Henderson. These were the Third Kentucky Cavalry, and the Eleventh, Seventeenth, and Twenty-sixth Infantry, commanded respectively by Colonels Jackson, Hawkins, McHenry, and Burbridge. General Crittenden was first directed to threaten the enemy's left by a demonstration against Hopkinsville, held by a thousand men. The enemy evinced activity on this flank, as on the other before General Thomas, and several slight engagements occurred during October. Late in the month a force of four or five hundred men threatened Colonel McHenry at Hartford. General Crittenden sent Colonel Burbridge from Owensboro with two hundred and fifty men, including infantry, cavalry, and artillery, to his assistance. With his own command, augmented by eighty men from McHenry's regiment, under Captain Morton, Colonel Burbridge encountered the enemy at Woodbury, and routed him, with a loss of about fifty killed and a large number wounded.   About the same time, Colonel McHenry defeated a band of the enemy at Morgantown.

The most formidable menace, however, was made late in November.   During the earlier portion of the month the augmentation of the enemy's forces at Hopkinsville and Russelville indicated, as was supposed, an effort to turn the right of the line.   On the 24th, General Breckinridge entered Rochester with about four thousand men, and at the same time a large force of cavalry advanced from Hopkinsville and occupied Greenville.   The indications of this movement, for so long a time before its execution, gave General Crittenden time to take such measures for defense that Breckinridge refrained from attack and retired to Bowling Green.   He had doubtless meditated the penetration of Crittenden's line, the destruction of the locks on Green river, and probably the interruption of McCook's communications.

On the 3d of December, General Crittenden was appointed as commander of the Fifth division, comprising the Eleventh, Thirteenth, and Fourteenth brigades.

Eleventh Brigade.
Colonel S. Beatty commanding.

19th Regiment Ohio Volunteer Infantry, Colonel S. Beatty.

59th Regiment Ohio Volunteer Infantry, Colonel J. P. Fyffe.

13th Regiment Kentucky Volunteer Infantry, Colonel W. E. Hobson.

9th Regiment Kentucky Volunteer Infantry, Colonel B. C. Grider.

21st Regiment Kentucky Volunteer Infantry, Colonel S. W. Price.

3d Regiment Kentucky Volunteer Infantry, Colonel T. E. Bramlette.

Thirteenth Brigade.
Colonel Charles Cruft commanding.

31st Regiment Indiana Volunteer Infantry, Colonel C. Cruft.

44th Regiment Indiana Volunteer Infantry, Colonel H. B. Reed.

17th Regiment Kentucky Volunteer Infantry, Colonel J. H. McHenry.

25th Regiment Kentucky Volunteer Infantry, Colonel James W. Shackelford.

Artillery.

Captain John Mendenhall's Regular Battery.

Captain Joseph Bartlett's Ohio Battery.

Fourteenth Brigade.

Colonel J. G. Jones commanding.

42d Regiment Ohio Volunteer Infantry, Colonel J. G. Jones.

11th Regiment Kentucky Volunteer Infantry, Colonel P. P. Hawkins.

26th Regiment Kentucky Volunteer Infantry, Colonel S. G. Burbridge.

Early in February, General Buell ordered the embarkation of Colonel Cruft's brigade to join General Grant. This brigade reached General Grant at Fort Henry after its reduction, and participated effectively in forcing the surrender of Fort Donelson. The brigade was then transferred to General Halleck. A few days later, General Crittenden embarked at Owensboro with the remainder of his division, descended the Ohio, and in company with Nelson proceeded up the Cumberland to Nashville.

Brigadier-General T. J. Wood was relieved of the command of the Fifth brigade, Second division, and ordered to Bardstown, Nelson county, Kentucky, on the 24th of December, 1861, to establish a camp of instruction for all arms of the service, represented by the troops at that place. He was directed to institute the most thorough system of discipline and instruction. General Wood displayed such energy, in compliance, that by the 15th of the following month the Sixth division was fully organized, and by order of General Buell he was assigned as permanent commander. This division comprised these brigades:

Fifteenth Brigade.

Colonel M. S. Hascall commanding.

17th Regiment Indiana Volunteer Infantry, Colonel M. S. Hascall.

58th Regiment Indiana Volunteer Infantry, Colonel M. S. Kerr.

26th Regiment Ohio Volunteer Infantry, Colonel E. P. Fyffe.

3d Regiment Kentucky Volunteer Infantry, Colonel T. E. Bramlette.

Twentieth Brigade.

Colonel C. G. Harker commanding.

65th Regiment Ohio Volunteer Infantry, Colonel C. G. Harker.

64th Regiment Ohio Volunteer Infantry, Colonel J. W. Forsythe.

51st Regiment Indiana Volunteer Infantry, Colonel A. D. Streight.

13th Regiment Michigan Volunteer Infantry, Colonel M. Shoemaker.

Twenty-first Brigade.

Colonel G. D. Wagner commanding.

15th Regiment Indiana Volunteer Infantry, Colonel G. D. Wagner.

40th Regiment Indiana Volunteer Infantry, Colonel J. W. Blake.

57th Regiment Indiana Volunteer Infantry, Colonel W. S. Hines.

24th Regiment Kentucky Volunteer Infantry, Colonel L. G. Grigsby.

Artillery.

5th Ohio Battery, Captain C. Bradley.

6th Indiana Battery, Captain George Estep.

10th Indiana Battery, Captain J. B. Cox.

The 3d Ohio Cavalry, Colonel Lewis Zahm, was subsequently added.

The plan of operations in contemplation at this period required the accumulation of supplies at Somerset, and General Wood was ordered, in conjunction with General Schoepf's brigade, of the First division, to employ his division in repairing the road from Lebanon to Somerset through Danville. A change of plan soon required the recall of the Sixth division to Lebanon, and its prompt movement thence by railroad to Munfordsville. Assisting in the repair of the railroad, it moved through Bowling Green and Franklin to Nashville, where it arrived March 6, 1862.

CHAPTER VIII.

OPERATIONS OF GENERAL NELSON, COLONEL GARFIELD, AND GENERAL CARTER IN EASTERN KENTUCKY.

WHEN General Nelson was ordered to Maysville to organize troops, it was anticipated that the insurgents would greatly annoy the loyal people in Eastern Kentucky, and unless opposed would penetrate the central portions of the state. Early in October it was ascertained that Colonel J. S. Williams had collected a force of two thousand men at Prestonburg, on the Big Sandy river, threatening Central Kentucky by way of McCormick's Gap. To repel this invasion, General Nelson moved from Maysville to Olympia Springs with all the troops in hand; the Second Ohio, under Colonel L. A. Harris, having previously marched to the latter place from Paris, and the Twenty-first Ohio, under Colonel Norton, from Nicholasville. From Olympia Springs, General Nelson advanced to McCormick's Gap, where he divided his command, sending Colonel Harris, with his regiment, a section of Konkle's battery, and Captain McLaughlin's company of Ohio cavalry, to West Liberty, and retaining under his own direction the Twenty-first Thirty-third, and Fifty-ninth Ohio regiments, under Colonels Sill, Norton, and Fyffe respectively, the Kentucky volunteers under Colonels Marshall and Metcalfe, the remainder of Konkle's battery, and a small body of cavalry, he advanced upon Hazel Green. Both places were occupied on the 23d, the former after a severe skirmish, in which Colonel Harris killed ten of the enemy, wounded five, and captured six, with a loss to himself of one wounded. Advancing from these points, the two columns united at Licking Station and followed the enemy toward Prestonburg. At the latter place, General Nelson again divided his command, sending Colonel Sill, with the Twenty-first Ohio, two battalions of Kentucky troops, and a section of Konkle's battery, by a detour to the right, to the rear of the enemy in position on Ivy Mountain. On the day following, he advanced with the remainder of his force on the direct road to Piketon. Pressing on, he encountered the enemy in ambush, on the mountain side at Ivy creek. After a spirited engagement, in which the Second and Twenty-first Ohio regiments, Metcalfe's battalion, and two sections of Konkle's battery participated, the enemy was routed, leaving thirty men either killed or badly wounded on the field. Nelson's loss was six killed and twenty-four wounded. This engagement occurred on the 8th of October. Pursuit was commenced immediately, but owing to the destruction of the bridges over the swollen streams and obstruction of the roads, General Nelson did not reach Piketon until the morning of the 10th, finding the place occupied by Colonel Sill, who, having met with little opposition, had arrived the night previous. The enemy retreated through Pound Gap, and General Nelson's command was soon withdrawn to Louisville.

After the withdrawal of Nelson's troops, the loyal people in the valley of the Big Sandy were again subjected to depredations by irregular bands of Confederate soldiers. This state of affairs demanded the return of the national troops to that region. Colonel L. P. Moore, commanding the Fourteenth Kentucky regiment at Catlettsburg, was directed to prepare for a speedy advance up the valley. Soon after, Colonel Lindsay commanding the Twenty-second Kentucky, was ordered from Portsmouth to join Colonel Moore and assume command of the two regiments. Pending the preparation for this expedition, General Humphrey Marshall invaded Kentucky through Whitesburg, with a force variously estimated as ranging from three to six thousand men, and intrenched himself near Paintville, on the road from that place to Prestonburg. To drive back these troops, General Buell organized the Eighteenth brigade, comprising the Fourteenth and Twenty-second Kentucky Infantry, and the Fortieth and Forty-second Ohio Infantry, three battalions of Woodford's Kentucky Cavalry under Lieutenant-Colonel Letcher, and an

independent battalion of Ohio Cavalry under Major McLaughlin, with Colonel J. A. Garfield as commander. Having received intructions from General Buell in person, Colonel Garfield proceeded to the mouth of the Big Sandy, arriving there
on the 22d of December. At this time the troops composing
his brigade were posted at Maysville, Catlettsburg, Paris, and
Lebanon, and were at once put in motion toward the enemy.
Colonel Garfield moved up the valley of the Sandy, from Catlettsburg with the Forty-second Ohio, Fourteenth Kentucky,
and McLaughlin's troopers, reaching the mouth of George's
creek on the 25th. The necessary repair of the roads delayed
his advance from this point until the 31st. On that day he
moved up the creek and passed toward Paintville. On the
6th of January, while en route, he was joined by Colonel
Bolle's West Virginia Cavalry, and also by three hundred men
of the Twenty-second Kentucky, who had marched from
Maysville. The day following, Colonel Bolles drove the
enemy's cavalry from a strong position at the mouth of Jen-
nie's creek, losing two men killed and one wounded, and inflicting upon the enemy a loss of six killed and many wounded.
Marshall here offered no further resistance, and abandoned his
intrenched camp upon the near approach of Garfield's troops.
Colonel Garfield here rested for two days, and during the time
was joined by the Fortieth Ohio regiment, and three battalions
of Woodford's Cavalry, the latter having marched from Lebanon. Having now his entire command in hand, he determined
to provoke a battle or press the foe still farther toward Virginia.
Accordingly, on the 9th, with his cavalry in advance, and his
reserve at Paintville, he moved toward Prestonburg. When
near this place, he ascertained that Marshall was some three
miles distant on Abbott's creek. Anticipating an engagement,
the next day he ordered forward his reserve under Colonel
Sheldon. The following morning, in making a detour in hope
of capturing the enemy, Colonel Garfield encountered his
cavalry at the mouth of Middle creek, opposite Prestonburg.
This force maintained a brisk skirmish while slowly falling
back upon the main body, which was strongly posted on the
hills near the confluence of the two branches of the stream,
two and a half miles distant. The ground occupied by Mar-

shall was so favorable for the concealment of his dispositions for defense, that Garfield was compelled to throw forward several detachments to draw his fire at different points, and thus disclose his exact position. These tentative movements proved to have been so judiciously directed, that with subsequent provision against a flank attack, the battle was conducted to a successful issue by the repeated reinforcement of the several detachments which first advanced against the enemy. The engagement was inaugurated mainly by two Kentucky companies on the right, and two Ohio companies under Captains Jones and Williams, from the Fortieth and Forty-second regiments, on the left. Those on the right were reinforced by Major Burke, with two companies from the Fourteenth Kentucky, and those on the left, first by Major Parker, with a hundred men from the Forty-second Ohio, and subsequently by Colonel Cranor with one hundred and fifty men from the two Ohio and Fourteenth Kentucky regiments. While these troops were hotly engaged, the enemy attempted to turn Garfield's right, but was foiled and driven back by Lieutenant-Colonel Monroe, with one hundred and twenty men from the Fourteenth and Twenty-second Kentucky regiments. At 4 P. M., Lieutenant-Colonel Sheldon reached the field from Paintville with the reserve. Thus strengthened, Colonel Garfield pressed the enemy from his position, but darkness prevented pursuit. Reaching the valley, Marshall burned his stores and hurried on in disordered flight. The disparity in numbers and losses in this engagement was remarkable. Colonel Garfield reports the number of his own troops actually engaged, to have been nine hundred; his loss, one killed and twenty wounded; while the force of the enemy was thirty-five hundred, and his acknowledged loss, one hundred and twenty-five killed, the number of wounded being unknown. Twenty-five prisoners were taken during the engagement, and others the next day by Colonel Letcher, in pursuit.

Not being able to supply his command at Prestonburg, Colonel Garfield returned to Paintville. While there, he was directed by General Buell to advance as soon as possible to Piketon, and drive the enemy from Kentucky. In obedience to this order, early in February he commenced the concentration of his troops at Piketon, sending them forward as his supplies would warrant, but before preparations could be made to advance from Piketon, Marshall withdrew entirely from Kentucky, established his headquarters at Gladesville, and evinced no purpose to re-enter the state. A month later, Colonel Garfield having learned that he was collecting the Virginia militia to defend the mountain passes, determined to move against him at Pound Gap. Accordingly, with six hundred infantry and one hundred cavalry, he advanced from Piketon, The Gap was held by Major J. B. Thompson with five hundred men, strongly intrenched. This force Colonel Garfield proposed to attack in front, flank, and rear, with the hope of capturing it, but owing to the failure of the detachment sent to the rear to cut off the retreat of the enemy, he only succeeded in routing and dispersing his forces. Having thus freed Eastern Kentucky from the presence and depredations of the enemy, Colonel Garfield was ordered to Louisville with his troops, and was assigned to the command of the Twentieth brigade, Sixth division, Army of the Ohio.

On the 26th of January, General Carter's brigade, augmented by the Sixteenth Ohio Infantry, Colonel De Courcey, and the Forty-ninth Indiana, Colonel Kay, Major Mundy's battalion of Kentucky cavalry, and Wetmore's battery, was ordered from Somerset to London, preparatory to a prompt movement upon Cumberland Gap. General Carter reached London with his command early in February, and took position at Cumberland Ford about the 10th of the month. This advance was regarded as the first step toward the penetration of East Tennessee by a large army, under General Thomas. This projected invasion having been abandoned, for reasons hereafter mentioned, General Carter was left in proximity to Cumberland Gap, to prevent a counter invasion from that direction. Wishing to ascertain the strength of the enemy, he sent Lieutenant-Colonel Mundy, with a detachment, to reconnoiter the position. Colonel Mundy reached Cumberland Gap on the 14th of February, and having driven in the enemy's pickets, he approached sufficiently near to discern the formidable character of the defenses, and draw the fire of the artillery. Subsequently, several reconnoissances were made in different directions, and one or two more expeditions, having more serious purposes, resulted in successful skirmishes, but in no way changed the relative positions of the contending forces.

CHAPTER IX.

GENERAL VIEW OF THE SITUATION IN THE CENTRAL THEATER OF WAR, FROM THE BEGINNING TO THE FALL OF NASHVILLE.

THE preceding narrative of facts, as related to the organization and operations of the divisions of the army separately, has failed to compass the broader features of the situation in Kentucky and Tennessee, previous to the capture of Nashville, and hence a general view is here introduced.

The recognition of the neutrality of Kentucky by the President, and the demand for troops in Eastern and Western Virginia, prevented early provision for large armies in the great central theater of military operations. The strategic importance of Cairo, Illinois, had not been overlooked, for soon after the fall of Sumter, it was occupied by national troops. But the accumulation of forces was slow, even at that point, though it was hedged in between the States of Missouri and Kentucky, then in such critical hesitation with regard to Northern or Southern alliance.

The insurgents, also, for a time, professed respect for the neutrality of Kentucky. But they were not, in consequence, less active in preparation for a bold policy, whenever the interests of their cause should demand the invasion of the state. Anticipating civil war as at least the probable result of secession, the Southern people really prepared for such a struggle before they attempted the withdrawal of the Southern States from the Union. And after the actual inauguration of war, while the loyal states contiguous to Kentucky and Missouri were sending most of their first equipped regiments to the East, the Confederate generals were massing their earliest Western volunteers on the northorn boundary of Tennessee.

Thus, when both the national and insurgent authorities declined further respect for the false position of Kentucky, President Lincoln could only throw a few raw regiments into the state, to repel a bold and apparently threatening invasion. General Anderson succeeded in defeating the effort of the Confederate general, Buckner, to capture Louisville, but during the period of his command in Kentucky, the state of affairs was considered critical in the extreme. In October, General W. T. Sherman assumed the administration of affairs, in room of the hero of Fort Sumter, under a weight of responsibility and surcharge of embarrassments, which rendered anxious and despairing the soldier who afterward was hopeful in conducting campaigns of boldest aggression. Apprehending the magnitude of the struggle, and seeing his slender forces distributed from Henderson to the Big Sandy river, and from Cincinnati and Louisville to London and Nolin, confronting hostile forces of supposed superior strength and of easy concentration for offense, he startled the authorities at Washington and the people at large by the announcement that he needed two hundred thousand men. This estimate for an army resulted in his speedy supersession by Brigadier-General D. C. Buell, through an order from Washington. The main efforts of both Anderson and Sherman had been directed to defense, and in this, each had been successful.

The earlier period of General Buell's command was devoted to the same end. But he assumed the direction of military operations under more hopeful circumstances. The insurgents had gained no advantages in Kentucky since their primal advance, and were now relatively weaker than when they first made revelation of aggressive purpose. He came from Washington under instructions to inaugurate offensive operations, and was hopeful of commanding the resources necessary for their success. His instructions pointed to the especial importance of sending a heavy column into East Tennessee. The rapidity with which new regiments were thrown into

Kentucky soon made it evident that General A. S. Johnston, who commanded the insurgent forces in the West, had lost the opportunity for the successful invasion of Northern Kentucky, if at any previous period he had had sufficient strength to warrant such an enterprise. This rapid increase of troops imposed upon General Buell the necessity of an offensive initiative in some direction, as soon as a distinctive army organization could be given to his forces.

The subsequent grandeur of the service rendered by the Army of the Cumberland, then called the Army of the Ohio, must be taken as full proof that he who first laid his organizing hand upon it, did his work well, and transmitted his personal influence upon it through all its accretions and battles to the end of the war. He transformed citizens into soldiers, by instruction, discipline, and drill; exacted from his officers the strictest attention to all their new duties; eliminated such as gave no promise of efficiency; reduced the baggage of his army, and consequently the wagons for its transportation, and soon was ready for active operations.

After a careful study* of the East Tennessee enterprise, he reached the conclusion that its success would require an army of thirty thousand men—twenty thousand for an advancing column, and ten thousand for the line of communications, which involved wagon transportation for two hundred miles, most of this distance through a barren and mountainous region. In room of this movement, which in his view was so beset with difficulties as to be altogether unpromising, if not impracticable, he suggested an advance against Nashville, by the march of a column to the left of Bowling Green, through Glasgow and Gallatin, co-operative with another which should ascend the Cumberland river on steamers, under convoy of gunboats, with dependence for supplies, after the conjunction of the columns, upon river transportation. Hoping that this plan would be approved at Washington, he held his forces in readiness for its execution, and rather than change his dispositions, having reference to its prosecution, he permitted Zollicoffer to threaten central Kentucky, from the north bank of

* General Buell's statement before the military commission.

the Cumberland river, near Somerset, for several weeks, making no adequate effort to dislodge him. However, in the absence of official approval at Washington, he held his forces in waiting to move against Nashville, and continued his efforts to provide sufficient transportation for the expedition into East Tennessee, in consideration of the probability of being required to conduct it. On the 29th of December, the attitude of Zollicoffer became so threatening as to demand an effort for his dislodgment from the north bank of the Cumberland. He sent General Thomas to accomplish this work, and on the 1st of January, renewed his request for permission to turn toward the capital of Tennessee. As General McClellan, the commander-in-chief, was ill at the time, the President directed him to confer with Major-General Halleck, in command in Missouri, with regard to the concerted action of their armies.* In compliance, he addressed, January 3d, a lengthy communication to General Halleck, giving estimates of Johnston's forces, at different points on his defensive line, and suggesting a plan for the co-operation of their armies very nearly similar to the one whose execution subsequently resulted in the capture of Forts Henry and Donelson, and the evacuation of Bowling Green, Nashville, and Columbus. His plan proposed an advance upon Nashville, through Kentucky, strong demonstrations against the flanks of Johnston's line, Bowling Green and Columbus, to issue in real attacks should Johnston weaken these points to strengthen others, and the ascent of twenty thousand men on the Tennessee and Cumberland rivers, under convoy of gunboats. On the 6th, General Halleck replied, that such was the demand for troops in Southwestern Missouri, that he would have but ten thousand men to form a movable column, and objected to the proposed plan as contemplating operations on exterior lines, but offered to make a demonstration from Paducah, toward Columbus, and expressed the hope that in a few weeks he could render material assistance.

As General Halleck proposed no definite co-operation, and as General Thomas' movement against Zollicoffer was pend-

---

* General Buell's statement before the military commission.

ing, General Buell was restricted to operations in his own department, and to thoughts of aggression with his own forces. He had not decided upon his first step in offense, when the victory of General Thomas at Mill Springs, over Generals Crittenden and Zollicoffer, resulted in the complete dispersion of their army. This victory, on the one hand, opened the way for the expedition into East Tennessee, as there was no longer a strong guard to the mountain fortress at Cumberland Gap and the contiguous passes, and rendered more inviting the movement upon Nashville, as it deprived Johnston's right flank of a heavy supporting column. But the failure of co-operation between Generals Halleck and Buell, induced the President and General McClellan to express to the latter their conviction that the so long-meditated movement into East Tennessee was of primary importance, and he again addressed himself to preparation to push an army, under General Thomas, in that direction.

Carter's brigade, accompanied by Wetmore's battery, was at once advanced from Somerset to London, and efforts were made to repair the roads and accumulate supplies and transportation. But again progress was slow; and on February 1st, General Buell advised the general-in-chief that he deemed the enterprise impracticable, and that he would abandon it and advance against Nashville. The fact that he had a day or two previous been advised by General Halleck that he had ordered an advance against Fort Henry, was doubtless a strong incentive to change the direction of his offensive operations, as the first step in his own plan was now upon trial. General Halleck gave no information as to his plans, and did not solicit co-operation. Nevertheless, General Buell determined that, unless restricted by orders from Washington, he would at least accomplish what he had prescribed for himself in his own plan, although the initial movement of it had been undertaken by another, and in every way that was possible contribute to the success of the aggression on the Tennessee river. He therefore disposed the greater portion of his troops for the advance upon Bowling Green, and sent Colonel Cruft's brigade and eight new regiments to join the column moving against Fort Henry. Having learned soon after that this fort had surrendered to Commodore Foote, and that the works at Fort Donelson had been greatly strengthened and its garrison largely reinforced, and fearing that his advance upon Bowling Green could not be sufficiently rapid to prevent such further reinforcements as would endanger the success of the effort to reduce it, he directed three divisions toward Fort Donelson, by water, and three toward Bowling Green. This force was sent to Fort Donelson in response to a request from General Halleck for aid and co-operation. The wisdom of General Buell's original plan was now apparent, though in consequence of its initiation on the rivers without the suggested co-ordinate movement, the enemy had thrown the largest portion of his forces from Bowling Green to Fort Donelson, instead of offering his main resistance at the former place, as General Buell anticipated in the event of his own advance simultaneously with General Halleck's column, as he had suggested.

Fort Henry was surrendered on the 6th of February. General Grant disposed his troops before Fort Donelson on the 12th. When the former fell, the latter was weak; but during the six intervening days, General Johnston had sent sixteen thousand men from Bowling Green, and when they arrived, the forces within the intrenchments were superior to those assuming a beleaguering attitude under General Grant. General Buell's forethought made provision for this emergency, as the troops that he had sent without solicitation from General Halleck, reached General Grant, with the fleet of gunboats under Commodore Foote, on the 14th. Had not General Buell sent these troops before he had been requested to do so, the issue at Donelson might have been very different, as with their efficient aid, success was at one time doubtful in the extreme.

With a strange lack of forecast and provision for probable contingencies, the Confederate general, Floyd, in chief command of the forces in the fort, had allowed General Grant's investing lines to close the roads leading to Nashville. Hardly had this been done before it dawned upon Floyd and his subordinates, Pillow and Buckner, that their safety lay in opening these only avenues of escape. Urged by this conviction, they made a bold and well-sustained effort, early in the morning of the 15th, to accomplish this paramount object. A heavy line of troops, with a similar one in near support, was hurled against the right of General Grant's line, resting upon the coveted roads. After a somewhat protracted and very fierce conflict, the right of the investing line was doubled upon the center, and the enemy was in possession of the roads. During this conflict, General Grant was with Commodore Foote on the gunboats, and upon his return he found his right wing in disorder. The enemy had been partially repulsed by Colonel Cruft's brigade of General Lewis Wallace's division, which had been improvised at Paducah, and mainly formed from the troops that General Buell had sent. Colonel Cruft had been thrown into the action by General Wallace, in response to the request of General McClernand, whose division was holding the right of the line. He maintained his position after all the troops on his right and left had fallen back, and he was then ordered to withdraw his command and occupy the slope of a hill to the rear. Here he was again heavily engaged, and though twice repulsing the enemy in his front, was forced to retire to a new line. Colonel Thayer's brigade of the same division was severely engaged also, and arrested the success of the enemy to the left of Cruft. The action of these brigades was essential to a reformation of the shattered troops. Later in the day, Cruft's brigade, in co-operation with two regiments, the Eighth Missouri and Eleventh Indiana, under command of Colonel M. L. Smith of the former, supported by other regiments from Wallace's division, by a gallant charge, under orders from General Grant, drove back the enemy into his intrenchments and reclosed the roads. Troops from McClernand's division advanced in support on their left, but their action in restoring the investment on the right had marked prominence. This success, coupled with the more decisive issue of General Smith's assault on the enemy's works on the left, was decisive of the general contest. For the next day, after the responsibility and disgrace of capitulation had been transferred from Floyd to Pillow, and from Pillow to Buckner, the latter reluctantly surrendered without conditions.

The primal success of the enemy in the morning really opened the roads for escape, but the hope of complete victory led the generals away from this first object and wrought their ruin.

The loss of this fort, commanding the navigation of the Cumberland river, and the surrender of a large army, except as the result of blundering management on the part of the generals in immediate command, puts under condemnation General Johnston's division of his forces. When, however, he resolved "to defend Nashville at Donelson," it is not probable that the loss of the greater portion of the army set for its defense, was regarded by him as a possibility. He doubtless anticipated the reunion of the sundered portions of his army, even if the larger one could not successfully defend the fort. The two fractions were each on interior lines, with respect to both Grant and Buell, and there were fewer contingencies to bar conjunction than there were to jeopard his whole army in the event of concentration against either. There had been no recent period when he could have safely assumed the offensive in any direction, and he had done well to make such impression of strength upon the generals opposed to him, as to prevent an attack by General Buell alone, or a combination of the armies of Grant and Buell, long before practicable. Neither General Johnston, nor General Buckner in previous command, had ever had such strength as warranted an offensive movement in force. When Buckner first occupied Bowling Green, after his pretentious but feeble movement upon Louisville, he had only four thousand men. By the 15th of October, there were about twelve thousand Confederate troops at that place, with no further increase until December. The highest number reported by the Confederate generals upon their defensive line, from Mill Springs to Columbus, was thirty-seven thousand. General Johnston, therefore, had been from the first too weak to attack Buell, and during the later months of the year too weak to resist him. In concentration, he would have been stronger than Grant, but General Grant had been beyond his reach, seated behind the Ohio river, upon whose waters a fleet of gunboats steamed in proud mastery. Besides, an advance against Grant would have uncovered Nashville to Buell.

There were objections quite as strong against concentrating against Buell, who had an army sufficiently large to overwhelm him, in offense or defense, and the withdrawal of all his river forces to Buell's front would have left them and Nashville at the mercy of Grant. Thus, as he had been too weak to concentrate for offense against either of his antagonists, he could offer only feeble resistance to both combined. And in view of actual events, the withdrawal of all his forces to a new line, when he saw the two armies converging upon him, would have been his safest course. The fact that he abandoned Bowling Green the very day that Grant appeared before Donelson, shows that he had no thought of resisting Buell at that point after he had sent away sixteen thousand men. And when, as he neared Nashville, he learned that Fort Donelson had fallen with its large garrison into the hands of General Grant, he ordered the evacuation of Columbus, and passing through the capital of Tennessee, he sought a new line and the heaviest possible concentration far to the South, in hope to regain what was then so plainly lost. Not being pursued beyond Nashville, he stopped for a time at Murfreesboro to gather together the troops that had held Bowling Green, Clarksville, and Nashville, the few that had escaped from Fort Donelson before the surrender, and those that had been collected from the dispersion at Mill Springs.

The victory at Mill Springs, the capture of Forts Henry and Donelson, and the enforced evacuation of Bowling Green, Columbus, and Nashville, form a series of successes, which gave the first marked prestige to the national arms, and in no small degree revealed the power of the national government to suppress the rebellion. The significance of these victories produced a profound impression in the South. To the more thoughtful, it suggested the possibility, if not the probability, of the ultimate failure of their cause. The frenzied dismay of the citizens of Nashville at the fall of Donelson, and the indefinite southward retreat of the legions which had so long stood between them and the national armies, was only the complex feeling of disappointment and discouragement which pervaded the Southern people, finding expression even in official utterances from Richmond. From the inception of the struggle, the Southerners had been exceedingly hopeful. The more intelligent could not have expected uniform success, but the masses anticipated the independence of the States Confederate in rebellion, as the result of a succession of victories. The issue of the first great battle of the war intensified this hopefulness. The disorderly retreat of the Army of the Potomac from Bull Run was jubilantly hailed as the typical issue of all succeeding battles. But, now, a succession of alarming disasters and defeats had made evident the realities and the possibilities of the gigantic struggle, which the South had so madly and so hopefully invoked—the national armies were now to be feared, whether in open battle or before intrenched positions. And their sweep far southward, with serried ranks and boldest step, while producing intense disappointments and dread, must have suggested, at least to sober minds, that the independence of the South was by no means assured.

In the North, the results of the first great central campaign were cheering in the extreme. The defeat at Bull Run had produced mortification and depression, and the useless sacrifice of life at Ball's Bluff had brought sadness to all loyal hearts. And hitherto, success and defeat had been so nearly balanced in the West, that the outlook had given no special promise. But, with this experience of positive disaster and uncertain prospects, there came a clearer discernment of the character of the conflict, and while there was less hope than at first of its speedy termination, the loyal people gave persistent support to war measures of gigantic compass. The importance, then, of these first great victories can not be measured by the mere capture of forts, cities, prisoners, and munitions, but by their inspiring moral effect as contrasted with the consequences of disasters of equal range. In a war of such proportions, involving so many occult causes of success and failure, ruling influences and events may not always be determined with positive certainty; but in searching for pivotal events, the philosophical historian would not be likely to

overlook the conduct and issues of the campaign which culminated so gloriously at Donelson.

CHAPTER X.

ADVANCE OF THE ARMY OF THE OHIO FROM NASHVILLE TO SA-
VANNAH, AND THE BATTLE OF SHILOH.

THE occupation of Nashville by the Army of the Ohio, and
of other strategic positions by the army under General Halleck, at that season of the year which invites military enterprise and the manifest urgency of renewed aggression before
the enemy could recover from recent defeats, forbade delay in
the formation of plans for new operations. General Johnston
had been hurled from his first chosen defensive line, and the
configuration of the region to which his standards pointed,
gave unerring indication of the location of his second. Mountains, rivers, and railroads determine the grand strategic points
and lines of defense equally with those of aggressive maneuver and supply, and palpable military possibilities gave
prophecy of the concentration of the western insurgent forces
at Corinth, Mississippi. Here the Memphis and Charleston
and the Ohio and Mobile railroads intersect, and thus form a
railroad center which sustains relations to the Mississippi and
Tennessee rivers and the railroad system of the South, especially with the great road connecting these rivers and Richmond, Virginia. Hence, this position was regarded by the
enemy as sustaining important relations to all proximate and
remote military operations, and as had been anticipated by
the generals in command of the Western national armies, all
the insurgent forces were speedily put in motion thither, as
the grand key-point east of the Mississippi in the solution of
their paramount Western problem—the maintenance of the
mastery of the lower portion of the Mississippi river.

In the preceding campaign, General Johnston had been

forced into error by public opinion in the South, in holding a long line against vastly superior armies, and now it became evident that aggression and resistance by the enemy was to be conducted with massed forces.

This attitude of the enemy demanded the intimate co-operation, if not the actual consolidation of the armies commanded by Generals Halleck and Buell. While their fields of operation were distinct, it was perhaps appropriate that these commanders should sustain a common relation to the chief at Washington. But now a common objective required that the two armies should be united under one field commander. The necessity of co-operation had previously existed, and there had been partial concurrence in their operations on the Cumberland river. Perceiving the necessity of the still closer union of their armies to meet the palpable concentration of the insurgent forces, Generals Halleck and Buell agreed upon a plan of operations early in March, whose execution would require their close association; and Savannah, on the east or right bank of the Tennessee river, had been designated as the point for concentration. So important an object was not, however, left to the voluntary agreement of the two generals, but was enforced by the President's war order No. 3, which consolidated three Western departments in one, under the command of Major-General Halleck, and threw upon him the responsibility for general results flowing from the various operations of the vast forces and resources in the West. General Halleck at once ordered General Buell to march his army to Savannah—a movement for which provision had been made in the plan of co-operation previously agreed upon.

At this juncture the Army of the Ohio comprised ninety-two regiments of infantry—exclusive of those which had been sent to General Halleck—with an aggregate of seventy-nine thousand three hundred and thirty-four men; eleven regiments, one battalion, and seven detached companies of cavalry, aggregating eleven thousand four hundred and ninety-six men; and twenty-eight field and two siege batteries, with three thousand nine hundred and thirty-five men. The grand total was ninety-four thousand seven hundred and eighty-three men.   Of this aggregate, seventy-three thousand four hundred and seventy-two men were in condition for the field, comprising sixty thousand eight hundred and eighty-two infantry, nine thousand two hundred and thirty-seven cavalry, and three thousand three hundred and sixty-eight artillery.

The First, Second, Fourth, Fifth, and Sixth divisions, commanded respectively by Brigadier-Generals Thomas, McCook, Nelson, Crittenden, and Wood, with a contingent force of cavalry, in all thirty-seven thousand effective men, constituted the main army, which, under the personal command of General Buell, was to join General Halleck in the projected movement against the enemy at Corinth, Mississippi.   The remaining thirty-six thousand effective troops were disposed by General Buell for the defense of his communications, the enforcement of quietness within his lines in Kentucky and Tennessee, and for two expeditions co-operative with the ruling movement— one, under General Morgan, to seize Cumberland Gap, and the other, under General O. M. Mitchell, to strike the Memphis and Charleston railroad south of Nashville.

Before starting to Savannah, General Buell organized the Seventh division of his army, and assigned Brigadier-General G. W. Morgan to its command.   This division comprised the troops under General Carter, at Cumberland Ford; the Eighteenth brigade, recently withdrawn from Eastern Kentucky, and several additional regiments which had been posted at various points in Kentucky.   General Morgan was instructed to operate against Cumberland Gap, and occupy East Tennessee, in the event of an open way thither; and should the offensive be impracticable, to hold the enemy in check.   Brigadier-General O. M. Mitchell, with his division, was ordered to move upon the " Memphis and Charleston " railroad through Murfreesboro and Fayetteville.   The Sixteenth brigade, Brigadier-General W. T. Ward commanding, was posted at the camp of instruction at Bardstown, Kentucky.   Brigadier-General Dumont was placed in command of the garrison at Nashville.   Colonel Duffield, in command of the Twenty-third brigade, including the Ninth Michigan, Third Minnesota, and Eighth and Twenty-third Kentucky regiments, was ordered from Kentucky to take post at Murfreesboro, Tennessee, to protect the road from Shelbyville to Lavergne, and reinforce either General Buell or General Mitchell, as circumstances might require. General Boyle's brigade, the Eleventh, composed of the Third, Ninth, Thirteenth and Twenty-first Kentucky, and the Nineteenth and Fifty-ninth Ohio regiments, and the Sixth Ohio battery, was assigned to General Crittenden's division; and Colonel Bruce's brigade, the Twenty-second, comprising the First, Second, and Twentieth Kentucky regiments, was attached to General Nelson's.

Having thrown forward a detachment of cavalry, to save, if possible, the bridges between Nashville and Columbia, on the 15th of March,* General Buell put McCook's division on the road in their rear, as the head of his infantry column. The Fourth, Fifth, Sixth, and First divisions, in the order mentioned, followed at intervals between the 15th and 20th. The cavalry saved all the bridges, except those over Rutherford's creek, four miles north of Columbia, and over Duck river at that place. Rutherford's creek was soon crossed, but the water in Duck river being forty feet deep, a somewhat protracted delay was unavoidable.

General Buell had no pontoons, and he was forced to take time to build a bridge or wait for the subsidence of the water. As the reduction of the water to a fordable stage involved an indefinite waiting, Johnson's brigade of McCook's division was employed in the construction of a bridge. But though the Thirty-second Indiana regiment was composed largely of mechanics, and the whole brigade worked energetically, the bridge was not completed until the 29th. At a later period of the war, when there were organized "mechanics and engineers," and every army commander regarded pontoon trains as essential as those for supply, the high water in Duck river would have hardly caused a halt; but as General Buell was situated, it was a serious matter to pass this river with his army and trains. As his delay at this point has such historical significance, the truth requires that this embarrassment should thus be mentioned, in connection with the fact that he was

---

* This was previous to the reception of an order from General Halleck to make the movement.

not under orders to hasten his march to Savannah. He had supposed that General Grant's army was on the east bank of the Tennessee river, as the place designated for the conjunction of the two armies was on that bank; and when on the march, he learned first that General Grant's forces were on the west bank, he was assured that there was security for them in the natural strength of their position.

General Halleck's original object in sending a column up the Tennessee by steamers, was to destroy the railroad connections at Corinth, Jackson, and Humboldt, and this expedition, at first, had no recognized relation to the subsequent union of the armies of the Ohio and Tennessee. This enterprise, under the direction of General C. F. Smith, was a failure, in consequence of the lateness of its inauguration, as the enemy's strength at the objective points was such as to preclude all effort to reach the railroad at either of them. After abandoning the object of his expedition, General Smith steamed down the river, and debarked his forces at Pittsburg Landing. General Smith did not select this point as one for the concentration of the two armies to move against Corinth, as he was at the time ignorant of any such purpose. Subsequently, when reinforcements were moved up the river with a view to the conjunction of the armies under Generals Grant and Buell for offense against Corinth, under the immediate command of General Halleck, they in great part took position at Pittsburg Landing. Thus, without General Buell's knowledge, the place of concentration was changed, and he was left to learn the fact while on the march.

When, before the bridge at Columbia was fully completed, it was ascertained that General Grant's army was on the west bank of the Tennessee river, General Nelson sought permission from General Buell to ford the stream, and move rapidly to Savannah. Though not fully sympathizing with his excitable division commander in his fear that the enemy would attack General Grant before the reinforcing army could reach him, General Buell gave him promise that, could he get his men safely over the stream, with his trains, and all his artillery and baggage, he should have the advance thenceforward to the Tennessee river. This fact, exceedingly trifling in itself, had significance of intensest interest and greatest moment. It gave the impetuous Nelson the head of Buell's army, whose speed in the advance, rapid beyond expectation and the requirement of orders, brought his division to Savannah the day before the battle of "Shiloh," or "Pittsburg Landing."

At 6 A. M. March 29th, Nelson's division, Ammen's brigade leading, plunged into Duck river, and following the tortuous ford, reached the opposite bank and the head of the army. The bridge was completed the same day, and the immediate resumption of the march was resumed. On the 31st, with an interval of six miles from the head of each division and the one following, to give room for troops, artillery, and trains, the Army of the Ohio moved toward Savannah. Only one route was practicable, a single narrow roadway, in poor condition for the ordinary travel of a sparsely inhabited region, and six miles was deemed requisite as the length of each division in unembarrassed movement. This road led through Mount Pleasant and Waynesboro, and General Nelson, passing beyond the latter place earlier than had been anticipated by General Buell, defeated the adoption of a measure that would have prevented the participation of the Army of the Ohio in the battle of "Shiloh." General Buell had not yet received an intimation that General Grant was in any danger, or that there was need of haste in the movement of his army, and desiring to have his forces in good shape to meet a comrade army, obtained permission from General Halleck to stop for rest at Waynesboro. The army commander had also under consideration the propriety of moving to Hamburg, above Pittsburg Landing, and thence to place of conjunction. Stronger evidence could not be adduced than this project of stopping at Waynesboro, that neither General Halleck nor General Buell, at this time, thought that there was anything actual, probable, or possible, in the situation at Pittsburg Landing, to demand the hurried advance of the Army of the Ohio. But General Nelson, ignorant of this proposal to halt at Waynesboro, and alive to the probability of an early attack upon General Grant, hurried through the place for rest and trimming up for a handsome introduction to the Army of the Tennessee, and by sweeping impetuously on the road to

Savannah, he both defeated the deflection toward Hamburg and the halt at Waynesboro; for before General Buell thought it necessary to give orders to Nelson, other divisions, to which the speed of the first had been communicated, were also beyond Waynesboro, and could not then be recalled.

That General Grant felt secure at this time is equally manifest. Telegraphic communications between him and Nelson were established on the 3d of April. The latter telegraphed that he could be at Savannah with his division on the 5th. On the 4th, General Grant* replied that he need not hasten his march, as transports to convey him to Pittsburg Landing would not be ready before the 8th. Nevertheless, Nelson hastened on, and it was well he did, for he gave motion to the whole army behind him, and General Johnston was even then on the march from Corinth, with his entire army, to crush General Grant before General Buell could give him assistance.

During the 4th and 5th, the rain fell continuously, the country was broken and the roads bad; but Nelson's division, by brigades, reached Savannah during the 5th, and Crittenden's division encamped at night a few miles distant. General Buell also reached Savannah on the 5th, but did not communicate with General Grant, as the latter had previously made an appointment for a meeting on the 6th.

A variety of facts support the assumption that neither General Halleck, General Grant, nor the division commanders on the field beyond Pittsburg Landing, had the remotest expectation that the enemy would advance in offense from Corinth with full strength. General Halleck proposed to command the united armies in their advance upon Corinth, and yet he was not to leave his headquarters at St. Louis, Missouri, until the 7th. On the 5th, General Sherman, though not the senior division commander, yet virtually so, from the confidence reposed in him by General Grant, telegraphed to the latter: "All is quiet along my lines now; the enemy has cavalry in our

---

* This fact has been asserted by General Buell in several papers published since the war. He has been equally explicit in declaring his ignorance of the establishment of the Army of the Tennessee, at Pittsburg Landing, instead of Savannah, until he reached Columbia, although he had inquired particularly of General Halleck.

front, and I think there are two regiments and one battery six miles out." Again: "I have no doubt that nothing will occur to-day more than some picket firing. The enemy is saucy, but got the worst of it yesterday, and will not press our pickets far. I will not be drawn out far, unless with the certainty of advantage, and I do not apprehend anything like an attack upon our position." General Grant telegraphed the same day as follows: "The main force of the enemy is at Corinth, with troops at different points east." "The number of men at Corinth, and within supporting distance of it, can not be far from eighty thousand men." "Some skirmishing took place between our outguards and the enemy's, yesterday and the day before." "I have scarcely the faintest idea of an attack (general one) being made upon us, but will be prepared, should such a thing take place." "It is my present intention to send them (Buell's three foremost divisions) to Hamburg, some four miles above Pittsburg, when they all get here."

It has been claimed, and doubtless with truth, that the position of General Grant's army before Pittsburg Landing was an exceedingly eligible one. Its surface was broken, and it was flanked on right and left by creeks that, in a great measure, forbade turning movements. But the location of the several divisions on the field did not indicate the expectation of a defensive battle more clearly than did the utterances of the commanders. General Sherman, with two brigades of his division, held the advance position near Shiloh Meeting-house, on the main road to Corinth. One of his brigades was on the right, guarding the bridge on the Purdy road over Owl creek; another was on the extreme left, guarding the ford of Lick creek, on the Hamburg road. General McClernand's division was in the rear of General Sherman; General Prentiss' division was between the direct, or right road to Corinth, and the brigade on the extreme left; and the two divisions of Generals Hurlbut and C. F. Smith, General W. H. L. Wallace commanding the latter, were near Pittsburg Landing, two or three miles in the rear. These divisions had thus their camps mainly on the roads leading toward the enemy's position at Corinth. They were widely separated, and did not sustain such relations to each other that it was possible to form quickly a connected defensive line; they had no defenses and no designated line for defense in the event of a sudden attack, and there was no general on the field to take, by special authority, the command of the whole force in an emergency.

While the national army was unprepared for battle, and unexpectant of such an event, and was passing the night of the 5th in fancied security, Johnston's army of forty thousand men was in close proximity, and ready for the bloody revelation of its presence and purpose on the following morning. General Johnston was already a day later, in attaining position for attack, than he had anticipated, and this loss of a day had brought the Army of the Ohio one day's march nearer to the conjunction with General Grant, to prevent which was the object of his advance. Usually the indications of approaching battle are so palpable that the men in the ranks, as well as officers of all grades, foresee the deadly struggle and nerve themselves to meet it. But in this case the nearness of the enemy in force was not known in the national army, and there was no special preparation for the conflict.

Early in the morning of the 6th of April, 1862, a Sabbath day of unusual brightness, cannonading in the direction of Pittsburg Landing was distinctly heard at Savannah. General Grant supposed that it indicated an attack upon his most advanced positions, and not waiting to meet General Buell as he had appointed, and not leaving any instructions or suggestions for his guidance in moving his army to the field, or even expressing a desire that he should give him support, he gave an order to General Nelson to march his division up to Pittsburg Landing, and taking a steamer, hastened toward the noise of battle. He did, however, advise General Buell, by note, that an attack had been made, whose occurrence he had not anticipated before Monday or Tuesday; apologized for not meeting him as he had contemplated, and mentioned the fact that he had ordered General Nelson to move with his division "to opposite Pittsburg Landing." The omission to request him to take any other divisions to the field, or even to hasten their march to Savannah, must be accepted as conclusive that General Grant did not at the time anticipate such a battle as would require the assistance of other portions of the

Army of the Ohio. General Buell was thus left free to manage his army; but being without any knowledge of roads, and having no steamers for his troops, he could do little, except to dispatch orders to the rear to hasten forward his nearest divisions—Crittenden's and McCook's. As the day wore on, the noise from the front more and more plainly indicated that a general engagement was progressing, and General Buell, to learn the true condition of affairs and procure transportation for his forces, seized a small boat and steamed up the river. He subsequently received a note from General Grant, addressed to the " commanding officer, advance forces, near Pittsburg, Tennessee," advising him that his forces had been engaged since early morning contending against an army estimated at a hundred thousand men, and that the introduction of fresh troops upon the field would inspire his men and dishearten the enemy.

As General Grant had mentioned in his instructions to General Nelson that he could obtain a guide at Savannah, the latter at once instituted a search for one. Failing in this, he sent Captain Kendrick of his staff, to discover, if possible, a practicable route to the battle-field. During the absence of this officer, the certainty of a general battle became manifest, increasing the anxiety of those who were so near and yet unable to reach the field. Incited by the distant cannonading, the nearest divisions pressed forward rapidly, the roads having been cleared of trains by General Buell's order, that the march of three additional divisions should be unimpeded.

About noon, Captain Kendrick returned, and reported that the road nearest the river was impracticable, on account of the overflow, but that the second was practicable for infantry and cavalry, but not for artillery and trains. By this time a guide had been secured, and the division was soon in rapid motion. As the battle-field was approached, the character of the conflict and its issues became apparent. The artillery, at work on the bluff above the landing, indicated the nearness of the foe, and the louder roar of cannon up the river, gave proof that the gunboats were battering the flank of the enemy, while the masses of fugitives, huddled in terror under the river bank, spoke plainly of broken lines and general demoralization. Moving steadily to the field through these proofs of disaster, Nelson's troops gave evidence of thorough discipline and courage. The rear of an army in successful action is often depressing to those going to the front, but such a scene as Pittsburg Landing presented at 5 P. M., when Nelson succeeded in crossing Ammen's brigade, was enough to appall the stoutest hearts. This brigade went into action at once, on the left of Grant's line, at the very crisis of the final effort of the enemy to break through to the river. It formed under the eye of General Buell, and upon ground of his selection. A short time previous, General Bragg, on the right of the line, had hurled his command against General Grant's left, upon whose stability rested the safety of his army. Bragg had partially succeeded, when two regiments of Ammen's brigade, the Sixth Ohio and Thirty-sixth Indiana, moved into position near a battery, then entirely without support. The enemy no doubt had anticipated a complete victory as the result of Bragg's assault. To gain the landing, it was only necessary to press back Grant's left flank one-eighth of a mile. This accomplished, and the position would have been no longer tenable. Fortunately, the ground was favorable for defense. It was very uneven, and through it extended a deep ravine, full of back water from the river. Near the river, this ravine was very deep, and barred attack on the extremity of the line. Thus, the ground placed Bragg at disadvantage, while the gunboats, fresh troops, and the persistent resistance of Hurlbut's division, effected his repulse, and the maintenance of the left saved the army. The night falling soon after this repulse, the fighting ceased, and both armies rested on their arms, with the consciousness that the conflict was to be renewed on the morrow. Having rendered efficient service during the later hours of the day, throughout the night the gunboats Tyler and Lexington threw their heavy shells, at regular intervals, into the lines of the enemy, whose roar and the heavy rain deprived the weary soldiers of both armies of needed rest.

The Army of the Tennessee had fought at great disadvantage from the fact that it had been attacked before it could be well formed, and the isolated divisions and brigades had been well enveloped before support could be rendered. But though roughly handled by the enemy, barring the immense number of fugitives, it had fought with great gallantry and persistence. At the close of the day, with thinned ranks and broken organizations, it held a short line round the hill, upon whose summit had been placed the heavy guns intended for offensive purpose, but at last essential to defense. General Sherman said, officially of his command, that " it had become of a mixed character." His central brigades had been attacked very early in the morning, and though other troops in the advanced positions had become vigorously engaged, it was not until about 8 A. M. that he " became satisfied for the first time that the enemy designed a determined attack on the whole camp." The divisions were hurried to the front, and throughout a day of hardest fighting all the divisions had been driven back from point to point, and all had been shattered. Nearly all of Prentiss' division, not killed or wounded, had been captured. General H. W. L. Wallace had been mortally wounded, and his division had become fragmentary. The divisions of McClernand and Hurlbut had maintained greater compactness, but had lost heavily. But the last line of the Army of the Tennessee before Pittsburg Landing was a demonstration of the unaccomplished purpose of the enemy.

Each army was yet hopeful of final victory. The success of the enemy warranted the hope of further advantage, and he had not heard of the presence of a portion of Buell's army on the field, and the proximity of such other portions as would on the morrow change essentially the conditions of the conflict.

General Beauregard, who had succeeded to supreme command after the fall of General Johnston, about 2 P. M. the previous day, jubilant over the palpable advantages gained, and assured of complete victory, sent such dispatches to Richmond as to evoke from Mr. Davis a message of congratulation to the Confederate congress, asserting the total defeat and rout of General Grant's army.

Late in the evening, General Nelson succeeded in crossing the remainder of his division, and during the night Crittenden's division reached the field on transports, which had been sent to Savannah at the request of General Buell, when he first met General Grant. McCook's division, by a forced march, reached Savannah late in the evening, and finding that no provision had been especially made for the transportation of his men, General McCook impressed boats as they touched the shore. It was known that this was the last division from the Army of the Ohio that could reach the field in time for the battle of the next day. But a fourth fresh division of General Grant's army, commanded by General L. Wallace, arrived at night from Crump's Landing. General Buell examined the ground in front of General Grant's line, and selected positions for his divisions, and gave directions for their formation. No regularly defined plan of battle was agreed upon between the army commanders. There was simply an understanding that they would assume the offensive the next morning, and that the Army of the Ohio should take the left of the field. The battle-field is an undulating table-land of very considerable elevation, breaking into ravines along the Tennessee river, and bounded on the south and west by Lick creek and Owl creek, which have sources in proximity, but in their divergence compass a wide space, mostly wooded, but only here and there so densely as to embarrass the movement of troops. Small farms and cultivated fields occasionally broke the continuity of the forest, but rather gave variety to the scene than suggested special dispositions of troops.

General Buell first formed General Nelson's division next to the river as the left of the battle front, and General Grant assigned Wallace's first division to the right flank near Snake creek, below the mouth of Owl creek. Between these extremes the remaining forces were formed—Crittenden's division on the right of Nelson's, with a space for McCook's on his right when it should arrive, and on the right of the position for this division the troops engaged the day previous, somewhat refreshed, extended the line to Wallace's left.

At 5 A. M. Nelson's division was formed in line of battle, without artillery or reserves, and moved forward. The skirmishers soon met the enemy's pickets and drove them rapidly for nearly a mile, too far for the security of his right, as Crittenden's division was yet some distance behind. Nelson was therefore halted, by General Buell's order, that Crittenden might advance abreast. This done, the two divisions moved forward again with a strong line of skirmishers in front and on the left flank. Nelson soon encountered the enemy in such force as not only to check him, but to force his slow retirement. His need of artillery* was extreme, and Mendenhall's regular battery from Crittenden's division was sent to his support, whose well-directed fire deterred the enemy from further advance.

The character of Nelson's onset revealed to General Beauregard the presence of reinforcements to General Grant. He says in his report of the battle, that " at 6 A. M. a hot fire of musketry and artillery opened from the enemy's quarter on his advanced line, assured me of the junction of his forces, and soon the battle raged with a fury which satisfied me that I was attacked by a largely superior force." The presence of Buell was indeed the prophecy of his defeat, as from the first, the enemy's assurance of victory was contingent upon the failure of the Army of the Ohio to reach the field during the conflict. This state of things, though dreaded previously, was unexpected, as he had received the night previous a special dispatch " that delay had been encountered by General Buell in his march from Columbia, and that his main forces therefore could not reach the field of battle in time to save General Grant's shattered fugitive forces from capture or destruction on the following day."† With this hope he had disposed his forces, the evening previous, for a renewal of the conflict. There had been fearful disorganization in his own army during the previous day. Many of his troops were fugitives in the rear, and added to the usual causes of disorder in desperate battle, there had been an overmastering temptation to many of his troops to straggle, to gather the rich spoils of the captured camps of five divisions. But notwithstanding this depletion of his army, from these causes and the severer casualties of deadly conflict, and the disappoinment of not

---

* His own was at Savannah.
† Quoted from his official report.

having crushed Grant before Buell could join him, he still
fought them both with such determination and persistence as
are usually born of hope.

At the time that the recession of Nelson's line was arrested,
McCook's foremost brigade, Rousseau's, moved into position
on the right of Crittenden.   This brigade extended the line,
but Rousseau's flank was for a time as much exposed as Crittenden's had been, as there was still a wide space between the
two armies.   Before, however, the enemy could take advantage of this exposure, Kirk's brigade reached the field and was
placed in reserve on the right flank.   Each brigade of Buell's
army was now required to furnish its own reserves, while
Boyle's brigade of Crittenden's division was designated as a
general reserve, and was so placed as to be facile of movement
whenever there should be need of support.   General Buell
also availed himself of the fragmentary forces of the Army of
the Tennessee, found in his rear.

The Army of the Ohio now offered a battle front one mile
and a half long, about half the distance between Nelson's left
and Wallace's right.   The left flank was covered with skirmishers, and was in some degree protected by the roughness
of the ground near the river.   The right had no assured connection with the Army of the Tennessee, but rested in a wood.
To strengthen the right, thus exposed to an enfilading or reverse
fire, Gibson's brigade of McCook's division on coming to the
field was placed in reserve in proximity.   In front of Nelson
was an open field, partially screened by woods, which extended
beyond the enemy's line.   Crittenden's left brigade and
McCook's right were covered by a dense undergrowth, while
in front of their right and left brigades respectively the ground
was open.   The ground, mainly level in front of Nelson, formed
a hollow before Crittenden, which fell into a small creek, passing in front of McCook.   The Hamburg road penetrated
the line near Nelson's left.   The enemy was in heavy force
beyond the open ground in Buell's front, in a line slightly
oblique to his line, having one battery so posted as to command Nelson's left, another to sweep his front and the woods
before Crittenden's left, a third bearing upon the junction
of Crittenden's right and McCook's left, and a fourth in the

immediate front of the latter. Beauregard had massed his forces on his right the evening previous, under General Bragg, to grasp the landing, and in consequence this flank was strong for defense in the morning.

As Nelson's division was well offered to the enemy in this complete formation, it soon became hotly engaged, as the introduction to the general action, from flank to flank. The enemy resisted all attacks most stubbornly, and in turn assaulted boldly and repeatedly with temporary success. In the second effort to advance the national line, Crittenden became most warmly engaged. Hazen's brigade, on Nelson's right, captured, in a charge, the second battery of the enemy, which had been exceedingly annoying. But in this act the brigade was subject to a cross fire of artillery from the adjacent batteries, conjointly with an infantry attack, and was forced back with the loss of the battery and a very large number of men. The enemy followed this advantage and advanced to the front of Crittenden's left, where he was repulsed and hurled back by Smith's brigade. In the meantime, Nelson was pressed by a strong force, with evident intent to turn his left, held by Ammen's brigade. This brigade fought gallantly to maintain a position second to none on the field, but at length began to give ground, and a decided advantage to the enemy seemed inevitable, as Nelson had neither artillery nor infantry to direct to its support, Hazen's brigade having been shattered, and Bruce's being needed in its own position. But the impending disaster was averted by Terrell's regular battery of McCook's division, which, having just arrived from Savannah, dashed into position, and by its rapid and accurate firing silenced the enemy's first battery, which was aiding the infantry force pressing Ammen. Subsequently, the enemy repeated the attack, and endangered both the brigade and Terrell's battery, the latter having lost very many gunners and being without adequate support. In this emergency, the Nineteenth Ohio, from Crittenden's division, and the Second Iowa and Fifteenth Illinois, from the Army of the Tennessee, were sent to Nelson's assistance. This reinforcement permitted the Sixth Ohio to become the special support of Terrell's battery, furnishing gunners in room of those he had lost. The enemy, however, did not at once relax his effort to turn the flank, but was finally forced back.   Then, by a flank attack by Nelson, and a direct one by Crittenden, aided by a concentric fire from the batteries of Mendenhall, Terrell, and Bartlett, he was driven beyond the position of his second and third batteries.   Afterward, the enemy assumed a new position some distance to the rear, and again opened with artillery, but his guns were soon silenced by Mendenhall, and were subsequently captured by Crittenden's division.   These successes decided the contest on the left, and Nelson swung round over the ground which had been lost the day before.

The action in the center of the general line, or the right of Buell's, was not less spirited or decisive than that on the left. The initial attacks, by the extreme divisions of the two armies, had been made almost simultaneously, and the intermediate divisions became involved in turn from both left and right. Thus, McCook followed Crittenden in attacking the enemy. This division met the same stubborn resistance, and made frequent charges.   Rousseau's brigade, having taken an advanced position early in the day, repulsed a charge as its introduction to battle.   It then gave a counter-blow, drove the opposing force some distance, and captured a battery.   The direction of Rousseau's advance left an opening between McCook and Crittenden, which the enemy perceived, and began to mass troops to occupy.   To prevent this, General McCook ordered Colonel Willich, commanding the Thirty-second Indiana, to drive back the enemy, and by the bayonet and bullet this was gallantly accomplished.   The remainder of Gibson's brigade followed Willich, and soon both brigades, Rousseau's and Gibson's, were in hottest conflict.   Willich's regiment at one time became wedged between other forces, and receiving their fire was compelled to withdraw.   This led to confusion, but order was soon restored.   Kirk's brigade reached the field just as Rousseau had exhausted his ammunition, and took his position, that he might replenish.   While Rousseau was absent, Gibson was severely pressed, as the enemy continued his movements to separate Crittenden and McCook.   His left regiment, the Forty-ninth Ohio, was involved in imminent danger and was compelled to change front twice under fire to prevent the turning of the position. Upon the return of Rousseau, his brigade, and two regiments of Hurlbut's division hitherto in reserve, went into line, when General McCook's whole division thus supported, advanced and drove the enemy beyond General Sherman's camps. The last severe fighting was purely defensive on the part of the enemy to hold his main line of retreat and cover his retiring columns.

Just as the fighting ceased, General Wood, with two brigades of his division, arrived, and one of them, Wagner's, joined in pursuit of the enemy. None of the troops followed far, as their extreme fatigue and the approach of darkness prevented. General Thomas' division was still in the rear. Being the last on the march, its approach had been retarded by the trains of the other divisions left on the road.

The losses of each army were heavy. According to official reports, General Grant lost fourteen hundred and thirty-seven killed, five thousand six hundred and seventy-nine wounded, and two thousand nine hundred and thirty-four captured. General Buell lost two hundred and thirty-six killed, one thousand eight hundred and sixteen wounded, and eighty-eight captured. The total loss in the two armies was twelve thousand one hundred and ninety. The enemy lost one thousand seven hundred and twenty-eight killed, eight thousand and twelve wounded, and nine hundred and fifty-seven captured; total, ten thousand six hundred and ninety-seven.

Early the next morning after the battle, Generals Sherman and Wood, with two brigades each, were sent forward by General Grant to discover the position of the enemy, if in position, or to pursue him, if in retreat. The movement was promptly made, and resulted in the discovery that Beauregard had withdrawn his infantry and artillery beyond Lick creek, and had left a large body of cavalry in his rear. General Sherman encountered this force and drove it some distance toward the main army, when he and Wood returned to camp. General Beauregard succeeded in removing the artillery, which he captured on the 6th, but lost guns and munitions on the 7th, and was compelled to leave his severely wounded men in hospitals near the field.

As was common during the war, especially at the beginning, each army commander greatly overestimated the strength of the other. General Beauregard computed General Grant's forces on the 6th, at forty-five thousand, and his reinforcements on the 7th at thirty-three thousand, claiming for himself about forty thousand at the commencement of the battle, and not over twenty thousand on the 7th. While General Grant during the battle, was led to believe that he was fighting one hundred thousand men, giving no other estimate after its conclusion, at least in his official report. He had on the field at the beginning of the battle about thirty-three thousand men, and General Buell gave him the second day about twenty thousand.

General Albert Sidney Johnston, the commander-in-chief of the insurgent forces in the West, died on the field, from a gunshot wound. G. M. Johnson, provisional governor of Kentucky, and General Gladden were mortally wounded, and four other general officers were wounded. General Grant lost but one general, W. H. L. Wallace, temporary commander of General C. F. Smith's division.

The battle of "Shiloh," viewed in reference to the antecedent plans and movements which produced it, the strength and losses of the armies engaged, and the persistent fighting of each, both when flushed with success and hopeless of victory, must be regarded as one of vast results as affecting the general struggle; also, as one unique in type as regards some at least of its prominent features.

The position of the Army of the Tennessee, on the west bank of the Tennessee river, awaiting the coming of the Army of the Ohio, for co-operation in offense against the concentrated forces of the enemy in position in proximity, certainly invited the attack. The invitation was accepted with such tardiness as prevented success. General Johnston did indeed intend to deliver battle on the 5th; but the fact that he did not, or could not as he had planned, proves that his forecast was at fault. General Grant did not anticipate battle before General Buell could join him, especially after he was known to be near, and General Johnston deferred his advance until it was possible for Buell to participate, although he also knew that he was in motion to accomplish this object. Thus this great battle was fought as the result of the mutual misapprehension of the commanding generals of the probabilities and possibilities to each. It was delivered too early for General Grant's plans and those of his chief, and too late for the success of General Johnston. The stern, soldierly character of the great majority of the men of the Army of the Tennessee saved it from overthrow when fighting under conditions of positive disadvantage. The opportune and essential aid of the Army of the Ohio was revealed in the type and issue of the second battle. It was an extraordinary experience in the history of war, that two armies, under separate commanders, should fight a successful battle without definitely recognized relations or specific plan,* each fighting almost alone on the same wide field, and yet each fighting for the other as parts of the same army.

The compact line of the Army of the Ohio, the absence of all stragglers, the space it occupied in the battle front, the way it was handled, and the manner of its fighting from flank to flank, give it a record for discipline and valor in its first great engagement that will not suffer in comparison with that of any other army on any other field of the war. The exact service it rendered on the bloody ground of "Shiloh" can not be a matter of doubt. The official report of General Buell, and those of the division, brigade, and regimental commanders, giving the details of the engagement on the left and center, bring into bold relief the distinguished gallantry and success of each unit, large and small; while the testimony from the officers of the Army of the Tennessee, and even those of the enemy, is equally emphatic. General Sherman used language of strongest compliment in his report. When General Beauregard had despaired of success on his right, and anxious to secure a safe retreat, had massed his forces on the Corinth road, near the "Shiloh Chapel," and having there made such impression upon the line as to threaten the isola-

---

* General Buell states in his official report, that he knew nothing of the position of General Grant's forces, except a few regiments that he put in position with his own troops.

tion of Wallace's division, McCook's division sprang to the front, and General Sherman thus speaks of its action: "Here I saw for the first time the well-ordered and compact Kentucky forces of General Buell, whose soldierly movement at once gave confidence to our newer and less disciplined forces. Here I saw Willich's regiment advanced upon a point of water-oaks and thickets in beautiful style. Then arose the severest musketry fire I ever heard, and lasted some twenty minutes, when the splendid regiment had to fall back." Again: "Willich's regiment had been repulsed, but a whole brigade of McCook's division advanced beautifully deployed, and entered this dreaded wood. I ordered my second brigade, then commanded by Colonel T. Kilby Smith (Colonel Stuart being wounded), to form on its right, and my fourth brigade, Colonel Buckland, on its right, all to advance abreast with this Kentucky brigade before mentioned, which I afterward found to be Rousseau's brigade of McCook's division. I gave personal direction to the twenty-four pounder guns, whose well-directed fire first silenced the enemy's guns to the left, and afterward at the Shiloh Meeting-house. Rousseau's brigade moved in splendid order steadily to the front, sweeping everything before it, and at 4 P. M. we stood upon the ground of our original front line, and the enemy was in full retreat. I directed my reserve brigades to resume at once their original camps. I am now ordered by General Grant to give personal credit where I think it is due, and censure where I think it merited. I concede that General McCook's splendid division from Kentucky drove back the enemy along the Corinth road, which was the great center of the field of battle, and where Beauregard commanded in person, supported by Bragg's, Polk's, and Breckinridge's divisions."

General Wallace, whose division, it will be remembered, held the extreme right, and had driven the enemy's left a great distance, thus speaks of the action of Willich's regiment, in its effect upon his own command, which at the time was in peril of complete isolation, as from the recession of General Sherman's right, his own left was exposed. General Wallace had previously made a most determined effort to turn the enemy's left by changing front by a left wheel, relying

upon the forces on his left for the support of that flank of his
division. But the supporting troops had given way, his own
reserves had been thrown to that flank, and dispositions had
been made to cover his retreat in the event of need. "Fortunately," he states, "before the enemy could avail themselves
of their advantage, some fresh troops dashed against them, and
once more drove them back. For this favor my acknowledg-
ments are especially due to Colonel August Willich and his
famous regiment."

From these statements it appears that while Wallace had
wheeled upon the enemy's flank, and his own left flank was in
peril, that troops from the Army of the Ohio gave it security,
and that consequently General Buell's forces were holding
the whole battle front to the left of the imperiled flank of the
extreme right division of the two armies. General McCook's
division, fighting in view of the two right division commanders of the Army of the Tennessee, deserved all the praise they
generously bestowed, but it was not more deserving than the
other two divisions of the army, Crittenden and Nelson's,
which defeated and routed the whole right of the Confederate
army.

The results of this battle repeated the significance of previous ones—that the war was one of vast proportions, and
that its duration might extend far into the future. At its beginning, hope of its early termination was entertained North
and South, but as it progressed, great battles, whether decisive
or not, seemed only to feed the energy and intensify the ruling
sentiments of the two sections. After "Donelson" the enemy
took position far to the south, to gather strength for a decisive
offensive blow, to restore prestige to his arms, and regain the
vast fertile region of country which he had lost. General
Beauregard had been sent to the West to assist General Johnston in the assumption of the offensive in Kentucky. When
that was impossible, the two generals gathered troops from all
quarters at Corinth. Bragg's veterans from Fort Pickens,
and Polk's forces guarding the Mississippi river at Columbus,
Kentucky, were called thither, and the governors of the States
of Tennessee, Mississippi, Alabama, and Louisiana were invoked for additional forces, that the speedy concentration of

a vast army might assure success. Their first object was to overwhelm General Smith, should he advance from the protection of the gunboats, and the second and greater one was to strike a sudden blow to crush the army under General Grant, in position before Pittsburg Landing, and in the direction of Savannah, before he could be reinforced by General Buell. Perhaps no battle of the war was projected with greater objects than that of "Shiloh." The aims were to crush, first, Grant, then Buell, and then take the offensive throughout the West. But the magnitude of the interests involved, did not find correspondence in the strength of the army gathered at Corinth, and the initial movement of the grand scheme was undertaken too late to succeed. To cover up the total failure of the plan, minor advantages were magnified in the report of General Beauregard, and an adroit apology was given for the withdrawal of the army from the battle-field. The leaders declared themselves satisfied with the result, and the press throughout the South expressed the hopefulness of final triumph which General Beauregard claimed for himself and his defeated army. But beneath this show of hope there must have been the profoundest disappointment. A hopeless defensive at once took the place of a bold aggression, freighted with the grandest anticipated results. "Shiloh" buried hopes which had stronger foundations than any of the admitted expectations of subsequent campaigns and battles. This battle was to the enemy not merely another proof of what "Mill Springs" and "Donelson" had palpably revealed—the persistence and pluck of the national troops—but it was the miscarriage of a new mode of warfare, for the quick destruction of two armies destined for conjunction and co-operation in room of the diffusion of their forces to defend territory. This fact gives broad significance to the issue of the battle of "Shiloh." A grand plan there failed through inadequate resources and comparative feebleness of execution. And failure from either cause, where the possibilities lying beyond initial success were so promising, meant the loss of the cause rather than that of a great battle. But the Northern people, though claiming a victory, measured its scope by the more palpable and immediate results. It was a victory because it was not a crushing defeat. The Confederate army was not so crippled that it could not safely withdraw from the field and enter upon preparations for battle on some other field. It did not therefore appear especially decisive. And this feeling, coupled with the sadness engendered by the multitude of the slain, and the sufferings of the far greater multitude of the wounded, was a heavy offset to the joy which the victory produced.

———

CHAPTER XI.

AFTER the failure of General Beauregard's grand offensive enterprise, the whole South was put upon a strain to prepare to withstand at Corinth the combined armies under General Halleck. Generals Van Dorn and Sterling Price, with their forces, were withdrawn from the scenes of campaigns and battles in the far West. And while these and other troops were concentrating at Corinth, General Beauregard threw forward toward Pittsburg, heavy detachments to resist all ordinary reconnoitering forces, and retard the advance of the national armies.

General Halleck arrived at Pittsburg Landing, April 11th, and lost no time in arranging for a vast concentration of armies to advance against Corinth, prepared for any type of resistance which might be offered. He called to him the divisions of Generals Davis and Asboth, made veteran by battles and marches in Missouri and Arkansas, and the Army of the Mississippi, under General Pope, fresh from its victories at New Madrid and Island No. 10. In the unification of his immense forces, General Halleck designated the grand units, as right wing, center, left wing, reserves, and cavalry, commanded respectively by Major-Generals George H. Thomas, D. C. Buell, John Pope, and J. A. McClernand, and Brigadier-General A. J. Smith. The "Right Wing" comprised four divisions of the Army of the Tennessee, and the First of the Army of the Ohio, under command of Major-General W. T. Sherman, and Brigadier-Generals T. W. Sherman, J. A. Davies, S. H. Hurlbut, and J. J. McKean; the center, the divisions of Brigadier-Generals McCook, Nelson, Crittenden, and Wood,

of the Army of the Ohio ; the left wing, the divisions of Brigadier-Generals E. A. Paine, D. S. Stanley, and S. Hamilton ;
the reserves, the divisions of Major-General L. Wallace and
Brigadier-General H. M. Judah ; and the cavalry division,
under the command of Brigadier-General G. Granger. This
plan of organization gave unity to the whole force without
materially changing the formation of the distinct armies of
which it was composed. Major-General U. S. Grant was announced as second in command.

For the moment, the general struggle was resting upon the
two immense armies concentered in Virginia and on the west
bank of the Tennessee river. Never, during the war, did
heavier masses, in the aggregate, confront each other, than in
the two opposing armies in the East and the two in the West.
The people of the country had not yet entirely given up the
idea that a few great battles would terminate the war, or at
least give such preponderance to one party or the other as to
foreshadow the final result. Hence, at no time before the end
was distinctly in view as contingent upon a single battle or
surrender, did two campaigns focalize more interest or hope
than those before Richmond and Corinth. But in the first
stages of a war, which, from the peculiar causes of its existence,
was not likely to terminate until one of the contending parties
should be exhausted, battles of marked decisiveness were not
probable, and the spring and summer of 1862, seemingly prophetic of decisive conflicts, passed away without materially
changing the relative strength of the warring sections.

General Halleck, though greatly stronger than his adver-
sary, studiously avoided either inviting or provoking a general
engagement, adopting the policy of gradual approaches by
parallels. And step by step, by short advances, fortifying each
new position, he slowly neared his objective. General Beauregard resisted each successive encroachment with greater
stubbornness and stronger forces, but never in such strength as
to precipitate a general battle, as for such an issue he was not
prepared.

On the 3d and 4th of May, General Halleck advanced his
whole line, and repeated this movement on the 7th, 17th, and
28th. These advances always involved heavy skirmishing,

and at times very sharp fighting by strong lines; and the national armies were not always the aggressors. May 9th, General Paine's division, in the advance of the Army of the Mississippi or left wing, was assailed by the enemy in heavy force, at Farmington, Mississippi. Paine was not reinforced, and having fought manfully for several hours, was able to withdraw in safety across Seven Mile creek, to General Pope's main line. Had not reinforcements been forbidden by the commander-in-chief, there might have been a heavy engagement, as the enemy, stimulated by the hope of capturing the isolated division, threw forward strong columns. The same day there was a similar effort, with similar issue, to capture an advanced detachment of McCook's division. The advance of the 17th brought on a spirited combat of respectable proportions on the right. General T. W. Sherman then drove the enemy across Bridge creek, and occupied the ground north of the creek on the Monterey and Corinth road. Whereupon, General Thomas directed General W. T. Sherman to reconnoiter the enemy's left. This movement resulted in driving back that flank some distance, and in a corresponding advance of the whole "Right Wing."

The advance of the 28th met far more opposition than any preceding one. The enemy then attempted to retake a position which had been wrested from him by the right wing, but was repulsed. He also attacked McCook's division in the center of the general line, but was defeated again.

This seeming boldness in aggression was only a feint to cover the retreat of General Beauregard's whole army from Corinth. The near approach of the national lines, now ready for the complete envelopment of his position, made it necessary for him to give battle in some form, retreat, or allow himself to be shut up by a siege. He chose retreat, though it is evident that he did not lightly esteem the advantages of the position which he was compelled to abandon. It was the vaunted "strategic position" of the campaign, but he was unable even in defense to cope with General Halleck's armies, and in leaving it, he hoped that there might be some compensation for its loss, by again changing the theater of the war in the West, and causing the diffusion of the forces in array before him.

The explosions at Corinth, early in the morning of May 30th, revealed General Beauregard's purpose and its accomplishment. For several days he had been sending off his munitions and stores, and during the night of the 29th he had so quietly and secretly withdrawn his army, that his own pickets at post did not know that they had been left, a sacrifice for the safety of their comrades. A reconnoissance verified the supposed significance of the explosions, and the "Left Wing," forty thousand strong, moved at once in pursuit, and General Buell, with McCook's, Crittenden's, and T. W. Sherman's divisions, followed in support. Although the railroad had been seriously damaged at Booneville by Colonel Elliott, in command of cavalry, having passed through Iuka to that point on the 29th, there was no such protracted detention at that place as to enable the pursuing forces to overtake the rear guard of the retreating army. General Beauregard halted at Okolona; the national cavalry, under General Granger, advanced to Baldwin and Guntown, and the campaign was terminated. Thus, Corinth, made historic as the objective of an imposing campaign, fell at last without general engagement or siege.

Soon after, Memphis, and all other points on the Mississippi river above that city, passed to the control of the national forces, and with them another section of the mighty river, as did also the whole region traversed by the "Memphis and Charleston Railroad," to the borders of East Tennessee. The possession of this vast region seemed at first a far greater advantage than it really was. To be utilized, it required a heavy elimination from the offensive strength of the Western armies. The insurgent army was not destroyed, nor even greatly diminished by losses, and hence the absolute strength of the rebellion was not diminished in proportion to the loss of territory. The impression prevailed that this was the case, but the subsequent diffusion of forces to guard it, and the facility with which, in consequence, the enemy first changed the theater of war and then assumed the aggressive to regain it, demonstrated the fact, that at that period of the war, the mere grasp of Southern territory was a waste of strength.

CHAPTER XII.

OPERATIONS OF GENERAL O. M. MITCHELL, GENERAL NEGLEY, GEN-
ERAL G. W. MORGAN, AND COLONEL DUFFIELD, AND THE EXPEDI-
TION TO DESTROY RAILROADS IN GEORGIA.

BRIGADIER-GENERAL O. M. MITCHELL, commanding the Second division, left Nashville about the middle of March and
advanced to Murfreesboro. General Johnston, in retreating
from one place to the other, had destroyed all the bridges to
prevent pursuit, and the repair of these on the railroad first
commanded the attention of General Mitchell. He built
twelve hundred feet of heavy bridges in ten days, when being
relieved at Murfreesboro by the Twenty-third brigade, under
Colonel Duffield, he moved forward to Shelbyville and there
established a depot of supplies. From Shelbyville, he made a
bold and rapid advance through Fayetteville to Huntsville,
Alabama. His van, consisting of Turchin's brigade, Colonel
Kennett's Ohio cavalry, and Captain Simonson's battery, entered Huntsville early in the morning of the 7th of April,
completely surprising the citizens of the town, capturing one
hundred and seventy prisoners, fifteen locomotives, one hundred and fifty passenger and freight cars, and other property
of great value to the enemy. Colonels Sill's and Lytle's
brigades and Loomis' and Edgarton's batteries followed
closely.

The next day, using the captured rolling-stock, General
Mitchell sent Colonel Sill eastward to capture Stevenson, the
junction of the Memphis and Charleston and Nashville and
Chattanooga railroads, and Colonel Turchin westward to seize
Decatur and Tuscumbia. Both expeditions were successful,
and thus, within a few days, one hundred and twenty miles

of this important railroad, connecting Corinth and Richmond, fell into his keeping. To hold what he had gained, detachments of troops were posted at the more important points, and the whole command was kept in constant readiness to move to any place on the line which the enemy might threaten or attack.

The necessity for a movement in force soon occurred, as General Kirby Smith advanced from Bridgeport against the detachment beyond Stevenson. As rapidly as possible, on the 29th of April, General Mitchell moved from Huntsville by rail to oppose him. On reaching his menaced detachment, four miles west from Bridgeport, he found that his troops had driven the enemy's pickets back across Widow's creek, the bridge over which had been burned. He then sent a portion of his force to reinforce the detachment in front of the enemy, to hold him there by a feigned effort to cross, while with the remainder he made a detour and advanced upon Bridgeport. The enemy at this point was surprised and thrown into confusion, and, mainly by the action of the artillery, was driven across the Tennessee river. The railroad bridge, reaching from the western bank of the river to the island, though fired by the enemy, was saved, but the one extending from the island to the eastern bank was destroyed.

Having routed one portion of Smith's force, General Mitchell made preparation to attack the other, which was guarding the crossing of Widow's creek before his own troops, anticipating that the report of cannon at Bridgeport would hasten their return to assist their comrades, and waiting their approach, he dispersed them also with his artillery.

Unofficial reports place the enemy's loss in this engagement at seventy-two in killed and wounded, and three hundred and fifty prisoners.

About the 10th of May, General Mitchell was placed in command of all the troops between Nashville and Huntsville. He at once ordered General Negley, who, with his brigade from the Second division, had been left at Columbia when the main army moved upon Savannah, to move from that place to Rodgersville, Alabama, held by a brigade of the enemy under General Adams. He also sent a force, in command of Colonel Lytle, from Athens, Alabama, to co-operate with him. Upon the near approach of these two columns— May 13th—the enemy dispersed and sought safety by crossing the Tennessee river, and the two commanders co-operating returned to their former positions.

The engagement at Bridgeport and the expedition against Rodgersville gave General Mitchell the control of that portion of Alabama lying north of the Tennessee river. This region he held firmly, making the impression, by his rapid movements, that his force was much larger than it really was. The seizure of the Memphis and Charleston railroad, and the complete occupancy of Northern Alabama, involved a series of bold and brilliant operations, which had important relations to those before Corinth and at Cumberland Gap, and also to the subsequent advance of the Army of the Ohio toward East Tennessee.

On the 29th of May, General Mitchell put in motion an expedition against Chattanooga, Tennessee. General Negley moved from Columbia to Fayetteville, and was there joined by Turchin's brigade, from Huntsville, and the Eighteenth Ohio, under Colonel T. R. Stanley, from Athens. From Fayetteville the column advanced through Winchester, Cowan, and the University Place to Jasper. When near the latter place, Colonel Hambright, commanding the vanguard, encountered a brigade of the enemy, under General Adams. After a sharp skirmish, General Adams fled, leaving behind him some twenty of his dead, as many who were wounded, twelve others as prisoners, and his ammunition and supply trains. From Jasper, General Negley advanced to the north bank of the Tennessee, opposite Chattanooga, arriving on the 7th of June. Colonel Sill's command had been sent to Shellmound, to attract the attention of the enemy and prevent his crossing the river at that point. During the evening of the 7th and morning of the 8th, General Negley bombarded Chattanooga, making a feint of crossing the river and assaulting the place, and then withdrew. This attitude drew General Kirby Smith from Knoxville to London, with a large portion of his command, on his way to relieve Chattanooga. Here he learned that General Negley had withdrawn from East Tennessee. General

Negley took position, on his return, at Shelbyville, and the co-operative forces resumed their former positions. The main advantage resulting was the intensification of the enemy's confusion, and the consequent derangement of his plans.

Brigadier-General G. W. Morgan arrived at Cumberland Ford, and assumed command of the forces in Eastern Kentucky, April 11th. The Cumberland Valley was destitute of supplies, the productions of the region having been exhausted by General Carter's brigade and the enemy. Forage had to be hauled at first from forty to fifty miles, and subsequently from eighty to ninety, over roads almost impassable. General Morgan concentrated his entire command at Cumberland Ford, consisting of the Twenty-fourth brigade (formerly the Twelfth), the Twenty-fifth, Twenty-sixth, and Twenty-seventh, commanded respectively by Brigadier-Generals S. P. Carter and J. G. Spears, and Colonels J. S. DeCourcy and John Coburn.* Some of the regiments were rearmed, and the artillery was increased from six to twenty-two pieces. Supplies and ammunition were brought forward, and a floating bridge was placed upon the Cumberland river.

Soon after his assumption of command, General Morgan ascertained, through a reconnoissance, that the defensive works at Cumberland Gap had been grouped on the enemy's left, and that the natural strength of the position was his dependence on the right. This gap is a deep depression in the Cumberland range, being the great gateway through the mountains for the roads of an extensive region. It is situated on the eastern side of the boundary line between Kentucky and Tennessee, and near the line separating Western Virginia from Kentucky and Tennessee. The eastern slope of the mountains is very abrupt, often presenting perpendicular heights of several hundred feet. The western slope is less steep, but is very much broken by spurs, knobs, and ravines. The ascent, therefore, on either side is exceedingly difficult. East of the Cumberland range, in close proximity, is a secondary parallel range, called Poor Valley Ridge. On the west there is another,

---

*The Twenty-seventh brigade, in June, passed to the command of Brigadier-General A. Baird.

inferior in height and extent. By personal observation, during a reconnoissance, General Morgan perceived a knob to the right of the fortifications, which commanded them, and sent at once for siege guns to be used from that point; but before they could be brought, the enemy fortified this eminence and defeated the plan. A subsequent reconnoissance, with Carter's and DeCourcy's brigades, without the expectation of even a skirmish, resulted in a spirited contest, brought on by an attack by the enemy. The loss was not heavy on either side, and except in demonstrating the difficulty and hazard of an attempt to carry the position by storm, the reconnoissance was fruitless.

General Morgan now determined to demonstrate on the enemy's left, and, if possible, force him to an open fight or to the abandonment of his fortifications. To conceal his purpose, and at the same time threaten Clinton, one of the enemy's depots of supplies, he posted General Spears, with three regiments, at the foot of Pine Mountain, on the road through Big Creek Gap, this road having been blockaded by the enemy for eighteen miles from the Gap toward Spears' position. This action induced the enemy to place at the Gap two brigades of infantry, two regiments of cavalry, and two batteries, under command of Brigadier-General Barton. So large a force having been detached from the main army, General Morgan proposed to leave Carter's brigade at Cumberland Ford, and with Baird's and DeCourcy's brigades cross Pine Mountain, and passing the Cumberland chain at Rogers' Gap, debouch into Powell's valley, and at the same time threaten Knoxville, Clinton, and Cumberland Gap. Before, however, this plan could be executed, General E. K. Smith, commanding the Confederate forces in East Tennessee, advanced from Knoxville, through Clinton, to Woodson's Gap, with about eight thousand men, having the double object of cutting Spears off and threatening Cumberland Ford, by detaching a brigade for the purpose.

On the 6th of June, with his whole command in hand, General Morgan moved upon the road leading through Rogers' Gap into Powell's valley. On the 10th, he sent two hundred men to burn the bridge at Lowdon, and this was accomplished without loss. By the 12th, two brigades were in the valley, and General Morgan had arranged to move against Cumberland Gap the next day with three brigades, Baird's, Spears', and De Courcy's, when telegrams from General Buell were received, which led him to order his command to countermarch to Williamsburg. In this movement, the siege guns blockaded the Gap, and De Courcy was delayed in leaving Powell's valley, and on the next day (the 13th) a rumor reached him that the enemy was evacuating Cumberland Gap. This rumor reached General Morgan, in conjunction with a telegram from General Buell, advising him that General Mitchell had been ordered to demonstrate against Chattanooga, and induced him to resume his movement against Cumberland Gap.

General Smith, en route to relieve Chattanooga, threatened by General Negley, heard at London of General Morgan's advance into Powell's valley, and also of Negley's withdrawal, and immediately retraced his steps, turning his main column toward Clinton to oppose Morgan, and sending General Barton to observe Rogers' Gap and the Knoxville road. On the 17th, General Morgan learned that Smith was moving toward Clinton, that Barton was approaching the valley on his right flank, that Rains with a force was at Baptist Gap, and that General Stevenson was in supporting distance, but determined nevertheless to move the next day directly upon Cumberland Gap. Accordingly, on the morning of the 18th, he marched his whole force rapidly up the valley, and reaching the fortifications late in the evening, found them vacant. Thus, this position of wonderful natural strength, and strongly fortified, was occupied by the national forces without an engagement. The generals of the opposing forces must certainly have regarded a direct movement upon such a position improbable, or else supposed that they would be able to prevent its success, should it be made. But while maneuvering somewhat remotely from their stronghold, with offensive rather than defensive intent, Morgan dashed upon it when there were no troops to utilize its defensive advantages.

On the 11th of April, Colonel Duffield, commanding at Murfreesboro, sent Lieutenant J. W. Childs, with a detachment of the Seventh Pennsylvania Cavalry on a scouting expedition toward McMinnville.   Ascertaining that the Confederate brigadier-general, J. P. M. Maury, was at his home, five miles beyond McMinnville, Lieutenant Childs proceeded thither, and captured him, taking him to Murfreesboro, whence he was forwarded as a prisoner of war to Nashville.

May 4th, Colonel John H. Morgan, returning from his attack upon General Mitchell's train at Pulaski, with about eight hundred cavalry, crossed the Nashville and Chattanooga railroad, moving toward Lebanon.   Brigadier-General Dumont, from Nashville, and Colonel Duffield, from Murfreesboro' (both having been in previous pursuit of him), reached the latter place the same day, and immediately gave chase, with detachments of Wynkoop's Seventh Pennsylvania, and Wolford's and Green Clay Smith's Kentucky cavalry regiments.   Arriving at Lebanon on the 5th, General Dumont surprised and attacked Morgan, and after a severe fight of an hour and a half, completely routed him, following in pursuit some eighteen miles.   During the engagement, the citizens kept up a galling fire upon the national troops, and while General Dumont was pursuing Morgan, sixty-five men, under Lieutenant-Colonel Wood, having secreted themselves in the Odd Fellows Hall, unexpectedly opened fire upon a small force under Colonel Duffield, who had been left to collect the wounded and care for them.   Having rallied his men, Colonel Duffield advanced, under cover of the house, to close range, and by a precise and rapid fire, forced the enemy to surrender. There were six commissioned officers in the party.   Morgan lost one hundred and fifty men captured, one hundred stand of arms, and over one hundred and fifty horses ; his loss in killed and wounded was not reported.   Colonels Wolford and Smith were both wounded, and there were six killed and twenty-three others wounded, and one captured, in Dumont's command.

In the month of April, at the suggestion of Mr. J. J. Andrews, a citizen of Kentucky, in the secret service of the government, General O. M. Mitchell organized an expedition for the destruction of the bridges on the " Western and Atlantic Railroad," between Chattanooga and Atlanta, Georgia.   The party consisted of Mr. Andrews, the leader; William Campbell, a citizen of Kentucky, and twenty non-commissioned officers and privates, from the Second, Twenty-first, and Thirty-third Ohio regiments,* selected because of their known bravery and discretion. Dressing in citizens' clothing, having only side-arms, and separating into squads, they set forth, April 11th. Twenty-two of the number reached Chattanooga, and, without being suspected, took passage for Marietta, Georgia, arriving there at midnight. The next morning they took passage for Chattanooga, and at Big Shanty (where there was no telegraph office or extra locomotive), while the conductor and engineer were at breakfast, detached the locomotive and three box-cars, and started for Chattanooga at full speed. Mr. Andrews had a schedule of the road, according to which they should have met but one train that day, but two extra trains had been put on, and in waiting at stations for these to pass an hour was lost, which gave the pursuers opportunity to overtake them. They made every possible effort to escape, cutting the telegraph wires, and placing obstructions on the track behind them, but all in vain. When the relentless pursuers, who had followed them, by hand-cars and a coal-engine, and afterward with a locomotive from a passenger train, were in sight, they leaped from their cars, a few miles south of Chattanooga, and sought safety by scattering in the woods. The population of the surrounding country joined in search for them, and all were captured—most of them in a day or two, two not for three weeks.

Private Jacob Parrott, of the Thirty-third Ohio, was fearfully flogged by a lieutenant to extort from him a confession as to the object of the expedition; but his fortitude was proof against suffering and threats. Mr. Andrews was tried as a spy at Chattanooga, condemned, and subsequently hung at Atlanta. Twelve of the party were transferred to Knoxville, and seven were there tried as spies and condemned,

---

* The names of the twenty were George D. Wilson, Marion A. Ross, Perry G. Shadrach, Samuel Slavens, Samuel Robinson, John Scott, W. W. Brown, Wm. Knight, J. R. Porter, J. A. Wilson, John Wollam, Jacob Parrott, Wm. Bensinger, E. H. Mason, Mark Wood, M. J. Hankins, D. A. Dorsey, Robert Buffum, Wm. Baddick, and Wm. Pettinger.

though in their trial it was clearly set forth by their counsel that the expedition was purely military. Soon after the trial, all at Chattanooga and Knoxville were transferred to Atlanta, where, without time to prepare, the seven condemned at Knoxville were hung. Fourteen were now left, and anticipating the fate of their comrades, they resorted to a bold measure to effect escape. When the door of their prison was opened by the jailer to bring them food, they seized him, then disarmed seven guards, and eight of them were beyond pursuit before an alarm was given, six being recaptured. Of the eight, six reached the national lines. The fate of the remaining two is unknown. The six recaptured were sent to Richmond, Virginia, and were finally exchanged as ordinary soldiers—an act which condemned as unjustifiable the execution of their comrades. Had acts similar to theirs, in type and intent at least, been similarly punished, the execution of captives would have been a prominent element in the history of the war. The bodies of those who were hung at Atlanta were subsequently removed and reburied at the National Cemetery at Chattanooga. This expedition was authorized by General Buell.

CHAPTER XIII.

THE ADVANCE TOWARD CHATTANOOGA FROM CORINTH, AND THE RETREAT FROM SOUTHERN TENNESSEE TO LOUISVILLE, KY.

THE withdrawal of the Confederate army from Corinth left General Halleck's combined armies without an immediate objective worthy of their collective proportions. This vast aggregation of forces was therefore resolved into its original parts, and separate fields were sought for the distinct armies of which it had been composed. The opposing Confederate army suffered similar disintegration. Neither of the belligerents proposed yet to abandon Northern Mississippi; but each resolved to enter upon active operations two hundred miles eastward. And again small armies began to operate upon fields so remote as to forbid all positive unity of purpose or harmony of action on either side of the grand hostile front, extending from the Atlantic ocean to the barren deserts of the West.

From the beginning of the war, the occupancy of East Tennessee in such force as to hold in permanent grasp that mountain region, with the great railroad coursing through it, which connected Richmond with the Mississippi Valley and the central Gulf States, had been regarded by the authorities at Washington and the Northern people as one of the most important military advantages that could be attained west of the Alleghany Mountains. For a time other objectives had attracted the Army of the Ohio far to the West and South. But as these had now been gained, this army was charged with a campaign having for its primal object the capture of Chattanooga, as the condition precedent to offensive movements east and south from that strategic position. The series of grand operations which terminated in the occupation of Corinth and Memphis, and the sweep of Mitchell's bold detachments eastward and westward from Huntsville, had wrested from the enemy the "Memphis, and Charleston Railroad" throughout its whole length. The possession of the roads passing from Stevenson, through Chattanooga, to Knoxville, and southward from Chattanooga and Cleveland to Dalton, Georgia, was scarcely less essential to the suppression of the rebellion than the opening of the Mississippi river to gunboats and transports which bore the national flag. And this was the prescribed object of the projected eastward march of the Army of the Ohio. To accomplish it easily, advantage was to be taken of the concentration of the Western insurgent forces in Northern Mississippi.

After such disastrous defeats as the enemy had suffered, and such consciousness of weakness as the refusal to give battle at Corinth evinced, the leaders in the South could not be ignorant of the vital character of their next efforts. Thus far in the West their attempts at offense and defense had alike failed. Their armies had been pressed back the depth of a state, between the Mississippi river on the west and the Nashville and Chattanooga railroad on the east, and without some interruption to this course of defeat their cause was hopeless. In this emergency they adopted the wisest measures, and by hiding them for a time under seeming passivity, they set to work with greatest energy and earnestness to gather strength for their execution.

If Chattanooga was vitally important to the national cause, both as regarded strategy and political considerations, it was not less so to the insurgents. They could assume the offensive from no other point with any hope of success—at least this place was a vital point in an offensive line. The very remoteness of Chattanooga from the recent theater of war, scarcely less than its inherent strategic value, called thither the Confederate forces to spring thence to Northern Kentucky.

This common aim incited the eastward march of the two armies, which were destined to severest conflict to the close of the war. General Bragg, who had succeeded General Beauregard, in Western command, put his columns in motion simultaneously with the movement of the Army of the Ohio. Each party thought to take advantage of the heavy concentration of the other in Northern Mississippi, so as to operate in East Tennessee without strong opposition.   But the advantage was with General Bragg with respect to the ruling contingency to each—the occupation of Chattanooga in force—as he had an open way behind the hills upon the south bank of the Tennessee, with communications established when he should get there; while General Buell's advance involved the supply of his army without communications, and a vital draft upon his strength to create them.

General Buell was informed that his army would return to Tennessee, while he was moving with two of his divisions, McCook's and Crittenden's, toward Brownsville, Mississippi, to support General Pope. He at once turned these divisions eastward, and sought General Halleck to confer with him in regard to the proposed campaign. It plainly involved problems which previous campaigns had not compassed, and for which, consequently, the conditions and experiences of anterior operations could not furnish a solution. Hitherto the national armies had not moved far from a secure base of supplies, and Pittsburg Landing and Nashville were both connected with Louisville, the primal base, by rivers navigable always during winter and spring, and so guarded by gunboats as to assure uninterrupted communications with this grand source of supply. The advance to East Tennessee from Corinth was conditioned upon the use of railroads for a great distance, either the one running east from Corinth, or those leading south from Nashville. And with Corinth or Eastport in the west, or Nashville to the north, as the main secondary base, without a large fraction of an army to guard communications, they would not be secure.   General Halleck preferred the Memphis and Charleston railroad as the channel of supply, while General Buell regarded the Nashville and Decatur, and the Nashville and Chattanooga roads, as far preferable. The objections to the Memphis and Charleston road were, that it crossed the Tennessee river by a long bridge, which had been destroyed, and that it ran from Corinth to Decatur parallel to the enemy's front, and was, in consequence, liable to interruptions from raids. The other road did not promise a line of supply free from perilous contingencies, but, on the whole, General Buell considered it the more eligible.*

This difference of opinion, with regard to lines of supply, induced disagreement as to the line of advance. General Buell desired to move through Middle Tennessee to McMinnville, and thence to Chattanooga, in accordance with his preference for Nashville as a secondary base; while his superior ordered him to march on the line of the Memphis and Charleston road, and to repair the track as he advanced. It would have been well had the forecast of the campaign compassed all the conditions of its conduct, progress, and issue; but in advance of actual experiment, provision for the ruling contingencies was not made. The necessity of all possible haste in transferring the army to East Tennessee was enforced in official instructions, but the prescribed condition of march—the repair of the railroad—barred rapidity of motion.

On the 11th of June, McCook's and Crittenden's divisions moved eastward—the former from Corinth, and the latter from Booneville. At the time, Wood's division was on the railroad east of Corinth, engaged in its reconstruction. General McCook reached Florence on the 15th, closely followed by General Crittenden, who had touched the line of march first at Iuka. In the meantime, General Wood had advanced beyond Tuscumbia, having left the repair of the railroad west of Tuscumbia to the supervision of General Nelson. To facilitate the march of the forces eastward, General Mitchell, and Captain Morton, of the engineers, had been directed to prepare the means of crossing the river at Florence and Decatur, and the former officer had been ordered to collect supplies at Athens. Ferry-boats having been provided at the places designated, Generals McCook and Crittenden commenced crossing their forces at Florence on the 22d, but the report of an attack upon Nelson caused a suspension of the movement, that support might be afforded him in the event of need. At

---

* General Buell has represented that General Halleck at first gave his consent to his plans, and afterward insisted upon the Memphis and Charleston road as the line of supply, and the more southern line of advance.

the same time, Major-General Thomas, having been first relieved from the command of the Army of the Tennessee, and then of the troops holding Corinth, and restored to the command of his former division in the Army of the Ohio, was ordered by General Buell to move from the rear to reinforce Nelson. The falsity of the rumored attack was soon ascertained, and then the crossing at Florence was resumed. The wagons and teams were first put over the river, and dispatched to convey supplies over a gap in the railroad north of Athens. On the 25th, the divisions of McCook, Crittenden, and Nelson crossed and moved toward Athens, reaching that place on the 29th. During this slow advance, supplies had been provided with great difficulty. They were conveyed from Corinth to Iuka by a few cars, drawn by a half-serviceable locomotive, thence to Eastport by wagons, and from that place to Florence on light-draught boats. The boats could carry only from thirty to forty tons over the shoals, and soon ceased running altogether, when supplies were conveyed from Waterloo to Florence by wagon trains on the north side of the river.

The embarrassments of the situation were now fully revealed. Since early spring, from various causes, General Buell's effective force had been greatly reduced. His own estimate was twenty-five thousand effective men for an offensive column, and sixteen thousand variously disposed at important points on the railroads in Middle Tennessee and Northern Alabama. He had no secure communications, and was still more than a hundred miles from Chattanooga with his main column. His outlying forces were scattered from Iuka to Stevenson, and many of his smaller detachments were remote from his line of march, and some on that line were exposed to attacks from the superior cavalry of the enemy, which since the evacuation of Corinth had been transferred to the north side of the Tennessee river, while guerrilla bands in Northern Alabama, Middle Tennessee, and Southern Kentucky had been largely multiplied. He was still under orders to repair the Memphis and Charleston road, and was urging its completion with the least possible delay; but distrusting its reliability when completed, he was also putting the roads to Nashville in running order, which still further diffused his forces. The offensive column, in advancing upon Chattanooga, could receive no accessions from the troops guarding the roads, as matters then stood, and on the whole the outlook was very unpromising. An immediate advance was impracticable, and in the event of the activity of the enemy, delay assured the miscarriage of the campaign.

June 29th, General Buell established his headquarters at Huntsville, and grappled with the difficulties in his way making prompt dispositions for the attainment of several important objects—the repair of the railroads leading south from Nashville, the location of the grand units of his army so as to conceal the purpose of the campaign, and at the same time render their subsistence and concentration as easy as possible, and to provide the means of crossing the Tennessee river at Bridgeport whenever the offensive column should be ready to dash on to Chattanooga.

As wagon transportation was not sufficient to carry supplies over the gaps in the railroads and beyond Bridgeport, General Buell became convinced that railroad connection with Nashville was one of the cardinal elements in the solution of the problem of the advance to Chattanooga. Another scarcely less vital matter was the defense of bridges, by stockades, that all possible contributions might be drawn to the aggressive forces. He therefore increased the force on the railroads with engineer and other troops, and hired mechanics, and instructed the military superintendent of railroads to hurry them to completion.

Apprehending an attack upon the detachments of Mitchell's division at Battle Creek, and on the Nashville and Chattanooga railroad, General Buell, early in July, ordered McCook and Crittenden's divisions to advance from Athens to Battle Creek, in order to show a strong front toward Chattanooga, and at the same time put strong detachments from these divisions on the Nashville and Chattanooga railroad. He left General Nelson at Athens, with instructions to put a large working party from his division on the Nashville and Decatur road. He directed General Wood to move his division across the river at Decatur, and on the north bank guard that important place, the ferry and the town. In the meantime, General

Thomas held the road from Tuscumbia eastward, with a heavy detachment at Eastport to protect supplies, and a strong cavalry picket at Russellville, to observe the enemy in the direction of Fulton. General Buell himself organized regular railroad guards, and reunited the regiments and brigades which had been broken up by General Mitchell's diversified operations, organized a brigade to move from the Nashville and Chattanooga railroad to McMinnville, ordered horses for his cavalry, and made other minor preparations for the contemplated movement into East Tennessee upon the opening of railroad communications and the accumulation of sufficient supplies. Generals McCook and Crittenden arrived at Battle Creek about the middle of July. The former put a brigade at work on the railroad from Stevenson to Decherd.

While these movements and preparations were going on, the enemy's cavalry became more active in Kentucky, and in the immediate rear of the army. Detachments in Kentucky and Tennessee were captured, and General Buell's communications far and near were endangered. This boldness was really more threatening than was at first apparent, as it was an indication of General Bragg's purpose to assume the offensive from Western Virginia to Corinth. After the refusal of battle at Corinth, it was not anticipated by the national commanders that the enemy would soon attempt general offense in the West. But with the change of commanders by the enemy, there was formed a plan of general aggression, whose foreshadows were now seen. When Colonel John H. Morgan appeared, early in July, in Kentucky, having swept from Knoxville through Sparta, Tennessee, he announced in proclamation that his cavalry force (of twelve or fifteen hundred men) was the vanguard of an army advancing for the liberation of the state. This was so like his usual boasting, that, in absence of other indications of such a movement, it was not accepted as evidence. Neither did the dash of Colonel Forrest, with his bold troops, from Chattanooga to Murfreesboro, without any other announcement than the destructive force of his movement, indicate of itself anything beyond a raid to interrupt General Buell's communications. And while no columns of infantry assumed an offensive attitude, and no rumors of a concentration of forces at Chattanooga were wafted northward, there was no thought of changing the plan of the East Tennessee campaign.

Provisions were made as soon as practicable, to save the communications from serious interruptions, but only with partial success. Generals Boyle and Green Clay Smith were active in resisting Morgan in Kentucky, but his movements were so rapid and adroitly concealed, that his blows could not be anticipated, and he effected great damage without receiving harm, as accurate intelligence of the combinations formed against him was communicated by his numerous friends. He therefore effected some damage, and drew to his colors many young Kentuckians, to whom his partisan warfare was exceedingly attractive.

Having crossed the Cumberland river at Celina, Morgan attacked and defeated Major Jordan, commanding a detachment of the Seventh Pennsylvania Cavalry, at Tompkinsville, Kentucky, July 9th. Moving thence by Glasgow, he threatened Bowling Green, and advanced to Lebanon, sending a detachment toward Lebanon Junction to destroy the railroad. Colonel A. Y. Johnson, commanding at Lebanon, made effort to gather reinforcements, but was forced to surrender, with the loss of a large amount of government property. Morgan then passed through Harrodsburg and Lawrenceburg, and threatening Frankfort by the way, crossed the Kentucky river, entered Versailles, and then demonstrated toward Lexington. Having destroyed portions of the railroads between Louisville and Lexington, Lexington and Frankfort, and Paris and Lexington, he advanced rapidly on Cynthiana, arriving there on the 17th. Lieutenant-Colonel Landrum defended the place gallantly but unsuccessfully, with three hundred poorly armed home guards and forty regular soldiers. By this time, Morgan perceived that he was in danger from various detachments moving to intercept him, and turned toward Tennessee, moving through Eastern Kentucky to Sparta, to be ready to co-operate with General Bragg in his advance.

Forrest was still more successful in a smaller circuit. Brigadier-General Crittenden and Colonel Duffield arrived at Murfreesboro on the 11th of July; the former to command the post, and the latter to command the Twenty-third brigade, destined for McMinnville. When relieved at Murfreesboro and Tullahoma, Colonel Lester, of the Third Minnesota regiment, had been in command of the post in the absence of Colonel Duffield, and owing to unpleasant feelings among the troops composing the garrison, he had scattered them somewhat widely in and about the town. For some reason not apparent, neither General Crittenden nor Colonel Duffield assumed command, and while there was a general lack of unity, harmony, and a proper disposition of troops for defense, Forrest, having advanced from Chattanooga through McMinnville, with a force variously estimated at from eighteen hundred to thirty-five hundred men, appeared before the town at dawn on the 13th. Dividing his force, he sent Colonel Wharton with two regiments against the force posted on the Liberty turnpike, and with the remainder dashed into the town. Wharton met a spirited resistance, but finally forced the detachment, consisting of five companies of the Ninth Michigan and a squadron of the Fourth Kentucky Cavalry, to surrender. Forrest overwhelmed the smaller force in the town and captured it, including General Crittenden. Soon after, Colonel Lester, without having offered very serious resistance at his post, on the east bank of Stone river, surrendered himself and nine companies of his regiment. The consequences of this disaster were very serious, the loss of a large garrison, munitions and stores, great damage to the railroad which had been opened the day before, and the postponement of the occupation of McMinnville.

To prevent further damage and dislodge Forrest from his communications, General Buell dispatched General Nelson with his division, from Athens, via Columbia and Nashville, to Murfreesboro. Nelson was delayed, first at Columbia, by the washing away of a bridge, and then at Nashville, by the destruction of bridges north of Murfreesboro by Forrest. These detentions gave the enemy time for more injury and leisurely withdrawal.

Simultaneously with the departure of General Nelson, General Wood, with two brigades of his division, was ordered to move from Decatur to Shelbyville. Subsequently, he took post at Decherd, to give greater security to the important bridge over Elk river, and guard the route from the mountains through Winchester into Northern Alabama. His third brigade was sent to Stevenson to construct defensive works to assure the safety of the supplies there accumulating for the projected advance to Chattanooga.

During the period of these changes, the enemy had been comparatively quiet where his chief activity had at first been anticipated—in front of General Thomas, between Iuka and Decatur. Some skirmishing, provoked by reconnoitering parties sent south by General Thomas, occurred, but there were no indications of the presence of heavy forces. A regiment of infantry and a squadron of cavalry, under Colonel Streight, moved about twenty miles south from Decatur, to escort some loyal mountaineers who wished to enlist in the national army. Colonel Streight, in the expedition, encountered only cavalry on local duty for purposes of observation and conscription. The absence of the enemy in force on the western portion of the line was another token of his aggressive purpose eastward. But General Buell's own aggressive drift, rather than the apparent attitude of the enemy, required that his rear division should move eastward. Accordingly, July 15th, General Thomas received orders to prepare to join the advanced forces as soon as relieved from guarding the railroad by General Grant's troops. At this time the main portion of the division was at Tuscumbia, but the remainder was scattered in detachments from Iuka to Decatur.

By the 21st, General Thomas was able to put his command in motion. Schoepf's brigade crossed the river at Decatur on the 23d. The next day, Fry's crossed at Florence, and proceeded to Pulaski, to look after the safety of Reynolds' Station and the trains running between there and Athens. While the remainder of the division was yet scattered in small detachments, a heavy force of irregular cavalry made a dash on the railroad between Tuscumbia and Decatur, and by surprising and capturing one detachment and frightening another from its post, interrupted communications and caused a withdrawal from the road. On the 27th, General Thomas crossed the river at Florence, with General Robert McCook's brigade, and advanced to Athens. Fry's brigade was then recalled from Pulaski, and the division marched toward Decherd. General Thomas left his command and proceeded to Huntsville, and after consultation with General Buell took the railroad for Decherd. The same day, Brigadier-General Robert L. McCook was killed by guerrillas, on the Hazel Green and Winchester road. He was riding at the time in an ambulance, prostrated by sickness. All the circumstances indicated that he was wantonly murdered, and General Buell instituted vigorous measures to inflict punishment upon those who were guilty. General McCook was a brilliant officer, and his death was universally deplored.

About this time General Buell made earnest request for more cavalry to protect his communications and pursue the raiding troopers of the enemy, in large bodies. He had tried stockades at bridges held by small detachments of infantry, and found these ineffectual, in conjunction with his cavalry, in giving security to his four hundred miles of railroad.

While at Murfreesboro, General Nelson constructed strong field works, so that a small force could hold the place. He then was ordered to McMinnville with his division, reaching there on the 5th of August. As the railroad between Nashville and Stevenson had been completed on the 28th of July, and the one from Nashville to Decatur on the 3d of August, the movement of troops to positions on the north of the Cumberland Mountains was in provision for an emergency, hitherto unexpected, but now threatening to arrest altogether the advance into East Tennessee.

For some time, General Bragg had been massing troops in East Tennessee drawn from Mississippi and other states. He had distributed his forces eastward from Chattanooga, carefully concealing his intention, strength, and main point of concentration. He reached Chattanooga on the 29th of July, and from that time rumors that he would assume the offensive became current. Reports at first, however, were contradictory as to his movements, strength, and purposes. At one time, it was asserted that he was crossing at Chattanooga, then at

Cleveland, and in turn at various other points. To elicit the truth if possible, General Buell sent reconnoitering parties in all directions, and in the absence of reliable information concerning the intentions of the enemy, made all possible preparations for defense. Fortifications were made at the most important points, so that they could be held by small garrisons when it became necessary to concentrate the army. Fearing that his department did not contain sufficient available troops to enable him to cope with General Bragg, he requested permission from Major-General Halleck, than commander-in-chief at Washington, to call upon General Grant for troops should his need become extreme.

At this juncture, the insurgents everywhere were exerting their entire strength. Their defeats in the West and on the South Atlantic coast had revealed to them the necessity of forcing into their armies all the able-bodied men in the South. This they had in great measure accomplished, while acting merely on the defensive for several months. And now large armies confronted General McClellan on the Peninsula of Virginia, General Morgan at Cumberland Gap, General Buell on the confines of East Tennessee, and General Grant in Northern Mississippi.

This attitude of the enemy, from the Atlantic ocean to the Mississippi river, was not revealed alone by the concentration on the foreground, but by the incessant action of his cavalry and guerrilla bands upon the communications of the national armies. The bold troopers, Morgan and Forrest, again dashed to General Buell's rear. The former captured the garrison at Gallatin, and at other points toward Nashville destroyed trains, and by burning one inside the tunnel south of Gallatin, wrought immense damage to it, and was only repulsed at Edgefield Junction, a few miles north of Nashville. While Morgan was dashing thus destructively upon the Louisville and Nashville railroad, doubly valuable at the season of low water in the Cumberland river, Forrest was in close support between Gallatin and McMinnville. General Buell's cavalry was too feeble to cope with the enemy's, and his effort to withstand Morgan and Forrest resulted in disaster. Since Morgan's first raid, he had withdrawn his cavalry forces from their service in detachments against guerrilla bands, and formed them into two bodies for more effective resistance to the regular cavalry of the enemy.   One of these bodies, composed of detachments of the Second Indiana, Fourth and Fifth Kentucky, and Seventh Pennsylvania regiments, he placed under the command of Brigadier-General R. W. Johnson, and sent it against Morgan's force from McMinnville on the 11th of August.   In moving against Morgan, Johnson got between him and Forrest.   Fearing the result, General Buell endeavored to support him with infantry, but failed.   Johnson pushed against Morgan at Gallatin, having sought him in vain at other points, in hope of capturing him before Forrest could render aid.   The attack was made, but resulted in the defeat and retreat of Johnson.   Morgan pursued so closely as to force him to battle, and after an unequal contest of a few minutes' duration, forced him to surrender himself and the small force then with him—about seventy-five men, who alone remained firm to the last.   General Johnson lost, besides, thirty killed and fifty wounded.   The remainder of his command escaped in small parties to Nashville.   This disaster eliminated a considerable portion of General Buell's cavalry at the time that the strength of this arm was most important.   After this occurrence, Forrest swept around Nashville, and Morgan remained north of Nashville, to prevent the repair of the railroad.   The enemy was equally active in the vicinity of Columbia, Clarksville, and McMinnville.   Major McGowan defeated and routed an irregular force of the enemy infesting Duck river, near Columbia; Colonel Rodney Mason surrendered to Colonel Woodward at Clarksville; Major J. H. Hart repulsed the enemy at Fort Donelson, and Colonel Wynkoop met a superior force and retired before it, when on a reconnoissance toward Sparta from McMinnville.

It was now probable that General Buell's campaign, planned for aggression, was to eventuate in defensive operations.   His army was well disposed for rapid concentration against General Bragg, should he advance from Chattanooga to the west or northwest.   Generals McCook and Crittenden were at Battle Creek; General Nelson at McMinnville; the divisions of Generals Thomas and Wood were on the Nashville and Chattanooga railroad, or near it; and General Rousseau's (recently General Mitchell's) was distributed on the other line, from Huntsville toward Nashville.

General Bragg's infantry forces, under his more immediate command, were massed at Chattanooga and Knoxville. Generals Hardee's and Polk's corps were at the former place, and General Smith's at the latter. This disposition of his army indicated a co-operative movement on separate lines of advance. The direct co-operation of these columns was not the result expected by General Buell, unless in concentration against his position, as he had not divined the purpose of his antagonist. His own dispositions looked to easy concentration against the enemy approaching across the mountains from Chattanooga, or through Northern Alabama, to turn his position from the south or west. To provide against an attack upon McMinnville, he directed General Thomas to repair the railroad from Tullahoma to that place, and throw forward a brigade to Pelham for observation. From the summits of the mountains, near Battle Creek, his signal officers were watching the movements of the enemy in the valley, toward Chattanooga, to give warning of an advance from that direction.

Deeming his forces insufficient to thwart the enemy, whatever might be his special plans, he requested General Grant to send him two divisions. General Grant refused, on the ground that he was himself under too great pressure to permit the reduction of his army. This attitude of the enemy in Mississippi was a part of the plan of general co-operation from Knoxville to Corinth; and the fact that it prevented the reinforcement of General Buell, gave proof of the completeness of General Bragg's preparations and the wisdom of his initial movement. For as the success of the general plan hinged upon the advancement of his central column to the north of the Cumberland Mountains, the prevention of reinforcements to General Buell was an essential condition of the success of his dominant movement.

The threatening bearing of General Smith before Cumberland Gap was an additional source of anxiety to General Buell. He was responsible, as department commander, for affairs in Kentucky. He therefore, in advance of a state of things which subsequently induced the creation of a new department, with General Wright in command, relieved General Nelson, August 16th, of the command of the Fourth division, and sent him to Kentucky to take charge of affairs in that state, and organize the fresh troops arriving for its defense. The raid of Morgan, in July, greatly alarmed the citizens of Cincinnati and Louisville, as it revealed how easily a bold raider could dash far behind the national army. So that General Buell was neither in advance by this step of a new alarm nor of the actual danger, as General Kirby Smith was even then in motion toward Central Kentucky.

When General Nelson was sent to Kentucky, General Thomas was relieved temporarily of the command of the First division, and ordered to McMinnville, to direct affairs at that important point. He assumed command on the 19th, and on that day General Bragg threw across the river from Chattanooga three thousand infantry and three hundred cavalry. Fearing that these troops might be followed closely by General Bragg's whole army, General Buell directed General Thomas to call Wood's division near to McMinnville, in readiness to support the troops already there should the enemy advance in force upon that place, or in that direction. To be nearer the new theater of operations, he transferred his own headquarters to Stevenson. General Buell regarded Nashville as General Bragg's objective, and made his dispositions to give battle before he could free himself from the embarassments incident to offensive warfare in a mountainous region.

His first object was to check the enemy before he could reach the Sequatchie Valley. Accordingly, upon receiving the first intelligence, on the 19th, of an advance, he directed General McCook, with his two brigades, to move up the valley from Battle Creek, to the Anderson and Therman road, and hold the enemy in check, if possible. In the event of being hard pressed, he was to fall back on the Therman road until he should form a junction with General Thomas, who would advance from McMinnville for his relief. He directed General Crittenden to move his division up the valley to the Tracy City and Altamont road, to support McCook and observe the old Nashville and Chattanooga road, which enters the valley at the point designated. Should he be compelled to fall back, he was to do so on the Higginbottom road, toward Tracy City and Altamont, until he should meet reinforcements. He instructed General Thomas to hold his command in readiness to advance from McMinnville at the shortest notice, either upon the Therman or Dunlap road.

In moving up the valley on the 20th, General McCook became fearful that the enemy would intercept him before he could reach the Therman road, and therefore retraced his steps to the mouth of Battle Creek, and then moved on the road leading up that stream for some distance, and then over the mountain, as there was no road nearer the enemy practicable for artillery.

Though it was now evident that General Bragg had assumed the offensive, his plan of operations had not been indicated. He had simply thrown his vanguard across the Tennessee river, with evident purpose of crossing Waldron's Ridge, intervening between Chattanooga and the Sequatchie Valley, but his proximate and ulterior objectives could only be revealed by the direction of his march after reaching the valley. Once in the valley he could turn down and sweep past McCook and Crittenden, and secure a route into Northern Alabama, get between General Grant and General Buell, and then pass toward Corinth or Nashville. If Nashville was his ultimate objective, he could adopt either of two routes—the one across the mountains to McMinnville, or the one up the valley to Pikeville, and thence directly to Nashville. If Kentucky was his destination, the latter route would form a portion of it through the valley and out of it.

At this time and for a few days later, General Buell could only act upon probabilities. The peculiar topography of the country gave great advantages to General Bragg, as he could, if he chose, avoid General Buell wherever he might concentrate. Should he throw his army before him at McMinnville, he could on a short line pass to Stevenson by Battle Creek. Should he concentrate against him in the valley, to prevent his taking this direction, there was an open way to him up the valley, and concealing his movements behind the mountains, he could get the start either to Nashville or Kentucky. A concentration at McMinnville would alone place the national troops before him, against an advance to either Nashville or Kentucky. The condition of resistance at that place, or at any other point on the same side of the valley to the northeast, involved no special risk, as General Buell would have his army near his communications, or on a short line to Nashville, should General Bragg be able to press him back. The only risk would have been in giving him the route into Northern Alabama, through Battle Creek and Stevenson.

On the 22d, General Buell established his headquarters at Decherd, to await the developments of the enemy. About the same time it was ascertained that General Bragg's whole army was on the north bank of the Tennessee. General Buell now fully abandoned his long-meditated advance against Chattanooga, and in manifest recognition of his defensive attitude, removed his depot of supplies from Stevenson to Decherd. General Bragg's ultimate objective was the fact of paramount importance to General Buell, but it was studiously concealed. In failing to perceive the intended direct co-operation of the Chattanooga and Knoxville columns, General Buell regarded Nashville as the paramount objective. In view of the past, this was bold; but it fell far short of his actual daring, and in keeping General Buell in the dark with regard to his proximate and remote movements, he gave actuality to the conditions of their success.

General Thomas differed from General Buell with regard to General Bragg's destination. On the 22d he said: "I have believed for a day or two that the demonstration in this direction is intended to cover the advance of his army toward Kentucky;" and recommended a concentration of the Army of the Ohio at McMinnville. He reconnoitered very thoroughly to the east and south of his position, sending parties to Altamont, Beersheba Springs, Dunlap, Spencer, Pikeville, Sparta, and other less important points, and thus ascertained that the enemy was not in force near him, nor even in the Sequatchie Valley, and then advised that Wood's division should be sent forward to Sparta, to intercept the advance of the main army; that another division should be left at Decherd, on the Nashville and Chattanooga railroad, and that the remaining forces should be concentrated at McMinnville, prepared to offer battle should General Bragg advance on that place, or meet him at Sparta or Allen's Ford should he pass by McMinnville. The movement of the enemy upon either Nashville or Louisville required that he should pass through McMinnville or Sparta, and General Thomas advised that provision be made to defeat him, whichever of these cities might be his objective. Even if Decherd should be his proximate aim, defense could be made by the army from McMinnville; and if matters should so eventuate as to permit a return to the original plan of invading East Tennessee, the proposed concentration would be a step toward it. In making these suggestions, General Thomas repeatedly expressed the opinion that General Bragg had no thought of moving into Northern Alabama.

On the 23d, believing that the enemy would advance on the Therman road, General Buell ordered the concentration of five divisions at Altamont, that he might there offer battle. He ordered Generals McCook and Crittenden to move up the Battle Creek road over the mountain, and onward through Pelham; General Schoepf, commanding the First division, to march from Elk river through Pelham, and General Thomas, with Ammen's division (the Fourth) and Wood's, to advance from McMinnville, on the Therman road. The day following, General Thomas received more explicit instructions with regard to the concentration, attack, route, and manner of retreat, should retreat become necessary. If the enemy was found in superior force. at Altamont, he was to force his way to Hillsboro, and if not in such force as to forbid success, he was to attack him and drive him back, and in the event of any reverse, rendering it necessary for his whole command to fall back, he should retreat through Manchester and Beech Grove, neglecting no opportunity to embarrass or check the enemy.

General Thomas reached Altamont on the 25th, but found no enemy there, and none nearer than Dunlap and Pikeville, a brigade being reported at each place. General Bragg was still struggling slowly over Waldron's Ridge, and General Thomas, deeming it improbable that he would attempt the passage of the mountain by way of Altamont, on account of the difficulties of the road and scarcity of water and forage, returned to McMinnville with the Fourth and Sixth divisions. General McCook's division reached Altamont on the 29th, and the day following moved to Hubbard's Cove, where his advance met and routed Forrest's cavalry,* endeavoring to join General Bragg by that route. The First division halted at Pelham, and the Fifth (Crittenden's) at Hillsboro. These movements developed the fact that General Bragg was not yet in threatening nearness, and that his purpose in advancing was not indicated fully. His dispatch of the 27th to his lieutenant-general, Van Dorn, in Mississippi, made known his purpose, and his assurance that General Buell was falling back. This purpose was to advance in four columns—one through Eastern Kentucky, a second by Cumberland Gap, another through Sequatchie valley to Kentucky, and the fourth against General Grant. And the recession of General Buell's forces from the line of the Memphis and Charleston railroad, invited him to move rapidly forward with his whole army.

General Buell did not start toward Nashville, as General Bragg supposed, on the 27th; but on the 30th he gave orders

---

* He had been repulsed the day before, in an attack upon Colonel Grose, near Woodbury. Forrest was defeated again, on the 29th, by a detachment under Captain H. R. Miller, of the Eighteenth Ohio, at "Short Mountain Cross-roads." The inclosure of a stockade had been completed, and the men were at dinner, a hundred yards from it, when Forrest fell upon them. It was then a question which party should reach the stockade first. Miller, however, by fighting as he ran, got into the stockade with a portion of his men, and with these he repulsed an assault, led by Forrest himself, with several hundred dismounted men. The men, cut off in the race, fought from the woods near by, and reached the stockade in safety, after the enemy withdrew. Forrest left behind him twelve dead, forty-one wounded, eight horses, and thirty guns

On the 30th, he suffered a fourth defeat. Passing to the left of General Wood's camp toward Woodbury, after leaving Captain Miller, he was soon after roughly handled by Colonel E. P. Fyffe, whom General Wood had sent with his regiment, the Twenty-sixth Ohio, to meet him. Colonel Fyffe attacked him when in line of battle, at the intersection of two roads, nine miles west of McMinnville, and by the suddenness and impetuosity of his attack, routed him without losing a man.

for the movement of his whole army to Murfreesboro, assuming, in advance of actual developments, or even a threatening approach of the enemy in any direction, that Nashville was the objective. After giving a lengthy order, defining the route and marching order of each division, and all the trains, he still hesitated with regard to the movement, and asked the advice of General Thomas with respect to it, on the 31st. His latest advices left him in doubt with regard to the strength and movements of the enemy. Heavy infantry forces had not yet been certainly discovered. General Thomas advised that as the movement had been begun, it would be best to continue it; but suggested a plan of operations from Murfreesboro, to attack and rout Bragg's army, giving in outline the various movements by which it could be accomplished. General Bragg had but five divisions of infantry, and General Buell had five before him, without dependence upon the forces on the Nashville and Decatur road, those in his immediate rear toward Nashville, or the two divisions approaching from General Grant's army.

As ordered, the several divisions and all detachments on the railroads were put in motion during the first three days of September, and united at Murfreesboro on the 5th. The troops of General Rousseau's division, posted on the Nashville and Decatur railroad, followed that road to Nashville. Two divisions from General Grant's army were on the march to join the retreating forces, as, in response to General Buell's call for troops, Brigadier-General J. C. Davis' division, General R. B. Mitchell commanding, and General Paine's division, General J. M. Palmer commanding, had been dispatched from Mississippi. The former reached Murfreesboro about the 1st, and the latter arrived at Nashville about the 12th.

General Buell made no halt at Murfreesboro, but ordered the movement of all his forces to Nashville. This action, supplementing the withdrawal from McMinnville and adjacent points, gave General Bragg free motion over the mountains and through the valleys and out of them, and the undisturbed choice of routes to Nashville or Kentucky. He chose the shorter line, to invade Kentucky, down the Cumberland river to Carthage, and thence through Scottsville and Glasgow to the Louisville and Nashville railroad.

At Murfreesboro, General Buell learned of the defeat of General Nelson's troops at Richmond, Kentucky, and also that General Bragg was moving so far to the East as to indicate a purpose to invade Kentucky. The danger northward was now fully apparent. The problem to solve was fraught with issues of stupendous importance. The only condition of favorable solution was the rapid advance of the Army of the Ohio to Louisville upon the demonstration that General Bragg was moving thither, and either beat him in the race, or move so close to his rear as to paralyze his offensive force northward. He therefore, on reaching Nashville, crossed the Cumberland, with McCook's, Crittenden's, Ammen's, Wood's, Rousseau's, and Mitchell's divisions, and pushed on toward Louisville, having assigned General Thomas to the command of Nashville, with his own, and Negley's and Palmer's divisions, by order issued September 7th.

In the meantime, General Bragg had crossed the Cumberland river at Carthage, and was moving rapidly toward Louisville, with a good start in the race, having left General Breckinridge behind, with a heavy force of infantry, cavalry, and artillery, to operate against Nashville and invest the place.

On the 12th, General Thomas was notified, by General Buell's chief of staff, that General Mitchell's division had been ordered to return to Nashville and report to him. The same day, General Bragg's troops tore up the railroad track between Franklin and Bowling Green, and on the day following, the head of his army, a brigade of cavalry, under Colonel Scott, appeared at Munfordsville, north of Green river. The railroad bridge over Salt river had been burned on the 9th. These developments induced General Buell to countermand the order sending Mitchell's division back to Nashville, and to order General Thomas, with his own and Paine's divisions, to leave Nashville early on the 15th, and join the main army by way of Bowling Green, but giving him permission to leave the latter division at Nashville, if he should not deem it safe to withdraw it.

The garrison at Munfordsville had been reinforced, from the

North, as early as the 8th, by the Seventeenth Indiana Infantry, under Colonel J. T. Wilder.   At 8 P. M. on the 13th, Colonel Wilder declined to surrender upon the demand of the enemy.   Early the next morning an assault was made upon him, which was repulsed with loss to the enemy.   During the day the garrison was reinforced by seven companies of infantry, under Colonel Dunham, from Louisville, and about one thousand men and Konkle's battery, under Colonel Owen, from Lebanon Junction.   The demand for surrender was repeated on the 14th, at 9 A. M., by General Chalmers, who represented that he had six regiments of infantry, a brigade of cavalry, a battalion of sharpshooters, and two batteries of artillery.   The garrison again refused to surrender, when the enemy withdrew and moved north.   On the morning of the 16th, the enemy again appeared, and an attack was made.   The fighting became general on the south line of defense, but no effort was made to carry the position by storm.   Late in the afternoon a flag of truce was received covering a note from General Bragg, which stated that the place was surrounded by overwhelming numbers, that reinforcements could not come, and then demanded the surrender of the post and garrison to save further loss of blood.   Colonel Dunham, then in command, by virtue of superior rank, sent his refusal by Colonel Wilder, who, from personal observations, learned that the force of the enemy was indeed overwhelming.   Having reported this fact on his return, a council of war was held, and General Bragg was requested to suspend hostilities until a decision was reached.   The council having decided that upon the verification of the assumed strength of the enemy the surrender should be made, and the fact of an immense force having been subsequently ascertained, the capitulation was made at 2 A. M. the 17th.   The terms permitted the garrison to leave with the honors of war, the retention of side-arms, private property, and four days' rations.   The officers and men were at once paroled.   The reluctance of General Bragg to assault, and the liberality of the terms, indicated that he did not consider the post worth the cost of carrying it by storm, while the proximity of General Buell's army forbade the hope of its reduction in any other way.   Besides, he could not have held the position, except upon the condition of a general engagement, and whatever might have been his expectations in the invasion of Kentucky, he certainly, from first to last, avoided this issue. He therefore disposed of Munfordsville as quickly and easily as possible, so as to give freedom of motion to his army, and put it out of the power of the garrison to reinforce General Buell, who might yet be able to force a general battle upon him.

General Thomas left Nashville on the 15th, with his own division, not considering it safe to withdraw Paine's, and on the 20th joined General Buell at Prewitt's Knob. At the time, General Bragg was here confronting General Buell, having for two or three days shown some disposition to deliver battle. His belligerent attitude, though involving skirmishing between the armies, may only have been a feint, as on the 21st he declined an engagement when formally offered by General Buell. It may have been that the arrival of General Thomas, with his division, changed a positive plan involving battle. On the 21st, while General Thomas, under instructions from General Buell, was disposing Crittenden's and Wood's divisions in order of battle, it was ascertained that the enemy was retreating. General Bragg not only left General Buell's immediate presence, but he deflected to the east of the Louisville and Nashville railroad, and gave an open way for the march of the Army of the Ohio to Louisville. To this city General Buell put his army in rapid motion, leaving General Thomas, for a day with his division, to protect the convalescent troops and stores until they could be sent to Bowling Green, held at the time by Colonel Bruce's brigade. On the 29th, the last portion of the army reached Louisville. General Bragg moved to Bardstown. Then both armies, in defiant attitude, took rest while preparing for impending hostilities.

CHAPTER XIV.

OPERATIONS OF GENERALS G. W. MORGAN AND WM. NELSON, IN KENTUCKY.

Soon after the occupation of Cumberland Gap by General Morgan, First Lieutenant W. P. Craighill of the engineers, under the general instructions of the President and Secretary of War, commenced the construction of such defensive works as would assure the safety of the position with the least possible number of men, making them formidable only against attacks from the south, while they should be so situated that should they again fall into the hands of the enemy, they might present no barrier to an attack from the north to regain them. The great obstacles to the retention of this important position were its distance from supplies and the character of the roads leading to it from Kentucky, and to overcome them, General Morgan proposed the construction of a military road to Crab Orchard, and Lieutenant Craighill was sent to Washington to lay the proposition before the Secretary of War. The project was approved, but the movements of the enemy rendered its execution impracticable.

In the general effort to drive the national armies from Southern soil and invade the North, the plan of the enemy compassed the invasion of Kentucky and the pillage of Cincinnati, by an army from East Tennessee, and indications of the movement soon became apparent. General Smith did not withdraw his forces from the vicinity of Cumberland Gap after its loss. General Stevenson's division remained in proximity, and other detachments were stationed at various points more or less remote. The enemy, for some time, made demonstrations against General Morgan, but he was prompt to resist all aggressions.

On the 5th of August, General Morgan sent Colonel De Courcy, with his brigade and a battery of artillery, to capture supplies collected by the enemy at Tazewell. Colonel De Courcy succeeded in seizing a large amount of forage, and some mules, horses, and tobacco, but was soon after attacked by Stevenson's division. A sharp conflict ensued, resulting in victory to De Courcy, with a reputed loss to the enemy of about two hundred in killed and wounded, but only a slight loss to himself, mostly in prisoners, who were captured on picket duty.

About the middle of August, the enemy began to reveal his purpose of invasion. On the 16th, General Stevenson presented himself before Cumberland Gap. Presuming that there would be co-operate movements, General Morgan sent Captain Martin's company of cavalry, with orders to move with the greatest speed possible, and observe the enemy at Rogers' and Big Creek Gaps. When within eighteen miles of the former, Captain Martin met the vanguard of General Smith's army advancing toward Kentucky. General Smith at once established himself at Barboursville, and sent General McCown, with a strong force, to Cumberland Ford. These dispositions of the enemy nearly enveloped Morgan's position, and positively cut him off from supplies. Anticipating the total exhaustion of his supplies on hand, before his communications could be restored, he put his troops on half rations at once, and made preparations to hold out to the last extremity. Although circumstances forbade hope of success, he nevertheless made effort to open the way for relief. He mounted about four hundred men of the Third Kentucky Infantry, under Colonel Garrard, on artillery, wagon, and extra cavalry horses, and sent them into Kentucky with Colonel Mundy's cavalry, to join a column organizing for the relief of his command. He afterward sent Colonel Childs with a battalion of the Third Tennessee Cavalry for the same purpose. Another battalion of this regiment, dispatched to the rear, was attacked by a superior force at London, and forced to return.

General Smith did not wait for the reduction of Morgan's position, as his strength enabled him to turn it with ease. He therefore left Stevenson's division to threaten from the south, and calling together his other forces, advanced into Central Kentucky. He thus advanced toward his objective, and at the same time barred the passage of reinforcements and supplies to Cumberland Gap. After the departure of the main army, General Morgan endeavored to provoke General Stevenson to give battle, but without success. He advanced to his position, repeatedly surprised and captured his outposts, watched the gaps, but could not bring on an engagement. These maneuvers resulted in a loss to the enemy, in the aggregate, of about one hundred men killed and wounded, but in no respect changed the situation. All the while, despite the issue of half rations and all efforts to draw supplies from the country, their diminution was rapid. The grain soon gave out, and it was apparent that the retention of the place could not last beyond the consumption of a few days' rations. It was not probable that the enemy would attack, and to hold out much longer, he would have no mules or horses to haul off his munitions. To wait for starvation to force surrender, would give the enemy ten thousand prisoners, twenty-two cannon, fourteen thousand small arms, and a large amount of ammunition. Influenced by these facts, it was decided, at a council of war held on the 14th, that the evacuation of the position was advisable. Accordingly, the next day, preparations were made for a safe retreat. The roads and mountain cliffs were mined to prevent pursuit, and the siege guns were disabled and hurled over the cliff. In the evening a large wagon-train, under escort of infantry and artillery, was started on the Manchester road, and on the following day and evening, the whole force was quietly withdrawn on the same road. What property could not be transported was destroyed, and the usual conflagration and explosions which herald an accomplished evacuation of a fortress, made known to the enemy that Cumberland Gap had again been vacated without an engagement or surrender. The enemy's pickets advanced, but having been repulsed, the army made the descent of the mountain in safety and even without molestation.

To avoid the enemy, known to be in force on the direct line to the Ohio river, General Morgan deflected to the north and east through Manchester, Booneville, Hazel Green, West Liberty, Grayson, and Greenupsburg. En route, he encountered General Morgan's cavalry, and was annoyed by them for several days, but suffered no check or serious loss. From Greenupsburg General Morgan moved through Gallipolis, Ohio, to the mouth of the Kanawha river, then up that river to Charleston, and after a short stay in Western Virginia, his command embarked for Vicksburg.

Two days after General Buell had ordered General Nelson from McMinnville, to take charge of affairs in Kentucky, the Department of the Ohio was reconstituted by general orders No. 112, war department, so as to embrace the States of Ohio, Indiana, Illinois, and Wisconsin, and a portion of Kentucky, and placed under the command of Major-General H. G. Wright. On reaching Kentucky, General Nelson was ordered by General Wright to proceed to Lexington and assume command of all the troops at that place and Lebanon, and all in the vicinity of those places. These troops mostly comprised new regiments, which had been hastily thrown into Kentucky from the adjoining states, principally from Ohio and Indiana. Many of the regiments had never been drilled as such, and officers and men were in a great measure without military training and experience. They were concentrated at Lexington, and formed into a division, with Brigadier-Generals M. D. Manson, Charles Cruft, and J. F. Jackson as commanders of brigades. Soon after assuming command at Lexington, General Nelson, knowing that the enemy was approaching in force from East Tennessee, sent forward Colonel Metcalfe, of the Seventh Kentucky Cavalry, with about four hundred men from his own regiment, and Colonel Childs' battalion, recently from Cumberland Gap, to take post at Big Hill and oppose the advance of the enemy. On the 23d of August, Colonel Metcalfe engaged a superior force, and at the beginning of the conflict the troops of his regiment became confused, and three-fourths of them fled. The other fourth, and the Tennessee battalion, however, fought bravely, and after repulsing the enemy, retired to the foot of the hill. Here Colonel Metcalfe rallied a large portion of his men, but upon the approach of the enemy they again fled, and the Tennesseeans, as before, stood firm, and so far restrained the enemy as to effect a safe retirement to Richmond. The enemy followed, and demanded the surrender of the town, but upon learning that Colonel Linck, from General Cruft's brigade, had arrived with reinforcements, withdrew. Soon after this occurrence General Nelson ordered General Manson, with his own brigade and General Cruft's, to march to Richmond, who, on arriving, established his camps two miles south of the town, and sent a portion of his cavalry forward to observe the enemy.

On the 29th, Lieutenant-Colonel Mundy, while scouting with a detachment of cavalry in the vicinity of Kingston, learned that the enemy was advancing in considerable force, and immediately informed General Manson of the fact, and the latter in turn forwarded the information to General Nelson at Lexington. General Manson then directed Colonel Mundy to make effort to hold the enemy in check, and ascertain his position and strength. He at the same time reinforced his pickets and prepared his brigade to advance at a moment's warning. At 2 P. M. he received information that his cavalry and infantry pickets were receding before a force estimated at five thousand men. General Manson then advanced with his brigade, leaving General Cruft's at Richmond. Having moved forward about a mile and a half, and dispersed the enemy's cavalry and artillery with his own artillery, he took possession of a high ridge, and formed his troops in line of battle on each side of the road, placing his artillery on the flanks, so as to command the road and the open country as far south as Rogersville. The enemy soon appeared with infantry, cavalry, and artillery, but after a sharp skirmish of an hour's duration, with a loss of one cannon and several men captured, he withdrew. General Manson then advanced to Rogersville, placed his command in bivouac, and sent Colonel Metcalfe in pursuit of the enemy, under instructions to ascertain his strength. He also directed General Cruft to post strong guards on the Lancaster turnpike, and on the road entering the town from the east, and hold the remainder of his brigade in readiness to move at notice. Colonel Metcalfe encountered the enemy six miles out, and after a slight skirmish fell back to Rogersville.

At 6 A. M. the next day, General Manson ordered General Cruft to his support, having learned that the enemy was again advancing. He then moved forward and met the enemy's vanguard about a half mile south of Rogersville, and taking position on a wooded elevation formed a line of battle, with the Fifty-fifth Indiana on the left of the road behind a fence, the Sixty-ninth Indiana on the right, the artillery on high ground to the left, and the Seventy-first Indiana in reserve. The skirmishers on the left opened the battle, and simultaneously the Sixteenth Indiana coming up took position in the woods on the left of the Fifty-fifth. After the fighting had continued for an hour, the enemy made a fierce assault upon the left, and the Seventy-first Indiana was ordered to its support. While executing this movement, the regiment was subjected to a galling fire, and Lieutenant-Colonel Topping and Major Conkling fell, the former mortally wounded and the latter killed. This reinforcement of the left did not relieve it from severe pressure, and seven companies of the Sixty-ninth Indiana from the right were also directed to its support. At this juncture, General Cruft reached the field with the advance of his brigade—the Ninety-fifth Ohio and a section of artillery. The Ninety-fifth was placed on the right behind the three companies of the Sixty-ninth, then warmly engaged, and were ordered to charge a battery which was posted on an eminence a short distance to the front. In making this charge, the regiment was thrown into disorder by the severe fire to which it was exposed, and then the enemy pressed the right from position. The left also was turned by a flank movement under cover of the woods, and driven back in disorder. Just as the rout became general, the remainder of General Cruft's brigade appeared. The Eighteenth Kentucky at once formed in line, and in a few minutes was compelled to fall back with heavy loss. The other two regiments of the brigade, the Twelfth and Sixty-sixth, were formed in line on a high position near Rogersville, a mile to the rear of the first line, and upon them the fragments of the routed troops were rallied. The ground here, however, not being considered favorable for defense, General Manson posted his cavalry and one gun on an eminence to check the enemy and withdrew to his position of the previous evening, and then formed again as in the morning, with his troops as much as possible under cover and his artillery on the flanks. As the enemy was advancing upon this new position, General Manson received an order from General Nelson, of August 30th, directing him to retire by the Lancaster road should the enemy approach in force. It was then too late for obedience, as a few minutes later the enemy attacked his whole line with great energy, and though his right was at first pressed back by artillery fire, he finally, though checked repeatedly, pressed General Cruft's troops back in great disorder. The left was then withdrawn and the whole force fell back to its camps in front of Richmond, the enemy pursuing closely. Here General Manson endeavored again to reform his command, and had partially succeeded, when General Nelson appeared and directed that a line should be formed near the town and cemetery. The troops had barely reached the position designated and formed in line before the enemy assaulted in overwhelming force. Resisting for a few minutes, the whole line crumbled, and its fragments drifted through Richmond and on to Louisville.

General Nelson's command consisted almost entirely of new regiments, and did not exceed six thousand five hundred. He lost two hundred killed, seven hundred wounded, and two thousand captured, and nine guns. The enemy's strength was twelve thousand infantry, four thousand cavalry, and fifteen guns. He lost two hundred and fifty killed and about five hundred wounded.

There was now no well-organized force to meet General Smith's army, and the excitement in Louisville and Cincinnati was intense. General Nelson took command at Louisville, and attempted to organize the new troops and the citizens who volunteered for the defense of the city. Multitudes from the adjacent populous regions hastened to Cincinnati to save the city from pillage.

After the battle of Richmond, General E. K. Smith moved

northward, with General Heath's division in advance, in boldest menace to Covington and Cincinnati. To defend these cities, new troops and citizens gathered in great numbers at Cincinnati, and an army had been formed of such proportions under Generals A. J. Smith, L. Wallace, and Gordon Granger, and though having approached very near to Covington, the Confederate general refrained from attack, and contented himself with distributing his forces in the eastern portion of Central Kentucky, to gather supplies and recruits, and there await the results of the movement of the armies of Generals Bragg and Buell toward Louisville.

CHAPTER XV.

CAMPAIGN OF PERRYVILLE, KENTUCKY.

GENERAL BUELL found at Louisville a large force of new troops, comprising the remnant of General Nelson's division, and regiments that had been hurriedly thrown into the city for its defense against the two Confederate armies in the state. He at once commenced the reorganization and re-equipment of his army. The new troops were mingled with his veterans, clothing was issued to all, and full preparations made for an active campaign against General Bragg. Three corps, each comprising three divisions, designated as First, Second, and Third, were formed, and Major-Generals A. McD. McCook and T. L. Crittenden and Brigadier-General C. C. Gilbert were announced as corps commanders.

On the 29th of September, Major-General Thomas received an order at the hands of Colonel McKibben, aid-de-camp to Major-General Halleck, commander-in-chief, assigning him to the command of the Army of the Ohio, but at his request General Buell was retained. The day following, General Thomas was announced as second in command.

General Buell, having completed his preparations for his movement against General Bragg, commenced his advance on the 1st day of October. General Sill's division, of General McCook's or the left corps, and General Dumont's, which had not been assigned to a corps, moved on the left toward Frankfort, to hold in check the army of General Kirby Smith. The remainder of the army moved directly on General Bragg's position at Bardstown. General McCook's corps advanced through Taylorsville, General Gilbert's through Shepherdsville, and General Crittenden's through Mount Washington, upon roads converging upon Bardstown from those places. Soon after leaving Louisville the head of each column engaged in skirmishing with the enemy's cavalry and artillery, the resistance constantly increasing as the army approached Bardstown. This was done to give time for General Bragg to withdraw his army, and this he accomplished a few hours before the heads of column approached the town. He retreated toward Springfield, and so close a pursuit was maintained that skirmishing with his rear-guard was not unfrequent. Inferring from information received, that the two Confederate armies would unite at Danville, General Buell directed General McCook, whose corps had arrived at Bloomfield, to march on Harrodsburg; he instructed General Thomas to move with Crittenden's corps on the Lebanon and Danville road, which passes four miles east of Perryville, with a branch road leading to that place, and in person proceeded with Gilbert's corps on the direct road to Perryville. Having learned soon afterward, that Smith's army had crossed to the west side of the Kentucky river near Salvisa, and was marching to form a junction with General Bragg at Harrodsburg or Perryville, he ordered General McCook to bear to the right and march on the latter place.

General Buell, with the central corps, arrived at a point within three and one-half miles of Perryville on the evening of the 7th, and having ascertained that the enemy held the place in force, directed that the corps should be disposed in order of battle. In compliance, General Mitchell's division was formed across the road, General Sheridan's on an elevation to the left, and General Schoepf's was held in reserve. In the meantime, the vanguard, under Captain Gay, consisting of cavalry and artillery, reinforced by two regiments, had, after heavy skirmishing, pressed the enemy's rear-guard a mile farther toward the town, and it was discovered that the enemy was concentrating for battle. General Buell at once dispatched orders for the other two corps to march at 3 o'clock the next morning and form on the right and left of the corps already in position. His orders required that each corps commander, upon the attainment of position on the field, should report to him in person, and expressed the expectation of attacking and carrying the enemy's position at Perryville the next day.

General McCook received his orders at 2½ o'clock the next morning, and had his column on the march at 5 o'clock. He reached his designated position at 10½ A. M., and formed his two divisions, Generals Rousseau's and Jackson's, on the left of General Gilbert's corps, connecting Rousseau's division with Gilbert's left. The order requiring an early movement of the troops and prescribing the preliminary arrangements for battle, did not reach General Thomas as soon as anticipated, in consequence of the fact that he had been compelled the night before to diverge from his direct line of march to obtain water for his command; his cavalry, nevertheless, was in front of the position to which he had been assigned, at daylight, and pushed back the pickets of the enemy. General Crittenden's corps came up later even than General McCook's, but two divisions were in position before noon. Upon being informed, early in the morning, that the enemy was in front of his position, General Thomas went forward to arrange for the formation of Crittenden's corps, and at noon sent an officer of his staff, Captain Mack, to inform General Buell of his arrival and position, and requesting instructions through him, assigning the presence of the enemy in his front as an excuse for not reporting in person. As soon as General Crittenden reached his assigned position, he sent a staff officer to General Gilbert to make inquiries with regard to his formation, and General Gilbert states in his official report that he went to General Crittenden's position to give the information in person.

The roads over which the army had advanced the preceding day were very dusty, and owing to this and the hot dry weather and scarcity of water, the troops had suffered exceedingly. During the night, Colonel Daniel McCook's brigade of Sheridan's division had been thrown forward from the center, to occupy the heights in front of Doctor's creek, a tributary of Chaplin creek, and about two and a half miles from Perryville. After a sharp skirmish, Colonel McCook succeeded at daylight in gaining the heights, and secured some pools of water in the bed of the stream, which afforded poor water for the thirsty troops. About two hours after the heights had been occupied, the enemy in considerable force advanced through the woods on the eastern slope and endeavored to regain the position. General Sheridan then ordered forward Laiboldt's brigade and Hescock's battery, instructing Colonel Laiboldt to advance two regiments and drive back the enemy. Stubborn resistance was offered, but after a severe conflict, in which both sides lost quite heavily, the enemy was forced across Chaplin river. In this action, Captain Barnett, with a section of his battery, and Lieutenant Taliaferro, with a section of Hescock's, forced the guns of the enemy from position.

The noise of this action incited McCook's corps to haste in gaining position, and near its close it arrived on the field, and General McCook at once directed General Rousseau to throw forward a line of skirmishers to examine the woods on the left and in front. He ordered Captain Wickliffe's company of cavalry to reconnoiter the ground to the left of the skirmishers, as acting Brigadier-General Gay was at the time making a reconnoissance in front and toward Perryville; directed General Jackson to post his two brigades on commanding ground, immediately to the right of the Maxville and Perryville road, and to hold them in column ready to move in whatever direction occasion might require; and ordered that Captain Loomis' battery should be posted on high ground, near Russell's house, to the left. He then indicated his line of battle, and directed General Rousseau to form it. Following these dispositions and the conflict in the center, there was a period of quietness, during which General McCook reported in person to General Buell, some distance in the rear, and General Gilbert went to General Crittenden's position. The force which had engaged General Gilbert's left had retired, and there were no other troops in view.

General McCook was instructed by General Buell to make a reconnoissance to Chaplin river, upon his return to his command; but during his absence, the troops were suffering so severely for water that General Rousseau ordered the right of his line forward a half mile to obtain a supply. Soon after, the enemy appeared in force, and having placed three batteries in position, opened fire. General Rousseau then moved his other two brigades abreast of his right, and responded to the enemy's artillery with Loomis' and Simonson's batteries. At this juncture, General McCook returned, and seeing no infantry, he directed that the batteries should cease firing and economize their ammunition. Learning that commanding ground for a portion of his line could be obtained a short distance to the left of the Perryville road (the one leading from Maxville), he ordered a portion of the Thirty-third Ohio into the woods in front to ascertain if the enemy was present in that vicinity, within a distance of six hundred yards from Chaplin river. Having gone forward himself, he called to him Generals Jackson and Terrell, "showed them the water, marked their line of battle," and ordered a battery to be posted on the line with strong supports. He further directed General Terrell "to advance a line of skirmishers cautiously down the slopes of the hill to the water, as soon as his line was formed," that the so much needed water might be obtained. The execution of this movement developed no enemy, except a body of cavalry, which appeared on the hills across the river, and fled upon receiving the fire of Stone's battery, posted to the left and rear of the position.

At half-past 1 o'clock, General McCook, not anticipating an attack, as no strong force of the enemy had been in view in his front, rode to the right of the line. But at 2 P. M. the enemy attacked the skirmishers of the Thirty-third Ohio, and then he ordered the remainder of the regiment, Lieutenant-Colonel Moore commanding, and the Second Ohio to their support. At this juncture, his line was formed, with Rousseau's right, near a barn on the right of the Maxville and Perryville road, and extending to the left on a ridge through a cornfield (the corn being cut and shocked), to the skirt of woods occupied by the Second and Thirty-third Ohio regiments; while the right of Terrell's brigade of Jackson's division held a wooded elevation running along to the left, overlooking a portion of Chaplin river, and his left formed a crotchet to the rear, in order to occupy the high ground to the left and rear. Starkweather's brigade and Stone's and Bush's batteries of Rousseau's division were posted to the left and rear of Jackson's left, on high ground, and Webster's brigade of Jackson's division was placed to the left of Russell's house and in the rear of the center of Rousseau's line.

Very soon after, the enemy fell upon the skirmishers of the Thirty-second Ohio. McCook's whole line became hotly engaged, while the chief force of the enemy was directed against his left. General Jackson was killed by the first fire, and by $2\frac{1}{2}$ P. M. General Terrell's brigade, composed of new troops, under an exceedingly heavy pressure by superior numbers, was forced back in confusion. General Terrell showed great bravery, and exerted himself to the utmost to hold his troops firm, but in vain. It was the traditional method of the enemy—an attack by a massed force on the end of a line—and an inferior force of raw troops soon gave way before it. Perceiving that his left had been turned, General McCook sent Lieutenant Hosea, of his staff, to request General Sheridan to secure his right. A half hour later, $2\frac{1}{2}$ P. M., he dispatched Captain Fisher to the nearest commander of troops for assistance. This officer met General Schoepf, who was advancing to the front with his division, who referred him to General Gilbert, who was with the column. He reported to General Gilbert that "McCook's whole command was engaged, his reserves being all in line, and that the safety of his corps was compromised." General Gilbert referred Captain Fisher to General Buell, but afforded no assistance. General McCook sent a third staff officer, Captain Hoblitzell, at 3 P. M., to General Schoepf, or the commander of the nearest troops, to ask for help. Having thus made effort to obtain reinforcements, he remained with his left until the enemy had been repulsed by Starkweather's brigade and the cross fire of Stone's and Bush's batteries, all suitably posted to secure this result, after Terrell's brigade had been driven back and the enemy had swung round in pursuit. The batteries alone held the enemy in check for some time. When having received reinforcements, he assaulted with great fury. The Twenty-first Wisconsin, lying in front of the batteries, then opened a destructive fire, but were forced back. The batteries and the remainder of the brigade were then assaulted, but here the enemy was repulsed again. He repeated his assaults with fresh troops, but was driven back each time with heavy loss, until the brigade and batteries having exhausted their ammunition, quietly retired to the line first selected, where, having obtained ammunition, they renewed the conflict.

Having witnessed the repulse of the enemy on his left, General McCook proceeded to his right, concerning which he had hitherto felt no uneasiness, to witness the issue of a terrible conflict there. While the battle had been raging on the left, General Rousseau's right and center brigades, commanded respectively by Colonels Lytle and Harris, had been hotly engaged, and had repeatedly repulsed the enemy, although his attacks had been made by superior numbers. Colonel Harris' brigade held its position against every assault, inflicting severe punishment upon the enemy, and presenting an unbroken front, even after its ammunition had been exhausted. It was finally withdrawn to the original line simultaneously with Starkweather's brigade. There was now an opening between Lytle's right and the central corps, while his left flank was exposed. General McCook ordered Colonel Webster to oppose the enemy, and in the vain effort he fell, mortally wounded. The enemy, in the meantime, having posted a battery in a favorable position, opened a destructive fire upon Lytle's right flank, and he too fell back. Even then the right, near Russell's house, could not be held, owing to the destructive fire of artillery and the heat of a burning barn in proximity. The enemy, with its recession, swung round in Lytle's rear. Fortunately, Loomis' battery, which, having previously exhausted its long-range ammunition, had been retired to a commanding ridge, about one hundred and fifty yards in the rear of Russell's house, under instructions to reserve its canister for close work, was now in readiness for such a fire as checked the enemy's advance. Soon after, Colonel Gooding's brigade, with Pinney's battery (Fifth Wisconsin), from Mitchell's division of the central corps, was near, and by the spirited action of infantry and artillery, the enemy was driven back and the position at Russell's was regained. This brigade lost four hundred and ninety men—nearly one-fourth of its effective strength. General Steedman's brigade, from Schoepf's division, followed Gooding's closely, and these reinforcements and night arrested the battle at this point. When

General Terrell's brigade gave way in the first onset, a portion of it fell back to the position of Stone's and Bush's batteries; and there, in the effort to rally his troops, this gallant commander fell, mortally wounded, and died a few hours later.

In the recession of the left, seven pieces of Parsons' eight-gun battery fell into the hands of the enemy, and at 6 P. M. four guns of Harris' Indiana battery were also lost.

About the time that General McCook was first attacked, General Sheridan advanced Captain Hescock's battery to a good position in front of a belt of woods, where he had an enfilading fire on the enemy's batteries on the opposite side of the valley of Chaplin river, and advanced six regiments to support it. The fire of this battery was severe, and the enemy attempted to dislodge it by establishing a battery at short range. But Hescock's shots were so well directed and effective, that the enemy abandoned this advanced position in a few minutes. The enemy then posted two batteries on Sheridan's right flank with infantry behind them, when General Sheridan, in obedience to orders, occupied the hill from which he had previously driven the enemy. The enemy again assaulted the position and advanced close to Sheridan's line, although suffering fearful losses from canister. Being now greatly pressed, General Sheridan called upon General Gilbert for reinforcements, and the latter ordered Schoepf's and Mitchell's divisions to close to the left and support him. Arriving at the scene of conflict, General Mitchell threw forward Colonel Carlin's brigade to relieve Sheridan's right from pressure. As Colonel Carlin ascended to the brow of the hill, he observed the enemy advancing in strong force, and he immediately charged, broke his line, and drove him beyond Perryville. Near the town, the Thirty-eighth Illinois, in the advance, captured three officers, one hundred and thirty men, some wagons, and two caissons with horses attached. Seeing that he was not supported on either flank, Carlin took advantage of the confusion of the enemy and safely withdrew. General Sheridan also drove the enemy for some distance, but having perceived that General McCook's right, having been left without support, had been turned, deemed it unsafe to advance far, and therefore turned his artillery upon the enemy across the valley, and thus relieved the pressure upon the left wing.

Though General Thomas had found the enemy in his front early in the morning, and had reported his presence as his excuse for not reporting to the commanding general in person, and although General Gilbert's corps had been engaged more or less from the earlier hours of the morning, and General McCook's corps had been struggling against overwhelming numbers, Gen. Thomas received no orders from Gen. Buell until 4 P. M., upon the return of Captain Mack. The verbal instructions through this officer were, that he should hold a division in readiness to reinforce the center if necessary, to reconnoiter his front to ascertain if the enemy had reinforced his left or was withdrawing, and report all information obtained. In compliance, the reconnoissance was made immediately, and developed the enemy; but though the fact was reported, no further orders respecting operations for that day were received. Owing to the absence of instructions requiring the advance of the right corps, it was not engaged during the day, excepting the cavalry in the morning, in the front, and Wagner's brigade of Wood's division, which became involved with General Mitchell's right, late in the evening.

In compliance with orders from General Buell, Generals Thomas, McCook, and Gilbert reported at his headquarters at night, to receive instructions for the next day. General McCook was directed to move his corps during the night and close up on General Gilbert's left, to hold this position and take advantage of any opportunity that the events of the day might present. Generals Thomas and Gilbert were ordered to make preparations to advance on Perryville at daylight the next morning, and attack the enemy's front and left flank, keeping their adjacent flanks well connected. The movements, as ordered, were made during the night and morning; but the advance troops in the morning discovered that the enemy had retired during the night; and was falling back to Harrodsburg, but had left no evidence of haste or disorder, save that his dead and wounded remained on the field.

General Buell reported his loss in this battle at nine hundred and sixteen killed, two thousand nine hundred and forty-three wounded, and four hundred and eighty-nine missing; total, four thousand three hundred and forty-eight. An exceedingly large number for the troops severely engaged, but one that attests their valor. Nearly all the losses were from McCook's two divisions, and the brigade sent from the center to his support.

The loss of the enemy in killed and wounded is not known. General Buell claims that from first to last, he captured from four to five thousand men, including the sick and wounded.

This battle, in some of its features at least, was the result of the mutual misconception of the situation by the commanding generals, and its initiation was palpably owing to the ignorance of General Bragg with regard to the actual concentration of eight divisions of the Army of the Ohio before him. General Bragg did not know this when he made an attack upon its left and center with three divisions. He had not, previous to the 7th, intended to give battle at Perryville, but owing to the pressure upon his rear, which arrested two of his divisions, Buckner's and Anderson's,* under General Hardee, he at that time determined to concentrate three divisions, Cheatham's and the two others mentioned of General Polk's command, and give battle before that town. On the 7th, Cheatham moved from Harrodsburg, General Bragg having sent Withers' division the day before to support Smith against the column formed of Sill's and Dumont's divisions advancing against him. Having learned subsequently that this force was retreating, he then proceeded to Perryville, and was present at the battle, though disclaiming the conduct of it beyond suggesting some changes in General Polk's dispositions. These facts, mentioned officially by General Bragg, indicate clearly that he expected to fight at Perryville only the more advanced portions of General Buell's army. He states explicitly in his report, that he declined battle on the 9th, because General Buell had received reinforcements during the previous day and night. With regard to the opening of the

* This was probably Hardee's division, in temporary command of Anderson; at least, the division which General Hardee had previously commanded.

battle, he made the following statements : " The action opened at half-past 12 P. M., between skirmishers and artillery on both sides. Finding the enemy indisposed to advance against us, and knowing that he was receiving heavy reinforcements, I deemed it best to assail him vigorously, and so directed."

On the other hand, General Buell did not seem to know that before General McCook became seriously engaged, General Crittenden's corps was in line of battle on General Gilbert's right. General Gilbert had been with General Crittenden while aligning his corps, and returned to his own before the action commenced, as he states in his official report. General Thomas' statement does not give the exact time when his line of battle was formed, but the fact of his own early presence on the field, and his early report of this fact to General Buell, through a staff officer, which report by order was contingent upon the assumption of position by Crittenden's corps, leaves no room to doubt that this corps was in readiness to participate in the action soon after 12 M. At this hour two of Crittenden's divisions, Smith's and Van Cleve's, were in position, and Wood's was two miles in the rear marching to the front. About 4 P. M. General Buell first learned that McCook's corps was seriously engaged and heavily pressed. He then ordered General Gilbert to send a division to its support, and directed General Thomas to hold one division in readiness to support the left. The execution of the order to General Gilbert gave two additional brigades to the support of General McCook near the close of the action. It does not appear, from any of the official reports from which this narrative has been drawn, that the order, announcing the intention to give battle on the 8th, and enforcing preparations for it, had been revoked, and from this fact, and the noise of musketry as well as artillery, which had announced the beginning and progress of a battle involving the center and left, there was a general expectation throughout Crittenden's corps that it too would participate in the action.

The testimony is very explicit from General Gilbert that General McCook called upon him for help (as his corps was upon the point of being compromised), when he was returning from General Crittenden's position, and that upon his second call he sent him one brigade and a battery, before he received an order from General Buell, through Major Wright, to send two brigades to his support. Thus the suddenness and impetuosity of the attack upon McCook did not permit him to delay for a moment in asking aid from the nearest troops, and it was General Gilbert who sent one of McCook's staff officers to General Buell, as he could not at first give him reinforcements. Thus, these two corps commanders conducted the engagement from their respective positions, to meet the attacks of the enemy, without orders from General Buell, and without any recognized plan of battle, or any apparent object, except to maintain their ground by repulsing the enemy.

Though General Bragg had withdrawn his army, General Buell still believed that he would deliver battle, and that Smith's army had joined him for that purpose. He therefore determined, that as the two Confederate columns had formed a junction, to await the arrival of General Sill's division, which he had ordered forward from Frankfort. In the meantime, he placed his army in position, his right four miles from Danville, his center on the Perryville and Harrodsburg turnpike, and his left near Duckville, on the roads converging to Harrodsburg. On the march from Frankfort, General Sill was attacked near Lawrenceburg by a portion of General Smith's army, but he repulsed the attack, and arrived at Perryville on the 11th. General Dumont's division remained at Frankfort.

On the morning of the 11th, a reconnoissance was made by three brigades of infantry from Crittenden's and Gilbert's corps, and by McCook's and Gay's cavalry, and discovered the enemy in force about three miles south of Harrodsburg, but he retired during the day, and his rear-guard was driven out of the town in the evening, with the loss of some stores, and about twelve hundred prisoners, mostly sick and wounded. The next day, General Buell ordered General McCook's corps to Harrodsburg, General Crittenden's to the left and rear of Danville, and General Gilbert's to a point midway between these towns, on the road connecting them, while a strong reconnoitering force advanced to the crossing of Dick's river, and ascertained that the enemy had crossed his entire army.

Two days later, it was known that the enemy was retreating south, and pursuit was at once ordered. General Wood's division marched at 12 o'clock that night, and engaged the enemy's artillery and cavalry at Stanford the next morning at daylight. The remainder of General Crittenden's corps, and all of General McCook's, followed General Wood through Danville and Stanford to Crab Orchard, and General Gilbert's corps reached the same point through Lancaster. The enemy resisted the head of each column with cavalry and artillery whenever he could find favorable positions, but he was steadily followed, and often attacked, as he moved on toward Cumberland Gap.

From Crab Orchard southward, the country is barren and rough, affording only meager supplies, and as there was now no prospects of forcing General Bragg to an engagement, McCook's and Gilbert's corps were halted at Crab Orchard, while Crittenden's, with W. S. Smith's division leading, followed on to London, on the direct road, and to Manchester, on the branch road. But nothing was effected beyond successful skirmishing with the enemy's rear-guard, and the capture of some prisoners and cattle. There being no promise of further advantage, the pursuit was not continued beyond London, and the Army of the Ohio turned toward Bowling Green and Glasgow, preparatory to a movement to Nashville. General Buell retired to Louisville, leaving General Thomas in chief command.

On the 26th of October, General Buell directed General Thomas by telegraph to concentrate the corps of Generals McCook and Gilbert at Bowling Green, and that of General Crittenden at Glasgow. In compliance, Generals McCook and Gilbert moved from Crab Orchard to Bowling Green—the former through Stanford, Lebanon, Somerville, and Cave City, and the latter on the same route, excepting through Campbellsville instead of Somerville. General Crittenden marched from London to Glasgow through Somerset, Columbia, and Edmonton. The cavalry remained at Lebanon to refit and otherwise prepare for active service.

It was not certainly known at this time what General Bragg's next movement would be. His successful retreat from Perryville proved the easy mobility of his army, and the direction of it warranted the fear that he would endeavor to attack Nashville before its feeble garrison could be reinforced. This was the expectation of General Buell when he turned his columns toward Bowling Green, but the authorities at Washington not only suggested, but ordered that his army should enter East Tennessee. This difference of opinion elicited a lengthy discussion, which terminated in the removal of General Buell from the command of the Army of the Ohio on the 30th of October.

The operations of Generals Johnston and Lee in Virginia and Maryland, and of General Bragg in Mississippi, Tennessee, and Kentucky, during the summer and autumn of 1862, compassed the broadest, if not the boldest, aggression of the Confederate armies during the war, and perhaps were expressive of their greatest actual strength, and freighted with the strongest hopes which the Southern people ever entertained subsequent to their first great defeats. In the forecast of these campaigns, it was assumed that General Bragg would unite the standards of four victorious columns at Louisville or Cincinnati, and that the commander of the eastern Confederate army should raise the symbol of their declared nationality on the dome of the national capitol. Then, should the fugitive or captive representatives of the national government refuse to recognize the independence of the Southern Confederacy, the two victorious armies were to co-operate in the invasion of the Northern States to compel an unwilling people to acknowledge its independence. While the murmurs of the people and the official complaints of the authorities at Washington were often repeated as General Buell advanced slowly toward Chattanooga and General McClellan halted before Richmond, the resources of the South were strained in preparation for the accomplishment of these grand objects. At this time, the national armies were holding the peninsula of Virginia in the East, and on the West, Cumberland Gap—a position of great strategic importance in both Northern and Southern regard—all Middle and West Tennessee, portions of Northern Mississippi and Alabama, commanding the resources, the rivers, and railroads of the vast region which had been wrested from the enemy, and their attitude was still one of absolute aggression. Suddenly they were thrown upon the defensive. The Army of the Potomac was defeated and withdrawn to Washington, the second battle was lost at Bull Run, and General Lee crossed the Potomac with his victorious legions. Then Kirby Smith turned Cumberland Gap, and soon after defeated at Richmond, Kentucky, the troops that had been improvised for the defense of Cincinnati and Louisville. Soon General Bragg, after sending hortatory orders to his lieutenants in Northern Mississippi to brush General Grant from their front and join him on the Ohio, scaled Waldron's ridge with his central column, and, finding an open way, hurried into Kentucky, proclaiming his advent as the redemption of the state from the despotism of the national government. These successes gave the brightest hour of the war to the South and the gloomiest one to the North—intensifying the opposition to it in the latter section, and imposing upon the government the most perplexing embarrassments. The conditions of the struggle seemed to have been changed entirely.

But promising as was the beginning of these campaigns to the South, like all others of similar character throughout the war, they resulted in failure, at least in respect to their dominant objects. When it was that General Bragg lost heart completely is not revealed, but he certainly gave evidence of some miscalculation, miscarriage, or waning hope, when he declined battle at Prewitt's Knob. He had previously moved in apparent disregard of the greater army which he had thrown to his rear, by leaping upon its communications, and yet his operations at the very moment of their seeming culmination lost their bold aspect, and thereafter the boastful commander of the western Confederate armies drifted about in Kentucky, neither in spirit or maneuver justifying the assumptions of his proclamations. His offensive campaign, a failure in its ruling objects,* was nevertheless successful in many subordinate ones.

---

* One of these objects, doubtless, was the permanent occupancy of Kentucky, and to give public expression to it, he went through the pretense of inaugurating a Confederate provisional governor in room of Mr. Johnson, killed at the battle of Shiloh. The representation of the state in

He gained territory of vast extent with its ungarnered corn, and military advantages which were only overcome by a campaign of nearly a year's duration, a great battle, and a vast expenditure of war material. He also made a heavy draft upon the resources of Kentucky. Her granaries supplied his armies while in the state, and doubtless for a time after they left it. Kentucky stores and looms provided clothing for his needy soldiers; the farms and stables of rich Kentuckians furnished his troopers with the best horses in the land. These were no inconsiderable results, and some were paraded as compensative, but after all they did not give cheer and hope to the Southern people as the only consequences of a campaign which, in its inception and primal progress, promised the recognition of the Southern Confederacy by foreign nations and even by the United States. Actual accomplishment fell far below Southern expectation, east and west. And when General Lee retreated from the battle-field of Antietam, General Bragg from Perryville, and General Van Dorn from Corinth, the Southern people saw plainly that the war was still to bring desolation to their section, and that the boldest strategy and the exertion of their full strength could only press back, temporarily, the national armies.

The general offensive attitude of the insurgents, their unexpected revelation of great strength, and the defeats of the summer, forced upon the government and the loyal people the alternative of the abandonment of the conflict or the enlargement of the national armies, first to repel invasion and then reassume the offensive with augmented vigor. There was too much at stake to yield to the claims of the insurgents, and the government and the people, under the pressure of a necessity which involved the life of the nation, made a draft for men and means proportionate to the compass of the emergency. During September and October, as the narrative has disclosed, the invading armies were all repelled and new offensive campaigns were projected. The main one in the West, looking to the reoccupancy of Middle Tennessee and Northern Alabama,

the Confederate congress required that there should at least be the semblance of a state government in alliance with the government at Richmond, and this object was attained by the same measure and an advance into East Tennessee and Georgia, found official expression in the order of the war department, recreating the Department of the Cumberland.

CHAPTER XVI.

THE CONCENTRATION OF THE ARMY OF THE CUMBERLAND AT NASH-
VILLE, TENNESSEE, AND SUBORDINATE CONTINGENT OPERATIONS.

WHILE General Buell's army was concentrating at Bowling
Green and Glasgow, he was relieved of command by Major-
General W. S. Rosecrans. This change occurred October
30th, in compliance with general orders No. 168, war department, dated October 24, 1862. This order gave General
Rosecrans the command of the "Department of the Cumberland," which embraced that portion of Tennessee lying east of
the Tennessee river, with a prospective enlargement from such
portions of Alabama and Georgia as his army might gain. By
the same order the troops of the department were designated
as the "Fourteenth Army Corps." This designation soon
gave place to the more appropriate and popular one, "Army
of the Cumberland,"—the name which the original portions
bore under Generals Anderson and Sherman.

In a day or two after General Rosecrans assumed command,
the concentration ordered by his predecessor was effected. The
commands of Generals McCook and Gilbert, each consisting
of three divisions, were at Bowling Green. The three divisions under General Crittenden, with the exception of Hazen's
brigade, which had not returned from the pursuit of the enemy,
reached Glasgow on the 3d of November. The cavalry had
also arrived at Bowling Green.

The question of an objective, unsettled by previous discus-
sions, was inherited by General Rosecrans. For a time, he was
urged* to advance directly into East Tennessee; but the dan-

---

* See his testimony before the "Committee of Congress on the Conduct
of the War."

ger to Nashville, which, having been held against Breckinridge's command by Negley's and Palmer's divisions, was now the objective of a new combination, and the importance of this city as a secondary base of supplies, induced him to make preparations to concentrate his forces there. The veteran portion of his army needed rest and re-equipment, and the new regiments needed discipline; but the activity of the enemy gave no time for the recuperation of the one portion or the training of the other. The purposes of General Bragg were not at once revealed, but the conjectured advance of his army toward Nashville was almost immediately indicated with certainty by the appearance of his forces at Murfreesboro. As, therefore, Nashville was in danger from the advance of the army withdrawn from Kentucky, conjoined with Breckinridge's force, there was reason to fear that General Negley would be compelled to surrender, unless speedily reinforced. To prevent this, General Rosecrans ordered an advance to that city on the 4th of November. General McCook then moved from Bowling Green through Franklin, Mitchellsville, and Tyree Springs, and having posted Carlin's brigade at Edgefield Junction, to keep the communications open and protect supply trains, reached Nashville with the remainder of his command on the morning of the 9th, thus accomplishing a march of seventy-two miles in about three days. General Crittenden, leaving Smith's division temporarily at Glasgow, proceeded, with Wood's and Van Cleve's divisions, through Scottsville to Gallatin. Here he was joined by Colonel Kennett, in command of the cavalry, who had advanced from Bowling Green through Franklin, Mitchellsville, and Fountain Head. Colonel Zahm's brigade leading, the cavalry entered Gallatin simultaneously with Harker's brigade of Wood's division. These two brigades, acting in conjunction, drove out of the town the rear-guard of Morgan's cavalry, capturing twenty men with their horses. Morgan had just returned from the vicinity of Nashville, having unsuccessfully assaulted Colonel Smith at Edgefield on the 5th, losing five killed and nineteen wounded.

Early in the morning of the 5th, Forrest had also provoked an engagement on the other side of Nashville, having attacked

General Negley's pickets, who were withdrawn under the guns of Fort Negley. Immediately after their withdrawal, General Negley advanced against Forrest and drove him seven miles, and returning, foiled an attempt of the enemy to cut him off.

The advance of McCook and Crittenden relieved Nashville from siege, to the great disappointment of the enemy, who had several times, during September and October, arrogantly demanded its surrender.

General Breckinridge did not have a sufficient force to reduce the city, and General Thomas had left a second division to defend it. With two divisions as a garrison, it was no easy matter to hold the place and gather supplies from the country; but this was successfully accomplished. Supplies could not be sent from the North after the army entered Kentucky in pursuit of General Bragg, as his cavalry held the road in General Buell's rear; but the garrison was maintained through a general system of foraging,* with large trains and strong detachments. Had General Breckinridge had a sufficient force to invest the town, he might have accomplished its reduction by starving the garrison. As it was, he could not get near, as the fortifications commenced by General Nelson, during the summer, and enlarged by General Negley, enabled the troops to keep him at a distance; and he had to content himself with feints, demands for surrender, and watching for opportunities to cut off foraging parties. General Bragg could not really spare Breckinridge's command from his main column, and had he not hoped that his Mississippi forces would be able to join him, bringing Breckinridge's troops with them, he would not perhaps have detached them to demonstrate against a place which would inevitably fall into his hands if he should succeed in defeating General Buell and establishing himself in Kentucky. When he began to despair of his ability to meet General Buell, he had changed the tone of his orders to his Mississippi generals, and presented the absolute necessity of their support, and urged them to free West Ten-

---

* The garrison was partly supplied by farmers living in the vicinity who willingly fed their enemies at good prices and prompt payment.

nessee and hasten to him, putting their hands upon Nashville as they came.   This was impracticable, without them, as General Breckinridge had no reinforcements, and the active garrison was ever ready for defense and almost ubiquitous in its foraging opperations.

General Negley did not confine himself altogether to the defensive, but made at least one offensive dash, with very favorable results.   Learning, early in October, that the enemy was concentrating at La Vergne, fifteen miles south, he sent out General Palmer, with eight hundred men—infantry and cavalry in equal strength, and four guns—on the direct road, and Colonel Miller, with eighteen hundred infantry, by a circuitous route, to the south of La Vergne.   General Palmer skirmished with the enemy as he advanced, and having provoked him to make a stand, after a fight of thirty minutes he was routed, with a loss of eighty killed and wounded, one hundred and seventy-five captured, with three guns and the colors of a regiment.

The system of pickets adopted by Lieutenant-Colonel Von Schrader was so complete, that during a nominal siege of two months, there were no surprises.

With Nashville gained, General Rosecrans turned his attention to the equipment and discipline of his army, and the establishment of railroad communications with Louisville, and demanded the earnest co-operation of his officers of every grade, in the accomplishment of these objects.

On the 7th of November, General Rosecrans announced, in general order No. 8, the reorganization of his army, assigning Major-General Thomas to the command of the "Center," comprising the divisions of Rousseau, Negley, Dumont, Fry, and Palmer; Major-General McCook to the command of the "Right Wing," and Major-General Crittenden to that of the "Left Wing."   Soon after he gave the divisions of Sheridan, Sill, and Woodruff* to General McCook, and those of Wood, Smith, and Van Cleve to General Crittenden.

The Louisville and Nashville railroad having been opened

---

*Generals R. W. Johnson and J. C. Davis subsequently commanded in room of General Sill and Colonel Woodruff, and General J. M. Palmer in room of General Smith.

to Mitchellsville, a point a few miles north of the south tunnel, which Morgan had greatly injured, a temporary depot of supplies was there established. The enemy had so damaged the road at the tunnel and between it and Nashville, that it required a period of several weeks to put it in running order. Until its completion, supplies for all the troops south of Mitchellsville were transported in wagons.

The completion and protection of the railroad, and the transportation of supplies, were intrusted to General Thomas, whose headquarters were established at Gallatin. Pursuant to orders, General Thomas relieved General Smith's division, at Glasgow, with Colonel Scott's brigade of General Dumont's division; sent Dumont with his other two brigades to Scottsville; occupied Gallatin with General Fry's division, for the protection of the railroad, and employed General Rousseau's division to forward supplies and assist in the maintenance of communications with Nashville. The divisions of Generals Negley and Palmer remained at Nashville.

While the command of General Thomas was thus located and employed, General Crittenden crossed the Cumberland river and disposed his troops at Silver Springs, and was there joined by General Smith, who had moved his division from Glasgow by way of Gallatin.

On the 9th, General Rosecrans established his headquarters at Nashville, an event which indicated the concentration of his army, and preparations for an advance. The enemy was active near his army, in efforts to intercept supply trains, annoy and capture outposts, and overwhelm feeble detachments, but as yet it was not known where General Bragg would concentrate his forces. Being superior in cavalry, his sporadic operations were often successful, and he succeeded, too, until late in the month, in veiling his grander objects. But ignorance of the ulterior designs of his antagonist did not prevent General Rosecrans from accomplishing his own, and gradually his forces were moved toward Nashville, even before railroad communications were established between that city and Louisville. General Crittenden moved on the 18th from Silver Springs, and leisurely concentrated his force at Nashville. General Dumont, with two brigades, advanced to Gallatin.

Scott's brigade moved first from Glasgow to Tompkinsville, and subsequently to Hartsville. Harlan's brigade was posted at Castalian Springs, and Colonel Hall was ordered forward from Munfordsville to Glasgow. General Paine reported to General Thomas, to take command of the troops guarding the railroad, and established his headquarters at Gallatin.

During the month of November the enemy had no marked success, even in his chosen mode of warfare. In most cases he was foiled in attempting to capture supply trains and outposts, and in several aggressive enterprises the national troops gained decided advantages. Several of these minor actions deserve mention.

November 12th, Colonel S. D. Bruce, with seventeen companies of infantry and about nine hundred cavalry, was ordered from Bowling Green to Russellville to clear that section of guerrillas. He marched from Russellville on the 29th, and routed about eight hundred of the enemy's irregular troops, and drove them beyond Clarksville, toward Charlotte.

About the 16th, Colonel Carlin sent a detachment, under Colonel McKee, from Edgefield, across the Cumberland river, into Cheatham county, to give attention to guerrillas. Colonel McKee captured forty-six men and thirty horses and mules, and returned to Edgefield on the 20th.

Two days later, General Morgan attacked Lieutenant-Colonel Lister, commanding the Thirty-first Ohio, at Cage's ford of the Cumberland river, and was handsomely repulsed. Colonel Lister had been posted there several days before by direction of General Thomas. Just before the attack, Morgan, in person, as it was afterward ascertained, and several of his staff, all in disguise, approached under a flag of truce. As they revealed no purpose which justified the use of this flag, Colonel Lister inferred that their real object was a reconnoissance with a view to capture his command. As the river was between him and support, he crossed over soon after Morgan left, and from the safer side awaited his coming. Morgan soon appeared again, and anticipating an easy capture, rushed upon Lister's vacant position, and was severely punished by the volleys of his intended captives from the opposite bank of the stream.

Colonel Kennett, acting chief of cavalry, left Hartsville on the 17th, and joined General Crittenden at Silver Springs. He subsequently took position in his front south of Nashville. On the 27th, he routed a large body of the enemy on the Franklin turnpike, and drove them fifteen miles.

The same day, General Kirk, with a portion of his brigade, drove Wheeler from La Vergne, capturing a small number of prisoners. From them, definite information concerning General Bragg's position, strength, and purposes was obtained. From this time General Rosecrans' plans had reference to a probable battle near Murfreesboro.

In the evening of the 27th, Colonel Roberts, of the Forty-second Illinois, captured a captain and squad of Morgan's men, with their equipments and horses; and about the same time, Major Hill, with a squadron of the Second Indiana Cavalry, recaptured a forage train, releasing the prisoners taken with it, and killing twenty of the force that had made the capture, by suddenly crossing the Cumberland river near Hartsville.

A few days later, Hartsville was made memorable by a serious disaster to the national arms. December 2d, Colonel Scott, of the Nineteenth Illinois, had been relieved of the command of the Thirty-ninth brigade by Colonel A. B. Moore, of the One Hundred and Fourth Illinois. This brigade had been stationed at Hartsville, by General Thomas, to guard a ford and observe the enemy on the Lebanon road. The position was elevated, and regarded as susceptible of easy defense. The brigade comprised the One Hundred and Sixth and One Hundred and Eighth Ohio Infantry, the One Hundred and Fourth Illinois, about two hundred and fifty men of the Second Indiana Cavalry, and one company of Kentucky cavalry, in all, about eighteen hundred men. The effective force, however, was twelve hundred, as two hundred had been sent to Gallatin, and four hundred were unfit for duty.

On the 6th, General Morgan, with a strong force of cavalry, infantry, and artillery, left Prairie Mills, eight miles south of Lebanon and twenty-five from Hartsville, and encamped the following night within five miles of the latter place. Morgan's strength has been variously estimated. Colonel Moore placed it at four thousand cavalry and two regiments of infantry. In "Morgan and his Captors," his strength is estimated at fifteen hundred men. General Bragg, in his congratulatory order after the engagement, states that he had twelve hundred men in action.

Morgan planned a complete surprise. He crossed the Cumberland and encamped so quietly the night of the 6th, and approached and formed his lines so adroitly the next morning, that he was almost in Moore's camps before it was known that he was near. The reports of his advance are so conflicting that it can not be ascertained with certainty how Morgan's proximity became known. Colonel Moore's videttes and pickets, from his fault in posting them, or their own in the performance of their duty, did not give warning of his approach. Still the surprise was not absolute. The "pickets" or "camp guard," or some frightened "negro," certainly made known that he was coming, but not in time for the formation of suitable plans to resist him. At the time he was discovered, he was marching toward a ravine at the base of the hill upon which Moore's command was posted. A frail skirmish line opposed his advance, and gave time for the hasty formation of a line of battle on the top of the hill. Morgan formed a compact line with his infantry and a portion of his cavalry dismounted, and moved steadily to the ravine, there securing a somewhat sheltered position, from which his fire was so effective that Colonel Moore deemed his position untenable, and approved of a movement to the rear. In effecting this, the command was thrown into confusion. Colonel Tafel, of the One Hundred and Sixth Ohio, assumed a position of his own selection, without orders. The One Hundred and Fourth Illinois, a portion of the One Hundred and Eighth Ohio, and the cavalry, resisted the enemy for a short time, and then Colonel Moore surrendered. Colonel Tafel and the commanders of isolated companies surrendered subsequently. The contest lasted an hour and a half. Colonel Moore lost fifty killed and one hundred wounded—the remaining fourteen hundred and fifty, two pieces of artillery, and arms, camp equipage and trains, corresponding to the strength of his command. General Bragg himself reported Morgan's loss at one hundred and twenty-five killed and wounded. A careful comparison of the conflicting reports of this action warrants the following conclusions: That Colonel Moore's outlook was at fault; that nothing had been done to strengthen his position; that there was confusion and absence of plan in the effort to resist the enemy, and that a portion of the troops failed to exhibit that subordination and bravery which characterized them in subsequent battles.

Another engagement occurred on the 9th, with different conduct on the part of officers and men, and consequently with different issue. On that day, Colonel Stanley Matthews, of the Fifty-seventh Ohio, with his brigade, composed of his own regiment, the Thirty-fifth Indiana, the Eighth and Twenty-first Kentucky, and a section of Swallow's battery, moved out upon the Murfreesboro road, with a large train, in quest of forage. Leaving the road, he passed to Stone river, and filled his wagons in a bend of the river, and just as the full train was ready to move toward Nashville, the sharp report of musketry was heard in his rear. This was the first intimation to Colonel Matthews that General Wheeler, with a force of cavalry, mounted infantry, and artillery, was between him and Nashville, and advancing to cut him off. The warning volley came from a few men of the Twenty-first Kentucky, who were guarding the wagons. He at once threw forward the Fifty-seventh Ohio and Thirty-fifth Indiana, and after a severe encounter with the foe, drove him so far as to admit the movement of his train toward Nashville, with his command so formed as to protect it; the Ohio and Indiana regiments were in front, and the Kentuckians on the flanks and in the rear. He ordered a brisk homeward movement, and as it progressed, Wheeler twice attacked the Kentuckians, but recoiled from their fire. He then advanced more cautiously upon the flanks of the command—a movement that involved the whole command in action, but resulted in the failure of the fourth attack. Wheeler then withdrew. Colonel Matthews lost five men killed, over thirty wounded, and six missing. Wheeler's loss was probably greater.

On the 11th, Brigadier-General D. S. Stanley, recently transferred from the Army of the Tennessee, and assigned as chief of cavalry in the Army of the Cumberland, moved upon the Franklin road with a strong force, encamping at night within four miles of Franklin. The next morning he engaged the enemy vigorously, and drove him from the place, killing five men, including a lieutenant, capturing twelve, and a large number of horses and valuable property, and losing but one man. He also destroyed mills and other property valuable to the enemy, and returned to his camp on the 13th. His men had in this operation their first experience with revolving rifles.

Late in December, General Morgan moved into Kentucky with a strong force, to destroy General Rosecrans' communications. On the 25th, Colonel Hobson, commanding at Munfordsville, attacked him six miles from that place and inflicted a loss of over fifty men. Moving north, Morgan captured the stockade at Bacon creek. At Muldraugh's Hill, he attacked and captured the Seventy-first Indiana. The fight here lasted ten hours, though the parties to it were unequal. At Elizabethtown, he captured the Ninety-first Illinois, surrounding the town and firing upon it, without giving warning or an opportunity to escape. He destroyed a large amount of property, in part belonging to his friends, and appropriated bountifully for his command. On the 26th, General J. J. Reynolds, commanding in room of General Dumont, moved in pursuit from Gallatin, by Scottsville and Glasgow, while Colonel Harlan proceeded with his brigade by rail. The latter overtook Morgan at the Rolling fork of Salt river, and defeating him, drove him toward Bardstown. Colonel Hoskins fell upon him as he was passing near Lebanon, capturing from his force one hundred and fifty men.

Morgan wrought great damage and suffered heavy losses. The most serious injury to the railroad was the destruction of the bridges at Bacon creek and Nolin, and the trestles at Elizabethtown and Muldraugh's Hill.

Meanwhile a counter raid was in progress. On the 21st, General Carter, with the Ninth Pennsylvania, Second Michigan, and part of the Eighth Ohio Cavalry, moved from Lebanon, Kentucky, toward East Tennessee, to injure the Tennessee and Virginia railroad. He advanced through Nicholasville, Big Hill, and Pine Mountain; crossed the Cumberland Mountain, forty miles northeast of Cumberland Gap, and moved thence through Southwestern Virginia and Jonesboro, Tennessee, to Carter's Station. He destroyed the bridges over the Watauga and Holston rivers and the railroad for several miles, on the 28th, and then returned to Kentucky, mainly on the route of his advance. While these subordinate operations were in progress, preparations for an offensive campaign were completed. The Louisville and Nashville railroad having been opened, and sufficient supplies having been accumulated to warrant an advance against General Bragg, at Murfreesboro, General Thomas moved to Nashville on the 22d of December, and concentrated there Rousseau's and Negley's divisions, and Walker's brigade of Fry's division, leaving the remaining two brigades of the latter and Reynolds' division on the line of the Louisville and Nashville railroad. General Rosecrans had previously placed the post of Nashville under Brigadier-General R. B. Mitchell, with Morgan's and McCook's brigades as garrison.

During the first two months of his command, General Rosecrans had been untiring in his efforts to assimilate with his army the fresh troops that had been attached, and had obtained from Washington power to make summary disposition of all officers who failed in duty from incompetency or other causes. And to simplify the designation of divisions and brigades, he changed the consecutive numbering throughout his army, and numbered the divisions as First, Second, and Third, in each grand unit, and the brigades in the same way in each division. He required that brigades in divisions, and divisions in the larger organizations, should be numbered from right to left, but that in reports they should be designated by the names of their respective commanders.

The department commander also instituted new measures in dealing with the non-military enemies within his lines—measures which impressed this troublesome class of persons with the power of the national government, and restricted them in aiding the enemy in arms with information or supplies.

It is probable that General Bragg did not anticipate an advance against his position at Murfreesboro, as he sent, at the same time, General Morgan into Kentucky, and General Wheeler into West Tennessee, thus depriving himself of the greater portions of his cavalry.   Their absence and the fact indicated by their absence, induced General Rosecrans to make an early movement.   On the evening of the 25th of December, he gave orders for his army to march the next morning.

CHAPTER XVII.

STONE RIVER CAMPAIGN.

WHEN General Rosecrans ordered the advance of his army, the dispositions of his antagonist were well known. Generals Polk's and Kirby Smith's corps were at Murfreesboro, with an advance at Stewart's creek and La Vergne; and General Hardee's corps was on the turnpike road between Triune and Eagleville, with detachments thrown forward to Knob's Gap and Nolensville. As it was the prerogative of the enemy on the defensive to choose his battle-field, General Rosecrans gave positive and contingent orders to the commanders of his "Right Wing," "Center," and "Left Wing." He directed General McCook to move with his three divisions—Johnson's, Davis', and Sheridan's—by the Nolensville turnpike to Triune; General Thomas, with Rousseau's and Negley's divisions, and Walker's brigade, to march on the Franklin and Wilson turnpikes to threaten Hardee's left, and then to cross by county roads to Nolensville; and General Crittenden to advance on the direct road to Murfreesboro. At Nolensville, General Thomas would be in position to support either wing, and General McCook was ordered to attack Hardee at Triune, as soon as the commander of the "Center" should reach Nolensville. Should General Bragg reinforce Hardee against McCook, then Thomas was to move to his support. If Hardee should retreat, and the enemy meet Crittenden in force, then Thomas was to reinforce the "Left Wing," and move upon the enemy's left flank, and McCook, after detaching a division to pursue Hardee or observe him, should then move to the rear of Thomas and Crittenden.

The movements ordered were begun on the morning of the

26th of December, 1862.   The advance of the right wing was
given to General Davis, who moved from camp at 6 A. M. toward Nolensville, on the Edmonson turnpike, to Prim's
blacksmith-shop, where he diverged on a common road leading through a broken country, rendered unfriendly to the
comfort and celerity of his command by the rain which fell in
torrents during the forenoon.   General Davis' cavalry escort,
Captain Sheerer's company of the Thirty-sixth Illinois, developed the enemy's pickets a few miles from camp—a fact
which showed plainly that though General Bragg may not
have anticipated the advance of the Army of the Cumberland,
he had made provision to gain early knowledge of all movements in his front.   Only slight resistance, however, was
offered until the head of the column reached the vicinity of
Nolensville, where it became necessary to form the division to
dislodge the enemy.   Post's brigade was deployed in line of
battle, and Pinney's battery so posted as to command the
town and the approaches from the southwest.   At this juncture, the enemy's cavalry was observed to be assuming position, and a battery opened fire, which Pinney's response soon
silenced.   Woodruff's brigade then formed on the right to prevent a flank attack, and Carlin advanced and dislodged the
enemy.

   General Davis here learned that he would be more strongly
opposed at Knob's Gap, and he at once disposed his weary
troops to carry that point also.   The enemy's lines were soon
discerned, extending upon a range of high rocky hills through
which the Nolensville and Triune turnpike passes in a depression known as "Knob's Gap."   The position was favorable
for defense and well guarded by artillery, which opened upon
Davis at long range, who put Hotchkiss' and Pinney's batteries
in action as speedily as possible.   Carlin's brigade then charged
the enemy's battery, captured two guns, and carried the heights
on the right.   Post's brigade carried the hills on the left, and
Woodruff's drove the enemy's pickets on the extreme right.
Night came with the termination of the conflict.   Johnson's
and Sheridan's divisions, having followed in supporting distance all day, came up, and the whole command bivouacked
for the night.

The "Left Wing" advanced on the Murfreesboro road, Palmer's division leading, and encountered the enemy a short distance beyond the former outposts. Spirited skirmishing was maintained all day, the obstinacy of the enemy increasing as the head of the column steadily advanced. At night, this wing bivouacked four miles north of La Vergne.

General Thomas' command advanced, with Negley's division in front. At Owen's store, Negley moved hurriedly to the left to support General Davis at Nolensville. At night, the troops were scattered from Brentwood to Nolensville.

The cavalry moved in three columns. Colonel Minty's brigade, under Colonel Kennett, the division commander, accompanied the left wing. Colonel Zahm's brigade proceeded on the Franklin road, as a protection to General McCook's right flank, and General Stanley, with the reserve brigade, also accompanied the right wing.

A dense fog, on the morning of the 27th, prevented the right wing from advancing to Triune as early as had been expected. A forward movement was attempted early in the morning, but the enemy having been encountered in apparent strength by General Johnson, General McCook deemed it hazardous to press an engagement on unknown ground, in fog so thick as to forbid the distinction of friend from foe, at the ordinary interval between opposing lines of battle. Heavy skirmishing and artillery action were maintained during the forenoon. At 1 p. m. the fog lifted, and Johnson, with Sheridan in immediate support, advanced to the town, where Hardee's corps had been in line of battle during the preceding night and morning. Later he had burned the bridge over Wilson's creek, and leaving some cavalry and a battery to contest the crossing, retired his main force. Upon Johnson's approach, his rear-guard fled, after the feeblest resistance to a line of skirmishers. Johnson then moved south a mile, and stopped for the night; the other two divisions were close in his rear.

As it was proposed that the wings of the army should advance without offering either to the enemy, in the absence of the support of the other and the center, General McCook's delay prevented the early movement of General Crittenden.

At 11 A. M., however, he moved forward—Wood's division in the advance, Palmer and Van Cleve following. General Hascall's brigade of the leading division drove the enemy from La Vergne, and the adjacent hills, and, supported by the other brigades of the division, forced the enemy over Stuart's creek, five miles beyond. Colonel McKee, of the Third Kentucky Infantry, saved the bridge, which had been fired by the retreating foe. Hascall also repulsed an attack of cavalry on his left flank, capturing twenty-five prisoners. From La Vergne, Colonel Hazen's brigade of Palmer's division moved on the Jefferson turnpike, and seized the bridge over Stuart's creek, and drove the enemy beyond. Van Cleve's division, after countermarching on the main road, followed, and encamped north of the creek. Wood's and Palmer's divisions passed the night at Stewartsboro, on the direct road.

During the day, General Thomas advanced Negley's division from Nolensville to Crittenden's right at Stewartsboro, and moved Rousseau's division to Nolensville, leaving Walker's brigade at Brentwood. The marching on the turnpikes was greatly retarded by the rain which fell on the 26th and 27th, but on the common cross-roads it was exceedingly laborious. Therefore the troops and trains of this command changed positions slowly.

The 28th being the Sabbath, there was no general advance. General McCook sent forward General Willich's brigade on a reconnoissance, to ascertain the direction of General Hardee's retreat. General Willich advanced seven miles on the Shelbyville road, and learned that he had retired to Murfreesboro. General Crittenden only deployed a few troops to guard against the onsets of cavalry, which were threatened during the day. General Thomas advanced Rousseau's division to Stewartsboro, and Walker's brigade to the Nolensville turnpike. General Stanley made a reconnoissance to College Hill, and confirmed the retreat of General Hardee to Murfreesboro.

General Stanley moved in advance of the right wing, on the 29th. The Anderson cavalry, the Fifteenth Pennsylvania, pushed the enemy, at full charge, for six miles. A heavy loss was suffered, however, late in the evening, in an unfortunate attack upon two regiments of infantry lying in concealment.

Major Rosengarten and six men were killed, and Major Ward and five men wounded. Colonel Zahm's brigade advanced on the Franklin road, and joined the reserve brigade at the crossing of Stewart's creek. The enemy's cavalry were met during the day in strong force, at Wilkinson's Cross-roads, and were driven across Overall's creek to the immediate front of General Bragg's line of battle before Murfreesboro. General Davis followed the cavalry, and bivouacked at Overall's creek; Johnson and Sheridan at Wilkinson's Cross-roads.

General Crittenden advanced with Wood's division on the left of the Murfreesboro road, and Palmer's on the right of it. Wagner's brigade of the former, and Grose's of the latter, were deployed in front, and drove the enemy's skirmishers before them upon their main line of battle. Late in the afternoon, these divisions halted about two and a half miles from Murfreesboro, their commanders having observed indications of an army in position in their immediate front. They at once deployed their troops in line of battle, and informed General Crittenden of their action and the probable situation. Up to this time the opinion had obtained in the national army that General Bragg would not accept battle at Murfreesboro. Acting upon this supposition, General Rosecrans ordered General Crittenden to occupy the town that night with one of his divisions, and encamp the other two miles outside. This order reached General Crittenden at dark, just as he reached the front. He at once made dispositions for its prompt execution, designating Wood's division for the advance. General Wood, believing that as this movement was to be made at night over unknown ground and against an army in position, it would result in total failure and heavy loss, earnestly protested against it. At first, General Crittenden refused to suspend his order to General Wood, and required his immediate advance, as he considered the order of his superior too positive to admit discretion. Subsequently, however, General Palmer having supported General Wood in a second protest, he suspended his order for an hour, and dispatched to General Rosecrans for instructions in the premises. Before the hour had passed, General Rosecrans came up and countermanded his own order, and recalled the troops to their former position. Even this movement was critical, as Colonel Harker's brigade had crossed Stone river, and had driven Breckinridge's advance upon his main line, and Hascall's brigade and Bradley's battery were in the river, advancing in rear. However, Colonel Harker's adroitness and the veil of darkness secured their withdrawal with only slight loss.

In the meantime General Van Cleve's division, which had moved from the Jefferson turnpike to the Murfreesboro road, came up and was posted in rear of General Wood's position. Colonel Hazen also came up from Stewart's creek, and was placed in line with his division. General Negley, who had marched from Stewartsboro on the right of Crittenden's command, went into position on General Palmer's right. Thus four divisions were in line of battle before the enemy.

General Rousseau remained at Stewartsboro, but detached Colonel Starkweather's brigade to the Jefferson turnpike bridge over Stone river. At night Colonel Walker reached Stewartsboro.

Very early in the morning of the 30th, General McCook was ordered to move forward and take position in line of battle on the right of General Negley. In compliance, Sheridan's division, preceded by General Stanley, with a regiment of cavalry, moved on the Wilkinson turnpike, closely followed by Johnson and Davis. As General Sheridan approached the enemy's position he was more and more obstinately opposed, and when his head of column had reached a point within two and a quarter miles of Murfreesboro, it became necessary that he and General Davis should deploy their divisions in line of battle. The left of Sheridan's division, when in line, rested on the Wilkinson turnpike. General Davis formed his division on Sheridan's right, and General Johnson held his in reserve. The direction of the line was such as to refuse Sheridan's right and Davis' whole front, and yet the latter was stubbornly resisted—a fact that revealed General Bragg's care of his left flank at this early stage of the conflict. As the line wheeled into position, Carlin's brigade of Davis' division had a severe conflict with the enemy, in which the eagerness of Colonel J. W. S. Alexander, commanding the Twenty-first Illinois, led him to charge a battery, which, when abandoned by its cannoneers, was successfully defended by supporting infantry. This attack served to fix definitely the troops in opposition at this point. In the attainment of position, General Sheridan lost seventy-five men, and General Davis nearly two hundred.

The left wing during the day maintained essentially the position assumed the previous evening. There was a slight change in Palmer's division, which was advanced a short distance, against spirited opposition. The pioneer brigade, under Captain Morton, was posted on Stone river to prepare fords.

In the center, General Thomas brought up three brigades of Rousseau's division, and stationed them in rear of Negley's line. Colonel Starkweather was left to guard a bridge on the Jefferson turnpike, and repulsed an attack by cavalry. Colonel Walker moved from Stewart's creek to La Vergne, and routed a portion of General Wheeler's cavalry, that had captured General McCook's train. He recaptured about eight hundred men, and all the train animals, the wagons having been burned by the enemy.

In the afternoon, General Stanley, with a portion of his cavalry, returned to La Vergne. The remaining portions of his command were posted on the flanks of the army.

It was now evident that the two armies were in close proximity, in readiness for battle. During the day there had been heavy skirmishing in front of the troops in position, and the right wing had met strong resistance in advancing to its assigned place, abreast the center. At intervals, from flank to flank, batteries had responded to batteries, and where the main lines were parallel, or nearly so, they had reciprocally felt the fire of musketry.

On the general battle front of the national army, Wood's division was next Stone river, Hascall's brigade forming the extreme left, Harker's the center, and Wagner's connecting with Palmer's left at the Nashville turnpike. Palmer's division was formed with Grose's brigade on the left, Cruft's on the right connecting with Negley, and Hazen's in reserve. Miller's brigade of Negley's division connected with Cruft, and Stanley's with Sheridan's left on the Wilkinson turnpike. Roberts' brigade of the latter division was on the left, Sill's on the right, and Schaefer's in reserve. Sill's brigade touched Woodruff's brigade on the left of Davis' line. Carlin's formed his center, and Post's his right. The formation of these two divisions of the right wing conformed to the general type, and had at least average strength. At first Johnson's division was wholly in reserve.

During the afternoon of the 30th, General McCook was informed by a citizen that the right of Davis' division, resting near the Franklin turnpike, was opposite the center of General Bragg's battle front, which fact he communicated to General Rosecrans; and to provide as far as possible against the palpable danger, he threw Johnson's division in position on the right of Davis. Kirk's brigade was formed on the right of Post, but thrown forward so as to hold the front edge of the woods, which gave strength to the position, and also to command the open ground between the opposing lines of battle. Willich's brigade was refused to the right and rear of Kirk, with a line facing south, and Baldwin's was entirely in reserve, near division headquarters, a mile or more distant.

General McCook's corps was now formed in a line broken at several points. General Davis' line formed a right angle with General Sheridan's, and faced the south very nearly. The trend of Kirk's line was more toward the east, and then Willich's stretched westward, facing south; and although Kirk was thrown forward to secure all the advantages of the position, the two divisions on the right, as a whole, formed a refused flank. General Rosecrans' report indicates his belief that his right did not trend in a proper direction, in facing "strongly toward the east, and that his own disadvantages of position and maneuver were fatally enchanced by the 'faulty position'" of his right wing. . The general trend of this wing, however, conformed to that of the enemy's line in its front, the latter leaning forward from the point opposite Sheridan's right, and the former bending back in correspondence. The enemy's line, from the river to the Franklin road, had been located for defense, and rested as far as practicable in woods, with open ground in front; and as the right wing of the national army, according to the plan of battle, was to await attack, its division commanders observed similar prudence in establishing their lines.

As General Bragg believed that his army was inferior in numbers to that of General Rosecrans, his first policy was to await an attack.   He therefore formed his army with his left wing, composed of Withers' and Cheatham's divisions, under General Polk, in front of Stone river, covering the direct roads leading from Murfreesboro to Nashville and Franklin, and his right wing embracing Breckinridge's and Cleburne's divisions, across the river on Polk's right.   He posted McCown's division, as the main reserve, in rear of his center, and a free brigade, under General Jackson, on his extreme right flank.   In this formation, Withers' division occupied the space from Stone river to the Franklin turnpike, or the whole front of the national army.   Cheatham's division formed a line of the same length, directly in the rear.   The right wing was similarly formed, with Breckinridge's division in front and Cleburne's in rear.

With his forces thus disposed, General Bragg awaited General Rosecrans' approach, until the evening of the 29th, then, apprehending from General McCook's advance on the Wilkinson turnpike that he would be flanked on his left, he transferred McCown's division from reserve across the river, to General Polk's left, with its right resting on the Franklin road.   In not receiving an attack on the 30th, the Confederate general was disappointed, and in the evening resolved to assail from his left the next day, and for this purpose moved Cleburne's division from the rear of Breckinridge to the rear of McCown, and gave the command of these two divisions to General Hardee.   He had then four divisions in double formation, in front of Stone river, their right resting on the river bank and their center on the Franklin turnpike, near which rested the right of McCook's corps.   He had no reserve but Breckinridge's command on the east side of the river, but considered this force available for support at any point in his line, as there were no indications of an attack upon his right.

General Polk was evidently in error in his official report, respecting the exact positions of the three divisions of the right wing of the national army, though correct as to the order of their alignment. He supposed, and so stated, that the left of Withers' division, resting on the Franklin turnpike, was opposite the right of Sheridan, whom he located "on a ridge of rocks, with chasms intervening, and covered with a dense growth of rough cedars"—the exact description of Davis' position—while Sheridan only touched the cedars with his right. As further proof of this misapprehension, General Polk stated that Alexander's assault in the evening of the 30th, was an attempt to capture a battery on the left of Withers' line, and hence opposite Davis, not Sheridan.

The battle front of each army was now continuous, save the separation of Breckinridge by the river. But such was the topography of the field, that the trend of the main lines was curved and broken in turn. Between the two armies there was open ground almost continuously. Some portions of the national line rested in strong defensive positions, as in the case of Davis' division and Kirk's brigade; but much of the line was on open ground. Sheridan's division was on open ground, except where its right touched Davis. Negley's division was uncovered, but had woods in rear. Palmer's was somewhat embowered by an oak grove.

General Rosecrans' plan of battle, as revealed in his official report and by his orders on the field, was as follows: General McCook was instructed to take an advantageous position on the right, and hold the enemy in check, if attacked; but if over-powered, to fall back slowly, refusing his right. If not attacked, he was to engage the enemy sufficiently to hold him in his front. Generals Thomas and Palmer were to open with skirmishing, and gain the enemy's center and left as far as the river. General Crittenden was to throw Van Cleve's division across the river, at the lower ford, to advance against Breckinridge, and to cross Wood's division by brigades at the upper fords, and support Van Cleve's right. If successful in driving back the enemy's right, General Wood was to place his batteries on the heights east of the river, and open on his center and left in reverse. Then General Palmer should press the enemy in his front, and General Thomas should sustain the movement in the center.

Each army commander, on the night of the 30th, was therefore equally intent upon executing an essentially identical plan of battle, with an initiative by each from his left flank. General Bragg proposed that Hardee should attack at daylight the left of the national army, and then he would bring his whole army into action from this initiative by a right wheel on Polk's right flank, at Stone river, as a pivot. To mask his movement from his left, General Rosecrans ordered that fires should be built for two miles beyond McCook's right flank. This expedient was adopted to make the impression that the national forces were massing on that flank, to throw General Bragg off his guard at the opposite extremity of his line, and thus assure the success of the movement against it, proposed for Crittenden the next morning. General McCook had previously felt uneasy in regard to his right flank, believing that it was greatly overlapped by the enemy, and had given stringent orders to his subordinate commanders to watch against surprise; and any invitation to increase the strength of General Bragg's left, magnified his fear for his right.

Early in the morning of the last day of the year 1862, the commanders of the confronting armies, of nearly equal proportions, put upon trial a common plan of battle, with the contingency to each of miscarriage in the event of being too late in initial offense. The advantage of this dominant contingency was gained by General Bragg, and General Rosecrans was thrown upon the defensive at the opening of the battle.

Soon after dawn, General Hardee, with two-fifths of General Bragg's infantry, wheeled in long circuit upon the right of the national army. When he first moved from position, McCown's division deflected to the left, opening an interval to the left of Withers' flank, which was quickly filled by Cleburne's line; then the two divisions wheeled upon McCook's right flank. Kirk's brigade first felt the shock of battle, as it was in proximity to the pivot of the column in motion. His line had been attenuated to secure a good position for a battery, and one of his regiments was in the rear. The enemy's onset was furious, expressing alike the importance of the movement and the initial courage and spirit of the Southern armies. Unfortunately for the national army, this flank of three brigades, when receiving an attack from two divisions of four brigades each, was not in ordinary condition for battle. The division commander was not on the line, nor near enough to give orders, and General Willich, commanding the brigade which had been posted for lateral defense, was absent from his command. This position of affairs forbade unity of action; in fact, these brave troops were thrown into confusion by circumstances over which they had no control. Generals Bragg and Polk claimed pretentiously, in their official reports, that these troops were surprised; and to some of them, no doubt, the blow was unexpected, at least from the quarter whence it came. Still the usual provision against surprise had been made. Skirmish lines were well offered to the enemy, and when General Kirk perceived the advancing column, he threw forward the Thirty-fourth Illinois to check it. This commander, who was mortally wounded, but lived to make a report, claimed that when he saw the strength of the column hurrying upon him, he called for help from Willich's brigade, which at that time was without a recognized commander. This brigade had been on the lookout for the enemy from an early hour, but had been ordered to breakfast by General Willich at the time of his starting to visit division headquarters. It does not appear from the reports that all the guns near the salient angle of this flank were in battery. In some cases the horses were detached. These circumstances, and the manifestly overwhelming strength of the enemy's lines, rendered the conflict exceedingly unequal. The reports of the commanders who battled upon these unequal conditions are so inharmonious that it is impossible to determine the order of the recession of these two brigades. It is, however, demonstrable that neither held position long, and that both in the sharp conflict suffered such losses as prove severe fighting or the maintenance of position, until withdrawal was impossible without great waste of life. Kirk lost five hundred men killed and wounded, and three hundred and fifty by capture. Willich lost a few less in killed and wounded, and more than double as many men by capture. General Willich was captured in an effort to join his brigade. Captain Edgarton was captured with his battery located near the salient angle of the line, and three guns were lost from Goodspeed's battery, posted to the right of Willich's brigade. So quickly were these two brigades dislodged, that Colonel Baldwin was informed of the fact by stragglers from their ranks, and had barely time, in conjunction with General Johnson, to form his troops and make a slight advance before the enemy was upon him.

The recession of Kirk's and Willich's brigades exposed General Davis' right flank to the enveloping lines of the enemy, and he at once ordered Colonel Post to change the front of his brigade nearly perpendicularly to the rear, and to dispose his regiments and battery to repel a flank attack. Pinney's battery was moved one-fourth of a mile to the right, and the Fifty-ninth Illinois sent with it for support; the Seventy-fourth and Seventy-fifth Illinois were posted in the edge of the woods behind a fence, and when the enemy revealed his overlapping lines far to the right, the Twenty-second Indiana was deployed beyond the battery.

Colonel Baldwin's position was at least one-fourth of a mile to the right of Post. His brigade was posted behind a fence on the margin of wooded ground lying in front, and presented four regiments and a battery in line, with one regiment in reserve.

These dispositions had hardly been made, before the enemy advanced against Baldwin and Post on the flank, and against Carlin, Woodruff, and Sill on the main battle front. The consequent action was the second distinct stage of the battle and was one of the fiercest of the day. The forces which had driven Kirk's and Willich's brigades from position, attacked Baldwin and Post; while the brigades of Loomis and Manigualt, of Withers' division of General Polk's front line, fell upon Carlin, Woodruff, and Sill. Baldwin maintained his ground for a short time, but he was soon flanked on his right and compelled to withdraw; but Post repulsed the enemy, and Carlin, Woodruff, and Sill hurled back the columns assaulting them. This repulse was so emphatic that General Polk threw forward the reserve brigades on his left to renew the attack, his first line having been so broken as to need radical readjustment.

In repelling the attack upon Sheridan's right, General Sill had the support of a portion of Schaefer's brigade, but with this additional strength he was barely able to drive back the foe.

General Sheridan's line compassed four regimental intervals and was consequently a strong one, or this first attack would have pressed back his right brigade, at least that portion which was on open ground. The lines of the two divisions being perpendicular to each other, the right angle formed by Sill's and Woodruff's brigades and prominently offered to the enemy, made that point exceedingly critical, as a direct attack upon either would enfilade the line of the other, and the withdrawal of either of the connecting flanks would greatly expose the other. In the subsequent attacks, therefore, the enemy made special efforts to break these lines at the point of connection.

Having formed Vaughn's and Maney's brigades in room of Loomis' and Manigualt's, General Polk soon made a second attempt to carry this position, but the issue was the same as before—a complete repulse. In conjunction with this assault in front, Cleburne's division fell again upon Post's line and was also repulsed. Some previous success of this division had been regarded by General Polk as the dislodgment of Davis' division, and he now referred the fire of Pinney's battery to one of Sheridan's, wheeled to the right, but this division was still before him. Its left flank was now slightly bent back in consequence of the turning of Sill's brigade on its left. In the first attack upon General Sill, the enemy had made effort to capture Bush's battery, which had been posted considerably in advance of Hiscock's and Houghtaling's, and in the second assault this object was manifest. General Sill was killed between the guns of this battery, and soon after his fall, the right of the brigade having been turned, it was retired to the position of the other batteries, and Colonel Grensel, commanding in room of General Sill, sent the Twenty-first Michigan to support Hiscock's, now in the front.

As soon as practicable after the repulse of Vaughn's and Maney's brigades, General Cheatham reorganized his shattered troops, and with four brigades made a third attack upon Davis and Sheridan. In the formation of Polk's corps in two lines, by divisions, the four brigades forming the left half of his corps, were under the command of General Cheatham, and the other four on the right were under General Withers. In this third attack Post's brigade was enveloped by General Hardee's victorious forces and was compelled to withdraw with the loss of one gun. His retirement exposed Carlin's right flank and rear, while resisting the enemy in his front. The flanks of both Woodruff's and Carlin's brigades were so bent that each commander thought himself isolated and entirely without support on either flank. The reports are not concurrent as to the order of the withdrawal of Carlin's and Woodruff's brigades, and Davis' and Sheridan's divisions, from the original battle line. The weight of testimony supports the hypothesis that Sheridan's right brigade was shattered and divided, while Woodruff was unmoved by the assaults upon him, except that his left was bent back for lateral defense, and that his brigade was the last of Davis' division to leave position. The conditions of the battle and the circumstances of withdrawal were such as to give different views to the several commanders, and their conflicting reports embarrass him who attempts to determine the exact order of events.

The regimental commanders of General Sill's brigade mention that they gave ground repeatedly on the right of the brigade, and assign as a reason that they were unsupported on their right. The reports from Woodruff's brigade claim that this brigade was unsupported on its left. The only fact which can explain this contradiction, and others occurring under similar circumstances, without impeaching the veracity of commanders, is, that under the pressure of attack covering the connecting points of regiments, brigades, or even larger organizations, the flanks naturally bend backward and inward toward their respective centers, and there is partial isolation at least, without an absolute loss of position.

There is the most positive testimony from the enemy, that the troops of Davis' division held their position in the cedar woods with great persistency. General Polk mentioned in his report that Vaughn lost one-third of his troops and every horse in the brigade but three, and that other brigades lost heavily. He claimed the capture of two guns from Sheridan, but these were from Carpenter's battery of Davis' division, and this fact is decisive of General Polk's mistake in reference to the position of General Davis. General Sheridan lost no guns from his first position.

Whatever may have been the exact order of the recession of Davis and Sheridan, it is certain that neither held position long after the third assault of the enemy. The conditions of their retreat, however, were different, though the cause of it was common—the battle line on the left of Sheridan was intact, while the brigades of Davis' division were exposed on all sides. Colonel Post, under the pressure of Cleburne's division, moved directly to the Nashville turnpike, in rear of the army. Colonel Carlin held his ground until the destruction of his brigade was imminent, when his regiments broke to the rear from his left flank. Hotchkiss' battery moved across open fields to wooded ground, where General Davis attempted to form a new line. As Carlin's broken regiments reached this position, they were disposed to support this battery. Woodruff retreated through the woods in his rear, and then turned and charged the pursuing enemy with such force that he regained his original position, but being entirely unsupported, could not hold it. Through false information as to the purpose of General Davis, and danger from the overlapping lines of the enemy, Carlin abandoned the new line before Woodruff reached it, and both brigades crossed the Wilkinson turnpike and joined a portion of Johnson's division, which, having made repeated efforts to withstand the enemy, had fallen back to the right of General Rousseau's division.

When General Sill's brigade yielded its position, General Sheridan changed the front of Roberts' to the right, to cover its retreat, and ordered its commander to charge the enemy. In obedience, Colonel Roberts advanced, but the enemy did not await his approach. This movement was doubtless coincident with Woodruff's charge, when he regained his position, and the action of these brigades expressed such positive offense, that the advance of the enemy was greatly retarded.

Having recalled Colonel Roberts to a new line trending across his first line of battle, General Sheridan soon found that this new position was untenable, and then he fell back to the Wilkinson turnpike, where he re-established his connection with Negley's right, and bending back his line twice at right angles, formed a new flank and covered Negley's rear.

General McCook's corps was driven from position after hard fighting against three-fifths of the Confederate army, eager to give complete success to the ruling movement of General Bragg's aggressive plan. General Hardee overlapped every flank offered to him, and yet his losses were so heavy that early in the day he asked for reinforcements, and did not press rapidly nor with remarkable power upon any of the improvised lines, and never so far gained the rear of a single brigade as to prevent an easy escape, and at last felt his way with great caution across the Wilkinson turnpike. General McCook gave personal attention to the maneuvers of Sheridan's division, and had his horse shot under him in proximity to his lines. As his other troops reached the right of General Rousseau, he made dispositions for their reorganization and alignment, so as to cover the communications of the army.

The third distinct stage of the battle involved a new disposition of all troops not on the battle front, and the fiercest fighting of Rousseau's, Sheridan's, Negley's, and Palmer's divisions—such fighting as palpably involved a crisis of the battle. The Confederate army continued to wheel, even to its pivot on the bank of Stone river, and the wave of battle was rapidly transmitted to that point.

Negley's and Palmer's divisions had made a slight advance early in the morning to feel the enemy, and to be in readiness to rush through his lines to the river, should General Crittenden's movement against Breckinridge across the stream prove successful. At 8 A. M., Crittenden's advance—Van Cleve's division—was in motion, and its leading brigades had crossed the river, while General Wood had withdrawn two brigades from position in preparation to follow. The noise of battle on the right had been heard all the morning, but as yet there had been no such indications of disaster to McCook as precluded the possibility of offense from the left flank, although it was probable that the right wing was severely engaged. When positive intelligence that the right had been turned was received, Beatty's and Price's brigade of Van Cleve's division were in line before Breckinridge, and Fyffe's brigade was in the act of fording. Immediately, General Rosecrans recalled this offensive movement, that he might reinforce his right. He moved Fyffe's brigade rapidly to the rear on the Nashville road to repel the enemy's cavalry that had fallen upon the trains and captured men and wagons. He sent Beatty's brigade to the right of Rousseau, and soon ordered to the same point Harker's, from Wood's division, which had been withdrawn from position in conjunction with Hascall's, in preparation to follow Van Cleve. Price's brigade, of Van Cleve's division, was left to hold the ford, and General Wood was allowed to hold Hascall's brigade as a mobile column. These dispositions were ordered about the time that the enemy moved against Negley.

When General Thomas perceived that General Sheridan had changed position, and knew that this change was the prophecy of unexpected conditions of battle for his command, he ordered General Rousseau to move two brigades to the right and rear of Sheridan, whose right flank was then exposed, though bent far back toward Negley's rear. Hardee's corps was now entirely upon the broken flank, which had been bereft of two divisions, and was moving with his divisions in eschelon to overlap Sheridan and take Thomas in reverse. Cheatham was wheeling upon his front with his four brigades, and Withers, with an equal force, was advancing against Negley and Palmer in front. This combination involved the action of the entire Confederate army, save the force under Breckinridge across the river. The object of Thomas in moving Rousseau to Sheridan's right was to support him should he be able to hold his ground, and cover his retreat should he be compelled to fall back. For a time, these dispositions checked the advance and success of the enemy, but they provoked a conflict which palpably brought on another crisis of the battle.

Three of the five divisions of the national army forming the battle front had been displaced, and the attack upon Negley was intended to dislodge another, and was consequently made with a fury and persistence born of such a purpose. Had there been immediate success, the center of the national army would have been broken at a time when the new dispositions of troops to restore the right were incomplete, and in all probability, total defeat would have ensued.

The first attacks upon Negley and Sheridan, involving Rousseau also, were repulsed. Negley had three batteries (Marshall's, Ellsworth's, and Schultz's), which were well posted, contributing largely to the defensive strength of this division. The brigades of Anderson and Stewart, under General Withers, assaulted Negley; while General Cheatham, with the left half of Polk's corps, moved repeatedly upon Sheridan, pressing his left especially, as its displacement would be fatal to Negley. Roberts' brigade, supported by Houghtaling's battery and a section from each of the other batteries, Bush's and Hiscock's, occupied a position south of the Wilkinson road. At the termination of this attack, General Sheridan having nearly exhausted his supply of ammunition, and Colonel Roberts having been killed, ordered his division to fall back, leaving Houghtaling's battery and two guns from Bush's in the hands of the enemy. This withdrawal opened a gap between Negley's and Rousseau's divisions, exposing the right flank of the former and the left flank of the latter. Into this space the enemy rushed, closely following Sheridan's retiring troops, and reaching the rear of these divisions. The condition of Negley and Rousseau was now exceedingly critical, exposed on flank and rear, and subjected to a cross fire of musketry and artillery at short range. While it was utterly impossible for them to maintain their positions, it verged closely upon an impossibility for them to secure new ones with safety to themselves and the army. In the emergency, General Thomas ordered both Negley and Rousseau to withdraw to form a new line. Each was covered at first by cedars. But the enemy was in their rear as well as front, and it was impracticable to give mutual support, as their insulation was too positive and the necessity of rapid movement too imperative. It was necessary also to form a temporary line to save the artillery, before a permanent one could be established. General Thomas, therefore, first directed that a new line should be taken running along a depression in the open ground in rear of the cedar woods, to be held until the artillery could be retired to the high ground near the Nashville turnpike, where the permanent line was to be established. Rousseau's division, leaving its position under a heavy fire, drew back to this depression, having first posted its batteries on the high ground farther to the rear. The exultant enemy soon emerged from the cedar woods, but then fell under the musketry of Rousseau's division at short range. Colonel Shepherd's brigade of regulars quivered under the onset of the enemy, now fully hopeful of an immediate and decisive victory; but this brigade, by the efficient support and co-operation of Scribner's and Colonel John Beatty's brigades, Loomis' and Guenther's batteries, and the pioneer brigade with Stokes' battery, withstood the attack. This short and decisive conflict saved the center and the army, but it cost Shepherd's brigade alone twenty-two officers and five hundred and eighteen men killed and wounded. When the enemy was here repulsed and driven back to the woods, the formation of a new line on higher ground was practicable.

General Negley was so completely unsupported on his right when Sheridan had withdrawn, that the safety of his division was compromised. The massed forces that had assaulted Sheridan were in his rear, and his division having been well offered to the enemy in the original formation, was now almost completely enveloped. To prevent capture he ordered his troops to cut their way through the enemy's lines to the ground designated for the realignment of the center. In passing Rousseau's division, he was partially relieved from pressure by the prompt action of Colonel Scribner, who wheeled the Thirty-eighth Indiana and Tenth Wisconsin so as to receive and repulse the force that was pressing Negley, and then covered his formation in the rear. In this dash to the rear through the enemy's enveloping lines, General Negley lost six guns. This hazardous change of position by General Thomas' command also received support from Colonel Samuel Beatty's brigade of Van Cleve's division, which, with the division commander, reached the right of Rousseau at the moment the latter was forming his temporary line. This brigade engaged the enemy at the time of his severest attack upon Rousseau's division, and clung to its right during the day.

The withdrawal of Negley's division from the front line involved Palmer's division in a conflict, whose conditions were identical with those of the divisions to its right. Hazen's brigade, which had exchanged places, from reserve, with Grose's, as the last brigade on the left of the continuous line of battle, was now in air, with almost a division interval between it and Wagner's brigade of Wood's division, which still held position on the river bank, which having been designated to form the rear of Crittenden's offensive column, was the only one that maintained original position. This flank had been hypothetically secured, in the plan of aggressive battle, by the anticipated enfilading fire of Wood's and Van Cleve's musketry and artillery from the east side of the river, but in actual defense it was vulnerable to an attack from Breckinridge, who could have crossed the river at any time, and the space between Hazen's left and the river gave an invitation to General Polk to wheel his right upon it. Perceiving this exposure of Palmer's left in defensive battle, General Wood had left Wagner's brigade on the river bank, and had held Hascall's, though once in motion to the right, in reserve opposite the space between Wagner's right and Hazen's left. The safety of this flank during the first half of the day was doubtless owing to the fact that General Bragg's plan restrained his right until the issue of his continuous attack from his left should be fully developed.

The attack upon Palmer was made with great fury, especially upon Cruft's brigade, which was in advance of Hazen. General Cruft was unable to withstand the enemy, in the open space to which he had advanced, and was pressed back to the woods. Here he fought desperately and successfully, until Negley dashed to the rear, in the emergency at the center. Then Cruft's right was in air, and though he repulsed Chalmers in front, he was soon enveloped by that brigade and Donelson's, and the forces which following Negley reached his rear. So complete was the insulation of Palmer at this juncture, that Colonel Grose, in reserve, changed front to the rear, and forcing back the enemy, made it possible for Cruft to draw back toward the new position assumed by General Thomas' corps. The fighting here, as along the whole line, was exceedingly severe. Hazen alone now held position, and even he was forced to change slightly to conform to the changes on his right. He moved a short distance to the left, until his left flank rested on the left of the railroad, and his whole brigade was in a strong position in woods, on high ground. As Cruft moved to the rear, he became hotly engaged, and Grose, who had fought facing the rear, again changed front, and supported Cruft and Hazen. Cruft's brigade lost heavily in maintaining position in great exposure, and in gaining connection with the center. The batteries of the division—Standardt's, "H" and "M" Fourth United States Artillery, under Lieutenant Parsons, and Cockerell's—rendered efficient service during this conflict.

Every brigade of General Bragg's four divisions on the west side of the river had been severely engaged, many of them in repeated assaults, and his losses had been very heavy. He had yet five brigades of infantry across the river, under General Breckinridge, and with these as his resource for farther aggression, he made a fourth and final combination, the object of which was to turn General Rosecrans' left as he had turned his right, and upon this contingency the success of his plan manifestly hinged, though he had not yet abandoned all aggression with his left.

General Breckinridge had hitherto been comparatively inactive, although he had been under orders for action. As early as 10 o'clock A. M., General Bragg had ordered him to send one brigade, and soon after a second, to reinforce or act as a reserve to General Hardee. Instead of prompt obedience, General Breckinridge informed his chief, first, that the national troops, in heavy force, were in the act of crossing the river, and then that they had crossed and were advancing against him. Simultaneously, General Bragg received intelligence of the advance of another strong force of infantry on the Lebanon road. To provide against this seeming aggression, the army commander directed General Breckinridge not to await an attack, but to advance, and ordered General Pegram, in command of cavalry, to develop the movement on the Lebanon road. When the report was received that there were no national troops on that side of the river, it was too late to reinforce Hardee from his extreme right, and besides by this time his left was too much exhausted to promise much by further aggression. Thus, the incipient offense from General Rosecrans' left flank, though seemingly a total failure, was not without very important results, as thereby Breckinridge was kept on the east side at a time when his help on the left might have enabled Hardee to reach the center and left of the national army. And this attempted transfer of troops from the right to the left of the Confederate army may be accepted as evidence that General Hardee had met stronger opposition from Generals McCook and Thomas than had been anticipated, and that at 10 o'clock the success of the ruling movement was doubtful.

The repulse of the enemy by General Thomas, and his successful establishment of a new line, had greatly changed the conditions of the conflict on the right. Recoiling from Thomas, Hardee could not safely overlap the new right flank of the army, now held by Beatty's brigade of Van Cleve's division. This gave time for the reformation of McCook's forces and the alignment of Crittenden's reinforcing troops. Fyffe's brigade of Van Cleve's division formed on the right of Beatty's, and then Harker's, of Wood's division, and beyond were portions of the three divisions of the right wing.

While General Breckinridge was transferring his first two brigades across the river, commanded respectively by Generals Adams and Jackson, there was a lull in the action on the left. During this quiet the enemy made his second combination to turn General Rosecrans' left, and counter preparation was made to hold it. General Wood now threw Hascall's brigade on the right of Wagner's and placed Cox's battery in Wagner's rear, to respond to the enemy's batteries across the river, and to repel attacks from that quarter, and posted Estep's battery in rear of Hascall. The high wooded ground at the railroad was regarded by the enemy as the key-point, and designated by him as the "Round Forest." Upon this spot he converged his lines, and made repeated assaults to carry it, resistance to which not only involved Hazen's brigade, which rested upon it, but those on Hazen's right and left. Colonel

Hazen had at that point the Forty-first Ohio, Ninth Indiana, and One Hundred and Tenth Illinois; his remaining regiment, the Sixth Kentucky, was engaged farther to the right. This was a small force to hold the key-point, when converging columns were directed upon it, even though well supported. While, however, this position was the main objective of the enemy, the adjacent forces were also heavily pressed. And General Palmer's first call for help from General Wood was to give support to troops to the right of Hazen. In response, the Third Kentucky was sent, and was soon terribly mangled, losing its commander, Lieutenant-Colonel McKee. General Polk repeated his assaults with great fury, and even desperation, as success at this point was now plainly the condition of victory. General Rosecrans, in his frequent rapid passage along his lines, was an observer of this conflict, and gave directions concerning it, and General Crittenden, with his division commanders, Generals Wood and Palmer, gave it the closest attention, throwing together all the available troops and batteries of the left wing to maintain this vital point.

The new dispositions in the center and on the right had now fully arrested Hardee's turning movement, and he had been forced to take the defensive by Rousseau and Van Cleve. The troops of the latter, pressing forward too eagerly under the emphatic order of General Rosecrans, had exposed a flank, and severe loss and a repulse had resulted. In this, Fyffe's brigade had been the greatest sufferer, but saved its battery (Swallow's), and was soon reformed for action. About the same time Harker's brigade was hotly engaged, and also some portions of the right wing on the right of Crittenden's troops.

By this time, General Bragg had abandoned all purpose of aggression, except from his right flank; and here the brigades of Jackson and Adams had been repulsed and shattered, and now two more, Preston's and Palmer's, were moved across the river and directed against the "Round Forest."

When the pressure of the first new combination fell upon Hazen, at his call, General Wood sent the Twenty-fourth Ohio, of Hascall's brigade. Hazen used the railroad cut for a rampart, and with the aid afforded maintained his position. To repel the later assaults, additional troops were concentrated.

In response to a second request for help from General Palmer, General Wood sent the Fifty-eighth Indiana, which relieved the Third Kentucky on the right of the railroad, its left resting on that road. The One Hundredth Illinois, from the same brigade, was sent to Hazen, and formed the right of his line, its right resting on the railroad. Colonel Hazen had called the Sixth Kentucky to the left of this road, and the Second Missouri, from Schaefer's brigade of Sheridan's, which, with the brigade, was in the rear of the "Round Forest," was associated with the One Hundredth Illinois in holding Hazen's right. The Fortieth and Ninety-seventh Ohio, of Wagner's brigade, were in position also, on the right of the railroad, in conjunction with the Sixth and Twenty-sixth Ohio, of Grose's brigade. In connection with these regiments, Estep's battery rendered efficient service, and afterward joined Cox's battery on the extreme left, where these batteries were supported by Wagner and the Twenty-sixth Ohio regiment, of Hascall's brigade. Having been bereft of half his brigade, Wagner became severely engaged in the extreme left, on the bank of the river. Not waiting for an assault, which was palpably foreshadowed, Wagner charged the enemy with great energy. The Fifteenth and Fifty-seventh Indiana regiments dashed against the enemy far in advance of our main line, but though successful against the enemy's infantry, they could not maintain the position under a heavy fire of artillery, and were compelled to fall back. In this charge the Fifteenth Indiana captured nearly all the men of a regiment that were not killed or wounded. The retirement of these troops from their perilous insulation was doubtless covered by the Fifteenth Missouri regiment, of Schaefer's brigade of Sheridan's division. The report of his successor in command, Colonel Laiboldt, declares that Colonel Schaefer was killed when about giving orders to this regiment, which, after deployment in a corn-field, was retreating to the position of the brigade at the railroad; and General Sheridan avers that he lost his last brigade commander when in the act of relieving from the pressure of the enemy Wood's division, which had given way. These were the only troops on the extreme left that gave ground to the enemy, and these only left an advanced position to resume their original place.

Of the entire battle line of the army in the morning, only Wagner's position at the river and the ground at the railroad were now held; the left of the continuous battle line was now resting much nearer the river than at the opening of the battle. Between the Nashville turnpike and the river were two brigades of Wood's division, Wagner's and Hascall's, and two of Palmer's, the regiments of which had been thrown together as emergencies were developed at different points by the assaults of the enemy, by the exhaustion of troops, or failure of ammunition. Hazen still held the left of the continuous line, but his brigade had been pushed to the left more than its length; its right in the morning rested between the Nashville turnpike and railroad, and at the end of the engagement the One Hundredth Illinois was between its right and the railroad. On the right of the Nashville turnpike, the battle line, bent back with a curve until its trend was nearly perpendicular to its original direction.

The assaults on our left cost the enemy immense losses. Some of the assaulting regiments lost more than half their strength; and none of these attacks were even temporarily successful. General Bragg admitted, in his official report, that General Polk made repeated attempts to turn General Rosecrans' left flank, with utter failure. He attributed his failures to the concentration of artillery of superior range, which seemed to bid him defiance, and which enabled his enemy to maintain the strong position on Stone river. This is strong testimony for the efficiency of the artillery posted on this flank of the national army. The infantry of Wood's and Palmer's divisions, as such, were not less efficient in repelling the enemy.

During the day, the enemy's cavalry passed entirely round General Rosecrans' army, and consequently provoked several conflicts and greatly disturbed the trains in the rear. A portion of Colonel Zahm's brigade rendered good service on the right of the army, in covering the infantry in retreat. In a hand-to-hand conflict, Colonel Minor Milliken, commanding the First Ohio Cavalry, was killed by a pistol shot while using his saber. Colonel Kennett's command first engaged the enemy in the immediate rear of the army, repulsing him and recapturing a train. Finally, there was a concentration of cavalry, under General D. S. Stanley, behind Overall's creek, where successful resistance was offered to a superior force. Here Colonel Walker's brigade, of General Fry's division, approaching from Stewartsboro, supported Stanley. The roar of Church's battery, in this engagement, excited grave apprehension at the front that General Bragg had thrown a strong force upon the communications of the army. Squadrons of troopers were active on the Nashville road, several miles to the rear, but beyond the capture of some stragglers, no injury was done.

After the enemy had been fully checked at all points, General Rosecrans readjusted his line of battle, extending his center and right in a northwesterly direction, nearly at right angles to their original trend, and refusing his extreme right on the left of the Nashville turnpike. In consecutive order, from right to left, were Davis', Sheridan's and Johnson's divisions, Walker's and Harker's brigades, Van Cleve's division, Pioneer brigade, and Rousseau's, Palmer's, and Wood's divisions. Negley's division constituted the reserve of the center, and Starkweather's brigade having reached the battlefield, was placed in reserve, in rear of Sheridan's left. The cavalry remained beyond Overall's creek. The enemy felt this line until late in the evening, when the two armies, after the long, exhaustive conflict, rested on their arms in close proximity.

Neither army commander had fully executed his plan of battle, although General Bragg had approached very nearly the completion of his. He had turned a flank of the national army, bent back the right to the rear of the center, but had failed to turn its left or reach its rear, and hence had not gained the extreme advantages which he had inticipated in assuming the offensive and had seemingly attained at the grand crisis of the battle. He had assaulted boldly and persistently from first to last, but had completely exhausted his army without gaining a decisive victory. General Rosecrans had fought a battle radically different from the one he had proposed for himself. Instead of turning the right of the Confederate army and taking its center in reverse, according to his plan, he had been forced into the most emphatic straits in maintaining the defensive from flank to flank. Both commanders had lost heavily; General Bragg by continuous assaults with massed forces, and General Rosecrans by resistance at each point to superior numbers, and by frequent recessions under the guns of the enemy. Their respective losses on this day are not given even approximately in official reports, but it may be assumed that the aggregates mentioned for the four days of battle were drawn mainly from the first. A battle whose emergencies of offense and defense involves the use of all reserves, must necessarily be a bloody one.

It is seldom that an engagement of such dimensions has left two commanding generals so much in doubt as to the course that either would adopt, and hence each determined to await developments, and each was ignorant of the purpose of the other. Of the two, General Bragg was the more hopeful; not because he had strength for further offense, but from his belief that such was the condition of the opposing army that its retreat was a necessity. And the question of retreat was doubtless at first an open one with General Rosecrans and his subordinate commanders.

General Rosecrans' report indicates that he was at first in doubt as to the propriety of attempting to remain on the field. He did not certainly know that the opposing army had been so reduced in strength and spirit as to have abandoned the offensive, and being aware of his own heavy losses in men and material—such material, too, as the defensive demands— and having his right flank bent back upon his line of communications after a battle which he had provoked by positive offense, he could hardly avoid hesitation in maintaining the defensive in that position. He thus mentioned his action and decision in his official report: "After a careful examination and free consultation with corps commanders, followed by a personal examination of the ground in rear as far as Overall's creek, it was determined to await the enemy's attack in that position, to send for the provision train, and order up fresh supplies of ammunition, on the arrival of which, should the enemy not attack, offensive operations were to be resumed."

During the night, Van Cleve's division, under command of

Colonel Samuel Beatty, General Van Cleve having been wounded early in the day, resumed its connection with the left wing; and a little before daylight, on January 1st, General Crittenden, with permission of General Rosecrans, retired his line a few hundred yards to higher ground. General Palmer then took the left, with Wood's division on his right. At this time the latter division was commanded by General Hascall, General Wood having been wounded on the 31st.

At noon on the 1st, Negley's division was moved to General McCook's support, in expectation of a second effort of the enemy to turn his right. General Bragg demonstrated heavily against the center, and right at several points with artillery and a show of infantry. This action, however, was only tentative, as he was still in doubt as to General Rosecrans' intentions, though expecting his retreat. In the afternoon, General Crittenden moved Beatty's division, supported by Grose's brigade, across the river, and formed a line of battle in front of Breckinridge, who had resumed his position on that side.

During the day the enemy's cavalry, under Generals Wheeler and Wharton, were busy in the rear to embarrass the passage of trains to and from Nashville, and to watch carefully for indications of the retreat of the army. A heavy force appeared at 2 P. M., in the vicinity of La Vergne, captured a portion of a train, dispersing the remainder, and then attacked Colonel Innis, commanding the First Regiment Michigan engineers and mechanics, holding a stockade on the hill south of the town. Colonel Innis twice refused to surrender upon formal demand, and successfully repelled every attack, although his little stockade was bombarded. At his call, Lieutenant-Colonel Burke of the Tenth Ohio first sent a detachment of cavalry to his support from Stewart's creek, and upon the failure of this force to give aid, he made a rapid march to La Vergne, arriving, however, after the withdrawal of the enemy. This conflict, the presence of the enemy's cavalry in heavy force on the communications of the army, attacking train guards and destroying wagons, and a multitude of frightened teamsters and demoralized soldiers straggling to the rear, produced the wildest confusion from Stewart's creek to the vicinity of Nashville. This excitement in the rear was in striking contrast with the comparative quietness reigning over the field, where each army was awaiting the action of the other, harmonizing in purpose now as fully as when opening battle upon the same plan.

During the forenoon of the 2d, there were indications that General Bragg would renew the offensive this time from his right. The movement of infantry and artillery was plainly visible from Beatty's position. Skirmishing was maintained between the two lines across the river, with occasional cannon shots. Colonel Beatty's line in front of General Breckinridge was formed with Price's brigade on the right, next the river; Fyffe's on the left; Grider's, formerly Beatty's, supporting Price, and Grose's supporting Fyffe. Drury's battery, Lieutenant Livingston commanding, was posted in the rear. At 3 o'clock P. M., the advance of strong columns following skirmish lines, revealed fully the purpose of the enemy.

This aggression had really a defensive object, as General Bragg had concluded that he must dislodge the force in front of his right, or he would be compelled to withdraw Polk's right across the river, since it was exposed to an enfilading fire from Beatty's position.

His hope of the retreat of General Rosecrans had been strengthened by the return of Wheeler and Wharton from the rear, with information indicating this movement. The former of these commanders was again in the rear of the national army, under instructions to ascertain definitely "whether a retrograde movement was being made." While there was any doubt respecting this expected and greatly desired withdrawal, it was imperative that General Polk's position should be maintained, and the condition of its accomplishment was the dislodgment of Beatty. He therefore formed as strong a combination as practicable, giving Breckinridge two thousand cavalry under Wharton and Pegram for his right, and added ten Napoleon guns to his artillery. This movement then was the expression of a vital object, involving even the stability of his main lines on the left side of the river. To veil his purpose as much as possible, General Bragg had opened his artillery upon General Rosecrans' center and right at noon, which had become quiet after a vigorous response in semblance of a tentative demonstration. His real object, doubtless, was to draw attention to his own center and left, that he might throw Breckinridge suddenly against Beatty, and gain the heights he deemed necessary for the defense of General Polk's right flank.

Impressed with the importance of his movement, General Breckinridge advanced with his forces massed and with great vigor. Artillery, in active contests on the other side of the river, had heralded an engagement considered by the enemy as decisive of the general conflict, and Breckinridge's onset was in correspondence with the magnitude of the interests compassed by his adventure. He received and disregarded the fire of Beatty's skirmishers, his first and second lines and artillery, and wheeling upon Price's and Grider's brigades, broke their lines and followed the retreating fragments to the river.

In the quiet that prevailed on the other side of the river, this contest drew upon it the attention of both armies. On the high ground on the opposite bank, were massed two brigades, Hazen's and Cruft's, of Palmer's division, and Negley's division, with their batteries. And when General Crittenden perceived that his left, across the river, was under great pressure, he asked Major John Mendenhall, his chief of artillery, what he could do with his guns to relieve Beatty, and the latter hurriedly massed all the guns of the left wing, except Drury's, and with them Negley's guns and Stokes' battery. This battery had been sent with the pioneer brigade to the left by General Rosecrans, when he first heard the noise of battle from that direction. As the engagement across the river progressed, Major Mendenhall, in the presence of Generals Rosecrans and Crittenden, posted battery after battery, until fifty-eight guns were ready to bear upon the enemy. At the culmination of the conflict, on the dislodgment of Price and Grider, these guns were opened upon the enemy, who in his eagerness of pursuit followed to the river, losing heavily under such a fire at every step, and finally receiving, in addition, volleys from the supporting infantry. At the river, Breckinridge recoiled and drew back his rapidly diminishing forces. At this juncture, Colonel John F. Miller, followed by a portion of Stanley's brigade, charged with his brigade across the river. Disregarding an order from a general officer, not his immediate commander, to desist from so hazardous an adventure, he dashed over and fell furiously upon the foe, already in rapid retreat. The right of Miller's line was supported by the Eighteenth Ohio, and portions of the Thirty-seventh Indiana and Seventy-eighth Pennsylvania, of Stanley's brigade. Moving on the opposite bank his left, by Grose's brigade, which had changed front and resisted the enemy, when Price and Grider gave ground, and in his rear were Hazen's brigade and portions of Beatty's division. Miller reached a battery in position, and charging with the Seventy-eighth Pennsylvania, Sixty-ninth and Seventy-fourth Ohio, and Nineteenth Illinois, the Twenty-first Ohio striking opportunely on the left, captured four guns, and the colors of the Twenty-sixth Tennessee regiment. The Twenty-first Ohio siezed the guns and drew them off, and the Seventy-eighth Pennsylvania gained the colors. Miller's hurried movement having disordered his lines, he here halted to readjust them, and was almost immediately relieved from position by Hazen's and Grose's brigades, and Davis' division. General Davis had first thrown one brigade from his position on the extreme right of the army, across the river, and afterward, having obtained permission from General Rosecrans, had followed with two brigades. General Davis, being the ranking officer on that side of the river, assumed command of all the forces nearly equal to a full corps in number. He assumed command just after Colonel Miller, under orders, passed to the rear with his brigade, and recrossed the river. General Davis at once threw forward skirmish lines. These soon encountered the enemy, who had somewhat recovered from his panic, and a sharp engagement ensued, in which artillery was freely used. During the night General Davis fortified his line and intrenched a battery.

Colonel Miller's movement had great prominence, in utterly defeating General Bragg's object in this engagement, which was to secure the heights commanding his lines across the river. General Rosecrans, being as yet on the defensive, had no thought of aggression from any point of his line, and hence it is not improbable that, had not Miller moved promptly to charge Breckinridge's forces, and had he not followed them in rapid pursuit, they might have reformed upon their object-ive, and held it.   As it was, Miller drew after him such a combination as prevented Breckinridge from holding the cov-eted heights, who having been carried beyond the hills, by his success at first, lost them altogether, his failure costing, in the various forms of casualty, an aggregate of two thousand men.

The weather on the 3d was unfavorable to active opera-tions against the enemy, and as General Bragg declined the offensive altogether, after the repulse of the preceding even-ing, there was quietness throughout the day.   At 6 P. M., Gen-eral Thomas interrupted the reigning stillness, by throwing forward Colonels Beatty's and Spear's brigades—the latter having come up during the battle—and driving the enemy from the woods in his front and his intrenchments beyond, severed his line in the center.   During the night, General Bragg retreated, as he stated in his official report, in conse-quence of his knowledge of reinforcements to General Rose-crans.   His information was incorrect, or else the coming of Spear's brigade was considered as giving a dangerous prepon-derance to the national army, or became an excuse for an act that other circumstances made imperative.   The 4th was spent in burying the dead, and on the 5th the army occupied Mur-freesboro.

General Rosecrans moved from Nashville with about forty-seven thousand men.   He fought the battle with an aggregate of forty-three thousand four hundred—thirty-seven thousand nine hundred and seventy-seven infantry, three thousand two hundred cavalry, and two thousand two hundred and twenty-three artillery.   He lost ninety-two officers killed, and three hundred and eighty-four wounded; one thousand four hun-dred and forty-one enlisted men killed, and six thousand eight hundred and sixty wounded, and about two thousand eight hundred missing.   Lieutenant-Colonel Garesche, his chief of staff, was killed by his side.   In addition to the field officers already mentioned as killed, eight colonels, five lieutenant-colonels, and five majors fell in immediate death, or died from wounds. The aggregate loss was over twenty per cent. The enemy gained about thirty guns, and lost three.*

General Bragg reported his strength at less than thirty-five thousand men, of whom thirty thousand were infantry and artillery. His losses, in the aggregate, including four general officers, two of whom were killed, were nine thousand killed and wounded, and one thousand missing.

General Rosecrans estimated the opposing army at over sixty thousand men, and General Bragg, in reciprocal error, conjectured that he fought an army of seventy thousand. The latter was superior in cavalry, while the former had five more brigades of infantry in action from first to last, but only two more seriously engaged on the 31st, and only three more on the field until late in the day.

A victory had been gained by the Army of the Cumberland, and in view of the primal success of the enemy, a great victory, but in respect to the broadest possibilities of battle, it was not emphatically decisive. The national army held the field, and had made an advance of thirty miles toward Chattanooga, with good ground for encamping, and a good depot for supplies at Murfreesboro; but General Bragg, though compelled to abandon the field after an initiative of battle which promised complete victory, had withdrawn his army in good order and fair condition, with freedom to retire at leisure to his next defensive line, that of Duck river, as the last of the advantages which he had gained by his advance from Chattanooga, in August, 1862. The victory, then, was simply the

---

*The colonels were Frederick C. Schaefer, commanding a brigade under General Sheridan, who fell near the railroad, in rear of the left; Minor Millikin, First Ohio Cavalry; Geo. W. Roberts, Forty-second Illinois; James Forman, Fifteenth Kentucky; Leander Stem, One Hundred and First Ohio; T. D. Williams, Twenty-fifth Illinois; S. P. Reed, Seventy-ninth Illinois; F. C. Jones, Twenty-fourth Ohio; J. G. Hawkins, Thirteenth Ohio, and F. A. Harrington, Twenty-seventh Illinois. Lieutenant-Colonels: John Kell, Second Ohio; M. F. Wooster, One Hundred and First Ohio; David McKee, Fifteenth Wisconsin; L. Drake, Forty-ninth Ohio, and P. B. Houssem, Seventy-seventh Pennsylvania. The Majors: S. D. Carpenter, Nineteenth United States Infantry; Henry Terry, Twenty-fourth Ohio; Adolph G. Rosengarten, and F. B. Ward, Fifteenth Pennsylvania Cavalry; and D. A. B. Moore, First Ohio Cavalry.

expression of a long stride toward the restoration of the status
of the preceding summer, in Middle Tennessee.

———

CHAPTER XVIII.

OPERATIONS DURING THE ARMY'S ENCAMPMENT OF SIX MONTHS
AT MURFREESBORO.

On the 5th of January, the Army of the Cumberland went into position in the vicinity of Murfreesboro. General Thomas, by direction, placed his divisions on the Woodbury, Bradyville, Manchester, and Shelbyville turnpikes; General McCook posted his forces from the Shelbyville road across the Salem turnpike to Stone river, where his right rested, and General Crittenden disposed his command from General Thomas' left so as to cover the Liberty and Lebanon turnpikes, resting his left on Stone river.

Thus located, attention was first given to the recuperation and reinforcement of the army. The slightly wounded were sent to Nashville and farther north as fast as possible, while the severely wounded were placed in the public buildings of Murfreesboro not occupied by the enemy as hospitals, and in large field hospitals in the vicinity of the town.

Until the railroad to Nashville was put in running order, wagon trains were the sole dependence for supplies. The contingencies of bad weather and bad roads, and the vastness of the daily demand, forbade a full commissariat or the rapid reclothing of the troops.

By authority of general order No. 9, war department, January 9, 1863, the troops of the Army of the Cumberland were organized into three corps d'armée, designated the Fourteenth, Twentieth, and Twenty-first, corresponding in the main to the former grand divisions of "Center," Right and Left Wings, without change of commanders. During the month of January, General Steedman's division, formerly under com-

mand of General Fry, moved from Gallatin and took post at
Antioch Church on Mill creek, near Nashville, and at La
Vergne, and General Reynolds' division advanced from the
same place to Murfreesboro.

The objects proposed for attainment, while the army was in
camp at Murfreesboro, were the fortification of the place, the
complete re-equipment and reorganization of the troops, general preparation for a summer campaign, the greatest possible
restraint to the enemy north of Duck river, and the greatest
possible injury to him south of that stream.

Soon after the occupation of Murfreesboro, the most elaborate fortifications were projected, and their construction commenced, and were completed during the six months of
comparative inactivity which followed. Earthworks of the
strongest type were thrown up on the high ground between
the town and Stone river, on each side of the railroad and
Nashville turnpike, and on the elevated ground north of the
river. These heavy works were commanded in turn by a succession of forts which offered vulnerable sides to the great
central fortress. And besides the heavy forts and intrenchments, there was a circumvallation in front of the extended
camps of the army. These defenses subsequently furnished
refuge for troops stationed for the protection of communications and the depot of supplies at Murfreesboro, but no
great army ever had an opportunity of repelling a greater
army through their friendly help.

January 25th, by order of the war department, Forts
Henry and Donelson were transferred from General Grant to
General Rosecrans, and subsequently the order was amended
to include Fort Heiman. This change placed the Cumberland
river in the care of General Rosecrans (being one of the two
channels of supply connecting his primary and proximate
depots) and appropriately threw upon him the responsibility
of maintaining the open navigation of this river.

No general engagement being imminent, the enemy's cavalry was exceedinly active in embarrassing the concentration
of divisions, and in expeditions against the communications of
the army. About the last of January, General Wheeler
having under his command his own cavalry and the troopers

of Forrest and Wharton, appeared at Triune, in rear of the army. Having received early intelligence of his movement, General Rosecrans directed General Davis, with his division and two brigades of cavalry, under Colonel Minty, to move by the Versailles turnpike to the rear of Wheeler. He also directed General Steedman to keep watch toward Triune. General Davis, upon arrival at the junction of the Versailles and Eagleville roads, dispatched Colonel Minty to move round by way of Unionville and Rover, while he advanced directly to Eagleville, reaching there on the evening of the 31st. At Rover, Colonel Minty captured a regiment numbering three hundred and fifty men. Afterward, the pursuing forces concentrated at Franklin to intercept the enemy. General Davis divided his command and moved upon different routes, and General Steedman advanced to Nolensville and thence to Franklin. But Wheeler eluded the infantry and cavalry, and appeared before Dover. Tenn., on the 3d of February. This post was held by seven hundred men under Colonel A. C. Harding, Eighty-third Illinois. Wheeler made repeated attacks, but was as often repulsed, with a total loss of two hundred men killed, six hundred wounded, and one hundred captured. Colonel Harding had thirteen killed, fifty wounded, and twenty captured. Shortly after dark, several gunboats convoying a large fleet of transports laden with troops on their way to reinforce General Rosecrans, arrived at Fort Donelson, when Wheeler at once retreated. Before morning, Colonel Lowe arrived from Fort Henry, and from all quarters efforts were made to intercept the enemy. Colonel Lowe sent his cavalry in direct pursuit, and General Davis, at Franklin, having been reinforced by five hundred cavalry, under General Morgan, made effort to cut him off in his retreat. He gave chase with Morgan's and Minty's cavalry, but Wheeler moved far to the west and avoided him altogether, crosssing Duck river at Centerville. All the troops that had been directed against Wheeler resumed their previous stations, except General Steedman's command, which remained at the front.

The troops that reached Fort Donelson, February 3d, comprised eighteen regiments of infantry and four batteries of artillery, having recently been designated the " Army of Kentucky," under the immediate command of Brigadier-Generals C. C. Gilbert, A. Baird, and George Crook, but under the general command of Major-General Gordon Granger, who was still at Louisville. · From Fort Donelson they steamed to Nashville. These forces, with two regiments of infantry and four of cavalry, which soon after joined them by rail and boat at Nashville, numbered in the aggregate about fourteen thousand men. The appearance of the fleet approaching Nashville was exceedingly imposing. The river below the city is tortuous, and the line of gunboats and steamboats, whose decks were covered with troops with arms and banners, revealing its winding length, formed a pageant of wonderful grandeur. The unfriendly citizens of Nashville were forced to contrast this revelation of power and splendor with the confusion and dismay which reigned when the retreat of Johnston's army through their streets left them defenseless.

The reinforcements gradually took position in the front. February 12th, General Gilbert moved with his brigade to Franklin; on the 24th, General Crook embarked with his and proceeded up the Cumberland to Carthage, Tennessee, where he debarked and took position, and on the 3d of March, General G. C. Smith advanced from Nashville to Brentwood with the cavalry of General Granger's command.

March 4th, General Rosecrans ordered a general reconnoissance to ascertain the strength of the enemy in his front. General Sheridan, with four brigades of infantry and Minty's cavalry, moved from Murfreesboro toward Rover. When near the latter place he turned toward Eagleville with the infantry, giving the direct road to the cavalry. Colonel Minty found four hundred of the enemy's cavalry at Rover; drove them upon another force of six hundred at Unionville, and having routed the whole, pushed them to Shelbyville, capturing fifty-two prisoners, some wagons and mules. He then joined Sheridan at Eagleville. General Steedman, with his entire command, moved from Nolensville, through Triune and Harpeth, toward Chapel Hill, meeting and driving back Roddy's cavalry.

The same day (March 4th), General Gilbert sent an expedition under Colonel John Coburn, of the Thirty-third Indiana, south from Franklin. The objects were to form a junction with a column moving toward Columbia from Murfreesboro, and the collection of forage to fill a train of eighty wagons. Colonel Coburn's command embraced his own regiment, the Thirty-third Indiana; the Eighty-fifth Indiana; the Nineteenth and Twenty-second Michigan; six hundred cavalry under Colonel Thomas J. Jordan, comprising a detachment from his own regiment, the Ninth Pennsylvania Cavalry, one from the Second Michigan, and another from the Fourth Kentucky; and Aleshire's Eighteenth Ohio battery. The total strength of the force was two thousand eight hundred and thirty-seven.

Colonel Coburn was directed by General Gilbert to advance the first day to Spring Hill, and divide his force on the second, sending one fraction to Rally Hill to meet the column from Murfreesboro, and the other toward Columbia, each to return to Spring Hill at night, unless the former should meet the expected column.

Colonel Jordan moved in advance of the infantry, and met the enemy about three miles from Franklin, moving north. Both forces quickly formed lines of battle, but Colonel Jordan was first in readiness for action, and Aleshire opened with his guns. After a sharp conflict for some hours, the enemy withdrew and retreated toward Spring Hill. The next morning the column advanced, but before reaching Thompson's Station the enemy was again found, and this time in position. There were rumors of other forces on the left flank, and some troops were in sight on high ground in proximity, in that direction. Colonel Jordan charged the enemy on a line of hills in front of the station, with his men dismounted, when a new position was taken on another range of hills beyond the station. Colonel Coburn pursued to the vicinity of the station, where the column was arrested by shells from a battery on a hill to the left, and soon by the fire of another on the right, which, from the direction of the advance, enfiladed the line. Colonel Coburn had, the day before and that morning, advised Gen. Gilbert of these indications and of direct information that he was meeting the enemy in strong force; yet, as his orders had not been modified, he determined to advance and charge the annoying battery on the right. He placed his own battery by sections on opposite sides of the turnpike and railroad, which are separated by a narrow space; placed the cavalry in immediate support, and disposed three regiments for the attack—his fourth, the One Hundred and Twenty-fourth Ohio, being in the rear to guard the train. The line advanced under the fire of both batteries, when suddenly they ceased firing, and the enemy's infantry was seen in motion to attack. The situation was now fully developed. There was infantry with the two batteries, while cavalry was reported on the left and rear. Colonel Coburn now resolved to retreat; but it was necessary first to repel the enemy. After some sharp fighting in front, the retrograde movement was commenced from the midst of large forces of infantry, cavalry, and artillery. Colonel Jordan was directed to collect his command and cover the retreat, who, soon seeing the infantry of the enemy moving to his rear to cut him off, ordered the battery to move to the rear, and dismounted the detachments of Majors Scranton and Jones to hold the enemy in check to enable Captain Aleshire to save his battery, and then effect a junction with the infantry regiments to the east. But the cavalry and infantry were here separated. The infantry regiments, by changing front to resist attacks from various directions, moved backward and to the east. The cavalry, artillery, and the One Hundred and Twenty-fourth Ohio, which, upon being threatened by the enemy, retreated with the train, followed the turnpike road. Colonel Jordan deemed it vain to attempt to resist the heavy masses of the enemy, and Colonel Coburn finding himself in a short time surrounded, surrendered the three regiments with him. The other forces escaped. His loss was forty killed, one hundred and fifty wounded, and thirteen hundred surrendered, including his wounded. The reported loss of the enemy was one hundred and fifty killed and four hundred and fifty wounded.

The enemy's force, under Generals Van Dorn and Wheeler, was fourteen or fifteen thousand strong, and the surrender, after Colonel Coburn had gone into the midst of this army and had been turned to the east of the road, was doubtless a necessity. He went forward against his own convictions, because his orders were not changed.   An earlier retreat might have saved his command.

The reports of Colonels Coburn and Jordan are conflicting as to the exact situation when the latter commenced to retreat. Colonel Jordan asserted that his retreat was necessary to save himself from being cut off by a force moving to his rear, west of the road, which was the direct line for the retrograde movement, and that the situation was then hopeless, as it was vain to resist an army.   Colonel Coburn had hope of saving his whole force if its unity had not been broken.

In the meanwhile, General Sheridan had taken position at the junction of the Chapel Hill and Shelbyville turnpikes, and General Steedman had pushed the enemy's cavalry, under Roddy, south through Chapel Hill and across Duck river, capturing sixty men and eighty horses.   General Steedman then intrenched himself at Triune.

Upon receiving information of Colonel Coburn's defeat and surrender, General Granger threw General Baird's brigade into Franklin from Nashville by rail, and followed in person.

March 6th, Colonel Jones' brigade, supported by Colonel Heg's, drove the enemy out of Middleton, when both brigades returned to Murfreesboro.

The same day, General Granger brought forward his cavalry, under General Smith, from Brentwood, to join a co-operative movement against General Van Dorn.   The next day, General Sheridan closed up on Franklin, and a brigade arrived from Nashville.   General Steedman was now threatened by some six thousand cavalry, but upon the arrival of two regiments from La Vergne, the enemy retired toward College Grove. Two days later, Colonel Minty moved to Franklin, and the day following, General Granger, with his own and Sheridan's and Minty's troops, advanced from Franklin and drove Van Dorn from Spring Hill.   At the same time, General Davis was thrown forward from Salem to Eagleville, to relieve General Steedman's front, and General R. S. Granger was posted at Versailles, in his support.   On the 10th, General Davis closed upon General Steedman at Triune, and General Gordon Granger drove Van Dorn across Rutherford's creek, near Columbia.   The day following, General Granger's cavalry having crossed the stream several miles above, advanced almost to Columbia, but the high water prevented the passage of the infantry and artillery. This movement terminated this general and complicated reconnoissance, when all the various commands engaged in it returned to their former respective positions. It was developed that the enemy was in strong resisting force at various points, but no special knowledge of General Bragg's aggregate strength was gained.

March 5th, General Rosecrans ordered Colonel H. P. Lyon to abandon Fort Henry and transfer the garrison to Fort Donelson. A few days later, Fort Heiman was also abandoned, and its garrison, under Lieutenant-Colonel Patrick, was withdrawn to Fort Donelson. The latter fort was strengthened to give greater security to the navigation of the Cumberland river.

During the spring and early summer, the Confederate generals, Morgan and Forrest, were very active, the former operating to the east of Murfreesboro and the latter to the west. Their frequent appearance in the vicinity of outposts of the army provoked several efforts to punish them for their audacity.

March 18th, Colonel A. S. Hall was sent from Murfreesboro, with the second brigade of General Reynolds' division, to look after Morgan to the northeast. He advanced beyond Statesville, and learning that Morgan was preparing to attack him he retreated to Milton, and posting his brigade on a hill in the vicinity, awaited his assault. Morgan's superior numbers gave him strong assurance of success, and though meeting a more stubborn resistance than he anticipated, assaulted Hall's command first on both flanks, and then in turn on left, right, and rear, but was repulsed throughout the engagement, which lasted three and a half hours. Morgan left four hundred men on the field, of whom over sixty had been killed. Colonel Hall had six men killed and forty wounded. This was the most decided failure that Morgan had yet made. His policy, always, was to attack only when he had such advantage as to assure his success, and he no doubt supposed, as the usual condition was palpable, he would attain the common result.

On the 1st of April, General Morgan was driven from his stronghold at Snow Hill by General Stanley. He left his dead on the field and fled toward McMinnville. General Stanley returned to Murfreesboro with forty prisoners and three hundred horses and mules.

On the 25th of March, General Forrest captured at Brentwood, after a short engagement, about four hundred men of the Twenty-second Wisconsin regiment, under Lieutenant-Colonel Bloodgood. He also captured, at a stockade south of Brentwood, a detachment of the Nineteenth Michigan. General Smith at the time was moving with about six hundred cavalry to the support of Colonel Bloodgood, and pursued the enemy. He overtook Colonel Biffle's regiment four miles from Brentwood, inflicted a severe loss upon it, and recaptured considerable property, but was compelled to retreat before Forrest's whole command.

April 7th, General Rosecrans organized a provisional brigade of seventeen hundred men for independent service, and assigned Colonel A. D. Streight to its command, with instructions to repair to Nashville and prepare to make an expedition into Alabama and Georgia to interrupt communications and destroy property of all kinds useful to the enemy. Having obtained a partial supply of unserviceable mules, Colonel Streight proceeded to Palmyra, and thence across to Fort Henry, gathering on the way as many serviceable animals as possible. At Fort Henry he embarked for Eastport, Mississippi. He left that point on the 21st, reached Tuscumbia on the 24th, and moved thence on the 26th for Moulton. Leaving that place at midnight on the 28th, he pressed forward through Day's Gap toward Blountsville. While passing through the Gap, his rearguard was attacked by Forrest's cavalry. The enemy followed him through Blountsville, Gadsden, and on toward Rome. He defeated Forrest repeatedly, but his men and his animals becoming jaded, he lost heavily by capture. With diminished ranks and in almost utter destitution of serviceable ammunition,* he moved on, and crossed the Chattooga river, in hope of destroying the bridge at Rome. But in this he failed, as the enemy pressed upon him so closely that his men became exhausted, and many having been already killed and captured,

---

* His ammunition had been injured by fording streams.

and there being no hope of accomplishing the object of his expedition, he surrendered to Forrest on the 3d of May. This enterprise was boldly conceived, and there was no lack of bravery and energy in its conduct, but the contingencies were not clearly apprehended, and the actual results did not compensate for the loss of so many men and so much material. But failure though it was, it was the type of enterprises which, undertaken under better conditions, resulted in brilliant success. It was a mistake to start with a half supply of poor animals, depending mainly upon captures to mount half his command at the start. This plan caused delay in starting, and the result was that the enemy was encountered in superior numbers soon after Colonel Streight had passed beyond the reach of support. The enemy's partisan leaders in their raids in Tennessee and Kentucky had citizens of these states for soldiers, could always depend upon the friendship and assistance of a large portion of the inhabitants, and, besides, were themselves thoroughly acquainted with the country, and consequently were hardly ever ignorant of the strength of the forces operating against them, or of the short routes to safety. The conditions of success were very different subsequently, when the national forces undertook to interrupt the enemy's communications and make destructive raids. Such enterprises were given an unheralded start, and were prepared for quick movement, or else had such strength as to defy ordinary opposition. These conditions were wanting in Colonel Streight's adventure.

On the 9th of April, General Stanley moved from Murfreesboro, through Triune, to support General Granger at Franklin, who was threatened by about nine thousand cavalry and two regiments of infantry under General Van Dorn. General Granger's forces numbered about five thousand infantry and two thousand seven hundred cavalry. His infantry were posted on the south bank of the Harpeth river, and General Smith's cavalry had been sent to reinforce the garrison at Brentwood. The enemy suffered severe loss in approaching Franklin, inflicted by the Fortieth Ohio Infantry, which resisted very stubbornly as it slowly retreated. General Stanley crossed the river and struck the enemy in flank, but was subsequently forced to recross. Having met such opposition before reaching Franklin, General Van Dorn retreated without making a general attack.

April 20th, General Reynolds, with four thousand infantry, and two thousand six hundred cavalry, under Colonel Wilder, made a reconnoissance northeast and southeast from Murfreesboro. He destroyed almost entirely the railroad from Manchester to McMinnville, a cotton-mill and two other mills at McMinnville, a small mill at Liberty, captured a large amount of supplies, one hundred and eighty prisoners, over six hundred animals, and returned to Murfreesboro with the loss of one man wounded.

At 1 A. M., on the 27th, Colonel Watkins moved out of Franklin, between the Columbia and Carter's Creek turnpikes, and surprised the Texas legion encamped within a mile of General Van Dorn's main force. He captured one hundred and twenty-eight prisoners, three hundred horses and mules, eight wagons, and all the camp and garrison equipage without losing a man. Colonel Campbell, with his brigade of cavalry, went out from Franklin on the 30th, to surprise the enemy on the Columbia and Jonesboro turnpikes. He killed fourteen men, wounded twenty-five, and captured thirteen.

May 21st, General Stanley started from Murfreesboro with a portion of General Turchin's cavalry division and one regiment of mounted infantry, to attack a force encamped in the vicinity of Middleton. His advance under Lieutenant O'Connell charged the enemy, and drove him from his camp and from another position, inflicting heavy loss. General Stanley brought in three hundred horses and seven hundred stand of arms, with other less valuable property.

Early in June, there was one of the peculiarly sad occurrences of war at Franklin, Tennessee. Two men, claiming to be officers, and wearing the uniform of a colonel and major, presented themselves to Colonel Baird, commanding the post, and stated that they were Colonel Anton and Major Dunlap, and authorized, by an order from General E. D. Townsend, assistant adjutant-general, at Washington, and another from General Rosecrans, to inspect outposts. Their conduct excited surprise, and Colonel Watkins soon concluded that they were spies. This supposition proved to be true, as upon inquiry at department headquarters, it was ascertained that there were no such inspectors in the national service. General Rosecrans at once ordered a drum-head court-martial, and their immediate execution, upon conviction, as spies. Learning that such a court had been ordered, they confessed that they were Colonel Lawrence A. Williams and Lieutenant Dunlap, of the Confederate army. The former had been in the army of the United States. They claimed that they were not spies, and solicited clemency. But the proof was positive, and General Rosecrans' order was imperative, and they were consequently hung June 9th, the day after their arrest.

The conduct of these men was somewhat inexplicable. It was supposed that it was their object to gain such knowledge of the post as would enable Forrest to dash on it and capture it. But Franklin was not an exceedingly important place, not being on the direct communications of the army, and one that could not be held by the enemy except with a large army. Why they should make such a venture to gain knowledge of its strength and defense, is incomprehensible; and if they had an ulterior object, it was not apparent.

During the six months of the army's encampment at Murfreesboro, which were filled up with numerous reconnoissances and "affairs of outposts," there was an earnest and protracted discussion between General Halleck, commander-in-chief, and General Rosecrans, with regard to an aggressive campaign, and from the first months of the year the latter was urged to advance against General Bragg, in position on Duck river. After General Grant had commenced his campaign against Vicksburg, General Halleck became more urgent, as he thought that the inactivity of the Army of the Cumberland would permit General Bragg to detach forces to Mississippi, to maintain the enemy's grasp of the Mississippi river. This was considered the more probable, as General Joseph E. Johnston was in command of a large department, including General Bragg's army, as well as the one operating in the State of Mississippi. General Rosecrans was restrained from active operations, as he claimed, first, by the character of the roads in Middle Tennesse in winter, and then by delay in the enlargement of his cavalry arm, and the lack of animals for transportation, and the want of forage. He also assumed the ground that military considerations forbade his advance while General Grant's campaign was in progress. That, should he force General Bragg to retire behind the mountains, he would give him an opportunity to send reinforcements to General Johnston in Mississippi, which he would not have should he be held on the line of Duck river, with the contingency of battle at any moment, and that, should General Grant fail, there would be a heavy combination against himself in Middle Tennessee, and that for this contingency the reserve army should not be far from its base. General Bragg however, did detach a portion of his troops, but fortunately they did not reach Mississippi until General Grant thrust his army between Generals Johnston and Pemberton, and had shut up the latter to a siege within his intrenchments at Vicksburg, so thoroughly established that no outside relief could reach him.

Thus the spring passed away before General Rosecrans deemed himself prepared to advance. His cavalry horses multiplied slowly, and his trains and forage attained the requisite proportions in the same degree. Still, by the 1st of June, the more special indications of an advance began to appear. General Ward's brigade was ordered forward from Gallatin, to take post at La Vergne. General Gordon Granger moved his command from Franklin to Triune. General Crook's brigade was transferred from Carthage to Murfreesboro, and attached to General Reynolds' division, the Fourth, of the Fourteenth Corps. The former Fourth division of that corps was transferred to General G. Granger, whose forces were constituted as the reserve corps, comprising three divisions, designated as First, Second, and Third, and commanded respectively by Brigadier-Generals A. Baird, J. D. Morgan, and R. S. Granger. General Rosecrans, however, still delayed, and about the 10th of June he invited a formal expression of opinion with regard to an advance against the enemy from his corps and division generals. He was sustained in his delay by his subordinates generally, though General Garfield, his chief of staff, urged upon him a speedy movement, for reasons both military and political, and chiefly upon the ground that he could advance with sixty-five thousand one hundred and thirty-seven bayonets and sabers, against an army of forty-one thousand six hundred and eighty men, as he estimated the strength of General Bragg's army.

By the 23d of June, the question of advance was fully solved, and orders were issued for the movement of the army. By this time the cavalry had been greatly enlarged, through accessions of regular cavalry and mounted infantry, and the grand fortifications at Murfreesboro afforded in their completion protection to General Rosecrans' accumulated supplies.

CHAPTER XIX.

TULLAHOMA CAMPAIGN.

In June, 1863, General Bragg's army was occupying a strong position north of Duck river. His infantry front extended from Shelbyville to Wartrace, and his cavalry rested at McMinnville, on his right, and Spring Hill and Columbia on his left. General Polk's corps was at Shelbyville, having a redan line covered with abatis in front. A detachment from it was thrown forward to Guy's Gap. General Hardee's corps held Hoover's, Liberty, and Bellbuckle Gaps. Chattanooga was the base, and Tullahoma was the chief depot of supplies.

General Rosecrans determined to concentrate the corps of Generals Thomas, McCook, and Crittenden on the enemy's right, covering this movement by a feint upon his left with General Granger's corps and the main portion of his cavalry. The execution of this plan was commenced on the 23d, by the advance of Granger's corps. The enemy's position was well chosen for either defense or retreat. He had in his front a range of hills rough and rocky, through whose depressions, called gaps, the main roads to the south passed. These gaps were held by strong detachments, with heavy columns within supporting distance. Such was the strength of the position at Shelbyville, that General Rosecrans anticipated stubborn resistance should he attack it, and in the event of success in assault, the enemy could cover his retreat, having a route to his rear, easily defended. He therefore proposed to turn General Bragg's right, and avoiding his intrenchments at Shelbyville altogether, provoke a battle on ground of his own selection, or force him to retreat on a disadvantageous line. This purpose involved the necessity of forcing the advanced forces from the gaps from the left to the right of the main position.

The movement of troops, in the first place, to Triune had been made to create the belief that a direct attack would be made upon Shelbyville; and now, in the actual advance of his army, he endeavored to keep up this impression. For this object, General R. B. Mitchell, commanding the First cavalry division, moved forward from Triune and drove back the enemy's cavalry upon his infantry line, skirmishing sharply at Eagleville, Rover, and Unionville. General Rosecrans also demonstrated with his cavalry from his left, and sent an infantry force to Woodbury, that the enemy might regard these movements as a feint to divert attention from the direct attack upon Shelbyville. The same day, June 23d, General Granger, with his own corps and General Brannan's division of General Thomas' corps, moved from Triune to Salem.

The next day the whole army was in motion. General McCook advanced toward Liberty Gap. His corps started on the Shelbyville turnpike, but the divisions at different points deflected to Millersburg, where Sheridan's and Davis' divisions bivouacked at night, while Johnston's advanced to the Gap. On approaching the position, Colonel Harrison, with five companies of his mounted infantry, the Thirty-ninth Indiana, was thrown forward to skirmish. Colonel Harrison having provoked resistance in front of the gap, General Willich's brigade was deployed, and advancing pushed the enemy's skirmishers upon their reserves, posted upon the crest of the hills on the opposite sides of the entrance to the gap. A demonstration in front developed the impracticability of carrying the position by a direct attack. Colonel Miller, with a portion of his brigade, was then brought up, and a line having been formed of such length as to envelop both flanks of the enemy, he was driven through the depression a distance of two miles. The whole division bivouacked between the hills to hold one of the gateways through the enemy's natural defenses.

During the day, General Thomas advanced on the Manchester turnpike, Reynolds' division leading, followed by Rousseau's and Negley's divisions. Colonel Wilder's brigade of mounted infantry, of Reynolds' division, encountered cavalry posted seven miles from Murfreesboro, and pressing them upon their reserves, drove the whole force through Hoover's Gap, a defile three miles long, and took position at its southern entrance. He was soon fiercely attacked by a large body of infantry, but held his ground until General Reynolds' joined him with his other two brigades, when the enemy withdrew, and the Fourteenth Corps rested for the night in another of the passes through the hills in front of the enemy.

General Crittenden, having left General Van Cleve's division to garrison Murfreesboro, moved, with Generals Wood's and Palmer's divisions, to Bradyville. General Granger, accompanied by Brannan's division, advanced from Salem to Christiana. General Stanley proceeded from Murfreesboro, on the Woodbury turnpike, to Cripple creek, with General Turchin's division of cavalry, and thence through Salem to reinforce General Mitchell, and formed a junction with him at the intersection of the Salem and Christiana roads. General Mitchell had advanced during the day from Rover through Versailles to Middleton, where he met cavalry, and in an engagement of considerable sharpness killed thirty men and wounded a large number.

The next day, General Crittenden advanced to Holly Springs. General Brannan joined General Thomas, from Christiana, and was placed in position in Hoover's Gap. General Reynolds skirmished all day with the enemy. At night, General Rousseau closed up in his rear, preparatory to an attack upon the enemy the next day at Beech Grove. General Stanley joined General Granger, with Mitchell's division and Minty's brigade, at Christiana, for operations on the right flank, having first driven the enemy's cavalry to Guy's Gap. Colonel Long, with a portion of his brigade, advanced to Lumley's Stand, and scouted to Track's Ford and Pocahontas. The remainder of Turchin's division accompanied General Crittenden.

Late in the afternoon, the enemy made an attack at Liberty Gap, with the evident intention of dislodging Johnson's division. General Johnson did not hold the southern entrance, as did General Thomas at Hoover's Pass, and this fact and the supposition of General Bragg, that General Rosecrans would throw the main portion of his army through this gap, induced the effort to regain it.

The enemy first attacked the center of Johnson's line, and being repulsed, next attempted to gain the hills, so as to command Johnson's flanks with infantry and artillery; but he was circumvented in his strategy, and repulsed in every attack, withdrawing entirely late in the evening, in the direction of Bellbuckle. The troops engaged were Willich's and Miller's brigades of Johnson's division, supported by Carlin's brigade of Davis' division, and all evinced distinguished gallantry. The losses in this action revealed its character. General Johnson lost two hundred and thirty-one killed and wounded, and the enemy one hundred killed, and seven hundred and fifty wounded.

On the 26th, General Thomas advanced toward Fairfield, and met the enemy in force on the heights north of Garrison creek. He drove him steadily, Generals Rousseau and Brannan operating upon his left flank from the hills north of the road, and General Reynolds against his front and left. Having assumed a new position, he made preparations to resist, and attempted from the hills to enfilade General Thomas' line, but was driven from position by a charge of Walker's brigade and the regular brigade, under Major Coolidge. He then retired before the rapid advance of the Fourteenth Corps, and covered his retreat with heavy skirmish lines, supported by artillery in rear and cavalry on the flanks. After pursuing some distance, General Thomas disposed his divisions so as to offer a battle front, extending from the Fairfield road to a point within five miles of Manchester. During the day, Generals McCook and Granger remained in bivouac, the former at Liberty Gap and the latter at Christiana. General Crittenden struggled on toward Manchester, over almost impassable roads, rendered so by the heavy rains, which had fallen every day since the army left Murfreesboro.

The position of the Fourteenth Corps, far in advance of Hoover's Gap, made practicable the concentration of the whole army on the enemy's left, to force him to fight to resist its further advance, or abandon his position altogether. Accordingly, on the 27th, General McCook withdrew from Liberty Gap, and having passed through Hoover's Gap, marched his corps, in rear of General Thomas, toward Manchester. Early in the day, General Thomas put his corps in motion—Rousseau's and Brannan's divisions to Fairfield, Negley's on their left in support, and Reynolds' directly on Manchester. The latter arrived at Manchester early in the morning, Wilder's brigade surprising the town and capturing forty prisoners. The enemy not having been found at Fairfield, the other divisions turned toward Manchester, where, about midnight, the whole corps was concentrated.

The reserve corps, preceded by the cavalry under General Stanley, advanced from Christiana to Guy's Gap, where the enemy was encountered. Colonel Minty's brigade, supported by Mitchell's division, drove him from the gap and pursued him to his intrenchments, four miles north of Shelbyville, where he again offered resistance. General Wheeler was in command, having with him Martin's division and a portion of Wharton's. Colonel Minty attacked him and forced him out of his intrenchments, and pushed him into Shelbyville. At this juncture, General Mitchell coming up, turned his right flank and cut him off from direct retreat, while Minty charged into the town and completed his total defeat. General Stanley captured Wheeler's artillery and about five hundred of his men, while nearly two hundred were either killed or drowned in attempting to swim Duck river. General Wheeler escaped with the remainder of his command by swimming the river. The movements of the day revealed the fact that General Bragg had withdrawn his army entirely from his first line of defense, and confirmed the success of the first grand feature of General Rosecrans' strategy. It now remained to force him, by battle or strategy, to fall back to his stronghold on the Tennessee river.

While the corps of Generals McCook and Crittenden were concentrating at Manchester, slowly in fact, but as rapidly as the rain and bad roads would permit, General Thomas, in compliance with instruction from General Rosecrans, commenced the movements which were designed to bring the campaign to a decisive issue. Early on the morning of the 28th, he sent Colonel Wilder with his brigade to break the railroad at some point south of Decherd, and Colonel John Beatty's brigade to Hillsboro, in support of the movement. He also threw forward toward Tullahoma, Rousseau's and Brannan's divisions, with some regiments from Reynolds' and Sheridan's, on their right and left flanks.

Colonel Wilder reached Decherd at 8 P. M., burned the depot and water-tank, and destroyed about three hundred yards of railroad, but retired upon the approach of the enemy's infantry. The next day he moved to the University, broke up the Tracy City railroad, and then dividing his force advanced toward Anderson and Tantallon. The enemy was found at these places in such force as to forbid attack, and the brigade was soon after united at University. On his return, he avoided Forrest at Pelham, and reached Manchester in safety about noon on the 30th.

On the 29th, there was an advance toward Tullahoma until the front of the army was within two miles of the place. Generals Thomas', McCook's, and Crittenden's corps closed in upon it, and General Stanley, with the cavalry, reached Manchester, completing the concentration of the army for the final movement against Tullahoma.

Early in the morning of the 30th, General Thomas learned, through a citizen, that General Bragg had evacuated the position. He at once ordered General Steedman, with his brigade and two additional regiments, to make a cautious reconnoissance and ascertain the truth or falsity of the report. The troops entered the town about noon without opposition, and captured a few prisoners. The fact having been communicated to General Rosecrans, he immediately disposed his troops for pursuit. Rousseau and Negley overtook the enemy's rear-guard at Bethpage bridge, and skirmished sharply. His forces, however, had possession of the heights across the river, and commanded the bridge by artillery protected by epaulements. The swollen streams, especially Elk river, performed a friendly office for General Bragg, as they formed behind him a barrier to a rapid pursuit. The cavalry, in some instances, forced the passage of the bridgeless river at the moment of engaging the enemy, but in the main, the pursuit, either by cavalry or infantry, was entirely fruitless. It developed the fact, however, that General Bragg had crossed the Cumberland Mountains, and that Middle Tennessee was again in the possession of the Army of the Cumberland.

During this campaign of nine days, the rain fell almost incessantly, and the ground over which the army moved was of such nature that the movement of artillery and trains was exceedingly slow, and the escape of the enemy without battle was mainly owing to this cause.

General Rosecrans lost in the campaign eighty-five men killed, four hundred and eighty-two wounded, and thirteen captured. General Bragg's loss in killed and wounded was not ascertained; but he left behind him as prisoners fifty-nine officers and one thousand five hundred and seventy-five men, eight field pieces, and three rifled siege-guns, besides the usual waste of material in a hasty retreat.

At the conclusion of this short but spirited campaign, the Confederate Army of the Tennessee and the Army of the Cumberland resumed in the main the attitude of the preceding summer, when each was gathering forces for aggressive movements. These armies had marched into Northern Kentucky and back again; had fought two battles and skirmished over large portions of Kentucky and Tennessee; and they gave themselves again to preparation for future conflicts, the one at Chattanooga, and the other with its camps disposed as before, from Winchester to McMinnville. In declining battle at Tullahoma, General Bragg invited the renewal of the old plan for the invasion of East Tennessee, and General Rosecrans' acceptance of it brought to his army the old work of repairing roads and building bridges, and the long waiting for the accumulation of supplies. This campaign then terminated with the complete restoration of the status of July, 1862—the Army of the Cumberland in possession of the line of the Tennessee and the railroads in Middle Tennessee, with Chattanooga as its objective. It was then decisive of the complete failure of General Bragg's aggression. While the preparations for another campaign were going on, the remoteness of the enemy precluded the usual infantry skirmishing and reconnoissances, which, in the interval between great battles, maintain active belligerency; but the cavalry had opportunity to revisit most of the places in Tennessee and Northern Alabama, from which the national forces had been withdrawn the previous summer. And this was done to the intense annoyance of the citizen enemies of the national government, as in the second coming of the Army of the Cumberland supplies were to be drawn from the country, in the absence, too, of the slightest presumption that the government was to be maintained and the Union restored through mere kindness to the people whose property and aid had been freely given to the Confederate armies.

The return of the Army of the Cumberland to Southern Tennessee and Northern Alabama was doubtless as unexpected as its first appearance the previous year. When it moved northward, the farmers of this region had been exhorted to repair their fences and plant their fields under the most positive assurance by the Confederate generals that no second invasion would ever interrupt their ordinary pursuits. But war, with a more dismal front and sterner power, was again at their doors.

During the early part of July, the cavalry was concentrated at Salem, Tennessee, preparatory to a general sweep to Huntsville, Alabama. On the 12th, General Stanley put his cavalry in motion. He sent Colonel Galbraith along the railroad to Fayetteville, to ascertain the condition of the road. He captured some prisoners, and learned that General Forrest's command was north of Elk river, moving south. He moved across to Pulaski, and then pursued a force of cavalry to Lawrenceburg, killing eight men and capturing ninety. The other forces of the cavalry, by various routes, concentrated at Huntsville on the 14th, and soon after diverged widely on their return to the rear of the army, bringing about three hundred prisoners, one thousand six hundred horses and mules, nearly one thousand cattle and sheep, and six hundred negroes. These minor operations were then suspended to enter upon another of the great campaigns of the war.

CHAPTER XX.

THE MOVEMENTS OF THE ARMY OVER THE MOUNTAINS AND TENNESSEE RIVER, AND BATTLE OF CHICKAMAUGA.

UPON the conclusion of the Tullahoma campaign, General Halleck urged General Rosecrans to advance against the enemy south of the Tennessee river. But there were difficulties in the way of an early movement, which General Rosecrans deemed insurmountable. In his judgment, three conditions were essential to the successful advance of his army. These were the repair of the railroad to the Tennessee river, ripe corn in the fields, and support to his flanks. For the actuality of the first, he was himself responsible; the second depended upon time and favorable weather; and the third rested with the military authorities at Washington, and the commanders of the armies east and west of him, on the line of the Tennessee river.

July 13th, the railroad bridge over Elk river was ready for trains, and on the 25th they were running to Bridgeport, Alabama. But corn does not ripen in Tennessee and Georgia in July, and the movement of General Burnside into East Tennessee was long deferred, and no promises had been given that the right flank of the Army of the Cumberland should have protection while advancing against Chattanooga. On the 5th of August, in disregard of General Rosecrans' assigned reasons for not moving his army, General Halleck gave peremptory orders for its advance. The former, however, deferred movement until the middle of the month. By this time his preparations were complete, and the fields promised the forage for which he had been waiting; but no further assurance had been given that he should have supporting forces on right or left.   As a partial protection to his right, he had sent, August 11th, Brigadier-General R. B. Mitchell's cavalry division, Colonel E. M. McCook commanding, from Fayetteville, Tennessee, to Huntsville, Alabama, and thence along the Memphis and Charleston railroad, to protect that road and guard the line of the Tennessee river from Whitesburg to Bridgeport.

At this juncture, the Fourteenth, Twentieth, and Twenty-first Corps, with the cavalry on the flanks, were mainly disposed on a line from Winchester to McMinnville, in readiness for the various movements involved in the plan of campaign. Sheridan's division, since the opening of the railroad to Bridgeport, had been on that road, with heavy detachments at Stevenson and Bridgeport.   A brigade had taken post at Pelham, and a detachment had been sent to Tracy City, on the 13th of August, to protect a depot of supplies established at that point—the terminus of the mountain railroad.

The reserve corps was in the rear, occupying all the country north of Duck river, with garrisons at Fort Donelson, Clarksville, Gallatin, Carthage, Nashville, Murfreesboro, Shelbyville, and Wartrace.   The army was dependent for supplies upon the railroad to Louisville, as during the months of summer and autumn the navigation of the Cumberland river is exceedingly precarious.   Nashville was a secondary base, and there were surplus supplies nearer the front to meet the wants of the army during any temporary interruption of the railroad.   But the assurance of full rations at the front depended primarily upon the maintenance of railroad connection with Louisville.   The thorough defense of this road required a force equal, at least, to one-fourth of the offensive strength of the army.   Looking to the rear, the problem of supplies demanded most earnest attention and most positive solution, and involved difficulties by no means light; and looking toward the enemy, who was resting in fancied security in a position invested by mountains, the barriers to advance, successful strategy, or attack, seemed exceedingly formidable.   General Rosecrans had maneuvered Bragg out of Tullahoma and across the Tennessee river; but as the topography of the region around Chattanooga was very different from the surroundings of his former position, his antagonist did not anticipate that he should again be compelled to abandon a stronger position by mere strategy. He doubtless felt safe from direct attack, and did not foresee that Rosecrans would throw his army upon his communications. But this bold venture was proposed for the Army of the Cumberland—bold under any circumstances, but especially so, when there were no active campaigns in progress, east or west, to prevent the enemy from concentrating heavy forces at Chattanooga or in Northern Georgia. General Rosecrans was not indifferent to the possibility of overthrow, but his orders deprived him of discretion, except as to the plan of campaign.

Chattanooga had long been the objective of his army, and yet he was under orders to move against it with inadequate forces, and under conditions which involved great peril. The position was too important to the enemy to warrant the hope that he would fail to exhaust his resources to hold it. Under any circumstances, General Bragg could concentrate his own forces, and with timely warning of a movement against him, he could draw reinforcements from remote points. It was impossible for Rosecrans to advance rapidly, and yet the concealment of his ultimate design was a ruling condition of his success. Apart from the exposure of his flanks in moving beyond the Tennessee river, the configuration of the country between him and his objective imposed the alternative of skillful maneuver or failure. The first barrier was the Cumberland range of mountains, which, trending in a southwesterly direction, touches the Tennessee river a few miles east of Bridgeport, and then stretches westward to Athens. Waldron's ridge, on the east, forms the second barrier on the line of direct approach from McMinnville. This mountain abuts the Tennessee river, nearly half-way from Bridgeport to Chattanooga, and by its abrupt ascent, bars passage on the bank of the stream. These mountains, with subordinate hills, were between Rosecrans and Chattanooga, and were in his way, should he make a direct advance on that place, or move past it on the north to reach the enemy's right flank. He could reach the river, by moving directly south across the Cumberland range, but beyond the river, two other mountain ranges interposed—Sand Mountain and Lookout Mountain. The northern extremities of these mountains confront each other, from opposite sides of Lookout valley, in the immediate vicinity of Chattanooga. Trending thence to the southwest, they cross all the lines of advance toward the communications of the enemy south of Chattanooga.

In view of the strength of Chattanooga against direct attack, General Rosecrans resorted again to maneuver to dislodge his antagonist. As the route to Bragg's right flank penetrated a mountain region almost destitute of forage and water, and involved a wider separation from his communications, he selected his lines of advance over the river and mountains west and south of his objective. He, however, so directed his first movements as to mislead the enemy with regard to his ultimate design, which was to threaten his communications, and force him to abandon his position, or give battle on equal terms. The movement in this direction compassed another great advantage, as it gave him the railroad to Bridgeport directly in his rear as a channel of supply.

The movement of infantry and artillery across the Cumberland Mountains was commenced on the 16th of August. Two divisions of the Twenty-first Corps—Generals Palmer's and Wood's—marched by different routes over the mountains into the Sequatchie valley. Two brigades of General Van Cleve's division, the third having been left at McMinnville, and Colonel Wilder's brigade of General Reynolds' division of the Fourteenth Corps, moved on the Harrison Trace road to Pikeville; while Colonel Minty's brigade of cavalry diverged to Sparta, to cover the left of the column. This disposition of General Crittenden's Corps was intended to conceal the general movement of the army to the south, by making the impression at Chattanooga that an effort would be made to turn the position from the north. The four divisions of the Fourteenth Corps moved upon Stevenson and the mouth of Battle creek—Generals Baird's and Negley's to the former place, and Generals Brannan's and Reynolds' to the latter. General Davis' division of the Twentieth Corps joined General Sheridan at Stevenson, and General Johnson's passed through Bellefont to Caperton's ferry. General Stanley, with Colonel

Long's brigade of cavalry, advanced to Stevenson. The river having been reached, the pontoons were kept in concealment at Stevenson until the places for crossing had been selected.

Soon after the left had reached the Sequatchie valley, Generals Hazen's and Wagner's brigades were thrown across Waldron's ridge into the valley of the Tennessee, and were there joined by the brigades of Minty and Wilder from Pikeville. These four brigades, numbering in the aggregate between six and seven thousand men, under the command of General Hazen, took position from Williams' island to Kingston, on the north bank of the river, but in heaviest force opposite Chattanooga and the mouth of North Chickamauga creek. The extent of front presented, the show of strength near Chattanooga, the vigorous shelling of the city by Wilder's artillery, the troops at Pikeville and in the Sequatchie valley—in fine, the bold expression of the whole movement—constituted a brilliant feint, and contributed largely to General Bragg's misconception of General Rosecrans' plan of aggression. A wrong interpretation of the meaning of this movement, or some cause not apparent, induced the enemy to offer no resistance to the passage of the river at Bridgeport and other places in the vicinity.

The army commenced crossing the river on the 29th of August, and by the 4th of September, all the troops were across, except those under Hazen, and a few brigades farthest in the rear. General Johnson's and Davis' divisions, and the cavalry, crossed at Caperton's ferry, and advanced over Sand Mountain to the base of Lookout Mountain, at Winston's Gap, where they were joined by Sheridan, who had crossed at Bridgeport. The divisions of the Fourteenth Corps passed over the river at four different points—Caperton's ferry, Bridgeport, mouth of Battle creek, and Shellmound—and crossing Sand Mountain on converging roads, united in Will's or Lookout valley, in the vicinity of Trenton. When General Crittenden had concentrated his corps, it passed down the Sequatchie valley, crossed at Bridgeport and the two points above, and moving up the river to Whitesides, deflected to the right from the direct road to Chattanooga, through a pass into Lookout valley. The cavalry preceded the Twentieth Corps to Winston's Gap, and reconnoitered in various directions, without finding the enemy in force. As the army of offense advanced, the reserve corps, as far as practicable, moved in rear to hold the important positions, and give support in the event of battle.

The passage of Sand Mountain involved the necessity of making and repairing roads; and when this had been done as far as practicable without too much delay, such was the steepness of the ascents on the different routes of advance, that teams were doubled often to move the artillery and wagons.

By the 6th of the month, these movements in the main had been completed, and the army lay along the western base of Lookout Mountain, from Wauhatchie, a point six or seven miles from Chattanooga, to Valley Head, thirty-five miles distant. To dislodge the enemy from Chattanooga, it was now necessary to carry the point of Lookout Mountain where it abuts the Tennessee river, or to cross the mountain through the gaps farther south and endanger his line of communications. The former scheme being considered impracticable, the latter was adopted, and orders were issued to scale the mountain from the center at Trenton, and the right at Valley Head, while the left should demonstrate directly against Chattanooga, until the action of the enemy was revealed.

On the 30th of August, information had been received through a loyal citizen who had been forced to leave Chattanooga, that General Burnside had occupied Knoxville, that the rebel general, S. B. Buckner, and the troops that had held Knoxville, had retreated to Loudon; and that fifteen thousand men were on the way from Mississippi to join General Bragg. And on the day the army reached Lookout valley there came a rumor that Buckner had joined Bragg, and that the latter would abandon Chattanooga. The probability of the truth of this report induced General Rosecrans to continue the movements whose object was the accomplishment of this result. Accordingly, on the 7th, Negley's division of the Fourteenth Corps commenced the ascent of the mountain, and reached the top at four o'clock in the afternoon. During the day, Colonel Harker, of Wood's division, made a bold reconnoissance under the guns of the enemy, on the front of Lookout Mountain, and found it guarded by a heavy force, which was then covering the withdrawal of the army from Chattanooga. But this fact came to light subsequently. The Twentieth Corps remained in camp on the 7th.

The day following, General McCook, on the right, ordered two brigades of Davis' division to cross the mountain into Broomtown valley to support the cavalry in reconnoissance toward Lafayette and Rome. General Negley seized Cooper's and Stevens' Gaps, the latter having been heavily obstructed, and then bivouacked his main column at the junction of the State road and the one from Cooper's Gap. The operations of the day elicited no opposition—a fact that plainly indicated that the enemy was withdrawing from Chattanooga. Captain Van Buskirk, Ninety-second Illinois Mounted Infantry, advanced with fifty men to within five miles of Summertown without opposition, and discovered that the signal stations of the enemy had been abandoned. Rumors from various sources concurred in supporting the belief that Bragg had retreated. To elicit the truth, General Rosecrans directed General Thomas to send Colonel Atkins, of the Ninety-second Illinois, to make a reconnoissance toward Chattanooga on the mountain road early on the 9th, and instructed General Crittenden to send a brigade up an almost impracticable path, called the Nickajack Trace, to Summertown, a hamlet on the mountain, to reconnoiter the front of the mountain, and to hold the main portions of his corps in readiness to support the troops on reconnoissance, to prevent a sortie of the enemy over the nose of Lookout, or to enter Chattanooga should the enemy evacuate or make feeble resistance. He ordered the cavalry on the right flank to push by way of Broomtown valley, and strike the enemy's railroad communications between the Resaca bridge and Dalton. But the fact of the evacuation was manifest to the troops on the north bank of the river in the evening of the 8th, and at 3:30 A. M., on the 9th, General Rosecrans was so informed. Thus, without a battle or heavy skirmish, the primary objective of the campaign, the "Gateway to Georgia," and the southern entrance to East Tennessee, fell into his hands, as the result of his strategy.

Thus far, this movement, justly considered perilous in view of the possibilities to the enemy, was remarkably successful. During its progress there had been a lull in active operations east and west, which allowed the interest of the government and the loyal people to converge upon the movement in Southern Tennessee and Northern Georgia. When it became known at Washington that Bragg was receiving reinforcements, the necessity of the conjunction of the armies under Generals Rosecrans and Burnside was clearly perceived. But, unfortunately, the perception of this necessity was too late for practical advantage. Burnside's advance was intended to be co-operative with that of Rosecrans, but the accomplishment of his work drove his enemy to the army before Rosecrans, while he was himself too remote and too much engaged with affairs east of Knoxville, to render aid at Chattanooga. The improbability of the union of the two armies in time for battle, intensified the uneasiness that was felt with regard to the advance into Georgia. The evacuation of Chattanooga, therefore, relieved the anxiety of the authorities at Washington and General Rosecrans; and now, all thought of pursuit, rather than of defense, against Bragg's reinforced army.

General Bragg's reasons for the abandonment of Chattanooga, as stated by himself, were these: He estimated the Army of the Cumberland at seventy thousand men, and the one under General Burnside, at twenty-five thousand. He regarded the movement of troops to Pikeville and Kingston as a menace to Buckner's rear, while Burnside was in his front with superior forces. Buckner was therefore first withdrawn to the Hiawassee river, and subsequently to the vicinity of Chattanooga. But with this accession, his army was inferior to the one which he was opposing. So when Rosecrans had crossed the river at Bridgeport, and was as near his main depot of supplies as he was himself, not being able to divide his army on account of its weakness to hold his position and protect his communications and depots, he was compelled to throw himself before Rosecrans to save his line of supply. But he did this with the hope of striking the columns of his enemy as they should separately debouche from the mountain gaps.

To accomplish this, he placed his army between Lee and Gordon's Mills and Lafayette, on the road from Chattanooga to the latter place. He thus faced the eastern slopes of the mountains, directly on the line of advance from Trenton. He claimed that his movements partially accomplished his purpose, as he threw Rosecrans off his guard by his rapid movement, apparently in retreat, but in reality for concentration opposite the center of his army, and that being deceived by the information of deserters and persons sent within his line, he exposed himself in detail.

General Rosecrans states, in his official report, that the receipt of evidence, gathered from all sources, led him to believe that General Bragg was moving on Rome. Accepting his retreat far southward as a fact, he continued the movements of his right and center across Lookout Mountain, as previously ordered, and directed General Crittenden to occupy Chattanooga with a division, and subsequently with a brigade; to call his troops from the north bank of the Tennessee river, and follow the enemy vigorously on the road to Ringgold and Dalton. When over the mountain, General McCook was required to advance rapidly on Alpine, interrupt the retreat of the enemy, and strike him in flank; and General Thomas was instructed to move upon Lafayette.

In obedience to orders, General Crittenden occupied Chattanooga with Wood's division about noon on the 9th, called to him his troops from the opposite bank of the river, and put his corps in motion toward Ringgold, his head of column reaching Rossville, five miles distant, in the evening. The same day, Negley's division, by direction of General Thomas, moved down the eastern slope of the mountain and debouched into McLemore's Cove. This nook is formed by Lookout Mountain and Pigeon Mountain, a spur from Lookout, which curves round at its origin to the east and then trends northward on the east side of Chickamauga river, maintaining parallelism with the stream, Missionary Ridge on the west, and Lookout itself. Negley met the enemy's troopers at the foot of the mountain and drove them several miles with a heavy line of skirmishers. On the right, Carlin's brigade of Davis' division moved upon Alpine, Georgia, and Heg's brigade of the same divison into Broomtown valley, in support of the cavalry. In the evening, General McCook received information of the retreat of the enemy and orders to advance in pursuit.

During the 10th, the three columns moved in pursuance of orders. Crittenden's corps, with the exception of Wagner's brigade of Wood's division, left to garrison Chattanooga, advanced in pursuit of the enemy on the Ringgold road. Palmer's division leading, through deficiency of supplies made a short march, and encamped at the crossing of the Chickamauga; but short as was the advance, the enemy's cavalry annoyed the head of the column, and in a bold dash rode over the front of the First Kentucky regiment and captured two officers and fifty men. The movement on the Ringgold road partially uncovered Chattanooga, by giving open ways to the enemy on the three roads coursing through the valleys between Lookout Mountain and the line of march. This fact, taken with another, that Bragg had retired his forces mainly on the road to Lafayette, induced General Rosecrans to modify his orders to General Crittenden, restricting his advance to Ringgold,* and requiring him to make a reconnoissance the next day on the route of the enemy's retreat.

The advance of the central column also discovered the enemy, contrary to expectations. Negley moved forward beyond Bailey's Cross-roads and skirmished hotly with the enemy until he reached the opening of Dug Gap, in Pigeon Mountain, through which the direct road to Lafayette passes—the designated route of the Fourteenth Corps. He found the gap obstructed and a line of pickets, indicating the proximity of the enemy in force. Negley was now between the gap in his front and Catlett's Gap in the same mountain, farther to the north, and was exposed to attack in front and on both flanks. His situation, viewed in reference to Bragg's purpose of crushing his enemy in detail, was exceedingly critical. As he had progressed he had received conflicting rumors, but at night he was assured that heavy forces were in proximity to him in the three directions of his exposure. Baird's division had passed the mountain during the day, and was encamped at the

---

* Statement in General Rosecrans' report.

debouche from Stevens' Gap, a few miles in his rear, assuring him support in the morning. The advance of the central column had not been as rapid as General Rosecrans had anticipated, and he expressed his disappointment to General Thomas in terms of implied censure. His impression was that the tardiness of General Thomas in moving toward Lafayette imperiled both flanks; but in the full revelation of the facts, it appeared as saving Negley's and other divisions of the center, and at the same relieving one or the other of the corps on the flanks from exposure to an overwhelming concentration of forces.

In the effort to defeat Rosecrans in detail, Bragg's first combination was directed against Thomas; and this fact doubtless saved Crittenden's corps, which was in air and in no state of preparation to resist the attack of an equal force, much less a great army. McCook's corps was at the same time in complete insulation at Alpine, and not far from Bragg's army. Thus far the movements of the three columns met the expectations and wishes of the rebel commander. Crittenden had diverged to the east on the Ringgold road; McCook had advanced far from support, and Thomas had moved directly toward his army. His army now comprised about fifty thousand men. He had been joined by two divisions from Mississippi, and his own estimate placed his infantry at thirty-five thousand men; and almost into the midst of this vast army Negley had penetrated. As soon as his head of column had appeared at McLemore's Cove, General Bragg had given orders for a movement in great force against him. At midnight on the 9th, he gave orders to General Hindman to advance with his division to Davis' Cross-roads, in Negley's front, to co-operate with Cleburne's division and a force of cavalry from Hill's corps. Cleburne being sick and Dug and Catlett's Gaps being heavily obstructed, General Hill failed in his part of the combination; but Hindman advanced and was at Morgan, three or four miles from Negley, early in the afternoon of the 10th. To prevent a miscarriage of the movement altogether, at 8 A. M. General Bragg ordered Buckner with his corps to join Hindman at Morgan's, three miles from Davis' Cross-roads, and very near to Negley. Bragg was very urgent in regard to the movement, as he had inferred that the three advancing columns were moving for concentration near his position. To assure success by giving strong support to the forces already in Negley's front, he directed General Polk to send a division of his corps to Anderson's, to cover Hindman during his operations. Fortunately for Negley and the army there was delay. Hindman proposed a change of plan, and in waiting for instructions the day passed away. General Bragg refused to modify his orders, and at midnight repeated them with emphasis. Negley, as has been seen, was still unsupported and in ignorance of the elaborate combination which had been formed to overwhelm and capture him, for in addition to the four divisions at Morgan's and Anderson's, Walker's corps was ordered to support Cleburne at Dug Gap.

The experience of the Twentieth Corps on the 10th was not different from that of the two to its left. Johnson's division crossed the mountain and reached the vicinity of Davis' position, and Sheridan's encamped on the western slope. On reaching Alpine, General McCook ascertained that the enemy had not retreated, as had been anticipated, and that he could not communicate with General Thomas, on the east side of the mountain. He had been ordered to communicate with that commander, on that day, at Lafayette. He had also been directed to advance on Summerville. In this unexpected state of things he abandoned the advance to Summerville to await developments, and sent messengers to General Thomas, by way of Valley Head.

In view of the developments of the day, General Rosecrans made dispositions for the morrow. He ordered General Crittenden to the front, with instructions to advance with his main force to Ringgold, and detach a brigade to reconnoiter toward Lee and Gordon's Mills. Pursuant to these orders, General Crittenden directed Harker's brigade of Wood's division to retire to Rossville, and then move on the line of the enemy's retreat. With Palmer's and Van Cleve's divisions he advanced toward Ringgold. Soon after Harker reached the Lafayette road, he became engaged with the outlying guards of the enemy, and upon report of the fact, General Wood, with Buell's brigade, went to his support. During the afternoon, these brigades advanced to the mills, and at nightfall the camp-fires of the enemy were in view toward Lafayette. Palmer and Van Cleve reached Ringgold early in the day, and there met the brigades of Wilder and Minty, which had driven out the garrison of the place. Hazen, with his brigade, joined the infantry column at Graysville, earlier in the day. These brigades had crossed the Tennessee river at the mouth of the North Chickamauga. In the afternoon, Wilder, supported by infantry, advanced toward Dalton. He drove the rebel cavalry before him to Tunnel Hill, and encamped in front of a heavy force. The enemy gave many indications of concentration, as his outlying forces were formed on all the roads. In fact, Crittenden had passed the right flank of a large army intent upon operations in an opposite direction, or something more than a skirmish might have occurred.

The fact of concentration was revealed with greater emphasis before the Fourteenth Corps. At 8 A. M., Baird reached Negley, and formed his division on his left. Soon after, it was ascertained that the obstructions had been removed from the gaps, and that the enemy was advancing through them in heavy force, while another column was approaching farther to the left. It was then apparent that the trains and even the command would be endangered should battle be accepted without change of position, and General Negley decided to withdraw as speedily as possible. He sent the trains toward the mountain, and followed with his own division, leaving Baird's to check the enemy, until he could assume a new position north of the Chickamauga, and in turn cover the withdrawal of Baird's line, and prevent a flank movement on the left. When Negley's division had gained position and formed in line of battle, Baird withdrew, step by step, first his skirmishers, then his main line, until he too had crossed the stream. The enemy pressed him as he retired, and he was compelled to fight, suffering and inflicting loss. He had hardly crossed the stream before the enemy appeared with heavy lines on the opposite side, and opened with his artillery, while a heavy force formed in line of battle on his left. Negley's artillery responded from a hill to the rear, and Starkweather's and Stanley's brigades

became warmly engaged, and so far checked the enemy, that
Baird was able to form a new line behind Negley. When this
was done, Stanley retired, and Starkweather, having covered
his withdrawal, with quickness and safety moved his troops to
the rear of the third covering line. Previously, Negley had
sent Beatty's and Scribner's brigades to the rear to protect the
trains against the enemy's cavalry. These timely, cautious,
and dextrous movements saved these insulated divisions, and
their safe retirement from the presence of an army may be
regarded as one of the pivotal events of the campaign. Having
completely foiled the enemy by their skillful withdrawal, Negley and Baird took a strong position in front of Stevens' Gap,
and were soon joined by the divisions of Brannan and Reynolds. These four divisions were disposed for defense by General Thomas: Negley on the right; then, in turn, to the left,
Baird, Brannan, and Reynolds—the whole line covering Stevens' and Coopers' Gaps. But these preparations for defense
were not necessary, as General Bragg had abandoned his effort
against the central column. He had joined Cleburne at Dug
Gap, at daylight, to await the noise of Hindman's guns, as the
signal for Cleburne's movement upon Negley's flank and rear.
During the early hours of the day, in his impatience at Hindman's delay, he had repeated his orders to hasten his movements. But when the signal guns were heard, Cleburne's advance was too late to reach the flank or rear of the force
devoted, in orders, to destruction. Chagrined that this combination had failed, General Bragg turned his attention to a
movement against Crittenden.

During the 11th, General McCook remained at Alpine, but
the cavalry in his front were active in the endeavor to ascertain the movements and purposes of the enemy. Believing
that co-operation with General Thomas through Broomtown
valley was impracticable, General McCook ordered all his
trains and material not necessary for his troops to be retired
to the summit of the mountain to await the result of the
reconnoissance sent by General Stanley toward Lafayette.

The events of the day made evident the fact that General
Bragg had concentrated his army to give battle. Before General Rosecrans had learned the nature and issue of Negley's

engagement he had received information which rendered it probable that a heavy force had been concentrated at Lafayette, and suggested to General Thomas to call General McCook to his support. When the report of the engagement in McLemore's Cove reached him, he emphasized his suggestion that McCook should be called to the center.

Looking to the concentration of his whole army, General Rosecrans directed General Crittenden to move the divisions with him at Ringgold to the Lafayette road, either to join Wood at Lee and Gordon's Mills, or to call Wood's troops to himself at some good defensive position farther north. The orders under which General Crittenden had conducted his movements during the day had not been interpreted as restricting his advance to Ringgold, but as giving him freedom to advance indefinitely, if it was apparent that the enemy had retreated to some remote point. As the head of his column was beyond Ringgold when he received the order requiring the movement of his corps to the Lafayette road, he had to recall Wilder from Tunnel Hill, and the supporting infantry, not far in his rear, before he could withdraw from Ringgold with his remaining forces, and delay was unavoidable. The order in question did not reach him until after night, and this, too, retarded his movement to the northwest.

General McCook remained at Alpine, ignorant of events at McLemore's Cove, but in constant receipt of information making certain the fact of Bragg's concentration at Lafayette. He was consequently uneasy with regard to his own corps, and anxious with regard to the other columns. The concentration of the enemy so near him was suggestive of the fact that his position was a false one, as he could not reach General Thomas should the enemy attack him immediately; neither could he get support from any source should Bragg fall upon him with his whole army. But in the absence of orders he did not deem it legitimate to either advance or retreat.

When General Bragg withdrew his forces from McLemore's Cove, he directed Polk's and Walker's corps to Lee and Gordon's Mills. He made this movement in hope that he could easily defeat Crittenden, whose corps he had learned was divided on the roads to Ringgold and Lafayette. His orders to his corps commanders, and those sent against Crittenden at Ringgold, on the night of the 11th, required that they should move to a common destination. But though brought face to face, two corps against one, no battle resulted. And Crittenden's escape from another combination, seemingly well formed, brings to view another pivot on which the army's safety turned.

Early in the morning of the 12th, Wilder's brigade and the supporting infantry returned to Ringgold, and the whole force was put in motion toward Wood's position. Wilder's brigade was directed to follow on the line of march and cover the left flank of the column. Palmer skirmished with the enemy during the day, and Wilder had a severe engagement at Leet's tanyard, in which the enemy lost fifty men killed and wounded, his own loss being thirty men. His superior guns made the difference, for he had no other advantage. Wilder joined the corps at Lee and Gordon's Mills after dark, where the union of the three divisions had been effected during the afternoon.

Neither General Thomas nor General McCook changed position on the 12th, but each gained additional evidence that the Confederate army was concentrated at Lafayette. The cavalry forces on the right, reconnoitering toward that place, were assured that an army was before them.

On the morning of the 13th, General Crittenden made dispositions for defense. He threw Cruft's brigade and Wilder's on his left to reconnoiter, and the Fourth cavalry, which had that morning reported to him, on his right, toward Mc-Lemore's Cove. Ignorant of the fact that two corps were in readiness to attack him, he sent Van Cleve, with one brigade, on a reconnoissance toward Lafayette. Van Cleve met the enemy, with cavalry and artillery, soon after leaving the mills, and skirmishing heavily, drove him three miles. This agressive attitude disconcerted General Polk, and instead of attacking, as he had been repeatedly ordered, he halted in defense and called for reinforcements. Polk had received three distinct orders to attack at daylight. Three exceedingly important considerations induced General Bragg to press his subordinate to prompt action.   There was opportunity, as he thought, to strike Crittenden "in detail," and he proposed to attack the troops in motion from Ringgold, and then those at the mills.   Having crushed Crittenden, he could then give attention a second time to those in the cove.   Besides this inviting prospect north and west of his position, the approach of McCook from the south made it important to attack promptly.   He promised his lieutenant-general the support of Buckner's corps, and gave personal attention to the movement, accompanying Buckner as he advanced in support. But he was again disappointed.   Polk did not attack, as he had ordered; and though there were three corps against one, he abandoned the policy of striking his enemy "exposed in detail," and gave orders for the concentration of his army on the right bank of the Chickamauga, to deliver battle from his right flank.

The proximity of the enemy to the mills excited the gravest apprehensions, although his strength in Crittenden's front was not known.   It was known, however, that it was possible for Bragg to throw his whole army against Crittenden, or throw it between him and Thomas.   Each possibility was portentious of overthrow.   In the emergency, General Crittenden was ordered to move two divisions to the right to cover the Chattanooga road in the valley, immediately east of Lookout, leaving Wood's division at the mills.   Wood was instructed to hold his position if possible.   At this juncture the advance of the reserve corps—Whittaker's and Mitchell's brigades of Steedman's division, and Daniel McCook's of Morgan's—were expected at Rossville, and Wood was directed to look to these forces for support should the enemy attack him.   His division was in great peril in its isolation before the whole rebel army— two brigades opposite the center of an army of nearly sixty thousand men, without direct support on the right, left, or rear, and on the direct road to Chattanooga from Bragg's position.   In the event of yielding his position, General Wood was directed to defend the road to Chattanooga, and the one over the "nose" of Lookout Mountain, at all hazards.   Into the chasm between Crittenden and Thomas, Wilder was thrown, with instructions to reconnoiter along Chickamauga and Chattanooga creeks, and join General Thomas with such rapidity as the safety of his brigade would permit.

There was no movement in the center on the 13th, except a slight advance of Reynolds toward Catlett's Gap. General Thomas was now awaiting the approach of McCook before leaving the protection of the mountain.

At midnight of the 12th, General McCook received the first intimation that he was to join General Thomas. During the early part of the day he received other communications, which more fully revealed the necessity of this movement. He at first prepared to send his trains under the protection of three brigades, General Lytle commanding, back on the route of advance, and with the remainder of his corps, to move along the eastern base of Lookout to Dougherty's Gap, the route that had been suggested. Subsequently, this route was abandoned as impracticable, and another was sought on the mountain to Stevens' Gap. But as citizens concurred in denying the existence of such a road, and having no guide, General McCook determined to move by way of Valley Head. He therefore ascended the mountain, through Henderson's Gap, on the night of the 13th. He was now safe from attack; but the problem of his conjunction with General Thomas in time for battle was one involving the fate of the army. The issue was in the balance while he crossed and recrossed the mountain during the next four days.

General Rosecrans now made effort to hold all the roads to Chattanooga east of the mountain, and concentrate his army upon them before the enemy. From the 13th to the 17th, General Thomas advanced his corps slightly from day to day. General Crittenden, with Palmer's and Van Cleve's divisions, moved to the Chattanooga valley on the 14th, and countermarched on the day following, when Van Cleve took position at Crawfish Springs, and Palmer on his right, at Gowen's ford. During the 15th, Minty reconnoitered the front, and reported that the enemy was in force at Dalton, Ringgold, Leet's tan-yard, and Rock Spring Church.

After ascending the mountain at Winston's Gap, General McCook, with Johnson's and Davis' divisions, followed a mountain road to Stevens' Gap, and there descended to General Thomas.   Sheridan marched down Lookout valley to Johnson's creek, and crossed over the mountain on the line of the advance of the Fourteenth Corps.   The cavalry, under command of Brigadier-General R. B. Mitchell, General Stanley having been relieved on account of sickness, followed the infantry on the mountain road.   General Mitchell stationed Crook's division at Dougherty's Gap, and sent McCook's division to McLemore's Cove.

Thus, on the 17th, the three corps were again in supporting distance of each other.   When McCook reached the cove, General Thomas closed up on Crittenden, whose right division moved to the left to give room.   It had been a matter of life and death to effect the concentration of the army.*   On the 11th, the heads of column had met Bragg's outlying detachments, and from all came the startling announcement that his army was concentrated preparatory to battle.   Subsequently, it was ascertained that reinforcements had been drawn from Mississippi, Georgia, and Virginia.   General Rosecrans then abandoned the offensive—an attitude which his army had sustained with marked success for nearly a year.   The change to the defensive was a sad revelation to the troops that had crossed the lofty Lookout in fancied repetition of their former pursuits of Bragg's army.   Happily, however, the compact union of the three corps of the Army of the Cumberland, so long and so perilously insulated, was effected before the enemy was ready to deliver battle.   When the necessity of concentration was perceived, the interval between Crittenden and Thomas, and between the latter and McCook, was greater than that between each and Bragg's army.   Why, with knowledge of this fact, the Confederate general did not strike either, in its insulation, is not fully explained by the assertion that his subordinate corps and division commanders were slow to do his bidding.   Bragg's effort to strike Crittenden was made on the 13th, and yet for four days thereafter, his corps was between him and Chattanooga, in closest proximity and without support.   No general perhaps, during the war, had such opportunities, and none so completely failed to avail himself

---

* Statement in General Rosecrans' Report.

of them. In the merest glance at his possibilities, in comparison with his achievements, the utter absence of generalship in the management of his army comes into boldest relief. No excuse or apology can be made for such blunders. There was not so much defect of plan, as unprecedented feebleness of execution. Indeed, his plans were in many respects admirable. They compassed a magnitude of means out of all proportion to the objects proposed, and yet the results were too meager to give praise to the advance of a line of skirmishers. If his corps and division generals would not obey him, he should have drawn their successors from the generals of brigades, rather than have allowed his policy of defeating his enemy " exposed in detail " to fail. But all his blunders had not occurred. When Rosecrans' united army was in defiant attitude across the Chickamauga, on the night of the 17th, having failed to crush either of the three corps of that enemy in their isolation, his plan compassing the leading features of a great battle was yet to fail, through the delay of its initial ruling movement.

The 17th did not close with General Rosecrans in ignorance of the movement of Bragg's army toward his left. The approach of heavy columns from the direction of Dalton had been observed by General Steedman, who had advanced to Ringgold in reconnoissance. The clouds of dust which Steedman saw south of Ringgold, had their counterpart within the range of vision from the signal stations of the national army, and the trending of these clouds told plainly the object of the enemy. General Bragg had been massing his forces on his right, with effort to conceal his purpose by apparent activity and strength on his left. But the coming of his reinforcements from Virginia, through Dalton, revealed his strategy, by the direction of their march.

The night of the 17th, General Bragg announced his plan and prescribed the movements of his army for execution on the following morning. His army comprised five corps, some of them improvised for the occasion. Their order from right to left was: Hood's, Walker's, Buckner's, Polk's, and Hill's. Hood was ordered to cross the Chickamauga at Reed's bridge, and sweep up toward Lee and Gordon's Mills, to reach Rosecrans' flank and rear; Walker was directed to cross at Alexander's bridge and join Hood, and Buckner was required to cross at Ledford's ford, and press upon Wood's position in front of Polk's corps; while the latter was to demonstrate on the line of direct approach, and if not met by too much resistance, to cross and attack any force he might meet. Hill's duty was to cover the left flank of the army, and in the event of the movement of the Union army to Wood's position, he was directed to attack its left flank. The cavalry was stationed at the gaps in Pigeon Mountain, to cover the left and rear of the army.* Had these movements been executed promptly as ordered, the larger portion of Bragg's army would have been on Rosecrans' left, and in the rear of his left, with a fair prospect of grasping all the roads east of the Chattanooga valley, as at the time fixed for the execution of the movement, General Rosecrans was not prepared to defeat it. It was a repetition of the initiative of the same commander at Perryville and Murfreesboro, only on a grander scale. The conditions here were different, and though he was nearer the rear of his enemy, and had designated heavier columns for his favorite movement, there were obstacles which gave more embarrassment than in his other battles. In preparing for battle on the 18th, he had overlooked causes of detention, and this mistake gave General Rosecrans time to throw his army to the left, between him and Chattanooga, upon the shortest roads thither. The roads designated for his columns were narrow and unsuited for the movement of artillery; a stream with few bridges and few fords was in his way, and the movement of a large army by the flank on transverse roads involves embarrassments which almost always cause detentions not anticipated. So that, at nightfall on the 18th, Bragg was by no means ready for battle on the 19th, having entirely failed to deliver it on the 18th, as he had planned. But his preparations were in advance of those of General Rosecrans, as he had the initiative and moved on shorter lines. Night marches alone could give partial finish to Rosecrans' provisions for the engagement now plainly imminent.

* His plan as given in his official report.

Early in the day, the clouds of dust trending to the northeast had made evident the character and purpose of the movement of the Confederate army by the right flank. At an early hour, there was a demonstration in Palmer's front, to the right of Crawfish Springs, and at noon, Polk slightly threatened Wood. This activity was intended to conceal the heavy movements down the stream. Minty and Wilder were on the watch at Reed's and Alexander's bridges, and it was not until late in the afternoon that the heads of column appeared before them. These two brigades resisted so persistently, that General Bragg mentioned their action as one cause of delay. Wilder inflicted a loss of one hundred and five men to Liddell's division, at Alexander's bridge. But he and Minty were finally forced back, and the enemy secured the crossings. The lower one, at Reed's bridge, was wrested from the enemy late in the evening, and burned by Colonel McCook, of the reserve corps. Wilder was driven across the Lafayette road, and neither Minty nor McCook were able to learn what forces crossed the stream late at night. General Bragg held the river from Wood's position to Reed's bridge, and under cover of the night and the forests, his movements were perfectly concealed.

As two corps of the enemy remained in position across the Chickamauga, and his cavalry was on the right bank, far up the stream, it was very critical to move the Army of the Cumberland by the left flank. Crittenden's corps was compelled to maintain position, both from policy and absolute necessity. And the movement of the infantry, from the right toward Crittenden, was accomplished with great caution and consequent slowness during the day, so that at 4 P. M. no troops had reached the rear of Crittenden, though it was well known that the enemy had forces far beyond Wood's position. At this hour, General Thomas was directed to relieve Palmer's and Van Cleve's divisions with Negley's, that Crittenden might place Palmer and Van Cleve on Wood's left, and with Baird's, Brannan's, and Reynolds' divisions, to take position at Kelley's, on the Lafayette road. These changes in the main were effected during the night, and at early dawn there were five divisions in front of the enemy, and others were in motion. McCook's corps bivouacked at Pond Spring, and at daylight resumed motion toward the left. This corps was yet far from the battle-field, but its presence there was practicable, and some of its brigades were to be deployed in line of battle, while subject to the historic fierceness of the primal attacks of Southern armies. McCook was placed in command of all the troops, including the cavalry on the right of Crittenden's corps.

The unexpected slowness of General Bragg's columns on the 18th did not change his plan of attack; and at daylight on the 19th, Buckner's corps and Cheatham's division of Polk's corps crossed the Chickamauga, and joined Hood and Walker, who had crossed during the evening and night previous. General Bragg's line of battle was formed with Walker on the right, Buckner on the left, Hood in the center, and Cheatham, with five brigades, in reserve. Buckner's left rested on the Chickamauga, a mile below Lee and Gordon's Mills, and Walker's right on the road leading west from Alexander's bridge.

At daylight, General Thomas, with Baird's division, reached Kelley's house, Brannan's following closely. The two divisions were immediately formed so as to cover the roads to Reed's and Alexander's bridges. Wilder's brigade had taken position the night before, on the west of the Lafayette road, some distance south from Kelley's, and General Thomas proposed to place the two remaining brigades of Reynolds' division, Turchin's and King's, between Baird, who was on the right of Brannan and Wilder, when they should reach the field. While these dispositions were being made on the left, General McCook reached Crawfish Springs with his head of column, and received orders from the general commanding to mass his corps at that point, and await further directions. The enemy was not demonstrative in any direction at the time, and the Twentieth Corps was held for direction to any part of the field, as emergencies should arise. Crittenden had been charged by General Rosecrans to hold his position with persistent firmness in the event of attack, as upon his retention of position, the success of the movement of the other two corps to the left depended. The quietness in his front was to him prophetic of danger. His fear of attack had also been induced by information which Minty had given him as he passed his front with his brigade early in the morning, that the enemy was in front of the left of his line. It was not yet known that General Bragg's army was west of the Chickamauga, forming for battle, and to relieve the doubtfulness of the situation, General Crittenden directed General Palmer on his left to send a brigade to reconnoiter the road to the north. Colonel Grose was sent on this reconnoissance, but, before he could return and report, the suspense was relieved by the noise of battle on the left.

Soon after General Thomas had taken position before Kelley's house, he was informed by Colonel McCook, who had bivouacked on the road to Reed's bridge, that he had succeeded, the night before, in burning the bridge after a brigade had crossed. Believing this brigade to be isolated, Colonel McCook suggested that an effort should be made to capture it. Deeming the suggestion worthy of experiment, and wishing to explore his front, General Thomas directed General Brannan to leave one brigade within supporting distance of General Baird, and with the other two reconnoiter the road to the burnt bridge, and, if practicable, capture the isolated brigade. General Thomas, sharing the prevailing ignorance of the exact movements of the enemy, had been forming his line in nearness to a heavy force. Although the armies had been maneuvering in closest proximity for twelve days, each army commander was ignorant of the special dispositions of the other, and a merely tentative advance became the initiative of one of the bloodiest battles of the war. General Bragg had hoped to conceal his effort to throw his army between General Rosecrans and Chattanooga. The latter had discerned the movement of troops to his left, but neither he nor any of his officers were aware that seven-tenths of General Bragg's army were on the west bank of the Chickamauga early in the morning of the 19th. Brannan's reconnoissance, however, developed the enemy, and brought on the battle, disturbing General Bragg's combinations and preventing the suddenness of his blow.

In compliance with instructions, General Brannan posted Croxton's brigade on the left of Baird, and with Vanderveer's and Connell's moved forward, diverging to the left.

Croxton also advanced and soon encountered the enemy—three brigades of cavalry under Forrest, that were covering General Bragg's right flank. In moving forward, Baird met hostile forces, and captured two hundred prisoners. In the meantime, Croxton had become hotly engaged, as Forrest had called infantry to his aid. When General Thomas first heard the noise of battle in the direction of Croxton's advance, he rode forward to learn the nature of the conflict. He found Croxton very heavily engaged, but holding his ground against superior numbers, and returned to direct General Baird to his support. General Brannan also sent the Thirty-first Ohio, Lieutenant-Colonel Lister commanding, to Croxton's left. When these dispositions had been made, the two divisions advanced and pressed back the enemy some distance. This done, the line was halted for readjustment, when General Baird learned that there was a large force on his right. He prepared for resistance by ordering King's brigade, on his right, to change front to the south. But before the change could be made, Liddell's division was upon him, and hurled King's and Scribner's brigades from position in disorder and with the loss of ten pieces of artillery. Starkweather's brigade was thrown before the enemy, but it too gave way. Fortunately, reinforcements were near to press back the enemy to the front and right of Baird's position, while General Brannan had been so far relieved from pressure that he could charge the pursuing forces, with portions of Vanderveer's and Connell's brigades. The charge was exceedingly gallant and brilliant—the Ninth Ohio, Colonel Kammerling, recapturing, with the bayonet, Gunther's battery of the Fifth artillery, which King had lost. The capture of these and other guns by the enemy was mainly due to the fact that the conflict occurred on ground thickly covered with forest trees and undergrowth, and consequently unfavorable for the rapid movement of artillery, as also for its effective use. This opening passage of arms was the type of the fighting, in its first stages, from left to right. Excepting a few insignificant fields, the whole region between the Lafayette road and the Chickamauga was thickly wooded, and divisions and brigades from each army were often hotly engaged, while in complete isolation in the densest woods; for when armies meet unexpectedly on such a field, methodical movements are impracticable, as also continuous lines, until there has been an immense waste of strength.

The reinforcements at hand, to retrieve disaster on the left, had come at the call of General Thomas, and through anticipation of their need by General Rosecrans. When General Thomas was first assured that he had developed the Confederate army in his front, he requested General Crittenden, whose corps was nearest him, and not engaged, to send him support. General Crittenden sent Palmer's division, which reached him almost simultaneously with Johnson's division of General McCook's corps, acting under orders from General Rosecrans. Reynolds' division of the Fourteenth Corps arrived soon after. As yet, General Bragg had not advanced his divisions to the chasm between Thomas and Crittenden. His object had been to swing round his compact lines and envelop Crittenden, supposing that Rosecrans' extreme left rested at Lee and Gordon's Mills. When his cavalry met infantry overlapping his right flank, General Bragg threw Walker's corps against Brannan and Baird, and was compelled subsequently to direct his reserves, and one division from his extreme left, to his right, where Walker's corps had been broken and routed. The time spent in the execution of these movements, and surprise from the unexpected conditions of the engagement, permitted three divisions to secure alignment on the right of Baird. The first movement of Brannan and Baird had been regarded by General Bragg as intended to turn his right flank, and until its security had been attained, other dispositions were suspended. This prevented the advance of his central columns upon the unoccupied ground between Thomas and Crittenden, and robbed him of his greatest advantage.

General Johnson, on arrival at Kelley's, was directed by General Thomas to form his division in line of battle and move forward. The division was formed with Willich's brigade on the right, Baldwin's on the left, and Dodge's in reserve. When the division was in readiness for motion, Palmer's was in proximity on the right. By direction of General Rosecrans, General Palmer had formed his division by brigades in echelon, on the march from the right—Hazen's on the left, then Cruft's and Grose's, the latter well refused. In moving forward, these two divisions met Cheatham's division of five brigades, called from reserve to restore the enemy's right. After an hour of severe fighting, Cheatham yielded ground and fell back some distance. In the meantime, Reynolds had formed to the right and rear of Palmer. Turchin's brigade was posted southeast of Kelley's, and King's brigade, destined for his right, was thrown to his left on Palmer's right, in response to a call for help from Palmer, whose troops had nearly exhausted their ammunition. Reynolds planted his batteries, Harris' and Swallow's, near the road, with the Seventy-fifth Indiana and the Ninety-second Illinois in support.

The line not being continuous between Generals Thomas and Crittenden, there was danger that General Bragg would still interpose a heavy force before reinforcements could arrive. Troops were in motion from the Twentieth Corps, who were to bridge this chasm, but none were yet near. At this juncture, through anxiety for the safety of Palmer's division, General Crittenden sought and obtained permission to send other troops to the left. He at once put Beatty's and Dick's brigades in motion, leaving the third brigade of Van Cleve's division with General Wood, at Lee and Gordon's Mills. General Van Cleve soon found position on the right of Reynolds, and almost simultaneously General Davis arrived with Carlin's and Heg's brigades of his division, and formed them on the right of Van Cleve, extending the line well toward General Wood.

General Davis had been instructed by General Rosecrans to turn the enemy's left flank, and the former, in compliance, formed his brigades, by regiments in echelon, to wheel to the left from General Van Cleve's right. Having first planted his batteries on high ground, in an open field east of the Lafayette road, and posted the Eighty-first Illinois to the right in their support, he commenced his movement to flank the enemy. He, however, advanced only a short distance before he met the foe, and became heavily engaged. At first he drove back the enemy, but soon, little by little, his two brigades gave ground, specially on the flanks of the line, until his right and left rested upon the road.   In this position, supported by Wilder's brigade of mounted infantry, he resisted successfully the superior forces of the enemy through several hours of severest fighting.

Generals Van Cleve and Davis were opportunely thrown before an immense concentration of forces formed to separate the two wings of the national army, and upon the latter especially the enemy's blows fell heavily.   After a protracted conflict, Dick's brigade of Van Cleve's division, on his left, gave way, and then he was in isolation, except as supported by .Wilder, and for a time severely engaged.   His left brigade, with great loss, its commander, Colonel Heg, falling, held position, but the Eighty-first Illinois, on the right of the batteries, was driven back.   At this juncture, the enemy was pressing front and flanks, and the unequal contest could not have been maintained, had not reinforcements arrived.   Colonel Harker first reported with his brigade, and was placed by General Davis in rear of Heg's brigade, with orders to pass through it and engage the enemy.   Soon after, Colonel Bradley's brigade of General Sheridan's division reached the field, and was similarly formed in the rear of Carlin's brigade, to relieve it by passing to its front.   Soon after, General Wood, having been relieved by Lytle's brigade, moved, with Buell's brigade of his own division, and Barnes' of Van Cleve's, from Lee and Gordon's Mills to Davis' right, and nearly simultaneously, Laiboldt's brigade of Sheridan's division came also to the relief of Davis.   These commanders and troops were in time to defeat an effort of the enemy to pass around Davis' right.   Colonel Buell felt the shock of battle as the enemy was pressing back the Eighty-first Illinois, and his brigade was somewhat shattered and driven back, but soon rallied, and with Laiboldt's and Barnes' brigades, forced back the flanking column and maintained the position, the enemy desisting soon after entirely.

The scene of this conflict was Vineyard's farm, extending east and west from the Lafayette road, and skirted on all sides by thick woods.   The troops of each army, in the alternations of advance and retreat, found friendly cover in the woods, while the open fields gave such exposure that they were thickly

strewn with the commingled dead and wounded of the two
armies. This farm and the surrounding woods was a distinct
battle-field. The struggle upon it, though an important element of a great battle upon a vast field, was, during the later
hours of its continuance, a separate battle, mapped upon open
field and forest, in glaring insulation, by the bodies of the slain.

On the other side of the chasm, on the left of this position,
there was the counterpart. The left arm of General Bragg's
combination against General Rosecrans' center and right, was
laid heavily on Davis' and Van Cleve's divisions; the right
arm fell with crushing force upon Reynolds' and Palmer's divisions. The recession of Dick's brigade exposed General
Samuel Beatty's right flank, and after a severe conflict, this
brigade was overwhelmed and driven from position. There
was then a wide breach in the right center of the national
army, and General Bragg called troops from the other side of
the Chickamauga, to double back the broken line toward each
flank.

The previous repulse of the enemy's right wing had been
so decisive that a complete lull had succeeded. This quietness
permitted the retirement of Brannan's and Baird's divisions
on the left of General Thomas' line to a commanding position
on the road to Reid's bridge. General Thomas made this
change to make his left stronger in anticipation of another
assault upon it. On his right, Turchin's brigade of Reynolds'
division had relieved Hazen's on Palmer's left, that he might
replenish his ammunition. General Palmer had also called
away from the support of Reynolds' batteries the Seventy-
fifth Indiana. These latter changes left King without immediate support; and when under great pressure he called for
help, General Reynolds was compelled to send him the Ninety-
second Illinois—the last regiment defending his artillery.
When Hazen had secured ammunition he moved his brigade
to the left of King's position, holding his left refused upon the
Lafayette road. By this time, Van Cleve had been driven
from line, and King and Hazen engaged the enemy as he
wheeled to double up the flank. As Palmer's division was
not heavily engaged at this juncture, Grose's brigade was sent
to their support. Scarcely had Grose moved to the right

before the enemy in heavy force fell upon Cruft and Turchin. The five brigades stood for a few minutes under a destructive fire, and were then borne back with broken lines. In this threatening emergency, General Thomas moved Brannan's division from his left to his disordered right. This timely reinforcement, the quick reformation of portions of Palmer's and Reynolds' divisions, and the most effective use of several batteries of artillery arrested the disaster. The action of the artillery was especially conspicuous in the repulse of the enemy. Portions of Standart's, Cockerill's, Cushing's, Russell's, Harris', and Swallow's batteries opened upon the enemy with grape from two groups of guns formed respectively from the artillery of Palmer's and Reynold's divisions. When the enemy was repulsed on the main road, his forces moved through the chasm, and were met and driven back by Negley's division, which had advanced from Widow Glenn's and by Brannan's, which wheeled upon him from the vicinity of Kelley's house. The whole right of General Bragg's army had been broken and repulsed, and his central forces, though more successful in maintaining lines, had suffered equal losses. His left—Polk's and Hill's corps and cavalry—beyond menace to Wood and a dash at Negley, had provoked no conflict. His right had been so disordered by the early assaults, that Johnson's division, though far advanced toward the Chickamauga and entirely unsupported on the right after Palmer had been driven back, was not again attacked until a fresh division could be brought from the right bank of the stream, opposite Lee and Gordon's Mills. At the time that Brannan had been moved to the right in the afternoon, Scribner's and Starkweather's brigades were advanced to Johnson's left in support, while King's regular brigade, the third of Baird's division, was left on the road to Reid's bridge to hold the ground previously occupied by two divisions. These changes were merely provisional, and General Thomas, as night approached, selected ground for a new and more compact line, and designated the respective positions of the five divisions which he had handled during the day. But before Johnson's division and Baird's two brigades could be withdrawn, they were attacked by Cleburne's fresh division, supported by Cheatham's, and a severe night conflict ensued, lasting for an hour, with heavy losses on both sides and final repulse of the enemy.

The successful defense turned upon the rapid movement of the whole army to the left. General Rosecrans' field position was at Widow Glenn's house, and as he was advised of actual or prospective emergencies, he directed troops to meet them. Early in the day, the enemy made an unsuccessful effort to cross the Chickamauga in Negley's front, when in position west of Crawfish Springs, and late in the day General Lytle's brigade of Sheridan's division posted at Lee and Gordon's Mills, by General McCook, when that point was abandoned by Wood's division, repulsed a similar effort. The movement by the left flank extended to the cavalry; and at night all the fords of the stream above Lee and Gordon's Mills were held by this arm. The field hospitals had been located in the vicinity of Crawfish Springs for the center and right of the army, and for the extreme left on the road to Rossville. The hospitals on the right, though beyond the flank of the infantry line, were covered by the cavalry on the line of the Chickamauga.

Both armies lost heavily during the day. The loss of officers in the Confederate army was exceedingly large. But heavy as were the losses, each army knew that the indecisiveness of the battle involved a renewal of the conflict on the morrow and a repetition of carnage. Neither army was willing to yield without further fighting, and yet to neither was there the assurance of ultimate victory; and as they lay on their arms in close proximity, there was to each the oppression of doubt with regard to the issue. General Bragg, however, had more troops in reserve, available for the next day, than General Rosecrans. Longstreet reached Ringgold in the evening, with several brigades. Breckinridge's division had not been engaged at all, and Hindman's and Preston's only slightly, while nearly all the brigades of the national army on the field had been fully engaged. General Rosecrans being on the defensive, was compelled, moreover, to diffuse his army more widely, not only to cover the two main roads to Chattanooga from the field, but those also in proximity to his flanks. His cavalry was on his right, upon the roads to Chattanooga, through the first valley east of Lookout Mountain, and his reserve corps, represented by three brigades, was before Rossville, guarding the roads which led thither from the south and east. It was not only necessary to watch against a movement toward Chattanooga on the roads converging to Rossville, but also upon the roads farther north; and Minty had been sent with his troopers early in the day to Mission Mills, north of east from Chattanooga.

But notwithstanding General Bragg's reserves, he had cause to feel uneasiness with regard to the work before him. He had been completely foiled in his strategy and tactics. He had expected to find Crittenden's corps on the left of the national army; but his own enveloping lines had been taken in flank, and the right half had been fearfully shattered. He had had marked advantage without marked success. At the opening of the battle, his army had been well in hand for offense or defense, while General Rosecrans had been compelled often to throw forward divisions and brigades without support on right or left; and the national army was now before him, with continuous lines, and having the choice of strong positions in the rear. Besides, this army was yet upon the roads to Chattanooga, which he had expected to grasp after he had doubled its left upon its center and pressed it back upon the mountain passes. In all his special expectations and dominant aims, General Bragg had been disappointed and defeated.

General Rosecrans attained a continuous battle front only at the close of the engagement. The conditions of this attainment, however, had been such as to produce an involution of divisions destructive to the unity of his corps. Such had been the antecedent positions of his three corps, and such the necessary haste of movement to the points most threatened by the enemy, that their organization could not be maintained. Thus, General Thomas had three divisions from his own corps, and one from each of the other two; and on the right center and right of the army, the remaining divisions of McCook's and Crittenden's corps were in regular alternation. This mixing of divisions gave an expression of improvision to the battle front strongly significant of the emergencies of its formation.

In forming a new line in the evening, General Thomas did not change the order of the divisions, but modified their relations so as to give greater compactness and strength to the front that should be offered to the enemy. The order from left to right, was Baird, Johnson, Palmer, Reynolds, and Brannan. Baird's division was well refused, facing the east; Brannan's was on the right, in echelon. The battle front coursed round the northeast corner of Kelley's farm, crossed the Lafayette road a little south of his house, and extended thence to the southwest. Baird's, Johnson's, and Palmer's divisions were east of the road, and Reynolds' and Brannan's were west of it. This new line was much shorter than the one maintained during the day, allowing greater strength and heavier reserves. The general formation was two brigades from each division, in double ranks on the battle front, and one brigade from each in reserve.

About midnight, after a conference with his corps commanders and other general officers, General Rosecrans gave orders relative to the battle front for the next day. General Thomas was directed to maintain his line as formed in the evening. General McCook was instructed to leave his grand guard in position until driven in by the enemy, and withdraw Sheridan's and Davis' divisions, and form a new line to extend from the Widow Glenn's to the right of General Thomas' line; and General Crittenden was ordered to leave out his grand guards also, and retire Wood's and Van Cleve's divisions to the rear of the junction of Thomas' right and McCook's left, to be able to direct support to either. It was also arranged that the cavalry should connect with McCook, and receive orders from him, and that Negley's division should be relieved from position on the right of Brannan and transferred to the left of Baird. General Thomas requested the transfer of Negley's division, as he anticipated that the enemy would renew his effort to turn his left flank.

Before daylight, the divisions designated for new positions, except Negley's, made the movements required; while those in position, as far as practicable, covered their fronts with barricades of logs and rails. General Rosecrans not having pointed out the exact localities for the divisions of the Twen-

tieth and Twenty-first Corps, Generals McCook and Crittenden made their own selection of positions within the range
permitted by their instructions. General McCook placed
Lytle's brigade of Sheridan's division to the right and rear
of Widow Glenn's, and Laiboldt's and Bradley's, Colonel Wal-
worth commanding, to the rear and right of Lytle, and the
two brigades of Davis' division, Carlin's and Heg's, in rear of
the line thus formed. Carlin's and Heg's brigades, in with-
standing the heavy columns of the enemy the day before, lost
two-fifths of their effective strength, and could not now muster
more than fourteen hundred men in the aggregate. Wilder's
brigade, which reported to General McCook by order of the
general commanding, was divided, two regiments being placed
on the right and two on the left of Sheridan. General Crittenden posted his two divisions on the eastern slope of Missionary Ridge, in readiness to support to the right or left.
Unfortunately, these dispositions did not subsequently command the approval of General Rosecrans, who ordered changes
during the morning.

General Bragg received reinforcements during the night,
and with them their commander, Lieutenant-General Longstreet. He transferred all his infantry to the west bank of
the Chickamauga, divided his army into two wings, and
placed General Polk in command on the right and General
Longstreet on the left. He ordered the former to attack from
his right at daylight, and to bring his divisions into action
consecutively to his left, and the latter to await developments
on the right, and then attack in similar manner. In giving
instructions to General Longstreet, General Bragg conveyed
the impression that he had had heavy skirmishing in getting
his army into line of battle. It was, however, such skirmishing as had shattered the right half of his army, and reduced
the strength of some brigades on his left at least one-fourth.

A heavy fog hung over the battle-field during the early
hours of the day, and General Polk did not attack as ordered.
General Bragg waited near the center of his army until his
patience was exhausted, and then proceeded to his right, to find
that the commander of that wing was not on the field, and
that the necessary preparation for battle had not been made.

During the progress of preparations, General Bragg ordered a reconnoissance beyond General Thomas' left flank, and was gratified to learn that the Lafayette road was open to his possession. This condition of affairs on the left of the national army was owing to the fact that Negley's division was still in position on the right of Brannan. The continued delay of Negley, caused General Thomas great uneasiness, as he feared the issue of an attack on his left flank, and was assured that it would not be long withheld. Baird's division could not cover all the ground, whose firm defense was essential to the security of the line. The troops had worked vigorously to construct barricades, but the flank could not be strong while the promised division was absent. And yet General Bragg was forming a combination against it, both in pursuance of a general plan and with special reference to its weakness.

Although the troops on the right had been moved to positions in the immediate vicinity of General Rosecrans' headquarters at Glenn's, yet, when he made a special examination of his lines, he decided to change the formation on the right. He wished to hold the space from Widow Glenn's house to Brannan's right with McCook's six brigades, including Wilder's, and keep Crittenden's corps wholly in reserve. He therefore ordered General McCook, early in the morning, to fill the space to be made vacant by the withdrawal of Negley's division, if practicable. But it was not practicable for General McCook to cover the space from Widow Glenn's house to Brannan's right, except with an attenuated line,* and as his effort to do so was not made as soon as anticipated, General Rosecrans called upon Crittenden to furnish troops to fill the

---

*General Rosecrans stated, in his official report, that McCook "was to close up on Thomas, his right refused, and covering the position at Widow Glenn's house." In his testimony before the court of inquiry, at Louisville, Kentucky, he stated that "the information on which the orders for the 20th were predicated, was that the position at Widow Glenn's house would be amply within the limits of our strength to cover, and keep Crittenden's corps wholly in reserve; but I am satisfied that the distance from that position to the right of Brannan was greater than we at the time supposed, and that the line was therefore attenuated. It was an apprehension that this might be the case, which led me to bring down Davis' division from the left side of the Dry valley, in the morning."

division interval which Negley was holding. In compliance, General Crittenden directed General Wood, with his two brigades, and Barnes', of Van Cleve's division, to relieve Negley, and directed General Van Cleve, with his remaining brigades, to take position in the rear of Wood, in reserve. General Rosecrans ordered General Davis to form his two brigades on the right, some distance to the north, and east of his original position. As this change exposed his right flank, General McCook posted Laiboldt's brigade of Sheridan's division to the right and rear of Davis', and held the remaining brigades in reserve. Other changes were in reserve for this portion of the line, which rendered it too weak to withstand the enemy.

In order to hasten General Negley to his left flank, General Thomas sent Captain Williard of his staff for him. Upon reaching Negley's position, this officer ascertained that two brigades were yet in line, and that the reserve brigade, General John Beatty commanding, alone was free to move. This, Captain Williard conducted to the left of Baird, and one brigade in thin line was the only support to the left flank, in room of a division of the previous day, and in the stead of the whole division promised for the coming battle.

At half-past 8 A. M. the character of the skirmishing in Baird's front plainly indicated that the enemy was preparing for an attack, and within an hour from that time, he made a furious assault upon the left of the general line, which was rapidly extended to the right. Against the left, the assault was made by Breckinridge and Cleburne. The left brigade of the division of the former struck the left of Baird's division, and the other two brigades soon overpowered Beatty's brigade. When this brigade was displaced, General Thomas' left flank was greatly overlapped. Upon the firmness of this flank depended the possession of the road to Rossville, to gain which was the primal object of General Bragg's combination on his right; in fact, it was the dominant object compassed by his general plan of battle for the day. Had General Negley's entire division been in line as contemplated by General Thomas, General Bragg's right could have been turned as on the previous day; for, as it was, Breckinridge's left brigade and Cleburne's division were so shattered, that it was not deemed safe to swing the overlapping brigades into Baird's rear.   This for a time saved General Thomas' left, especially as other divisions on the left of Cleburne were repulsed with equal emphasis, as General Bragg's imposing attack swept from his right to his left.   For an hour he maintained the conflict with great vigor, in great part with fresh troops, but his whole right was broken as on the previous day.   General Cleburne reported the loss of five hundred men in a few minutes, and Breckinridge's left brigade was almost annihilated, having lost its commander, General Helm, and two colonels killed and two colonels wounded.   Generals Cleburne and Stewart mentioned in their reports the effect of the national artillery as the most destructive in their experience.   Thus this second battle opened auspiciously for the national army.   The left in the initial conflict was again triumphantly successful, but disaster on the right, and a second attempt to overwhelm the left, for several hours threatened the complete overthrow of the whole army.   In the maintenance of the left, Stanley's brigade of Negley's division rendered timely assistance, after Beatty's was shattered.   Although the action on his right had not progressed as General Bragg had anticipated, and General Longstreet had consequently been delayed in movement, yet when the latter did advance to attack, he found only isolated fragments of a battle line before him. This state of things resulted from a combination of circumstances.   As the promised division had not been sent to General Thomas, he repeated his requests for reinforcements, especially after the opening of the action.   These calls and the quietness of the enemy on the right, induced General Rosecrans to believe that General Bragg was moving his army to his right. So strong was this belief, that he finally decided to withdraw his own right altogether.   At 10.10 A. M. he ordered General McCook to make dispositions looking to the movement of his troops to the left, and soon after gave him a specific order to send two brigades of Sheridan's division to General Thomas with all possible dispatch, and the third as soon as the line could be sufficiently withdrawn to permit it.   He also directed General Crittenden to send the two reserve brigades of Van Cleve's division to the same destination.   These orders put in motion to the left every brigade in reserve except Wilder's.

Another misapprehension was still more favorable to the enemy. General Rosecrans having received information that Brannan's line was refused, on the right of Reynolds, he ordered General Wood to " close up on Reynolds and support him."

Regarding this order as too explicit in requirement, and too imperative in tone to warrant any discretion as to obedience, General Wood withdrew his division with promptness. His left was aligned with Brannan's right, and he saw no way to close upon Reynolds but to withdraw from line and pass to the left, in the rear of Brannan. Having advised General Mc-Cook that this change would be made, General Wood moved his division rapidly from line. Brannan was not out of line, Reynolds was not under pressure, and Wood moved from line at the very moment of the enemy's attack. General Davis threw his reserve brigade toward the wide vacant space, but the heavy columns of the enemy were soon upon it, and Davis' two small brigades were speedily enveloped. His troops resisted bravely, but assaulted in front, flank, and rear, they were lifted from position and hurled in fragments toward Missionary Ridge. The attack and issue were too sudden for Laiboldt to move to his assistance, and the latter was quickly routed. Buell's brigade of Wood's division, the last to leave position, was severed as it retired, and Brannan was struck in flank. Lytle's and Bradley's brigades of Sheridan's division, at the time in quick motion to the left, were halted, and aided by Wilder's brigade, offered gallant but vain resistance, and the vain effort cost, in addition to other losses, the life of the chivalrous Lytle. These brigades, and Beatty's and portions of Dick's, of Van Cleve's division, also in motion to the left, were broken and swept over the ridge to the west. The rapid movement of Brannan's batteries threw General Samuel Beatty's brigade into utter disorder, and in this condition it was involved in the confused retreat of all the troops on the right of Brannan. The suddenness of the displacement of the lines of infantry exposed the artillery in their rear to capture, and many guns fell into the hands of the enemy without dispute. Brannan's right flank, in swinging back under fire, was thrown into temporary confusion. But his left being secure, order was soon restored, and he was able to maintain position until a lull in the conflict gave him opportunity to gain a new position.

For a time after the disaster on the right, there were but five divisions in line against the whole rebel army. These divisions were all firm, but the enemy was concentrating on both flanks of the line, which lay across the Lafayette and Chattanoooga road. And soon, under the inspiration of partial victory, and the hope of complete triumph, most vigorous and persistent assaults were made, whose successful resistance under the circumstance, makes the closing struggle of this great battle one of the most remarkable which has occurred in modern times—one of the grandest which has ever been made for the existence of army or country. From noon till night, the five divisions which had previously constituted "Thomas' line," and such other troops as reached him from the right, under orders, or drifted to him after the disaster, and two brigades from the reserve corps, successfully resisted the whole Confederate army. General Wood, with Harker's and Barnes' brigades, and the greater portion of Buell's, reported to General Thomas in due time. The three brigades of Negley's division, Beatty's, Stanley's, and Sirwell's, reported separately. The Forty-fourth Indiana, from Dick's brigade, and the Seventeenth Kentucky, from Beatty's brigade of Van Cleve's division, were the only regiments that, without orders, diverged from the line of retreat, and reached General Thomas in time to participate in the final conflict.

General Rosecrans, believing that the day was lost, went to Chattanooga " to give orders for the security of the pontoon bridges at Bridgeport and Battle Creek, and to make preliminary dispositions, either to forward ammunitions and supplies, should the army hold its position, or to withdraw the army into good position should it become necessary."

Entertaining the same opinion as to the issue of the battle, Generals McCook and Crittenden followed the general commanding to Chattanooga, to report for instructions. All communication between General Thomas and the generals and troops in retreat having been cut off for a time, the approach of hostile columns in the direction of expected reinforcements first revealed to General Thomas the condition of affairs on the right, although he did not learn the extent of the disaster until late in the day.

The issue of the first attack from his right did not deter General Bragg from a renewal of effort to turn General Thomas' left, and gain the Rossville road. His second assault was made with stronger lines and greater impetuosity, and this time with partial success. General Thomas had not yet been reinforced, except by Barnes' brigade, which had been reported by General Wood, and placed in support to General Baird.

In preparation for this new effort, General Bragg moved General Breckinridge farther to the right, and placed Walker's corps between him and Cleburne. In this combination, Breckinridge was to wheel to the left and envelop General Thomas' exposed left flank. His division advanced in co-operation with other divisions on his left, and was soon able to move southward on the Lafayette road, and take in reverse the main line near Kelley's. This movement was well devised, except that no support was provided for Breckinridge in his insulation in the rear of the national army. He advanced boldly, but was met and overwhelmed by the reserve brigades of Johnson's, Palmer's, and Brannan's divisions, Willich's, Grose's, and Vanderveer's, which were in fortunate freedom for this most threatening emergency. His division was driven in route round Baird's left flank, to join the broken ranks of Walker's corps and Cleburne's division, which had been repulsed in every attack upon Baird, Palmer, and Johnson. These assaults were furious and persistent, but without impression upon the firm defensive line. As in the morning a complete cessation of the deadly strife followed these repulses, and none of the divisions on the left were again engaged until late in the evening, when they were withdrawing under orders.

This lull on the left permitted the return of Stanley's and Vanderveer's brigades to the right. Barnes' brigade of Van Cleve's division was posted by General Thomas on the left of Baird, in provision against another effort to turn the left flank.

The transfer of Stanley and Vanderveer to the right was opportune, as a conflict was there imminent, which, for the vigor and frequency of charge and countercharge, and successful resistance to vastly superior numbers, is perhaps without parallel in the war.

Soon after the rupture of the main line on the right of Brannan, which caused him to throw back his right, he found it necessary to change his position altogether. His division had been previously engaged on all parts of the line, having made frequent charges to restore broken columns and turned flanks, and in consequence had been greatly reduced, but its severest fighting was yet to come. In withdrawing from the right of Reynolds, General Brannan selected a position to the right and rear of the one which he abandoned—a strong position of defense, but at the time it was taken was unprotected by troops on the right or left. The position was admirable for defense, and time was given by the enemy for the division to construct barricades. Brannan's withdrawal exposed Reynolds' right flank, and made a broad chasm between the two divisions. Upon this intervening space, General Wood, with Harker's brigade and a portion of Buell's, took position, though not at first in connection with Brannan on the right or Reynolds' on the left. The presence of these troops in this wide interval, well advanced toward the enemy, retarded his movements, and thus gave time for some preparation for the impending conflict,

The position assumed by General Brannan was a high knoll on the curving ridge, trending eastward from the Dry Valley road, and then northward on the east of that road. In harmony with other ridges of the region, its summit was notched by depressions, and its slopes indented by projecting spurs. The position was strong, but easily turned, as on the west there was a depression which afforded easy passage round it. This ridge, from the Dry Valley road to Kelley's or the Lafayette road, was wooded, and every way advantagous for a defensive line whose flanks were secured by reserves.*

---

* The ridge held by Generals Wood, Brannan, and Steedman, was called by the general officers of the enemy "Horse Shoe Ridge," on account of the circular trend of the crest, and Brannan's rounded summit was called by them "Battery Hill."

While the enemy persisted in his effort to turn the left flank of the army, General Thomas gave attention to that portion of his line; but when Bragg's exhausted right wing was entirely withdrawn from action, he was called to the right by the noise of musketry in that quarter. He had no knowledge, at the time, of the displacement and rout of the right wing of the army, nor of the consequent changes in the positions of his own troops next to the breach. He knew nothing of Brannan's change of position or of the movements of Negley. Two brigades of the latter had been for a time under his own eye (Beatty's and Stanley's), and he had sent orders to the division commander to mass a large number of guns on the eastern slope of Missionary Ridge, to keep the ground to the left and rear of Baird, where the enemy was partially successful in turning his left flank. General Negley had posted his artillery in the rear of Reynolds and Brannan, but had finally drifted to the Dry Valley road, and thence toward Rossville, with his guns and supporting infantry. But all this was unknown to General Thomas, as he rode to the right to ascertain the cause of the firing in the rear of his own line.

As he emerged from the woods bordering the Rossville road, he met Captain Kellogg, of his staff, who informed him that in his effort to reach General Sheridan, to conduct his division to the left, he had been fired upon in the rear of Reynolds' position by a force advancing cautiously, with skirmishers thrown out. This officer reported also that troops had been in view for some time from Wood's position, and that they were supposed to be Sheridan's division. To ascertain the facts in the case, General Thomas proceeded to Harker's brigade, and gave orders that should these troops fire after seeing the flag, that their fire should be returned, and their further advance resisted. Meeting General Wood near by, he was confirmed in the opinion that they were the enemy. But as Harker soon became engaged, all doubt was removed, and it was then evident that the right of the army had been turned, though the extent of the disaster was not foreshadowed, as these troops were not recognized as the representatives of the whole left wing of the Confederate army, which, after rest and reformation, was advancing to renew the conflict. In the emergency, General Thomas directed General Wood to form his troops on the left of Brannan, of whose position he had been informed, and gave notice to Reynolds that the enemy was in his rear. In compliance, General Wood formed his line slightly in advance of Brannan's, for the sake of a better position, and General Reynolds drew back his right brigade so as to face the force threatening his rear.

There was scarcely time for the execution of these movements before the left wing of the Confederate army fell upon Wood and Brannan. It is impossible to compute with accuracy the number of troops with these generals. Portions of their respective divisions had been previously severed and lost, and there were troops with them representing at least two divisions : General Beatty of Negley's division was acting with a fragmentary force, and a large portion of Stanley's brigade, Colonel Stoughton commanding, Colonel Stanley having been wounded; the Twenty-first Ohio regiment from Sirwell's brigade of the same division; and the Seventeenth Kentucky, Colonel Stout, and the Forty-fourth Indiana, Lieutenant-Colonel Aldrich, from Van Cleve's division. But this isolated line, composed of the fragments of brigades and regiments, about four thousand men in all, repeatedly repulsed the most furious attacks of Longstreet's massive lines. But its insulation invited the enemy to other than direct assaults; and soon a strong force was seen passing around Brannan's right flank to his rear, to take in reverse the line which had resisted unbroken, every direct attack. The advance of this column evolved the dominant crisis of the battle. Having been repulsed by the left of the national army, even after his success against its right, General Bragg now moved heavy columns to the rear of a slender line of heroes, many of whom had already, in destitution of ammunition, clutched their muskets for the desperate use of the bayonet.

In giving personal direction to the movements on the right, General Thomas took position in the rear of Wood's line. With no line of troops intervening, he now saw the foe advancing in a direction to strike him before he could reach his troops. Fortunately there were reinforcements equally near. The noise of the conflict had penetrated the murky clouds which overhung the bloody field, and reaching General Granger far to the left and rear, suggested the need of his troops where the battle was so hotly raging. Accordingly he had moved forward rapidly, in disregard of the enemy's effort to arrest his progress, and at the moment of greatest need reported to General Thomas with two brigades. As the enemy moved down the northern slope of the ridge toward the rear of Brannan and Wood, Whittaker's and Mitchell's brigades of Steedman's division, with a fury born of the impending peril, charged the foe and drove him over the ridge, and then formed line of battle from Brannan's right to the hill above Villetoe's, in front of Longstreet's left flank. In gaining this position there was heavy loss; but if the issue of battle has ever given compensation for the loss of valuable lives, it was in this action, for the opportune aid of these two brigades saved the army from defeat and rout.

At 3 P. M., General Longstreet, despairing of carrying the position without reinforcements, called upon General Bragg for assistance from his right. He was informed that the troops of their right wing "had been so badly beaten back" that they would be of no service on the left. Ascertaining thus that the right of his own army was in little better condition than the original right of the national army, Longstreet hesitated to put into the fight his reserve division, and renewed the assault with the troops that had been repeatedly repulsed. In this charge, the rebel General Hindman commanding on the extreme left, gained a temporary advantage, which induced Longstreet to put his reserve division into the action in hope of sweeping the hills before him. But before he could get Preston's large division into line, Hindman was driven from the hill above Villetoe's, upon which he had planted his banners, by Steedman's brigades. The reserve division, however, was not withheld, and Longstreet renewed the action with his whole force. Brannan had with him about twenty-five hundred men, and on his right were the two brigades of Whittaker and Mitchell. And yet from his center to Steedman's right, there were ten brigades of the enemy in line, and Gracie's brigade of Preston's division, on the right, went into action with two thousand and three effective men. With this immense preponderance of strength, Longstreet assaulted with frequency and vigor, but was continually repulsed. The forces before Wood were relatively as strong as before Brannan and Steedman, and were repulsed in every attack. His position was favorable for defense, as the configuration of the ground was equivalent to a parapet. The troops could advance and deliver a plunging fire from the brow of the hill, and by a slight recession while loading, were entirely covered from the bullets of the enemy. The conflict involved the use of the musket solely. Wood had no artillery, and the enemy could not use his to advantage.

Late in the afternoon there were indications that Longstreet would throw his troops between Wood and Reynolds, and Hazen's brigade of Palmer's division was transferred to the intervening space. Hazen was sent because he had ammunition, and at the time the general destitution created more alarm than the previous assaults of the enemy had done. Some unauthorized person had ordered General Thomas' corps ammunition train to Chattanooga, and many of the division trains had been separated from the troops they were intended to supply, and had gone to the rear. On the whole line, the average to the man was not more than three rounds, and in some commands there was less than this. It was common to search the cartridge-boxes of those who fell. Steedman's train afforded a few rounds in addition, but this was soon exhausted, and his own men were at the last entirely destitute. Whenever ammunition failed entirely, the order was given to fix bayonets and hold the hill with cold steel. When Hazen attained position between Reynolds and Wood, he became engaged in severest conflict, and from Reynolds to Steedman the battle raged with unabated fury; but the enemy was gallantly repulsed at every point until night-fall, and in the final attacks, this was accomplished in no slight measure with the bayonet and clubbed muskets.*

---

* The Confederate commanders not only admitted the defensive valor of the national troops, but the spirit and rigor of their offensive returns. General Hindman, who commanded ten brigades on the left of the ene-

About 4 p. m., General Garfield, in company with Captains Gaw and Barker, whom General Thomas had sent to the rear for ammunition, reached the field from the direction of Rossville. Lieutenant-Colonel Thurston, chief of staff to General McCook, about the same time joined him from the right. From these officers the first definite information concerning it was received, and their arrival attested the possibility of communications with General Thomas from the Dry Valley road. Soon after, General Thomas received a dispatch from General Rosecrans, " directing him to assume command of all the forces, and with Crittenden and McCook to take a strong position and assume a threatening attitude at Rossville," where rations and ammunition would be sent, and that from that point he should send all the unorganized troops to Chattanooga.

Upon the return of the officers sent for the ammunition, the division commanders were notified through Major Lawrence, chief of artillery, that a supply would be distributed; and when this had been accomplished, orders were issued for the withdrawal of the army by divisions. General Reynolds was instructed to commence the movement, and as General Thomas went to meet him to point out where he wished him to form a line to cover the retirement of the troops on the Lafayette read, he met a force that had gained the woods in the rear of Reynolds. As this general's head of column was near, he directed him to form his division at right angles to the road, with his right resting upon it, and charge the enemy in his immediate front, though the rear of the army. The charge was made with great vigor, and the enemy was completely routed. Turchin's brigade drove this daring force entirely beyond Baird's left, capturing more than two hundred prisoners. This brigade, and Colonel E. A. King's, which, after his fall, was commanded by Colonel Robinson, was posted by General Thomas on the road leading through the ridge to the Dry Valley road, to hold the ground while the troops from the right and left passed by. Soon after, Willich's brigade, Johnson's reserve, took position on high ground, near the Trans-

---

my's line, with his right resting opposite " Battery Hill," and his left on the Dry Valley road, declared that " he had never seen Federal troops fight as well," while " he had never seen Confederate troops fight better."

verse road. The three divisions on the left, Palmer's, Johnson's, and Baird's, were attacked as they left position; but though the fighting was severe, there was little confusion, and no very serious losses—a result which was due in some measure to the brigades which General Thomas had posted to cover the movement. Wood, Brannan, and Steedman, on the right, withdrew from line without molestation, except an attack on the junction of their lines, so emphatically had the left wing of the Confederate army been repulsed.*

During the night, General Thomas formed a new line at Rossville, and was joined by Generals McCook and Crittenden, who resumed command of their respective corps. This point was important only as commanding the roads leading from the battle-field, and from Ringgold, to Chattanooga. There was need to check the advance of the enemy, and dispositions were here made to this end. General Thomas placed one brigade of Negley's division in the gap, and the other two on the ridge to the right; Reynolds' division between Negley's right and the Dry Valley road; McCook's corps, between this road and Chattanooga creek; Crittenden's, on the left of Negley, covering the roads from the east; and Granger's troops, Baird's and Brannan's divisions, at various points in rear of the main line. The position was strong against a direct attack, but could be easily turned by a heavy concentration against the right in Chattanooga valley, and General Thomas advised General Rosecrans to withdraw the army to Chattanooga.

The battle of Chickamauga and the movements which preceded it, present features of marked distinctness. This fact is evident from the reports of the generals-in-chief and other gen-

---

* The heaviest losses in the withdrawal of the army were from captures, mainly from Baird's division, which left position, under a heavy assault; from Steedman's division, and the Twenty-first Ohio regiment, the latter being between Brannan and Steedman. This regiment maintained ground, in greatest exposure during the afternoon, and by its revolving rifles and gallant fighting, made the impression upon the enemy that its position was held by a heavy force. At dark, portions of the Twenty-first, the Eighty-ninth Ohio, and Twenty-second Michigan, the latter two from the left of Whitaker's brigade, were captured.

eral officers of the opposing armies; but, nevertheless, the campaign of which the battle itself was the culumination, and the conduct of the battle, have elicited much antagonistic criticism in both sections of the country. Despite, however, all partisan representations, the pivotal events may be clearly apprehended.

General Bragg was compelled to withdraw from Chattanooga, but his reinforcements were so near that he deemed it safe to concentrate his forces at Lafayette. From this point he had command of his communications and lines of retreat, and General Rosecrans could not at once concentrate against him. His plans were elaborate, but he failed in every distinct object, except in making the impression that he was retreating to some remote point, to induce his antagonist to "expose himself in detail." Admitting his failure directly, or by implication, in his official report he made prominent his possession of the battle-field, the number of his prisoners, captured guns and small arms, and the failure of his subordinates to execute the details of his plans as his justification as a strategist and tactician. If Negley's and Baird's divisions had been overwhelmed in McLemore's Cove, or had Crittenden's corps been broken and routed while with attenuated lines it covered Chattanooga, or had Bragg delivered battle from the same position on the 18th, the results of his strategy might have been the total defeat of the Army of the Cumberland and the repossession of Chattanooga. As it was, General Rosecrans "exposed himself in detail" without injury, and threw his army before Chattanooga on ground which General Bragg had selected as an open field for maneuver; and the latter, instead of hurling the national army in disordered mass upon the mountain passes through which it had gained his front, followed that army to Chattanooga with just such speed as it permitted, leaving behind him, from the casualties of battle, two-fifths of his forces. No wonder that his generalship was criticised, and that the Southern people complained that the battle of Chickamauga gave no results commensurate with the resources it represented or the losses it entailed. His strategy failed, and his tactical dispositions by no means compassed the possibilities of the battle-field; but the spirited and persistent assaults of his troops during two days of conflict have seldom been surpassed.

At the time that it was ascertained that the Confederate army was concentrated at Lafayette, at least forty miles, and mountain ranges, separated the extremes of the Army of the Cumberland. The union of the three corps before battle was a condition of safety. So was the attainment of position for the action of the 19th in the acceptance of battle on the Chickamauga. The conditions of the conflict on the 20th were in no small measure promising to General Rosecrans; but the movements on his right in the morning gave the advantage to the enemy, and so imperiled the army that its salvation was almost miraculous. It was unfortunate that Negley's division was left in line on the right during the night, and until the troops of the Twentieth and Twenty-first Corps had taken position, and that he was not sooner relieved in the morning. General Thomas was thus left without his division, upon which he depended for the security of his left flank. The battle having been opened before heavy reinforcements reached him, his previous and subsequent calls for support lost their true significance. Negley's transfer was finally too late for the emergency on the left, and the movement of his division by brigades was fatal to its subsequent unity and efficiency. The motion of the two brigades of Sheridan's division and the two of Van Cleve's to the left, followed by the withdrawal of Wood's division from the line at the very moment of the enemy's attack, exposed equally the troops in motion and the few left in position. The latter were not able to resist the enemy until the former were out of reach of the blow, and then the right was defeated in detail. The recession of the line from Reynolds to Sheridan, and its compact formation on the hills, where General Thomas with a part of the army saved the whole of it, effected at the proper time would have been eminently judicious; but the attempt to make this change so late in the day was perilous in the extreme. The fact that that position was held against all attacks by a slender force, reveals the strong probability, if not certainty, of Bragg's total defeat, had the whole national army stood on the line of final defense. Again, the stability of the right was affected by the want of co-operation on the part of the cavalry, which resulted in part at least from the indefiniteness of orders.*

After the troops had been displaced on the right and were in motion toward Chattanooga, it was possible for them to have joined General Thomas in time for participation in the final conflict. Generals Negley, Sheridan, and Davis met on the Dry Valley road, near the northern opening of McFarland's Gap; and there were sufficient troops with them, in all probability, to have changed the issue of the battle had they been thrown against the left flank of the enemy at Villetoe's. Not far from McFarland's house there was a gap opening eastward, through which a road passed to the rear of General Thomas' line, and on this these troops could have passed to his assistance, had they been so directed, if the Dry Valley road, leading directly to General Thomas' right flank, had not been open to the very front and flank of the enemy. Most of the divisions, in the withdrawal in the evening, passed through this lateral gap, which opened the way to the rear of Brannan's position. And yet, after delay in conference, and after Colonel Thruston, of General McCook's staff, had borne a request from General Thomas, that they should move to his right flank, General Negley and General Sheridan proceeded toward Rossville with their troops; while General Davis, accompanied by Colonel Thruston, advanced with a fragmentary force which had been collected, on the Dry Valley road, toward Villetoe's, but was too late for effective service. General Sheridan moved through Rossville, and reached the vicinity of General Thomas' left flank; but he, too, was too late to attack

---

* General Rosecrans, in his testimony before the court of inquiry at Louisville, stated that the cavalry had orders to communicate with General McCook and "close on his right. The senior officer of the cavalry was told that he must take orders from him, though attend to their own business." At General McCook's call, the cavalry did not close on his right. General Mitchell, commanding the cavalry, excused himself for not closing to the left, upon the order of General McCook, in consequence of the fact that he had been directed by General Rosecrans to cover Crawfish Springs with his force. This apparent conflict of orders deprived the infantry forces on the right of the support of the cavalry in their efforts to rally after the line was shattered.

the enemy, and General Thomas was ignorant of his movement. There was no general officer of high rank on the line of retreat to comprehend the situation and provide for its possibilities. The general in command on the extreme left of the rebel army was in constant dread of an attack in flank and rear by infantry and cavalry during the later hours of the day. Fearing this, Longstreet kept troops in reserve as long as possible; and when the brigades of Whittaker and Mitchell hurled his troops from Brannan's rear and flank, he supposed that he was meeting again the troops that he had fought in the morning near Widow Glenn's. These facts show that the enemy not only knew of no bar to the further participation in the battle of those forces that had been displaced on the right, but that their conjunction with those to the left was expected.

The official reports of the two commanding generals do not give the strength of their respective armies, and each claimed that he fought superior numbers. There is, however, no reason to doubt that General Bragg's army was the larger.

General Bragg had on the field eleven divisions of infantry and four of cavalry, comprising thirty-five brigades of infantry and ten or twelve of cavalry. The reported aggregate strength of five divisions of the former, of three brigades each, was twenty-four thousand one hundred men, an average of sixteen hundred and six to each brigade. Giving this strength to the remaining twenty brigades of infantry, would make an infantry aggregate of fifty-six thousand two hundred and ten. The reports of the general officers of the cavalry are too indefinite to furnish a basis for an approximate estimate of the strength of that arm. It is highly probable, however, that the four divisions comprised about fifteen thousand men. And thus, from actual and inferential data, it may be assumed that General Bragg had an army of seventy thousand men.

General Rosecrans had in the action thirty brigades of infantry, five of cavalry, one of mounted infantry, and thirty-three batteries. In all, he had one hundred and thirty-five regiments of infantry, twenty-one of cavalry, and five of mounted infantry. The average of fifteen brigades of infantry whose strength was reported, representing the four corps, was fifteen hundred and sixty men. If this should be accepted as the average strength of brigades throughout the army, its aggregate was fifty-six thousand one hundred and sixty men. It may then be assumed that General Bragg's army was superior by twelve or fifteen thousand men.

During the afternoon of the 20th, General Bragg must have had more than double as many men as General Thomas. He employed all his infantry and five or six brigades of cavalry, and a large portion of the latter arm was fought as infantry.* General Thomas had about eighteen brigades of infantry, exclusive of Colonel Daniel McCook's brigade, which resisted the rebel cavalry on the right flank of the Confederate army on the road to Rossville, and formed no part of the battle front. All but two of his brigades had been greatly reduced by hard fighting for a day and a half, and could not have averaged more than one thousand men. His force then did not, on his final line, probably exceed twenty thousand men, allowing four thousand to General Steedman's two fresh brigades.

As the statement appears in many histories of the war, and even in some of recent publication, that General Thomas with his single corps saved the army at Chickamauga, it is imperative to refute this error, as it does great injustice to the officers and men of the other corps. The preceding narrative gives an indirect refutation, but this prevalent mistake should be explicitly corrected. Generals Crittenden and McCook had each eight brigades on the field, and General Granger had three. And of these nineteen brigades, twelve were with General Thomas in the final conflict. Five brigades of McCook's corps were cut off on the right, but not more than two from Crittenden's, counting fragments. Palmer's division of Crittenden's corps, and Johnson's from McCook's, were with General Thomas throughout the battle, and General Wood of the former corps, with two brigades of his own division and one from Van Cleve's, went to him on the second day. Granger's three large brigades constituted nearly one-

---

* Even General Longstreet fought five hundred troopers on foot, on his left, late in the evening, who had come from the cavalry force in rear of their "left wing."

fourth of the entire force on the final line. More men left the field from General Thomas' own corps, the Fourteenth, than from General Crittenden's. Four regiments of Wilder's brigade of Reynolds' division were on the right of the breach; a large portion, more than a moiety, of Negley's division was led or driven from the field (Beatty's brigade, through the emergencies of battle and orders of General Negley's adjutant-general, joined the divisions on the right, and at night were found by General Beatty, at Rossville), and Brannan lost a portion of one of his brigades through orders of a general who left the field before the final crisis of the battle. The glory of the final conflict is then the common inheritance of the army, as it was won by the valor of troops representing the four grand units.

General Bragg's losses were exceedingly heavy. He admitted in his official report a loss of two-fifths of his army. His left wing comprised, on the morning of the 20th, twenty-two thousand eight hundred and eighty-five men, exclusive of cavalry. General Longstreet reported his losses in the aggregate, exclusive of one brigade not reported, at seven thousand eight hundred and fifty-six. Of these, one thousand and eighty were killed, six thousand five hundred and six were wounded, and two hundred and seventy captured. His loss in one day of battle, and chiefly in the afternoon, was thirty-six per cent. This fact justifies General Bragg's admission. A very large number of Confederate officers fell. Two major-generals were wounded, three brigadiers were killed and three were wounded, and one of the latter was captured.

General B. H. Helm's Kentucky brigade went into this fight one thousand seven hundred and sixty-three strong, and came out with four hundred and thirty-two, General Helm being among the killed. Bate's brigade lost six hundred and eight out of one thousand and eighty-five. A Mississippi brigade lost seven hundred and eighty-one, and came out with but two regimental officers uninjured, and several other brigades lost fully half their number.

The reported aggregate loss of the Army of the Cumberland was sixteen thousand three hundred and thirty-six, including one hundred and thirty-two officers killed, five hundred and ninety-two wounded, and two hundred and seventy missing; fifteen hundred and fifty-five enlisted men killed, eight thousand eight hundred and twenty wounded, and four thousand nine hundred and eighty-five missing. As many of those reported as missing were among the slain, the number of the killed exceeded two thousand. The loss from Baird's division was twenty-two hundred and thirteen; from Brannan's, twenty-one hundred and forty-four; from Palmer's, thirteen hundred and forty-nine; from Johnson's, sixteen hundred and twenty-nine; from Steedman's two brigades, seventeen hundred and thirty-two;* from Wood's two, ten hundred and thirty-five; and from Sheridan's and Davis' divisions, more than forty per cent. The remaining divisions of the army lost less heavily, though none suffered lightly. Among those who fell were Brigadier-General Lytle, Colonels E. A. King, Heg, and Baldwin commanding brigades, and Colonels W. G. Jones, Bartleson, Alexander, Gilmer, and McCreary. The loss in material was immense, fifty-one guns, fifteen thousand small arms, wagons and ambulances in great numbers, and ammunition and stores in large quantities.

On the morning of the 21st, there were indications that the enemy was advancing against the position at Rossville. Colonel Minty having reported the advance of a strong force of infantry and cavalry, General Thomas directed him to withdraw from the front and take position on the left flank of the army. Soon after, the enemy approached cautiously on the direct roads from the battle-field. No purpose however, was revealed, to attack the army, and all the tentative demonstrations were easily repulsed. It being evident to General Thomas that the enemy could easily concentrate on his right flank, and by turning it, could cut him off from Chattanooga, he advised General Rosecrans to concentrate his forces at Chattanooga. Adopting the suggestion, General Rosecrans authorized a withdrawal from Rossville, and General Thomas at once made preparations for its accomplishment. Having called together the corps commanders, he gave them such instructions as would preclude confusion in making the move-

---

* This loss was forty-four per cent. between 2 P. M. and dark.

ment. He first sent all the wagons, ambulances, and surplus artillery carriages forward; then stationed Brannan's division half-way to Chattanooga, to cover the troops on the direct road, and having thrown out toward the enemy strong skirmish lines, supported by Baird's division and Minty's cavalry, he commenced the movement from the left at 9 P. M. It was made by divisions, in supporting distance, one after another from left to right. The withdrawal of the army was effected without the loss of a single man, and at 7 A. M. the next day, the troops were in position around Chattanooga, from the river on the north to the river on the south. General Bragg excused himself for allowing this quiet withdrawal of the national army on the ground that his own army was less than half as strong, and greatly exhausted. This statement may be regarded as proof that his victory was only nominal in his own estimation.

But whatever were the immediate and more local consequences of the battle, in its remoter relations and significance, it has claims to historic grandeur. The Army of the Cumberland, without support on either flank, had leaped across the Tennessee river and the contiguous mountains, and yet escaped destruction, though the armies of the enemy east and west were made tributary to a combination of forces to accomplish this end. Paroled prisoners from Vicksburg, regular troops from Mississippi and Georgia, a veteran corps from Lee's army in Virginia, and Buckner's corps from East Tennessee joined Bragg on the bank of the Chickamauga, not simply to retake Chattanooga, but to annihilate the Army of the Cumberland. Nearly half of Bragg's army consisted of recent reinforcements, sent to Northern Georgia, while the authorities at Washington, perplexed with the military situation, were resting under the delusion that General Bragg was reinforcing Lee. But this heavy draft upon the resources of the Confederacy was burdened with the fatality which clung to all the grander efforts of the insurgents in the West. And General Bragg's broken and exhausted army was a symbol of the fast coming exhaustion of the Confederacy itself. The issue of the battle was not thus defined to the consciousness of the Southern people, but was doubtless one of the most emphatic disappointments of the struggle, and intensified the gloom produced by previous defeats. A vast army, representing a large fraction of the military strength of the Confederacy, had only gained a barren victory, if a victory at all, in room of anticipated results of widest compass. The utterances of Mr. Davis can not be taken as a just expression of the hopes of the Southern people. They were usually too extravagant to represent the sober thoughts of the people. Still, it can not be doubted that he had general sympathy in the conviction, publicly expressed, that the total overthrow of General Rosecrans, which was regarded as assured, would virtually terminate the war.

Instead of the annihilation of the Army of the Cumberland, the recapture of Chattanooga, and the attainment of far grander ulterior results, which had been anticipated as the fruits of the battle of Chickamauga, General Bragg, with a shattered army, followed slowly and cautiously his retreating foe, to invest, at Chattanooga, the army which he had failed to crush on the field of battle, hoping, through starvation, to wrest from General Rosecrans the original objective of this campaign.

CHAPTER XXI.

SIEGE OF CHATTANOOGA.

The incipient fortifications left by General Bragg were speedily strengthened by General Rosecrans, as portions of a complete circumvallation. General Rosecrans, however, made no effort to hold Lookout Mountain, the railroad, or river below Chattanooga. His aim was to hold his bridges at the town, and present strong lines to the enemy. For a day or two, General Bragg threatened to attack, but soon posted his forces to besiege and starve the army which he had failed to overwhelm in battle. His lines extended from Lookout Mountain across Chattanooga valley to Missionary Ridge, and along its base and summit to the Tennessee river above the town. General Longstreet insisted upon a flank movement instead of a siege. He suggested to his chief, to cross the river above Chattanooga, and make himself so felt in the rear as to force General Rosecrans to evacuate the position and fall back to Nashville, and then, if not able to continue the northward movement from inadequate transportation, to follow the railroad to Knoxville, destroy Burnside, and from there threaten Rosecrans' communications in the rear of Nashville. General Bragg, however, did not deem this suggestion feasible. His transportation was not considered adequate, and, in his view, purely military considerations forbade the step. He thought that the interruption of Rosecrans' communications with Bridgeport, south of the river, promised better results, and he disposed his army to accomplish this object. He confided the holding of this important route to General Longstreet, and threw his cavalry across the river to operate against the transportation of supplies by wagons over the mountains from Bridgeport. He judged wisely that his superiority in cavalry, and the length and condition of the roads, rendered wagon transportation a precarious means of supply for the army shut up in Chattanooga. His success was assured, if he could maintain his hold upon the river and the shorter roads to Bridgeport.*

The situation of the beleaguered army was critical from the first. General Rosecrans expressed his fears to the President, the day after the battle, that he should not be able to hold Chattanooga. Two days later, however, he assured the President that his army could not be dislodged, except by very superior numbers, but requested that his communications should be covered, and that reinforcements should be sent to him. General Halleck had previously ordered General Burnside to move to his support. This had been done before it had been perceived that the enemy was concentrating forces from all quarters in Northern Georgia. The issue of the battle, and the situation at Chattanooga, induced the detachment of troops from the Army of the Potomac, and orders to Generals Hurlbut and Sherman to give assistance. But the movement of troops from points so remote gave no promise of immediate relief, and as the enemy was on the direct line of approach, their passage from Bridgeport to Chattanooga was of itself an intricate problem. It was scarcely less difficult of solution than that of supplying the army at Chattanooga, until the coming of reinforcements and the establishment of adequate means of transportation.

Having attained secure position at Chattanooga, General Rosecrans disposed his cavalry on the north bank of the Tennessee river, from Washington to Caperton's ferry, to observe the enemy and protect trains in passage from Bridgeport to Chattanooga. Crook's division kept watch for fifty miles up the river, while McCook's stood guard at the crossings above and below Bridgeport. General Crook could only watch at the main fords, while the intermediate ones were numerous. At one of the latter, on the 1st of October, Wheeler crossed

---

* These different plans are fully presented in the official reports of the two generals.

with a large force of cavalry, and moved toward the communications of the army. As soon as advised of the fact, General Rosecrans directed General Crook to collect his command and pursue, and ordered Colonel McCook to move from Bridgeport to Anderson's Cross-roads. Wheeler, however, had the start, and intercepted and nearly destroyed a large train of wagons loaded with supplies, near the place to which McCook had been ordered to move. Colonel McCook, upon the reception of the order, sent instructions to Colonel Campbell, commanding his second brigade, to join him at Jasper, and started up the valley, with the troops in hand, the First Wisconsin, and the Second and Fourth Indiana regiments, and a section of artillery. An incessant rain delayed the movement, and as McCook approached Anderson's, on the 2d, he saw the smoke of the burning wagons. He hurried forward, and encountering a portion of Wheeler's troopers, charged with the First Wisconsin and Second Indiana, and drove the force past the burning wagons upon the main body, which was one mile north of the cross-roads, in line of battle. These two regiments dislodged the enemy from several positions, and pursued for two miles, when he was found, in a strong position across a creek, behind a barricade of rails. McCook carried the position by assault, and attacking repeatedly, the enemy was driven across the Sequatchie valley. In this action the saber was freely used. The following morning the pursuit was continued to the top of mountain beyond Dunlap, where the rear-guard of the enemy was again attacked, with successful result. McCook captured, from first to last, twelve commissioned officers, including Major Green of Wheeler's staff, and ninety-three enlisted men, and killed seven officers and several enlisted men. He recaptured eight hundred mules, and saved some of the wagons. The enemy destroyed three hundred wagons and a large number of mules. The force of the enemy engaged was Martin's division, under the personal command of Wheeler. General Wheeler had previously divided his force, and sent Wharton's division to McMinnville, by a detour to the north.

In the meantime, General Crook, with Minty's and Long's brigades, and Colonel Miller's mounted infantry, lately Wilder's, had ascended the mountain south of Smith's Cross-roads, and was in rapid pursuit toward McMinnville. He overtook Wharton's rear-guard in descending the Cumberland Mountains, on the 3d of October. Pursuing rapidly, he succeeded in surrounding a brigade, but through the coming of reinforcements and darkness, the brigade escaped. In the action, Crook lost forty-six men killed and wounded; the loss of the enemy was not ascertained. Pursuit was resumed the next morning, but Crook could not reach McMinnville in time to save its garrison and stores. The troops holding the place surrendered without offering any resistance, and when General Crook arrived, he found that a large amount of public and private property had been destroyed, and that the enemy was in rapid movement toward Murfreesboro. Pursuing without delay, he overtook Wheeler's rear-guard two miles from the town. Stubborn resistance was offered to give free motion to the main column, but a saber charge by the Second Kentucky, led by Colonel Long, dislodged the force. Pursuing rapidly, General Crook compelled Wheeler to halt and give battle. A spirited engagement ensued lasting until dark, the enemy yielding two positions and suffering loss. Wheeler then moved rapidly toward Murfreesboro to destroy the railroad at that point. He sent squads acquainted with the country, to cut the telegraph wires between Murfreesboro and Nashville, hoping to be able to follow and destroy the railroad also. For the double purpose of avoiding ambush and saving the railroad, General Crook crossed over from Readyville to the Liberty turnpike, to interpose his force north of Murfreesboro. This movement turned Wheeler toward Shelbyville, saved Murfreesboro from pillage, and the railroad at that place and northward, but did not prevent the interruption of telegraphic communications.

On the 6th, the corp-commander, General Mitchell, with McCook's division, reached Murfreesboro, and the following night the whole command bivouacked seven miles from Shelbyville. In moving forward to the town the next morning, it was ascertained that Wheeler had divided his forces into three columns, directed severally to Wartrace, Shelbyville, and Unionville. General Mitchell sent McCook with his division to Unionville, and Crook with his toward Farmington, as the column which had sacked Shelbyville had moved upon a road leading to that place.   General Crook found Davidson's division encamped on Duck river.   The mounted infantry were in advance, and as the enemy seemed to be in confusion, they charged without dismounting.   Having driven the foe a short distance they dismounted, and Colonel Long's brigade passed to the front.   Colonel Long made a furious charge, drove the enemy thirteen miles, killing and capturing large numbers. When Davidson reached a position against which the cavalry could not operate, the infantry drove him in rout toward Farmington.   Here resistance was offered, the enemy being in position in a dense cedar thicket.   General Crook had with him only Long's and Miller's brigade; Minty's was unexpectedly in the rear.   The enemy was greatly superior, and was in a position which could not be attacked by cavalry.   Opening with artillery, he attacked the mounted infantry, in effort to turn both flanks.   Captain Stokes could find position for only one of his guns, but this he used so effectively that he threw the enemy's artillery into confusion.   At this juncture Colonel Miller charged, broke through the enemy's line, and captured four pieces of artillery, but General Crook's force was too small to take advantage of this success, as Wheeler had united his command against him.

On the morning of the 8th, General Crook moved toward Pulaski, having learned from scouts that Wheeler had retreated in that direction.   The other division, General Mitchell accompanying, moved on roads to the right.   Wheeler's command was at this time greatly disorganized; many of his troops had deserted, others were roaming over the country, and those under their colors were scattered on the lines of retreat.   He, however, moved with great speed toward the Tennessee river, and succeeded in crossing not far from Rodgersville.   He left two regiments at Sugar creek to cover his retreat.   These, Lieutenant-Colonel Patrick, of the Fifth Iowa, charged with the sabre, killed ten, wounded nine, captured seventy, and scattered the remainder in the mountains.

The cavalry divisions were united at Rodgersville, October 9th, where fifty-two thousand dollars' worth of cotton belonging to the Confederate government was destroyed.   On the

11th, the command was put in motion toward Stevenson, Alabama. At Huntsville, in the evening, it was ascertained that the rebel general, Roddy, had crossed the river and was moving toward Winchester and Decherd. Pursuit was commenced at daylight on the 12th, via New Market, and late at night the enemy was encountered, but the darkness was too dense for opportunity to press him beyond a skirmish. The next morning the fact was revealed that Roddy had counter-marched, and was hastening to recross the river. He was pursued for a day, but the impossibility of overtaking him being evident, the command was again turned eastward. Roddy's movement was doubtless intended to be co-operative with Wheeler's, and the direction of his march indicated that the quick disposition which had been made of the main column was entirely unexpected. General Bragg had placed his hope of forcing General Rosecrans from Chattanooga upon the possibility of so deranging his communications that his army could not be supplied so far from his base. His plan contemplated the movement of three columns of cavalry upon the long line of railroad, whose maintenance intact was the ruling condition of the continued occupancy of Chattanooga by the national army. Wheeler's defeats, and his hurried re-crossing of the Tennessee river so far to the west, admonished the leaders of the other columns that their co-operation was impracticable. Hence, Roddy sought safety on the southern bank of the river. And General Lee, who, with a large force of cavalry, reached Courtland, Alabama, the day that Wheeler recrossed, learned that his own advance would not be permitted. That Wheeler's raid was disastrous, his own report, which does not compass all the truth, plainly reveals. He put his losses far below the computation made by the general officers who followed him through Tennessee, but spoke in severe terms of the incapacity of many of his officers, and the shameful conduct of a portion of his men. General Crook estimated his losses at two thousand men and six pieces of arti ery. He left on the field at Farmington eighty-six dead and one hundred and thirty-seven wounded. One entire regiment deserted, and scattered through the mountains.

General Crook lost fourteen killed and ninety-seven

wounded. Among the slain was the gallant Colonel Monroe, of the One Hundred and Twenty-third Illinois, who fell in leading his regiment at Farmington.

In this campaign, marches were made on several days, ranging from forty to fifty-seven miles, the saber was justified as the weapon for cavalry, and a remarkable revelation of endurance was made. Many of the men were in need of clothing, and they had but three days' rations in twenty of almost incessant rain, hard marching, and frequent fighting.

Meanwhile, the situation of the army at Chattanooga became exceedingly critical. At the commencement of the occupation, there were large trains in good condition, and the prospect of transporting supplies was somewhat promising. But early in October the rain began to fall. With its continuance, the roads became almost impassable. The destruction of hundreds of wagons and animals by Wheeler was nearly fatal to the army. The remaining animals, from necessity, were pressed beyond endurance. The roads rapidly grew worse; the mules became exhausted by constant motion and lack of forage; each successive trip to Bridgeport compassed a longer period of time, and each trip reduced the number of wagons and the weight of their contents; at each succeeding issue the ration was diminished; the artillery horses, being least useful in the emergency, were deprived of forage and fell dead in great numbers day by day; and the alternative of surrender, or retreat with great peril and certain loss of all material, seemed only delaying its demand for the desperate election of the army. The thought of surrender could not be entertained, as no large army had yet lowered its colors at the demand of the foe, and the Army of the Cumberland could not be the first to experience this humiliation; and the shortest rations, as long as actual starvation could be averted, could not force that army to turn its back to the enemy. So, with full appreciation of the situation, it bravely awaited the issue.

Early in October, General Hooker, with the Eleventh and Twelfth Corps, took position on the Nashville and Chattanooga railroad. His troops, disposed from Nashville to Bridgeport, gave security to the communications between those points. But this did not give immediate relief to the army at Chattanooga. The Eastern troops had moved by railroad, and were without transportation. They were not needed at Chattanooga, as beyond an imposing but harmless cannonading from the crest of Lookout Maintain, the enemy was not demonstrative. But if they had been essential to the defense of the place, their going was impracticable; and if their advance had not been barred, their presence would have been the harbinger of starvation. It was some relief to the national army to know that reinforcements were so near; and this fact, coupled with the imminence of starvation, was a spur to the origination of a method to open the river and utilize it as a channel of supply. The enemy had firm hold of Lookout Mountain, and his batteries and sharpshooters commanded the river, the roads on the south bank, including the railroad, and the shortest road north of the river. This mastery of the shortest communications forced the supply trains to move from Bridgeport, up the Sequatchie valley, and over the mountains, to Chattanooga, a distance of sixty miles, and at the same time gave Bragg the power to interpose such forces as would overwhelm Hooker should he attempt to approach Chattanooga on the south of the river. In anticipation of an open river, steamboat-building had been commenced long before, at Bridgeport, and a steamboat captured at Chattanooga had been repaired. General Rosecrans had in view the opening of the river, and the erection of storehouses on Williams' Island, situated opposite the termination of Lookout valley, and gave orders to General Hooker to concentrate such portions of his command at Bridgeport as the safety of the Nashville and Chattanooga railroad would permit, and hold himself in readiness to move toward Chattanooga. He also gave orders for the construction of pontoons for a bridge down the river. On the 19th, he directed Brigadier-General W. F. Smith, his chief engineer, to reconnoiter the river in the vicinity of Williams' Island, with a view to making the island a cover for a steamboat landing and store-houses. That day he was relieved as commander of the Army of the Cumberland.

This change was the offshoot of another of broader compass. All through the summer there had been an evident lack of co-operation in the movements of the three armies, whose fields of operation were penetrated by the Tennessee river. Orders from Washington had, to some extent, required indirect or remote co-operation. But the Armies of the Tennessee, the Cumberland, and the Ohio, being not only organically distinct, but without defined relations, their operations had been directed to widely separated objectives, under circumstances which were adapted to defeat even indirect co-operation.

To secure the future intimate co-operation of these three armies, which in consequence of the issues of their recent campaigns was especially imperative, the Military Division of the Mississippi was created by the President, and General Grant assigned to its command. The posture of affairs at Chattanooga doubtless precipitated this measure as the expression of a radical change of policy in the central theater of war. The President and his counselors feared that General Rosecrans could not extricate himself from the embarrassments which environed him, and that he would abandon his position before reinforcements could reach him. The general's dispatches did manifest that he was not sanguine that he could hold Chattanooga, unless the assistance which he suggested could be afforded; but in no way did he indicate that he thought of withdrawing, except as an absolute necessity, and on the last day of his command of the army, was intent upon maturing the scheme which subsequently was the means of opening the river and the roads on the south bank.

The President's order of October 18th, which created the Military Division of the Mississippi with General Grant in command, placed General Thomas at the head of the Army of the Cumberland. He assumed command formally on the 19th, and General Rosecrans having dictated a farewell to his army, left for Cincinnati before it was generally known that he had been relieved.

At the time of this change of commanders, the Army of the Cumberland comprised the Fourth, Eleventh, Twelfth, and Fourteenth Corps and three divisions of cavalry. In compliance with the President's order of September 28th, the Fourth was formed on the 9th of October, by the consolidation of the Twentieth and Twenty-first, and at the same time the Reserve Corps was attached to the Fourteenth.   The compression of four corps into two necessitated a corresponding reduction in the number of brigades and divisions.   Under the new organization, there were three brigades in each division, designated as the First, Second, and Third, and three divisions in each corps, similarly distinguished.   Major-General Gordon Granger was assigned to the command of the Fourth Corps, and his division commanders in the numerical order of divisions were Major-Generals J. M. Palmer and P. H. Sheridan and Brigadier-General T. J. Wood.   The commanders of the First, Second, and Third divisions of the Fourteenth Corps were respectively Major-General L. H. Rousseau and Brigadier-Generals J. C. Davis and A. Baird.

The dominant problem was that of supplies.   Upon its solution rested the fate of the army.   To this General Grant's first order and General Thomas' first act as army commander pertained.   General Grant telegraphed to General Thomas: "Hold Chattanooga at all hazards.   I will be there as soon as possible.   Please inform me how long your present supplies will last and the prospect for keeping them up."   The response was: "Two hundred and four thousand and sixty-two rations in storehouse.   Ninety-six thousand to arrive to-morrow, and all trains were loaded which had arrived at Bridgeport up to the 16th; probably three hundred wagons.   We will hold the town till we starve.   The same day, October 19th, the day the command of the army was formally relinquished by General Rosecrans, General Thomas directed General Hooker to hasten the concentration of his command and his preparations to move, in accordance with the previous instructions of General Rosecrans.

General Grant reached Chattanooga on the 23d in the evening, and the projected plan for securing a lodgment of troops on the left bank of the river, at Brown's ferry, as the initial step in opening the river and shorter roads to Bridgeport, was at once submitted to him.   The day following, in company with Generals Thomas and Smith, he made a thorough reconnoissance north of the river, with reference to the feasibility of the plan proposed. Agreeing with those who had matured the scheme, he authorized its execution. Fortunately, the preparations were far advanced and their completion required little time. General Smith was charged with the enterprise and directed to perfect the necessary arrangements.

General Thomas at once gave specific instructions to General Hooker with regard to the advance of his troops in co-operation with the movement from Chattanooga. He was directed to leave General Slocum, the commander of the Twelfth Corps, with one division, to guard the railroad from Murfreesboro to Bridgeport, and to concentrate the Eleventh Corps and one division of the Twelfth at Bridgeport, in readiness to cross the Tennessee river; move first to Rankin's ferry and afterward to Brown's ferry. He was advised that two brigades of Palmer's division of the Fourth Corps would move on the north side of the river to Rankin's ferry, and that there would be co-operation at Brown's ferry also. These instructions were given at 2.30 P. M. on the 24th, and General Hooker replied promptly that he would move by daylight on the 27th.

The night of the 26th was fixed for the expedition from Chattanooga. The plan of operations was elaborated with great care, and involved the nicest adjustment of co-operative movements as a condition of success. By the river, the distance from Chattanooga to Brown's ferry is nine miles; but across the peninsula, less than half as far. The direction of the river, after curving round a high hill directly west of the town, is to the southwest until it touches the base of Lookout. From that point it trends northwest to Williams' Island. The course of the river defines to the view, from the top of Lookout Mountain, a peninsular hill of singular shape, not unlike the moccasined foot of an Indian, which, in harmony with the conceit, bears the name of Moccasin Point. Brown's ferry is opposite the narrowest part of this hill, south of west from Chattanooga. As a pontoon bridge was to be thrown at this point, General Smith concluded that it would involve less risk of failure to float his boats and a portion of his troops, and land them on the left bank of the river, than to transport them across the peninsula, and operate from the right bank in laying the bridge. Each course suggested disastrous probabilities. In pursuing the former, his boats must pass the enemy's pickets, stationed for seven miles along the left bank of the river, and land under their fire; and in attempting the latter, the enemy might be able to concentrate a sufficient force to prevent the laying of the bridge. His decision to float the boats was made in view of two probabilities—one, that his movement could be made so quietly as not to be perceived by the pickets; and the other, that should the enemy's camp be alarmed, a concentration of troops would not be made at his place of landing. Accordingly, he divided his forces, embarking fifteen hundred picked men under General Hazen, and sending General Turchin with his own brigade, the remainder of Hazen's, and three batteries of artillery under Major Mendenhall, to take position in the woods above the ferry, in readiness to move down to cover the landing on the opposite bank, and cross in support as quickly as practicable, or cover the other troops, in the event of disaster.

The boats moved from Chattanooga at 3 A. M. on the 27th. A slight fog veiled the moon, and the boats, directed by Colonel T. R. Stanley, glided noiselessly with the current. Hugging closely the right bank, they rounded Moccasin Point and moved unperceived to the place of landing. The boats had been called off into sections before starting, and each section was placed under an officer, who knew beforehand his exact place of landing. As the foremost section neared the shore at its appointed place at early dawn, the surprised pickets fired a harmless volley and fled. In quick succession the several sections landed, and the men leaped upon the bank and ascended the adjacent hill to meet and drive back a small force that had hurried forward in response to the warning volley. There was a sharp engagement for a moment, and then all was quiet. The boats first brought over the remainder of Hazen's troops, and soon after Turchin's brigade. Hazen took firm hold of the hill above the gorge through which the Bridgeport road passes to the ferry, and Turchin the one below it. As soon as skirmishers could be thrown sufficiently forward to prevent a surprise, detachments with axes went vigorously to work felling trees and constructing barricades and abatis. In two hours the defenses were such as to bid defiance to the enemy. This accomplished, the pontoon bridge was speedily thrown under the skillful supervision of Captain P. V. Fox, First Michigan Engineers. Although the force engaged was exposed to a vigorous cannonading by the enemy's batteries on the front of Lookout Mountain, General Smith's loss was six killed, twenty-three wounded, and nine missing. The loss of the enemy was probably not less, as six of his dead were left on the field, and six prisoners were captured. Twenty beeves and two thousand bushels of corn were added to the slender rations of the troops. These supplies of hardly appreciable value to a large army under ordinary circumstances, were of very considerable moment at a time when soldiers gladly gathered the fragments of crackers and grains of corn which fell to the ground in transfer.

The conditions of success in the expedition were numerous and intricate. Had any one of the responsible officers failed in his special duty, the movement might have miscarried, but there was no serious default. There was such brilliancy of plan and execution as to call forth the following notice from General Thomas: " To Brigadier-General W. F. Smith, chief engineer, should be accorded great praise for the ingenuity which conceived, and the ability which executed the movement at Brown's ferry. The preparations were all made in secrecy, as was also the boat expedition, which passed under the overhanging cliffs of Lookout, so much so, that when the bridge was thrown at Brown's ferry on the morning of the 27th, the surprise was as great to the army within Chattanooga, as it was to the army besieging it from without."

Though this success was a source of great mortification to General Bragg, he did not at first discern its full significance. And while he was wasting powder and shells in bombarding the floating bridge, Hooker was moving eastward to give the full revelation of what the lodgment at Brown's ferry was the prophecy—an open river and short lines of supply.

Pursuant to orders, General Hooker put his command in motion toward Chattanooga early on the 27th, crossing on a pontoon bridge which had been thrown the day previous. He advanced to Whitesides, and thence deflected into Lookout valley. At 3 P. M. his head of column was at Wauhatchie, and as he knew that Longstreet could strike him at pleasure, farther advance was made with caution. Many circumstances favored Longstreet. His points of observation were so numerous and elevated that he could discern all the movements of Hooker's troops, while such was the topography of the valley that he could conceal his own. Between Lookout and Raccoon Mountains there were several sharply defined hills, separated by deep depressions. Through the upper depression the railroad passes to the base of Lookout, where it touches the river, and farther down, the wagon road to Chattanooga deflects to the right through another, while the road to Brown's ferry courses along the western base of these hills.

The road to Kelley's ferry, a few miles farther down the river, turns to the left, where the Chattanooga road turns to the right. The enemy held the hills commanding these roads, and it was anticipated that he would dispute their possession.

The approach of a large force from Bridgeport in a few hours after the lodgment of the national troops at Brown's ferry, must have revealed to General Bragg that the co-operative movements were designed to raise the siege of Chattanooga. It must have been apparent, also, that to prevent such a result, he must either crush Hooker or interpose a very heavy column between him and Brown's ferry. Why this was not done is as inexplicable as the loss of his advantages before the battle of Chickamauga. He did indeed offer resistance to Hooker's advance beyond Wauhatchie, but it was too feeble to prevent it, and another failure was added to the numerous preceding ones.

The head of column of the Eleventh Corps, when a short distance north of the railroad, received a volley of musketry from the adjacent hills. As the exact nature of the attack was concealed by the dense woods, General Howard, by direction of General Hooker, threw a brigade on the right and another on the left. The enemy then fled, and burnt the railroad bridge over Lookout creek in his flight. A few of Howard's men fell at this point, and others were killed as from time to time the column was exposed to the batteries on Lookout Mountain. At 5 P. M. the troops halted for the night, and went into camp about one mile from Brown's ferry.

General Geary's division of the Twelfth Corps remained at Wauhatchie, three miles distant, so as to hold the road leading to Kelley's ferry. Pickets were thrown out from each camp; but no effort was made to maintain continuity of line, the force being too small to afford substantial communications for such a distance, and the troops were divided, as it was deemed important to retain positions which commanded the two roads.

During the first watches there was no alarm; but about midnight, a regiment that had advanced toward Lookout was involved in a skirmish, and an hour later the roar of musketry from Geary's position announced an assault, but not a surprise, as the isolated division was in line of battle before the enemy approached. Fearing that Geary might be overpowered, General Hooker directed General Howard to double-quick Schurz's division to his support. When this division had proceeded a short distance, it received the fire of the enemy from the central hills, which was the first intimation of his presence in such close proximity. In the emergency, Tyndale's brigade was ordered to charge, and the other brigade to hasten forward.

Soon, Steinwehr's division came up to Tyndale's position, when it was discovered that the enemy was occupying another hill in the rear of the one held by the troops which had fired upon Schurz. Smith's brigade of Steinwehr's division was at once ordered to carry the hill with the bayonet. This small brigade marched up the steep acclivity, receiving, but not returning the fire of the enemy; drove a greatly superior force from the intrenchments on the summit, captured prisoners, and scattered the rebels in all directions. Tyndale encountered less resistance, and soon pressed the enemy from his front.

In the meantime, the noise of battle from musketry firing, and occasional discharges of artillery, was of such character as to indicate the progress of a fierce struggle at Wauhatchie. The reinforcements failed to reach Geary, and for nearly three hours he resisted the furious assaults of superior numbers. At last he assumed the offensive, and breaking Longstreet's line, drove his troops from the field.

The enemy had doubtless observed the distance between Howard and Geary, and had interposed his troops in the hope, no doubt, of crushing them in turn. The night attack expressed the enemy's consciousness of the emergency, and his plan to meet it was well devised, but his columns had too little weight to assure success.

General Hooker's loss in killed and wounded was four hundred and sixteen. Among the severely wounded were General Green, and Colonel Underwood, of the Thirty-third Massachusetts. The estimated loss of the enemy was much greater, as one hundred and fifty of his dead were buried in Geary's front, and more than one hundred were captured.

To strengthen Hooker's grasp of the valley, Whittaker's and Mitchell's brigades of Davis' division were moved over the river. The problem of supplies was soon solved. The steamboat which had been repaired at Chattanooga passed the enemy's batteries on Lookout the night of the 28th, and the one at Bridgeport was soon in motion up the river loaded with rations for the army. A good road was soon made from Chattanooga to Brown's ferry, and thence to Kelley's, and work was commenced on the railroad from Bridgeport east. The question now was not how long should the Army of the Cumberland hold Chattanooga, but how long should the rebel banners be permitted to wave on Lookout Mountain and Missionary Ridge. This change of problems had been produced by measures commenced by General Rosecrans, continued under General Thomas, elaborated by General Smith, and which, having been approved by General Grant, were executed by his authority.

CHAPTER XXII.

BATTLES NEAR CHATTANOOGA.

The Confederate leaders and the army commander were sanguine of the success of the siege of Chattanooga up to the very moment of its failure. General Bragg had, for a time, just ground for sanguine expectations, as the elements were his allies. At the time of greatest promise, the oracular Confederate President appeared on Lookout Mountain, and from " Pulpit Rock," as he looked down exultingly upon the beleaguered army, predicted its total ruin. But the loss of Lookout valley, the river, and the direct roads to Bridgeport virtually threw Bragg upon the defensive. It is true that he maintained his lines on Lookout Mountain and Missionary Ridge, and through the intervening valley, in semblance of besieging effort, until the army with which he had so often battled, leaped from its intrenchments and hurled him and his oft-defeated army from their lofty battlements. But he made no movement of actual offense against Chattanooga during the time the Army of the Cumberland was preparing to assume the boldest aggression.

For four weeks Chattanooga was the scene of the most comprehensive activities. In the rebound from the constraint of investing lines, the menace of starvation, and the foreshadows of direct disaster, the Army of the Cumberland displayed new vigor and spirit, while the resources of the military division were made tributary to the concentration of forces to operate offensively. All the troops of the Army of the Cumberland that could be spared from the rear, especially cavalry and artillery, were ordered forward, and General Sherman, long before ordered to Chattanooga, but delayed hitherto by repairing roads, was directed to move the Fifteenth Corps as rapidly as possible, paying no further attention to the roads than the swift movement of his troops required.   General W. F. Smith, chief engineer, and General J. M. Brannan, chief of artillery, of the Army of the Cumberland, were charged with preparing the fortifications for heavier guns than those with the army, and the latter was empowered to send for as many guns of heavy caliber and such ammunition as should be needed.   To facilitate the movements of troops, General Smith was directed to construct pontoons for two additional bridges.   The coming of troops, supplies, and munitions, and the din of preparation for a battle, known to be imminent, would have made Chattanooga historic, without the clash of arms which soon electrified the continent, or the previous battle involved in gaining possession.

Battle-fields become a part of history equally with the story of the conflicts enacted upon them.   They are mapped on stone and steel, and delineated in pen pictures, appear in historic narration in intimate association with the deeds of heroes.   Not alone do the topographical features which suggest plans of battle and dominate tactical combinations become historic, but those also of mere grandeur and beauty, whenever the hosts of war commingle in deadly strife, where nature has been lavish of her gifts.   Even the name of him who may perchance offer his humble cot for the fire of war to burn, or its enginery to level, has association on the historic page with him who commands an army.   And in all that is grandly concomitant with grandest battle, Chattanooga is pre-eminent.

The town is surrounded with almost all the types of the grand and beautiful in nature.   Mountains far and near, rising from water and plain, sharply defined by low valleys and the river curving at their feet; subordinate hills with rounded summits and undulating slopes, and broad plains delicately pencilled here and there by winding creeks and rivulets, are the prominent features of nature's amphitheater, in the center of which is Chattanooga.

Looking to the southwest, Lookout Mountain,* with bold

---

* This mountain rises two thousand eight hundred feet above the ocean, and one thousand four hundred and sixty-four above the Tennessee river.

front and craggy crest, is seen rising abruptly from the river and the valleys on either side; to the west Raccoon Mountain appears, trending from its river front far to the southwest, parallel with Lookout; to the north, Waldron's Ridge forms the sky line far to right and left; to the east, Missionary Ridge, with indented summit, more humbly takes position, hiding the lofty ranges far beyond; to the south, the east, and to the northeast, stretches the plain where the armies were marshaled for the assault of Bragg's army on Missionary Ridge; and to the southwest, twice across the river, lies the valley from which Hooker crept slyly up the mountain steeps, covered with trees and shrubs, standing and fallen, and with huge fragments of stone, which during the ages have dropped from the ledges overhanging the crest, to give battle on a field suited to the stealthy belligerence of the Indian, but adverse in every phase to the repetition of all the precedents of modern warfare. But this battle-field defies description, and he who would fully appreciate either battle or field, must read the story of the one as he looks down from Lookout Mountain upon the magnificence of the other.*

---

* Historians have made effort to transmit to the future the significance of the names which distinguish the natural features around Chattanooga. It is no pleasant task to leave groundless the many pretty conceits which have so long passed for facts; but he who would write the truth, must not hesitate to dissipate a myth or disclose a false hypothesis. With only occasional allusion to the various interpretations of Cherokee names, which have so long been accepted as true, their actual meaning, as derived from John Ross, the celebrated Cherokee chief, and from Lewis Ross, his brother, are here given.

"Chattanooga," originally was the name of a small Indian hamlet, situated near the base of Lookout Mountain, on the bank of Chattanooga creek. It means, in the Cherokee language, "to draw fish out of water," and hence was applied to the collection of huts, which were occupied by Indian fishermen. The humble hamlet disappeared, and its name, at first suggestive and appropriate, was inherited by the town of the white man, with meaningless application. A somewhat similar name was applied by the Cherokees to the cliffs, rising boldly from the river above the town, which was derived from "Clanoowah," the name of a warlike but diminutive hawk, which was supposed to embody the spirit of the tribe. These cliffs were the favorite nesting-place of the bird, and hence a name was given which expressed this fact, and which, perhaps, has suggested the myth, that "Chattanooga" means "eagle's nest."

By a strange misapprehension of the situation, after the coming of Hooker, and the establishment of reliable and adequate lines of supply, General Bragg detached Longstreet's corps, and sent it to East Tennessee to overwhelm Burnside, and regain what had there been lost, with the ulterior object of returning to strike a heavy blow upon Grant's left flank. It is believed that this movement originated with the Confederate President, during his visit of exultation and prophecy. But by whomever suggested or ordered, it was a palpable blunder. If made upon the supposition that Bragg would yet be strong enough to maintain the siege of Chattanooga, it rested upon a conjecture, without warrant from any approximately just apprehension of the posture of affairs at Chattanooga; if upon the supposition that his investing lines would not soon be changed to defensive use, the reason for the movement was equally remote from the truth. The Confederate commander could not have been ignorant of the fact that Longstreet fought a reinforcing column in Lookout valley, and he ought to have known, that as he had drawn

---

The Cherokee name for Lookout Mountain did not mean an outlook, but "to look at," and embodied some Indian's fancy, that this mountain was looking at Raccoon Mountain, across the intervening valley. Its present name, however, is infinitely more appropriate; for as an outlook, it is unrivaled, seven states being in view.

Missionary Ridge was called by the Indians, Missionaries' Ridge, from the fact that the missionaries, in passing from their station, at the present site of the "Mission Mills," to Chattanooga, the landing-place for their supplies, crossed it. It was theirs, because they used it.

Taylor's Ridge, near Ringgold, Georgia, made classic for another mountain fight of Hooker's, was so named because Richard Taylor, the second chief of the tribe, during the latter portion of his life, used this ridge in the same way. By a modification of this conception of the relation of persons to places, the Cherokees gave a name to one of their missionaries, who, on preaching tours, frequently crossed the mountains, a name which signified "the one who crosses the mountains."

Will's Valley was named for William Webber, who lived in it, and whose common name was "Will." Webber's Falls, in the Arkansas river, above Fort Smith, derived its name from this man, who, after the removal of the Cherokees to the West, settled at the falls.

Brown's ferry bears the English name of a prominent Cherokee.

The meaning of "Chickamauga" was not known to the Cherokees, and was supposed by them to be a word from the Chickasaw language.

troops from Mississippi to fight the battle of Chickamauga, the victorious army at Vicksburg could be easily transferred to Chattanooga. And yet, in the face of possibilities and probabilities that would have deterred a prudent commander from the first diminution of his strength, other portions of his army were subsequently started to Longstreet's support.

As soon as it had been ascertained with certainty that Longstreet's corps had been detached, General Grant became eager to attack the enemy on Missionary Ridge, to compel him to retain his remaining forces, and recall those that he had detached, as he feared for Burnside, and could help him only indirectly, if at all. Accordingly, on the 7th of November, he instructed General Thomas to attack and carry the north end of Missionary Ridge on the following morning. And having carried this point, to threaten and attack, if possible, the enemy's communications between Cleveland and Dalton. To render the movement possible, he ordered that mules should be detached from the wagons, the horses from the ambulances, and private horses of officers should be taken, if necessary, to move the artillery.

General Thomas and General Smith agreed in the opinion, that the army was not in condition for battle, unless in defense. And after a thorough reconnoissance of the ground, and a full consideration of the condition and paucity of the animals, and the inadequacy of his forces, General Grant decided that the movement was " utterly impracticable until Sherman could get up." * But the considerations which induced the general commanding to order it, in the first place, found expression through the activity of the army in preparation for the operations which were to drive Bragg from his position before Chattanooga, and open the way for support to Burnside.

Having revoked his order for an immediate movement against the enemy, General Grant busied himself with the formation of a plan of operations for his combined armies, and urged General Burnside to maintain his position at Knoxville, until a battle could be fought and a column moved to

---

* Statement in his report.

his assistance.   His plan proposed primary movements by Hooker and Sherman—the former against Bragg's left, on Lookout Mountain, and the latter against his right on the northern extremity of Missionary Ridge.

General Sherman reached Bridgeport with his leading divisions on the 15th, and hastened to Chattanooga to confer with General Grant.   After his arrival, Generals Grant, Thomas, Sherman, and Smith made a thorough reconnoissance of the region north of the river, which disclosed the fact that there were good roads from Brown's ferry to the mouth of the North Chickamauga, north of the first range of hills, which Sherman could use, with good prospect of concealing his movement to the place designated for his crossing, to reach the right flank of the enemy.   His troops would be in plain view of the enemy at the ferry, but their subsequent concealment by the hills, would leave him in doubt as to their destination, whether to Knoxville, or to some point on the north side of the river, to participate in operations at Chattanooga.   It was observed, also, that the north end of Missionary Ridge was imperfectly guarded, and that the bank of the river, from the mouth of the North Chickamauga to his main line, was watched only by a small picket of cavalry. These facts determined General Grant's plan of operations, the first object of which "was to mass all the forces possible at one given point, namely, Missionary Ridge, converging toward the north end of it."   This ruling object induced a change of the first plan, so far as it contemplated Hooker's attack upon Lookout Mountain, that Howard's corps might give weight to the proposed assault upon the northern extremity of the ridge.   This reconnoissance, made upon the north bank of the river, and conducted in such way "as not to excite suspicions on the part of the enemy," did not develop the fact that Bragg's right flank, at least the extremity of his main line, did not rest upon the summit farthest to the north, but was to rest in battle upon the third one to the south, which was a much stronger position, separated from the second by a deep depression—a circumstance which greatly modified the conduct of the battle.

Having formed his plan, General Grant announced it to his army commanders on the 18th, and mentioned the 21st as the time for its execution. It required that Sherman, with his own troops, and one division of the Army of the Cumberland, should effect a crossing of the Tennessee river, just below the mouth of the South Chickamauga, on Saturday, November 21st, at daylight, his crossing to be protected by artillery on the heights to the north, and after crossing the river, to carry Missionary Ridge from its northern extremity to the railroad tunnel. It contemplated that Thomas was to co-operate by concentrating his troops on his left flank in the valley, leaving only the necessary force to hold the fortifications on the right and center, and one division as a movable column, and after Sherman had carried the ridge to the tunnel, and the conjunction of their forces had been effected, by advancing as nearly simultaneously with him as possible, to sweep the enemy from position. It proposed that Lookout valley should be held by Hooker, with Geary's division and the brigades which had been detached from the Fourth Corps to co-operate with him in his advance from Bridgeport, and that Howard's corps was to be held in readiness to act with either Thomas or Sherman.

Upon its announcement, the army commanders and their respective subordinates addressed themselves to the preliminary movements. General Thomas at once directed General Howard to take position between Brown's ferry and Chattanooga, and the two brigades of the Fourth Corps, Whittaker's and Grose's, recalled from position down the river to fill the place of Howard's corps in the valley. He also designated General Davis' division of the Fourteenth Corps, Major-General J. M. Palmer commanding, as the support to General Sherman, and ordered Colonel Long, with his brigade of cavalry, to first move on Sherman's left, and when no longer needed, to cross Chickamauga Creek and make a raid upon the enemy's communications. These movements were all made before the 21st.

A heavy rain-storm, which commenced on the 20th and

continued through the 21st, delayed General Sherman, and necessitated the postponement of the battle till the 22d. On the 22d, General Grant proposed further delay, as two of Sherman's divisions had failed to cross the river at Brown's ferry in consequence of the parting of the bridge. At this juncture, General Thomas suggested that Howard's corps should be sent, if needed, to take the place of the divisions that were behind, and that the latter, with Hooker's troops, could form a column to attack the enemy on Lookout Mountain, or at least divert his attention from the movement against his right flank. He thus counseled against further delay, fearing that the enemy should become advised of the plan of operations, and greatly desiring that Hooker should make the movement which he proposed for him. These suggestions were in part approved, though the engagement was postponed as General Grant had proposed. On the 22d, Howard's corps was moved over the river to Chattanooga, and posted between Sheridan's and Wood's divisions in the line to lead the enemy to believe that Sherman's troops, whose passage of the river at Brown's ferry was in plain view, were reinforcing the town rather than moving up the river on the north bank.

During the 22d, rumors reached the national lines that the more recent movements of the enemy's forces indicated their withdrawal. Deserters reported that troops had been sent to McLemore's Cove.* This fact, and the detachment of forces to march to General Longstreet's support in East Tennessee, produced the impression in the Confederate army that a retreat was meditated by General Bragg. In view of the statements of deserters and a formal notification from General Bragg to remove all non-combatants from Chattanooga, sent on the 20th, General Grant directed General Thomas to order a reconnoissance in front of Chattanooga, that General Bragg might not withdraw his army in quietness, if such was his intent. Under the general direction to ascertain the truth or falsity of the report of General Bragg's retreat, General Thomas organized a movement, which in expression and un-

---

*This movement was induced by the appearance of General Ewing's division of General Sherman's command, at Trenton, in Will's valley.

expected issue was a suitable prelude to the grand battle of which it constituted the initial aggression.

General Bragg could not have been ignorant of the vast concentration of national forces at Chattanooga, and how then he could have felt so secure in his position, or so free to leave it, as to weaken his army to give support to General Longstreet in aggression, or even to save him from destruction, is unaccountable. His greatest weakness was in the length of his lines, and there was extreme hazard in the attempt to hold them with diminished forces. He had with him, after General Longstreet's departure, two corps of infantry, comprising eight or nine divisions, holding, it is true, a position of great strength; but there were nevertheless such advantages to an army of superior strength, having impregnable fortifications and shorter lines, as should have deterred him from detaching any of his remaining forces for any purpose. This, however, he did, and some of his troops in motion toward General Longstreet were recalled in time to participate in the battle.[*] There is concurrent testimony from various Confederate sources, to the fact that General Bragg expected General Grant to detach forces to support General Burnside in East Tennessee; but yet, after he knew that none had been sent to follow General Longstreet, he still dared to weaken his army before Chattanooga.[†]

The enemy's first line of pickets rested a short distance east of the Western and Atlantic railroad, passing in front of the hill which was crowned with Fort Wood, a fortification of marked elevation and strength. Between this fort and the railroad, the ground at first descends abruptly, but soon gently and smoothly, and blending with the slopes of other hills, forms a broad area, suited for the review of an army or its formation for actual battle. Upon this space, about noon on the 23d, several divisions formed in line of battle, in plain view from all the commanding positions held by the enemy. The order from General Thomas to General Granger required that

---

[*] Statement in General Grant's report.

[†] This fact is stated in the narrative of the "Richmond Dispatch," and also in a letter, descriptive of the battle, written by a member of General Hardee's staff.

he should throw forward one division of his corps supported by another, in the direction of Orchard Knob, " to discover the position of the enemy, if he still remain in the vicinity of his old camps." General Wood's division having been designated to lead, first deployed before the fort. Then General Sheridan's moved to the right and rear of General Wood; General Howard's corps formed in mass in rear of these two divisions, and General Baird's division took position on the right of General Sheridan, refused in echelon. General Johnson's division was in arms in the intrenchments, in readiness to give support whenever assistance might be needed. These movements were regarded by the enemy as indicating the extension of the national lines to obtain wood,* or as a mere pageant, and he made no special preparation to resist them.

Orchard Knob, in the direction of which the movement was ordered, is situated half-way from Chattanooga to Missionary Ridge. It rises abruptly to a considerable elevation above the plain. Between it and the lines of the national troops the ground is low, and being at the time covered in part with trees and bushes, was favorable for the concealment of defenses and forces. Along the western base of Orchard Knob, as also over its rocky summit, and for a half mile to the southwest, the enemy had barricades of logs and stones. His line of rifle-pits extended for more than a mile to the north, following the curvature of Citico creek, while across this little stream there were two parallel lines stretching still farther northward. In front of these, which were for the grand guards, were insulated defenses for the picket reserves.

About 2 P. M., General Wood moved rapidly forward, with Hazen's brigade on the right, Willich's on the left, and Beatty's in reserve. This pageant, and yet more than a pageant, attracted the attention of both armies, and in its developments revealed to each the nearness of a general battle. If General Bragg had previously fancied that his position was so strong as to preclude attack, he now had cause to apprehend that the trial of its strength was at hand. And it was

---

* This supposition was mentioned by prisoners, and was stated in a terse narrative of the battle in the " Richmond Dispatch."

soon evident to the national commanders that the enemy was still in position, and that his withdrawal was improbable, except when forced from plain, hill, and mountain.

General Wood's troops, in harmony with the grandeur of the scenery, the pageant which heralded their advance, and the inspiration which the consciousness of making the initial movement of battle in view of contending armies is adapted to create, pressed rapidly forward. His compact lines, marred by no straggling to the rear, swept from position, first the pickets and their reserves, and then moved, without halt or slackened pace, to the attack of the strong line on the hill. Willich meeting with less resistance than was anticipated in the defense of so important a position, at once hurled the enemy from the base and summit of Orchard Knob. Hazen did not so soon carry a lower hill to the right, as the troops holding it fought in a manner better suited to the surroundings and issues of the conflict. But though resisting bravely, they were soon forced by the bayonet to yield position, leaving for capture the Twenty-eighth Alabama regiment and its flag. General Wood lost one hundred and twenty-five men killed and wounded—a fact which attests the gallantry of the quick dash which secured an important position, and gave the type of the grander assaults by which one of the most dicisive victories of the war was gained.

As soon as General Wood had driven the enemy from position, General Sheridan moved his division to the right of General Wood, and refused it on a series of small hills trending to the southwest. The hills occupied by Generals Wood and Sheridan comprise nearly all the high ground between Fort Wood and Missionary Ridge, and afforded a good base for operations against the enemy's main lines beyond. From the summit of Orchard Knob, these lines, first and second, were plainly visible running along the base and summit of Missionary Ridge, as also the intervening ground over which the national forces were to pass in the final assault.

At 4 P. M., General Wood was instructed by General Thomas to hold and fortify the position which he had unexpectedly gained, and was informed that General Howard's corps would form on his left. In compliance with instructions, both General Wood and General Sheridan threw up intrenchments in their, front, and the former constructed an epaulment for a six-gun battery on Orchard Knob, in which Bridges' battery was placed during the night. As soon as practicable, the Eleventh Corps advanced to form on General Wood's left, and met resistance from the double line of rifle-pits on the north of Citico creek. As, while General Wood was advancing, General Howard had thrown forward Battery A, Fourth Artillery, to cover his left flank, so now, in reciprocal assistance, the former sent Colonel Manderson, with two regiments, to strike in flank the force across the creek. Manderson's fire soon relieved General Howard's right from pressure in front, and the corps attained position.

Thus a most important advantage was gained by a mere tentative movement to discover the position of the enemy— an advantage upon which hinged the final decisive assault of the battle. And not only did this advance on the 23d give the central column a good position from which to assault on the 25th, but it caused General Bragg to transfer Walker's division, General Gist commanding, from Lookout Mountain, to sustain his right against what seemed a most threatening demonstration.

After Orchard Knob had been gained by the national troops, and a long battle front had been formed, with that summit as the center, General Bragg was compelled to elect between a strong left flank on Lookout Mountain and the strengthening of his right, which covered his depot of supplies across the South Chickamauga, at the expense of his left. In removing Walker's division to the right flank, the Confederate commanders were not ignorant of the resulting contingencies, as General Stevenson signaled from the summit of the mountain, at 11 P. M., his conviction that if an attack was intended, it would be upon that position. This action, then, on the 23d, had most intimate relations to General Hooker's success, on the front of Lookout Mountain, the next day.

During the 23d, another of General Sherman's divisions crossed the river, at Brown's ferry, but the bridge again parted, leaving Osterhaus' division, General Woods commanding, on the left bank. As General Sherman had three divisions in hand, General Grant decided not to delay operations any longer. And as it was improbable that his Fourth could cross in time to participate in his movement against the northern extremity of Missionary Ridge, General Thomas advised General Hooker that if it should fail to cross, he should endeavor with it and his own troops, " to take the point of Lookout Mountain." Later, he informed him that General Grant still hoped that General Woods could cross; but if he could not, in time to join General Sherman, that the mountain should be taken, if a demonstration should develop its practicability. That General Sherman's division might not be prevented, if it was possible for it to cross in time to join him, General Hooker sent a staff officer to the river to ascertain the fact that the bridge could not be joined. As soon as this officer reported, General Hooker made dispositions for his movement, to result either in demonstration or actual attack. Thus it appears that another modification of General Grant's pre-announced plan hinged upon the failure of one division to cross the river, though the consequent movement resulted in turning Bragg's left flank.

At 4 A. M. General Hooker reported that he was ready to advance against Lookout Mountain. His command, Geary's division of the Twelfth Corps, Osterhaus' of the Fifteenth, and two brigades of Cruft's division of the Fourth, were all strangers to each other, representing three corps, and allowing Geary's division to go back to recent relations, three distinct armies. But officers and men were true soldiers, and made the acquaintance necessary for unity of action as quickly as the combinations of the battle-field placed them side by side.

General Hooker sent Geary's division and Whittaker's brigade of Cruft's division to Wauhatchie, to cross Lookout creek, and then to sweep down its right bank, to clear it of the enemy and cover the crossing of the remaining forces. He ordered Grose to seize the common road bridge just below the railroad crossing and repair it, and directed Woods to move up his division from Brown's ferry, under cover of the hills, to the point designated for crossing the creek, and support the batteries—one, Battery "K," First Ohio Artillery, on a high hill without trees, a little north of the stream, and the other, Battery "K," First New York Artillery, on a hill to the rear of the other. He also sent a portion of the Second Kentucky cavalry up the valley to Trenton, to observe the enemy and give warning of danger from that direction. The picket line of the enemy was on the right bank of the creek; the picket reserves were in the valley beyond, and the main force of the enemy was encamped on the mountain side.

On the front of Lookout Mountain, intermediate between base and summit, there is a wide open space, cultivated as a farm, in vivid contrast with the natural surroundings of wildest types. The farm-house, known as Craven's or "the white house," was situated upon the upper margin of the farm. From the house to the foundation of the perpendicular cliff or palisade, which crops out from the rock-ribbed frame of the mountain, the ascent is exceedingly steep and thickly wooded. Below the farm the surface is rough and craggy. The base of the mountain, next the river, has a perpendicular front of solid rock, rising grandly from the railroad track, which, though in part cut through the deep ledges, does not perceptibly mar nature's magnificent architecture. Over the top of this foundation front the narrow road passes, which, in the western valley, throws off various branches, leading west and south. East and west from Craven's farm the surface is broken by furrows and covered with shrubs, trees, and fragments of stone. On the open space the enemy had constructed his defenses, consisting of intrenchments, pits, and redoubts, which, extending over the front of the mountain, bade defiance to a foe advancing from the river. At the extremities of the main intrenchments there were rifle-pits, epaulements for batteries, barricades of stone and abatis, looking to resistance against aggression from Chattanooga or Lookout Valley. The road from Chattanooga to Summertown, an elegant village for summer resort, winding up the eastern side of the mountain, is the only one practicable for ordinary military movements within a range of many miles. So that, except by this road, there could be no transfer of troops from the summit to the northern slope, or to the valley, east or west, to meet the emergencies of battle, and this road was too long to allow provision from the top for sudden contingencies below.

At 8 A. M. Geary crossed the creek, captured the pickets of the enemy, and then crept up the mountain side until his right, which was his front in the ascent, touched the base of the palisaded summit. The fog which overhung the mountain top and upper steeps, and the dense woods, concealed the movement. Then, with his right clinging to the palisades, he swept round toward the mountain's front. Simultaneously with Geary's first movement, Grose attacked the enemy at the bridge, and having driven him back commenced its repair. The noise of this conflict called the enemy's nearest forces from their camps. They formed in front of their intrenchments and rifle-pits, and one detachment advanced to the railroad embankment, which formed a good parapet and admitted a sweeping fire upon the national troops advancing from the bridge. To avoid the loss of life inevitable in a direct advance, General Hooker directed Osterhaus, now commanding his division, to send a brigade to prepare a crossing a half mile farther up the creek, under cover of the woods. A portion of Grose's brigade having been left at the bridge to attract the attention of the enemy, the remainder followed Woods' brigade to assist in the construction of the bridge. In the meantime, additional artillery had been posted, which, with the batteries first planted on the hills west of the creek, enfiladed all the proximate positions of the enemy. A section of 20-pounder Parrotts had also the range of the enemy's camp on the mountain side; and on Moccasin Point, Brannan's guns were in position to open a direct fire upon the front of the mountain.

At 11 A. M. Woods completed the bridge, and soon after, Geary's division and Whittaker's brigade, in line, sweeping the mountain from base to palisade, came abreast. The batteries then opened fire, and Woods and Grose crossed the creek and aligned their troops on Geary's left as it swept down the valley. The troops of the enemy, in the first positions, that escaped the artillery fire, ran into the infantry lines, so that quick overthrow occurred to all the troops that had taken position in the valley and near the western base of the mountain. Many were killed, more were wounded, and the remainder were captured, and then the line moved onward toward the mountain's front.

The booming of the heavy guns with interludes of light artillery and musketry fire, announced to friend and foe in the distant lines that an action was in progress where battle had not been expected. Quietness reigning throughout the other hills and valleys compassed by the long lines of the contending armies, the contest on the mountain side, revealed by its noise, but as yet hidden from sight, commanded the profoundest attention and interest of far more than one hundred thousand men. Those not held by duty or the constraint of orders, in crowds sought the elevated outlooks, and with glasses and strained vision, turned their gaze to the woods, fog, and battle-smoke, which concealed the anomalous contest. As the increasing roar of musketry indicated the sweep of the battle to the east, the anxiety for its revelation on the open ground became intense. Soon through the clefts of the fog could be seen the routed enemy in rapid motion, followed by Hooker's line, with its right under the palisade and its continuity lost to view far down the mountain. Whittaker held the right, under the cliffs, and below were the brigades of Cobham, Ireland, and Creighton; and this line hurled the enemy from position after position, climbing over crags and bowlders for attack and pursuit, and reached at noon the point where orders required a halt for the readjustment of lines and a more cautious approach toward the Summertown road. But as on the following day, in the assault made by other portions of the Army of the Cumberland, the restraint of orders did not arrest the pursuit of the flying foe, so now these victorious troops swept on. With a plunging fire from above and behind they rolled up the enemy's line, and lifting it from its intrenchments made no halt until the middle of the open ground was gained. Here the enemy met reinforcements and made a more determined stand. Soon, however, Grose's brigade of Cruft's division, and Osterhaus' command, having gathered up the captured on the lower ground, closed on the left, and then the enemy was driven from all his defenses on the open ground, and with broken ranks retreated down the eastern descent of the mountain.

The heavy Parrotts and the Tenth and Eighteenth Ohio batteries, under Captain Naylor, on Moccasin Point, rendered important aid to the assaulting forces, by preventing the concentration of the enemy's troops. But the potent cause of the victory was the fact that brave men reached the flank and rear of the enemy's defenses.

The heavy fighting ceased at 2 P. M. General Hooker's troops had exhausted their ammunition and it could not be supplied in the ordinary way, as no trains could reach them. Besides this want of ammunition, as a bar to further fighting, the fog which had overhung the mountain during the day, settled down densely over the enemy. But for these obstacles, and the fact that the enemy could now concentrate heavily to prevent the insulation of his troops on the mountain top, an effort would have been made to seize the Summertown road. Hooker, therefore, waited for ammunition and reinforcements. At 5 P. M. Carlin's brigade of the First division of the Fourteenth Corps crossed Chattanooga creek, near its mouth, and ascended the mountain to Hooker's right. The troops of this brigade carried on their persons ammunition for Hooker's skirmishers, in addition to the ordinary supply for themselves. Severe skirmishing was then maintained until nearly midnight.

As General Sherman's movement had been regarded as the leading one compassed by the general plan of operations, the engineer department, under the management of General W. F. Smith, had been pressed to the utmost activity to provide means for crossing his army to the south bank of the Tennessee. Lieutenant Dressen had collected all the pontoons between Brown's ferry and Bridgeport, and Captain P. V. Fox had been engaged in preparing boats for a new bridge. The river at the point selected for crossing, at the time of measurement, was thirteen hundred feet wide, and two bridges were proposed, and one also at the mouth of the South Chickamauga, one hundred and eighty feet in length. As it was expected that the enemy would contest the passage of the river if aware of the purpose to effect it, every precaution had been used to keep the projected bridges a profound secret. The pontoons had been hauled on by-roads to the North Chickamauga creek, eight miles above Chattanooga, and were there launched and concealed in readiness to be floated down to the place of crossing. The citizens in the vicinity had been put under guard to prevent them from giving information to the enemy. As Saturday, the 21st, had been designated for Sherman's attack, the boats and a brigade to man them were in readiness on the night of the 20th. Subsequently, the causes which delayed Sherman for a time threatened failure to the bridges, as the high water and driftwood which parted the bridges at Chattanooga and Brown's ferry, created the apprehension that the bridges could not be thrown, and that if thrown, they could not be maintained as long as needed.

But when General Sherman was ready to cross, a bridge was promptly thrown. At midnight on the 23d, one hundred and sixteen boats, with a brigade, left the North Chickamauga and floated quietly to the place of crossing. They were landed on the enemy's side of the river, at points above and below the mouth of the South Chickamauga, and were first used to transport troops from the opposite shore. By daylight two divisions were over, and the throwing of a bridge and the construction of a bridge-head were under vigorous prosecution. According to previous arrangements, General J. H. Wilson took the steamer Dunbar from Chattanooga to aid in the transportation of troops. This steamer's help was the more essential, as in consequence of the greater breadth of the river from high water, but one bridge could be thrown. Just as the last boat was connected, General Howard, with Buschbeck's brigade of Steinwehr's division and a small cavalry escort, reached the position. His unresisted advance from Chattanooga developed the fact that the enemy had yielded the river and the greater portion of the valley between the river and Missionary Ridge. At General Sherman's request, General Howard left his brigade to skirmish on the right flank of his line in its advance, and returned to Chattanooga with his escort.

The bridge was finished at 11 A. M., and at 1 P. M. General Sherman moved forward with three divisions in echelon, the several heads of column being covered with skirmishers and supporting forces. Meeting with no serious resistance, the advancing columns soon passed the foot hills, and at 4 P. M.

occupied the two northernmost summits of Missionary Ridge. Artillery was used on the right of the line late in the afternoon, but beyond this and slight skirmishing, the lodgment near the right flank of the enemy involved. no action. There was now one summit between General Sherman and the tunnel. Had he gained this, his distinct part of the battle, as first planned, would have been performed. General Grant had expected that he would be able to carry the ridge to about the tunnel before the enemy could concentrate against him, but the intervening hill was the one upon which Bragg's right flank rested.

The crest of Missionary Ridge is divided into distinct summits throughout its whole length by numerous depressions. The deepest of these, between the Tennessee river and Rossville, separates the second summit, which General Sherman had gained from the third, which was the strongest position for lateral defense within Bragg's lines. Here Cleburne's famous division was placed. The top of the hill was broad enough for a strong force, and yet sufficiently narrow to permit the formation of strong lines. Heavy barricades, or rather fortifications, constructed of logs and earth, covered the troops on the first defensive line, while the higher ground to the south gave room for successive supporting columns.* A somewhat thickly planted forest gave additional protection to the enemy. It was the strength of this position rather than ignorance of the strength of the combination against his right flank that induced General Bragg to yield the first two hills to General Sherman. Their abandonment shortened his line, while the depression on his right, and the slopes east and west, placed his enemy under his guns on every practicable line of attack.

At night, General Grant announced to General Thomas that General Sherman had carried the ridge to the tunnel, and advised him that General Sherman had been instructed to advance at daylight the next morning, and that his own attack should be simultaneous and co-operative, either to carry

---

* Subsequently, Cleburne's position became the salient of the line of the right wing, when troops were thrown to the rear to confront General Sherman's left, which rested on the Chickamauga.

the rifle-pits and ridge in his front, or move to the left, as the presence of the enemy might require.   He also gave directions with regard to General Hooker's action, requiring that if his position on the mountain could be maintained with a small force, and the ascent to the summit should be impracticable from it, that he should move up the valley and ascend by the first practicable road.

After receiving these instructions, General Thomas, in a formal order, congratulated General Hooker and his troops upon their glorious victory, and thanked them for their valorous conduct.   He then directed General Hooker to be in readiness to advance into Chattanooga valley, hold the Summertown road, and co-operate with the Fourteenth Corps by supporting its right, informing him that General Grant had ordered General Sherman to move along Missionary Ridge in the morning with the Army of the Cumberland co-operating.

Before daylight the next morning, anticipating the withdrawal of the enemy from the summit of Lookout Mountain, General Hooker dispatched several parties to scale the palisades.   Some daring soldiers from the Eighth Kentucky were the first reach the top and unfurl the national banner.   When the morning light first kissed its waving folds, the whole army apprehended the completeness of the victory which had been won the day before.   And as cheer responsive to cheer prolonged the expression of joy and exultation, there was a partial utterance of the inspiration, which, at the setting of the sun, found historic revelation through an assault most glorious in conception, execution, and issue.

The evacuation of the mountain top did not give full proof that the enemy had left Hooker's front, and the low-lying mist during the early hours of the day prevented the measures necessary to develop the situation.   The fog lifted between 9 and 10 A. M., and the retreat of the enemy was then apparent. His left flank had been turned, and the forces which had held the mountain fortress and the valley to the east had been transferred to Missionary Ridge.   General Bragg's defensive line was now only half its original length, and he no doubt still entertained the hope of successful resistance, at least such

as would afford him the safe withdrawal of his army. One*
of his subordinates, at least, advised him to retreat without
further battle; but the necessity or practicability of this step
was not obvious to him, and he made preparations to maintain
his position upon Missionary Ridge.

General Bragg now had his entire army on Missionary
Ridge. Cleburne's and Gist's divisions were on the extreme
right opposed to General Sherman; his left was held by Stewart's division; his center, by Breckinridge's old division, and
portions of the commands of Buckner and Hindman, under
General Anderson; and the divisions of Cheatham and Stevenson, fresh from defeat on Lookout Mountain, were in motion
toward the right. The two parts of his army before Generals
Sherman and Thomas, were commanded respectively by Generals Hardee and Breckinridge.

It was evident early in the morning that General Grant
had misapprehended the degree of General Sherman's success
the evening previous. The ridge had not been carried to the
tunnel, and hence the condition precedent to the co-operation
of Thomas and Sherman in a general attack was yet wanting.
And as the battle had been delayed to enable General Sherman to get into position on the northern extremity of Missionary Ridge, so now the co-operative movement was deferred
that he might carry the one summit between him and the tunnel.
General Thomas' troops were therefore restrained from action
until late in the day, except in the movement of General
Hooker's column toward the enemy's left flank, and the transfer of three divisions to General Sherman.

General Sherman opened the battle of the 25th, in an independent movement, soon after sunrise, by the advance of
Corse's brigade from his right center.

General Corse moved down the southern slope of the second
hill gained the night before, and under a destructive fire as-

* General Hardee's "staff officer" asserted, in his letter, that his chief
advised the withdrawal of the army after the loss of Lookout Mountain,
and in the account of the battle in the Richmond Dispatch, it is stated
that General Bragg gave orders for this movement, and afterward decided
that he had not time to make it, and then massed his forces on Missionary Ridge.

cended toward Cleburne's fortified position.   He gained a
lateral elevation, about eighty yards distant from the enemy's
defenses, and held it firmly.   Advancing repeatedly from this
position, he was as often driven back, and in turn repulsed
every attack of the enemy.   Back and forward, in the alternations of offense and defense, the struggle was long continued
without decisive advantage to either side.   In the meantime,
General Morgan L. Smith's division advanced along the eastern base of the hill, and Loomis' brigade, supporting Corse
on the left, was sustained by the two reserve brigades of General John E. Smith's division.   Morgan L. Smith pressed his
attack to the enemy's works, but gained no permanent lodgment.

The character and issue of this contest was observed by
General Grant from Orchard Knob, and at 10 A. M. he directed
Howard's corps, in position on the left of General Thomas'
line, to General Sherman's support.   This corps, upon arrival,
was formed on the left of Sherman's line, with its own left on
Chickamauga creek, in room of troops that had previously
been sent to the right, to support the attacking column.
General Sherman then had six divisions—three of his own
under General F. P. Blair, Steinwehr's, and Schurz's of
Howard's corps (the Eleventh), and Davis' division of the
Fourteenth Corps.

Pending General Sherman's first series of attacks, there had
been some activity on the right flank of the national army.
Early in the morning, General Thomas had directed General
Hooker to move with the force that he had led from Lookout
valley, except two regiments to hold the mountain, on the
road to Rossville.   Later, he had ordered him to advance
upon the enemy's works, in conjunction with Palmer's corps—
the Fourteenth, using General Sheridan, on the right of the
Fourth Corps, as a pivot.   General Hooker advanced to Chattanooga creek rapidly, but was there delayed to restore a
bridge which the enemy had destroyed in his flight from the
mountain.

It was evident from the issue of the first conflict on the left
of the national line, and from the importance of the position,
that General Bragg would maintain his right flank if possible.

General Sherman was threatening not only to turn that flank, but was also menacing his rear and his depot of supplies at Chickamauga Station. When General Grant gave open emphasis to his determination to turn his right flank, by sending General Howard's corps to General Sherman, General Bragg sent his floating divisions, Cheatham's and Stevenson's, to General Hardee. Thus, both commanding generals massed heavily in the vicinity of the tunnel—General Grant, to give weight to his ruling attack, and General Bragg, to maintain his right against the vast concentration to turn it, deeming his left and center fully secured by the left half of his army. Between the two wings of the Confederate army there was now a chasm, corresponding to the interval separating the columns under Generals Sherman and Thomas.

Soon after General Howard had attained position, General Sherman renewed his effort to turn the enemy's right flank. Corse's* and Buschbeck's brigades again pressed forward, and when the right of their line became exposed, the brigades of John E. Smith advanced in support. The extreme right of the line thus extended, reached well toward the depression or gorge in the western slope, through which the railroad passes to the tunnel. In this gorge, in complete concealment, General Hardee massed a heavy force, and then throwing it upon Smith's brigades drove them in disorder down the hill. This success, however, was only temporary, as this assaulting force was in turn taken in flank by Corse's and Loomis' brigades, and then there was a return to the previous status: Corse's brigade holding the lateral hillock first gained in the morning, with Loomis and Buschbeck in support.

When General Grant perceived that the troops that had advanced almost to the enemy's defenses near the tunnel, had been driven down the slope, true to his purpose of massing forces against the northern extremity of Missionary Ridge, he ordered Baird's division from line on the right of Johnson's to move to General Sherman's support. This order gave General Sherman seven of the thirteen divisions before the enemy.

---

* General Corse having been wounded, Colonel Walcutt assumed command of the brigade.

When Baird moved to the left, General Thomas had eight brigades in line between Chattanooga and the ridge, and General Hooker had seven as far removed on his right as was General Sherman on his left. At noon, when General Grant ordered Baird's division to General Sherman, it could not have been his intention to make an independent movement from his center, since to give overwhelming strength to the turning column on his left, he had detached nearly half of the central forces which were under General Thomas in person. The strength of his left under General Sherman, compared to that of his center under General Thomas was then as seven divisions to eight brigades.

General Baird moved as ordered, following the road on the bank of the river until he had reached the rear of General Sherman's right. He was then informed by the latter that he did not need him, and he then returned to the center and formed his division on the left of Wood. He was ordered to this position to lessen the interval between General Thomas' left and General Sherman's right. His division was in line at 2½ P. M.*

In the meantime, General Hooker had attained position on the enemy's left flank. As soon as the stringers of the bridge across Chattanooga creek were in position, General Osterhaus threw over the Twenty-seventh Missouri, and soon his entire division, which was followed by the remaining forces. The leading regiment was deployed to skirmish and cover the rapid advance toward Rossville. General Hooker directed the Missourians to engage the enemy briskly as soon as he should be met, and when the skirmishing became spirited, he ordered General Osterhaus to move Woods' brigade to the right and Williamson's to the left. Finding his flanks thus endangered, the enemy retreated beyond Rossville. General Hooker then disposed his troops to sweep Missionary Ridge toward the north. He directed General Osterhaus to cross to the east side, General Cruft to advance on the summit, and General Geary on the western slope and edge of the valley. While General Hooker was forming to advance and turn the enemy's

---

* Statements in General Baird's official report.

left flank, other movements were ordered which broke his center and routed his army.

Soon after Baird's return, General Grant ordered an advance from the center. His order expressed the third radical departure from his pre-announced plan. In it, no movement against the enemy by the central forces in independent action had been prescribed, and yet one had already been successfully made. And now, though the instructions for this day required that General Thomas should move in co-operation with General Sherman, an independent assault was ordered. General Grant had waited for Sherman's success in turning the enemy's right flank since early morning; during the afternoon he had expected General Hooker to move against his left. The day was now nearly gone, and some new measure was necessary, or the sun would set with General Bragg in possession of Missionary Ridge. Four insulated divisions were in line in front of General Bragg's center, now held by less than four divisions, as a portion of Stuart's, on the extreme left, under the personal direction of General Breckinridge, had been directed against General Hooker. Wood's and Sheridan's divisions were in the position attained on the 23d, Johnson's was on the right of Sheridan, and Baird on the left of Wood. These divisions were formed by brigades, from right to left, in the following order: Carlin's and Stoughton's of Johnson's; Sherman's, Harker's, and Wagner's of Sheridan's; Hazen's, Willich's, and Beatty's of Wood's, and Turchin's, Vanderveer's, and Phelps' of Baird's. Two lines of skirmishers covered the battle front, and such troops as were designated as reserves were massed in rear of their respective organizations.

Between 3 and 4 P. M. six successive cannon shots from the battery on Orchard Knob gave the signal for the advance. General Grant's order required that the enemy should be dislodged from the rifle-pits and intrenchments at the base of Missionary Ridge. The statement is made in his official report that it was his design that the lines should be readjusted at the base for the assault of the summit; but no such instructions were given to corps or division generals. Neither does it appear from his report whether he meditated an independent assault of the summit from his center, or one co-operative with Sherman on the left, or Hooker on the right, as the original plan prescribed for the former or as the issues of the day suggested for the latter.

As soon as the magnificent lines moved forward, the batteries of the enemy on the ridge opened upon them with great activity. General Brannan's large guns in Fort Wood, Fort Cheatham, Battery Rousseau, and Fort Sheridan, and four light batteries on the intermediate hills, which had not been silent hitherto, gave emphatic response. Their fire was first directed to the enemy's inferior intrenchments, and when this endangered the advancing lines, their missiles were thrown upon the summit. This change of direction was soon necessary, as leaping forward at the signal, the eager troops in rapid movement first met the enemy's pickets and their reserves, then his troops occupying the intervening woods, and finally his stronger line in his lower intrenchments, and drove all in confusion to the crest of the ridge. In vain had General Bragg made effort to strengthen his lower line. The advance of the national troops had been so rapid and their movement had expressed such purpose and power, that the very forces that had so often repeated their furious assaults at Chickamauga lost courage and made no soldierly effort to maintain their position, though supported by at least fifty guns, which, at short range, were fast decimating the assaulting columns.

Having executed their orders to the utmost requirement, holding the enemy's lower defenses, the four divisions stood under his batteries, while the troops they had routed threw themselves behind the stronger intrenchments on the summit. General Bragg's right flank had not been turned as first proposed, and General Hooker's attack on his left, though successful, was too remote to affect immediately the central contest. To stand still was death; to fall back was not compassed by orders, and was forbidden by every impulse of the brave men, who, with no stragglers to mar the symmetry of their line or make scarcely a single exception to universal gallantry, had moved so boldly and so successfully upon the foe. There are occasional moments in battle when brave men do not need commanders, and this was one. The enemy held a position of wonderful strength several hundred feet above them.　He had two lines in one behind earthworks, where nature had provided a fortress.　These men, however, did not stop to consider the enemy's position or strength, but from a common impulse of patriotism and the inspiration of partial success, leaped forward and dashed up the hill.　The color-bearers sprang to the front, and as one fell, another bore the flag aloft and onward, followed by their gallant comrades, not in line, but in such masses as enabled them to avail themselves of easier ascent or partial cover.　They advanced without firing, though receiving a most destructive fire of artillery and musketry, from base to summit.　The officers of all grades caught the spirit of the men, and so eager were men and officers throughout the line, that the crest was reached and carried at six different points almost at the same moment.　The enemy was hurled from position with wonderful quickness; his artillery was captured, and in some cases turned against him as he fled.　General Hooker soon swept northward from Rossville, and then the Army of the Cumberland held Missionary Ridge the whole length of its front.　General Hardee's forces, opposite General Sherman, alone maintained position.

To this general result, each of the four central divisions and those with General Hooker contributed, in co-ordination and harmony unprecedented in an improvised attack.　Each one was successful, though each was not equally prominent in success.　From General Bragg's declaration that his line was first pierced on his right—that is, to the north of the house which he occupied as his headquarters—and from the observation of those occupying elevated positions, there is no room to doubt that General Wood's division first reached the summit.　Sheridan's and Baird's, on the right and left, almost simultaneously gained the crest.　General Wood's troops enfiladed the enemy's line to the right and left as soon as they broke through it, and the other divisions pressed against other points so quickly, that General Bragg's effort to dislodge the troops who first gained his intrenchments by sending General Bate to the right, miscarried at its very inception.　After portions of the several divisions had gained the crest, many isolated contests were conducted with spirit by the enemy, but the fragments of his line were speedily brushed away.

The impulse to carry the summit of the ridge was seemingly spontaneous, though not entirely simultaneous, throughout the four divisions, and from different points several brigades passed beyond the limit fixed by General Grant's order, before there was any concerted action toward a general assault. The division commanders did not arrest their troops, and for a time the corps generals did not give official sanction to their advance. The impression, indeed, so far prevailed, that the movement would not be authorized, that Turchin's, brigade, on the right of Baird's division, was halted when far up the ascent, and Wagner's brigade, on the left of Sheridan's division, was recalled from an advanced position by a staff officer who was returning to General Sheridan from General Granger, with the information that General Grant's order required only that the enemy's intrenched line at the base of the ridge should be carried. Soon, however, it was apparent to all, that the eagerness of the troops had created a necessity superior to the limitations of orders, and this conviction gave unity and energy to an assault, whose transcendent issue justified its otherwise unauthorized execution.

To prevent defeat, Generals Bragg, Hardee, Breckinridge, and others of inferior rank, exerted themselves to the utmost. General Bragg, in the center, was nearly surrounded before he entirely despaired and abandoned the field. General Breckinridge resisted General Hooker, as he ascended the ridge at Rossville, availing himself of the fortifications which had been constructed by the national army after the battle of Chickamauga. His first resistance was quickly overcome by the Ninth and Thirty-sixth regiments of Grose's brigade. General Cruft's division was then formed in four lines on the summit, and with the lateral divisions abreast, moved rapidly forward, driving the enemy in turn from several positions. Many of his troops, that fled east or west, were captured by Osterhaus or Geary, and those who tried to escape northward, fell in Johnson's hands. As soon as General Hardee heard the noise of battle to his left, he hastened to join his troops under General Anderson, on the right of their central line.

But before he could cross the chasm corresponding to the interval between General Sherman's right and General Thomas' left, Anderson's command was thrown into a confused retreat. He then hurried Cheatham's* division from the vicinity of the tunnel, and formed it across the summit to resist Baird's division, which had advanced northward, after carrying its entire front, in the assault. In a severe contest, in which Colonel Phelps, a brigade commander, fell, General Baird pressed this fresh division northward from several knolls, but was finally compelled to abandon the conflict by the peculiar strength of a new position and the approach of darkness.

The victory was gained too late in the day for a general pursuit. General Sheridan's division and Willich's brigade of General Wood's division pursued the enemy for a short distance down the eastern slope. Later, General Sheridan advanced and drove the enemy from a strong position, captured two pieces of artillery, numerous small arms, and several wagons from a supply train.

During the night General Hardee withdrew his forces from the position which he had persistently held against General Sherman.

While General Grant had been hurrying his preparations for the battle, his anxiety for Burnside had been intensified by unavoidable delays. He knew that Burnside's supplies would not permit him to refuse terms of surrender much beyond the 3d of December, and it was by no means certain that he could resist Longstreet as long as his supplies would last. Now that General Bragg had been defeated, General Grant gave attention equally to the pursuit of the routed enemy and the relief of his lieutenant at Knoxville; and during the evening of the 25th, gave orders looking to the accomplishment of both objects. He directed General Thomas to recall the

---

* General Hardee's staff officer said: "At this juncture, matters looked terrible, and I will never forget the look of anguish written on poor General H——'s face. He sent me hurriedly to make some changes in his other divisions, yet intact, and to hurry one forward to stem the tide of defeat." General Bragg's report mentions Cheatham's division as the one performing this service.

Fourth Corps to prepare for forced marches to Knoxville, and in conjunction with General Sherman to pursue the enemy with his available troops. Accordingly, General Thomas ordered Wood's and Sheridan's divisions to return to Chattanooga, and Generals Hooker and Palmer—the latter with two divisions—to move in pursuit of the enemy.

These generals moved on the morning of the 26th, as ordered, Hooker leading. On reaching the West Chickamauga, Hooker found that the bridge had been destroyed and that the water was too deep for fording. Pontoons had been ordered for such emergencies, but none were up, and the columns were delayed until a temporary bridge could be constructed. After some hours, the men crossed the bridge, the horses swam the stream, and pursuit was resumed without artillery. At Peavine creek there was another stop from similar cause. A bridge was here constructed as quickly as possible, and the troops crossed and moved forward. At this creek the road forks, the right branch leading to Ringgold, the left to Graysville. Hooker took the former and Palmer the latter. Carlin's brigade leading, toward Graysville, soon heard the noise of men and wagons in motion. As the proximity of the enemy was thus revealed, dispositions were made to intercept him if possible. At 9 P. M. his rear-guard was overtaken, and upon receiving a volley from Stoughton's brigade, fled in all directions. The troops proved to be a remnant of Stewart's division, that Hooker had handled so roughly on the ridge the evening previous, and in flight left behind them three Napoleon guns, their colors, and a large number of small arms.

The pursuit was continued, and at 11 P. M. a brigade of the enemy was routed at Graysville, and one gun and a number of prisoners were captured.

On the following morning the two columns advanced to Ringgold. The artillery was still behind, as the pontoon bridges had not been thrown, but the enemy was nevertheless closely pursued. Before reaching the East Chickamauga creek, many captures were made, and the enemy was driven from the bridge and pursued into the town. But a stand was made, beyond where the railroad passes through the gap in Taylor's ridge. General Hooker was still without artillery, but he determined to feel the enemy at once. Accordingly, skirmishers advanced, and Woods' brigade deployed in their rear under cover of the railroad embankment. The skirmish line of the enemy was soon driven upon the main line, and the exact position of a battery which had been very active was ascertained. To silence the battery by picking off the gunners, the Thirteenth Illinois regiment was thrown forward to seize some houses at suitable distance for this purpose. This movement provoked the enemy to advance against Woods' line. His skirmishers fell back, and the main line repulsed the enemy most handsomely, and followed into the gorge. Cleburne's division was engaged, and its dead and wounded were abandoned as it gave ground. In the meantime, Osterhaus had detached four regiments under Colonel Williamson to move a half mile to the left, ascend a hill, and turn the enemy's right. The enemy was found in heavy force, and Colonel Creighton with four more regiments was sent still farther to the left. Attacks were then made by both Williamson and Creighton, but despite the display of great daring, the troops of both were repulsed with heavy loss. Creighton's brigade held position on the side of the ridge, well sheltered in a depression, and Williamson's returned to the railroad. The enemy having been developed in force in a strong position, troops were moved to support those who had been engaged, and the action was arrested in waiting for the artillery. Between 12 and 1 P. M. the guns came upon the field and were put in position, and other dispositions were made to renew the attack. The heavy guns were planted to enfilade the gorge, and a regiment was sent to ascend the hill on the right, to throw a plunging fire upon the enemy below. But the enemy had succeeded in delaying pursuit, which was the object of his resistance, and upon the opening of Hooker's guns, withdrew, attempting to burn the bridges beyond the town. He was so closely followed, however, that the bridges were saved.

General Grant having reached the field, gave orders to discontinue the pursuit. But in the afternoon, to make the impression of purpose to pursue, Colonel Grose was sent forward with his brigade toward Tunnel Hill. Grose soon encountered the enemy's cavalry and drove the force upon the infantry.　Ascertaining that there was a strong column in a strong position, he returned to Ringgold.

General Hooker lost, according to his report, sixty-five killed and three hundred and seventy-seven wounded; Colonel Creighton and many other officers fell.　The enemy left one hundred and thirty dead upon the field, and two hundred and thirty as prisoners; his wounded was not computed.

Very early on the morning of the 26th, General Davis was ordered by General Sherman to cross his division on the pontoon bridge at the mouth of the Chickamauga and pursue the enemy, and General Howard was ordered to repair a bridge two miles up the creek and follow.　The repair of the bridge threatening too much delay, the latter moved down the stream, and crossing his corps on the pontoon bridge, moved on toward the depot of Bragg's army at Chickamauga Station.　Davis, in advance, reached that point at 11 A. M., in time to witness the burning of the depot building and the greater portion of the supplies.　A short distance beyond, the enemy was found partially intrenched, but was speedily forced to retreat; General Davis pursued and at dark overtook the enemy, when a sharp conflict ensued, but the darkness covered his escape.　In the morning, Davis reached Graysville, and found himself in rear of Hooker's command, which he followed to Ringgold.

General Howard advanced through Parker's Gap, farther east, and detached a column to destroy railroad communications between Bragg and Longstreet.　Having destroyed a large section of the railroad between Dalton and Cleveland, the detached forces joined the corps.

These movements terminated the pursuit of the enemy. Burnside's condition was exceedingly critical, and General Grant deemed his relief and the continued possession of East Tennessee more important than the farther pursuit of Bragg. He therefore directed General Sherman to give his troops a rest of one day before starting to raise the siege of Knoxville. In consideration of the importance of promptly relieving Burnside, General Grant committed the enterprise to Sherman, giving him Howard's and Granger's corps, and Davis' division of the Fourteenth, in addition to the three divisions of his own.

The destruction of railroad by Howard's troops, added to the results of Long's raid, effectually prevented the passage of troops by rail from Bragg to Longstreet, or from the latter to the former, if their future plans should require such transfer. Colonel Long having moved on the flank of General Sherman's forces, as directed, crossed the river on the 24th, on the pontoon bridge, and reached Tyner's station on the Knoxville road that night, destroying supplies and rolling-stock at that point. Colonel Long then proceeded to Ooltawah, and captured several wagons loaded with forage. At Cleveland he destroyed a copper-rolling mill, and a large depot of commissary and ordnance stores. From Cleveland he moved rapidly to Charleston, hoping to capture a large wagon train which had been detained there by the parting of a pontoon bridge. Learning, however, that the bridge had been connected, and that the train was beyond his reach, as there was a large force of the enemy on the opposite shore, he returned to Cleveland. Then, having damaged the railroad for several miles toward Dalton, he moved in safety to Chattanooga.

General Grant ordered General Hooker to remain at Ringgold until the 30th, to cover General Sherman's movement toward Knoxville, and keep up the semblance of pursuit.

The official reports of the commanders-in-chief of the two armies do not give their strength. It is probable that General Grant had sixty thousand men in action, and General Bragg forty thousand. The former had thirteen divisions, including two detached brigades, and the latter had eight, with perhaps a corresponding diminution.

General Bragg's loss in killed and wounded is not known. He lost by capture six thousand one hundred and forty-two men, forty-two guns, sixty-nine gun-carriages, and seven thousand stand of small arms. His loss in material was immense, part of which he destroyed in his flight, but a large fraction, which was uninjured, fell to the national army.

The aggregate losses of the armies of the Cumberland and Tennessee were seven hundred and fifty-seven killed, four thousand five hundred and twenty-nine wounded, and three hundred and thirty missing. These losses were small compared with those of other battles of similar proportions, and exceedingly small in view of the fact that the enemy generally resisted behind intrenchments.

These engagements, in general issue, were exceedingly decisive, both in their proximate and more palpable results, and in their remote and more occult consequences. The blood of " Chickamauga," " Wauhatchie," " Lookout Mountain," " Missionary Ridge," and " Ringgold," and even that of anterior battles, had been directly shed in decision of the question whether a national or Confederate army should hold Chattanooga—a position inviting to each for defense or aggression. Fortified in its outer lines by ranges of mountains, after the battle of Chickamauga, it had been made strong in its inner lines by a broad and high circumvallation, manifold forts and redoubts, and heavy guns. Situated at the confluence of many streams, the diverging valleys suggested aggressive marches, and especially as the gateway to Georgia it was the natural base for an overland bisection of the Gulf States. This martial throne, dominant of strategy far and near, had been the objective of the Army of the Cumberland for nearly two years, and as the result of a battle compassing all the elements of the most brilliant warfare, it fell in perpetuity to its possession, when this grand army cheered in proudest triumph on the crest of Missionary Ridge. The mere possession of Chattanooga, while Bragg's lines stretched over mountain, plain, and hill, from the river on the southwest to the river on the northeast, was of little moment. But the Southern leaders and people knew that a national army at Chattanooga, with full mastery of river, railroads, and diverging routes of aggression, was a direct menace to the existence of the rebellion. And the issue of the battle which gave the Army of the Cumberland the fruits of all its conflicts in Kentucky, Tennessee, and Georgia, produced a startling surprise throughout the South. It is true that there were some in the South who said that the loss of Lookout Valley was equivalent to the loss of Chattanooga. But, as Bragg had detached Longstreet's corps after this loss, and held his lines, notwithstanding the gathering of Grant's forces at Chattanooga, the hope was entertained, that if he could not retake the place, he could at least neutralize it as a base for offensive operations, and the Southern people were not prepared for the rout of his army from a position deemed impregnable. And his own official acknowledgment of the total defeat and panic of his army was couched in language which made prominent his own surprise at the issue. He said, " The position ought to have been held by a skirmish line against any assaulting column." This statement, though expressive of his opinion of the strength of his position, was by no means true. No skirmish line could have held Missionary Ridge against even a small portion of the brave men who dashed up the steep acclivity. Besides, it was not altogether surprising that his troops were routed. The moral forces were with the assaulting column. The peculiar features of the field revealed to the enemy the transcendant array of the national troops. The battle had opened with the splendid charge of Wood's division, and Lookout Mountain had been wrested from his hands in such a way as to change the martial tone of each army. Those assaulting Missionary Ridge had Chickamauga to avenge, and Lookout Mountain to surpass. And the dashing, yet firm and resolute sweep of the assaulting column for more than a mile, expressed in advance the resistless character of the attack. When more than a half-hundred battle flags, forming the foremost line, approached the crest, the Confederate soldiers knew that they would wave over their defenses, or those who bore them, and a moiety of the twenty thousand men who followed, would fall. The men who fled before this revelation of strength and fiery inspiration, had proved themselves brave on other fields, and were perhaps less to blame than their impassive general, who had failed to perceive the ruling conditions of the battle. The loss of more than twenty per cent. in the two central divisions, in a contest of less than an hour, shows that the enemy did not yield his position without a struggle. There was a panic, but its cause was not mere fear, but the overwhelming impression that resistance was useless.

HISTORY

OF THE

ARMY OF THE CUMBERLAND.

CHAPTER XXIII.

CAMPAIGN IN EAST TENNESSEE AND MINOR OPERATIONS IN THE DEPARTMENT OF THE CUMBERLAND.

GENERAL BURNSIDE had been informed that he should have help as soon as practicable, when first it was known that General Longstreet had been sent against him. General Grant said to him that he could hardly conceive the necessity of retreating from East Tennessee. But as the issue at Chattanooga, though glorious in its coming, had been delayed, it became imperative at once to make effort to raise the siege of Knoxville.

November 29th, General Howard marched from Parker's Gap to Cleveland, taking the lead in the movement upon Knoxville. He was followed immediately by General Sherman's three divisions, under General F. P. Blair, and General Davis' division of the Fourteenth Corps. On the 30th, General Granger left Chattanooga with two divisions of the Fourth Corps for the same destination.

Brigadier-General Elliot, who had recently been appointed chief of cavalry in the Department of the Cumberland, and who had concentrated the troops of his first division at Sparta, moved in conjunction with the infantry forces. Colonel

Long's brigade moved to the head of the column, and on the 2d of December, the Fifteenth Pennsylvania and Tenth Ohio Cavalry left Chattanooga for Kingston. Colonel Spears' brigade, that had been previously stationed on the north bank of the Tennessee river above Chattanooga, also moved toward Knoxville. General Sherman's command embraced more than eight divisions of infantry, while five were left to garrison Chattanooga. Supplies for the troops in motion were sent up the river on the steamer Dunbar, but the main dependence was upon the country.

On the 30th, General Howard advanced from Cleveland to Charleston, on the Hiawassee river. As he approached the town, the enemy's cavalry retreated toward Athens. They had previously partially destroyed the railroad bridge, and had made effort to destroy the pontoons also. But a large number of the boats were saved, and during the following night the railroad bridge was repaired and planked over, so that in the morning the Eleventh Corps passed over, followed by the rear forces. The head of column reached Athens the next evening. The march of the infantry was resumed on the 2d and Colonel Long hurried on to Loudon to save the bridge, if possible. He, however, found the enemy in such force that he could not make a dash, as had been anticipated. The town was well fortified, and was held by infantry and artillery, under General Vaughan, and he could only skirmish until General Howard should get up. The latter reached the position on the 3d, but the enemy had evacuated it the night previous, having first destroyed the bridge, three locomotives, and from sixty to seventy-five cars containing commissary stores, clothing, and ammunition. The pontoon bridge had also been partially destroyed. Notwithstanding the immense destruction of supplies, three days' rations were found uninjured. From this point, Colonel Long was sent with picked men to communicate with General Burnside. On the 4th, Colonel Hecker's brigade crossed the river, skirmished with the cavalry, and took possession of four rifled cannon, which the enemy could remove, and captured a flag. Here General Howard found about thirty wagons partially destroyed, which he repaired for use in forming a temporary bridge, in anticipation of crossing the Little Tennessee river at Davis' ford. The route by this ford was not the one which had been designated, but it was ascertained that time could be saved, and the march shortened by advancing upon it rather than upon the road to Morgantown, and General Sherman permitted General Howard to use it.

Before leaving Loudon, General Howard received an order to command the left wing of the army, while the center and righ twere placed respectively under Generals Granger and Blair. These divisions of the army were to act independently, but to march to each other's support when called by the noise of battle.

December 5th, General Howard crossed the Little Tennessee river, at Davis' ford, by means of an extemporized bridge formed of wagons and movable trestles, and reached Louisville at dark. At night, the three heads of column communicated at Marysville. Here information was received that Longstreet had raised the siege of Knoxville, and retreated eastward. He assaulted Fort Sanders, the key to the position, on the 29th, and was repulsed with heavy loss. Aware, subsequently, of the proximity of Sherman's army, he sought safety in timely retreat. All the forces were now ordered to halt, and the day following, General Sherman met General Burnside at Knoxville. It was then agreed that the Fourth Corps should remain and the other forces return to Chattanooga.

The countermarch was commenced on the 7th. A halt was made at Athens, with the various columns so disposed as to cover a movement of Colonel Long, who had gone toward North Carolina to cut off one of Longstreet's trains. Upon his return, the infantry forces marched to Chattanooga. Howard's corps and Davis' division resumed their old relations in the Army of the Cumberland, and Sherman's divisions returned to the West.

Though the march to East Tennessee involved no serious fighting with Longstreet's command, which was lost to General Bragg in his emergency at Chattanooga, it nevertheless thoroughly accomplished its object, as it forced the former from Knoxville toward the East, in what proved to be perpetual separation from the Confederate Army of the Tennessee. It was a hard march, as the troops commenced it immediately after a series of engagements, and Sherman's forces after a long march from the West. The latter had " stripped for the fight" at Bridgeport, and they, with many from other commands, were destitute of suitable clothing for a winter campaign. Besides, their supplies were drawn mainly from the country, and in a hurried movement this source is exceedingly precarious. Supplies were sent up the river in boats it is true, but the army was not always near the river; and, on the whole, the circumstances were such as none but veteran soldiers would easily overcome. The mills were seized in advance, and run night and day; and a broad belt of country in the march and countermarch paid exhaustive contributions. There were some excesses which were reprehensible, especially as the march was through a region whose inhabitants were mainly loyal. General Davis' division, by its order on the march and its restraint from pillage, elicited special praise from General Sherman. In this commendable and conspicuous bearing, this division represented the Army of the Cumberland, which, throughout its existence, was systematically restrained from pillage and irresponsible foraging.

The objects now were to hold all the territory which had been gained, to maintain and perfect communications, reinforce, recuperate, and reorganize the army, and accumulate supplies and material, all looking to offensive movements, as early as practicable. The enemy was in no condition for aggression on a grand scale, but great vigilance and skillful dispositions were necessary to maintain communications and prevent cavalry raids and guerrilla depredations.

Upon the withdrawal of the troops from Ringgold, General Hooker resumed the occupation of Lookout valley. General Cruft was directed, with his two brigades, to stop on the way and bury the national dead on the battle-field of Chickamauga,* and then to take position on the railroad between

* War's visage, despite the glory of heroism and victory, and all the gentle courtesies which enemies may extend at all times, except when the rage of battle brooks no restraint, is grim and forbidding; but when the ordinary usages of civilized and Christian nations in the conduct of

Whitesides and Bridgeport. Colonel Watkins' brigade of the First division of cavalry was directed to take post at Rossville; and the Ninety-second Illinois Mounted Infantry was sent to Caperton's ferry, to guard and observe at that point. A pioneer brigade, composed of detachments from various regiments, Colonel G. P. Buell commanding, was employed in the construction of a double-track macadamized road over the nose of Lookout Mountain, to serve as a communication between Lookout valley and Chattanooga, without dependence upon pontoon bridges. Beyond this primary use, this road was essential to overland communications with Bridgeport. The repair of the railroad commanded immediate attention, but as two long and high bridges were to be built—one over the Tennessee river at Bridgeport, and the one over Falling Water, near Whitesides—much time was required.

When the army returned from East Tennessee, the Eleventh Corps went into camp at Whitesides; two brigades of Davis' division, east of Missionary Ridge, near Rossville; and the third at the mouth of the North Chickamauga. General Elliott was ordered to establish his headquarters at Athens, and post pickets at Calhoun, Columbus, and Tellico Plains.

During the months of November and December, there were several brilliant contests in resisting the enemy's cavalry, repressing guerrillas, and scouting to the front to ascertain the strength and movements of the enemy. And in most cases the national troops were victorious.

November 2d, Brigadier-General R. S. Granger, command-

---

war are ignored, then are its features forbidding in the extreme. The carnage and suffering are appalling when cool reflection and the kindly sympathies have play; but all strong terms are inadequate to express the wanton barbarities of war, either in cruelty to the living or dishonor to the dead, and on both counts the leaders of the rebellion must be convicted. Andersonville and other prisons, where starvation and want of room for captives entailed the intensest suffering and fearful mortality, and Chickamauga, with its hundreds of unburied dead, give proof of the most revolting inhumanity. General Bragg accepted an exchange of prisoners who were wounded, but he denied burial to multitudes of the slain. The national dead upon that part of the field occupied by General Longstreet were buried; but very many on their right, where General Polk commanded, lay upon the ground for two months.

ing at Nashville, sent a mixed command, under Lieutenant-Colonel Sculley, First Middle Tennessee Infantry, to look after Hawkins, and other guerrilla chiefs, near Piner's factory. Sculley met them, and having routed the party, pursued to Centerville. At this point, as he was crossing the river, Hawkins attacked in turn, but was again routed, and his partisans were dispersed. His loss was from fifteen to twenty killed, and sixty-six prisoners.

November 4th, Major Fitzgibbon, of the Fourteenth Michigan Infantry, fought near Lawrenceburg the guerrilla bands of Cooper, Kirk, Williams, and Scott. After a hand-to-hand contest, Fitzgibbon defeated them, killing eight, wounding seven, and capturing twenty-four men. Among the captured were a captain and two lieutenants. The victor had three men slightly wounded, and eight horses killed.

On the 13th, Captain Cutler, with one company of mounted infantry from the garrison at Clarksville, and a section of Whitmore's battery, had a contest with Captain Gray's company of guerrillas, near Palmyra. He killed two, wounded five, and captured one. The same day, fifteen prisoners were captured near Lebanon, and forty by Missener, near Columbia.

On the 16th, General Payne sent parties from Gallatin and La Vergne. Five guerrillas were killed, and twenty-six were captured, also horses, cattle, sheep, and hogs, which had been collected for the Confederate army.

The next day, Colonel Coburn sent an expedition from Murfreesboro against the enemy's irregular cavalry. A detachment of the Fourth Tennessee Cavalry captured nineteen guerrillas and twenty horses, without loss.

On the 21st, an expedition was sent down the Tennessee river, which destroyed nine boats for local use, some of them being sixty feet long. They were wrested from the enemy.

On the 26th, the First Tennessee Cavalry and Ninth Pennsylvania Cavalry, under Colonel Brownlow, attacked Colonel Murray, at Sparta. He killed one man, wounded two, and captured ten. Extensive salt-works were destroyed, and some horses and ammunition were taken.

The same day, Captain Brixie's scouts encountered a party

of guerrillas near Bathsheba Springs, capturing fifteen or twenty, and dispersing the remainder.

December 12th, Colonel Watkins, with two hundred and fifty men, from the Fourth and Sixth Kentucky Cavalry, made a dash upon Lafayette, Georgia, and captured a colonel of the Georgia home guard, six officers of the signal corps, and thirty horses and mules, and returned to his camp at Rossville, without loss. On the 27th, the colonel sent Major Willing, with one hundred and fifty men from the same regiments, to McLemore's Cove and Lafayette. The major captured one lieutenant, sixteen men, and thirty-eight horses and mules.

On the 15th, General Dodge captured a small party of cavalry, under command of Major Joe Fontaine, General Roddy's adjutant, not far from Pulaski, Tennessee. This party had made a reconnoissance on the Nashville and Chattanooga and Nashville and Decatur railroads, which doubtless had some relation to projected movements or raids. It suggested greater vigilance along these important roads.

December 27th, General Wheeler, with fifteen hundred men, appeared at Calhoun, Tennessee, with evident expectation of capturing a train under escort of Laiboldt's brigade. Colonel Laiboldt charged this force, and routed it speedily, and Colonel Long, with one hundred and fifty men, having come from the opposite side of the river, in support, moved in pursuit, believing that a small force had been cut off from the main body. By a saber charge, this force was scattered in all directions. One hundred and thirty-one prisoners were taken, including five officers, one a division inspector and one a surgeon. The number of killed and wounded was not ascertained. Colonel Long lost two killed, twelve wounded, and one missing. Wheeler commanded in person, and anticipated rich booty with slight trouble, but failed in his object, with heavy loss.

CHAPTER XXIV.

GENERAL VIEW OF THE STATUS OF THE CONFLICT AT THE CLOSE
OF 1863.

THE year 1863 was crowded with disaster to the insurgents. They were victorious in some of the great battles in Virginia, but lost fearfully in the battle of Gettysburg. So that, at the East, where only they had been at all successful, their strength was relatively less than at the beginning of the year. In the West, their losses in men, material of war, and territory were immense. In their effort to maintain their hold upon the Mississippi river, they lost two armies, and when subsequently the " Father of Waters " flowed "unvexed to the sea," and the supremacy of the national navy upon this great river and its tributaries was unquestioned, all contiguous portions of the insurgent states were at the mercy of the national armies. At the close of the year the central offensive line was resting upon the northern limits of Alabama, Georgia, and North Carolina. The loss of so much territory, the complete division of what remained by the navy moving at pleasure upon the Mississippi river, and the immense diminution of men and means, gave new conditions to the campaigns of the next year.

Besides the effect of numerous defeats during the year, two proclamations of the President of the United States greatly alarmed the insurgents. On the 1st day of January, 1863, he proclaimed freedom to all the slaves in the revolted states, and in the last month he promised pardon to all below a given grade, in the insurgent armies.

As a sequence of the freedom of the slaves, and as a war measure of great moment, arms were soon put in their hands.

At first, however, the enrollment of the freedmen as soldiers was only occasionally undertaken by individual department commanders in absence of any general plan or explicit authority from Washington. Though slavery directly and indirectly was the dominant cause of the war, there was manifest reluctance for nearly three years to lay hands upon it, and after its abolition was decreed, the national authorities hesitated to make soldiers of those whose bondage they had broken. The slaves had aided the enemy not only by their productive labor, but also by the construction of defenses, and contributed to the strength of the rebellion in greater measure, than they had previously given political weight to the Southern States, in Congress. The more moderate and far-seeing men of the South anticipated, from the first, that sooner or later the African race would be involved in the war. And later than many of this class anticipated, and a growing party in the North demanded, the President pronounced the freedom of the negroes in the seceded states. Their enlistment as soldiers was so plainly a legitimate consequent that it was not long delayed. Both measures were repugnant to the traditional and inveterate prejudices of the Southern people, and of many in the North as well. In the official utterances of the Confederate President, the reprehension of the civilized world was invoked upon those who proposed these measures, and the total destruction of the Africans in America was predicted. But the argument in their support was so simple and forcible that serious opposition to either soon ceased in the North. As the slaves were a source of strength to the rebellion, the logic of war first declared them contraband, and then demanded their employment as soldiers. The fact that their freedom was contingent upon the overthrow of the Southern Confederacy, not only justified their grasp of the musket, but enforced its obligation. And the results vindicated the policy, as colored regiments greatly augmented the national armies for the campaigns of 1864.

The President's offer of pardon to the masses in the Confederate armies, had marked effect. It gave assurance that peace could ensue without the entailment of penal criminality upon those in arms against the government below the rank of brigadier-general, and hence removed the necessity that mere desperation should keep them under the standards of treason. And as this promise of amnesty involved no hard conditions, and was made at a time of general despondency in the South, and when such was the depreciation of Confederate money, that no poor man could give even partial support to a family from his pay as a soldier, it prompted numerous desertions. Desertion being added to the drain of active campaigns, the diminution of the insurgent armies became alarming to the leaders. But they still claimed that the independence of the Southern States was assured, and on this ground, in part justified a conscription of widest compass. The people did not bear this patiently. Murmurs of discontent became general. Occasionally there was open protest and severest criticism. But as nothing but counter-revolution could remedy the evil, and as this step plainly led through anarchy to submission to the general government, the relentless conscription of young and old, and the sweeping appropriation of private property was endured. As a result, sullenness and discouragement took the place of cheer and hope in their armies, and outward restraint rather than moral force kept multitudes in the ranks; while the certainty of pardon, in the event of the failure of the rebellion, induced those not ready to desert to weigh the cost of protracting a contest when success was extremely doubtful. But the leaders, after a year of gigantic reverses, standing upon the threshhold of new campaigns with diminished armies, as boldly as ever declared that subjugation was impossible. President Davis, in his annual message to his congress, announced that " grave reverses had befallen the Confederate armies," and that the hope of a speedy termination of the war, entertained at the beginning of the year, had not been realized, and yet asserted that peace could only come with the acknowledgment of the independence of the Confederate States. Even after General Lee's defeat at Gettysburg, the fall of Vicksburg and Port Hudson, and the retreat of General Bragg's army over Cumberland Mountains, M. T. Maury assured the world, in a paper published in the " London Times," that the prospect of success to the South was brighter than at any former period of the war. Whether this assurance was real or assumed, on the part of the leaders, and whether they had to any great extent the sympathy of the masses in their avowed hopes, such was the power of the Confederate government and the momentum of the rebellion, that armies of fair defensive proportions were maintained, and some of the Southern generals even entertained projects of aggression.

The events of the year as affecting the national cause, viewed from a military or political stand-point, were cheering in the extreme. The victories of the national armies and the support of war measures as evinced by the elections, equally indicated that the crisis of the nation's destiny had been safely passed. The strength of the rebellion had culminated, and the general situation gave encouragement to the government and those who supported it, to strike blow after blow until the final one should be given. The elections declared the nation's approval of the President's proclamation of freedom to the slaves, and the policy of making them soldiers, and universal freedom was now as firmly established as a condition of peace as the surrender of the Confederate armies.

The maintenance of the full strength of the national armies was now the grand problem. The term of enlistment of very many regiments would expire early in 1864. Their retirement during active operations would endanger the success of all plans of aggression which might be formed. In fact, the speedy suppression of the rebellion turned upon their retention in the service, and yet there was no law to hold them. Fortunately for the country her citizen soldiers were equal to the emergency, and their voluntary re-enlistment, more stringent drafting, and the enrollment of the freedmen, gave promise of adequate armies.

It was evident at the close of the year that the Army of the Cumberland was again to confront its old enemy, the Army of the Tennessee. After its defeat at Chattanooga, this army took position at Dalton, with a heavy detachment at Buzzard's Roost, and forces also at the strong positions between Dalton and Atlanta. The Western and Atlantic railroad courses through the hills and mountains of Northern Georgia, which give marked advantage to an army acting on the defensive, against another dependent upon the railroad for supplies.   And before the exact character of the next central campaign could be determined, the Confederate generals exerted themselves to give additional strength to the fortresses which nature had provided.   Whether they should be able to take the offensive or not, their past experience suggested the propriety of making provision for defense as far to the rear as practicable, while maintaining a strong defensive front.

CHAPTER XXV.

OPERATIONS IN THE DEPARTMENT DURING JANUARY, FEBRUARY, AND MARCH, 1864, AND PREPARATIONS FOR AGGRESSION.

AT the beginning of the year 1864, and during the first months of the year, the troops of the Army of the Cumberland were disposed from Knoxville to Bridgeport, and on the railroad from the latter place to Louisville, Kentucky. The attitude of the army was mainly defensive. In fact, it was in no condition for aggression. At least ten thousand animals had died during the siege of Chattanooga, and those which survived were so reduced in strength as to be unfit for service. The army, too, was temporarily weakened by the absence of numerous regiments that had been granted furloughs upon re-enlistment; and previous to the completion of the railroad between Chattanooga and Bridgeport, it was hardly possible to supply the troops at rest on the defensive line, including the Army of the Ohio in East Tennessee. Thus restrained from active operations, its chief duty was preparation for future aggression.

As the primary step, it was imperative to make Chattanooga a reliable proximate base of supplies for an army advancing toward Atlanta. The Confederate army being in winter-quarters in Northern Georgia, could destroy all the productions of that region which it did not consume or transport. So that the accumulation of supplies at Chattanooga, and the continued maintenance of railroad communications with Nashville and Louisville, were conditions of a southward advance; and the practicability of making Chattanooga a base for offensive operations, hinged upon the capacity of a single railroad.

Two railroads from Nashville meet at Stevenson, Alabama, but from their junction to Bridgeport, and thence to Chat-

tanooga, there is only a single track. As the bridges at Bridgeport and Falling Waters were not completed until the 14th of
January, half the winter was gone before there was the slightest
accumulation of supplies; and though subsequently this single
railroad was pressed to its utmost capacity, such were the immediate wants of the armies, and so numerous were the veteran regiments passing over the road, that the large storehouses which had been built at Chattanooga were very slowly
filled.

During the first half of January, the enemy was not active.
General Thomas sent scouting parties in all directions, but no
indications of aggression were discerned. Apart from the exhaustion which the preceding campaigns had produced, a
change of commanders was doubtless one cause of inaction.
Soon after his defeat before Chattanooga, General Bragg had
been removed from command in Georgia, and General Joseph
E. Johnston, while charged with the administration of a military division corresponding in extent to the one which had
been created for General Grant, assumed personal command of
the forces immediately south of Chattanooga. His presence
at Dalton indicated his appreciation of the importance of the
center of his line, either to regain what had been so recently
lost, or to neutralize Chattanooga, as far as possible, as a base
for aggressive operations.

By this time, the foreshadows of the campaign which General Grant had projected began to appear. Mobile was his
next objective, with Atlanta and Mongomery as important
intermediate points.* Not being ready to advance upon the
direct line to his objective, he proposed a movement from
his right flank by General Sherman, while General Thomas
should make effort to hold Johnston's forces at Dalton, and
General Foster, commanding in East Tennessee in room of
General Burnside, should neutralize Longstreet's army. The
objects proposed for General Sherman were the destruction of
the railroads from Vicksburg to Meridian, and the capture of
Mobile, should its practicability be developed as he advanced.
But before he was ready to move, rumors were current that

---

* Statement of plan by General Badeau, in "Life of General Grant."

Longstreet was receiving reinforcements from Virginia. This deranged the plans with regard to the center and left. General Thomas was desirous of recalling his troops from East Tennessee, to be able to demonstrate strongly against Dalton; but it now became necessary that he should have regard to the contingency of sending additional troops to General Foster.

General Longstreet's attitude had been ambiguous since his abandonment of the siege of Knoxville, upon the approach of General Sherman, in December. His presence was a menace, even in absence of operations of direct offense; and as it was possible for reinforcements to reach him from Dalton and from Virginia, an effort to regain the mountain fortresses of East Tennessee was probable, especially if General Johnston could entertain the hope of keeping the war out of Georgia by carrying it to the North. Any plan of aggression on his part would involve the possession of a route to the northeast of Chattanooga, and for a time such a course was plainly indicated or feigned.

When, on the 15th of January, General Wood advanced to Dandridge and drove the rebel cavalry from the town, an offensive return was provoked, which for a time threatened to change General Grant's plans very materially. Though General Wood was joined by General Sheridan's division and McCook's cavalry at Dandridge, it was not deemed safe to hazard a general engagement. For two days there was skirmishing, and late in the afternoon of the 18th, there was a brisk conflict mainly between McCook's cavalry and Longstreet's advance. Three Ohio regiments—the First, Ninety-third, and One Hundred and Twenty-fifth—were holding the front as pickets, and were severely pressed by a tentative advance of the enemy, but they fought bravely to cover the preparations for a retreat. McCook, by a saber charge, cleared the field and captured two steel rifle-guns, and over one hundred prisoners. This action and the darkness permitted the safe retreat of the national troops. They fell back, first to Strawberry Plains, and subsequently to Marysville, followed by Longstreet.

Simultaneously with this movement, General Roddy crossed the Tennessee river near Florence, Alabama, with two brigades of cavalry. General Dodge, commanding troops of General Sherman's army at Pulaski, Tennessee, received information on the 20th, that he was preparing boats and concealing them with the evident purpose of crossing his command for a raid upon the railroads. General Grant at once advised General Thomas of the fact, and directed him to organize an expedition to drive Roddy back, and destroy his boats and all material which could be used in effecting the passage of the river. But he was across two days before these instructions were communicated, and General Thomas could only make arrangements to defeat his purpose. He directed the detachments guarding the roads to watch against attacks, and ordered General Crook commanding cavalry at Huntsville, Alabama, to advance against Roddy and drive him across the river.

Colonel H. O. Miller, Ninety-second Indiana, commanding one expedition, defeated Johnson's brigade near Florence on the 26th, killing fifteen, and wounding and capturing a large number. Among the prisoners were three officers. His own loss was ten wounded. General Gillem also sent parties from the line of the Northwestern railroad against Roddy, as soon as he heard that he had crossed the river. These parties returned on the 30th with Lieutenant-Colonel Brewer, two captains, three lieutenants, and twenty men as prisoners. Having thus met forces between him and the railroad in all directions, Roddy recrossed the river, having effected no damage that compensated for his losses.

January 27th, the cavalry under General Elliott, in a brilliant action at Mossy Creek, East Tennessee, defeated General Martin, commanding two divisions of cavalry, Morgan's and Armstrong's, and followed his routed forces until darkness terminated the pursuit. Campbell's and La Grange's brigades were engaged, and they put the enemy to rout by a saber charge, capturing one hundred and twelve prisoners, including two regimental commanders and seven other officers, two rifled guns, eight hundred small arms, Morgan's battle-flag, and two regimental flags, which the enemy had previously captured from the national troops, and killed and wounded over two hundred men, exclusive of prisoners. Morgan's division was thoroughly broken, and Armstrong's was thrown into rapid retreat. Guerrillas were also active. January 20th, one hundred and fifty guerrillas attacked Tracy City, and having three times summoned the garrison to surrender, were handsomely repulsed.

The next day, Colonel T. J. Harrison, Thirty-ninth Indiana Mounted Infantry, sent two hundred men on an expedition to Sparta, Tennessee, to look after the guerrillas infesting that region. This party in five subdivisions scoured the country occupied by the bands of Curtis, Ferguson, Bledsoe, and Murray. Remaining out several days, they killed four men, wounded five or six, and captured fifteen, including a captain and lieutenant. They also captured thirty horses and twenty stand of arms.

On the 24th, Colonel Boone, commanding the Twenty-eighth Kentucky Mounted Infantry, with four hundred and forty-six men, moved through McLemore's Cove, crossed to Broomtown valley, and proceeded through Summerville, across Taylor's ridge, to Dirt Town. Beyond the latter place he destroyed a camp of the Georgia militia, captured fifteen men, including Captain Hubbard, and returned without loss.

Upon the completion of the railroad from Bridgeport to Chattanooga, General Thomas transferred the working parties to the road leading to Knoxville, and on the 24th directed General Stanley, commanding the First division of the Fourth Corps, to dispose his command from Chickamauga Station to the Hiawassee river, to protect the workmen on the road. As it had been suggested that troops might be sent to East Tennessee to support Foster against Longstreet, these troops were thus in readiness to meet this contingency while guarding the railroad, and watching against the direct movement of troops from Dalton to Longstreet.

As deserters concurred in asserting that General Johnston was sending troops south from Dalton, General Thomas directed General Palmer to make a reconnoissance with a portion of his command to ascertain, if possible, whether these representations were true. The latter having accomplished his office by developing a strong force at Tunnel Hill, returned to Chattanooga.

February 10th, General Grant directed General Thomas to prepare for an advance to Knoxville, with such forces as could be spared from the protection of Chattanooga and its communications, to assist General Foster to drive Longstreet from East Tennessee.   Such a movement was no part of the original plan, but concurrent reports had convinced General Grant that there had been a heavy concentration of troops under Longstreet to secure East Tennessee, and he determined to prevent it, and relieve that flank from pressure.   General Foster had prepared to assume the offensive if he could get at least ten thousand men from General Thomas.   It was deemed safe to diminish the forces at Chattanooga, as there was reason to believe that Johnston had detached heavily from Dalton to reinforce Polk against Sherman in Alabama, as well as to strengthen Longstreet for offense against Foster in East Tennessee.

The Army of the Cumberland was not in condition to enter upon a winter campaign, and General Thomas found it difficult to make such preparations as he deemed essential.   His army was greatly diminished by the absence of regiments having re-enlisted as veterans.   Artillery horses and train animals had not been supplied in room of the thousands that had died from starvation during the siege, and he advised a postponement of the movement until the railroad would be in running order to Loudon.   On the 12th, however, the day previous to the one designated for starting, he was informed by General Grant that a conversation with General Foster, who, on account of ill-health, had been superseded by General Schofield, and dispatches from the latter, induced him to doubt the propriety of moving against Longstreet, and suggested that should he not be required to go into East Tennessee, he should make a formidable reconnoissance toward Dalton, and if possible occupy that place, and repair the railroads to it. This order was given on the 17th, and at the time there was some probability that it might be successful, as it was supposed that Johnston had weakened his center, especially to strengthen Polk against Sherman.   Two days later, however, General Thomas received information that Johnston had in hand six divisions, comprising from thirty to forty thousand men, and that no troops had been sent away, except one brigade of infantry. This intelligence did not, however, induce General Grant to recall the movement, though it rendered General Thomas hopeless of success.

The troops were put in motion toward Dalton, February 22d. General Thomas threw General Stanley's division, General Cruft commanding, with such cavalry as he could safely withdraw from Calhoun, Tennessee, forward on the Spring Place road, and Johnston's and Baird's divisions, with cavalry in advance and on the right flank, directly to Ringgold. At night, Cruft's division was at Red Clay, with Long's cavalry in advance, having been instructed to observe the enemy well toward Dalton, and give timely warning of any effort to turn Cruft's left flank, or to notify him to advance should Johnston retire. The other divisions were at Ringgold, in position on the ridge west of East Chickamauga, with a regiment of mounted infantry on each flank, and Carlin's brigade thrown toward Taylor's ridge.

During the evening, General Palmer advised General Thomas that he had received intelligence that Johnston had dispatched Cheatham's and Cleburne's divisions to reinforce General Polk, who was falling back before General Sherman, in Alabama. All available troops were now moved up to dislodge General Johnston, should this report prove to be true. Davis' division advanced to Ringgold on the 23d, and General Matthias was directed to send six regiments from Cleveland to support General Cruft, at Red Clay. Colonel Long advanced toward Dalton, on the Spring Place road; first drove in the enemy's videttes, and when within four miles of Dalton, attacked and routed from camp a regiment of infantry. The enemy then forming in force, he withdrew to Russell's Mills. Cruft's division advanced to Lee's house, on the road from Red Clay to Tunnel Hill. The four divisions were now well concentrated in the vicinity of Ringgold, and after a thorough reconnoissance on each flank, General Palmer advanced, on the 24th, to develop the enemy's strength at Tunnel Hill. After skirmishing three or four miles with Wheeler's cavalry, he gained possession of the town, when the enemy formed a new line, and opened with his batteries from a hill, one mile beyond. General Palmer then withdrew, and encamped three miles to the northwest. The following morning he decided to feel the enemy's position more fully. Baird's division was south of Taylor's Ridge near Ringgold, and Cruft's was well closed up on its left. Davis'* and Johnson's divisions were in the advance toward Tunnel Hill, with Harrison's mounted infantry in front, and Boone's on the left flank, and Long's brigade, supported by Grose's brigade of Cruft's division, was at Varnell's station, on the Dalton and Cleveland railroad. These pairs of divisions were ordered to advance on different lines, the former upon Tunnel Hill, and, if practicable, directly upon Dalton; the latter, with Long's cavalry, to move down the valley, along the eastern base of Rocky Face Ridge, to threaten the right and rear of the enemy.

In compliance, the troops on the right advanced in three columns. After the right and left had moved some distance, the center advanced, but was soon checked by a battery of Parrott guns planted on the summit beyond the town of Tunnel Hill, and skillfully handled. The right and left columns, Morgan's and Hambright's brigades, again advanced, and flanking this battery, forced its retirement. Davis' division, with Johnson's in support, pursued and found the enemy at Buzzard's Roost, a gap in Rocky Face Ridge, whose precipitous acclivities and salient summits forbade assault. Baird and Cruft also encountered the enemy as they moved down Rocky Face valley. Giving ground at first, he soon offered resistance upon a central hill. An attack was here necessary to develop his strength; and General Turchin, with four regiments, the Eleventh, Eighty-ninth, and Ninety-second Ohio, and the Eighty-second Indiana, was directed to advance. Advancing boldly, these troops pressed back the enemy and reached the summit, but were unable to hold it, as the routed troops met reinforcements, and returned in overwhelming force. The conflict was sharp, but it was too unequal to be maintained, and Turchin yielded the hill. Spirited skirmishing and cannonading were continued until nightfall, when the national troops were withdrawn. Colonel Harrison spent

* General Davis' division had previously closed up from the rear.

the night at a gap six miles south of Buzzard's Roost, nearly opposite Dalton, whence he was driven the following morning by Cleburne's division, one of the two that had been dispatched to Alabama.

As it had been ascertained that General Johnston was holding his strong positions with forces superior to his own, General Thomas deemed it futile to attempt to dislodge him, and that it was even impracticable to maintain his threatening attitude. The country was stripped of provisions, and his transportation was not sufficient to supply his command. He therefore advised General Grant of his embarrassment, and suggested the abandonment of the enterprise. In reply, General Grant urged him to maintain his position, and make the impression upon Johnston that an advance into the heart of the South was intended, until the fate of General Sherman should be known. Compliance, however, was not considered practicable, and as it was known that Johnston had recalled his divisions from Polk's support, orders were issued for the withdrawal of the troops. Baird's division was posted on a line of hills north of the town of Tunnel Hill, to cover the retirement of Johnson and Davis, and then took permanent post at Ringgold. Davis' division returned to his former position near Rossville. Two brigades of Johnson's division were posted at Tyner's Station, and the third at Graysville, with a strong guard at Parker's Gap, to protect Baird's left flank. Cruft's division returned to Ooltawah and Blue Springs, the commander sending a detachment to Cleveland to guard his supplies, where Colonel Long also took post to patrol the left flank of the army. Colonels Harrison and Boone were stationed at Leet's tanyard, to observe the enemy toward Lafayette.

This movement to Dalton involved a loss of more than three hundred men killed and wounded. Among the wounded was Colonel Mihalotzy, of the Twenty-fourth Illinois, who died a few days later at Chattanooga. The enemy's loss was probably two hundred. As a reconnoissance it was successful, though there were no such results as General Grant mentioned as probable. It seemingly recalled the two divisions that General Johnston had sent against General Sherman, but as the latter had retreated from Meridian on the 20th, six days previous to their return, the demonstration had no effect upon their movements. The chief advantages were the development of the strength of General Johnston's position before Dalton, and the suggestion to General Thomas of a plan to turn it by a movement through Snake Creek Gap. He was so impressed with the feasibility of this plan, that upon his return to Chattanooga, he requested permission from General Grant to make preparation to accomplish it.

Having disposed his troops for defense, General Thomas addressed himself to preparation for the spring campaign. He ordered General Butterfield to make a careful examination of the Nashville and Chattanooga railroad, and Captain Merrill, chief engineer of the department, to examine other roads, to ascertain the minimum force necessary to hold them securely. He also ordered a thorough examination of the railroad to Tunnel Hill, with a view to its repair, as an important step in provision for an advance.

These examinations resulted in a more economical protection of railroad communications, by means of a system of block-houses at the bridges and other important points, which became an element of power to the close of the war. And the conclusion having been reached that six thousand infantry and two thousand cavalry could hold securely the railroads to Nashville, General Thomas recommended that the railroad guards, as far as practicable, should be drawn from the local Tennessee militia.

The month of February closed with the military situation by no means developed. General Sherman destroyed railroads extensively in Mississippi, but otherwise his expedition was not compensative. It was not known what Longstreet would do, whether give further trouble in East Tennessee, return to Virginia, or join Johnston. Neither were General Johnston's plans at all indicated. One day would bring rumors from deserters, and from sources more reliable, that he was under orders to withdraw his army from Dalton, followed on the next by contradictions from sources equally entitled to credence. But ignorance of the purposes of the enemy did not prevent preparation for aggression. Reconstruction of railroads was pressed westward and southward, and material and supplies were accumulated as rapidly as possible. Steamboats and large storehouses were built. Horses were provided for the artillery, and efforts were made to recuperate those of the cavalry worn down by hard winter service. Eight companies of the First Michigan Engineers and Mechanics, and two regiments of colored troops, were ordered to commence the construction of block-houses and other defenses along the line of the Nashville and Chattanooga railroad, and the first Missouri Engineers and Mechanics were detailed for similar duty on the Nashville and Decatur railroad. In anticipation of a campaign designed to bisect the Gulf States east of the Mississippi river, the secure defense of railroad communications from Chattanooga to the North with the least possible draft upon the strength of the aggressive columns, was a matter of great moment. With strong block-houses at all the bridges, and with earthworks, in addition, at all of the more important points, a comparatively small force could hold the roads securely—at least, could prevent all damage that could not be quickly repaired. One of the greatest embarrassments to Generals Buell and Rosecrans, had been the necessity of scattering their troops in heavy detachments on their lines of supply. The plan now adopted promised better security, both to the railroads and to the troops guarding them, while employing a small portion of the force formerly assigned to this service. Besides, it transferred the cavalry almost entirely from the rear to the front, and relieved the veteran infantry from guard duty, as new regiments and local militia could be trusted to hold the block-houses and earthworks.

At the beginning of March there were indications that General Johnston was receiving reinforcements at Dalton, and General Grant was not free from apprehension that Longstreet's army might join him, in addition to other forces, for an attack upon Chattanooga. To provide against such a contingency, the two divisions of the Fourth Corps in East Tennessee were ordered to be constantly ready for quick movement to support General Thomas. On the 3d, Wagner's brigade of Sheridan's division was moved to Calhoun, Tennessee, to relieve the first brigade of the first division of cavalry, Colonel Campbell commanding, that it might take post at Cleveland. Five days later, Colonel Daniel McCook, commanding second brigade of Davis' division, was ordered to Lee and Gordon's Mills, to give strength to the front, and observe the enemy upon a line of former approach. The same day, Colonel Harrison was driven from Leet's tanyard by a strong force of cavalry. This advance, coupled with rumors that Johnston had been joined by ten thousand men from South Carolina and by Roddy's cavalry, that Longstreet's cavalry was in motion toward him, and that his troops were under orders to carry three days' rations on their persons, intensified somewhat the apprehension that an offensive movement was meditated. There were no changes of troops, however, except that McCook's division of cavalry was ordered to Cleveland, since it was not yet deemed safe to withdraw the Fourth Corps from East Tennessee, as Longstreet's action was still uncertain.

On the 17th of March, General Grant, having been appointed lieutenant-general, in command of the entire army, advised General Thomas that Major-General W. T. Sherman had been assigned to the command of the Military Division of the Mississippi. The assumption of general command by General Grant gave the contemplated campaign into Georgia a closer relation to operations against General Lee's army in Virginia than had previously existed between movements east and west.

Soon after his assignment to the command of the military division, General Sherman went to Chattanooga to confer with General Thomas with regard to future movements. At this conference, General Thomas suggested that the armies of the Tennessee and Ohio, under the respective commands of Major-Generals McPherson and Schofield, should demonstrate against Johnston's position before Dalton, by the direct roads to Buzzard's Roost, and from Cleveland, while he should throw the entire Army of the Cumberland through Snake Creek Gap, which he knew to be unguarded, and fall upon Johnston's communications between Dalton and Resaca, and thereby turn his position completely, and either force him to retreat toward the east, through a difficult country poorly supplied with provisions and forage, with a strong probability of the total disorganization of his army, or attack him, in which event he felt confident of being able to beat him, especially as he hoped to gain position in his rear before he should be aware of his movement. General Sherman objected to this suggestion, for the reason that he desired the Army of the Cumberland to form the reserve of the united armies, and to serve as a rallying point from which the two wings, the armies of the Tennessee and Ohio, could operate.

The union of the armies of the Cumberland, Tennessee, and Ohio in a campaign from Chattanooga as a base, having been determined upon, preparations of the grandest dimensions possible were at once inaugurated with vigor. The most difficult problem was that of supplies. Its solution turned upon the capacity of a single railroad track from Stevenson to Chattanooga, and thence toward Atlanta. There was steamboat transportation from Bridgeport to Chattanooga; but there was dependence alone upon the track from the former place to Stevenson. As the accumulation of supplies at Chattanooga had hitherto been slight, General Sherman restricted railroad transportation to dead freight, and forbade passage to citizens or private property. He also forbade the further issue of rations to the destitute citizens of the country. The people complained of these measures; but such was the necessity for the accumulation of supplies, that he persisted in their maintenance, against the protests of the citizens; remonstrances from Washington, and what under other circumstances would have been the demands of humanity.

During the month of April, again, as before the battles in November, Chattanooga was the scene of the greatest activity. Troops were constantly coming up from the rear and moving to position in the front. The quartermaster and commissary departments were pressed to extreme exertion building steamboats, erecting and filling vast storehouses, bringing forward artillery and cavalry horses, mules, and cattle; while the railway was almost constantly trembling under the long trains heavily loaded with supplies and munitions.

General Johnston, in the meantime, was not idle, though he was restrained in his preparation for an offensive movement, which it was expected in the South he would be able to make

in such force as to change the theater of war again to the
North. He waited for preparation for well-sustained aggression, and thus lost an opportunity for partial success. Cleveland was the weak point in the national line. General Thomas
could not hold this vital point strongly while the Fourth Corps
remained with General Schofield, and this corps could not be
safely withdrawn until it was known that Longstreet had
abandoned East Tennessee. But before Johnston was well
prepared even for defense, the opportunity was lost for forcing
any concentration of troops which was not required by General Sherman's plan of operations. General Johnston was
fully alive to the importance of successful aggression to change
the tone of feeling in the South, and sought such reinforcements as he thought were necessary. A little later he learned
that he needed more troops than were available in all the
South, upon the plan of defense which was adopted. In the
light of subsequent events, it is plain that in failing to give
adequate reinforcements to Johnston, while General Grant's
armies were widely separated and weakened by the temporary
absence of veteran regiments, the Confederate authorities at
Richmond rendered impossible the aggression for which they
subsequently clamored. In December previous, General Beauregard suggested, as the only hope of success, that Richmond
and other important places should be fortified and garrisoned
for defense, and that an immense army should be concentrated
against Grant, at Chattanooga, or thrown in bold offense from
Knoxville. Later, General Johnston's suggestions were somewhat similar, but were unheeded by Mr. Davis and his advis-
ers. The Western army remained in diffusion, until concentration, as a necessity of defense rather than a condition of
aggression, was hurriedly effected. Longstreet's army was
sent to General Lee, and from all of the troops that so long
menaced Knoxville, only Martin's division of cavalry joined
General Johnston; while almost all the national troops that
wintered in East Tennessee were free to join the combination
against him. The impracticable President had entertained
visions of successful aggression from Dalton, but had been,
from choice or necessity, so sparing in provision for such enterprise, that the thought of it, except in wildest vagary, could

not be entertained. To require Johnston to advance with less than fifty thousand men against a combination of armies, which in defense would greatly exceed one hundred thousand, was to exact defeat. The fact that the Confederate President did not discern this, revealed his incapacity as a revolutionary leader, and his subsequent criticisms of his ablest general, for the non-accomplishment of a palpable impossibility, manifested the inveteracy of his self-conceit and his utter misapprehension of the situation in Georgia. His general had no choice of methods, but was confined to the defense of his positions between his enemy and the campaign region south of Resaca. Had he been able to assume the offensive, he could not have reached any vital point in the rear of Chattanooga, without a long detour, in dependence for supplies upon a devastated country, or on wagon transportation from a remote base. In his weakness and his restriction from movement by mountain barriers right and left, he could make no flank movements or threatening dashes, with infantry or cavalry; and any expectation of a general advance from Dalton, except with an immense army, through East Tennessee or Northern Alabama, Bridgeport or Decatur—was groundless.

Having now, from necessity, accepted the defensive, General Johnston could only make effort to embarrass Sherman's communications with his cavalry, and await the approach of the armies combining against him. He threw his cavalry into Northern Alabama, in constant menace, but accomplished no interruption to communications. General Thomas sent General Geary, with two regiments and one piece of artillery, on a steamboat, to destroy the boats used by the cavalry in crossing and recrossing the river, as far to the west as possible. General Geary was only partially successful; he destroyed a great many boats in going and coming, but was prevented by forces on each side of the river from going a great distance.

On the 29th of April, a tentative advance was made by General Baird, having reference to the general movement of the united armies. He sent three hundred cavalry, under General Kilpatrick, supported by Vanderveer's brigade, to feel the enemy's position at Tunnel Hill. These troops encountered the enemy and drove him some distance, when developing a greatly

superior force, they were compelled to withdraw. At Davis'
house the enemy pressed them, when they turned and repulsed
him handsomely. The day following, General Johnston gave
indications of greater strength in front of Ringgold, and General Thomas instructed General Baird to call upon General
Johnson for help in the event of an advance against his position.

During the month, important changes were made in the
Army of the Cumberland. The reorganization of the Fourth
and Fourteenth Corps having been of recent date, they remained
intact, except some changes in general officers. On the 11th,
the cavalry, under the general command of Brigadier-General
W. L. Elliott, was organized into four divisions; Colonel Ed-
ward McCook, and Brigadier-Generals Kennard Garrard, Jud-
son Kilpatrick, and A. C. Gillem, commanding respectively, according to numerical designation. There were three brigades
in each division, and an average of three regiments in each
brigade. On the 15th, orders were received from Washington,
requiring the consolidation of the Eleventh and Twelfth Corps
as the Twentieth, under the command of Major-General
Hooker. Major-General Gordon Granger was relieved from
the command of the Fourth Corps, and Major-General O. O.
Howard assigned, and Major-General P. H. Sheridan having
been transferred to the Army of the Potomac, Major-General
John Newton was assigned to the position made vacant by his
vacation of the command of the Second division, Fourth Corps.

There were now in the Army of the Cumberland a large number of re-enlisted troops. During the winter and spring there
re-enlisted eighty-eight regiments of infantry, three of mounted
infantry, sixteen of cavalry, eighteen batteries of artillery, and
twenty-six detachments of all arms, and eight thousand one
hundred and thirty-six recruits in the aggregate were added to
these organizations while on furlough. The importance of the
re-enlistment of these troops can not be overestimated. Without them and the " veterans " of the other two co-operative
armies, the Atlanta campaign could not have been safely undertaken ; the war would have been greatly postponed, and its
issue might have been different. The slow movement of the
draft, and the provisional measure of short enlistments could

not have furnished such troops as were demanded in the spring of 1864. Without the veterans, aggression could not have been entertained, and the feeble armies, during the summer, might have been compelled to relax their grasp upon the heart of the rebellious states. It is then the plainest duty of the historian to mention the regiments and other organizations, whose members, in whole or in part, re-enlisted as " veteran volunteers," and ever after bore the grandest name which the war originated. Of the regiments and batteries whose organization was maintained under re-enlistment, were the Thirteenth, Fifteenth, Seventeenth, Nineteenth, Twenty-first, Twenty-sixth, Thirty-first, Thirty-third, Thirty-sixth, Fortieth, Forty-first, Forty-ninth, Fifth-first, Fifty-fifth, Sixty-first, Sixty-fifth, Sixty-ninth, Seventy-first, Seventy-fourth, and Eighty-second Ohio Infantry ; the First, Third, and Fourth Ohio Cavalry, and batteries " B," " C," " F," and " G," First Ohio Artillery ; the Twenty-second, Thirtieth, Thirty-first, Thirty-fifth, Fortieth, Forty-second, Forty-fourth, Fifty-first, Fifty-seventh and Fifty-eighth Indiana Infantry ; Seventy-ninth Mounted Infantry, and Thirteenth Indiana battery ; the Tenth, Twenty-first, Thirty-sixth, Thirty-eighth, Forty-second, Forty-fourth, Fifty-first, Fifty-ninth, and Sixtieth Illinois Infantry, and batteries " H "and " I," Second Illinois Artillery ; the Fourth, Eighteenth, Twenty-first, and Twenty-third Kentucky Infantry ; the Second, Third, Fourth, and Sixth Kentucky Cavalry, and the Twenty-eighth Kentucky Mounted Infantry ; the Forty-sixth, Seventy-third, Seventy-ninth, and One Hundred and Ninth Pennsylvania Infantry, and the Seventh Pennsylvania Cavalry ; the Forty-fifth, Fifty-eighth, and Sixtieth New York Infantry, and the New York Independent Battery ; the Tenth and Thirteenth Michigan Infanty ; the Fourteenth Michigan Mounted Infantry, and the First Michigan battery ; the Thirteenth Wisconsin Infantry, and the Fifth Wisconsin battery ; the Fifteenth Missouri Infantry, and battery " G," First Missouri Artillery ; the Second Minnesota Infantry ; the Fifth Iowa Cavalry ; the Eighth Kansas Infantry, and Third Maryland Infantry. Of the detachments, there were representatives in greater or less numbers from the Fifth, Seventh, Eleventh, Eighteenth, and Twenty-fourth Ohio Infantry, and the Tenth Independent battery; the Tenth, Fifteenth, Twenty-seventh, and Thirty-seventh Indiana Infantry; the Twenty-first, Twenty-second, and Twenty-seventh Illinois Infantry, and battery "C," First Illinois Artillery; the Eighth Kentucky Infantry; the Seventy-ninth Pennsylvania Infantry; batteries "F" and "M," New York Artillery; the First Michigan Engineers, and battery "E," First Michigan Artillery; the Third Wisconsin battery; the First Missouri Engineers; the Tenth Maine Infantry, and battery "3," Maine Artillery; battery "F," Fourth United States Artillery, and battery "K," Fifth United States Artillery.

On the 1st of May, the Army of the Cumberland was well in hand, awaiting orders to advance. The Fourth Corps, Major-General O. O. Howard commanding, was at Cleveland. The Fourteenth, Major-General J. M. Palmer commanding, was before Chattanooga, and the Twentieth Corps, Major-General Joseph Hooker commanding, was mainly in Lookout valley. The divisions of the Fourth Corps, in numerical order, were commanded by Major-Generals D. S. Stanley and John Newton and Brigadier-General T. J. Wood; those of the Fourteenth, Brigadier-Generals R. W. Johnson, J. C. Davis, and A. Baird, and those of the Twentieth, Brigadier-General A. S. Williams and J. W. Geary and Major-Generals D. Butterfield and Lovell H. Rousseau. The division of the latter, and other troops of infantry, cavalry, and artillery, assigned as garrisons, comprising thirty-two regiments of infantry, nine of cavalry, and thirty-nine batteries, were disposed at all important points from Chattanooga to Nashville, on the direct road, and at Clarksville and Fort Donelson. The cavalry comprised four divisions, under Brigadier-General W. L. Elliott—the first, Colonel McCook commanding, was with the Fourth Corps, at Cleveland; the second under Brigadier-General Garrard, was ordered to report to General McPherson, commanding the Army of the Tennessee; the third under Brigadier-General Kilpatrick, was at Ringgold, and the Fourth, under Brigadier-General Gillem, was at Nashville. The army for the field comprised 54,568 infantry, 3,238 cavalry, and 2,377 artillery, with 130 guns; total, 60,773 effective men.

CHAPTER XXVI.

THE TURNING OF DALTON.

THE first of May, 1864, was a crisis of the war. Two of the largest armies hitherto assembled East or West were in readiness to move against the enemy at the bidding of the Lieutenant-General. The local objectives of these armies were distinct, but the common general object was the immediate suppression of the rebellion. It was proposed to accomplish this grand aim, by crushing General Lee's army covering Richmond and General Johnston's standing before Dalton. These two armies embodied the life of the rebellion.

Generals Grant and Sherman were to move on lines too remote to admit direct co-operation, but they proposed to be mutually helpful by simultaneous aggression. General Grant was to forbid the transfer of troops from Virginia to Georgia, by vigor of attack, and General Sherman was to engage Johnston in such a manner that he could not send supporting columns from Georgia to Virginia. Volunteers were invited for one hundred days, to hold the important points in the rear of the two great armies, that all the available veteran troops East might be massed against General Lee, and all in the West concentrated at Chattanooga, that General Sherman, with three armies in one, should dash upon General Johnston at Dalton. Campaigns, East or West, had never been undertaken under conditions of similar promise, and the loyal people were hopeful of early and complete success.

The conditions of the Georgia campaign were exceedingly favorable to General Sherman, as compared with the ruling features of all preceding campaigns in the central theater of war. The superiority of the national army at Chattanooga had been far greater than in any previous battle in this region, and in some of the anterior engagements, as at Chickamauga, the enemy had been superior. But General Sherman's preponderance of strength was greater than General Grant's when General Bragg was hurled from Lookout Mountain and Missionary Ridge. Then the strength of the opposing armies was perhaps as three to two; it was now to be as two to one. Besides, General Johnston could not now have, as his predecessor had always had, when on the defensive, the advantage of interior lines. The possession of Chattanooga and Cleveland, with roads converging at Dalton, gave direct lines for General Sherman's first advance, and with the railroad and river from Knoxville to Decatur well guarded, and a fortified line of supply from the north, he could move southward without endangering flank or rear, so long as he could so engage the enemy as to keep him before him. In the projected campaign, neither General Sherman nor General Johnston could have the advantage of interior lines, only so far as the defensive could give to either, shorter lines for maneuver and array, within a limited range only. The general line of maneuver being north and south, forbade great advantage of lines to either.

But General Johnston had other advantages. He had choice of positions and could always resist behind battlements with good management, and in giving ground would be constantly gathering to him his reserves; while General Sherman, in advancing, would be compelled to detach more and more from his offensive forces to guard his constantly lengthening line of supply. So, therefore, the relative conditions of the campaign were by no means expressed by the comparative proportions of the opposing armies.

The 2d day of May was first named by General Grant for the advance of the great armies, but finally the 5th was announced in orders. General Thomas, however, commenced his dispositions and movements on the 2d. On this day, General Davis' division joined General Baird's at Ringgold, and General Butterfield's advanced from Lookout valley to Lee and Gordon's Mills. During the day, General Baird sent infantry and cavalry detachments to reconnoiter toward Tunnel Hill, and developed the enemy in force at that point.

May 3d, General Johnson's division closed upon the other two of the Fourteenth Corps at Ringgold. On the day following, the Fourth Corps, with McCook's division of cavalry on its left flank, advanced to Catoosa Springs, and Butterfield's division advanced to Pleasant Grove, and General Williams' division to Lee and Gordon's Mills. The next day, General Geary's division, having marched across the mountain from Bridgeport, closed up on the other divisions of the Twentieth Corps at Leet's tanyard, completing the concentration of the Army of the Cumberland.

General Sherman originally designed that the Army of the Tennessee, Major-General McPherson commanding, should advance from Decatur by Gunter's Landing and Lebanon, Alabama, to Lafayette, Georgia; but subsequently, he ordered it to move upon Chattanooga. This army was not as strong as had been anticipated, as two of its veteran divisions under General A. J. Smith were detained by the protraction of General Banks' expedition west of the Mississippi river. With two corps, General McPherson attained position at Lee and Gordon's Mills on the 6th, and the same day the Army of the Ohio, Major-General Schofield commanding, reached Red Clay. At the close of this day the armies representing the controlling strength of the contending powers in the West, lay confronting each other on the eve of one of the greatest campaigns of a war, made memorable in the annals of the world by the magnitude of armies, the frequency of great battles, and immense compass of military operations.

General Sherman's three armies for offense now numbered nearly one hundred thousand men. There were sixty thousand seven hundred and seventy-three men in the Army of the Cumberland; twenty-four thousand and sixty-five in the Army of the Tennessee; and thirteen thousand five hundred and fifty-nine in the Army of the Ohio. The Army of the Cumberland comprised fifty-four thousand five hundred and sixty-eight infantry, two thousand three hundred and seventy-seven artillery, three thousand two hundred and twenty-eight cavalry, and one hundred and thirty guns; the Army of the Tennessee, twenty-two thousand infantry, one thousand four hundred and four artillery, six hundred and twenty-four cavalry, and ninety-six guns ; and the Army of the Ohio, eleven thousand one hundred and eighty-three infantry, six hundred and seventy-nine artillery, one thousand six hundred and ninety-seven cavalry, and eighty-two guns. The grand aggregates were eighty-eight thousand one hundred and eighty-eight infantry, four thousand four hundred and sixty artillery, five thousand five hundred and forty-nine cavalry, and two hundred and fifty-four guns. General Johnston's army embraced forty-four thousand nine hundred infantry, artillery, and cavalry ; two corps, commanded by Lieutenant-Generals Hardee and Hood, and four thousand cavalry, by Major-General Wheeler.

General Sherman proposed first to carry Tunnel Hill, and then threaten a direct attack upon Johnston's main position before Dalton, while McPherson's army should move through Snake Creek Gap to operate against Resaca. He accordingly gave orders, May 6th, requiring General Thomas, on the day following, to move his center, the Fourteenth Corps, directly upon Tunnel Hill; his right, the Twentieth Corps, to Trickum, and his left, the Fourth Corps, to Lee's house, in support of the Fourteenth: General McPherson to advance with his army first upon Ship's Gap and Villanow, and thence to Snake Creek Gap, and through it as soon as practicable; and General Schofield to move forward to Catoosa Springs, feeling toward General Thomas' left flank.

The Army of the Cumberland moved on the 7th, in compliance with orders. The enemy made a show of resistance to General Palmer, with infantry and artillery, at Tunnel Hill, but on the appearance of General Howard's corps upon his left, his troops fled to Buzzard's Roost. General Hooker, upon reaching Trickum, threw out detachments toward Buzzard's Roost on the left, and Villanow on the right, to observe the enemy. General Kilpatrick's cavalry remained at Gordon's Springs, in readiness to establish communications with the Army of the Tennessee, expected at Villanow on the morning of the 8th.

The next day, Harker's brigade of Newton's division of the Fourth Corps advanced along Rocky Face ridge to a point within a mile and a half of the enemy's signal station.

Meeting here with obstructions forbidding farther advance, Harker made preparations to hold the position. Skirmish lines were then thrown forward from Wood's, Davis', and Butterfield's divisions, and the enemy was pressed into his intrenchments at Buzzard's Roost, or "Mill Creek Gap,"* and the three divisions advanced to the entrance.

As General McPherson was now moving upon Snake Creek Gap, it was imperative that a strong feint should be made, to create the impression that it was the intention to carry the position by assault. Accordingly, General Geary was directed to scale Chattooga Mountain with his division, if practicable, at the point known as Dug Gap, where the road from Lafayette to Dalton ascends from Mill Creek valley. Chattooga Mountain is separated from Rocky Face ridge by Mill Creek at Buzzard's Roost, and from that point trends southward.

At the point selected for Geary's ascent, the mountain side is steep and rough, and the summit is crowned with a palisade of rocks, with occasional openings that admit passage to the top. With the One Hundred and Nineteenth New York deployed as skirmishers, and Buschbeck's and Candy's brigades formed on right and left, in two lines of battle, Geary moved up the mountain. Midway, his skirmishers became hotly engaged, but the enemy was pressed upward until the main lines reached the base of the palisades. After resting for a few minutes, to recover from the exhaustion produced by excessive heat and protracted exertion, an effort was made to reach the summit. A few men only succeeded, and they were either killed or forced back. The position was such that defense was easy, even by rolling stones from the summit. A second attempt, however, was made, soon after the first failed, but with similar issue. General Geary then brought McGill's rifled battery to bear upon the enemy in his front, to cover an effort of the Thirty-third New Jersey to reach the summit a half mile to the right, where the enemy made less show of strength. As in the other cases, a few men gained the crest, and their shouts invited the advance of the whole line, but

---

* So designated by General Johnston.

again there was emphatic failure.   By this time, General Hardee was present with reinforcements, and further effort would have been madness.   Geary 'ost heavily, but his action being regarded by the enemy as the initiative to carry the position by assault, it was in some degree compensative, as such impression was the object of the movement.   Night and the third repulse coming together, the division was withdrawn to the valley, out of reach of the enemy's guns.

During the afternoon, Johnson's and Baird's divisions were advanced to Davis' support, and Butterfield's was ordered to join General Hooker.   General Kilpatrick communicated with General McPherson, and then moved to Trickum.   McCook's division was thrown on Schofield's left flank, to cover the extremity of the general line, until General Stoneman should come up.   The position for General Garrard's cavalry division was to be with General McPherson, but it was yet in the rear, en route from Pulaski, Tennessee.

The next day, the Army of the Cumberland was somewhat heavily engaged on the east, north, and west of Buzzard's Roost.   The action was intended as a feint, unless it should be ascertained that General Johnston was withdrawing his army.   Such, however, was the position, by nature and art, that emphatic feints subjected the national forces to great exposure, and there was considerable loss throughout the line. The character of the feints may be inferred from the fact that General Johnston reported that five assaults upon "Rocky Face Mountain" were repulsed on the 9th of May.   His troops holding Buzzard Roost were Stewart's and Bate's divisions, supported by Stevenson's and Anderson's.   The defenses for infantry were at right angles to the roads, and batteries, covered with abatis, were placed on the adjacent summits to throw a converging fire upon the valley, which was flooded by means of well-concealed dams.   Carlin's brigade, supported by the remainder of Johnson's division, felt the enemy's lines on the west; Morgan's brigade of Davis' division, on the north, and Grose's brigade of Stanley's division, on the east.   The loss in killed was slight, but a great many were wounded.   The heaviest loss, in comparison with the number of troops engaged, was in McCook's division on the extreme left. Under instructions from General Schofield, Colonel McCook made demonstrations on all the roads leading to Dalton on the east. Colonel La Grange, commanding his second brigade, encountered Wheeler, with twenty-two hundred men, on the road from Varnell's Station. He was at first successful, and pressed Wheeler back to intrenchments near Poplar Place, but was there repulsed with heavy loss. He and fourteen officers were captured, and one hundred and thirty-six of his men were either killed, wounded, or captured. Wheeler's loss was supposed to be greater. During the day, Hooker's corps was at Trickum to support McPherson in passing through Snake Creek Gap.

The action the next day was less severe, though the feint was vigorously maintained with a view to prevent any concentration against General McPherson. To give him support, Kilpatrick's cavalry was ordered to join him, and Williams' division of the Twentieth Corps was sent to his rear. In the evening, General Hooker was directed to send a division on the following day to widen the road through the gap, to facilitate the passage of troops and trains.

General McPherson passed through Snake Creek Gap, and reached the vicinity of Resaca at 2 p. m. on the 9th. Finding the place "fortified and manned," and no roads through the forest to the railroad, while his flank was exposed to attack from the direction of Dalton, he withdrew to the debouche of the gap through which he had passed. During the afternoon of the 9th, General Johnston learned that two corps of the national army were in the gap, and sent General Hood to Resaca with three divisions.

When General Sherman learned that McPherson had not touched Johnston's communications and had withdrawn to the gap, he made a change of plan. He desired, from the first, to hold Johnston at Dalton, and entertained the hope that McPherson's movement would so interrupt his communications that he would be forced to give battle at Dalton—an issue that was preferred to operations "far down into Georgia." His instructions to General McPherson were to secure Snake Creek Gap, and from it make a bold attack on the enemy's flank or his railroad at any point between Tilton and Dalton. He said: "I hope the enemy will fight at Dalton; in which case he can have no force there that can interfere with you; but should his policy be to fall back along the railroad, you will hit him in flank. Do not fail in that event to make the most of the opportunity, by the most vigorous attack possible, as it may save us what we have most reason to apprehend—a slow pursuit, in which he gains strength as we lose it. In either event, you may be sure the forces north of you will prevent his turning on you alone. In the event of hearing the sounds of heavy battle about Dalton, the greater necessity for your rapid movement on the railroad. If broken to an extent that would take some days to repair, you can withdraw to Snake Creek Gap, and come to us or await the development, according to your judgment or the information you may receive." As soon as he learned that General McPherson had failed to accomplish any of these objects, except to attain position at the debouche of the gap, he determined to attack with his armies through the gap, and issued orders for the movement.

It was plain to General Sherman, as it had been to General Thomas, in February, that no effort should be made to dislodge the enemy from Buzzard Roost, by direct attack; but he continued the feint, in order to still hold Johnston at Dalton, that he might throw his armies upon his rear. Snake Creek Gap made it easy to turn Dalton, by an army strong enough to uncover its communications, or to detach sufficient forces to risk an engagement with the enemy's whole army. Through this gap all the fortresses north of Dalton could be evaded, and the army in passage be under the cover of the mountains. Had Johnston's army been strong enough for division to hold the positions north of Dalton, and the lower mouth of the gap, he could have defied a hundred thousand men. But as his safety demanded the concentration of his army on his lines of retreat and supply, he was compelled to leave the passage undefended, and make roads for the quick transfer of his army from Dalton to Reseca; should his antagonist use the gap for a flank movement. General Sherman's orders to effect this measure required the concentration of his armies in Snake Creek Gap, on the 12th.

When General Johnston first learned that General McPherson had retired from Resaca, he recalled Hood's three divisions, and on the 11th his army was again concentrated at Dalton. On the morning of the 12th, he was confronted by Howard's corps and Stoneman's cavalry, the remainder of the national forces being in motion to concentrate in Snake Creek Gap. Stanley's division was before Buzzard's Roost Gap; Newton's was holding the north end of Rocky Face ridge, and the roads around it; Wood's was in reserve on Tunnel Hill, and Stoneman's troopers were on Newton's left flank. From the signal station on the ridge, the movements of the enemy were plainly visible. About 10 A. M. a heavy column was seen to advance toward Newton's left, as if to turn it. The menace was of such positive expression that Wood's division moved to Newton's support. But the enemy, after driving back Newton's skirmishers, withdrew. General Johnston's object, doubtless, was to ascertain whether the national forces had withdrawn from his front, as he had heard the day previous that Resaca was again threatened. The evening before, he had ordered General Polk, who had just arrived with Loring's division, to defend the place with that division, and Canty's brigade. But as his safety depended upon his knowledge of General Sherman's movements, his reconnoissance was directed to this end. During the day, he was so fully assured of the flank movement, that, by a night march, he transferred his infantry and artillery to Resaca, leaving his cavalry to cover his rear.

This result was not in harmony with the plans and expectations of General Sherman, his object being to hold Johnston's army at Dalton, until his own armies could pass through Snake Creek Gap; but the opportunity to accomplish it was lost between the 9th and the morning of the 13th. On the 9th, Resaca was held by Canty's brigade. The day following, General Hood was there with three divisions. On the 11th, Canty's brigade again held the place, and from the evening of the 11th until the morning of the 13th, General Polk was there with Loring's division in addition to Canty's brigade.

General McPherson passed through Snake Creek Gap on the 9th, and was on that day with his army within a mile of Resaca, and from the 9th to the 13th, he was south of the gap. On the 11th, Hooker's corps was in supporting distance, and on the 12th, Palmer's corps and Schofield's two divisions were close in the rear of Hooker.

Johnston remained in ignorance of Sherman's grand flank movement until the evening of the 12th, and then he was at Dalton with his army. After the national armies had gained Snake Creek Gap, he was unable to ascertain how many troops passed through it. An army, there, could pass as secretly as a brigade. He said in his official report, that "Rocky Face Mountain, and Snake Creek Gap, at its south end, completely covered for the enemy the turning of Dalton." His ignorance, then, of the movement until the evening of the 12th, was a condition of its success. Had McPherson's army and the forces in his rear, on that day, moved rapidly into position between Resaca and Tilton, Johnston would have been thrown from his communications, or been compelled to give battle upon conditions of great disadvantage.

It was unfortunate that Resaca was not gained at the same time that Dalton was turned, as the campaign did not furnish a similar opportunity to defeat Johnston, or press him from his communications. The grandest possibility between Tunnel Hill and Lovejoy's Station invited a prompt advance in force from the debouche of Snake Creek Gap. General Thomas' plan differed from the one adopted by General Sherman. He proposed that the Armies of the Tennesse and the Ohio should hold General Johnston at Dalton, by a feint upon his position at Buzzard's Roost, while the Army of the Cumberland, sixty thousand strong, should pass rapidly through Snake Creek Gap, and fall upon Johnston's communications between Dalton and Resaca, and thus cut him off from his communications, and either drive him eastward into a mountain region, or force him to give battle on unequal conditions. General Sherman's first plan proposed to demonstrate against Resaca, so as to hold him at Dalton to give battle, or induce General Johnston to abandon Dalton, and then strike his army in flank, while in motion between that place and Resaca.

This first series of operations in offense and defense gave the types of the campaign. The offensive compelled a choice between the direct attack of fortified positions and the flank movement. The adopted methods of defense were the maintenance of fortified positions as long as practicable, a constant outlook for opportunities to strike insulated columns, and retreat when necessary to save communications. General Johnston's leading idea was to fight under cover, and thus reduce the national army until he could meet it on equal conditions of battle, and at Dalton, and almost daily while he held command, he gave it revelation. General Sherman's leading object was to entrap or force his enemy into battle under circumstances which would not neutralize his superior strength, and of this, his zigzag lines of aggression were the expression.

CHAPTER XXVII.

BATTLE OF RESACA.

EARLY on the morning of the 13th, General Howard discovered that General Johnston had withdrawn from Dalton, and he at once occupied the town, having driven his cavalry from it. He then moved in pursuit, and skirmishing as he advanced, encamped eight miles toward Resaca. In the morning, General Johnston reached Resaca, Loring's division having moved out to check General McPherson and give time for the formation of Hood's and Hardee's corps upon their arrival from Dalton. He formed his army, now stronger by several thousand men than at Dalton, with Polk's corps on the left, resting on the Oostanaula river below the town, Hardee's in the center, and Hood's on the right, his right flank resting on the Connasauga river.

At 8 A. M., Hooker's corps, preceded by Kilpatrick's cavalry, moved out upon the Resaca road, in support of McPherson, who was advancing against the town. Kilpatrick encountered Wheeler and drove him nearly to the town, when, being wounded, he turned over the command to Colonel Murray. Palmer's corps moved from Snake Creek Gap, two miles northeast of Hooker, and then moved parallel with the Resaca road, under orders to proceed as far as the railroad. On reaching the vicinity of the railroad, his skirmishers encountered those of the enemy, strongly posted on the hills, immediately west of the railroad, and warmly engaged them until nightfall. Butterfield's division of Hooker's corps moved forward to support Palmer's right. Schofield's two divisions advanced upon Palmer's left. Howard advanced to the vicinity of Resaca, and when communications were established throughout the line, it was found that his right was but a mile from Schofield's left.

General Johnston's position was a strong one, with Camp creek in front, and heavy intrenchments in the immediate vicinity of the town—the strongest to defend the bridges across the Oostanaula, and cover the retreat of his army. His outer defenses consisted of detached redoubts, and extensive rifle-trenches, and the ground beyond was favorable for defense. His army was disposed partly in the inner defenses, but mainly on the high hills north and west of the town, which were fortified.

Before delivering battle, General Sherman ordered a pontoon bridge to be thrown across the Oostanaula at Lay's ferry, in the direction of Calhoun, Sweeny's division of the Fifteenth Corps to cross and threaten that place, and Garrard's division of cavalry to move from Villanow toward Rome, to cross the Oostanaula, and if possible break the railroad below Calhoun and above Kingston. On the 14th, General McPherson crossed Camp creek, near its mouth, and forced Polk's corps from the hills commanding the railroad bridges from the west, and secured a lodgment close to his works. This done, it became necessary to swing round the whole line formed the previous evening, from Hooker's left to the extreme left. This movement was made with the right of Johnson's division, which was the right of the Fourteenth Corps, as a pivot, and each division advanced until it encountered the enemy.

As Johnson's right was in proximity to the enemy, the divisions to the left met the enemy in succession. Baird's division was in line on Johnson's left, and Davis in reserve. General Howard, in compliance with orders from General Thomas, moved in the morning, to form his corps on the left of Schofield, and advance upon the main roads to Resaca. Newton's division, followed by Wood's, moved toward Schofield's left, and Stanley's toward the enemy's extreme right, on the Fulton and Resaca road. When Newton gained Schofield's left, Wood changed direction to the left, upon a road between Newton and Stanley.

Carlin's brigade of Johnson's division was the first to encounter the foe. General Carlin crossed Camp creek and advanced some distance over the open ground in front of the enemy's position, under a severe fire of artillery and musketry. The passage of the creek disordered his lines somewhat, and being hopeless of holding the enemy's works should he succeed in an assault, he withdrew, and found shelter and a parapet at the bank of the stream. Here he maintained position all day, and delivered a desultory but destructive fire. General King, perceiving Carlin's repulse, halted his brigade to the left and rear. The ground over which the left of Baird's division and the right of Schofield's line advanced, was thickly wooded, rendering it difficult to maintain lines, and the troops farther to the left having gained ground, those having been delayed moved forward rapidly as they emerged from the woods upon the open space before the enemy's intrenchments; but such was the severity of the musketry and artillery fire to which they were exposed, that they were soon compelled to retreat. Some isolated squads had passed Camp creek, and were driven back; others were so delayed by the miry banks that they could not withdraw with the main line, and were compelled to seek cover at the stream. To cover the retreat and re-formation of Turchin's brigade, and Schofield's right, Mitchell's brigade of Davis' division, in reserve, moved quickly to the left, and was severely engaged, while the broken lines were reformed upon the high ground west of the creek. As the lines of advance of Howard's corps were converging, the three divisions made close connection before reaching the enemy's position, and as the convergence of the roads shortened the battle front continually, the greater portion of Newton's division fell in rear of Schofield's right, in reserve, and when his left carried the position in its front, Newton moved to the relief of his left center, and grasped firmly all the ground that had been gained. In the meantime, Wood came abreast of Newton, and drove the enemy from his rifle-pits, and Stanley formed his division on Wood's left, with one brigade across the Fulton road, to protect his flank. These movements were all slowly made, in consequence of dense woods and rough ground, and the resistance of the enemy. But an advanced line was gained, and from it artillerists poured a fire so destructive as in some cases to drive the enemy temporarily from his works.

General Johnston, fearing that the lines of investment were closing around him, determined to assume the offensive, and if possible turn General Sherman's left flank. General Stanley soon observed indications of the movement. As General Howard had no reserves to direct to the endangered flank, he communicated in person with General Thomas and secured immediate assistance from the Twentieth Corps. In compliance with orders, General Hooker promptly dispatched Williams' division, under the guidance of Colonel Morgan,* of the Fourteenth Colored regiment, and preceded it to the point of danger. Williams moved rapidly on the most direct route, and arrived on the extreme left just as that flank had been turned and pressed back. Stanley had exhausted all his reserves in extending his line against the overlapping of the enemy. Simonson's battery, by effective execution, was retarding the advance of the enemy to double up the line, when Williams deployed his division and advanced to the support of the battery. His terrific fire first checked and then routed the enemy, and completely defeated this attempt at flanking. The other divisions of the Twentieth Corps, Geary's and Butterfield's, followed Williams, later in the evening, and McCook's cavalry passed to Hooker's left.

The enemy's troops engaged against the left flank were Stevenson's and Stewart's divisions and two brigades of Walker's—a strong column in view of the length of Johnston's lines and the relative inferiority of his army. Another fact evinced his estimate of the importance of the movement. After its failure he gave orders for its repetition the next morning, but was subsequently led to revoke them, when he learned that the national infantry were crossing the Oostanaula river, near Calhoun, on a pontoon bridge. To provide against this menace to his rear, he dispatched General Walker to Calhoun.

Such advantages had been gained during the day as promised success in forcing Johnston to abandon his position, and

---

* Colonel T. J. Morgan was volunteer aid to General Howard.

orders were issued for a general advance the next morning. Notwithstanding this aggressive purpose, the troops covered themselves with the usual defenses. There was no change in the line, except that Schofield was directed to withdraw from the center and pass to Hooker's left.

There was delay in making the attack in the morning, to await the result of a reconnoissance by General Geary, from the left flank. Full preparations were not completed until noon. At this hour the Twentieth Corps advanced—Geary on the right, Butterfield on the left, and Williams in reserve. Before the enemy's works were reached, General Hooker directed General Williams to deflect to the left to cover and protect that flank, again threatened by the enemy, as General Johnston, having learned that there was no immediate danger from infantry at Calhoun, had repeated his order to General Hood to advance against the national left. Facing to the east, Williams' division moved to the point menaced—Knipe's brigade on the right, Ruger's in the center, and Robinson's on the left. The ground traversed by the advancing columns was hilly, with woods and open spaces alternating. Williams' brigades formed lines on a series of hills west of the railroad and running parallel to it; batteries were planted with supports to command the ground in front of the line.

The enemy before Hooker, occupied intrenched hills, having spurs extending in all directions, and batteries were so placed on the higher points as to enfilade assaulting lines. Geary's and Butterfield's divisions advanced with spirit, and though receiving a heavy fire from artillery and musketry, carried the nearest hills. Then Butterfield's division—Ward's, Coburn's, and Wood's brigades—supported by Ireland's brigade on Geary's left, drove the enemy from a battery, which from a ruling position was pouring an exceedingly destructive fire; but another line of intrenchments was so near that the captors could neither remove the guns nor remain with them. But, withdrawing to tenable ground, they covered the guns so fully with their fire that the enemy could not approach them, and during the remainder of the day the guns remained between the lines. They were taken during the night by a detachment of the Fifth Ohio under Colonel Kilpatrick.

In the meantime, the entire line became engaged, from How-

ard's right to Hooker's left; while throughout the whole front
of the "Army of the Cumberland," heavy skirmishing and
artillery action was maintained.   General Howard, being
nearest the assaulting corps, kept up a constant fire of artillery and musketry, and in one instance made a positive attack,
and although he did not succeed in holding any point of the
enemy's line, he prevented the diversion of troops from his
front, to sustain their comrades before General Hooker, against
whose left they were maintaining the offensive with great determination.   Near the railroad, in front of Williams, he
massed his forces and advancing as much as possible under
cover, made repeated assaults, but was unable to disturb the
line.   Williams' artillery was used with most destructive effect
in the repulsion of these assaults.   In front of Williams' right
and Geary's left, there was a long cleared field, compassing
two hills and a ravine, and extending to a wooded hill, upon
which rested the enemy's main line.   This field was flanked
on the right by wooded hills, which extended to the captured
battery.   About 5 P. M. Stevenson's division left the main line
and charged in column to gain possession of these lateral hills.

This movement, if successful, would have insulated one-
half of Geary's division, which had been concentrated under
Colonel Cobham, in the rear of the guns wrested from the
enemy.   But Stevenson was repulsed mainly through the concentration of fire from Williams' right and Geary's left.   His
leading regiments were almost annihilated.   On both sides,
artillery charged with canister and schrapnel was freely used.
Stevenson's repulse closed the general contest.   This attack
of Stewart's and Stevenson's divisions was made after General
Johnston had decided to evacuate Resaca, but his order forbidding the assault was not received in time to prevent it.

During the night of the 15th, General Johnston abandoned
Resaca.   It was observed by those on the outlook the preceding day, that he was sending his material to the rear.   He
had lost positions on his right and left, and had been pressed
throughout his lines by two days of fighting, and the exposure
of his communications in the event of a flank movement,
which had been foreshadowed, made his retreat necessary.   He
had attacked the brigade across the river below Resaca on the

15th, and had been repulsed, and as General Sherman's front now presented defenses as well as his own, the transfer of heavy forces across the river was plainly practicable. He therefore retreated before embarrassments crowded upon him.

The action at Resaca, though presenting different features from the one before Dalton, was not essentially different in type or result. In the latter one, the two armies more fully confronted each other, and there was more fighting and heavier losses. The champaign region of Georgia was now before General Sherman, offering freedom for maneuver and strategy, which the mountain region had denied.

As the aggregate monthly losses of the Army of the Cumberland were reported by General Thomas, it is impossible to ascertain definitely the casualties at Resaca. The Twentieth Corps lost seventeen hundred and forty-six men, and the other two corps lost nearly as many in the aggregate. General Johnston's losses were also heavy, especially when he assumed the offensive.

CHAPTER XXVIII.

ADVANCE TO THE ETOWAH RIVER, THE TURNING OF ALLATOONA, BATTLES NEAR NEW HOPE CHURCH.

RESACA was occupied by the Army of the Cumberland on the morning of May 16th, and General Sherman gave orders for rapid pursuit. There was delay, however, in passing the river, as it was necessary to throw a pontoon bridge at Resaca and at points above. During the day, the Army of the Tennessee crossed at Lay's ferry, and Howard's corps at Resaca. As in the pursuit the Army of the Cumberland was to follow the enemy's line of retreat, General Howard moved forward toward Calhoun. His progress was slow, as stubborn resistance was offered by the rear-guard of Johnston's army.

The next day, the three armies advanced. Palmer's corps followed Howard's; Hooker's having crossed above, moved on the left. On his left, was the Army of the Ohio, and the Army of the Tennessee advanced on lines on the right of the central army. Stoneman's cavalry was on the extreme left, and Garrard's on the extreme right, under instructions to reach the enemy's rear if practicable.

Early in the day, General Howard found the rear-guard of the enemy, formed of cavalry and artillery, and at times supported by infantry. Three lines were presented at short intervening distances, and generally behind barricades in woods, with open ground in front. When the first line was pressed from position, the troops forming it passed to the rear of the third and reformed. Thus, not only was the rear of the army covered, but two of the three lines of the rear-guard itself. The Fourth Corps advanced in two columns abreast, and pressed the enemy so strongly in the evening that a battle seemed imminent. The skirmish lines were reinforced until they had the weight of lines of battle, and artillery was freely used. The action terminated as darkness approached, and during the night, General Johnston abandoned a position which he had intrenched. His reasons were, that a portion of Polk's corps was yet in the rear; that, as he thought, the expiration of service of the regiments in the national armies confronting him that had not re-enlisted, would soon reduce their strength, and he hoped that some blunder would give him an opportunity to strike a blow without risking a general battle, or to enter such a contest with advantages to counterbalance the inferiority of his army.

General Sherman's object now was to compel Johnston to fight north of the Etowah river, divide his army, or give up Rome or Allatoona. In the event of his attempt to hold both these places, he proposed to break his line at Kingston; or should he concentrate at Kingston, to break his railroads right and left, and "fight him square in front." To give support to the cavalry on the right, he directed General Thomas to send a division from Resaca toward Rome, and Davis' had been put in motion.

On the 18th, the armies moved forward without change of order, and at night the Fourth and Fourteenth Corps encamped near Kingston. At 8 A. M. the next day, the central column, Stanley's division leading, advanced toward Cassville. Midway to that place the enemy opened upon Stanley with a six-gun battery, from an eminence, but yielded, under the pressure of an attack with infantry and artillery. Moving in pursuit nearly four miles, Stanley was again arrested. This time there was a formidable combination before him, and the enemy was observed to be advancing in two lines of battle. General Howard promptly deployed his corps—Stanley's and Wood's divisions in front, and Newton's in support of the left. As soon as the enemy observed these dispositions, his lines were halted and their front covered with barricades. When Howard's artillery opened, the first line retreated in some confusion, and the Fourth Corps advanced and occupied the position. Here a junction with Hooker's corps was made, which had engaged the enemy during the day on the direct road from Adairsville to Cassville. Skirmishing was maintained until dark, when the three corps bivouacked in close proximity. During the day, General Schofield approached Cassville, and General McPherson moved from Woodland to Kingston.

As reports had reached General Sherman that General Johnston had been reinforced, he thought it probable that he would now give battle in the vicinity of Cassville, and in such expectation he threw his armies from their parallel lines of march, toward the head of the central column. His cavalry was on right and left, in effort to break the railroad in Johnston's rear to force him to battle, or to subject a portion of his army and trains to capture, before he could cross the Etowah river. General Schofield was under instructions to support the cavalry on the left, in the accomplishment of this object, and during the day, McCook's division of cavalry had a brilliant passage of arms with Stevenson's division of infantry.

It was General Johnston's purpose to give battle at Cassville. He had been joined by French's division of Polk's corps, and the lines which Howard first encountered were Hood's, who had orders to attack. His lieutenant, however, under the impression that the columns on the east had turned his position, refrained until it was too late to overpower the head of column. Even after this failure, General Johnston meditated delivering battle, but was dissuaded by his lieutenants, Polk and Hood, though General Hardee gave counter advice. During the night he crossed the Etowah with all his trains, and moved to his strong position at Allatoona Pass. This step was a matter of subsequent regret to him, though it is probable that his sorrow would have been more profound, had he engaged Sherman's three armies at Cassville.

Pending these greater movements, General Davis with his division captured Rome. His orders did not require him to go so far from the line of march, but as circumstances, in his judgment, justified the step, and having advised General Thomas of his purpose, he passed beyond all co-operation with the cavalry, and hurried Mitchell's brigade in advance, on the 17th, drove back the rebel cavalry, and deployed within range of the artillery, on De Soto hill, on the west side of the Oostanaula. McCook's brigade and Morgan's moved forward, and the enemy, at first assuming the aggressive, was driven within his fortifications. The next morning the city was abandoned in too much hurry to destroy machine-shops and iron-works of great value, and vast quantities of stores and cotton, and six pieces of artillery. General Davis lost in killed and wounded one hundred and fifty men.

BEYOND THE ETOWAH.

General Sherman did not pursue beyond the Etowah. The rough hills and gorges around Allatoona presented such obstacles to maneuver and attack as to deter him from a direct advance. He chose rather to make a detour to the right, to turn Allatoona, or throw his armies upon Johnston's communications at Marietta or the Chattahoochee river. He accordingly gave orders for a few days of rest, and time to repair the railroad to Cassville, and accumulate supplies at Resaca.

At this period, General Johnston was calling to him infantry from the Southwest and cavalry from Mississippi, and General Sherman was making effort to maintain his relative superiority. His losses and constantly lengthening line of supply were reducing his offensive strength, and he called all available troops from the rear. May 23d, he ordered General Blair, with two divisions of infantry of the Seventeenth Corps, and Long's brigade of cavalry of Garrard's division, to move on Rome and Kingston, from Huntsville, Alabama.

On this day, he put his armies in motion south of the Etowah. The Army of the Tennessee crossed the river at the mouth of Conasene creek, on a bridge which had been saved from destruction, and advanced toward Dallas by Van Wert. General Thomas crossed four miles south of Kingston, and moved through Euharley and Stilesboro. General Schofield crossed near Etowah cliffs, and kept on the left of General Thomas. Each army had supplies for twenty days in wagons.

McCook's division of cavalry preceded the central columns, and reached Stilesboro in the afternoon, and finding the enemy there in force, with cavalry and infantry, skirmished until dark. Hooker, Howard, and Palmer encamped south of Euharley creek. Kilpatrick's division, Colonel W. W. Lowe commanding, was left to guard the line of the Etowah—an important duty, as Wheeler's cavalry had been sent to interrupt communications north of that river. Garrard's division was covering General McPherson's right flank.

At daylight on the 24th, by direction of General Thomas, General Hooker sent Geary's division to Euharley creek, to hold the Alabama road toward Allatoona, and cover the left flank of the corps, until relieved by General Schofield. The remainder of the Twentieth Corps was directed to advance to Burnt Hickory, preceded by McCook's cavalry. The cavalry commander, upon arrival, was instructed to picket strongly the roads leading toward Alatoona, and cover the movements of the army. McCook reached Burnt Hickory at 2 P. M., having skirmished with the enemy for several miles. In this skirmish he captured a rebel courier, bearing dispatches from General Johnston to a division commander of cavalry, requiring him to observe the movements of the national forces toward Burnt Hickory, and advising him that his army was moving toward Dallas and Powder Springs. Later in the day, General Garrard informed General Thomas that in moving upon Dallas, he had been attacked by Bate's division, the advance of Hardee's corps. Thus, from two sources, the fact was ascertained that General Johnston had divined General Sherman's purpose in time to throw his army before him near Dallas. At night, the Fourth and Twentieth Corps encamped at Burnt Hickory; the Fourteenth, impeded by trains, halted some distance in the rear.

The next morning, the march was resumed. McCook's cavalry moved on the road to Golgotha, followed by Butterfield's division. Hooker's other two divisions, and Howard's corps, advanced on roads running south of Butterfield's line of march. General Howard sought roads to the right, to avoid the main roads, upon which the trains of Johnson's division and the Twentieth Corps were advancing. Baird's division was left at Burnt Hickory, to protect trains and the rear of the army. The divisions of the Army of the Cumberland, marching upon four roads, were under orders to converge upon Dallas, as it was not expected that Johnston's army would be met nearer than that place. But at 11 A. M. Geary's division, the central one of the Twentieth Corps, came upon the enemy in considerable force. A cavalry outpost had been previously found near Owen's Mill, where a burning bridge had caused some delay. After crossing this bridge, General Geary had deployed the Fifth Ohio as skirmishers in advance of Candy's brigade, and when within four and a half miles of Dallas, this regiment became heavily engaged, and soon after, a charge was made by the enemy. Candy's brigade was then rapidly deployed, and after a sharp conflict repulsed the foe. General Geary immediately extended his skirmish line, formed Candy's brigade in line of battle, and brought up Ireland's and Buschbeck's in support. Advancing again, the division drove the enemy a half mile. From prisoners, it was now ascertained that Hood's corps was in front, and that Hardee's was not far distant, in the direction of Dallas. The situation was now critical, as no supporting forces were near. General Hooker, who was with his central division, now directed that it should be formed upon a hill affording advantages for defense, that the skirmish line should be extended, and make a show of strength by maintaining an aggressive fire, and that barricades should be constructed. He sent orders immediately to Williams and Butterfield to hasten to Geary's support, and informed General Thomas of the posture of affairs.

As Williams and Butterfield were several miles distant, they did not reach Geary's position until late in the afternoon. Upon arrival, their divisions advanced against the enemy with Geary's in reserve, under instructions from General Sherman to drive him beyond New Hope Church, a point where roads from Marietta, Dallas, and Ackworth meet.

Though the country was hilly and covered with trees and undergrowth, Williams' and Butterfield's division, dashed at the enemy at double-quick, and drove him back a mile and a half, to New Hope Church; but here they received his artillery fire at short range, and were arrested. Geary moved to the front again, and though the attack was vigorously made, the enemy was not dislodged. General Johnston had thrown his army directly across General Sherman's line of advance, and was ready for defensive battle. His position was a strong one, and his troops were under cover. The engagement which defined his position resulted in heavy losses to both armies.

When General Sherman first learned that the enemy was before him in force, he divined that he was on Johnston's right flank, and proposed to turn it. With this object in view, he directed General McPherson to move to the left, if he could not dislodge the eneny in his front. But General McPherson did not move to the left as projected, and the opportunity t' pass round General Johnston's right to Ackworth and Marietta was lost.

General Hooker at night intrenched a line in close proximity to the enemy. The Fourth Corps, ordered by General Thomas to his support during the day, came up by divisions in the evening and after night, and formed on his left. Davis' division of the Fourteenth Corps, having left Rome on the 24th, was now in supporting distance; but Johnson's and Baird's divisions, having been delayed by the trains on the roads in advance of them, were still in the rear.

The following day was spent in the concentration of the armies. General McPherson's army advanced to Dallas, and General Schofield's was directed to the left of General Thomas, to turn Johnston's right flank. Garrard's cavalry formed the extreme right, Stoneman's the left, and McCook's covered the rear.

The Twentieth Corps maintained the position assumed the previous evening. The Fourth was slightly changed by swinging round to occupy a line of hills, trending at right angles to Hooker's line. This change of front threatened the enemy's right flank more directly. General Schofield, on Howard's left, covered the road leading from Allatoona to Dallas, by New Hope Church. Both Howard and Schofield skirmished into position; and so close were they to the enemy that not only their skirmishers, but their main lines maintained a continuous fire.

In the forenoon, General Davis, by direction of General Thomas, made a reconnoissance to Dallas, to determine the position of Johnston's left flank and open communications with General McPherson. He advanced on the Burnt Hickory road with Morgan's brigade in front, drove the enemy's pickets through the town, and deployed his division on the east of the Marietta road. Soon after, the Army of the Tennessee came abreast, and was formed in lines extending across the Villa Rica road.

During the day, McCook, on the left, struck a column of cavalry in flank, broke it in two, and captured fifty-two prisoners. From his prisoners he learned that Wheeler's cavalry corps was on Johnston's right flank. In the afternoon, Johnson's division of the Fourteenth Corps came up in the rear of the Fourth Corps.

The opposing armies were now in closest proximity. Hardee's corps was on Johnston's left, Hood's on his right, and Polk's in the center. The batteries of the two armies were placed on the commanding positions in the opposing lines, and nothing was needed to precipitate the work of death but a word from either of the commanding generals.

As General Johnston had twice withdrawn his army under circumstances not radically different, General Sherman did not feel confident that he would maintain his position even for a day, and gave such orders as would compass the issues of battle or the retreat of the enemy. He directed General McPherson to connect his left with Hooker's right, so that he could then move his whole line by the left flank beyond Johnston's right, and interpose between him and the railroad. In addition to McPherson's movement, a strong demonstration by Hooker and Howard, and a positive attack upon Johnston's right flank, were ordered.

The effort to turn this flank commanded the personal attention of Generals Sherman and Thomas, in addition to General Howard, who was ordered to furnish the assaulting column. In the beginning, General Sherman designated the point in the enemy's line upon which the assault should be made, but Generals Thomas and Howard, upon special examination, perceived that there the enemy could bring a cross-fire of artillery and musketry to bear upon the approaches, and General Howard was directed to move his column to the left, beyond all the troops in line, and endeavor to strike the enemy's flank.

General T. J. Wood's division of the Fourth Corps was

selected to make the assault, to be supported on the left by General R. W. Johnson's division of the Fourteenth Corps, and by General McLean's brigade of General Schofield's Twenty-third Corps, on the right. The column was formed in the rear of the extreme left of the Twenty-third Corps— Wood's division in column of six lines deep, Johnson's on the left, with a brigade front. After moving a mile to the east, General Howard supposed that he had reached the enemy's flank, and directed General Wood to wheel his command so as to face the south, and advance. The enemy's works were soon discovered, and upon examination of their strength, the column was moved another mile to the east. Here, Generals Howard and Wood reconnoitered the ground, and ascertained that the line of works did not cover the whole division front, and preparation was made for attack. Johnson's division was slightly refused on Wood's left, with Scribner's brigade in front, and McLean's brigade was sent to a point in full view from the enemy's works, a little to the right of the place of attack, to attract his attention and draw his fire.

At 5 P. M. the entire column marched briskly forward, Hazen's brigade of Wood's division leading, and having driven back the enemy's skirmishers, assaulted his main line with great vigor. Hazen at first was without support from John-son's division on his left, and was so heavily engaged that General Wood was compelled to move up his supporting lines. Scribner's brigade was also hurried forward on Hazen's left, but, before getting abreast of Hazen, was struck in flank from the opposite side of a creek on the left. Colonel Scribner halted, to throw out troops to cover his flank, at the crisis of the assault, and it was soon evident that it had failed. The Confederate general, Cleburne, threw his reserves and an en-filading fire upon Wood's left flank, and forced it back, and his right at the same time was subjected to a cross-fire of ar-tillery and musketry, and was also without support, as McLean had not shown himself to the enemy nor opened fire. As both of Wood's flanks were melting away under a most de-structive fire, General Howard ordered the withdrawal of the column. The retirement was made with such deliberation as permitted the removal of the wounded. General Johnson

withdrew to the left and rear of the main line, and General
Wood to a ridge farther to the front and right.   General
McLean withdrew entirely, and left the two divisions in com-
plete isolation.

General Wood lost over fourteen hundred men killed,
wounded, and missing.   General Johnson's loss was slight in
comparison, but was himself severely wounded.   The reported
loss of the enemy was four hundred and fifty.

Two advantages resulted from this unsuccessful assault,
though dearly purchased.   A position was secured far on the
enemy's right, which was of importance to subsequent movements, and it was clearly developed that Johnston's right
would be found in strength wherever a column might go to
turn it.   At night, Wood and Johnson intrenched their respective positions.

During the day, the enemy came out of his works in front
of Newton's division, but was handsomely repulsed by Wagner's and Kimball's brigades.   Colonel Daniel McCook's brigade of General Davis' division seized a mountain pass in
the rebel center, and held it against a night attack by troops
from Polk's corps.

General McPherson found it impracticable to move to the
left, in compliance with General Sherman's orders.   General
Johnston was meditating offensive action, and pressed the national lines throughout their length in search for an opportunity to strike an effective blow.   Each commander was watching for an advantage, and yet each was " duly cautious in the
obscurity of the ambushed ground."   During the 28th, there
was brisk skirmishing from flank to flank.   General Sherman
was waiting for McPherson's movement to the left, to make
effort to turn General Johnston's position, and the latter was
planning a battle for the next day.   At night, General Hood
was instructed to attack the national left the next morning at
dawn, and the remainder of the army was ordered to join in
the action, successively from right to left.

General Hood advanced, but finding an intrenched flank,
refrained from attack and asked for instructions.   As this
delay defeated the surprise, that was intended, in the initiative, Hood was recalled.   But in the evening General John-

ston attacked McPherson, as he was in effort to leave position to close up on the center of the national line. Fortunately the Army of the Tennessee had not moved far from the defenses, and repulsed Hardee's corps with great loss. As a feint, to cover the assault upon McPherson, the enemy demonstrated in front of Stanley and Newton, and at intervals during the day there was artillery action and skirmishing throughout the battle front.

As General McPherson did not change position, there were only slight changes at other points in the line. A brigade of Stanley's division was thrown between Schofield and Wood, and Colonel J. G. Mitchell's brigade of Davis' division was placed in position about half-way toward General Hooker. The chasm here was three miles wide. Colonel Mitchell intrenched thoroughly, and cut roads to his rear to facilitate the closing up of the right wing upon the center at New Hope Church.

The purpose to move the whole line to the left was not abandoned by General Sherman, though the repeated attempts of General McPherson to leave position, during the last days of the month, invited the enemy's attacks.

During the month of May, the Army of the Cumberland lost about nine thousand men. Sixty-six officers and ten hundred and ninety enlisted men were killed; three hundred and one officers, and six thousand four hundred and fifty-one enlisted men were wounded, and eight officers and eight hundred and fifty-eight men were missing from the three corps of infantry. Colonels A. S. McDougall, One Hundred and Twenty-third New York, and John H. Patrick, Fifth Ohio, fell at New Hope Church, and Colonel Gilbert, Nineteenth Michigan, was mortally wounded; Lieutenant-Colonel E. F. Lloyd, One Hundred and Nineteenth New York, was killed at Resaca. The army captured one thousand four hundred and seventy-seven prisoners, and received five hundred and fifty deserters.

As General Sherman had held his armies before General Johnston, near Dallas, he had not made effort to ascertain with what force Allatoona was held, to turn which stronghold was his primary object in moving his armies to the right. He had ordered General Blair to move to that point, but on the first of June he was still far in the rear. But as at this time General McPherson effected his own dislodgment from the position that had been so closely watched by the enemy, and the united armies could move by the left flank, General Sherman ordered General Garrard to move to the east end of Allatoona Pass, and General Stoneman to the west with, instructions to fight cavalry with cavalry, and infantry with dismounted cavalry.

As General McPherson's army, by divisions, approached New Hope Church, the divisions of the Twentieth Corps moved to the left of Johnson's division, which had held the extreme left since the 27th of May. Davis' division relieved Hovey's of the Twenty-third Corps, and Baird's advanced from Burnt Hickory to Johnson's rear. Schofield's troops passed to Hooker's left. At night, Garrard and Stoneman were at Allatoona.

On the 2d, Hooker moved to the left of Schofield, and Baird moved to Johnson's left, when Hooker, Schofield, and Baird moved on a right wheel, drove back the enemy's skirmishers, and threw General Johnston farther from the roads leading to Ackworth and Allatoona; and yet, in front of the new positions on the left, finished defenses were found. The movements of the day were embarrassed by a rain-storm, which flushed the creeks and softened the ground.

During the 4th and 5th, the national line was gradually extended to the left, and by successive steps was advanced to Johnston's immediate front. From first to last, each army fortified as it advanced, and the field-works from Dallas far toward Ackworth revealed to the future the proximity and nature of the belligerence of the two armies. When at last General Johnston perceived that General Sherman's movement to the left had given him an open way to Ackworth, he abandoned the position and threw his army upon the mountains and hills north and west of Marietta.

The Army of the Cumberland rested on the 5th, and on the next day moved leisurely into position southwest of Ackworth: Hooker's corps, near the junction of the Sandtown road with the one leading from Burnt Hickory to Marietta; Palmer's on his left, and Howard's at Durham's house, three miles from Ackworth. McPherson was now on the left and Schofield on the right. As all the troops had been under fire for several consecutive days, though there had been no general battle, a rest until the 10th was declared. During this period, the repair of the railroad was hastened, and Allatoona was fortified as a secondary base of supplies.

June 8th, General Blair reached Ackworth with nine thousand men, having left fifteen hundred as a garrison at Allatoona. This reinforcement restored the grand aggregate of the armies again.

CHAPTER XXIX.

OPERATIONS NEAR KENESAW MOUNTAIN, INCLUDING THE BATTLE
AT KULP'S HOUSE, ASSAULT OF THE MOUNTAIN, AND THE FLANK
MOVEMENT.

JUNE 9th, General E. M. McCook, commanding the First
division of cavalry, made a reconnoissance in front, and having
driven back the enemy's pickets, formed a heavy line three
miles in front of General Hooker, and observed the enemy in
force on Pine Mountain. General Johnston's army now
rested with its left on Lost Mountain, its center at Gilgath
Church, and its right extended across the railroad. On the
10th, Palmer's corps advanced southeasterly and confronted
Pine Mountain, and skirmishing, gained an eminence within
artillery range. Howard's corps, with Hooker's in rear, came
abreast. The next day, Palmer and Howard advanced slightly,
and moved by the left flank until Palmer's left touched Mc-
Pherson's right at the railroad. General Johnston's position
was now fully discovered. His lines extended over a series of
hills from Kenesaw Mountain to Lost Mountain, with Pine
Mountain fortified in front. Before him, the ground was so
broken by ravines and so densely wooded as greatly to embarrass the advance of the national armies.

Two days of constant rain prevented all motion; but on
the 14th, active overations were resumed. The Fourteenth
Corps, carrying with it the left of the Fourth, advanced a
mile. The right of the Fourth still rested in proximity to
Pine Mountain, with the Twentieth Corps closed compactly
upon it. During the day, Lieutenant-General Polk was
killed upon the mountain by a cannon shot from one of the
guns of Simonson's Indiana battery. The advanced position

being now well turned by the forward movement of the left of the national line, was abandoned the following night, and the troops withdrawn to the main line of intrenchments between Kenesaw and Lost Mountain.

It was not known that General Johnston had a second intrenched line, and that he might not have time to construct one, General Sherman ordered an advance of his armies the next day. General Schofield was directed to threaten Lost Mountain; General McPherson to turn Kenesaw Mountain on the left, and General Thomas to press the center with a view to its rupture. General Schofield carried a line of works in his immediate front, which had been left exposed by the abandonment of Pine Mountain. General McPherson gained a hill on his left front, and General Thomas advanced a mile and a half in the center; but as in all other cases, General Johnston had his key-points well fortified and strongly defended. Newton's and Geary's divisions, supported by the remaining divisions of the Fourth and Twentieth Corps, carried an intrenched skirmish line and advanced nearly to the main line. General Howard, deeming it unsafe to assault without a reconnoissance, restrained Newton; but Geary penetrated the abatis and maintained a conflict under the enemy's guns until dark, losing five hundred and thirty-four men. During the night, the two corps intrenched a line a short distance from the enemy, and in the morning cannon responded to cannon, while the usual skirmishing prevailed between the armies. It being now evident to General Johnston that an assault could be made with fair prospect of success, he abandoned six miles of good field-works and fell back to an intrenched line on the Marietta side of Mud creek.

Early on the morning of the 17th, General Thomas ordered an advance of his army. The Fourth and Twentieth Corps and the right of the Fourteenth moved over the abandoned fortifications in a southeasterly direction, and encountered a skirmish line in front of a series of hills extending southwest from Kenesaw Mountain. The ground was so favorable to the enemy that it was not until night that his skirmishers were driven across Mud creek, and during the night he made two attempts to dislodge the skirmishers of the Fourth Corps intrenched on the west side of the stream. The next morning Generals Wood and Newton threw forward a strong line of skirmishers, and partially surprising the enemy, secured a portion of his main line. General Harker, of Newton's division, without waiting for orders, deployed two regiments to hold the position. Perceiving the advantage, General Howard ordered General Newton to move up his entire division in support. General Wood gained the ridge across the creek on the right and intrenched, and General Baird moved his division promptly on General Newton's left. As soon as it was dark, Newton's division intrenched within less than one hundred yards of the enemy's works. The advantage gained was decisive. General Johnston's new line was nearly perpendicular in direction to his old one, and that portion of the latter which he had lost was so related to the former that a successful assault was practicable. This General Thomas ordered for the next day, but the enemy withdrew before morning.

Early the following morning, General Thomas ordered an advance to ascertain how far General Johnston had receded. The Fourth Corps, Stanley's division leading, moved forward, and driving the enemy across Nose's creek, halted on the west bank; the Twentieth Corps crossed the creek late in the day, and formed with its left in proximity to the right of the Fourth; and the Fourteenth advanced toward Kenesaw Mountain and rested in line in proximity to its base, touching with its right the left of the Fourth. General Johnston's position was now well defined. Hood's corps was covering Marietta on the northeast; Loring's was holding Kenesaw Mountain, and Hardee's extended from the mountain to the road from Lost Mountain to Marietta. His lines were in view running along the base of the large mountain over the small one, and thence on the hills to the southwest. The large mountain was his salient, and from it right and left he drew back his flanks to cover Marietta and his communications. The position was one of great strength, thoroughly intrenched, and covered against approach by entanglements of every type.

Through three weeks of rain, General Sherman had been pressing the enemy from position to position, but it was now apparent that General Johnston must maintain his ground or defend Atlanta much nearer its gates. That he might reach round his army toward his communications, General Sherman determined to move his armies by the right flank, but not at first to uncover his depot of supplies at Big Shanty, and while he put the Army of the Cumberland in motion to the right, he held the Army of the Tennessee east of the railroad, in readiness, at call, or when the noise of battle should reveal the necessity to move also to the right.

On the morning of the 20th, General Wood's division and one brigade of General Stanley's moved to the right to relieve General Williams' division, that the latter might co-operate with General Schofield whose advance was resisted on the Sandtown road. During the forenoon, General Stanley, with Whittaker's and Kirby's brigades, crossed Nose's creek and intrenched a line, and in the afternoon Whittaker carried a wooded hill in his front and Kirby a bald one before him. The former barricaded at once, and held his position against repeated and furious assaults of the enemy, but the latter having been less prompt in constructing defenses, was driven back. At dark, the extended right of the Fourteenth Corps touched the left of the Fourth, and Williams' division was in connection with General Schofield's left.

The next morning, General Newton's division was relieved by a division from General Palmer's corps, when it moved to the right of General Wood. This accomplished, General Howard ordered Kirby's brigade and Nodine's, the left brigade of General Wood's division, to regain the hill which Kirby had lost the evening previous. It had been intrenched by the enemy during the night, and his artillery bore upon it, but these brigades carried it handsomely and intrenched its crest, under the fire of two of the enemy's batteries. General Wood then pushed two regiments to the front and right, and gained an eminence which commanded a long intrenched skirmish line, and permitted the advance of the right of the Fourth Corps a distance of five hundred yards. General Hooker advanced with his left abreast of General Howard's right, against all the resistance the enemy could offer. This movement was so threatening, that General Johnston transferred Hood's corps from his right to his left, leaving only

Wheeler's cavalry in front of the Army of the Tennessee, and made three unsuccessful assaults during the night to dislodge General Wood.

The removal of this corps from General McPherson's front was so thoroughly covered by the activity of Wheeler's troopers, that he was led to believe that there was a concentration rather than a vacuum behind their bold front. But though General Johnston succeeded in hiding the uncovering of his right, and the heavy concentration on his left, his subsequent aggression resulted in signal defeat. He gained, however, in defensive strength at the very point it was most needed, and defeated the combination to turn his left, and in fact defeated for a time all efforts to dislodge him. General Sherman's plan proposed that General McPherson should, " at the first possible chance, push forward on the line of the railroad and main Marietta road, break through the enemy and pursue him, or secure a position on the commanding ridge over which these roads pass," while the movement of the Army of the Cumberland toward General Schofield, who was searching for the enemy's left flank, should cause him to lengthen his line " beyond his ability to defend," and give an opportunity to break it, by a quick and energetic blow. This maneuver entirely failed in its final development through the transfer of Hood's corps from the right to the left, so secretly that it was in battle against Hooker's corps, on the Powder Spring road, before it was ascertained that it was not still before McPherson.

The movements ordered by General Sherman for the 22d, had reference to preparation for attack upon Johnston's left flank. He directed General Schofield to cross Nose's creek, and turn the head of his column up toward Marietta until he reached Hooker, and deploy south of the Marietta and Powder Spring road; while General Hooker was ordered to get possession of the ground, if practicable, up to Mrs. Kulp's, and deploy with his right resting on the Powder Spring road. This accomplished, the remainder of General Thomas' line was to be advanced in conformity. General McPherson was instructed to press the enemy in his front, to cover Big

Shanty, and hold his rear massed in readiness to support General Thomas, should he become heavily engaged.

At 3 A. M. on the 22d, Cobham's detachment of Geary's division drove the enemy from the hill a mile in front of the center of the Twentieth Corps. The whole division soon followed, and intrenched a commanding ridge, reversing the works of the enemy, and covering artillery as well as infantry lines. Subsequently, Williams' division advanced to Geary's right, and Butterfield's to his left, each skirmishing into position. The corps did not form a continuous line, but each division occupied a hill with slopes to right and left, and between Williams' left and Geary's right there was a swampy ravine. Williams' right rested on the Powder Spring road, at Kulp's house, and his division was formed with Ruger's brigade on the right, Knipe's in the center, and Robinson's on the left. In front of Robinson, who held a lateral hill, slightly refused, there was an open space extending to Geary's front. The ground was open before Knipe, except in front of his left, and almost entirely wooded in Ruger's front. General Williams' placed Winegar's and Woodbury's batteries before his center and left so as to command all the open ground. When the Twentieth Corps had attained this advanced position, General Howard moved his line forward in correspondence.

At 3 P. M., General Williams was informed that Hood's corps was massed before him. Reporting the fact to General Hooker, he was directed to deploy his division and construct breastworks without delay. He had, however, no time to construct defenses, and barely enough for array, before the enemy was seen to emerge from the woods beyond the open space in his front and dash toward his lines. The formation in triple lines and the peculiar shout of the troops forming them, alike, presaged an assault. The movement was begun with the enemy's usual spirit, but Woodbury's canister swept the open ground with such destructive effect that the enemy was soon thrown into confusion and retreat. A portion of the column was driven directly back, and the remainder was forced by volleys from Knipe's line and Ruger's left, to seek cover in a ravine and dense clump of trees and underbrush, on Knipe's left front.

A second column moved directly against Robinson's position, but being exposed in the open ground to a direct fire from Winegar's battery, and an enfilading one from Geary's guns on the left, was also thrown into confusion and rout. As a final effort, the rebel troops who had taken shelter in the ravine and woods, having been reinforced from the rear, attempted to turn Knipe's left flank by a stealthy advance under cover; but the movement having been perceived, Winegar's battery and Geary's artillery again opened. The Sixty-first Ohio of Robinson's brigade advanced to support the endangered flank, and the concentric fire of artillery and musketry soon completed the repulse of the enemy. While Hood's attack was in progress, heavy cannonading was maintained throughout the front of the Army of the Cumberland.

In the repulse of Hood's attack, General Hooker's artillery was so remarkably effective, that General Johnston admitted in his official report that his troops, Stevenson's and Hindman's divisions, were compelled to withdraw by the fire of fortified artillery. His loss was exceedingly heavy; General Hooker's very light. General Williams, who alone was directly assailed, lost only one hundred and thirty men, including nineteen captured on the picket line by the sudden advance of the enemy. Major D. C. Becket, of the Sixty-first Ohio, was killed.

As soon as the character of the attack upon General Hooker was developed, General Thomas made provision for his support. The reserve regiments of the Fourth Corps were immediately thrown to the right, and as soon as practicable, Butterfield's division was relieved by Stanley's, and moved to the rear of Williams' right. These dispositions were sufficient for defense, but the transfer of Hood's corps to General Johnston's left flank, necessitated a new combination, either to turn his position or break through his lines. General Thomas suggested that General McPherson should attack Marietta from the east side of Kenesaw Mountain; but General Sherman decided to attack General Johnston's fortified lines near his center, and on the 24th, directed Generals McPherson and Thomas to make preparations to assault on the 27th—the former near Little Kenesaw, and the latter about a mile to the south, in front of the Fourth Corps.

General Thomas designated Davis' and Newton's divisions to form the assaulting column, and during the night of the 25th, Davis' and Baird's divisions having been relieved on the left of the Army of the Cumberland by General McPherson's troops, moved to the rear of the Fourth Corps. On the morning of the 27th, Morgan's brigade of Davis' division occupied the intrenchments thrown up by Whittaker's brigade of Stanley's division. Stanley moved to the left to support Newton, and Baird held his division in direct support on Davis' right. Hooker's whole corps was held in readiness to support Palmer's and Howard's.

At 8 A. M. the preparations were complete. The brigades of Colonels Daniel McCook and J. G. Mitchell were massed in rear of the intrenchments held by Morgan's brigade, as there was no cover for formation in front. Their point of attack was a salient in the enemy's works, conforming to a projection in the ridge, around whose summit his fortifications were built, and was selected in consequence of the absence of obstructions in front. Newton's division was formed with Harker's and Wagner's brigades in line, slightly separated for better cover, and Kimball's in echelon with Wagner's. For fifteen minutes all the artillery available, poured a concentrated fire upon the points of attack, and then the columns moved forward. From the moment that McCook's and Mitchell's brigades bounded over their intrenchments, they were subjected to a galling fire of artillery and musketry. The distance to the enemy's works was about six hundred yards, and the ground was rough and partially covered with trees and undergrowth; but disregarding the fire of the enemy and the difficulties of the way, these brigades advanced rapidly until they were under the guns of the enemy. They reached his works, but such was their strength, and the spirit of the heavy forces behind them, and such their own exhaustion, that they were compelled to halt. At this juncture, their situation was exceedingly critical. To carry the works was impracticable; to retreat, threatened almost total destruction, and the maintenance of position likewise involved great hazard and loss. As, however, it was soon ascertained that it was possible to so far restrain the fire of the enemy by a vigorous response that defenses could be constructed, General Thomas directed

General Davis to hold the position and fortify it. Intrenching tools were at once sent forward, and works were thrown up within a few yards of the enemy. The loss in the advance and during the day was very great. Colonel McCook fell early mortally wounded; Colonel Harmon, the next in rank, was soon after killed, when the command fell to Colonel Dilworth. Lieutenant-Colonel James Shane and Major John Yager of Mitchell's brigade received fatal wounds, and from both brigades a very large number of officers and men were killed and wounded.

The conditions of Newton's assault were somewhat different, and so was the result. His troops were less exposed in the advance, but the formidable obstructions and entanglements held them to a terrific fire under circumstances that forbade its restraint. As a consequence, he was compelled to withdraw his division altogether as soon as it was evident that the assault could not be successful. At the moment of making a second effort to advance, General Harker was mortally wounded, and in his brigade and in Wagner's the loss was very great. Some were killed on the enemy's parapet.

The aggregate loss to Davis and Newton, in nearly equal division, was fifteen hundred and eighty killed, wounded, and missing. The compensation was the lodgment of troops in proximity to works too strong to be assaulted, and the infliction of a loss to the enemy of two hundred and thirty-six men, including one hundred captured. The officers and men engaged in this assault " went to their work with the greatest coolness and gallantry," as General Thomas testified, but their valor and sacrifice brought no adequate reward.

During the progress of the action in the center, Generals McPherson and Schofield demonstrated strongly on the enemy's flanks. The former threw a portion of his army against a spur of Little Kenesaw, and though he attained position near the enemy, did not disturb his line. The latter gained some advantage at Olley's creek, as opening the way for another flank movement to the right.

Thus far in the campaign, Generals Sherman and Johnston had each kept up the most persistent belligerence to keep the other from detaching troops to Virginia. But on the 28th, General Grant authorized General Sherman to make his movements without reference to the retention of General Johnston's forces where they were. This independence and the necessity of active offense induced immediate preparation for an effort to reach General Johnston's communications. As the accomplishment of this project necessitated the temporary abandonment of the railroad, General Sherman proposed, should the development of his movement cause General Johnston to abandon Marietta, to swing in upon the road in his rear, but should he hold that position, to strike it between him and the Chattahoochee bridge.

The Army of the Cumberland lost during the month five thousand seven hundred and forty-seven men—sixty-seven officers killed, two hundred and fifty-nine wounded, and eight missing, and eight hundred and seventy-three enlisted men killed, four thousand three hundred wounded, and forty missing. The army captured seven hundred and forty-two prisoners, including thirty-seven officers, and received five hundred and two deserters at Nashville and Chattanooga.

During the month, the enemy's cavalry in small parties, assisted by guerrillas and disloyal citizens, was exceedingly active along the railroad south of Dalton, but wrought no damage beyond slight interruptions and the destruction of a few cars. On the 10th, the "District of the Etowah" was created, with General Steedman in command, who was charged with the protection of the line of supply south from Chattanooga. Soon after, the district commander sent Colonel Watkins' brigade of cavalry to Lafayette, and a few days later it was attacked by General Pillow with about two thousand men. Colonel Watkins refused to surrender, and with four hundred men defended the town until reinforced by Colonel Croxton, commanding the Fourth Kentucky Mounted Infantry, whose vigorous attack routed the enemy. Pillow's loss was about three hundred men, including eighty captured. Watkins and Croxton lost sixty. On the 28th, Brigadier-General Smith's division of the Fifteenth Corps arrived at Chattanooga, and was soon after disposed to protect the railroad north from Allatoona.

As these troops gave assurance of secure communications, and as supplies had been accumulated in such quantity as to warrant the temporary abandonment of the railroad, General Sherman gave orders, July 1st, for the movement of his armies to the right, to turn the position he had failed to carry by assault. His orders required that General Thomas should hold his intrenchments and observe the enemy until General McPherson should pass to the right in menace to Johnston's rear. General McPherson moved his army on the 2d, and the night following General Johnston withdrew his army, and when morning dawned, was far on his way to other intrenchments. In the pursuit, the Army of the Cumberland first converged upon Marietta, and then moved on the direct roads to Atlanta. The enemy's rear-guard was overtaken four miles from Marietta, and driven forward to Ruff's station, where his forces were found in strong earthworks, constructed long before in provision for retreat. The lines of the Army of the Cumberland were speedily formed, and at midnight were again in closest proximity to the enemy. General Sherman urged his army commanders to extreme activity and vigor to press the enemy in confusion upon the bridges across the Chattahoochee. But General Johnston was secure against direct attack. His forecast of the possibilities of the unequal warfare had been so exhaustive that his steps from one intrenched position to another had all been anticipated. He held his' works at Ruff's station and on his left flank against General McPherson, until Hood's and Loring's corps were across the Chattahoochee, and then placed Hardee's corps in his intrenchments on the right bank of the river to cover the bridges.

General Sherman's plans were soon formed, though their execution was deferred to give rest to his armies, perfect his communications, and accumulate supplies in proximate depots, that he might be free from daily dependence upon the continuity of his communications in the next stage of his campaign. He proposed to make the next advance from his left, and the initial dispositions were such as at the same time to protect his communications against an anticipated cavalry raid north of Marietta. While holding the main portion of the Army of the Cumberland firmly against Hardee's corps in his defenses, and feigning with the Army of the Tennessee and Stoneman's cavalry far down to the right, he threw Garrard's cavalry to Roswell, and disposed the Army of the Ohio, and portions of the Fourth Corps, to secure and fortify the crossings from Roswell to Paice's ferry. Between the 6th and 9th, two heads of column crossed the river, one at Roswell and the other at Phillips' ferry; and to give security to the crossings, strong defenses were thrown up on the enemy's side of the river.

CHAPTER XXX.

ADVANCE UPON ATLANTA, AND BATTLE OF PEACHTREE CREEK.

ACTING upon the belief that two corps were across the river, and intrenched, General Johnston withdrew Hardee's corps the night of the 9th, and the smoke of the burning bridges was the first revelation of his action. He selected as his next line, Peachtree creek and the Chattahoochee below its mouth, and placed his army on the high ground south of the creek in waiting to attack the national armies whenever they should attempt to cross. Should he be unsuccessful in preventing their passage, he proposed to delay their approach to Atlanta until his defenses between the Marietta and Decatur roads could be intrusted to the state troops, and then sally out with his whole army, and strike the flank most exposed. He was under the impression that his method of defense, covering continually, not only his main line, but his skirmishers, with intrenchments, had enabled him to inflict losses fivefold greater than his own, and that such had been the reduction of General Sherman's superiority that he could now safely deliver offensive battle, especially as he had the fortifications of Atlanta for refuge in the event of defeat, which, in his estimation, were "too strong to be assaulted, and too extensive to be invested." But as his estimation of the reduction of General Sherman's strength was radically erroneous, there was no ground for his faith in his ability to meet him in general battle. He confessed a loss of ten thousand killed and wounded of infantry and artillery, and though General Sherman's loss in the same arms were probably one-half more, the relative strength of the armies had not materially changed since the battle of Resaca, and now, as then, he had fifty thousand against a hundred thousand men for an open battle. In the defense of fortifications, he was relatively stronger, as he had gradually received accessions of militia, to be used only in constructing and holding intrenchments, so that his purpose to act offensively before Atlanta was formed in ignorance of the fact that General Sherman had maintained a hundred thousand men on his offensive front, against all his losses and the demands of an ever-lengthening line of supply.

To General Sherman, the outlook from the Chattahoochee was promising in the main, but there were contingencies productive of no slight anxiety. He had been able thus far to maintain his communications against all the forces that General Johnston could detach against them; but Forrest, the bold raider, had given remote menace from East Tennessee, and the possibility of a dash by him from Mississippi was not yet entirely removed. And he looked anxiously, though hopefully, to Major-General Canby, commanding the newly created military division of West Mississippi, to so engage the enemy's forces in the West and Southwest as to prevent their approach to his rear. Before him, the city of Atlanta, his next objective, was in view. Its importance as a railroad and manufacturing center, and the moral effect of its successful defense, might justly be regarded as overmastering incentives to the enemy to fortify, and to fight to hold it. To sever its railroad connection with the states west, and cut off supply and reinforcement from that quarter, General Rousseau, with a mounted force, was in motion from Decatur, Alabama, to Opelika, and Stoneman had been sent to strike the same road nearer Atlanta. But another general advance could not be delayed in waiting for the issues of remote operations, and with the completion of preparations for it, there came, as an incentive to prompt motion, the announcement from General Grant that the transfer of Confederate troops from Virginia to Georgia was not improbable, and that provision for such a contingency should be made.

On the 16th, the date of General Grant's dispatch, General Sherman gave orders for the advance toward Atlanta on the following day. McPherson's army had been previously transferred from the extreme right to Roswell; Schofield's was across in front of Phillip's ferry, and Howard's corps on the south side, before Power's ferry.   The next morning, General McPherson crossed at Roswell, and moved toward the Augusta railroad, east of Decatur; General Schofield advanced toward Cross Keys, and Palmer's and Hooker's corps passed the river on pontoon bridges, at Paice's ferry, covered by Wood's division, which marched down the left bank of the river from Power's ferry, and subsequently rejoined the Fourth Corps, and with it moved toward Buckhead.   Garrard's cavalry acted with General McPherson, and Stoneman's and McCook's watched the river and roads below the railroad.

The movement was a right wheel, with Palmer's corps of the Army of the Cumberland as a pivot.   The night of the 17th, the Army of the Cumberland rested on Nancy's creek, a tributary of Peachtree creek, having pressed back the enemy's skirmishers from the bank of the Chattahoochee. The next day it advanced until Palmer's right rested at the junction of Nancy's and Peachtree creeks, and Howard's corps at Buckhead.   General Schofield approached Decatur, and General McPherson broke up a section of the Augusta railroad a few miles east of the town.   The line was now a long one, but the movements prescribed for the 19th were designed to unite the armies before Atlanta, or in that city.

Early in the morning, Woods' division leading, the Fourth Corps reached Peachtree creek on the Buckhead and Atlanta road, finding the bridge burned and a heavy fortification on the high ground beyond, manned with infantry and artillery.   In the afternoon, General Wood constructed a bridge and forced the passage, and drove the enemy from his defenses. General Stanley crossed the north fork of the creek some distance to the left, against strong opposition.   To the right, Davis' and Geary's divisions fought their way over the stream. General Geary covered the construction of a foot-bridge with a heavy artillery fire, and gained a strong position beyond. General Davis first threw over Dilworth's brigade, which soon became warmly engaged, and after a sharp conflict repulsed the enemy.   Mitchell's brigade moved promptly in support, and participated in the action near its close.   All the troops on the south side intrenched during the night.

Early the next morning the remaining divisions of the Army of the Cumberland passed the stream. This army was now compactly formed, and was under orders to advance to develop the enemy's purpose with respect to Atlanta. Between General Thomas' left and General Schofield's right there was, however, a wide interval, and General Sherman ordered two divisions of the Fourth Corps to move to the left to connect with General Schofield. Their movement to the left did not fill the interval nor greatly diminish its length, but changed its location in the general battle front, and gave the preponderance of strength to the left wing. When Stanley and Wood had moved to the left and faced toward Atlanta, in harmony with General Schofield's column, there was still an interval of nearly two miles* between the right of their line and General Thomas' left on the Buckhead road.

When General Williams crossed the creek, he advanced beyond General Geary to an eminence abreast of one Johnson had taken for his division on the left of the Fourteenth Corps, and separated from it by a depression. Here he halted, by direction of General Hooker, as he was near an extensive intrenched outpost of the enemy, and his front was covered by dense woods and thickets. At 10 A. M. General Geary moved forward to the hill on the left of General Williams, and formed his division several hundred yards in advance. Later, General Newton advanced and attained a good position in open ground on the Buckhead road, a division interval from Geary's left. General Hooker for a time held Ward's division opposite this interval, but concealed behind a hill. The resistance offered to the skirmishers that covered the advance of these divisions, and other circumstances, indicated the presence of the enemy in strong force, and both Newton and Geary made dispositions for defense. The former placed two brigades in line—Wagner's, Colonel Blake commanding, on the left of the road, and Kimball's on the right—and held Bradley's in column for support. Between the two deployed brigades, he placed a four-gun battery, and constructed slight rail barricades. General Geary formed his division with Candy's brigade on the left,

* Statement in General Howard's report.

Jones' on the right, and Ireland's massed in rear of Jones'. As the ground in front of Jones was wooded, but open before Candy and on his left, General Geary planted his guns on Candy's line. Here also barricades of rails were constructed.

A new army commander had been observing the movements of the national forces since the 17th, as on that day General Johnston, by order of the Confederate President, had given his army and his immediate projects to General Hood. General Johnston had proposed to himself attack General Sherman's armies as they should cross Peachtree creek, in hopes of pressing them in confusion upon the creek and the river beyond, but he had not anticipated such favorable conditions as now existed. He had determined to assume the offensive against Sherman's combined armies, and to make flanks to turn, by breaking lines; but his successor had been permitted to see the wide separation of the two smaller armies from the Army of the Cumberland, and then to see the latter cross Peachtree creek bereft of the two divisions which extended its flank between the forks of the stream, and then advance with its shortened left flank thrown forward almost to the hills upon which his forces were massed for sudden attack, while its right was wedged in between his works and the creek. And now to add surprise to exposure, that his success might be assured, he called in his skirmishers in semblance of entire withdrawal, and sent soldiers into the national lines, under the pretense of capture, who should say that there were no heavy bodies of their troops within two miles. So when, after formation, the most exposed divisions threw forward their skirmishers to develop the state of things in their front, there was no resistance, and no enemy in view until the moment that the massed forces were ready to spring from concealment, in boldest attack. The blow was well concealed, and it was well delivered under the most favorable conditions. It was nevertheless as complete a failure as any assault of the war.

At 3 P. M. the enemy in masses rushed from the woods. A division attacked Newton in front; another passed his left flank altogether, and thrust itself between Peavine and Peachtree creeks, and a third attacked his right flank. As the menace to his left flank involved the greatest danger, General Newton first repulsed the column on his left, and drove it to the woods, with Bradley's brigade and his reserve artillery. Wagner's and Blake's brigades next repelled the front attack, and drove back the enemy with heavy loss. The latter changed front at right angles, and engaged the enemy's third division. While this division had advanced between Newton and Geary, in evident belief that then there was a complete opening in the line, and had faced to the east to engage Newton, Ward's division advanced from cover, and the heavy skirmish line, far in advance, composed of the Twenty-second Wisconsin and One Hundred and Thirty-sixth New York, Lieutenant-Colonel Bloodgood commanding, held the enemy in check until the whole division had reached a hill to the right and rear of Newton. The unexpected appearance of this division and its destructive fire threw the enemy into confusion, and he fell back with shattered ranks. General Ward then advanced to another eminence abreast of Newton and Geary, and formed his division so as to connect with the right of the one and the left of the other. The hill he occupied commanded the open space for six hundred yards in front, and the enemy for a time refrained from attack. During this interval, General Ward fortified his position. The enemy first attacked the right of Geary's line, then passed round to attack him in flank and rear. Williams' division not being fully abreast, this advantage was possible. Geary was therefore compelled to change front to the right with almost all of his division, and extend his line to connect with Williams, leaving only five regiments, with his artillery, on his first line. When the noise of severe battle was first heard by General Williams, he was in the act of moving artillery to his skirmish line, to dislodge the enemy from his fortified outpost; but warned by the heavy volleys of musketry on his left, he deployed his division at double-quick—Knipe's brigade on the right, Robinson's on the left, and Ruger's in reserve—to await the development of the attack. He placed his batteries by sections, to command his front and flanks, and held three sections in reserve. Hardly had these dispositions been made before the enemy advanced upon Williams in great force, and having driven in his skirmishers, with his line of battle under cover of the thickets and undergrowth, approached very near without being seen. His attack, as in other cases, was direct in part, but heavy masses swept down the ravines to right and left. Hearing heavy firing on his right, General Williams sent the Twenty-seventh Indiana to reinforce Knipe's right. This regiment and the Forty-sixth Pennsylvania speedily checked and drove back the enemy, and held the ground until the close of the action. On the left, the attack was more threatening, because made with stronger columns; but Robinson's brigade, the artillery, and Geary's line upon the other hill, poured a destructive fire upon the enemy, and here, too, he was completely repulsed. This first attack swept from Newton's position to Colonel Anson McCook's brigade of Johnson's division of the Fourteenth Corps; but though signally repulsed, General Hood did not desist, and soon again, from Newton to Johnson, the battle raged furiously.

The second general action was commenced upon Newton's left in effort to double up the line by taking it in reverse as well as in flank. This time General Thomas sent the artillery of Ward's division, and in person urged the artillery horses to the greatest possible speed to meet the emergency, and then directed their action. These guns, and all of Newton's, with all kinds of metal most destructive at short range, opened upon the heavy assaulting columns, and they were again repulsed. Again the battle raged to the right; but as the national line was now compact, the enemy exhausted himself in direct attacks. His infantry assaults, as at first, extended from Newton to Johnson, and further to the right his fortified artillery was most active, but charge after charge from left to right was repulsed, until at 6 P. M., when he abandoned his effort to turn or break the line. In this action, artillery was used with fearful effect, and so skillfully was it posted, and so bravely defended, that the enemy did not reach a single gun.

When it is considered that four divisions and one brigade, in open field, repulsed an attack of the army which was intended to initiate such offense as should destroy Sherman's armies, the grandeur of this victory becomes apparent. Not General Hood alone, but General Johnston also, was defeated in the "Battle of Peachtree Creek." A new policy demanded by the authorities at Richmond, and by the Southern people, and a plan of battle elaborated by an able general and put upon trial under conditions far more favorable than had been anticipated, was defeated by less than half of the infantry and artillery of the "Army of the Cumberland." Four divisions, and a third of another, parried a blow intended to initiate the ruin of three armies, comprising more than five times as many men, and the significance of the miscarriage should have been accepted as the prophecy of the doom of the rebellion. The national troops fought great odds, introducing aggression as the policy of a new commander, to stop the further advance of General Sherman and save Atlanta. It was seemingly a grand opportunity, but the issue was positive defeat and immense loss. An opportunity for the enemy, it was an emergency for the exposed flank and the fraction of the national army subjected to attack. But there were those in chief and subordinate command, who, by personal direction and vigor, inspirited the troops made veteran by participation in numerous battles. Generals Thomas and Hooker were with their troops at the points of extreme danger, and officers and men in proportionate service contributed to the emphatic repulse of the enemy in a combination planned for grandest effect.

General Hood lost from three to five thousand men. He left over six hundred dead on the field, and several hundred of his men were captured. Ward's division captured seven battle flags and two hundred and forty-six prisoners.

The total loss of the Army of the Cumberland was sixteen hundred. Colonel Cobham, One Hundred and Eleventh Pennsylvania; Colonel Logie, One Hundred and Forty-fourth New York; Lieutenant-Colonel Randall, One Hundred and Forty-ninth New York, and many other officers were killed; and Lieutenant-Colonel W. H. H. Brown, Sixty-first Ohio, and Major Lathrop Baldwin, One Hundred and Seventh New York, were mortally wounded. A number of field and line officers were severely wounded. General Newton's loss was only one hundred, though his division was on the flank and in extreme exposure.

Generals Stanley and Wood were somewhat heavily engaged during the afternoon and evening, the enemy using artillery freely. They drove in his outposts, and came up in sight of intrenchments, with the usual skirmish line in front. Late in the evening, General Stanley captured a portion of the pickets, drove in the remainder, and worked up close to the enemy.

The night following, the enemy withdrew from General Newton's left. The next morning, General Wood advanced his right a mile and a half, and during the day, the Army of the Cumberland, from left to right, advanced close to the enemy's works. Heavy skirmishing was maintained; batteries were put in position and kept in continuous action wherever there was probability of effect, and the new front was strongly intrenched.

In the night, the enemy retired to the immediate defenses of the city; comprising a strong line of redoubts, connected by curtains, covered by abatis and cheveau de frise. The next morning, General Thomas advanced his line and intrenched as close as practicable to the enemy's works. The Fourteenth Corps fortified a line west of the railroad, the Twentieth Corps from the railroad to the Buckhead road, and the Fourth Corps from that road to General Schofield's right—the contraction of the line now permitting the reunion of the three divisions in continuous front. General Thomas' position was strong, affording commanding points for batteries within easy range of the city, and bearing directly upon the fortifications of the enemy. Constant skirmishing and cannonading were maintained. General McCook's cavalry was thrown on General Thomas' right, along Proctor's creek, and covering the Macon and Turner's Ferry roads.

On the 22d, while the Army of the Tennessee was changing position to close in upon Atlanta, General Hood put upon trial General Johnston's suggestion to sally from the fortifications and strike the most exposed flank. This time he gained a temporary advantage, but in the final issue was defeated with heavy loss.

General McPherson was killed early in the engagement, while making dispositions to save his left flank.

The same day, General Rousseau arrived at Marietta, having

accomplished his raid through Alabama and Georgia. He suggested the expedition, and had organized and commanded it by permission of General Sherman. He destroyed over thirty miles of railroad, several trestle-bridges, many station-buildings, and quantities of supplies and materials. He met and defeated General Clanton at the Coosa river, and another force at Chehaw station, and having suffered a loss of about forty men from a command of twenty-five hundred, reached the theater of war at a time when cavalry reinforcements were much needed.

CHAPTER XXXI.

SIEGE OF ATLANTA.

AFTER the 22d, the situation at Atlanta conformed in the main to the type of the campaign developed north of the Oostanaula. The two armies presented to each other fortified fronts, each inviting the attack of the other. The stronger not being able to secure a general battle on fair terms, was restricted again to a choice between assault and flank movement. As the issue of previous assaults did not warrant the attempt to carry the defenses of Atlanta, the alternative of a movement by the flank was inevitable. The railroad on the east having been greatly damaged by General Garrard to Covington, and nearer Atlanta by the Army of the Tennessee, there remained but one railroad—that from Macon to Atlanta—which had not been greatly damaged. If this road were held by the national forces or damaged beyond use, General Hood could no longer remain in the city. General Sherman resolved to change the Army of the Tennessee from the left to the right, and to reach toward the Macon road from his right flank, and at the same time throw his cavalry in two heavy columns upon it—five thousand under General Stoneman to pass to the east of the city to McDonough, and four thousand under General McCook to the west to Fayetteville, to meet at Lovejoy's Station and there destroy the road effectually. This accomplished, General Stoneman had permission to make effort with his own division to liberate the prisoners—two thousand at Macon, and twenty thousand at Andersonville. The object of these movements was to force the enemy to come out of Atlanta to fight or be invested, or force him to extend his lines to the south, and choose between Atlanta and East Point.

The cavalry started on the 27th. General McCook crossed the Chattahoochee at Riverton, and moved rapidly on Palmetto station, on the West Point road. Here he destroyed a section of the track two and a half miles long, and advanced to Fayetteville. There he burned a hundred bales of cotton, destroyed two railroad trains, burned a train of four hundred wagons, killed eight hundred mules, saving a large number, and captured two hundred and fifty prisoners. He then moved to Lovejoy's Station to meet General Stoneman. He there burned the depot and having commenced the destruction of the railroad, only desisted when there was such an accumulation of the enemy that he was forced to defend himself. Hearing nothing of General Stoneman and being strongly opposed on the east, he turned south and west to Newnan, on the West Point road. At Newnan he encountered an infantry force that had been stopped on its way to Atlanta by the break he had made in the road at Palmetto. The pursuing cavalry and the infantry now hemmed him in completely, and he was compelled to drop his captives and fight. He cut his way out with a loss of five hundred, and reached Marietta in safety with the remainder of his command.

General Stoneman went farther and fared worse. He sent Garrard's cavalry to Flat Rock, and moved through Covington, down the Ocmulgee, to East Macon. In endeavoring to return, he was hemmed in and captured with seven hundred of his command, the remainder escaping. General Garrard engaged successfully two divisions of cavalry at Flat Rock, and then returned to Atlanta. These cavalry expeditions in the main were failures, and made no impression upon the situation at Atlanta.

On the 27th, General Howard was assigned to the command of the "Army of the Tennessee" by order of the President, and General Stanley, by seniority of rank, to the command of the Fourth Corps. At this time the Army of the Tennessee was in motion to the right, and the next morning went into position on the right of General Thomas, with its line trending to the south. As a support to this movement, General Davis' division was ordered to make a detour to Turner's ferry on the Chattahoochee, and thence to Howard's right, to take the enemy in flank should he sally forth as on the 22d. This change of the Army of the Tennessee was so threatening that General Hood threw two corps upon it—Hardee's and Lee's—with great impetuosity. Attacking again and again, they were repulsed with immense loss. To create a diversion during the progress of this action, there was heavy skirmishing on the whole front of the "Army of the Cumberland;" but Davis' division, General Morgan commanding, was unable, through absence of a direct road, to reach the enemy's flank in time to participate in the action.

General Morgan was not only embarrassed in not finding such roads as had been anticipated, but he was left in ignorance of the object of his movement—his orders, which were received late in the morning, not being explicit as to his duty nor definite in description of the road which he was to pursue, and the consequence was, that the movement so far miscarried that he did not reach his camp until very late at night. The next day he was joined by General Ward's division of the Twentieth Corps, when the two divisions advanced, and driving back the enemy, ascertained that he had strong intrenched lines in their front. Strong reconnoissances from the Fourteenth and Twentieth Corps developed the fact that General Hood's lines were still strong on his right, although he had greatly extended his left.

On the 30th, the picket line of the Twentieth Corps was advanced to high ground, and captured one hundred and twenty of the enemy, including eight officers. The dash was a bold one, but the ground was permanently held. The next day General Davis made a reconnoissance toward the Macon railroad, and found the enemy within a mile, posted in earthworks, from which his artillery opened with canister. It was the old story of extension and counter-extension of lines and intrenchments, and the weaker army having inner lines could keep fully abreast, and at the same time have easy concentration for sally or defense.

During the month the Army of the Cumberland lost forty commissioned officers, one hundred and sixty wounded, and seventeen missing; five hundred and forty-seven enlisted men killed, two thousand five hundred and ninety-two wounded, and three hundred and forty-four missing—total, three thousand seven hundred and nine. General Hooker was relieved of the command of the Twentieth Corps, at his own request, and General Williams was assigned to temporary command. The President gave General Stanley the permanent command of the Fourth Corps.

On the first of August, General Schofield moved from the left to relieve Davis and Ward, and the "Army of the Cumberland" was holding the left of the investing line. The Fourth Corps refused its left to cover the Buckhead road; two divisions of the Twentieth were in the center and two divisions of the Fourteenth between the railroad and Turner's Ferry road; Garrard's division was on the left of the Fourth Corps, guarding the approaches from Decatur, and Roswell's and Kilpatrick's divisions, having been relieved on the line of the Etowah by McCook's, was on the railroad from Chattahoochee bridge to Marietta. When Davis and Ward gave room for Schofield on Howard's right, and then moved to the right of Schofield, the former was on the left in line, and the latter refused, to form a strong flank.

After the failure of General Hood's third effort at aggression, he relapsed into the defensive, and General Sherman was again forced to choose between assault and the "turning movement." The investing line had been moved far to the west and south, and yet Hood's left flank had not been found. The supposition was that the main portion of his army was on his left, extending his intrenchments as far or farther than General Sherman's, and that his main works on the north of Atlanta were held by state troops or a slender line of regular troops. General Sherman's armies had been on a strain for three months, in frequent battles, and perpetual skirmishing and watching. But though the enemy had been roughly handled during July, his army was yet as much out of reach as at any period of the campaign. General Sherman decided to again extend his line still farther to the right, so as at least to reach the Macon railroad with artillery at short range, and force General Hood to fight or abandon the city. In the execution of this plan it was necessary that his right flank should be kept exceedingly strong, while his line throughout its length should have such firmness as would insure its safety and at the same time menace Atlanta from the north so strongly as to prevent an overwhelming concentration against the advancing right flank.

On the 3d, Johnson's and Baird's divisions of Palmer's corps were moved to the right in support of Schofield, while Ward's division moved to the right of the Fourth Corps, and assisted in covering the space previously held by the Fourteenth. The Fourth and the Twentieth now held a line of intrenchments five miles long. During the day, while General Schofield was rushing to reach the railroad, there was great activity along the whole line from General Thomas' left to General Howard's right, in skirmishing and cannonading, to relieve the pressure upon the right flank in its aggression. General Schofield succeeded in getting two divisions, one of his own, and General Baird's, across the head of Utoy creek. General Baird formed his division on the right of General Hascall's, with his right swung back toward the creek.

The next morning, General Baird readjusted his line in expectation of supporting the divisions of General Schofield in an assault. But no movement was made of a general character, and late in the day General Palmer directed him to feel the enemy's works in his front with a brigade. He designated Colonel Gleason's brigade for this service, which advanced in double lines with skirmishers in front. Colonel Gleason carried the first and second line of rifle-pits, and approached so near the enemy's main line, as to develop its location and character, and drew from it an artillery and musketry fire. At night he withdrew his brigade, but held with shirmishers the outer line of rifle-pits which he had carried.

The next morning at 8 A. M. General Baird's division was in line ready to advance. He was instructed to pay no attention to his connections on his left, as General Cox's division was to fill the space between him and General Hascall, and was informed that the latter was already so near the enemy that he would not advance during the day. He was promised support on his right by the other two divisions of his own corps, although he was not yet in communication with them. Regarding his orders to advance as imperative, he threw forward skirmishers in double the usual strength, and moved forward in perilous insulation. As he advanced, he found that the enemy had reoccupied the inner line of rifle-pits which Colonel Gleason had carried the evening previous. This line he again carried against stubborn resistance, capturing one hundred and forty prisoners. He was then within short musket range of the enemy's main works. He could advance no farther, unless he assaulted without support, but held the position, refusing two regiments on his right, and intrenched himself as rapidly as possible under the fire of musketry and artillery. The main lines were now four hundred yards apart, while only thirty yards separated the skirmishers. Baird lost in this engagement, five officers, and seventy-eight enlisted men killed and wounded. Lieutenant-Colonel Myron Baker, commanding Ninety-fourth Indiana, was killed.

Soon after General Baird attained position near the enemy, General Davis' division, General Morgan commanding, formed on his right, and later, General Johnson's division took position in the rear of Morgan. As on the 3d, there was great activity along the line of the left to divert attention from the advance on the right.

Thus there was just sufficient extension and action on the right to advise the enemy of what was intended, without gaining any advantage that promised ultimate success. The line had only been extended by one division. General Sherman's orders required that the attack on the right should be pressed, and he had given promise that if it was too hard pressed, Generals Thomas and Howard should attack somewhere, but the indications were emphatic that General Hood was rapidly extending his intrenchments toward East Point, and yet General Sherman was so shut up to counter-movement, that he said to General Thomas in the evening, "We will try again to-morrow, and proceed to the end."

Accordingly, the next morning a new effort was made to reach beyond the enemy's left flank. The Fourteenth Corps, under command of Brigadier-General R. W. Johnson, by virtue of seniority, General Palmer having been relieved at his own request, held its own line and that occupied by the Twenty-third Corps, and the latter moved to the right, beyond what appeared the day before to be the left flank of the enemy. General Schofield then threw forward Reilly's brigade, but it was found impossible to penetrate the obstructions before the enemy's parapets. General Schofield then made a still larger circuit to the right, for the purpose of "breaching" his line at a point not protected by abatis, but he found his lines extended beyond the main Utoy creek. While General Schofield was operating against General Hood's left, the latter evinced great activity on his right. He felt General Thomas' line from right to left, and was so demonstrative against General Stanley, as to make it evident that he was either looking for a weak point to assault, or was endeavoring to ascertain the strength of his line, as throwing light upon General Schofield's movements. General Hood was now holding his works north of the city by state troops, supported by movable divisions of regular troops. The main portion of the army was on his left, extending his defenses to hold the Macon railroad. General Sherman's line was also greatly attenuated, and as a compensation for it, the defenses on the north were made exceedingly strong, and from them shells were constantly thrown to the city.

In the evening of the 6th, General Sherman said to General Schofield: "There is no alternative but for you to continue to work on that flank with as much caution as possible, and it is possible the enemy may attack us, or draw out." To General Thomas, he said: "Instead of going round East Point, I would prefer the enemy to weaken, so we may break through at some point, and wish you to continue to make such effort. I will instruct General Howard to do the same at the head of Utoy creek, his right." But General Thomas did not deem it prudent to assault such works, as there was a certainty of great loss, and with such a column, as he could form from his attenuated line, there was little probability of success. His response was: "I will keep the attention of the enemy fully occupied by threatening all along my front; but I have no hopes of breaking through his lines anywhere in my front, as long as he has a respectable force to defend them. My troops are so thinned out that it will be impossible to form an assaulting column sufficiently strong to make an attack sure." In the emergency, General Sherman ordered heavy rifled guns from Chattanooga to "batter the town."

On the 7th, General Hood withdrew his troops from the intrenchments assaulted by General Schofield, which, though strong and well protected by entanglements, formed no part of his main line, and their abandonment did not greatly endanger his possession of the Macon railroad. During the day the Fourteenth Corps advanced, carried a line of rifle-pits in front of the position previously occupied by the Twenty-third Corps, and established a line close to the enemy's works. The loss of the corps was seventy men killed, and four hundred and thirteen wounded. One hundred and seventy-two prisoners were taken.

From the 8th to the 10th, General Sherman continued his effort to reach the Macon road, by the extension of his line to the right. He thought it impossible that the enemy could reach much farther in that direction, but it was finally ascertained that his well-fortified line extended from the Decatur road, on the east of Atlanta, to East Point, a distance of fifteen miles. And as the farther attenuation of the investing line was not considered safe, and as the enemy's works were too strong to be assaulted, General Sherman began to cast about for a new plan. In the meantime, the heavy guns were at work throwing solid shell into the city with great frequency, night and day, in expectation that their agency would reduce the value of Atlanta as a "large machine-shop and depot of supplies."

On the 11th, General Sherman received intelligence through General Garrard, that General Hood was collecting an immense force of cavalry to operate upon his communications. It was important to General Hood to cut short General Sherman's supplies, but in the effort to do it, by breaking his railroad far to the north, he was depriving his own communications of protection. As soon as General Sherman learned that Wheeler, with eight or ten thousand troopers, was moving to the north, he determined to throw his cavalry upon the railroad south of Atlanta.

The news from the north on the 14th gave confirmation to

previous reports of Wheeler's intended raid. Early in the morning of that day he attacked a party guarding a large herd of cattle near Calhoun, dispersed a portion of the guard and captured a large number of the cattle, some portions of which were recaptured by Colonel Faulkner, who pursued upon receipt of the news. At 3 P.M. General Steedman, at Chattanooga, was informed that Wheeler was going toward Dalton. He at once relieved all the troops that could be spared from the garrison to prepare to move to Dalton. Being delayed by trains running on unusual time, General Steedman did not reach the vicinity of Dalton until midnight; and having been informed that the garrison had surrendered, he awaited daylight, and then moved forward and engaged the enemy's skirmishers. Hearing firing in Dalton, and learning that the garrison was still holding out, he dashed into the town and cleared it of the enemy. He remained for a day, and learning that the enemy had moved off, through fear for the bridges over the Chickamauga, he hastened back to Chattanooga. Colonel Laiboldt had held his position against a superior force, and General Steedman's quick relief gave him final safety.

From Dalton, General Wheeler moved north, injured the railroad slightly at Graysville, threatened Cleveland with a detachment, and then turned to the northeast. Soon after, however, he changed his course to meet in Middle Tennessee another cavalry force under General Roddy. The latter had crossed the Tennessee river, near Decatur, to strike the Nashville and Decatur railroad. General Wheeler's primary object was to damage the Nashville and Chattanooga railroad. About the same time, the enemy was active near Fort Donelson, thus giving a third intimation of purpose to disturb the communications of the national armies before Atlanta. There was, however, less force in the raiding columns or more in the troops defending the railroads than had been anticipated, as little injury was effected. The failure resulted from the combined opposition of General Rousseau, commanding at Nashville, General Steedman at Chattanooga, and General R. S. Granger at Decatur.

General Granger sallied forth from Decatur and encountered Roddy near Athens, Alabama, which place he was besieging. The garrison had been upon the defensive previously, but upon his arrival the barricades were removed, and the enemy was attacked and routed. General Granger then marched up the Nashville and Decatur railroad to Pulaski, to intercept Wheeler, who was moving to the west, followed by General Rousseau. From Pulaski he moved upon Linnville with three regiments of infantry, expecting General Starkweather to join him with a brigade of cavalry in time to give battle. He met his advance and drove it back, but his cavalry did not arrive in time to engage the enemy. During the night, Wheeler abandoned the line of the railroad and moved in the direction of Lawrenceburg. Granger then left his infantry to guard the railroad, and assuming personal command of his cavalry went in pursuit; and overtaking the enemy as he was leaving Lawrenceburg, he fell upon Wheeler's rear-guard and harassed him as he retreated. At this juncture, General Rousseau ordered General Granger to halt and form a junction with his own force. For a time the order was not obeyed, upon the supposition that General Rousseau was ignorant of the fact that he was up with the enemy and was retarding his retreat. A second order was received, requiring him to discontinue the pursuit and move upon Athens to intercept Roddy. The result was that both Wheeler and Roddy succeeded in crossing the Tennessee river without loss or embarrassment. The enemy thus escaped serious punishment, but utterly failed to interrupt General Sherman's communications.

Having despaired of flanking Hood out of Atlanta, on the 16th General Sherman announced his new plan of operations, but suspended them first to learn the results of a raid by Kilpatrick to Fairburn, and subsequently until his cavalry could make one more effort to break up General Hood's communications and compel him to fight or abandon the city. General Kilpatrick drove back Jackson's division of cavalry from Fairburn on the 15th, destroyed the station and public buildings, and the telegraph and railroad for about three miles.

CHAPTER XXXII.

THE FLANK MOVEMENT CULMINATING IN THE BATTLE OF JONESBORO AND THE FALL OF ATLANTA.

PENDING General Kilpatrick's movements the shelling of Atlanta was actively maintained, and feints of various kinds were employed by General Stanley on the left to confuse the enemy and lead to the belief that a movement was intended in that direction; but when, after General Kilpatrick's return, it was ascertained that the damage to the railroads was not such as to greatly embarrass the enemy, General Sherman repeated his order for the grand movement by the right flank, which involved the necessity of raising the siege of Atlanta, and using his armies against the communications of the enemy rather than against his intrenchments around the city. To take the place by siege would require too much time, and to take it by assault would cost too many lives. His sick, and all surplus supplies, wagons, and incumbrances, having been sent to the intrenchments beyond the Chattahoochee, the Fourth Corps was, on the 25th, withdrawn to the high ground, in the rear of the Twentieth Corps, to cover the retirement of the latter to the farther side of the Chattahoochee, to hold the railroad bridge and the bridges at Paice's and Turner's ferries, and guard the material there accumulated. Garrard's cavalry covered the movement of the Twentieth Corps to the rear, and that of the Fourth Corps to the right, to take position on the high ground along Utoy creek. This change was effected on the 26th with but slight molestation, and the night following, the Fourteenth Corps, now in permanent command of Brevet Major-General J. C. Davis, was withdrawn from position and formed on the right of General Stanley, on Utoy creek. The same night the Army of the Tennessee moved rapidly by a circuit toward Sandtown. General Schofield alone remained in position.

The next day the Fourth Corps advanced to Mount Gilead Church, and, forming line of battle on the road to Fairburn, skirmished with the enemy's cavalry. The Fourteenth Corps remained in position, as it was necessary that one corps should cover another until out of reach of the enemy. General Garrard's cavalry operated upon the rear and left of the armies during these movements, and Kilpatrick's having crossed the Chattahoochee, at Paice's ferry, and recrossed at Sandtown, was charged with similar service on the right. The Twentieth Corps, at the Chattahoochee, passed to the command of Major-General H. W. Slocum.

On the 28th, the Fourteenth Corps passed the Fourth at Mount Gilead, and reached its designated camp, near Red Oak, late in the afternoon. General Morgan's division, in the advance, skirmished with the enemy's cavalry during the day. The Fourth Corps followed, and the two corps encamped in line across the West Point railroad, facing east. The Army of the Tennessee was on the same road above Fairburn, and General Schofield was on this road below East Point. Shortly after dark, orders were received to destroy the railroad, by heating and twisting the rails and burning the ties. The work of destruction was continued through the night and a portion of the following day, by each army, and twelve and a half miles of the road were thoroughly dismantled. But this was not the road of most importance to the enemy. The Macon road passes to Jonesboro, from Atlanta, on the ridge dividing the waters of the Flint and Ocmulgee rivers, and offered a good position as a strategic base for ulterior movements, and on the 30th the armies advanced eastward to reach it, more directly in rear of Atlanta.

The Fourth and Fourteenth Corps moved to Couch's house, formed a line trending to the northwest, and went into camp. The leading divisions of each corps skirmished with infantry and cavalry, and at night it was ascertained that there was a force of the enemy at Morrow's mill, on Crooked creek, three-fourths of a mile from General Stanley's left. General

Thomas was in communication with General Howard beyond Renfrew's, but not with General Schofield on the left. General Garrard was guarding the left and rear, at Red Oak, and General Kilpatrick was on General Howard's right.

General Sherman having ascertained that General Howard was near Jonesboro, directed General Thomas to send Stanley's corps toward Rough and Ready, in connection with Schofield, and to send forward a strong detachment from the Fourteenth Corps to " feel for the railroad." In compliance, General Baird, with his own division, and Mitchell's brigade of Morgan's division, was sent forward from the center, and an early advance discovered that the enemy's trains were in motion on a road to the east toward Jonesboro, and later in the day it was ascertained from captured stragglers that Hardee's and Lee's corps had passed.

In the afternoon General Baird's leading detachment reached the railroad about four miles from Jonesboro. Although greatly in advance of other columns, General Baird determined to hold the railroad by strengthening Colonel Carleton's party in the advance, and sending Colonel Gleason's brigade forward in support. The Fourth Corps formed a junction with the Twenty-third, at the railroad, and rested on the road southeast of Rough and Ready, in a barricaded line facing Jonesboro. Carlin's division, formerly Johnson's, moved to Renfrew's to cover the trains, and late in the afternoon was ordered to support General Howard, who had been attacked by Hardee's and Lee's corps. Carlin moved as ordered, but did not reach the field until after General Howard had completely repulsed the enemy.

The situation was now partially developed. Two corps of Hood's army were at Jonesboro. It was not known that Stewart's corps had left Atlanta, but as the army was in force at Jonesboro, General Sherman determined to move against that place, and if Stewart was not there to thrust his forces between the two portions of Hood's army. Deeming it probable that the third corps would abandon Atlanta, he directed General Thomas to order General Slocum to make a reconnoissance toward Atlanta to determine the state of affairs, and also to send a cavalry force toward Decatur to observe the enemy in that direction.   Circumstances now indicated a speedy solution of all problems having connection with Atlanta.

General Sherman's orders for September 1st required all the forces to turn upon Jonesboro.   General Howard was already before it, and General Davis, with Morgan's and Carlin's divisions, joined Baird's on the railroad, and the whole corps was soon on Howard's left.   Generals Schofield and Stanley, having a longer march, and owing to railroad destruction and other causes, were greatly delayed.   General Garrard was still in the rear, and General Kilpatrick was sent down the west bank of Flint river to threaten the railroad below Jonesboro, and General Blair's corps of the Army of the Tennessee was sent in the same direction.   This immense combination had been directed against Hardee's corps alone, which had been left behind to cover the retreat to a point where the dissevered army could be reunited.

After occupying the position vacated by General Blair's corps, General Davis directed General Carlin to send a brigade to explore the ground toward the railroad upon which General Stanley was advancing. The reconnoissance was made by Edie's brigade of regulars, and was strongly resisted by the enemy. It was, however, pressed until a commanding hill beyond Moker's creek was carried, from the front of which the enemy's works could be attacked with advantage.

At this juncture General Thomas reached the head of column, to whom General Davis reported the condition of affairs, and suggested a plan of operations.   Having received permission to make the attack directly before the hill which Edie had gained, General Davis pushed his troops in column to that point, and deployed for action.   Carlin's second brigade was formed on the right of Edie's.   General Morgan crossed the creek and connected the left of his division with Carlin's right.   General Baird formed his division in rear of Carlin's left, which rested on the railroad.   General Morgan's movement was executed over rough ground, and in exposure to the enemy's artillery. About the time that the formation of the Fourteenth Corps was completed, General Stanley's head of column appeared on Carlin's left, and Grose's and Kirby's brigades of Kimball's division were deployed, under instructions to push the enemy vigorously on the left of the railroad.

The troops of the Fourteenth Corps designated for the attack, were General Carlin's two brigades and General Morgan's entire division, and were formed in double lines, and as nearly contiguous as the ground would permit. The distance to the enemy from Morgan's division, when deployed, was about one thousand yards; the intervening space was open, but swampy, and cut with ditches. The distance to the enemy's works in General Carlin's front could not be determined, as a dense thicket interposed. The defenses of the enemy were in the woods on a ridge, at various distances from the edge of the wooded ground, but in no case exceeding one hundred yards. Morgan's division was formed by brigades in column of regiments in echelon, from left to right—Lum's, Mitchell's, and Dilworth's—and were ordered to assault with the bayonet alone.

At 4 P. M., after a heavy cannonade from Prescott's and Gardner's batteries on Carlin's ridge, the troops moved forward, but owing to the thickets in Carlin's front, and the swampy ground and ditches before Morgan, their progress was slow, and there was difficulty in maintaining alignments and direction. When the whole line had advanced to the slope of a hill, and an open field within three or four hundred yards of the enemy's position, it was halted for readjustment, the ground offering some protection. Thus far the enemy's fire had been only slightly felt, except by Edie's brigade, which was some distance in advance of the troops on the right, and had already carried a projection of the enemy's works, and was exposed to a most galling fire. To give Edie support, or rather to relieve him from position in the line, Este's brigade of Baird's division was thrown forward, and took part in the general attack which followed. The other two brigades of Baird's division were retained on the left, to push the advantage on that flank, should a general assault prove successful.

At 5 P. M., the rectified lines again moved forward, and the attack was quickly and vigorously made along the whole battle front. There had been so many unsuccessful assaults made by both armies during the campaign, that the enemy regarded this attempt to carry his intrenchments, so strongly defended, as an exhibition of folly and harmless audacity. But it was soon revealed that the most determined resistance could not arrest or defeat the bold assault.

Morgan's division carried its entire front, and gloriously reversed the issue of its assault near Kenesaw Mountain on the 27th of June. The brigades of Mitchell and Dilworth there clung to the hillside under the enemy's guns, having failed in assault; here they leaped the fortifications, and under sword and bayonet held captive the troops set for their defense.

Este's brigade was successful at once on its right, the Tenth Kentucky and Seventy-fourth Indiana gaining the intrenchments in their front; but the Fourteenth and Thirty-eighth Ohio, on the left, met such obstructions, as compelled them to halt. They, however, held their ground under a fire of fearful effect. Colonel Este, who had been in the charge on his right, now turned his attention to his left, and meeting with Colonel W. T. C. Grower, Seventeenth New York, of General Morgan's left brigade, requested him to put in his regiment, which he did with great gallantry and success, though he was himself one of the first to fall. Joined by this regiment, Este's left carried the works in front, and captured a large number of prisoners. Moore's brigade, Carlin's left, encountered such obstructions as held it in check for a time, but finally joined the remainder of the assaulting troops in the enemy's works.

Equal success on the part of the Fourth Corps might have resulted in the capture of Hardee's command; but Kimball's and Newton's divisions were so delayed by the thick undergrowth, and the enemy's skirmishers, that they did not get before his main lines until 5 P. M., and then Grose and Kirby only succeeded in breaking through the entanglements in front of his barricade, while Newton, who was compelled to make a larger circuit, passed beyond the right flank of the enemy, when it was too dark to take advantage of his position.

Although Hardee's corps was neither captured nor annihilated—a conjectured result, had the troops on the left reached the field earlier—the action was the most brilliant and successful of its type during the campaign. All other assaults of main lines by either army had resulted in failure, and, as a general rule, the defensive in positive battle had been successful; but here a strongly intrenched line was carried, with the capture of nearly a thousand men, including one general officer, and many of inferior grades, also eight guns, and seven battle flags. During the night, about one thousand men in addition either surrendered or were captured.

The contest closed so late in the evening that pursuit was impossible, and the troops bivouacked in the enemy's works connecting with the Fourth Corps at the railroad. During the night, Hardee fell back to Lovejoy's Station. The next morning the national forces followed, except the Fourteenth Corps, left behind to bury the dead and collect the material abandoned by the enemy. The troops in pursuit reached the vicinity of the station at noon. The Fourth Corps formed line of battle, and made preparations to attack the enemy who was busy fortifying a line across the railroad, a mile north. The necessity of resistance at this point had not been anticipated, and the enemy was extemporizing defenses. General Stanley's line was formed with Wood's division in the center, and Newton's and Kimball's on the right and left. As his attack was to be co-operative with the Army of the Tennessee, he waited for General Howard to fix the time, and at $3\frac{1}{2}$ P. M. as directed, advanced his line. Upon reaching the immediate vicinity of the enemy, he did not deem it advisable to attack at the railroad, as Hood's artillery swept this point completely. Supposing that the Army of the Tennessee would so hold the enemy by attack, that he could reach his right flank, General Stanley advanced his center and left. The ground, however, was so unfavorable, on account of roughness, streams, and marshes, that Wood's and Kimball's divisions did not get near the position until nearly 6 P. M. While General Wood was selecting a point for attack, he received a wound which obliged him to relinquish his command. However, his left brigade, Knefler's, charged and carried the enemy's works, but could not maintain its hold, as it was subjected to an enfilading fire on both flanks. Kimball's column was exposed to a sweeping artillery fire, and the ground before them being open, the order to charge was countermanded. Both divisions in-trenched. General Sherman did not deem it advisable subse-quently to press the attack, as he was led to believe that Hood had halted merely to cover the roads to McDonough and Fayetteville, and that it was then too late to intercept Stewart's corps, reported to be in retreat from Atlanta upon McDonough.

Pending the movement south of Atlanta, General Slocum strengthened the position at the Chattahoochee, and watched the enemy closely toward Atlanta. The explosions during the night of the 1st called forth a special reconnoissance. As Colonel Coburn, commanding the advance, approached the city on the 2d, he was met by the mayor, who made to him a formal surrender of the place. After entering Atlanta, Colonel Coburn exchanged a few shots with Ferguson's cavalry, act-ing as a rear-guard of the retreating army, and captured one hundred men. General Slocum soon after occupied the city with seven brigades, and found twenty pieces of artillery and several hundred small arms; but General Hood had destroyed almost all valuable material which he could not remove, in-cluding eight locomotives and eighty-one cars loaded with ammunition and supplies. The explosion of the ammunition had been heard at Jonesboro, and was the first indication of the total abandonment of the place. As General Sherman had interposed between Stewart's corps at Atlanta, and Hardee's and Lee's on the Macon road, the retreat of the former was the only condition of safety.

The losses in the engagements south of Atlanta amounted in the aggregate to twelve hundred men. Fifteen hundred of the enemy were captured, and he left three hundred dead on the field of battle.

September 3d, General Sherman announced the conclusion of the campaign, and gave orders for the return of his armies to Atlanta, to rest and recuperate until the enemy's move-ments or some new plan of his own should call them again to action. As the enemy remained in his intrenchments at Love-joy's Station, General Sherman did not withdraw his army at once. Both commanding generals sent their trains to the rear; and thus indicated a mutual disposition to widen the breach between them for a time at least.

On the 5th, the Fourth Corps quietly withdrew from position and joined the Fourteenth at Jonesboro, at daylight on the 6th. Though the general withdrawal was impeded by a rain-storm and consequent bad roads, it was successfully conducted. The enemy manifested a disposition to annoy the two corps at Jonesboro, but there was no action beyond the exchange of a few shots. The next day, the army moved to Rough and Ready, the enemy refraining from pursuit, and went into camp on the 8th, on the outskirts of Atlanta—the Fourteenth Corps on the right of the Campbellton road, and the Twentieth and Fourth Corps to the east in reserve. Pickets were thrown out well to the front upon commanding positions. Thus, Atlanta was gained after a campaign of four months, involving strategical and tactical combinations on a grand scale, but without a general decisive battle. General Sherman did not risk a general assault, and the Confederate generals did not offer battle with a broad front, except with intrenched lines; but there were many engagements of great severity, and constant skirmishing on a scale that produced great waste of life.

The fall of Atlanta was hailed by the Northern people as a result of great moment. The noise of cannon all over the land, orders of congratulation from Washington and army commanders gave expression to the general appreciation of the campaign and its issue. The moral effect of the consummation was indeed great North and South, and yet, as no army had been destroyed or signally defeated, the possession of Atlanta was only a partial solution to the war problem in the West. The march southward of Sherman's armies, despite the heaviest concentration that could be made in resistance, the destruction of extensive manufactories of materials of war, and the palpable diminution of the central insurgent forces, were grand results indeed; but the Confederate Army of the Tennessee was not annihilated, and until it and the one in Virginia should be, the end of the war could not come. The end was indeed foreshadowed by the fact that the national armies could force their way into the South anywhere, subject to the one condition of supplies. But this war, beyond most wars, was a conflict of ideas, and the persistence of the parties to it revealed the overmastering force of the antagonistic opinions. The protraction of the war had intensified the original antagonisms, and had, besides, involved the two sections in debt to such an enormous extent that financial ruin was inevitable in the defeat of either. The success of the North would restore the Union and place its debt upon the whole country. The success of the South would be a division of the country, with a burden of debt to each portion of crushing weight. So that now, not only the primal causes of the war and the extreme reluctance of a proud people to yield to an enemy, but financial considerations, precluded peace so long as the South could maintain armies. The campaigns of the summer had made a heavy draft upon the strength of the Confederate armies; but the two which unfurled their banners before Grant and Sherman in May were intact, though one had been shut up in Richmond and the other had been battled and flanked out of Atlanta. General Canby and Admiral Farragut had neutralized Mobile, though the former had been bereft of the corps intended for its complete reduction to reinforce the Army of the Potomac. There were troops yet in the Gulf States, east of the Mississippi, to raise Hood's army to its maximum strength, though their accretion would reveal the desperate straits of the insurgents. There were forces beyond the Mississippi, whose isolation hitherto, through the viligance of General Canby, had prevented a more potential combination against General Sherman in Georgia. These troops were raiding in Missouri, and by predatory warfare were doing local mischief without affecting the general issue. The rebellion, then, was palpably resting upon the armies of Lee and Hood. The former, by political considerations, if not by purely military ones, was restricted to the defense of the Confederate capital. Hood's army alone had freedom of motion, and to determine how best to use that freedom was to the insurgent leaders the great problem of the hour.

The aggregate casualties of the Army of the Cumberland, during the campaign, from the 1st of May to the 6th of September, were as follows: One hundred and ninety-six officers and two thousand eight hundred and forty-five men enlisted were killed; eight hundred and ten officers and fourteen thousand nine hundred and seventy-three enlisted men were wounded; one hundred and four officers and two thousand six hundred and three enlisted men were captured—in all, twenty-one thousand five hundred and thirty-four men. During the campaign forty-three thousand one hundred and fifty-three were reported sick to Major George E. Cooper, surgeon United States army, medical director of the department. Of these, twenty-six thousand one hundred and eighty-four were sent to the rear; two hundred and seven died from disease, and one thousand and sixty-seven died from wounds. Almost all others, sick or wounded, were returned to duty.

General J. M. Brannan, chief of artillery, reported the capture of four guns by the Twentieth Corps, at Resaca, in battle, and four left by the enemy in his fortifications; ten guns captured by General J. C. Davis, at Rome; twenty left by the enemy in Atlanta, and eight captured by the Fourteenth Corps, at Jonesboro. He also reported the expenditure of 86,611 rounds of artillery ammunition, 11,815,299 rounds of infantry ammunition, and the loss of 1,439 artillery horses.

During the period the army captured 8,067 men from the enemy and received 2,162 deserters, as reported by Colonel Parkhurst, provost marshal general of the department. These statistics reveal the cost of war.

CHAPTER XXXIII.

THE MARCH OF THE OPPOSING ARMIES TO THE NORTH AND THE EVOLUTION OF NEW CAMPAIGNS.

WHEN General Sherman, August 13th, informed General Halleck that he would make the circuit of Atlanta with his armies, he suggested that it might be prudent to break up the railroad to Chattanooga, and shift his armies to West Point and Columbus, and there make his base for the fall campaign. To this General Grant replied, advising that there should be no backward movement, even if his roads should be so cut as to preclude the possibility of supplies from the North, and said : " If it comes to the worst, move South as you suggest." After General Sherman had taken the city, without overthrowing the army which had so long defended it, he was occupied with the question of its use in future operations. That he might hold it for purely military purposes, he banished the citizens, giving them choice to go North or South; and as the defenses constructed by the enemy were so extensive that only an army could utilize them, he established an inner line of works, which, held by an ordinary garrison, would protect his depots. That he might accumulate supplies for future enterprise, he restricted the railroads to persons connected with the army, and the transportation of military stores. But underlying these essential preparations, even to hold Atlanta defensively, there was the grand problem of farther aggression. To hold Atlanta and the long railroad to his primary base, and have forces to advance, in the manner of his previous movement, required an impracticable augmentation. As the enemy was now free to detach heavily, to break his communications, he was compelled to send troops to the rear, and, besides this draft, he was constantly losing regiments by expiration of term of service. Despairing of being able to cling to the railroads in advancing from Atlanta, he, in common with General Grant, was looking for a southern base to which he might leap, without intervening communications. General Grant suggested that General Canby should act upon Savannah, and General Sherman upon Augusta. General Sherman in reply expressed his willingness " to move upon Milledgeville, and compel Hood to give up Macon and Augusta, and then turn upon the other," if he could be assured of finding provisions at Augusta or Columbus; but without such assurance he would risk his army by going far from Atlanta. The country, in any direction southward, would supply an army that could maintain motion and freedom to forage, but the contingency of slow maneuvers or stopping to dislodge an intrenched enemy, coupled with constraint in foraging, was the barrier to a campaign having a remote objective. The questions of the direction and object of an advance, though discussed at length by Generals Grant and Sherman, remained unsettled until General Hood's movements gave a turn to affairs which had not been anticipated by either.

Soon after the fall of Atlanta, the Southern President left Richmond to confer with his western generals with regard to the next campaign, and to use his eloquence to rouse the people from despondency. His removal of General Johnston from command had not averted disaster. He had watched the closing in of the national lines around his capital, but the conditions of warfare were there inveterately defined, and he sped to the West to give shape to some new enterprise in solution of the problems imposed by the issue of the preceding disastrous campaign.

It would have been well had he called General Johnston to Palmetto, and this he doubtless would have done, had his sole object been to give a successful issue to a new campaign; but even in this supreme moment, personal considerations were dominant, and the justification of his removal of his ablest western general from command, took rank with the projects which involved the fate of the Confederacy. He now needed judicious counsel, for another campaign of dire issue would be fatal. Nearly one hundred thousand national troops were holding Atlanta, and preparing to utilize all the advantages gained in the previous campaign. It was not possible to increase Hood's army promptly to such an extent as to justify direct offense in open field, much less against Atlanta. The Confederate leaders were then restricted to the continuance of the defensive, wherever General Sherman should invite defense, or to some diversion that would retard or avert the blow which he was meditating. It was decided that Hood's army should be thrown upon General Sherman's communication, and the forces under Smith and Magruder called over the Mississippi river for conjunction in Northern Alabama; that the united armies, gathering recruits as they advanced, should sweep through Tennessee and Kentucky, and stand a hundred thousand strong upon the banks of the Ohio. Critics have been swift to condemn Hood's advance to the North, and considered as an independent movement, it is seemingly, at least, open to criticism; but regarded as a part of a comprehensive plan, it is not apparent that his army could have been used to better advantage. That the expectation of gathering a vast army on the Tennessee river was the inspiration of Hood's movement, which in itself promised no mean results, is plainly true; for before he had crossed the Chattahoochee, the Confederate President sent an order (which General Canby intercepted) to Smith and Magruder to cross the Mississippi river with their forces. The assumption of the practicability of their conjunction with Hood, is the explanation of Mr. Davis' prophetic declarations in speeches throughout the South, that should the absent soldiers return to their colors, General Sherman should be forced into a retreat as disastrous as that of Napoleon from Moscow, and the Confederate army would advance in triumph to the Ohio river. The precedents of the war were against the plan itself, as even in the first flush of the rebellion all aggression with remote objectives had resulted in failure; while in no case during the conflict, had a Confederate army been thrown with ultimate advantage upon the communications of a national army whose aggressive pressure could not be resisted. Latterly, all defense in the West had been unsuccessful, and the disparity of aggregate forces forbade all sober-minded Southerners the hope that any plan could be devised whose execution would arrest, much less avert the downfall of the rebellion.

General Hood remained at Lovejoy's Station, quietly recuperating and reinforcing his army, until the 20th of September, when those on the outlook informed General Sherman that he was in motion. General Sherman's first thought was that he was drawing back to Macon, and would send reinforcements to Richmond. The next day, however, it was apparent that General Hood had only shifted his army to Palmetto Station, and was there intrenching. This movement, and the appearance of Forrest with a force of six or eight thousand men in Tennessee, were the first steps in the execution of the new plan of operations. General Sherman now surmised that General Hood had resolved to throw his army on his flanks, to prevent the accumulation of supplies, and made dispositions to thwart him. He sent General Newton's division to Chattanooga, and ordered General Corse to unite his division at Rome, to act against any force that might threaten Bridgeport from the direction of Gadsden. Having provided for the defense of these important points, he left the disposition of Forrest to the district commanders—Generals Steedman, Granger, and Rousseau.

A raid from Forrest into Middle Tennessee had been expected by those in the rear, though not by those in the front. About the 12th of the month, General Granger received through his scouts information, which he deemed reliable, that such was his purpose, if the corps of General A. J. Smith had been removed from West Tennessee. He therefore expressed his convictions to General Sherman, and asked if Smith's corps had left Tennessee. General Sherman directed General Thomas to inform him that he need feel no uneasiness about Forrest, as he had gone to Mobile. Notwithstanding this positive assurance that there was no danger, General Granger sent a force to reconnoiter in the direction of Forrest's anticipated approach. In obedience to his order, Lieutenant-Colonel Elliott, commanding the Sixth Tennessee Cavalry, advanced toward Florence, and having returned to the main road, after a short detour, found himself in the rear of a cavalry force of eight or ten thousand men. And thus was positively revealed the first of a series of aggressive movements on the part of the enemy, which gave a new complexion and unexpected issues to military operations in Tennessee and Georgia.

September 25th, it was supposed that General Hood was moving toward the Alabama line, and this opening of the way for a march to the sea, turned General Sherman to the consideration of a movement thither without an intermediate base of supplies. General Grant, however, suggested that his attention should first be given to affairs in his rear, and appreciating the situation in Tennessee, and knowing that desperate efforts would be made to force Sherman to relax his grasp upon Georgia, ordered all the spare troops in the West to Nashville, that no further reduction of forces at Atlanta might be necessary. On the 28th, General Sherman said to General Grant: "I want Apalachicola arsenal taken, also Savannah, and if the enemy does succeed in breaking my road, I can fight my way to one or the other place, but I think it better to hold on to Atlanta and strengthen to my rear, and therefore I am glad that you have ordered troops to Nashville." And to President Lincoln, he said: "It would have a bad effect, if I am forced to send back any material part of my army to guard roads, so as to weaken me to an extent that I could not act offensively, if the occasion calls for it." Clinging thus to Atlanta, he was nevertheless so apprehensive with regard to his communications, that he sent General Thomas to the north to provide for their security, having previously ordered General Morgan's division to Chattanooga, and a brigade of the Army of the Tennessee, and the cavalry from Memphis, to Eastport, to operate against the flank of any force going into Tennessee by any of the fords near Florence. General Thomas started on the 29th, and the same day there came to General Sherman the first intimation that Hood was crossing the Chattahoochee. The day following it was known that a portion of his army was across, and by the first of October the movement was well developed, except in respect to its ultimate object. The direction of the march did not indicate an advance to Blue Mountain, but toward General Sherman's communications, and citizens reported that Rome was General Hood's destination. In doubt of his purpose and destination, General Sherman made provision for two contingencies—the enemy swinging across to the Alabama line and thence into Tennessee, or striking the railroad south of Kingston. In the one case, he proposed to send back to Chattanooga all the troops from Kingston north, and with all south of Kingston to move to the sea-board, and in the other, he would turn upon Hood and attack him.

To ascertain the direction of the enemy's march before putting his own armies in motion, General Sherman sent General Garrard to Powder Springs, General Kilpatrick to Sweetwater, General Howard to reconnoiter to Fairburn, and General Cox, commanding the Twenty-third Corps in absence of General Schofield, to send a division to Flat Rock. His object, in addition, was to get the bridges over the Chattahoochee, and then place his armies between them and General Hood. But the latter was indifferent to all such designs, as he had cut loose from all connections in his rear. General Sherman regarded his movement as ostentatious, but it was one of desperation rather, and right boldly did he and his army dash on to the issues involved. He was vigorously executing his part of the grand combination which had been projected, to change, if possible, the theater and the issue of the war in the West. Having crossed the Chattahoochee, he threw Stewart's corps upon the railroad north of Marietta, and with the remainder of his infantry forces, moved toward Dallas, his cavalry, under Wheeler, being already in Northern Georgia. Stewart reached the railroad, and commenced its destruction, October 2d, and citizens reported that it was General Hood's purpose to attack Acworth and Allatoona, afterward Rome, and in the event of repulse, to retreat to Blue Mountain, Jacksonville, and Selma. General Sherman now ordered General Stanley to move with ten days' rations to Ruff's Station, and open communications with General Elliott, who, with his cavalry divisions, was over toward Sweetwater and Nose's creek. The next day, he ordered all his remaining forces, except the Twentieth Corps, which was left to hold Atlanta and the railroad bridge over the Chattahoochee, to follow Stanley. In the evening of the 4th, the advance of the latter encamped near Little Kenesaw Mountain. General Hood's infantry was then advancing upon Allatoona, having captured the garrisons at Big Shanty and Acworth, and destroyed the track of the road for several miles. The same day, General Elliott found the enemy between Dallas and Big Shanty, occupying the old works of the national army, in more force than could be dislodged by dismounted cavalry.

General Sherman had been convinced of General Hood's audacity too late to protect his communications, and was now anxious with regard to his depot of supplies at Allatoona. He had previously ordered General Corse to reinforce the garrison from Rome, should the enemy approach from the south; and this provision saved the place. General Corse reached Allatoona with a few regiments, on the 4th, and the next morning he was attacked by French's division of Stewart's corps. General Sherman, while signaling his presence at Kenesaw Mountain, and his purpose to give the earliest possible support, witnessed the repeated repulse of the enemy. The gallant resistance of the garrison, and the movement of General Cox to his left, induced General French to withdraw entirely during the afternoon, having lost at least a thousand men. This was not a promising initiative for General Hood, and its probable bearing upon his plans was added to other circumstances of positive character to conceal again, for a few days, his ultimate purpose. French's division remained in the rear of the army, and offered such resistance to General Elliott, that it was impossible to ascertain in what direction the enemy's standards were pointing. From the 5th to the 10th, it was not known whether they were pointing northward or westward.

During this period, General Sherman again proposed to General Grant to break up the railroad to Chattanooga, and move with wagons to Savannah, entertaining the opinion that Hood would move to the West. But on the 10th, learning that he was marching toward Rome, he ordered his generals to move upon Kingston with a view to support General Corse at Rome, should the enemy approach in force. General Hood crossed the Coosa river twelve miles below, in feint upon

Rome, to cover another dash upon the railroad and his march northward. General Sherman's forces were concentrated in the vicinity of Kingston on the 11th, but again General Hood's movements were in doubt, as he disappeared from the vicinity of Rome without indicating where he was going. General Sherman, on the 12th, made effort to develop his movements, by sending Garrard's division* and the Twenty-third Corps across the Oostanaula, while a brigade from Hazen's division moved down the Coosa from Rome. In the meantime, Hood moved rapidly toward Resaca with his whole army. Here, again, provision had been made to reinforce the garrison, as, in compliance with General Sherman's contingent orders, the troops at Cassville, Colonel Watkins' brigade of cavalry, and General Baum, with three hundred and fifty infantry, moved forward before the place was invested. Colonel Watkins left his horses on the left bank, and placed his men in the intrenchments on the other side. General Hood demanded the surrender of the place on the 11th, under the threat that no prisoners would be taken if he should be compelled to carry the works by assault. But though General Baum refused to capitulate, and General Hood had a heavy force, probably two corps present, and threw a line around the town from the river above to the river below, he may have been deterred from attack by the uncertainty of the issue, or may have considered the temporary possession no compensation for the cost of taking it.

While halting before Resaca, General Hood sent detachments to destroy the railroad toward Dalton, and having himself withdrawn on the 12th, he demanded the surrender of the latter place the next day. Colonel Johnson, commanding the Forty-fourth Colored regiment, was convinced that resistance was useless, and accepted terms. The garrison at Tilton was also captured. Early in the day, General Schofield had reached Dalton on his way to join General Sherman, but not being able to go farther, and learning that the enemy was advancing, he returned to Cleveland with his train and what

---

* General Garrard drove a brigade of the enemy through the entrance to Chattooga valley, and captured two guns.

public property it was practicable to save. From Dalton, General Hood, with Lee's and Cheatham's corps, passed into Snake Creek Gap. Stewart's corps destroyed the railroad to Tunnel Hill. General Sherman reached Resaca on the 14th, and disposed his forces to strike the enemy in flank, or force him to fight by shutting him up in Snake Creek Gap. He sent General Howard to the southern entrance, and General Stanley, with his own and Davis' corps, by Tilton, to the northern entrance. But though General Howard skirmished to hold General Hood in the pass until General Stanley should reach his rear, his effort was ineffectual, as he retreated to the north before Stanley could intercept him by closing the Gap. Having emerged from the pass, General Hood had freedom of motion north and west. On the 16th, General Sherman threw his columns to Lafayette to cut off his retreat, but he was able to unite his forces in time to attain a safe position between the Coosa and Lookout Mountain.

Reference should here be made to operations by which Forrest was expelled from Tennessee. This bold trooper crossed the Tennessee river at Waterloo, September 20th, and two days afterward appeared before Athens, Alabama. Colonel Campbell, commanding the post, after skirmishing with the enemy for a short time, withdrew from the town to the fortifications. This step exposed the public buildings and stores, and Forrest immediately applied the torch. The next day he invested the fort, which had been constructed for defense by a small force, and opened with his artillery. Colonel Campbell responded with spirit, and refused two calls to surrender, but finally, through a personal interview with Forrest, was induced to conclude that resistance was useless. Forrest adopted the policy, which in many instances was successful, to make a show of force to induce surrender, when there was no intention to attack, or at least a great reluctance to do so, in view of inevitable loss or uncertain issue. The garrison surrendered consisted of four hundred and fifty men of the One Hundred and Sixth, One Hundred and Tenth, and One Hundred and Eleventh Colored regiments, and one hundred and thirty men of the Third Tennessee Cavalry. A half hour later, the Eighteenth Michigan and One Hundred and Third Ohio arrived, and were surrendered after an engagement. This was an auspicious beginning for Forrest, but fortunately proved to be his only important success.

From Athens he advanced toward Pulaski, and destroyed the Nashville and Decatur railroad for several miles. At Pulaski, General Rousseau was awaiting his coming with such force that Forrest withdrew after a skirmish. The same day, the 29th, one of his detachments appeared on the Nashville and Chattanooga road, north and south of Tullahoma, cut the telegraph wires, and injured the track. The road was soon repaired, but the party having touched it, was the advance of Forrest's main force, which passed Fayetteville the night following, moving toward Decherd. Having learned, however, that heavier forces were before him than he wished to meet, he changed direction and divided his forces. General Rousseau had moved by rail, the day previous, to Tullahoma, and General Steedman had crossed the Tennessee river, and was advancing north upon the road with five thousand men, and in the face of the two columns, Forrest turned back, sending Buford with four thousand men to Huntsville, and moving himself with three thousand toward Columbia. Buford reached Huntsville the night of the 30th, and made an ineffectual demand for the surrender of the place. Remaining during the night, he repeated his demand with similar issue the next morning, and then moved off toward Athens. Here he made an attack at 3 P. M., and was repulsed by the Seventy-third Indiana, Lieutenant-Colonel Slade commanding, which had been sent thither by General Granger to regarrison the post, immediately after Colonel Campbell's surrender. Buford anticipated an easy victory, but was twice repulsed, and was pursued after withdrawal, by a small party of General Granger's cavalry. He crossed the Tennessee, at Brown's ferry, on the 3d of October.

General Forrest succeeded no better. He reached Columbia on the 1st, but refrained from attack. He remained in the vicinity until the 3d, and then moved in the direction of Mount Pleasant, destroying five miles of railroad between Cartersville and Spring Hill. By this time, four columns were converging upon him, under the direction of General Thomas. General Morgan's division having arrived at Huntsville the night of the 1st, moved through Athens to secure the crossing at Bain-bridge; General Rousseau was on his way from Nashville with four thousand men, who had been hastily mounted; Croxton was advancing through Lawrenceburg, and General Washburne, with three thousand infantry and fifteen hundred cavalry, was passing up the Tennessee river, under instructions to leave his infantry at Johnsonville and join General Rousseau at Pulaski, with his cavalry. In addition to these dispositions, Lieutenant-Commander Forrest, commanding the naval force on the Up-per Tennessee, was requested to send gunboats to Florence, if the stage of water would permit. This combination might have resulted in Forrest's capture, had not the high water in Elk river detained Morgan, who did not reach Rogersville until the night of the 4th, while Forrest passed through Laurence-burg the same night, and crossed at Bainbridge on the 6th, his rear forces having been reached by Washburne's advance. But if Forrest was neither captured nor defeated, the main line of railroad was saved from serious damage, and to break it was doubtless the chief object of his raid.

As soon as General Thomas was advised of Hood's north-ward march, he made dispositions to offer resistance on the line of the Tennessee river, and especially to defend Chatta-nooga and Bridgeport—the most important points on the direct line of supply. He first directed General Rousseau to destroy all ferry-boats and other means of crossing the river below Decatur, and then take post at Florence, Alabama, and ordered General Morgan to return to Athens. When the direction of General Hood's march was clearly indicated, he directed General Croxton, with his brigade of cavalry, to cover the crossings of the river from Decatur to Eastport, and hur-ried Morgan's division from Athens to Chattanooga, Steed-man's from Decatur to Bridgeport, and Rousseau's from Flor-ence to Athens. The garrisons at Decatur, Huntsville, and Stevenson were not reinforced, that there might be the heavi-est concentration possible, should the enemy advance toward Chattanooga or Bridgeport.

The northward march of Hood's army, on General Sher-man's communications, created an intense alarm all over the North, from which the highest military circles were not free.

As a consequence, all available troops in the Department of the Ohio, and all, in fact, far and near, were directed to General Thomas; and so threatening was the emergency in the estimation of the lieutenant-general, that he advised the withdrawal of all the forces on the railroad "from Columbia to Decatur, and thence to Stevenson." General Thomas, however, did not adopt the suggestion, and subsequent events justified his action.

When, on the 13th, General Thomas ascertained that Hood's advance was at Lafayette, Georgia, he directed General Wagner, in command at Chattanooga, to call in all the detachments from Tunnel Hill, north, and make preparations to hold his important post. Accordingly, a very large number of guns were mounted in the fortificatious, which had been made exceedingly strong by Colonel Merrill, with his engineer regiment and the forces left as a garrison, while all the outlying troops were concentrated for the defense of the town and supplies.

Upon General Schofield's return from Dalton to Cleveland, General Thomas directed him to assume command at Chattanooga, and add to the garrison all the troops within reach.

But though General Hood was so near, he had no thought of putting his army between the mountains, south of Chattanooga, at least while General Sherman was in his immediate rear, and soon moved westward to avoid battle and pursue the accomplishment of the ultimate object of his march to the north. As soon as he turned westward, General Thomas sent General Schofield, with Morgan's and Wagner's divisions, up Will's valley to watch against the approach of the enemy toward Bridgeport, but soon recalled him, having gained knowledge of General Hood's movement upon Gadsden.

When General Sherman learned that Hood had turned westward, he proposed to follow him wherever he might go, but did not believe that he meditated the invasion of Tennessee, though the declarations of the Confederate President and General Hood gave assurance of this design. The pursuit of Hood was maintained by various routes to Gaylesville, and there General Sherman halted his armies to await the repair of the railroad and the developments of the enemy. He stationed the Army of the Tennessee near Little river, to support the cavalry and observe the enemy toward Will's valley; the Army of the Ohio at Cedar Bluffs, to feel forward to Center and in the direction of Blue Mountain; and the Army of the Cumberland at Gaylesville. While in this region the armies drew their supplies from the country.

Although General Hood had not achieved the grand results which the sanguine President had predicted, he had nevertheless been so far successful as to perplex the national commanders and give hope to the insurgents. He had not forced General Sherman into a disastrous retreat, but he had drawn him to the north, not in abandonment of Atlanta and his fortified positions, but with nearly all his forces. He had twice thrown his armies between General Sherman and his base; had maneuvered with skill; had captured the garrisons at Big Shanty, Acworth, Tilton, and Dalton; had destroyed nearly thirty miles of railroad, and, except in his attack upon Allatoona, had received no harm. He had moved in boldest disregard of railroads and communications, contrary to the precedents of the previous campaign, and, in fine, his northward march had been brilliantly executed. The resulting problems were freighted with the gravest issues. The insurgents were now too far exhausted to bear the overthrow of his army in its perilous adventure to the north, and yet Hood held boldly to his plan, as though assured of success. A new base, with railroad communications, was in preparation for him in Northern Mississippi, under the direction of General Beauregard, now in supreme command in the West, not for defense, but for aggression of the boldest type, whose explanation is found in the expectation that the trans-Mississippi forces would swell Hood's army for its resistless sweep through Tennessee and Kentucky. General Canby's dispatch to General Sherman, dated October 18th, gives evidence of the effort to reinforce Hood's army from the West; as, without heavy reinforcements, aggression, in the face of General Sherman's armies, was palpably impossible. No doubt the minor object was to decoy General Sherman from the Chattanooga and Atlanta railroad, and the undoing of the campaign on that line; but the main one was the invasion of Tennessee and Kentucky. Subsequently, General Sherman's movement to the south so changed the situation that this invasion was attempted without the trans-Mississippi forces.

While the rebel generals were preparing to invade Tennessee and Kentucky, General Sherman was engrossed with the project which he first suggested as a contingency when about to make the circuit of Atlanta, in August, and which he had since repeatedly brought to the attention of General Grant. At Atlanta, Allatoona, Kingston, and now, while awaiting, at Gaylesville, the repair of the railroad, he made suggestions to General Grant, from day to day, concerning the "march to the sea." He was unwilling to follow Hood farther west, as in this way, it had been planned that he should be decoyed from Georgia. By the 20th of October his plans for a counter-movement were well matured, and his utterances and orders foreshadowed their early execution. He proposed to leave General Thomas in command of the military division in his absence—which at first he thought would be ninety days, as in that time he could go to the sea and return—giving him as an army for defense the Fourth Corps, the garrisons in Tennessee and Alabama, and the new troops that had been ordered to Nashville. For himself he would retain the Fourteenth, Fifteenth, Seventeenth, Twentieth, and Twenty-third Corps, and a cavalry corps of three divisions, comprising twenty-five hundred men each, under the command of Brevet Major-General J. H. Wilson, recently sent by General Grant to be chief of the cavalry of the military division. These troops were to be trimmed to perfect efficiency. The railroad was to be repaired to Atlanta, for use in preparation for the march beyond, and then to be destroyed.

Telegraphic communication between Chattanooga and Atlanta was established October 20th, and on the 28th the railroad was in running order. In the meantime General Hood assumed the offensive. Advancing from Gadsden, he appeared before Decatur on the 26th and made an attack, but not with such force as indicated a purpose to storm the place—his three corps of infantry being near, and his cavalry being disposed on the south bank of the river, from Guntersville to Eastport. General Thomas sent two regiments to General

Granger, from Chattanooga, and instructed him to hold his post at all hazards. This was a feeble reinforcement, but he had no other spare troops to throw before the enemy. The divisions of Morgan and Wagner had been recalled from Tennessee by General Sherman, and for the defense of the line of the Tennessee river there were the usual garrisons, and General Croxton's brigade of cavalry spread out on the north bank. In the emergency General Sherman ordered General Stanley to report with his corps to General Thomas, and, by order, placed the latter in command of all troops and garrisons in his military division, not in his own presence, contingent upon his separation from his division " by military movements or the accidents of war."

On the 27th, General Hood intrenched his position before Decatur, skirmished during the day, but used no artillery, though he put guns in position. Under the cover of darkness, he drove in General Granger's pickets with a strong force, and established a new line within five hundred yards of the town. The next day, General Granger made a successful sortie. His troops advanced, under cover of the guns of the fort, down the river bank and round to the rear of the enemy's rifle-pits, and by a bold charge cleared them, killing a large number of men and capturing one hundred and twenty. A battery above the town was also captured by the Fourteenth United States Colored troops, Colonel T. J. Morgan commanding, but the position being too much exposed to be held, the guns were spiked and the regiment under orders retired to the fort. In the charge, Colonel Morgan lost forty men killed and wounded, including three officers killed. This resistance to the establishment of his investing lines, and his lack of provisions, induced General Hood to withdraw his forces altogether at 4 A. M. on the 29th. He could neutralize the place by passing to the west and meet his supplies, while he could secure crossings at less cost down the river; and these considerations doubtless induced his withdrawal. He lost several hundred, perhaps more than a thousand men, while inflicting a loss of eighty, and kept his troops in action in almost utter destitution of provisions.

General Hood has not reported his objects in the various

movements of his campaign, and hence his purpose in operating against Decatur has not been authentically revealed.
All circumstances, except his own statement of his plan, lead
to the belief that he expected to cross the Tennessee river at
Decatur and move rapidly upon General Sherman's communications in Middle Tennessee, and cut off his supplies entirely.
The press in the South, and his own officers, entertained and
expressed the opinion that this extreme aggression was meditated. The opposition of General Granger's small force at
Decatur was so positive, even showing the purpose of offense,
that he was deterred from the effort to carry the position by
assault. There was a diversity of opinion among his general officers as to the wisdom of his withdrawal from Decatur,
as it involved the abandonment, for a time, of his advance to
Nashville.

During the 29th, General Croxton discovered that the enemy
was crossing the Tennessee river at the mouth of Cypress
creek, two miles below Florence. He concentrated his forces
as far as practicable, but was unable to regain the north bank.
Having been informed of this turn of affairs, General Thomas
directed General Hatch, at Clifton, commanding a cavalry
division of General Howard's army, and under orders to join
General Sherman in Georgia, when ready for the field, to move
to General Croxton's support, and urged both commanders to
keep the enemy from crossing other forces, if possible, until
the Fourth Corps could arrive from Georgia and get into position to meet him. It was, however, too late to defend the line
of the Tennessee river, as Hood was master of too many
crossings; and when General Wood's division, the advance of
the corps, arrived at Athens, on the 31st, General Thomas
ordered General Stanley to unite his command at Pulaski and
await further instructions. The same day, General Schofield
was ordered to move from Resaca, Georgia, to Columbia, Tennessee, to combine with General Stanley and the cavalry to
resist the advance of the enemy into Middle Tennessee. That
an invasion was meditated had become evident from Southern
newspapers, and prisoners and deserters from Hood's army
bore testimony to this purpose. The conjecture that he could
not supply his army on the Tennessee or north of it was now

plainly groundless, as he had established communications by the repair of the Ohio and Mobile railroad, and supplies were coming to him from Selma and Montgomery, through Corinth, and thence eastward to Cherokee Station, on the Memphis and Charleston railroad. And while he had thrust the heads of infantry columns over the river at Florence and at points above and below, he had sent Forrest with his bold troopers up the Tennessee river to break up General Thomas' line of supply by the river and the Northwestern railroad.

Forrest appeared at Fort Heiman, an earthwork on the west bank of the Tennessee, about seventy-five miles from Paducah, where, three days later, he captured gunboat No. 55, and two transports, having previously burned the steamer Empress. On the 2d of November, he planted his batteries above and below Johnsonville, the western terminus of the Northwestern railroad, and an important depot of supplies. His guns blockaded the river, and shut in before the town three gunboats, eight transports, and about a dozen barges. The garrison comprised a thousand men from the Forty-third Wisconsin and the Twelfth United States Colored regiment, and a detachment of the Eleventh Tennessee cavalry, under the command of Colonel C. R. Thompson, of the Twelfth Colored regiment. The naval forces, under Lieutenant E. M. King, attacked the enemy's guns below the town, but though repulsed after a severe conflict, they recaptured a transport having on board two 20-pounder Parrott guns and quartermaster's stores, and forced Forrest to burn the gunboat captured on the 31st of October. On the 4th, the enemy opened fire upon the gunboats from the opposite bank. The guns on boats and land responded briskly, but were soon disabled, and for fear that they would fall into the hands of the enemy, both gunboats and transports were fired. The flames reached the stores on the levee, and property worth a million of dollars was consumed. It was fear rather than necessity that caused this waste, as Forrest withdrew soon after altogether, having delivered a furious cannonade. He crossed the river above the town, by means of extemporized flat-boats, and moved toward Clifton, with evident design of co-operating with the main army.

On the evening of the 5th, General Schofield reached Johnsonville with a portion of his command, having moved rapidly by rail, in compliance with instructions from General Thomas to save the gunboats and supplies. Having left a sufficient force to defend the place, he then proceeded to join General Stanley at Pulaski, to assume command of the forces before the enemy. He was assigned to this position, by reason of his rank as a department commander, though General Stanley was his senior as a major-general.

General Hood was now free to invade Tennessee, as the low stage of water in the river prevented the effective use of the gunboats against his pontoon bridges, and General Thomas could not offer a strong army on the north bank. He was also free to move to the southwest should General Sherman concentrate his armies against him; but General Sherman was unwilling to do this. His preparations for his march through Georgia were nearly completed, and he was unwilling to take a step backward, to pursue Hood. He made provision, however, for reinforcing General Thomas, by calling two divisions, under General A. J. Smith, from Missouri, and by sending back General Wilson, and the cavalry of McCook's and Garrard's divisions to give a good remount to Kilpatrick's division, retained by himself.

General Hood's threatening attitude called forth a fresh discussion of General Sherman's projected march between him and General Grant, but induced no change of plan. The conclusions reached were these, that turning back would undo the work of the preceding campaign, give up the territory which had been gained, and fulfill the predictions of Mr. Davis with regard to the effect of Hood's advance to the North, and that he could not be overtaken if followed; and on the other hand, going forward would destroy the railroads of Georgia, inflict immense damage, and produce a most potent moral effect, in illustrating the vulnerability of the South. In his last communication to General Grant, General Sherman said: " If we can march a well-appointed army right through this territory, it is a demonstration to the world—foreign and domestic—that we have a power which Davis can not resist. This may not be war, but rather statesmanship. Nevertheless it is overwhelming to my mind, that there are thousands of people abroad and in the South who will reason thus: If the North can march an army right through the South, it is proof positive that the North can prevail in this contest, leaving only its willingness to use that power." This moral effect was, indeed, the justification of the movement, as General Sherman proposed to use the territory which he had gained in Georgia as a track simply for his march, and not hold any part of Georgia except his objective on the Atlantic shore, while he left behind him one of the two great armies upon which the existence of the rebellion depended. It is true, however, that even in his last dispatches before starting, he expressed the conviction that Beauregard and Hood would be forced by public clamor to follow him. He retained for himself from his three armies the Fourteenth, Fifteenth, Seventeenth, and Twentieth Corps, and one large division of cavalry, in all sixty thousand infantry, and five thousand five hundred cavalry, and one piece of artillery to every thousand men.

CHAPTER XXXIV.

THE RESISTANCE TO GENERAL HOOD'S ADVANCE FROM THE TEN-
NESSEE RIVER, CULMINATING IN THE BATTLE OF FRANKLIN.

THE responsibility of repelling General Hood was now
thrown upon General Thomas, and the most stupendous interests turned upon his success.   Not in figure, but in fact, the
territory gained by all the battles in Kentucky, Tennessee, and
Georgia was in jeopardy.   The peril was not such as is inevitable when two equal armies meet in battle, but such as is
intertwined with the contingencies of improvising an army
against a bold invasion.   It is true that General Thomas expressed himself hopefully in his last dispatch to General Sherman, but his assurance was based upon the fact that General
Smith's forces were then due at Nashville, and the expectation
that his cavalry would be speedily remounted, and that the
coming of the promised reinforcements from the North would
not be delayed.   In these expectations he was disappointed,
and the situation in Tennessee was most unpromising during
the month of November.   General Hood's army was stronger
than when, under General Johnston, in May, it boldly confronted a hundred thousand men.   His three corps of infantry,
under Generals Lee, Cheatham, and Stewart, comprised from
forty to forty-five thousand men, and his cavalry corps from
ten to fifteen thousand, under Forrest, one of the boldest generals in the South.   Against this compact army, at least fifty
thousand strong, General Thomas had a movable army of
twenty-two thousand infantry and four thousand three hundred cavalry.   He had, in addition, the garrisons at Chattanooga, Bridgeport, Stevenson, Huntsville, Decatur, Murfreesboro, and Nashville, and the detachments in block-houses

on the railroads; but it was not considered safe to withdraw the troops from either of the two railroads leading from Nashville to the Tennessee river, until General Hood should indicate his line of advance. General Hood, with the exception of Forrest's raid in West Tennessee, confined himself to operations near Florence, during the first half of the month. His main reason for clinging to the Tennessee river was doubtless the uncertain attitude of General Sherman in Georgia. He may have still hoped that reinforcements from the other side of the Mississippi might join him as previously anticipated. But though refraining from positive offense, he was preparing for it. His forces which crossed the Tennessee river on the 29th of October, drove back General Croxton and covered the laying of a pontoon bridge. Lee's corps soon after crossed and intrenched, having cavalry in front. November 4th, General Croxton was driven across Shoal creek, but the enemy advanced no farther. General Hatch, with his division of cavalry, joined General Croxton on the line of Shoal creek on the 7th, and these officers then watched closely and reported the movements of the enemy. Wishing to ascertain the enemy's strength in his front, General Hatch crossed the creek on the 11th, and drove back the enemy's cavalry upon the infantry, and ascertained that there was a large force on the Waynesboro road. The next day telegraphic communication between General Sherman and General Thomas was severed; and as soon as it was thus known that General Sherman had started on his great expedition, there was the most anxious watching in Hood's front, in the endeavor to ascertain how the "march to the sea" would affect the situation in Tennessee. The alternative to General Thomas and his little army was the defensive in Tennessee, or the offensive in Alabama, accordingly as Hood should advance or retreat, and all were eager for the development of his intentions. Generals Hatch and Croxton watched closely for decisive indications, and although the high stage of water in the Tennessee delayed a general advance, it was soon evident that such a movement was meditated. To delay Hood's advance as much as possible, General Hatch obstructed the roads crossing Shoal creek, and sent rafts down the swollen river to break his bridges. Reports were current, subsequently, that his bridges did part, and from this or other causes, he did not complete the transfer of his army to the north bank until the 19th, when his movement was completely developed. Colonel Coon, commanding General Hatch's right brigade, crossed Shoal creek, which still separated the opposing cavalry, had a severe conflict, and did not return until he had discovered the advancing infantry. The possibility of General Hood following General Sherman was now at an end.

Up to this time General Thomas had hoped that the enemy would be so delayed, that he could concentrate his forces to give battle south of Duck river, but this was now plainly impossible. General Smith had not arrived, new regiments had not come as fast as old ones had been discharged upon expiration of terms of service, and the dismounted cavalry had made but little headway in securing horses, arms, and accouterments. His only resource then was to retire slowly, and delay the enemy's advance, to gain time for reinforcements to arrive and concentrate. It was hoped that the state of the roads would prevent the advance of infantry, but Hood appreciated the effect of delay, and pressed forward. He advanced on the 19th, on the Waynesboro and Butter Creek roads, with his cavalry mainly on his left. The direction of his advance indicated that he would strike Columbia, rather than Pulaski, and General Thomas authorized General Schofield to move to the former place, if Hood's approach to that point should be developed. General Hatch concentrated his division at Lexington, and on the 21st, withdrew to Lawrenceburg, where he was attacked the following morning.

A severe fight continued through the day, but General Hatch held the position against a heavy force of cavalry, with nine pieces of artillery in action. The same day, General Schofield commenced the removal of the public property from Pulaski, preparatory to falling back to Columbia, and moved with the divisions of Generals Cox and Wagner to Lynnville, the latter covering the passage of the trains. The next day General Cox advanced ten miles toward Columbia, and General Stanley, with the divisions of Generals Wood and Kimball, reached Lynnville. Colonel Capron was before the enemy on the Mount Pleasant road, and Generals Hatch and Croxton covered the movemeɪt from Pulaski, the latter having a severe fight at the junction of the roads to Pulaski and Campbellsville, maintaining his position and retiring at leisure by night to Campbellsville.

In the meantime, General Thomas made dispositions looking to the defense of the line of Duck river, and the Nashville and Chattanooga railroad. He ordered the two brigades of General Ruger's division of the Twenty-third Corps to move from Johnsonville—one by rail through Nashville to Columbia, and the other by road through Waverly—to occupy the crossings of Duck river at Williamsport, Gordon's ferry, and Centerville. General Granger was instructed to withdraw his command from Decatur, Athens, and Huntsville, and reinforce the garrisons of Stevenson and Murfreesboro, to protect the Nashville and Chattanooga railroad. He sent Colonel Von Schrader, his inspector-general, to Chattanooga to assist in the organization of the detached troops belonging to General Sherman's army, and another officer—Lieutenant M. J. Kelley—to Paducah, to hasten the coming of General Smith. His engineers were busy with the construction of fortifications at various points, especially at Nashville, while effort was made to provide pontoon trains in room of those which had gone to Savannah.

General Hood's rapid advance from Florence had been made with the hope of cutting off General Schofield from Columbia, and barely failed in this object, as the national troops gained the place by a night march. General Stanley, having been informed after midnight that Colonel Capron had been driven from Mount Pleasant by an infantry force, roused his corps and hastened toward Columbia, twenty-one miles distant. General Cox started at the same hour, and reached Columbia in time to save Capron from defeat and the town from capture. When within three miles of Columbia, General Cox crossed to the Mount Pleasant road and intercepted the enemy's forces, which were pressing Capron back upon the town. As the divisions of the Fourth Corps arrived, they formed in line of battle south of Duck river and intrenched. General Hatch was attacked at Campbellsville by cavalry supported by infantry. Colonel Wells, commanding first brigade, at first repulsed the enemy, but subsequently the whole command was compelled to retire to Lynnville; there the fighting was continued until after dark, when General Hatch withdrew to Columbia.

With a view to check the enemy and hold the place, heavy works were thrown up before Columbia, and the cavalry, General Wilson commanding in person, was disposed to watch against turning movements up and down the river. Hatch's division and Croxton's brigade were stationed on the Shelbyville road, six miles east of Columbia, and Capron's brigade at Rally Hill, on the Lewisburg turnpike. Colonel Stewart, with three regiments from Hatch's division, was sent to the right to the fords between Columbia and Williamsport; Capron's brigade, and the Eighth Iowa and Seventh Ohio Cavalry regiments were here formed into a provisional division under command of General R. W. Johnson.

During the 24th and 25th, the enemy skirmished before Columbia, but showed nothing but dismounted cavalry, until the 26th, when his infantry appeared, and during that day and the next he pressed the lines, but made no assault. General Schofield constructed an interior line of works, but these were soon regarded as untenable, as the enemy manifested an intention to pass round the position. An effort was made to cross to the north bank the night of the 26th, but failed on account of a severe storm and entire darkness. The night following, the movement was accomplished, and General Schofield left General Ruger to hold the crossing at the railroad bridge; placed General Cox's division before the town, and directed General Stanley to station his corps on the Franklin turnpike, in readiness to meet the enemy should he attempt to cross near Columbia. These dispositions were made by General Schofield in hope that he could hold the line of Duck river, until reinforcements should arrive; but the promised reinforcements had not reached Nashville. General Thomas had received twelve thousand raw troops, and had sent North, either on final discharge or to vote, fifteen thousand veterans. General Smith had not come, and only one thousand cavalry had found horses and the front. General Thomas had obtained permission to call upon the governors of the Western States for troops, but was cautioned to use such troops sparingly.

The 28th was passed in quietness, at Columbia, though there were palpable indications that quietness there meant activity in another quarter. At noon the enemy's cavalry appeared at various fords, between Columbia and the Lewisburg turnpike, in such force as to indicate plainly the purpose to cross. General Hood's cavalry was especially massed at Huey's Mills, eight miles above Columbia, and having there driven in General Wilson's pickets, began to pass over the river. At 2.10 P. M. General Wilson notified General Schofield of the enemy's movements, and informed him that he would concentrate his cavalry at Hunt's creek, on the Lewisburg turnpike, expressing the belief that the enemy would swing in between them and strike the road to Franklin, at Spring Hill.

General Wilson's cavalry detachments, at the various fords, held their respective positions as long as possible, but all were finally driven back, and it was then evident that three divisions of cavalry—Chalmers', Buford's, and Jackson's—had crossed Duck river. By 7 P. M. General Wilson had concentrated his command, as far as practicable, at Hart's Cross-roads. Major Young, of the Fifth Iowa Cavalry, commanding detachments, was intercepted, but cut his way through the enemy's lines with trifling loss. During the night General Wilson ascertained that General Forrest was moving toward Franklin, and also that General Hood's infantry forces were expected to cross before morning. In view of the palpable peril, he advised General Schofield to withdraw to Franklin, and suggested that his command should be at Spring Hill by 10 A. M. the next day. When General Thomas was informed of the probable state of things at Columbia, he directed General Schofield to withdraw to Franklin, as soon as he should gain certain knowledge of the reported movements of the enemy. And very soon afterward, at 3.30 A. M. on the 29th, he directed him to withdraw from Columbia, as by this time he was convinced that General Hood had turned General Schofield's position.

The situation at Columbia on the morning of the 29th, and during that day, was exceedingly critical. General Hood's infantry forces were crossing the river during all the early hours, at Huey's Mills, on a road leading directly to Spring Hill; his cavalry forces had very early cut off all communication between Generals Schofield and Wilson, and were pressing the latter back upon Franklin, on the Lewisburg turnpike, General Wilson having chosen this line of retreat as the one upon which he could best resist General Forrest, and cover the retirement of the infantry on the direct road from Columbia to Franklin.

To develop the facts fully, before withdrawing altogether from Columbia, General Schofield directed General Wood to send a brigade up the river to watch the enemy; ordered General Stanley to move with two of his divisions to Spring Hill, to hold that point and cover the trains and spare artillery; left General Cox to guard the crossing at Columbia, and ordered Ruger's division to take position on the turnpike, in rear of Rutherford's creek, leaving one regiment to hold the ford at Columbia, near the railroad bridge—this bridge having been partially destroyed and all the others entirely.

General Wood sent Post's brigade early, to reconnoiter up the river; and at 8 A. M. General Stanley moved toward Spring Hill with Wagner's and Kimball's divisions. Before reaching Rutherford's creek, four miles distant, he learned that the enemy was crossing infantry and trains above Columbia, and was moving to the north on a converging road which touched General Schofield's line of retreat at Spring Hill. Apprehending that the forces that Colonel Post reported to be crossing the river might make a flank attack upon the troops between Duck river and Rutherford's creek, he halted Kimball's division and formed it facing east, and then proceeded to Spring Hill with Wagner's division. When within two miles of the place, at 11.30 A. M., he was informed that the enemy's cavalry was approaching from the direction of Rally Hill. The noise of firing east of the village immediately called the division to rapid motion, and the town was gained in time to meet the enemy, who was driving back a small force of national toops, composed of infantry and cavalry. Colonel Opdycke immediately deployed his brigade and drove back the enemy's cavalry, when General Stanley threw forward the division to hold the town and protect the trains. Opdycke's and Lane's brigades were deployed to cover such space as served to park the wagons, and Bradley's was advanced to hold a wooded knoll nearly a mile to the east, which commanded the approaches from that direction.

At the time these dispositions were made, it was not known that heavy forces of infantry were near ; but this fact was soon after developed by a fierce assault upon General Bradley. The nature of the attack, confirming the first reports of the advance of the Confederate army to the east of Columbia, gave demonstration of the greatest peril, not only to General Stanley, but to the four divisions behind him. General Hood's columns had now passed General Schofield's left flank, and were enveloping a single division, twelve miles in his rear, or twelve miles in advance, when he should face to the north to retreat.

When the enemy's infantry attacked General Bradley from the east, his cavalry on the west of the town threatened the railroad station, and then fell upon a small train, composed of some baggage-wagons, at Thompson's Station, three miles north. About the same time, General Stanley received a dispatch from General Schofield, confirming the reports that had first indicated the strategy of General Hood, and led him to fear that a heavy force was enveloping his position. He could not therefore reinforce General Bradley, lest he should thereby expose his trains to capture or destruction.

General Bradley repulsed two fierce attacks, but in the third his right flank was overlapped by the enemy's line, and he was compelled to fall back to the town, where his shattered brigade was rallied and reformed. The enemy followed, but fell under the fire of eight pieces of artillery, at good range for spherical case shot, and was also taken in flank by a section on the turnpike, south of the town. A portion of the attacking troops then fled to the rear, and other portions sought cover in a ravine between the opposing lines. General Stanley reported Bradley's loss at one hundred and fifty men killed and wounded, and the enemy's at five hundred. General Bradley received a severe wound while encouraging his men to resist the last attack, and the command of the brigade passed to Colonel Conrad.

As darkness fell, the enemy's lines were extended until a corps of infantry was in order of battle facing the Franklin road. Two other corps were near a little later, one deployed also, and Forrest's troopers were on the main road, both north and south of Spring Hill. It seemed hardly possible in this posture of affairs that General Schofield's forces and trains could elude this involution by General Hood's army, and yet this result was achieved without a serious contest.

During the day, the enemy covered his movement past General Schofield's left to his rear by earnest efforts, as General Schofield believed, to force a crossing and lay a pontoon bridge at Columbia, that he might thus secure a passage for his artillery, which was impracticable at Huey's Mills. His repeated attacks were all repulsed by General Cox, and at 3 P. M. General Schofield became satisfied that the enemy would not attack on Duck river, but was moving two corps directly to Spring Hill. He then gave orders for the withdrawal of all the troops when darkness would cover the movement, and with General Ruger's division hastened forward to open communications with General Stanley. At dark, he brushed away the enemy's cavalry from the road, three miles south of Stanley, and joined him at 7 P. M. Whittaker's brigade of Kimball's division followed Ruger's closely from Rutherford's creek, and upon arrival was posted parallel to the turnpike, where the enemy's left rested within eight hundred yards of the road, to cover the passage of the troops still in the rear. General Schofield, leaving the management of the march and the safety of the trains to General Stanley, then moved again with Ruger's division to clear the road to Franklin. As he approached Thompson's Station, the enemy's cavalry disappeared, and then the road was open from Columbia to Franklin, though an army of at least fifty thousand men was in closest proximity to it, and along its front four divisions and an immense train were at rest or in motion, and yet there was only slight skirmishing here and there, and occasional picket-firing. There was momentary expectation that this great army would take a step forward, and press troops, artillery, and trains from the road in confusion and rout; but still the movement went on without interruption by the enemy.

Having cleared the road at Thompson's Station, General Schofield returned to Spring Hill to make arrangements and dispositions to avert his extreme peril. He did not anticipate the possibility of his getting his army out of the reach of the enemy that night, and feared that he would be forced to fight a general battle the next day, or lose his wagon train. In the emergency he had dispatched a staff officer to Franklin to bring forward the command of General A. J. Smith, which he supposed had reached Franklin.

At 11 P. M. General Thomas, believing that General Schofield had, in obedience to his order of 3.30 A. M., withdrawn from Columbia earlier in the day, telegraphed to him at Franklin to withdraw from that place also, should the enemy attempt to get on his flank with infantry. As General Smith's troops had not yet arrived at Nashville, he considered it necessary, should the enemy advance quickly upon General Schofield, to concentrate his forces at Nashville.

General Cox left Columbia at 7 P. M., followed by General Wood, and the latter by General Kimball. There was some delay at Rutherford's creek, as the bridge was inadequate for the emergency, but nevertheless the divisions, one after another, arrived at Spring Hill—the foremost of the three at 11 P. M. The enemy's pickets fired into the column frequently, but when they did not come upon the road, the national troops gave no response. The enemy was so close to the road, that when a column was not moving upon it, it was difficult for a single horseman to pass.

The danger did not end with the arrival of the last division at Spring Hill. It was 1 A. M. before a train of eight hundred wagons, including artillery and ambulances, could move toward Franklin, in rear of Cox's division, as at starting the wagons had to pass singly over a bridge. This caused delay, and consequently peril, as an attack was inevitable, unless the train and troops could be put on the road and in motion before daylight. General Stanley was advised to burn at least a portion of the wagons, to avoid an attack, but he determined to save all, if practicable. At 3 A. M. an attack upon the head of the train, north of Thompson's, was reported, and all wagons on the road were stopped until General Kimball could rush forward to clear the road, and General Wood deploy his division on the east of the road. The attack was repulsed by Major Steele, with stragglers that he had gathered together, and then the train, bereft of ten wagons burned by the enemy, moved on, with Wood's division on the right and Wagner's in the rear. At 5 A. M. the last wagon crossed the bridge, and then all was in motion. The enemy's cavalry was on the hills to the right for awhile, and made one or two dashes, but these were easily repulsed by Wood's skirmishers, with the help, at one time, of a section of Canby's battery. Colonel Opdycke's brigade formed the rear-guard, and though skirmishing with the pursuing forces of the enemy, kept them so well in check as to save the weary and lame from capture. Rarely has an army escaped so easily from a peril so threatening. It has been accepted as true that General Hood ordered one corps general and then another to attack the national troops when passing so near the front of his army, at Spring Hill; but these generals disobeyed the orders, so plainly imperative from the situation itself, as well as from the voice of the commander-in-chief. From whatever cause the failure resulted, the opportunity of the campaign was lost to the Confederate army.

General Schofield, with the head of his column, reached Franklin before daylight, and he immediately made preparation to pass the Harpeth river, as he had been ordered by General Thomas to fall behind this stream. The railroad bridge was fitted as rapidly as possible for the passage of wagons, and a foot-bridge was constructed, which also proved adequate for them. General Schofield's aim was to get his train and artillery over the river before the enemy could attack him, but he nevertheless instructed General Cox to put the troops in line around the town, as the several divisions should arrive. The Twenty-third Corps formed the left and center—Cox's division on the left with its left flank on the river, Ruger's on its right, and Kimball's completing the circuit to the river on the right. Wood's division crossed to the north bank to be directed to the support of either flank in the event of a turning movement, and Wagner's was left in front to check the enemy, should he form his army to attack. Colonel Opdycke reached the heights two miles south of the town at noon, and was ordered to halt to observe the enemy. Croxton's brigade of cavalry was pushed back by infantry on the Lewisburg turnpike, and at 1 P. M. Colonel Opdycke reported heavy columns of infantry advancing on the Columbia and Lewisburg roads, when the division was withdrawn to the more immediate front of the army on the Columbia road. Colonel Opdycke, at his own notion, came inside the main line, and halted his brigade on the Columbia road in rear of the junction of the right and left flanks of Cox's and Ruger's divisions of the Twenty-third Corps.

The line as formed, was about one mile and a half long, inclosing the town, except on the north where the Harpeth river was the boundary, with its flanks touching the river. The line rested on a slight elevation, or series of low hills, which encompassed the town. The troops threw up breastworks, and a slight abatis was also constructed in places. The artillery of the Twenty-third Corps was on the north side of the river, and a portion of it placed in Fort Granger—a fortification previously constructed so as to command the railroad, which leaves the town near the river, and runs in parallelism with it for some distance. The batteries of the Fourth Corps were held on the south side, some of them having been placed on the line and others in reserve. The Sixth Ohio Light Artillery and the First Kentucky battery were in position on the right and left of the Columbia road, before the battle opened. Battery "M," Fourth United States Artillery, and battery "G," First Ohio Light Artillery, were placed with the left brigade of the Twenty-third Corps, and Bridge's battery, Illinois Light Artillery, was posted in the center of Strickland's brigade of Ruger's division. The position was a good one for defense, and the undulations of the ground in front exposed the enemy in approaching. The key-point was Carter's Hill on the Columbia road, and was opposite the center of General Hood's army, which was advancing on the Lewisburg, Columbia, and Carter's Creek turnpikes.

General Croxton resisted the enemy's infantry on the Lewisburg road until 2 P. M., when, having learned that Forrest was moving to his left, as if to cross at Hughes' ferry, he crossed at McGarock's ford. He had hardly gained the north bank before it was reported that the enemy's cavalry were endeavoring to cross at several points above Franklin. General Wilson now threw his whole force before General Forrest, and held him in check during the day and following night, in some cases driving back detachments after they had succeeded in crossing the river. Had General Forrest succeeded in crossing with his whole force, he could have caused a heavy detachment of forces from the little army to protect the trains already in motion toward Nashville, in anticipation of the withdrawal of the army from Franklin at 6 P. M., should General Hood make no attack.

At the time that General Croxton was forced to cross the river, General Hood's infantry began to appear in great force in front of Wagner's two brigades, but it was not believed by the ranking generals of the national army, until 4 P. M., that he would attempt to carry the position by assault. But at this hour his army emerged from the woods, in splendid array, heavily massed on the Columbia road, two corps in front and one in reserve, and soon brushed away the two brigades of Wagner's division, posted in extreme exposure on the plain, opposite the massive center of the Confederate army. General Wagner had been instructed to check the enemy with these brigades, without involving them in an engagement with superior forces, but had, notwithstanding, directed their commanders, Colonels Conrad and Lane, to hold their position as long as possible. Conscious of their extreme peril they threw up barricades, and when General Hood finally advanced against them with his main lines, uncovered by skirmishers, their effort to check him precipitated a conflict so unequal as to have been hopeless from the first. When broken by the attack of an army, they fell back in great haste and disorder, and formed a shield for the enemy following upon their steps. The veteran troops mainly succeeded in reaching the main line of the national army, but a large portion of the raw troops were captured. The pursued and the pursuers broke through the intrenched line in company, carrying away portions of Reilley's brigade, on the right of General Cox's division, and Strickland's, on the left of General Ruger's. And thus, without conflict on the immediate front of the national army or on the parapet, General Hood gained a lodgment at the key-point of the position, and commanded the direct approach to the bridges. He had gained this advantage, almost without firing a shot, after the rout of Conrad and Lane, and without receiving one, except that a portion of the troops of the brigade of the latter, having loaded guns, wheeled and fired as they crossed the intrenchments. Such an advantage, to an army of more than double the strength of the divisions holding the position, according to the precedents of war, was decisive of complete victory. But in this case it was not, though at first it seemed to be entirely so. The enemy's center, made strong to thrust itself through the national line, had gained its immediate objective, and commenced at once to use two captured batteries in enfilading the national line, right and left, to double each fraction upon the flanks, and grasp the bridges between them. Two of the three brigades of Wagner's division, the only troops south of the river not in the main line, were so shattered that they could not be rallied for the emergency, and every moment of delay in attacking the enemy's forces that had gained the center, permitted their reinforcement from his rear lines. The teams from the captured batteries galloped to the rear, and intensified the impression that the disaster was fatal. Conrad's brigade had entered the intrenchments near the Columbia road, and on the right of this road the enemy gained at the first dash three or four hundred yards of the line. Lane's brigade had crossed the parapet several hundred yards to the right, without disturbing the troops at that point, and its volley had a marked effect upon the enemy. Toward the breach, the enemy's heavy central lines began at once to press, and to it his lateral lines were turned, in seemingly overwhelming convergence. To General Hood, the advantage so easily gained, promised the capture or destruction of the national army, and he and his army were inspired to quickest action to maintain and utilize it for this grand achievement. And he certainly could have maintained his hold of the national line, and used it for extreme success, had time been given him to thrust into the breach his rapidly-advancing and massive rear lines; and as it was, he began to gain ground right and left from the Columbia road.

When General Stanley first heard the noise of battle, he was with General Schofield, at his headquarters on the north bank of the river, a fifteen minutes' ride from Carter's Hill, and was entertaining the conviction, from the strength of the position and the former course of the enemy, that an assault was entirely improbable. But as soon as an attack was indicated to him and others, in their distant view, he rode rapidly to his troops, and reached the left of Opdycke's brigade to find that a disaster, seemingly prophetic of the overthrow of the army, had came with the first onset of the enemy. In quick provision for the emergency, he approached this one reserve brigade, to order it to charge the enemy in the breach; but seeing its gallant commander in front of its center leading it forward, he gave no orders, for none were needed, and taking position on the left of the line, the corps and brigade commanders, with common purpose to hurl back the enemy and restore the continuity of the line, cheered as they led this heroic brigade. When Colonel Opdycke had first seen the enemy within the intrenchments, he turned to his men from the front of the center of his brigade, to find they had already fixed bayonets for the encounter, which they plainly foresaw would be desperate and decisive; for they were veterans who had charged the enemy on other fields, and yet they had never been called by orders, soldierly instincts, or patriotism to such a conflict as was now plainly before them. Their commander saw, in this unbidden act of preparation, and in their eyes and attitude, the response to his own purpose, and his ringing order, "First brigade forward to the lines," was in harmony with the stern will of every officer and man of that brigade. And when he dashed on the breach, he gave expression to the courage and purpose of every man in that self-appointed forlorn hope, while those near General Stanley shouted: "We can go where the general can." Opdycke rode forward until he reached the enemy, followed closely by his brigade. He first emptied his revolver, then clubbed it in the hand-to-hand conflict, and as the deadly struggle raged more fiercely, he dismounted and clubbed a musket. His men fought as did their leader, and with bayonets baptized in blood, they hurled the enemy from the intrenchments and saved the army. This was one of the supreme moments of battle which heroes recognize, and by which only the bravest of the brave are inspired to deeds of daring, transcendent from motive and momentous results. Four regimental commanders fell in the charge, but other officers of similar temper maintained the gallant leadership. Colonel Oydcke, foremost in the charge and throughout the ensuing conflict in the intrenchments, escaped injury. General Stanley also escaped for a time, but in leaving this brigade to look after other dispositions, was pierced in the neck by a bullet, and was compelled to leave the field.

Colonel Opdycke's brigade recaptured eight pieces of artillery, and with them four hundred prisoners; wrenched ten battle-flags from the hands of the enemy, and left the ground behind them strewn with a greater number, which dropped under their blows. The number of prisoners and battle-flags, shows most plainly that General Hood was holding the position with an exceedingly strong force.

The recaptured guns again changed the direction of their missiles of death, while the sheet of flame from Opdycke's brigade and others in reach revealed to the enemy the necessity of other charges upon new and less promising conditions, or the abandonment of the conflict. Opdycke's charge regained nearly all the line that had been lost, but the enemy still held a small salient to the right of the Columbia road, and to maintain this point and widen the breach, General Hood and his subordinate commanders exerted themselves to the utmost. In counter effort, small portions of Conrad's and Lane's brigades were directed to Opdycke's support. The enemy's first heavy line in his front was not more than fifty yards distant, and in addition to a direct fire from this line, he was subjected to an enfilading one from the troops still in the intrenchments on his right. It was next to impossible for his brigade to maintain position under this deadly cross-fire, but yet, in twenty minutes, through the vigorous support of troops on right and left, the enemy was entirely expelled, and the continuity of the line re-established. Then, in seeming retribution for General Schofield's escape at Spring Hill, and his own dislodgment from his hope-giving grasp of the key-point of the national line, General Hood repeated his assaults with the expression of frenzied vengeance and valor. His subordinates, with a recklessness of life in keeping with the charge of Opdycke and his heroic brigade, led their columns to the muskets of the national troops, charging repeatedly, mainly at Carter's Hill, and only desisted with the fall of night. In leading a charge, General Cleburne, the most dashing division commander in the Confederate army, fell upon the parapet in front of Opdycke's brigade, and in the whole contest, five other generals were killed, six wounded, and one captured—a fact which reveals how the columns of the enemy were led; while the loss of thirty-three battle-flags manifests the strength of the columns which gained the national lines.

The defensive fire was so rapid from 4 P. M. to nightfall that it was difficult to supply the troops with ammunition. One hundred wagon-loads of artillery and infantry ammunition were used from the Fourth Corps train alone, and this expenditure wrought fearful havoc in the ranks of the enemy, whose boldness placed them much of the time at short range.

Firing, of more or less severity, was maintained until nearly midnight, the enemy continuing his activity to determine the time of the withdrawal of the national army, and to embarras such a movement.

General Hood buried seventeen hundred and fifty men on the field. He had three thousand eight hundred so disabled as to be placed in hospitals, and lost seven hundred and two captured—an aggregate of six thousand two hundred and fifty-two, exclusive of those slightly wounded.

General Schofield lost one hundred and eighty-nine killed, one thousand and thirty-three wounded, and one thousand one hundred and four missing—an aggregate of two thousand three hundred and twenty-six. More than half of this loss was from Wagner's division, from the exposure of Conrad's and Lane's brigades, and from the charge and subsequent fighting of Opdycke's brigade.

The battle of Franklin, for its proportions, was one of the

grandest of the war. The salient features of this battle were the position and action of the two brigades posted in front of the main line, and the gallantry of the third, after the enemy had carried the intrenchments on Carter's Hill.

The reports of Generals Schofield, Stanley, and Cox declare that it was not the expectation that the brigades in front should resist until they should be compromised in an engagement with superior forces, and that General Wagner was so instructed. Nevertheless, the two brigade commanders were instructed by General Wagner to hold their position as long as possible, and having been thus impressed with the necessity of extreme resistance, they did not abandon their position until forced to do so by the bayonets of the enemy, and then their hurried retreat brought disaster to their own army. Their resistance, if not prudent, was exceedingly gallant, and veterans and new troops alike displayed the highest qualities of soldiers in confronting in actual conflict an army of three corps, and deserve mention in history as brave and heroic, under circumstances of extreme trial and peril.

With regard to the second prominent feature of this battle, it may be said that seldom in the history of war has a single brigade* made itself so conspicuous in saving an army, and its transcendent action must be accepted as proof that its previous training and experience, and the manhood of its members had given the morale—the *elan* requisite for such an emergency. It was no new experience for Colonel Opdycke to ride in a charge in advance of his men, for this he did in developing the enemy in front of General Thomas' right, after the great disaster at the battle of Chickamauga. He charged, too, with a demi-brigade on Missionary Ridge, and with his regiment, the One Hundred and Twenty-fifth Ohio, on Rocky Face Ridge, and the officers and men of his brigade were meet for such a leader. And General Stanley, sick as he was, manifested his appreciation of the emergency as well as his personal gallantry, in descending from the command of a corps to take the left

---

* This brigade comprised the One Hundred and Twenty-fifth Ohio; the Twenty-fourth Wisconsin; the Thirty-sixth, Fourty-fourth, Seventy-third, Seventy-fourth, and Eighty-eighth Illinois regiments.

of a brigade, in an action plainly decisive of the battle. For beyond all power of generalship to mold the battle or control its issue, the simple charge of Opdycke's brigade stands in boldest relief.

The enemy having been repulsed and the trains transferred to the north bank of the Harpeth river, the problem to solve was the safe withdrawal of the army to Nashville. It was still in General Hood's power, having great superiority in both infantry and cavalry, to cross the river above General Schofield's position, and unless prevented by battle or withdrawal, to throw his army between Franklin and Nashville. As to the propriety of withdrawal, there was no question, either with the general officers at Franklin, including General Schofield, or with General Thomas. So that the movement to the rear, meditated before the battle, was commenced as soon as the quietness of the enemy permitted. During the early part of the night the artillery was transferred to the north bank, and at midnight the army crossed the river without loss or special hinderance. General Wood retained his position until 3 A. M., and then moved northward as the rear-guard of the army. General Hood perceived the retirement early, and though following closely, wrought no damage. General Wood had destroyed the bridges before leaving position, and his division in rear of the army, with Wilson's cavalry on its flanks, was able to beat back General Hood's head of column, which he could not under the circumstances make strong in time, even to greatly harass so strong a force. With the exception of a brush between Hammond's brigade of cavalry and some portion of Forrest's command at Brentwood, the enemy provoked no engagement, and the army marched quietly to Nashville. The rear column reached that city at 1 P. M., and the different corps were assigned to positions on the defensive line which General Thomas had selected. The Twenty-third Corps, under General Schofield, was assigned to the left, extending to the Nolensville turnpike; the Fourth Corps, General Wood commanding, in room of General Stanley, disabled by his wound, took position in the center; and the corps from the "Army of the Tennessee," General A. J. Smith commanding, having arrived the day before, held the right, with its flank touching the river below the city.

In view of General Hood's superiority of force, his operations thus far had fallen behind just expectations. He had allowed General Schofield to pass safely before his army, after he had touched his communications, while he was yet at Columbia, and he had met most disastrous defeat at Franklin, in assaults that could not be repeated with greater vigor. The consequent depression in his army was doubtless excessive. Thus far, none of the grand results of his northward march, as announced with prophetic emphasis by Mr. Davis, had been achieved, although General Sherman had swept southward from Northern Georgia and on toward Savannah, with sixty-five thousand men; and the Confederate army, of which so much had been expected, was now far from its base, thus far defeated in the accomplishment of its great aims, with the consciousness that the conditions of ultimate success were passing day by day beyond the range of possibilities. To go back would express total defeat; and before General Hood was a fast-increasing army, posted on a strong defensive line, with a deep river behind, and its key-points fortified early in the war; and as he could not at once go round Nashville, he sat before the city and extended his lines in semblance of a siege, which should last until General Thomas should be fully ready to throw him upon the defensive.

General Thomas had hoped to deliver battle at some point farther to the south; but his reinforcements had come too slowly, and his cavalry horses had come as tardily as his accessions of troops. His forces were not fully in hand, and those that had fought their way from Columbia were physically exhausted beyond the ordinary experience of veterans on long marches and months under fire. During the seven days of Hood's advance from the Tennessee, he had hurried his preparations for the battle now palpably imminent. On the 29th of November, he had ordered General Milroy to abandon Tullahoma and retire to Murfreesboro, leaving a garrison in the block-house at Elk River bridge. The same day, he had ordered General Steedman, with a provisional division of five thousand men, composed of detachments from the corps with

General Sherman and a brigade of colored troops, to move to Nashville. Nashville had been placed in a state of defense; additional fortifications had been constructed under the direcsion of Brigadier-General Tower, and the whole had been manned by the regular garrison, reinforced by a provisional force, under Brevet Brigadier-General Donaldson, chief quartermaster, composed of the employes of the quartermaster and commissary departments. No other forces were now expected, except the brigade of General Cooper, of Ruger's division, which having watched the fords of Duck river, below Columbia, was now marching to Nashville by a detour to evade the enemy. With the cavalry remounted, and this heterogeneous force organized, General Thomas proposed to assume the offensive and dispute with General Hood the possession of Tennessee.

CHAPTER XXXV.

THE arrival of General Steedman with his command from Chattanooga, December 1st, in the evening, completed the concentration of forces, which had been so unexpectedly delayed. Three lines of defence had been abandoned because the promised troops had not appeared in Tennessee. And now that the concentration had been effected, the improvised army contained three corps, each one of which represented a distinct department; a provisional division made up of detachments from almost every organization, large and small, embraced in the sixty-five thousand men, then on " the march to the sea ;" an infusion of raw infantry regiments ; the greater portion of the cavalry of the Military Division of the Mississippi, but still largely dismounted; and colored soldiers, who were to have their first opportunity in the central theater of war, to fight by brigades.

General Thomas had held General Steedman's command, on the line of the Nashville and Chattanooga railroad for two reasons—one, the complications in East Tennessee, of which a narrative will be given in another chapter ; and the other, the probability that General Hood would strike that important railroad south of Nashville. Having arrived, General Steedman took position about a mile in advance of the left center of the main line, and east of the Nolensville turnpike. General Wilson, with his cavalry, had previously taken a strong position at Thomson's Chapel, on the Nolensville turnpike, covering the space between General Schofield's left and the Cumberland river.

General Hood being still greatly superior in cavalry, there

was danger that he would detach a large portion of it to interrupt the vital communications with Louisville. To guard against the passage of his cavalry over the Cumberland, above Nashville, General Hammond's brigade of cavalry was sent to Gallatin on the 2d, to watch the river as far up as Carthage. And the day following General Thomas threw all the remaining cavalry across to Edgefield, and then General Steedman's command covered the space between General Schofield's left and the river.

General Hood's infantry did not approach Nashville until the 3d, when General Thomas' outposts were driven in, and soon after the enemy began to establish his main line. The next morning his salient was seen on Montgomery Hill, within six hundred yards of the center of the national line. General Hood's investing lines occupied the high ground on the southeast side of Brown's creek, extending from the Nolensville turnpike, across the Granny White and Franklin turnpikes, in a southwesterly direction, to the hills south and southwest of Richland creek, and down that creek to the Hillsboro turnpike. From his right, on the Nolensville road to the river, above the city, and from his left, on the Hillsboro road to the river below, his cavalry were posted. Intent upon completing and strengthening his line, General Hood made no response to the fire of artillery, which opened upon him from several points. It was doubtless necessary, too, that he should be economical in the use of his ammunition, as it was difficult for him to replenish from his base at Corinth.

Although not active at Nashville, General Hood was enterprising in other directions. He sent Bate's division of Cheatham's corps to reduce Murfreesboro and other minor points in the vicinity, and on the 4th the block-house, at Overall's creek, five miles north of Murfreesboro, was attacked by this force. But such was the strength of the block-house constructed for the defense of the railroad bridge, that although seventy-four artillery shots were fired against it, the garrison held out until General Milroy arrived with reinforcements from Murfreesboro, consisting of three regiments of infantry, four companies of cavalry, and a section of artillery. General Bate was then attacked and driven away. During the 5th,

6th, and 7th, having been reinforced by a division from Lee's corps, and twenty-five hundred cavalry, General Bate demonstrated heavily against Fortress Rosecrans, near Murfreesboro, held by eight thousand men, under General Rousseau. The enemy declining to make a direct attack, General Milroy was sent against him on the 8th, with seven regiments of infantry. He was found on the Wilkinson turnpike behind rail barricades, which were carried by assault—General Milroy capturing two hundred and seven prisoners and two guns, and suffering a loss of thirty men killed, and one hundred and seventy-five wounded. The same day Buford's cavalry, after shelling Murfreesboro, entered the town, but were driven out by a regiment of infantry and a section of artillery. The whole force then moved to Lebanon and down the bank of the Cumberland river to Nashville, threatening to cross, to interrupt the Louisville and Nashville railroad.

A portion of the enemy's cavalry, under General Lyon, succeeded in crossing the Cumberland river above Clarksville, on the 9th. The object of the movement was to reach the Louisville and Nashville railroad, at some point in Kentucky, and to prevent its accomplishment General Thomas directed General McCook, who was in Kentucky, to remount Watkins' and La Grange's brigades of cavalry, and to look after Lyon with these brigades.

During the first half of December, General Grant felt great uneasiness with regard to the situation in Tennessee, fearing that General Hood would pass round Nashville and march into Kentucky reproducing the scenes and issues of the summer and autumn of 1862. Believing that General Thomas should have delivered battle immediately after the engagement at Franklin, he urged him thereafter, from day to day, to attack General Hood. General Thomas, on the other hand, thought it advisable to remount his cavalry and make other preparations, that he might be assured of victory, before assuming the offensive, and at the same time gain the full results of victory by a vigorous pursuit of the enemy, when defeated and routed. He was confident of final success, and was vigilant in guarding the river with his cavalry, and secured the services of the gunboats of the Eleventh Division of the Mississippi Squadron, under Lieutenant-Commander Leroy Fitch, to patrol the river above and below the city. During the first eight days of the month, General Wilson had raised his cavalry to good strength, by the influx of new horses and by ransacking the corrals for convalescent animals, and in this time much had been done to supply the army with the transportation essential to successful pursuit, and with pontoons for the full rivers. But delay for any cause was displeasing to General Grant, as besides the supposed danger to Kentucky, the troops under General Canby on the Mississippi river, intended for co-operation with General Sherman, were detained to prevent the trans-Mississippi Confederate forces, from joining General Hood, and on the 9th of December at the suggestion of the lieutenant-general, an order was issued by the President, relieving General Thomas, and placing General Schofield in command. General Thomas himself preferred to be relieved rather than be responsible for a battle fought under unfavorable conditions. The order relieving him, however, was subsequently suspended; but there was no respite to the urgent communications requiring the deliverance of battle without delay.

General Thomas at first hoped to be ready for battle on the 7th, but on account of delay in remounting his cavalry, he was not ready until the 9th. But with the completion of his preparations there came a sleet which rendered the movement of troops for any purpose, especially for battle, an impossibility. Reconnoissances on the 11th and 13th—the first by Colonel J. G. Mitchell, and the second by Colonel A. G. Malloy—developed the fact that infantry could move only with the greatest difficulty upon the surface of the uneven ground. On the 9th, General Thomas ordered General Wilson to move his command to the south side of the river to take position between the Hillsboro and Harding turnpikes, to be in readiness to participate in the attack, projected for the next day; but even this movement could not be executed upon the ice with cavalry, except with horses shod expressly for such a surface. As the refusal of General Thomas to give battle, after a peremptory order on the 6th to attack without waiting

longer for a remount for his cavalry, called for the order relieving him from command, with General Schofield as his successor, so his unwillingness to attack upon the ice first
elicited an order from General Grant, on the 11th, to delay no
longer for weather or reinforcements, and then another on the
13th, directing Major-General John A. Logan to proceed to
Nashville, reporting arrival at Louisville and Nashville. And
on the 15th, General Grant reached Washington, on his way
to Nashville to take command in person.

However, by midday on the 14th, the ice had so far melted
that General Thomas resolved upon attacking the enemy the
next day, and at 3 P. M. he called together his corps commanders to announce to them his plan of battle, and give
them instructions with regard to the specific action of their
respective commands in its execution. The following is the
text: "Major-General A. J. Smith, commanding detachment
of the Army of the Tennessee, after forming his troops on
and near the Harding pike in front of his present position, will
make a vigorous assault upon the enemy's left. Major-General Wilson, commanding the cavalry corps Military Division
of the Mississippi, with three divisions, will move on and support General Smith's right, assisting as far as possible in carrying the left of the enemy's position, and be in readiness to
throw his force upon the enemy the moment a favorable
opportunity occurs. Major-General Wilson will also send one
division on the Charlotte pike, to clear that road of the enemy
and observe in the direction of Bell's landing, to protect our
right rear until the enemy's position is fairly turned, when it
will rejoin the main force. Brigadier-General T. J. Wood,
commanding Fourth Corps* after leaving a strong skirmish
line in his works from Lawrens' Hill to his extreme right, will
form the remainder of the Fourth Corps on the Hillsboro
pike to support General Smith's left, and operate on the left
and rear of the enemy's advanced position on Montgomery
Hill. Major-General Schofield, commanding Twenty-third
Army Corps, will replace Brigadier-General Kimball's division of the Fourth Corps with his troops, and occupy the
trenches from Fort Negley to Lawrens' Hill with a strong
skirmish line. He will move with the remainder of his force

---

* Gen. D. S Stanley was absent on account of wounds received at Franklin.

in front of the works, and co-operate with General Wood, protecting the latter's left flank against an attack by the enemy.   Major-General Steedman, commanding District of Etowah, will occupy the interior line in rear of his present position, stretching from the reservoir on the Cumberland river to Fort Negley, with a strong skirmish line, and mass the remainder of his force in its present position, to act according to the exigencies which may arise during these operations. Brigadier-General Miller, with troops forming the garrison of Nashville, will occupy the interior line from the battery on hill 210, to the extreme right, including the inclosed work on the Hyde's Ferry road.   The quartermaster's troops, under the command of Brigadier-General Donaldson, will, if necessary, be posted on the interior line from Fort Morton to the battery on hill 210.   The troops occupying the interior line will be under the direction of Major-General Steedman, who is charged with the immediate defense of Nashville during the operations around the city.   Should the weather permit, the troops will be formed to commence operations at 6 A. M. on the 15th, or as soon thereafter as practicable."

General Thomas modified this plan, by ordering General Steedman to make a most positive feint against the enemy's right, to divert his attention from the dominant movement against his left, and also by calling General Schofield's corps, first to the reserve, and afterward directing it to move upon General Smith's right, after other movements had been successfully accomplished.

The weather and the ice, which from the 9th had prevented General Thomas from assuming the offensive, had also for six days barred all activity on the part of the enemy, who was meditating a movement* round Nashville from the consciousness that he could not successfully assault the army intrenched before it.   The morning of the 15th being favorable for the tactical dispositions required by General Thomas' plan of operations, the two armies were thrown into deadly conflict,

---

* This statement is not supported by official testimony, but upon the declarations of prisoners and citizens within General Hood's lines.   He, too, was delayed by the ice-covered ground.

to contest not only the possession of Tennessee, but to decide the supremacy of the national arms in all the West.

At 4 A. M. on the 15th, the provisional division composed of troops from corps and other organizations of General Sherman's army, under command of Brigadier-General Cruft, moved forward and relieved the Fourth and Twenty-third Corps, occupied their exterior line of works, and picketed the front of this line from the Acklin place to Fort Negley, commanding the approaches to the city by the Granny White, Franklin, and Nolensville turnpikes. At the same hour, General J. F. Miller occupied the works with the garrison of the city, from Fort Negley to the Lebanon turnpike, covering the approaches by the Murfreesboro, Chicken, and Lebanon turnpikes. Brigadier-General Donaldson, with his command, occupied the defenses from General Cruft's right to the Cumberland river, commanding the approaches by the Harding, Hillsboro, and Charlotte turnpikes. General Steedman was instructed to support General Wood's left, when his corps should take position, and make a vigorous demonstration in his front to cover the grand effort to turn the enemy's left flank.

About daylight the other commands began to move to their several positions as prescribed in the modified plan of battle. General Smith advanced his second division, Brigadier-General Garrard commanding, on the Harding turnpike, and deployed to the left of that road; he threw forward his first division, Brigadier-General J. McArthur commanding, on the Harding and Charlotte turnpikes, and formed it on the right of Garrard; his third division, Colonel J. B. Moore, Thirty-third Wisconsin commanding, he held in reserve opposite the junction of the right and left flanks of the other two divisions. Owing to the divergence of the roads upon which he moved, and the stubborn resistance of the enemy, McArthur did not get into position until 8 A. M. He silenced a batttery, and skirmished heavily as he advanced.

General Wood formed the Fourth Corps, with the Second division, Brigadier-General Elliott commanding, on the right; the First division, Brigadier-General Kimball commanding, in the center; and the third division, Brigadier-General S.

Beatty commanding, on the left. Elliott's right was refused, in echelon with Smith's left. The other divisions were formed in similar manner—the right of each in echelon—to facilitate the wheel of the whole line to the right, on the left of the Fourth Corps as a pivot. The formation of the Fourth Corps was a double battle-line—the first deployed, and the second in column, by division, opposite the intervals in the first. The front was covered with a line of skirmishers, and a similar force remained in the works in the rear.

The Twenty-third Corps, when relieved from position on the left of the Fourth, moved to the right of Wood. The Third division, Brigadier-General J. D. Cox commanding, excepting one brigade left to support General Steedman, moved by the Hillsboro turnpike, and formed in the rear of Elliott's right; the Second (recently General Ruger's), Major-General D. N. Couch commanding, advanced on the Harding turnpike, and took position in rear of Garrard's left.

When the infantry on the right had given room for the movements of the cavalry, General Wilson at once assumed position. The Fifth division, Brigadier-General E. Hatch commanding, took position on the right of McArthur, of Smith's corps. General Croxton, with his brigade of the First division, formed on the right of Hatch. The Seventh division, one brigade mounted, Brigadier J. F. Knipe commanding, was held in reserve, to render aid wherever emergency might demand. The Sixth division, Brigadier R. W. Johnson commanding, one brigade mounted, was ordered to move by the Charlotte turnpike, to clear that road of the enemy, and keeping connection with Croxton by skirmishers or patrols, to push as far as Davidson's house, eight miles from the city, so as to cover the remainder of the corps from the enemy's cavalry, and look well to the guns of the enemy at Bell's landing, commanding the Cumberland river, and the force supporting them.

A dense fog hung over the two armies during the early morning, which, with the undulations of the ground, concealed the movements of the national army, though from these causes the evolutions were also greatly retarded. When, about noon, the fog lifted, there was doubtless to General

Hood an unexpected revelation. He had thus far in the campaign monopolized the offensive, and during the days of enforced inaction, he had been maturing his plans to turn Nashville and move into Kentucky. This would have been an exceedingly rash adventure, and after his experience at Franklin, where three divisions beat back his army, with the help of extemporized intrenchments, he could not, even in the wildest forecast of the consequences of an attempt to carry Nashville, with its elaborate fortifications, held by an army of equal strength, decide to take such a risk. Neither could he stay long before the city, and supply his army. It was imperative that he should move in some direction, and in his desperate extremity, he no doubt meditated an early advance into Kentucky, hoping, despite all the dangerous contingencies, that he could at least escape destruction. He had not anticipated the necessity of so soon acting on the defensive, and even when he saw an army deployed before him in aggressive attitude, he did not expect an attack upon his left flank. The troops opposite his right, during the twelve days of his nominal investment, alone had made the pretense of aggression, in contesting the defenses which General Steedman had constructed when he was before Wilson, on the left of the national line. And now, while the strength of the Army of the Cumberland was on his left, he was to be still further misled by a feint, which, from its spirit and force, might easily be mistaken for a positive assault.

When the combination to turn General Hood's left had been fully completed, Brigadier-General Whipple, chief of staff to General Thomas, bore an order to General Steedman to advance against his right, in semblance of actual assault. General Steedman had previously formed a column for this movement, composed of three strong detachments—the first under Colonel T. J. Morgan, embracing his own regiment, the Fourteenth Colored, the Seventeenth, Forty-fourth, and a detachment of the Eighteenth; the second under Colonel Thompson, including his own regiment, the Twelfth Colored, and the Thirteenth and One Hundredth; and the third under Lieutenant-Colonel Grosvenor, of the Eighteenth Ohio, composed of his regiment, the Sixty-eighth Indiana, and the Second battalion of the Fourteenth Army Corps; and in addition, the Eighteenth Ohio and Twentieth Indiana batteries. At 8 A. M. the detachments of Morgan and Grosvenor, the former commanding both, moved forward from the Murfreesboro turnpike to Riddle's hill, drove in the enemy's pickets, and assaulted his works, between the turnpike and the Nashville and Chattanooga railroad. These troops gained a lodgment in the works, but were exposed, while holding them, to a severe fire from General Hood's massed forces on that flank, and General Steedman withdrew them. The charge was so gallantly made, that General Hood was so deceived as to its ultimate aim, that he drew troops from his center and left to give strength to his seemingly endangered flank.

Soon after this action on the extreme left, the forces on the opposite flank moved forward on the Harding and Hillsboro roads with resistless force, in executing the grand initiative of the battle. McArthur's division moved rapidly behind its skirmishers, who were soon sharply engaged, and gradually wheeling to the left, the direction of the line, was parallel to the Harding road. Advancing thence a short distance, the division was before a detached earthwork of the enemy, situated on the top of a hill, and inclosing four brass guns. This fort was covered by a stronger one, some four hundred feet to the right, and containing the same number of guns. In the meantime, Hatch's division of cavalry, with its left connected with McArthur's right, had swept round on a longer curve and was in readiness to co-operate in assaulting the forts. Hatch had previously engaged Ecton's brigade of infantry beyond Richland creek, and had driven it past Harding's house, near which Colonel Spalding, commanding the Twelfth Tennessee Cavalry, charged and captured forty-three prisoners and the headquarter-train of Chalmers' division. Hatch's right brigade, under Colonel Coon, having diverged too far from the direction of the general movement, was now moved by the left flank till it joined his other brigade on the flank of the four-gun redoubt, which covered the extremity of the enemy's line. Here, by direction of General Hatch, Coon's brigade dismounted to charge, planting its battery—" I," First Illinois Artillery—so as to enfilade the enemy's line. Four batteries then opened upon the guns in the redoubt and soon silenced them, and Coon's brigade charged the supporting infantry force, and though under the fire of the second redoubt, captured the four guns. The skirmishers of McMillen's and Hubbard's brigades of McArthur's division were also charging from an opposite direction, and entering the redoubt at the same moment contributed to the successful issue. One hundred and fifty prisoners were taken with the guns.

The two divisions immediately moved to the right, cavalry and infantry vieing with each other in the effort to carry the stronger redoubt on a hill whose acclivity greatly increased the hazard of an assault. This position, however, was carried in the same manner as the other. Coon's brigade, armed with the Spencer rifle, supported by two fresh brigades, charged up the hill and drove the enemy from position; while McArthur's brigades were in such close proximity, in a sweeping charge, as to lay claim to the guns and two hundred and fifty prisoners.

During these successful movements, by the direction of General Thomas, General Schofield moved his corps to the right of General Smith, and formed it for battle. This change became necessary, as the latter had moved farther to the left than had been anticipated, and the enemy's true flank had not been found. General Schofield was directed to attack his flank, which rested upon a group of hills near the Hillsboro turnpike, that the cavalry might operate in his rear. In order to preserve continuity of line, General Smith threw Ward's brigade of his reserve division to the front, to fill a space of a half mile between his right and Schofield's left; and to give full space to General Schofield, General Hatch moved to the right, across the Hillsboro turnpike, and with his other brigade attacked the enemy on another range of hills, drove him from it, and captured a battery in the valley beyond. In the meantime, Generals Schofield and Smith advanced their lines. Colonel Hill's brigade of McArthur's division carried a small earthwork containing two guns, but lost its commander in the assault. Colonel Wolf's brigade of Garrard's division crossed the Hillsboro turnpike and gained the works on the left. General Schofield moved to the right of the two redoubts first captured, crossed the Hillsboro road and a valley beyond, and carried a series of hills overlooking the Granny White turnpike—one of the two remaining lines of retreat available to the enemy. The charge was made by General Cooper's brigade of Couch's division. The enemy here made his first attempt on his left to give a counter-blow. He had previously massed a heavy force on his left to hurl it against General Thomas' right flank. When General Cooper had crossed the valley to carry the hills beyond, this force appeared in his rear in the low ground. General Couch then sent Mehringer's brigade against it, and though the enemy was of superior strength, Colonel Mehringer checked him until Doolittle's and Casement's brigades of Cox's division advanced in his support. The engagement was continued with sharp fighting until dark.

The action of the Fourth Corps was equally successful. As soon as General Smith became engaged on General Wood's right, the latter moved his corps toward Montgomery Hill, the salient of the enemy's defensive line. This position was very strong, being an irregular cone rising about one hundred feet above the general level of the country. The ascent, except on the left and rear, is quite abrupt, and was covered with forest trees. The intrenchments concealed the hill a little below the crest, and the approaches were covered with abatis and sharpened stakes firmly planted in the ground. During the formation of the corps for assault, the guns in position expressed defiance, and in response and menace General Wood's guns opened with vigor. As the corps advanced, it swung to the left, in order that the more easy ascent should be in front of Beatty's division, which had been required to furnish an assaulting column, of which Colonel Post's brigade was designated for the front and Colonel Streight's for immediate support. At 1 P. M. Colonel Post dashed up the hill and over the intrenchments on the summit, and held the enemy's stronghold. This action was anterior to the more positive success of Smith and Wilson on the right, and opened the way for General Schofield to move to the right of General Smith. When the Twenty-third Corps was transferred to the right, General Thomas directed General Wood to throw his reserves on his right, to extend his line to as great an extent as was compatible with the security of his front. In obedience, General Wood put the reserve brigade of each division on his right, and then engaged the enemy with his entire corps. He brought three batteries into play and pressed forward a strong skirmish line, but at first made no threat of assaulting. Soon, however, he made preparations to carry the enemy's works in his front; moving his right division, whose right had extended in rear of General Smith's left, farther to his own left, and then advanced it and his central division, so as to bring Kimball's division opposite a fortified hill near the center of General Hood's main line. Placing two batteries so as to throw a converging fire upon the hill, he used them vigorously for an hour, and then ordered General Kimball to charge with his whole division. With loud cheers, the division ascended the hill and leaped over the intrenchments, capturing several pieces of artillery, stands of colors, and a large number of prisoners. At the same time, General Elliott carried the intrenchments in his front, and General Beatty crowned the enemy's works before his division with captures of artillery and prisoners. In this general advance, the right of General Wood's line became involved with the left of General Smith's, and conflicting claims for the fruits of victory were preferred. At 5 P. M. General Wood received an order from General Thomas to move to the Franklin turnpike, two and a half miles distant, and facing southward, to drive the enemy across it. The corps moved as directed, but the night fell too soon for it to reach its destination, but it bivouacked on a line parallel to the Granny White turnpike connecting with General Smith's left.

On the extreme left, other advantages were gained after the feint of the morning. Colonels Morgan and Grosvenor pressed the enemy from Raine's house and held the position, using the buildings for defense. Colonel Thompson, with his detachment, advanced across Brown's creek, between the Murfreesboro and Nolensville turnpikes, and carried the left of the front line of fortifications on the latter road, holding his ground firmly. In this succession of aggressive movements, the colored troops were prominent and successful.

During the day the enemy had been driven from his original

line of works, and forced back to a position on the Harpeth hills, and his left had been completely turned, though he still held two lines of retreat—one on the Granny White road, and the other on the direct road to Franklin. Seventeen pieces of artillery had been taken from him, also twelve hundred prisoners and several hundred small arms. The cavalry had cleared its front, covered the extremity of the infantry line, enveloped the enemy's left flank and taken it in reverse, and had only failed in the extreme possibility of reaching the Franklin turnpike in rear of Hood's army. General Wilson at dark directed General Hatch to bivouac on the Hillsboro road, to cover General Smith's right flank. He placed General Knipe's division on Hatch's right; Hammond's brigade had reached the six-mile post on the Hillsboro road, and turned thence up a branch of Richland creek for three miles, bivouacking on the Granny White turnpike. General Johnson's division had moved far to the right during the day, to co-operate with the gunboats in dislodging the enemy from Bell's landing, and bivouacked in the vicinity, in prospect of co-operating with Lieutenant-Commander Fitch in an attack the next morning. General Croxton had moved on Johnson's left for several miles, and having turned to the left, rested for the night at the six-mile post on the Charlotte turnpike. The brigade of dismounted cavalry took position on the Hillsboro turnpike, to cover Hatch and Hammond against a possible advance of the enemy's cavalry on that road.

The whole army bivouacked with assurance of complete victory on the morrow. The authorities at Washington and the people of the country, after ten days of impatience at General Thomas' delay in preparation for a battle now so gloriously begun, were in full sympathy with the troops lying on their arms before the defeated enemy. General Grant, on his way to Nashville from City Point, Virginia, stopped at Washington, while General Logan, farther advanced toward the same destination, halted at Louisville. Official congratulations from the President, Secretary of War, and Lieutenant-General sped their swift way to General Thomas and his army. The defeat, total and immediate, of one of the two great armies upon which the existence of the rebellion depended was now assured, and the reaction from the historic uneasiness which had obtained throughout the country with regard to the situation at Nashville to the extreme of hopefulness with respect to the immediate issue and the ultimate consequences of the battle, was one of the most marked revulsions of opinion and feeling during the war. The army had felt no uneasiness, and now looked forward with calm assurance to the result which had been anticipated during all the days of peparation for battle.

During the night, General Hood drew back his center and right to a stronger position, his right then resting on Overton hill, and his left remaining on the Harpeth or Brentwood range. His line extended along the base of the hills, his artillery was massed at points most available for its effective use, and his troops spent the night in fortifying the position. The battle-front now presented by the enemy was on its left nearly perpendicular in trend to the right of the national line, the latter having so far wheeled to the left that its direction was nearly at right angles to its original linear course. This relation of the army lines made General Schofield fearful with regard to his right flank, and during the night he requested reinforcements from General Smith, who sent to him Colonel Moore's division. Before daylight, Colonel Moore was in reserve on General Schofield's right.

As General Hood's retreat was now probable, General Thomas gave orders for movements on the 16th having reference to attack should he accept battle, and to pursuit should he retreat. Each corps was ordered to move forward rapidly at 6 A. M. until the enemy should be met. As General Hood's left remained in proximity to General Schofield's line, he did not move early in the morning. The Fourth Corps advanced promptly as ordered toward the Franklin road. The enemy's skirmishers were soon encountered, but were speedily driven back, and the Franklin road was gained. Here the corps was deployed—Elliott's division across the road facing southward, Beatty's on the left, and Kimball's in reserve behind Elliott. It then advanced rapidly three-fourths of a mile, and met a strong skirmish line behind barricades, the main line being plainly in view a half mile beyond. Simultaneously with the movement of the Fourth Corps, General Steedman advanced on the left, and General Smith on the right. The former soon found that the enemy had left his front, and pressing forward, took position between the Nolensville turnpike and General Wood's left, his own right resting on the railroad, and his left on the Nolensville road. To cover his rear against dashes of cavalry, he ordered Mitchell's brigade of Cruft's division from the defenses, to occupy Riddle's hill. General Smith advanced with two divisions, Garrard's and McArthur's, going into position under the fire of the enemy's artillery, about eight hundred yards from his main line. The Twenty-third Corps was still at right angles with this his new offensive line, facing eastward. General Smith's right was opposite very strong intrenchments of the enemy—in fact, was at the base of the hill upon which they rested. He simply held position until 1 P. M., waiting for General Schofield, who was to take the initiative against General Hood's left. There being an interval between his left and General Wood's right, the latter threw into it Kimball's division, and completed the continuous alignment of the infantry from left to right. In the meantime, the artillery from all parts of the line kept up a measured fire, and even muskets were used freely to induce the enemy to expend his limited ammunition.

Pending the movements of the infantry to perfect their array, General Wilson was active in the formation of the cavalry on the right. Early in the morning, Hammond's pickets on the Granny White turnpike had been attacked and driven back; but in compliance with orders, General Hammond had strengthed his line and regained his position. During this action, Hatch's division had been directed to the enemy's rear, passing to Hammond's left. The country being hilly and covered with a dense forest, was impracticable for the movement of cavalry, mounted, and hence the whole force was dismounted and pushed forward. General Croxton moved to the front to support either Hatch or Hammond, and General Johnson, who had ascertained early in the morning that the enemy had abandoned Bell's landing, had been ordered to move across to the Hillsboro turnpike. By noon, the cavalry formed a continuous line from General Schofield's right to the Granny White turnpike. General Thomas' object now was to turn both flanks of the enemy. His flanks were stronger than his center, but success in turning either or both promised better results than to break through his center, as they covered his lines of retreat. Could one or the other be turned, there was the possibility of reaching his rear and cutting off his retreat, and could both be turned at once, he would be thrown in confusion on his only line of retreat through the Brentwood Pass, and the probability would be doubly strong of cutting him off. Having rode along his line from Wood to Schofield, he ordered the latter and Smith to attack the enemy's left, and the former and Steedman to move against Overton hill.

The Brentwood hills, rising about three hundred and fifty feet above the level of the country, consist of two ranges trending from their northernmost summits, on the one hand to the southeast, and on the other to the southwest, and terminating on opposite sides of the Brentwood Pass, through which the direct road to Franklin courses, and situated about nine miles from Nashville. These hills were the background for General Hood's army; his battle line coursed over the detached hills in front, covered in great part with native forests. Overton hill commanded the Franklin turnpike, running along its base, and was intrenched around its northern slope, half-way from base to summit, with a flank running round its eastern descent, and the approaches were obstructed by abatis and other entanglements. This position was exceedingly strong, and the troops holding it had been heavily reinforced during the forenoon.

General Wood sent Colonel Post to reconnoiter the position, who reported that the northern slope was most favorable for assault. As before, his brigade was chosen to form the head of the assaulting column, with Streight's in support. General Steedman designated Thompson's brigade of colored troops, and Grosvenor's, to co-operate in the assault. As preparatory to the advance of these columns, Major Goodspeed, chief of artillery of the Fourth Corps, was ordered to pour a converging fire upon the enemy's batteries, and continue it as long as it could be done with safety to the advancing troops. At 3

P. M. the assaulting columns moved up the steep ascent, covered with a strong line of skirmishers, to draw the enemy's fire and annoy his gunners. The instructions required that the columns should move steadily until near the intrenchments, and then to dash up the ascent and leap the abatis and parapets. The movement promised success until the moment of final issue. The leading men in each column reached the parapets, and a few had gained the works, when the enemy's reserves opened a fire so destructive as to drive back both lines with heavy loss. The colored soldiers suffered equally with the veteran white troops, and with them shared the glory of a gallant but unsuccessful assault. The survivors were reformed at the base of the hill, in readiness for another attack; but Colonel Post was not for the third time to lead, as had received a severe wound.

The advance on the right soon followed the attack upon Overton hill. It had been anticipated that the Twenty-third Corps, facing east, would first advance; but there was so much delay that General McArthur requested permission to carry the strong position before him and General Schofield equally, and although General Thomas desired him to wait until he could hear from General Schofield, and went himself to the right, McArthur, fearing that an opportunity would be lost, directed Colonel McMillen to charge with his brigade and take by storm, the hill upon which rested the left flank of the main line of the enemy. McMillen was directed to ascend from the west, while the other brigades of the division should attack in front, when he should be half-way up to the summit. Colonel McMillen ordered his men to refrain from firing a shot, and from all cheering, until they had gained the works. The One hundred and Fourteenth Illinois, Ninth Indiana, and Eighth Minnesota formed his first line, and the Seventy-second Indiana and the Ninety-fifth Ohio his second. A heavy line of skirmishers moved rapidly forward, and as it advanced, the artillery, in sympathy, gave roar after roar with quick repetition, while between these sheets of flame and smoke, in the stern silence of desperate valor, the brigade moved up the hill. Hubbard, "eager in emulation," started directly up, followed by Hill's brigade with another leader, and all by Garrard's division. The enemy opened with musketry, and the death-dealing short-range missiles of his artillery; but on, without halt or waver, moved the columns, and soon the position was carried, with three general officers and a large number of lower grades, and a corresponding number of men as prisoners, and twenty-seven pieces of artillery, and twelve stands of colors. The shout of these divisions in victory called forth responsive cheers from those charging on right and left. Wilson, with his dismounted troopers, swept eastward, and, with Coon's brigade, gained the hill, against which the Twenty-third Corps was advancing. Soon after, Doolittle's brigade of Cox's division crowned a fortified position on the right of the salient of the enemy's left flank, the division capturing eight guns and from two hundred and fifty to three hundred prisoners. The noise of Smith's victory moved Wood and Steedman to renew their assault upon Overton hill—their entire commands rushing forward and sweeping all before them, on the summit and beyond as they moved in rapid pursuit. Beatty's division crowned the hill, and captured four pieces of artillery, a large number of prisoners, and two stands of colors; Kimball's cleared the intrenchments in its front, and captured a large number of prisoners and small arms; and Elliott's carried the line throughout its front, and captured five guns and several hundred prisoners and small arms. This general charge was resistless, and the enemy was hurled from every position in utter rout and demoralization. The success of the first day was the inspiration of the second, and officers and men vied with each other in personal daring and persistent, steady courage. General Hood must have regarded his second position stronger than his first, or he would not have attempted to hold it, for all other conditions of the second battle were much more unfavorable to successful resistance than those of the first. The prestige was with the national army, and, on the second day of his last battle, he ought to have known that a victorious iniatitive by a Northern army had more significance than when attained by a Southern one. The Northern armies seldom lost a battle which had a promising beginning, and they often gained them, after the Southern people had been electrified by the rash assumption of victory by their generals, when afterward, on the same field, their initial success was turned into positive defeat, by the pluck and persistence of Northern soldiers.

When General Wilson's command had gained their saddles, which unfortunately was delayed in consequence of the fact, that they had gone far from their horses, as those leading them made slow progress over the broken ground and dense forests, Hatch and Knipe hurried in pursuit. General Hatch was directed to move on the Granny White road and make effort to reach the Franklin turnpike that night. He had, however, proceeded but a short distance, when he met Chalmers' division, strongly posted across the road behind a barricade of rails. Dismounting a portion of his command, he deployed on both sides of the road. While his skirmishers were advancing, Colonel Spalding charged, broke the line, and scattered the force in all directions, capturing Brigadier-General Rucker, for the time in command of the division. The cavalry then bivouacked for the night—Hatch, Knipe, and Croxton on the Granny White road, and Johnson on the Hillsboro road, near the Harpeth river.

The Fourth Corps followed the enemy on the Franklin turnpike, and the frequent discharges of its artillery increased the confusion of the retreat. At dark the corps bivouacked a mile from the village of Brentwood. The line of retreat revealed the fact that General Hood's army had abandoned itself to a most disorderly withdrawal. Small arms and accouterments were strewn thickly along the road, while no effort was made to carry off the wounded or dispose of the dead. The army was not only defeated, but it was broken and crushed, and had the conditions of pursuit proved favorable, even the fragments would have been gathered in capture.

The action of the 15th removed from all in the North the fear of disaster at Nashville, or the invasion of Kentucky. That of the 16th announced the overthrow of the rebellion in the West, and foretold its speedy utter annihilation. There was now no formidable Confederate army between the Mississippi river and Virginia. One of the two armies, upon whose organic life, strength and activity the rebellion rested, was fleeing southward in disorganization and dismay. On no other field of the war had two armies of equal proportions fought with similar issue. Drawn battle or indecisive victory had usually resulted. But now, the Confederate Army of the Tennessee, which had fought with historic honor at Donelson, Shiloh, Perryville, Murfreesboro, Chickamauga, Lookout Mountain, Missionary Ridge, Resaca, New Hope Church, Kenesaw Mountain, Peachtree Creek, Atlanta, Jonesboro, in all the minor battles of "the hundred days under fire," and at Franklin and Nashville, found its grave on a field in close proximity to its first line of defense. Neither was its demoralization rife before its last conflict. There were too many officers and men captured with swords, guns, and colors, within their intrenchments, to warrant the supposition that this historic army, with its traditions of valor and unity on every previous field, came far north in the mere semblance of the boldest aggression, to throw down its arms in shameless disregard of its glorious antecedents. There was, indeed, less loss of life to the victors than usual, but may not this result find explanation in the nice adjustment of strategic and tactical combinations and the almost unprecedented vigor of assault. Successful assaults are never as costly as those which fail, all other things being equal. Thompson's brigade of colored troops lost twenty-five per cent. of its strength in thirty minutes, on the slope of Overton hill; but had not the gallant leader of the main column fallen at the critical moment when a leader's presence and heroism is the ruling condition of successful assault, the soldiers who fell on the parapets and within the enemy's lines might have lived to plant their banners in room of those of treason and rebellion. The story is half told, and the philosophy of the victory is half revealed, by the declaration of a captured general officer, "that powder and lead were inadequate to resist such a charge." The other half of the history of the battle, and the cause of victory, come to light in the palpable co-operation of the chief subordinates with the commander-in-chief in the execution of a definite plan of battle, and the personal supervision of the vital movements by General Thomas. There were no exposed flanks, and no opportunities for stunning offensive returns.

There was only one unsuccessful assault, and that was upon the strongest position of the enemy, manned by the heaviest concentration on his line. No battle of the war manifests more complete prevision of contingencies, or more full provision for emergencies and possibilities. This battle moved on gloriously from its initial feint to the final charge, in the revelation of the highest type of generalship and the highest martial virtues of an entire army. Its immediate fruits were four thousand four hundred and sixty-two prisoners, including one major-general and three brigadiers, and two hundred and eighty officers of lower grades, all the wounded upon the field, fifty-three pieces of artillery, thousands of small arms, and twenty-five battle-flags.

General Thomas and the officers and men of his army were fully alive to the importance of vigorous pursuit. But it had been impossible to make full preparations before the battle, and the bridges on the line of retreat being at the mercy of the enemy, the difficulties in prospect were by no means slight. It was the season of rain, and there were bad roads, and the rivers and creeks which crossed the line of pursuit were full, as well as bridgeless in prospect. In the conduct of the pursuit, General Thomas was put under orders and exhortations, as he had previously been to fight the battle before he considered himself prepared and the conditions promising. During the evening of the 16th, he gave orders for the movements of the next day, and in one single direction to a staff officer he failed to express what he intended. Being roused from rest in his tent, by an officer who was to receive instructions regarding the movement of the pontoon train, he directed it upon the Murfreesboro road instead of the one to Franklin. He did not discover his mistake until the next morning, when he asked as he was riding on the latter road, if the train had passed to the front. It was immediately recalled from the wrong road, and hurried forward, but nevertheless a serious delay resulted.

Having given orders for the care of the wounded, and the collection of the captured and abandoned property, General Thomas commenced the pursuit early in the morning of the 17th. The Fourth Corps pushed on to Franklin through

Brentwood, and the cavalry followed the Granny White road to the junction of the two roads, and then General Wilson hurried past the infantry. In moving upon Franklin, General Wilson kept General Knipe's command on the direct road, and sent Generals Hatch and Croxton to cross the Harpeth above the town.

General Knipe found the enemy strongly posted at Hollow Tree Gap, four miles north of Franklin, and charging him, front and flank, carried the position, and captured four hundred and thirteen men and three flags. At Franklin, he again made a show of resistance, but upon Johnson's approach on the south bank of the river, he retreated toward Columbia.

Beyond the town, Generals Knipe and Hatch moved in parallel columns on the Columbia and Carter's Creek roads, while Johnson followed Knipe, and Croxton advanced on the Lewisburg road. The extreme flanking columns were instructed to press round the flanks of the enemy's rear-guard, composed almost entirely of infantry, while a strong line of skirmishers should attack in the rear—the object being to break up the last organized force which was covering the fugitive and broken columns in rapid retreat. This rear-guard, however, proved very efficient and subtle, preventing any successful flanking, and skirmishing with spirit in the rear, while moving rapidly. Late in the evening, the enemy took a strong position in the open field, about one mile from the West Harpeth. The rapid movement of the cavalry had thrown them into some confusion and intervolution with the enemy, which, with the fog and falling darkness, caused some doubt as to the fact that the force in front was the rear-guard of the enemy. The consequent hesitation gave the enemy opportunity to form his line and post his batteries. As soon as the true state of affairs was ascertained, General Wilson ordered Hatch and Knipe to charge both flanks. The batteries from both sides opened briskly, when Lieutenant Hedges, commanding the Fourth United States Cavalry, with his regiment in column by fours, dashed forward in a saber charge, and broke through the battery. Hatch's division and Hammond's brigade, dismounted, charged at the same time, and the enemy was completely routed. Lieutenant Hedges was three times captured, but escaped at last. The pursuit was vigorous, notwithstanding the darkness. General Hatch, with the Tenth Indiana Cavalry, forded the West Harpeth, and struck the enemy in flank. Being pressed on all sides, the enemy abandoned his guns, and fled in disorder, under cover of the darkness. This rearguard was Stevenson's division of Lee's corps, under Forrest.

The Fourth Corps reached Franklin a little after noon, but the river had risen so rapidly after the cavalry had crossed, that the infantry were delayed to extemporize a bridge. General Steedman followed General Wood, and encamped near by on the north bank of the Harpeth; the other two corps were in the rear. Trains followed, with rations for ten days, and a hundred rounds of ammunition to each man.

Early on the 18th, General Wilson pursued and endeavored, with Johnson's and Croxton's commands, to strike the enemy at Spring Hill, but he had passed on over Rutherford's creek, destroying the bridges behind him. The roads, even the turnpikes, had become exceedingly bad from the heavy rains and their use by the enemy, and in consequence the pursuit was greatly retarded. General Wood crossed the Harpeth in the morning, and joined General Wilson at night at Rutherford's creek.

The difficulties of the pursuit were now fully apparent, and anticipating the failure of all efforts to intercept Hood's army with his own in direct advance, General Thomas, on the 18th, ordered General Steedman to march his command to Murfreesboro; that passing through Stevenson by rail, he should take the troops of General R. S. Granger, including the former garrisons of Huntsville, Athens, and Decatur, and proceed to the latter place. His instructions required that he should reoccupy the important posts on that line, abandoned at the time of General Hood's advance, and with the remainder of his forces cross the Tennessee river, and threaten the enemy's communications west of Florence.

On the morning of the 19th, Generals Wilson and Wood advanced to Rutherford's creek, whose deep swift current formed a better rear-guard for the enemy than his dispirited infantry and cavalry. During the day, several efforts were made to cross the stream, but all were fruitless. The rain continued and the pontoon train was still in the rear. While the leading columns were thus detained, General Smith reached Spring Hill, and General Schofield crossed the Harpeth at Franklin.

The next morning, General Hatch formed a floating bridge from the debris of the railroad bridge, and crossing with his division advanced rapidly to Columbia, to find that the enemy had succeeded, the evening previous, in passing Duck river and lifting his pontoon bridge. General Wood also crossed by various expedients and encamped near Columbia.

The pontoon train reached Rutherford's creek at noon on the 21st. A bridge was immediately thrown, and the troops and trains passed over and moved to Columbia. The weather now changed from excessive rain to extreme cold; and this greatly retarded the throwing of the bridge over Duck river. The rapid subsidence of the water caused repeated alterations in the length of the bridge, and protracted the delay. General Wood, however, crossed in the evening of the 23d, and encamped two miles south of Columbia. The cavalry crossed the next day and the pursuit was resumed; but by this time General Hood had reformed his rear-guard, and this accomplishment was one of the conditions of his escape. All his best troops had been thrown to his rear, and the interval between his disorganized forces and their pursuers had been greatly increased. Such, too, was the topography of the country, that a small force could compel the deployment of the leading troops, with loss of time. Another difficulty was the impossibility of moving the cavalry off the turnpike on the flanks of the infantry column, as General Thomas had directed, on account of the softness of the soil. As a consequence, the infantry fell in rear of the cavalry; and in this order Generals Wilson and Wood moved toward Pulaski. The former encountered the enemy in the vicinity of Lynnville, and the country being open he was driven rapidly. At Buford's Station, while Hatch was pressing directly forward, Croxton struck the enemy's flank, when he was thrown into rapid retreat. A number of prisoners were captured, and General Buford was wounded.

The enemy moved hurriedly through Pulaski, closely followed by Colonel Harrison's brigade. Harrison's quick movement compelled the enemy to leave the bridge over Richland creek, and hurrying forward he found him intrenched at the head of a ravine through which the road passed. Here his infantry leaped quickly from the intrenchments, brushed back Harrison's skirmishers, and captured one gun of Smith's battery—"I," Fourth United States Artillery. The enemy retained the gun, but left fifty prisoners when Hatch and Hammond moved upon his flanks. On the 26th, the pursuit was continued to Sugar creek, where the enemy was again found in intrenchments, but which he abandoned upon the development of a line of attack.

Here the pursuit was abandoned, as it had been ascertained that General Hood's infantry forces had effected the passage of the Tennessee river at Bainbridge. The gunboats under Admiral Lee had reached Chickasaw, Mississippi, on the 24th, and soon after captured two guns from a battery at Florence. General Steedman reached Decatur on the 28th, having met resistance in crossing the river at that place.

When the pursuit terminated, General Thomas gave orders for the disposition of his forces in winter cantonments, on the line of the Tennessee river, having ulterior aggressive aims. His orders located the Fourth Corps at Huntsville and Athens, Alabama; the Twenty-third Corps at Dalton, Georgia; General Smith's corps at Eastport, Mississippi, and General Wilson's cavalry at Huntsville and Eastport. On the 30th, he announced in orders the conclusion of the campaign, and congratulated his army upon its eminent success.

This was the last invasion of the State of Tennessee by the Confederate Army of the Tennessee, composed largely of troops from that state, many of whom, in the final rout, scattered in all directions, and never again stood under their banners. Indeed, the banners of this army, as such, were never again borne in battle. Exclusive of the multitudes who wandered from his army, General Hood lost by capture thirteen thousand one hundred and eighty-nine men, including seven general officers, sixteen colonels, and nearly one thousand of lower grades, and two thousand by formal desertion. He lost seventy-two pieces of serviceable artillery, seventy stands of colors, and immense quantities of small arms, wagons, pontoons, and other material. If, to the fifteen thousand men reported as prisoners and deserters, there should be added his losses in battle and the never-reported desertions, it is safe to conclude that scarcely one-half of his army recrossed the Tennessee river. The portion of it which did cross, was too dispirited to give further support to the sinking cause.

In the whole campaign, General Thomas lost, in all the forms of casualty, about ten thousand men, a large portion of this aggregate having been slightly wounded.

This campaign, as also the Atlanta campaign, had intimate relations with the operations of General Canby on the Mississippi river. Twice had the Confederate President ordered the armies under Generals Smith and Magruder, west of the great river, to cross to the east—once to aid General Johnston against General Sherman, and again, to join General Hood in his projected advance through Kentucky. General Canby's success in preventing the transfer of these forces in the two cases, eliminated from each the ruling condition of success. He achieved this result by holding the best crossings with strong detachments, and keeping a floating army, in conjunction with the gunboat fleet, in constant motion up and down the river.

CHAPTER XXXVI.

MINOR OPERATIONS HAVING RELATIONS MORE OR LESS INTIMATE WITH THOSE OF THE MAIN ARMY DURING NOVEMBER AND DECEMBER.

GENERAL STEEDMAN knew, upon reaching Decatur, that it was too late to embarrass the enemy in crossing the Tennessee river, but he determined to move toward his line of retreat south of the river. He had been joined at Stevenson by Colonel W. J. Palmer, of the Fifteenth Pennsylvania Cavalry, with a force composed of his own regiment and detachments from the Second Tennessee, and the Tenth, Twelfth, and Thirteenth Indiana Cavalry, in all about six hundred and fifty men. At 8 P. M. on the 28th, Colonel Palmer moved from Decatur toward Courtland. He encountered the enemy at a point two miles distant, and attacking with his advance of thirty men pressed him back. The force was Colonel Wines' regiment of Roddy's command, and this commander was resisting to cover his artillery, but against thirty men, yielded his position and two pieces of artillery. Colonel Palmer the next day divided his force, sending Colonel Prosser with the detachments on the main road, and moving with his own regiment on the Brown's Ferry road. Colonel Prosser soon met Roddy's whole force drawn up in two lines, and without hesitation charged, broke his lines, captured forty-five men, and drove the enemy through Courtland.

At Leighton, on the 30th, Colonel Palmer learned that General Hood's pontoon train of two hundred wagons had passed through the day before en route for Columbus, Mississippi. General Roddy was in the rear to protect this train, and although Colonel Palmer felt safe in disregarding him in making an effort to capture it, it was necessary that he should shun another cavalry force under General Armstrong, which was also near.   Making the venture, he moved to the rear of a portion of Roddy's command, and captured Colonel Warren and other prisoners.   At Russellville, another portion was met and routed, and Palmer then pressed on after the train and soon captured it, consisting of two hundred wagons and seventy-eight boats with appointments complete.   Such was the condition of the roads and the teams that it was not considered safe to attempt its removal from the presence of the enemy, and hence it was destroyed.   Then having heard that a supply train was moving from Barton Station to Tuscumbia, Colonel Palmer moved to capture it.   On the 1st of January, this train, consisting of one hundred and ten wagons and five hundred mules, was also taken in Itawamba county, Mississippi, and mules enough saved to mount one hundred and fifty prisoners. Losing one man killed and two wounded, Colonel Palmer returned to Decatur.

In the meantime, General Steedman had been ordered to Chattanooga.   He put his sick men and his artillery on transports, and started his infantry by rail, under General Cruft. When the force reached Huntsville, Colonel Mitchell's brigade was hurried forward to Larkinsville, to intercept, if possible, General Lyon, who, with a portion of his command, was in retreat from Kentucky.   His expedition had proved disastrous in the extreme in its general issue.   He captured Hopkinsville, but was met near Greenbury by General McCook, who had been detached from the main army to protect the Louisville and Nashville railroad, and to pursue this raiding force.   Colonel La Grange first met Lyon with his brigade.   Engaging him with spirit, after a short conflict he threw his troops into confusion and rout, capturing one gun and some prisoners. General Lyon then made a detour through Elizabethtown and Glasgow, and crossed the Cumberland river at Burksville, and thence proceeded through McMinnville and Winchester to the Memphis and Charleston railroad.   On the 7th of January, General Cruft's command was disposed to capture him or drive him across the Tennessee river at the approaches to Bellefont, Larkinsville, and Scottsboro; but he succeeded in eluding all the detachments on the watch, and crossed the Tennessee river.

He was finally intercepted and captured, with one hundred of his men and his remaining gun, at Red Hill.   He, however, escaped, having shot the soldier in charge of him.

As General Thomas was in command of all the troops within the limits of the Military Division of the Mississippi, the operations in East Tennessee were subject to his direction.   There had been complications there during the summer and early autumn, and General Schofield had left his corps at Atlanta, to give attention to affairs in that region.   General J. H. Morgan had been killed by General Gillem's troops, but infantry had been subsequently sent there, and when General Hood was menacing Tennessee from Florence, General Breckinridge, supported by Duke and Vaughn, appeared before General Gillem at Bull's Gap.   At this period, General Gillem, commanding three regiments of Tennessee cavalry and a battery, was acting under the immediate instructions of Governor Johnson, having been detached for this duty.   On the 13th of November, General Breckinridge, with a force estimated at three thousand men, attacked and routed the fifteen hundred under General Gillem, capturing about one third, including his battery.   General Gillem had repulsed two attacks of the enemy, but reinforcements having come, he concluded to withdraw, and while retreating was attacked in rear.   There was a lack of co-operation between General Gillem and General Ammen, which General Thomas considered the cause of the disaster.   General Gillem fell back upon Knoxville with the remainder of his force, followed closely by General Breckinridge.

In the emergency, General Thomas directed General Steedman to hold troops in readiness to support General Ammen, at Knoxville; and General Stoneman, in command of the Department of the Ohio, in the absence of General Schofield, ordered a concentration of forces in Kentucky, to advance from Lexington to Cumberland Gap, either to repel the enemy, should he advance into Kentucky, or to advance into East Tennessee, should he continue to operate there.

On the 18th, General Breckinridge withdrew from the vicinity of Knoxville, and General Ammen, reinforced by fifteen hundred men from Chattanooga, reoccupied Strawberry Plains the same day.   About the same time, General Stoneman left

Louisville to take the direction of affairs in East Tennessee, and on his way received his instructions from General Thomas, at Nashville. He was directed " to concentrate the largest force possible against Breckinridge, and either destroy his force or drive it into Virginia, and, if possible, destroy the salt-works at Saltville, and the railroad from the Tennessee line as far into Virginia as he could go without endangering his command." On the 6th of December, General Thomas repeated his instructions upon the receipt of information that General Breckinridge was retreating.

General Stoneman had been delayed in consequence of the deficiency of his command in the essential appointments for the service proposed. On the 9th, he was ready for active operations. His command comprised the infantry and dismounted cavalry under General Ammen, General Gillem's force, and the mounted troops under General Burbridge, forty-two hundred men. He first sent the Fourth Tennessee and Third North Carolina regiments to Paint Rock, to hold the pass over the mountains into North Carolina. December 9th, he moved two regiments of Ohio artillery from Strawberry Plains to Blair's Cross-roads, and with General Gillem proceeded to that point the next day. At Bean's Station these forces were joined on the 11th by General Burbridge's command. Hitherto the commander alone knew the service and destination of the troops, but here the men were supplied with all the ammunition and rations that they could carry on themselves and horses. On the 13th, at daylight, General Gillem reached the north fork of the Holston river, opposite Kingston. Here was General John Morgan's command, under his brother, in the temporary absence of General Duke. After a sharp conflict, General Gillem crossed the river and totally defeated the enemy, capturing Morgan and a portion of his command, and killing or dispersing the remainder. During the afternoon, Burbridge was pushed on to Bristol, in the endeavor to intercept Vaughn, who had held Greenville for some time with a force estimated at twelve hundred men. At night, Generals Stoneman and Gillem followed, arriving at Bristol early on the 14th.

Fearing that Vaughn would pass in the night and join

Breckinridge, Burbridge was sent to Abingdon with instructions to send a regiment forward to strike the railroad at some point between Saltville and Wytheville. When General Gillem had completed the destruction of Bristol, which General Burbridge had commenced, he moved to Glade Springs, followed by Burbridge. At 2 A. M. on the 16th, General Stoneman learned that the Twelfth Kentucky Cavalry, sent forward from Abingdon, after threatening the salt-works, had destroyed two trains which had brought Breckinridge from Wytheville with reinforcements, and decided to press on to Wytheville, destroy it and the salt-works on New river, and give attention to the destruction of Saltville on his return. He therefore put his forces in motion eastward, and soon General Gillem overtook Vaughn at Marion, and attacking, routed him, pursuing rapidly to Wytheville, capturing his trains, artillery, and one hundred and ninety-eight men, and destroying the town. General Burbridge reached Mount Airy the next day, where Buckley's brigade was dispatched by order of General Stoneman to destroy the lead mines twenty-five or thirty miles beyond. Nothing now remained but the destruction of Saltville, and General Stoneman, by a quick return, interposed his command so that General Breckinridge was cut off and forced to retreat into North Carolina. The two main columns were then ordered to converge upon Saltville. When they were near, and General Stoneman was waiting for General Burbridge, he sent Colonel Stacy with his regiment, the Thirteenth Tennessee, to dash into the town and commence the work of destruction with all possible noise. The brilliant dash of Stacy put the enemy into retreat, and then the celebrated salt-works with all their machinery and supplies were destroyed.

This expedition brought defeat to the enemy at every step, and destruction to important manufactories of the material of war, to vast quantities of material of every kind, and to railroads and rolling-stock. General Burbridge destroyed five trains filled with supplies, a thousand stand of arms, a vast amount of fixed ammunition, and a large number of wagons and ambulances, and captured seventeen officers and two hundred and sixty privates; Buckley ruined the lead-works in

Wythe county; Major Harrison, of the Twelfth Kentucky
Cavalry, captured two railroad trains, destroyed all the railroad
bridges from Glade Springs to Marion, and the large iron-
works at the latter place, and captured several hundred fine
horses; General Gillem's brigade, reinforced by the Eleventh
Michigan and the Eleventh Kentucky Cavalry, drove Vaughn
beyond Wytheville, destroyed that town, all the railroad
bridges from Marion to Reedy creek, vast amounts of stores
and supplies of all kinds, several hundred wagons and ambulances, two locomotives and several cars, and captured ten
pieces of field artillery, and over two hundred prisoners. This
command made an average march of forty-two and a half
miles per day, completing its work of destruction on the 22d
of December. Then General Burbridge returned to Kentucky
by way of the Big Sandy valley, and General Gillem to Knoxville.

CHAPTER XXXVII.

THE MARCH TO THE SEA, AND THE CAPTURE OF THE CITY OF
SAVANNAH, GEORGIA.

GENERAL SHERMAN's forces selected for his march to the sea-coast comprised sixty thousand infantry and five thousand five hundred cavalry, and one piece of artillery for every thousand men. These troops had been so thoroughly sifted that they really represented a much larger army than this aggregate, with the usual percentage of ineffective men. They were organized into right and left wings; the former embracing the Fifteenth and Seventeenth Corps, under the command of Major-General O. O. Howard, and the latter the Fourteenth and Twentieth Corps, under Major-General H. W. Slocum. The Fifteenth and Seventeenth Corps, from the Army of the Tennessee, were commanded respectively by Major-Generals P. T. Osterhaus and F. P. Blair, and the Fourteenth and Twentieth, from the Army of the Cumberland, were commanded respectively by Brevet Major-General J. C. Davis and Brigadier-General A. S. Williams. The appointments were ample beyond precedent, as selection had been made from the material of the Military Division of the Mississippi; in fact, each corps had complete army appointments, that each might have the independence of a separate army.

The last ten days of October and the first days of November had been devoted to preparation. Supplies had been accumulated at Atlanta in such quantities that there were forty days' rations of beef, sugar, and coffee, twenty days' of bread, and a double allowance of salt for forty days. The amount of ammunition was ample for all possibilities. There was little forage, only for three days in grain; but it was known that the lines of march penetrated regions abounding in corn and fodder, and also in substantial supplies for men, and those delicacies in great abundance which do not often fall to soldiers. All the material at Atlanta not needed for the expedition was sent to the rear, or devoted to destruction with a large portion of the city. The garrisons north of Kingston moved to Chattanooga, and the rails were lifted from the railroad track from Resaca north; but those between Resaca and the Etowah river were left in place in view of the probable occupancy of the country as far forward as the line of that river.

November 11th, General Corse, in obedience to orders, destroyed the bridges, foundries, mills, shops, machines, and all property useful in war, at Rome, Georgia. The next day, the telegraph wires extending northward from Kingston were cut, and the several corps moved rapidly toward Atlanta. On the 14th, the four corps and cavalry were grouped around that city, and on the 15th, the Fifteenth, Seventeenth, and Twentieth Corps moved out upon their respective lines of march, and that night the conflagration of a large portion of Atlanta gave emphatic announcement that the grand movement had begun.

As the great objects of this expedition were an illustration of the weakness of the Confederacy behind its defensive and offensive lines, and the diminution of its remaining resources by the destruction of railroads and all property useful in war, the lines of march diverged widely. Besides, there was another end to be secured by this broad divergent front in moving from Atlanta—the concealment of the ultimate objective, that the enemy might not know where to concentrate his forces. The right wing, with Kilpatrick's division of cavalry on its right flank, marched by Jonesboro and McDonough, under orders to make a strong feint upon Macon, and then turn eastward and rendezvous at Gordon on the 23d. The Twentieth Corps advanced by Decatur, Stone Mountain, Social Circle, and Madison, to turn southward to Milledgeville, under instructions to tear up the railroad from Social Circle to Madison, and burn the railroad bridge over the Oconee in the same period. On the 16th, the Fourteenth Corps advanced upon Milledgeville, through Lithonia, Covington, and Shady Dale.

On the 23d, the right wing and the cavalry reached Gordon and the left wing Milledgeville; and this first stage of the campaign was the realization of all anticipations. General Sherman had interposed his army between Macon and Augusta, and the enemy, in his doubt as to his destination and his utter inability to oppose him wherever he might go, was paralyzed completely. He had not, in the eight days, shown any great strength at any point, and it was evident that no strong force was opposing either of the two main columns. His cavalry, under General Wheeler, which had been dispatched as a corps of observation, had engaged General Kilpatrick several times, and General Cobb's militia and regular troops, from Macon and Savannah, had sallied from the former place to receive severe punishment from Walcutt's brigade; and besides these feeble demonstrations there had been no opposition, and it was manifest that no serious resistance could be organized in Central Georgia. The veteran troops were either with General Hood, in Tennessee, or in the large cities on the seaboard, and General Sherman's plans had been discerned too late for any troops in force to be directed to his front. When General Beauregard, who was at Corinth directing the great concentration of forces which was to march in triumph to the Ohio river, learned that General Sherman with a large army was marching southward from Atlanta, he committed to General Hood the conduct of the Tennessee campaign, and hastened to Georgia to arouse the people, by frantic proclamations, to resist this overwhelming invasion. His own second great plan of aggression from Corinth, Mississippi, was now, as far as he was personally concerned, as palpabale a failure as was his first, when he evacuated Corinth in May, 1862, with an army embracing all the available Confederate troops in the West. Appeals of similar fervor and futility were issued by the Confederate authorities at Richmond, including the President and Congress—at least by the congressional representatives from Georgia—and from the governor of the invaded state. While there was a veteran army between the homes of the people and the invader, there was some basis for appeal; but now the hopelessness of the situation was so apparent that the people were paralyzed with fear and despair, and noisy proclamations were as impotent as the cry of women and children.

The orders for the second stage of the campaign sent the two wings on parallel lines toward Millin, and Kilpatrick to destroy the railroad between Milledgeville and Augusta, and then to hasten to Millin, to rescue the prisoners supposed to be there confined. On the 26th, the heads of columns of the left wing gained Sandersville, and then swept eastward toward the Georgia Central railroad, and the right wing moved from Gordon, on the line of the railroad. December 2d, the central columns of the two corps were at Millin, and the extreme corps were abreast. Immense damage had been done to the railroads, mills, cotton-mills, and gins, and some fighting had occurred on the flanks, especially by the cavalry—Kilpatrick having had several brushes with Wheeler, but had been victorious, whether in offense or defense. The heads of columns had also been slightly annoyed, but not to an extent to greatly embarrass their movements. The greatest obstacles on the way to Millin were the Ogeechee and Oconee rivers, and an army behind these streams might have been successful in resistance, but the enemy's slender forces were easily dislodged, and the army passed over without delay. There had been no rescue of prisoners from the enemy, as all had been removed from Millin too soon.

Instructions for the third and last stage required the convergence of the wings upon Savannah—the left wing and the Seventeenth Corps moving on parallel roads, and the Fifteenth Corps deflecting to the right, on the right bank of the Ogeechee, to cross at Eden Station. General Wheeler followed the columns on the east bank, but their rear was protected by Kilpatrick's cavalry and Baird's division of the Fourteenth Corps. As the army approached Savannah, the country became more marshy, and the roads more obstructed by fallen trees, especially where the roads crossed the swamps on causeways that traverse the lowlands, which are overflowed artificially for the culture of rice. When within fifteen miles of the city, the columns were confronted by earthworks and artillery, in addition to the ordinary obstructions of the roads and causeways. But these defenses were easily turned, and on the 10th of December, the enemy was driven within the fortifications of Savannah, and its investment in great part accomplished. The right and left wings closed in with connected lines near the main defenses of the city. The left of the Twentieth Corps rested on the Savannah river, and the right of the Fourteenth Corps connected with the left of the Seventeenth, beyond the canal, near Lawson's plantation. General Slocum held the bridge of the Charleston railroad and the river itself, and General Howard controlled the Gulf railroad and the Ogeechee down toward Fort McAllister. Thus General Sherman held firmly all the railroads centering in Savannah, and the two rivers forming the main channels of supply, and all the roads leading out from the city, except the Union causeway, over which the road to Hardeeville and Charleston passes from the shore of the river opposite the town.

General Slocum grasped the Savannah river firmly with his left flank, at a point about five miles from the city, and planted batteries so as to command the channel. He was scarcely in position, when Captain Gildersleeve, of the One Hundred and Fiftieth New York, in command of a foraging party, captured the steamer Ida, having on board Colonel Lynch of General Hardee's staff, bearing dispatches to the gunboats up the river. This boat was burned, to prevent recapture by the gunboats patrolling the river below. Near General Slocum's left flank were two river islands, Hutchinson and Argyle, whose possession was essential to his complete mastery of the river. These he promptly seized. During the evening of the 16th, Colonel Hawley, of the Third Wisconsin, from Carman's brigade, by order of General Williams, sent over two companies of his regiment to Argyle Island, and the next morning six more. While he was crossing with the latter, he discovered three steamers descending the river. He hastened across, while Winegar's battery from the Georgia shore opened upon them. The boats were driven back, and in turning the two gunboats disabled their armed tender, which fell into Hawley's hands, at the head of the island. The next day, General Geary, commanding First division Twentieth Corps, was directed to occupy the upper end of Hutchinson Island with a detachment, to prevent the approach of the enemy's gunboats. A sunken battery was also established on the Georgia shore, whose guns commanded the river above and below the island, and ranged over the island to the Carolina shore.

The defenses of the enemy had by this time been thoroughly developed by reconnoissances along the whole front of the investing lines, and it was apparent that by means of irrigating canals, traversing the rice plantations, the whole region could be so flooded as greatly to embarrass the advance of assaulting columns. It was equally apparent that there were but two ways to take the city, by assault between the rivers, or the completion of the investment by closing the road to Charleston, which was General Hardee's only avenue of escape, and force a capitulation by starvation.

Before, however, attempting either an assault or the completion of the investment, General Sherman made a successful effort to open communications with the fleet known to be in waiting for his coming, to secure supplies by the passage of the boats on the Ogeechee river, to the rear of his encampments. He was not yet in need, as he had large herds of cattle, and his trains were filled with supplies, which had been gathered on the march from Atlanta and with what had been loaded in that city, and there was an open country for foraging in his rear. Still he deemed communication with the fleet to be of paramount importance. The barrier to this was Fort McAllister, a redoubt on the right bank of the Ogeechee, holding heavy guns, and to its reduction he addressed himself, while he intrusted the immediate investment to his subordinate commanders. On the 13th, General Kilpatrick was sent over the Ogeechee on a pontoon bridge, under instructions to reconnoiter Fort McAllister and the inlets in that vicinity, and if practicable to take the fort; subsequently he was directed by General Sherman to examine St. Catherine's Sound and open communication with the fleet. General Kilpatrick having reported that Fort McAllister was manned by two hundred men, and the bridge over the Ogeechee, known as "King's Bridge," having been repaired in an incredibly short time by Colonel Buell and his regiment—the Fifty-eighth Indiana, famous in the Army of the Cumberland for such exploits—General Hazen, commanding the Second division of the Fifteenth Army Corps, was ordered to be in readiness to move against the fort. Early on the 13th, General Hazen crossed King's bridge, and deployed his division before the position, with its flanks resting on the river. Having at 3 P. M. signaled his readiness for assault to General Sherman, who, with General Howard, had taken post at Chase's rice-mill for observation and direction, he received orders to make the attack. In compliance, General Hazen assaulted at 5 P. M.; his troops broke through the abatis and leaped over the parapet, announcing their victory by shouts and the elevation of the national flag. While observing Hazen's operations, General Sherman caught sight of a steamer, which came to herald the proximity of the fleet at the very moment that the Ogeechee was opened for its use. Supplies were now assured, and the reduction of Savannah was the immediate problem for solution.

The day following, Generals Sherman and Foster, the latter commanding the forces in South Carolina, met Admiral Dahlgren in conference, and arranged for co-operative movements against Savannah. Siege-guns were to be brought from Hilton Head; the fleet was to bombard the lower forts, and the investing forces were to carry the landward defenses of the city. At this time General Sherman thought that he could reach the "Union Causeway"—General Hardee's only way of escape from his left flank—by throwing a column across the Savannah river. He therefore returned from the fleet, with announced determination to assault the lines of the enemy as soon as the promised siege-guns should arrive.

On the 17th, General Sherman demanded the surrender of the city; but on the next day received a positive refusal from General Hardee, who reminded him that his investment was not complete, that his guns were four miles from Savannah, and that there would be no justification for capitulation while he had an open road to Charleston. He had probably less than fifteen thousand men, a force that was inadequate for successful defense against the armies and fleet that were converging upon him, but the issue proved that the necessity of surrender did not exist.

The problem of reducing Savannah was not the only one which now engrossed the attention of General Sherman, as a greater one had been devolved upon him by General Grant—one in comparison with which the other was merely incidental. This was the movement of General Sherman's army, to assist in the reduction of Richmond. But as this enterprise was contingent upon the accumulation of vessels sufficient to transport fifty or sixty thousand men, the operations against Savannah were continued as though its capture was paramount, except that the ulterior objective induced General Sherman to refrain from throwing one of General Slocum's corps across to South Carolina.

Pending the opening of the Ogeechee and the coming of the siege-guns, there was some activity on the left flank of the army, and General Slocum was urgent to throw one of his corps into South Carolina, to close General Hardee's only avenue of escape. On the 15th, Colonel Hawley crossed to the Carolina shore from Argyle Island, with five companies, drove the enemy from Izzard's plantation, and made a reconnoissance of the country two miles farther. Being isolated, he thought it prudent to return, and in doing this he was vigorously pressed by the enemy, but recrossed to the island in safety. Upon his return, he was reinforced by the Second Massachusetts regiment, and on the next day the remainder of the brigade, Colonel Carman commanding, and a section of artillery, crossed to the island and took position on the eastern point near the South Carolina shore. During the night, Colonel Carman received orders from General Williams to cross to South Carolina and take position near the river, threatening the Savannah and Charleston road. This was not accomplished immediately for want of small boats, and barges could not be used on account of low tide. In the meantime, General Wheeler appeared on the opposite shore, and opened with his light guns upon Carman's troops, the latter responding during the 17th and 18th, but made no effort to cross.

In view of these revelations, General Sherman abandoned the idea of closing the road to Charleston by operations from his left flank, as the enemy held the river opposite the city with iron-clad gunboats, and could, as was conjectured, de-stroy pontoons between Hutchinson Island and the Carolina shore, and isolate any force sent from that flank.

Upon the abandonment of this movement, General Slocum was ordered to get the siege-guns into position and make preparations for assault. The approaches to the city were upon the narrow causeways, which were commanded by artil-lery; but nevertheless the reconnoissance from the left wing had convinced General Slocum and his subordinate command-ers that the works in their front could be carried. Two of General Howard's division commanders were confident they could attack successfully, though the conditions of assault on their portion of the line was less favorable than on the left.

In abandoning the purpose to close the Charleston road from his left flank, General Sherman did not forego the at-tempt to shut it from another direction, as it was then threat-ened by one of General Foster's divisions from the head of Broad river, and on the 19th he set sail for Port Royal to arrange with General Foster for a movement upon the cause-way, so vital to General Hardee. His instructions, at depart-ure, to Generals Howard and Slocum were to get ready, but not to strike until his return.

At daybreak on the morning of the 19th, by order of Gen-eral Williams, commanding the Twentieth Corps, Colonel Carman threw the Third Wisconsin, the Second Massachu-setts, and the Thirteenth New York regiments, under Colonel Hawley, to the South Carolina shore. These troops landed without opposition, and advancing to Izzard's mill, skirmished into a good position. The enemy expressed his appreciation of the position, which he had lost, by charging with his cav-alry to regain it, but suffered repulse. During the afternoon and evening, Colonel Carman sent forward the remaining reg-iments of his brigade, and assumed command at Izzard's mill. His position was a strong one for defense, but the ground be-fore him presented marked obstacles to an advance. His front was a rice plantation, traversed by canals and dikes, the fields being overflowed to the depth of eighteen inches. To move forward under these circumstances, it was necessary to follow the dikes, and these were easily defended. During the night he intrenched his line, which extended from the Savannah river, on his right, two and a quarter miles, to an inlet near Clyesdale creek.

The next morning, in obedience to orders from General Jackson, his division commander, Colonel Carman detailed twelve companies under Colonel Hawley, and directed in person a reconnoissance to determine the relation of his line to Clyesdale creek. This creek was reached, with loss of one man. Works were then constructed for a regiment; two companies were left to hold them, and with the remainder of the force an effort was made to reach the Charleston road. This movement had been anticipated by the enemy, and a strong force had been thrown before Carman. As he could not advance without crossing a canal under fire, he withdrew, but remained sufficiently near the road to observe the passage of vehicles of all descriptions, in motion toward Charleston. During the afternoon he was shelled by a gunboat, and at 4 P. M. he was reinforced by three regiments. He was so near the enemy's pontoon bridge, at Savannah, that from 7 P. M. to 3 A. M. he could distinctly hear the retreating army crossing upon it. This noise was also heard by General Geary from his position below Hutchinson's Island. These facts were duly reported.

Thus, under the mantle of darkness, during a moonless and windy night, General Hardee withdrew his entire force along the front of a brigade of the investing army. The approach of this brigade to his only line of retreat may have hastened his withdrawal; but his final haste, whatever its immediate cause, was his salvation, and his stay at Savannah for ten days with such possibilities in his rear, vindicates him from the charge of abandoning his post before there was absolute need.

General Sherman returned on the 22d, to find the city of Savannah in the quiet possession of his army. General Hardee had destroyed as much of his material as the security of his retreat permitted; but he left his guns unspiked, three steamboats, his railroad rolling-stock, twenty-five thousand bales of cotton belonging to the Confederate government, and vast quantities of other public property of great value, uninjured.

Except the failure to capture General Hardee's army at Savannah and release the prisoners at Millin, the march from Atlanta to that city was a triumphant success—the full realization of all anticipated possibilities. It illustrated with fearful emphasis the weakness of the rebellion, for no force able to resist one of General Sherman's thirteen divisions was met on the way. It left a track of desolation forty miles wide; broke up the railroad system of Georgia and of the South, by the destruction of three hundred miles of track, all workshops, station-houses, tanks, and warehouses; crippled the industries of the empire state of the South, by burning all the mills and factories on the broad belt of ruin, and made otherwise a heavy draft upon the resources of the people, in consuming and transporting supplies in immense quantities, and by the destruction of twenty thousand bales of cotton. The general significance of these results spread gloom and despair over the South. Coupled with the victory at Nashville, "The March to the Sea" brought near the collapse of the rebellion. The death-throes of treason, organized in magnitude most grand, were subsequently in harmony with its proportions and persistence; but all doubt of its quick destruction was now removed. When General Lee should surrender, the end would come; and to hasten this result, the victorious Western armies were under orders to move northward by sea or land, as circumstances should determine.

CHAPTER XXXVIII.

MARCH THROUGH THE CAROLINAS, FROM SAVANNAH TO GOLDSBORO AND RALEIGH; THE BATTLES OF AVERYSBORO AND BENTONVILLE.

Soon after the occupation of Savannah by General Sherman, the movement of his army by sea was abandoned, and its march through the Carolinas was adopted instead. General Sherman had indicated to General Grant, in his letter of December 16th, his preference for the overland movement, and in subsequent communications emphasized his choice. And in view of the apparent advantages of this approach to Virginia, General Grant authorized General Sherman, December 27th, to move his army northward through the Carolinas as soon as practicable. It was anticipated that this movement would prevent, in great measure, the union of the fragments of the defeated Confederate armies in the West and South, while it would repeat and intensify the effect produced by the march from Atlanta to Savannah. The plan adopted, compassed the permanent occupancy of Savannah by troops from a distance, that General Sherman might keep his army intact to be able to resist General Lee until General Grant could give him help from Virginia, should that general abandon the capital of the Confederacy to oppose him.

The river defenses of Savannah, with slight modifications, were deemed adequate. Forts Pulaski, Thunderbolt, and McAllister were put in complete order. The forts bearing upon the approaches by water were dismantled, and their heavy guns sent to Fort Pulaski and Hilton Head. The obstructions, including torpedoes, were removed from the adjacent waters, and Admiral Dahlgren had the channels staked out and indicated by buoys. Preparations were promptly commenced and energetically prosecuted, that the army might move northward by the 15th of January.

A portion of General Sherman's forces did move before the 15th of January; but rain, swollen rivers, and flooded low-lands so delayed co-operative columns, that they did not cross the Savannah river until the first week of February. On the 14th, General Howard, with General Blair's corps, crossed from Beaufort Island to the main land, flanked the enemy at Gordon's Corner, and followed him to Pocotaligo, and on the following morning took possession of the vacant fort at that place. This movement was a feint upon Charleston, to deceive the enemy as to General Sherman's first and second objectives, which were Columbia, South Carolina, and Goldsboro, North Carolina.

A pontoon bridge had been thrown at Savannah for the passage of the left wing, and the Union causeway had been repaired; but the flood in the river had borne away the bridge and submerged the causeway, and General Slocum was compelled to move up the river to find a crossing. Jackson's and Ward's divisions of the Twentieth Corps crossed at Purysburg, and on the 19th were at Hardeeville, in com-munication with General Howard at Pocotaligo. The Four-teenth Corps, and Geary's division of the Twentieth Corps, which had been relieved from garrison duty at Savannah, by General Grover's division of the Nineteenth Corps from Vir-ginia, did not leave Savannah until the 26th of January. These troops then moved up to Sister's Ferry, and succeeded in crossing the river during the first week of February. In the meantime, the Fifteenth Corps, General John A. Logan commanding, had crossed the river and lowlands, and joined General Howard at Pocotaligo.

General Sherman's forces were now in readiness to enter upon a campaign which involved strategic combinations of widest range. When the northward march was first indicated, Generals Bragg, Beauregard, and Hardee were intent upon concentrating all fragments of armies far and near to oppose it. Generals Beauregard and Hardee were in Charleston, and General Bragg was in North Carolina.

North Carolina was open to attack from the coast, and

thither General Schofield's corps of twenty-one thousand men from the West and other forces were to move. General Sherman had an offensive army of sixty-five thousand men, and forces in his rear to hold Savannah and garrison such other fortified places as should fall into his hands. Acting aggressively on a broad field, with possible objectives in front, or right or left, their antagonist could conceal his purposes, and strike vital points uncovered by invitation of feints in other directions. The disposition of his forces from Sister's Ferry to Pocotaligo menaced equally Charleston, Columbia, and Augusta, and which was General Sherman's immediate objective, the Confederate generals could not discern with certainty. And if they could have ascertained his aims, he could change them with pleasure with crushing effect. Having passed by Augusta in his march from Atlanta that he might menace that city with his left flank while feigning against Charleston with his right, to concentrate between the divided forces of the enemy upon Columbia as his first objective, he proposed that his two wings should shake hands where secession first found positive expression through the convention of South Carolina, and then stride on to Goldsboro and Richmond.

The inevitable delay at Savannah was favorable to the enemy, as it had given time for a sweeping conscription in the states immediately threatened, for the fragments of Hood's army to move far toward the Carolinas, and for Wheeler to obstruct the roads before General Sherman's columns, and destroy the bridges that could not be utilized for defense. These obstructions, the depth of the rivers, and the breadth of the immediate lowlands on their margins, doubtless gave hope to the enemy that the invasion of the Carolinas would be greatly delayed, if not defeated. But though the obstacles were almost insurmountable, General Sherman's victorious troops did not hesitate to make causeways in the deep cold waters for miles, nor to make roads through the swamps of South Carolina in midwinter, and made a march not inferior to the celebrated passage of the Alps, except in the low lines of advance.

The infantry forces of the enemy occupied the line of the

Salkehatchie river, while Wheeler's cavalry hovered around the heads of column or on the flanks of the two wings. The left wing, with Kilpatrick on its left flank, moved upon Barnwell, threatening Augusta; the right wing, accompanied by General Sherman, moved westward to the Salkehatchie, touching the river at Beaufort and Rivers' bridges, flanking Charleston, and neutralizing the elaborate fortifications of that city, which had so long defied the heavy guns of iron-clads and land-batteries. The bridges of the Salkehatchie were defended with spirit, but in vain; and General Howard soon forced the passages, when the enemy retired to Branchville, burning all bridges behind him. These movements spread alarm everywhere. The Confederate forces were feeble at best, and there were now so many possibilities to General Sherman, all fruitful of ruin, that extreme uncertainty and foreboding of crushing disasters palsied the courage of troops and citizens. They could only guess at General Sherman's objective, and so many were possible and his strategy so bewildering that no positions were held with adequate strength for temporary resistance, and Columbia was uncovered almost entirely.

General Sherman threw the Fifteenth and Seventeenth Corps on the Orangeburg road—the latter by Binnaker's bridge over the south fork of Edisto, and the former by Holman's. Having reached Orangeburg, the right wing moved on the direct road to Columbia. The enemy was driven from all points where resistance was made, and on the 16th, the head of column approached the capital of South Carolina. The left wing advanced steadily by Barnwell and Lexington as the general direction, and destroyed the Charleston and Augusta railroad for several miles. After a well-sustained menace to Augusta, General Slocum gathered his forces and touched the Saluda river above Columbia simultaneously with the arrival of General Howard on the bank of the river opposite the city.

General Sherman's maneuvers resulted in marked success. Throwing his columns in diverging lines from Savannah, and then converging them upon Columbia, he caused the evacuation of Charleston, and drove General Cheatham, moving eastward with the remnant of Hood's army, to the north of his projected line. It now remained to reach Goldsboro through repetition of the same confusing strategy; but the conditions of its success were now greatly changed, as the garrisons of Charleston, Columbia, and Augusta could be united with the Western troops and other forces on the Atlantic coast, and endanger isolated columns. Besides, a great strategist, General Joseph E. Johnston, had been appointed to the command of all the forces available to resist General Sherman, in tacit recognition of the fact that his management of defensive campaigns promised better results than that of any other general who could be assigned to command in the Carolinas; but General Johnston's conduct of the defensive was now to be subject to conditions radically different from those of the Atlanta campaign. His army, as before, was inferior to that of General Sherman's, and was composed of fragmentary troops, whose morale was in harmony with the condition of the cause which they represented; and, besides, he was to meet his old antagonist, with an army whose spirit had risen, if possible, with its successive triumphs, and not now, as before, restrained in maneuver by connection with a railroad as its only channel of supply. General Johnston could therefore have no hope of success, unless he could strike unsupported columns and defeat General Sherman in detail; and past experience did not give promise of such an opportunity.

In advancing from Columbia, General Sherman, as before, covered his real object by a menace in a different direction. He now directed General Slocum to threaten Charlotte, North Carolina, to create the impression that he would strike that point on his way to Virginia, while in reality directing his army to Goldsboro. Accordingly, General Slocum resumed motion on the 17th, crossed the Saluda at Mount Zion Church on the 19th, and Broad river at Freshley's mills the day following, and arrived at Winnsboro on the 21st. On this march the left wing and cavalry destroyed several miles of railroad north and south of Alston. The right wing, General Sherman accompanying, left Columbia on the 20th, on the direct road to Winnsboro, and destroyed the railroad between the two places. Eighty squares in Columbia were left in ashes from a conflagration whose origin and progress has been a matter of historical controversy.

From Winnsboro the two wings again diverged. General Slocum moved to the north with his troops well spread out and then turned east, crossed the Catawba, and advanced to Sneedsboro. The cavalry on his left demonstrated toward Charlotte, and then followed to Sneedsboro. The right wing, in the meantime, advanced to Cheraw—the Seventeenth Corps entering that place on the 2d of March. The enemy offered some resistance, but did not retard a single column. Wheeler's cavalry and the forces from Charleston appeared at times before the columns. The other forces, including Cheatham's from the West, were directed to Charlotte, under the impression that this was the objective.

From Pedee river the two wings moved toward Fayetteville, crossing near Sneedsboro and at Cheraw—the corps moving on separate roads, and the cavalry maintaining position on the left flank. On the 9th of March, General Hampton surprised one of General Kilpatrick's brigades, and gained a temporary advantage over his whole force. General Kilpatrick barely escaped capture on foot. The enemy, however, stopped to plunder the camps, and this gave time for the national cavalry to rally; and having done this, General Kilpatrick charged and recaptured his camps and repelled all subsequent attacks. General J. G. Mitchell, with his brigade of infantry, reached the scene of conflict just as the enemy abandoned his effort to regain his lost advantage.

On the 11th, the Fourteenth and Seventeenth Corps arrived at Fayetteville and skirmished with Hampton's cavalry, which covered General Hardee as he withdrew from the town on the bridge spanning Cape Fear river, which he succeeded in burning. It was anticipated that General Hardee would contest the possession of this place, but he abandoned it without resisting and with it a vast amount of public property, including an immense arsenal. At Fayetteville, General Sherman was met by the army tug Davidson, Captain Ainsworth commanding, and the gunboat Eolus, Lieutenant-Commander Young, with the first intelligence of the fall of Wilmington, and he then dispatched orders to Generals Schofield and Terry to move upon Goldsboro.

The march through South Carolina had left a track of desolation more than forty miles wide. That state's special guilt in taking the initiative in secession, was assumed by officers and men as the justification of its devastation. As many of the Southern people who were originally opposed to secession, blamed South Carolina for precipitating the movement, and having themselves experienced the terrible retributions of the war which resulted, desired that South Carolina should feel war's heavy hand before peace should come, it was not strange that the national troops in marching through the state which originally suggested secession, and studiously endeavored to induce the Southern States to withdraw from the Union, should leave behind them the fearful evidences of vengeance achieved. But it was easier for the veterans of the war to find justification for sweeping desolation in their own feelings than it is for others to find grounds for its historical vindication.

As General Johnston had now lost a large number of important places without losing their garrisons, and had been joined by several thousand troops from the West, it was now possible for him to unite all to resist General Sherman between Fayetteville and Goldsboro. Altogether they did not constitute an army equal to General Sherman's, yet, when united, were formidable against either wing or a smaller fraction. Referring to these forces, General Sherman thus wrote: "These made up an army superior to me in cavalry, and formidable enough in artillery and infantry to justify me in extreme caution in making the last step necessary to complete the march I have undertaken." In a letter to General Schofield, of March 12th, he said that General Johnston might concentrate at Raleigh from forty to forty-five thousand men, and wrote: "I can whip that number with my present force, and with yours and Terry's added, we can go wherever we can live." To General Grant, the same day, he wrote: "Joe Johnston may try to interpose between me and Schofield about Newbern; but I think he will not try that, but concentrate his scattered armies at Raleigh, and I will go straight at him as soon as I get my men reclothed and our wagons reloaded."

General Sherman's maneuvers, after leaving Fayetteville, were, in type, a repetition of his former strategy. He moved his cavalry toward Raleigh, and followed immediately with four divisions of the left wing, and more remotely with four of the right, throwing all his trains and the four remaining divisions farther to the east. He commenced these movements on the 15th. At 3 A. M. General Kilpatrick advanced on the direct road to Averysboro to make the feint on Raleigh, and then strike the railroad near Smithfield. General Slocum followed with four unincumbered divisions. General Howard held four divisions in trim to march to General Slocum's help should there be need. The trains of the left wing, with two divisions, moved on the direct road to Goldsboro, and the trains and two divisions of the right wing, toward Faison Station on the Wilmington and Goldsboro railroad. General Sherman accompanied the left wing.

The heavy rains made quagmires of the roads, and it became necessary to corduroy them for the artillery. So much of this work had been done in the swamps of South Carolina, that great facility had been attained, and the army moved on without serious delays. During the evening of the 15th, General Kilpatrick met a strong force of infantry near Taylor's Hole creek, under the command of General Hardee. He skirmished with the rear-guard and captured some prisoners, among whom was Colonel Rhett of the heavy artillery. The next morning General Slocum advanced his infantry columns to the vicinity of Averysboro, and found General Hardee intrenched on a narrow neck of swampy land between the Cape Fear and South rivers. General Hardee's position was in front of the point where the Goldsboro road through Bentonville leaves the main road leading in the direction of Raleigh. This was the first positive resistance which had been offered by infantry in strong force north of Savannah, and was doubtless intended to retard General Sherman's advance, until General Johnston could prepare for still stronger opposition at some point farther north or east. At this time the conjecture was that he would concentrate at Raleigh, Smithfield, or Goldsboro; but his point of intended concentration was much nearer than either of these towns. But the execution of General Sherman's plan, wherever General Johnston might offer battle, required that General Hardee should be dislodged. Without this, the feint on Raleigh could not be sustained or even fully initiated, and the ultimate reunion of the columns, as contemplated, could not be effected, as General Hardee barred the diverging road to Goldsboro.

General Slocum was therefore ordered to advance against General Hardee, whose position was not strong, except from intrenchments and the softness of the ground before it, which scarcely admitted the deployment and advance of infantry, and rendered the movement of horses almost impossible. Notwithstanding this obstacle, General Slocum advanced, Williams' corps leading and Ward's division deployed. General Ward's skirmishers soon developed Rhett's brigade of artillery, acting as infantry, behind slight intrenchments, whose trend was at right angles to the road, and was sustained by a battery, which enfiladed the line of direct approach. Direct attack being perilous, General Williams threw a brigade on the left of the enemy's line, when the quondam artillerymen, in complete rout, fell back to a stronger position. This success opened the way for a general attack, to accomplish which Jackson's division formed on the right of Ward and General Davis' two divisions of the Fourteenth Corps on his left. General Kilpatrick was directed to reach out beyond Jackson's right flank and grasp the Bentonville road. One brigade of cavalry gained the road, but was attacked furiously by McLaw's division, and driven back. After this repulse, General Slocum's whole line advanced, pushed General Hardee within his intrenchments, and pressed him there so heavily that during the following dark and stormy night he retreated. The next morning, General Ward followed through Averysboro, but soon rejoined the main force, in motion on the Goldsboro road, which the engagement had opened. General Slocum lost about eighty killed and four hundred and eighty wounded. The enemy left one hundred and seventy-eight dead on the field, and lost one hundred and seventy-five men and three guns by capture. The number of his wounded was not ascertained. General Ward's pursuit developed the fact that General Hardee had retreated toward Smithfield.

The night previous, General Kilpatrick crossed South river, and on the 17th advanced toward Elevation, on the east bank. General Slocum built a bridge over the swollen stream, and then advanced on the Goldsboro road. General Sherman continued with the left wing, and encamped with the head of column, on the night of the 18th, on the Goldsboro road, twenty-five miles from Goldsboro, and five from Bentonville, at a point where the road from Clinton to Smithfield crosses the one to Goldsboro. General Howard reached Lee's store, a few miles distant, the same night, and the two wings were sufficiently near to give support in battle, and were upon roads which united a short distance to the east.

Up to this time, General Sherman had anticipated an attack upon his left flank; but he was now led to believe that General Johnston would not attack, as it was supposed that he had retreated to Smithfield, and he gave orders for the two columns to move upon Goldsboro—General Howard, on the new Goldsboro road, by Falling Creek Church, to give the direct road to General Slocum. His object was to concentrate his forces at Goldsboro as soon as practicable, and he moved to General Howard's head of column, to open communication with Generals Schofield and Terry—the former coming to meet him from Newbern, and the latter from Wilmington, having conjointly from thirty to thirty-five thousand men. It was not known that General Johnston's whole army was in immediate proximity, but it was supposed that only cavalry would be met on the way to Goldsboro.

Scarcely had General Carlin's division of the Fourteenth Corps, in the advance of the left wing, wheeled into the road to push on to Goldsboro, when Dibbrell's division of cavalry was met, whose stubborn resistance indicated that there was support, or that its courage had given a new type to the conflict of cavalry with infantry. Being under orders to press on, and supposing that cavalry alone was in his front, General Carlin engaged the enemy vigorously, and soon the responsive roar of artillery announced the opening of a battle which General Johnston was delivering, in expectation of crushing the Fourteenth Corps at least. But the magnitude of the conflict was not yet apparent. As the resistance of the enemy became more stubborn, Colonels Hobart's and Miles' brigades were deployed, the former on the right, and Colonel Buell was sent, by order of General Slocum, some distance to the left to develop the enemy's line. The resistance offered by the enemy was supposed at first to be done by cavalry, and General Slocum so reported to General Sherman, who had gone to the right to join General Howard, whose columns were moving toward Goldsboro.

As resistance increased, General Morgan was directed to move to the right of Carlin in support. The former threw General Mitchell's brigade to the right of Miles' brigade and the road, and General Fearing's to the right and rear of Mitchell—both in double lines. The Seventy-eighth Illinois of the former was sent forward to skirmish. Under this stronger formation, both division generals were directed to press the enemy closely, and compel him to reveal his position and strength.

General Slocum soon became convinced that he had before him a force more formidable than a division of cavalry. While still in doubt as to the strength of the enemy, a deserter came to him, who had been a national soldier, who gave information that General Johnston had, by forced marches, massed his entire army in his front. This statement being supported by actual developments, induced General Slocum to prepare for defense, and immediately ordered General Williams to throw his train to the right, gather his forces, and hasten to the support of General Davis. He then sent a messenger to General Sherman to announce that there was evidence that an army was before him.

The direction of General Hardee's retreat from Averysboro, had led to the belief that the way to Goldsboro was open. And this was the impression that General Johnston desired to make by all his movements. General Hardee meanwhile had changed direction not far from Averysboro, and by a detour, had united his command with the other forces concentrated and intrenched near Bentonville. Apparently, the coveted conditions of the battle assured the success of General

Johnston's strategy, for two divisions in isolation were within his reach; two more were distant a few miles, and the four divisions of the right wing, intended for the support of the left, in the event of battle, were in rapid motion toward Goldsboro, far to the right. General Williams' defeat, in prospect, was to follow that of General Davis, and the other corps and detached divisions were to be defeated in turn, and the trains destroyed. The plan miscarried, mainly, from two unexpected causes—the resistance of two divisions until the Twentieth Corps could give support, and the lack of complete concert of action in General Johnston's army, composed of the commands of Generals Bragg, Hardee, S. D. Lee, and Cheatham.

When General Slocum first ordered the Twentieth Corps to move quickly to the field, it was his intention to form it on the right of the Fourteenth, but when he became fully convinced that General Johnston's army was in his front, he directed General Williams to form his corps, as the several fractions should reach the field, on the left of General Davis. Robinson's being in the advance, was the first to come up, and was placed in support of Carlin's division.

Anticipating that Colonel Buell would need support in his movement, General Carlin was directed by General Davis to move Hobart's brigade to the left, and place Robinson's brigade in its place in the line, and support a battery, located on the main road, which had been responding to the enemy's artillery.

Colonel Buell, in advancing as directed, soon struck the enemy's intrenchments, which he assaulted furiously. After a somewhat protracted struggle, resulting in heavy loss, Colonel Buell was forced to withdraw his brigade, which had been badly broken, when the enemy sallied from his works in strong force in pursuit, and pressed him back, until checked by Hobart's brigade, which offered most stubborn resistance.

When the action commenced, the small train of the corps, in charge of General Vanderveer's brigade, was moved to the right, until this brigade had reached the right of General Mitchell, where the troops were formed in double lines, with their right resting on a swamp. This was a timely disposition, as the advance of the enemy against Colonel Buell was merely an incident in General Johnston's plan of aggression, which was to wheel his whole line upon its left to envelop and capture General Davis' two divisions. Colonel Hobart, first, after Colonel Buell, felt the force of this general attack, but he was not entirely encompassed, as Buell's attack had broken the continuity of the enemy's movement, and General Johnston's troops on the right of the point assaulted by Buell failed to move forward promptly. This failure gave time for General Davis to make such dispositions as were essential to his safety, and afforded General Slocum opportunity to bring up his reserve artillery and locate it with reference to the arrest of the enemy and the formation of a new line to the left and rear.

The front attack upon Hobart and Robinson on his right, was so vigorous as to involve them speedily in the severest conflict, and soon after in retreat upon the artillery, put in position far to the rear, on the main road. The recession of these brigades exposed the artillery on the right of Robinson, three pieces of which were captured, and also caused the retirement of Miles' brigade between Mitchell's left and the road. There were now only two brigades, Mitchell's and Vanderveer's, on the original line, and the flank of the former was in air.

At this juncture, General Davis rode to his right and ordered General Fearing's brigade to move to the left, forming line of battle as it advanced, and facing the Bentonville road. This brigade moved quickly and was soon lost to view in the thickly wooded swamp. General Morgan now directed General Mitchell to throw his second line on his left, but this movement had been anticipated by the brigade commander in provision for the stability of his left flank. Mitchell's brigade was now in single line, bent at right angles in the center.

The full weight of the enemy's attack was soon after felt by all the troops on the field. The forces that had driven back Carlin's division and Robinson's brigade, pursued toward the batteries in the rear, and heavy columns assaulted Mitchell and Vanderveer with great impetuosity. General Slocum had been active in forming a new line near his artillery, which covered the re-formation of the troops that had been driven back on the left.   To this result General Fearing rendered timely co-operation, as he advanced against the flank of the columns in parallelism to the road, and brought upon himself a counter attack by overwhelming numbers.   Wounded himself, and his brigade decimated, he persisted in holding his position for a time, but was finally compelled to give ground, to the exposure of Mitchell's flank.   In the emergency, General Morgan threw Vanderveer's second line to Mitchell's left; but his line thus extended, was soon overlapped, and the two brigades, in single line, were exposed to attacks in front and rear, as they were cut off from all support and from all communication with the corps commander, and each brigade was separately surrounded.   Repulsing the enemy in front repeatedly, they leaped their barricades and reversing the direction of their fire repelled the enemy from their rear.   In this state of affairs, General Davis put into the action his escort and a train-guard of four companies under Lieutenant-Colonel Topping.   General Hoke and a part of his division were captured in the rear of Mitchell and Vanderveer, but as a guard could not be spared from the engagement, the prisoners passed round Vanderveer's right flank and escaped.

In the meantime, the new line had been formed at right angles to the road, at the batteries, and Fearing's brigade and portions of Carlin's division faced the road, but not in connection with Mitchell's left.   The general line was now bent twice at right angles—an improvised formation, but the most effective possible for defense; for the enemy's columns of attack to the left of Mitchell's salient angle were taken in flank in assaulting either the line parallel to the road or the one at right angles to it, while batteries enfiladed the road between the two angles of the line, and to some extent covered the opening between Mitchell and the troops on his left, and also swept a wide open space to the left of the road.   The firmness of Mitchell and Vanderveer contributed largely to break the offensive force of General Johnston's army.

Late in the evening, Cogswell's brigade of the First division, Twentieth Corps, moved into the space between Fearing and

Mitchell, and drove the enemy back until nearly all the lost ground was recovered.

Viewed in relation to the magnitude of the army, successfully resisted by eight brigades of infantry, and Kilpatrick's division of cavalry, which held position on the left and rear, the objects and hopes of the enemy and the character of the fighting by Morgan's division, this engagement takes rank amongst the great decisive battles of the war. The defense, under such unequal conditions, was triumphantly successful, and General Johnston here failed in the only special aggressive effort against General Sherman in his march from Atlanta to Raleigh. That the issue turned upon the action of the brigades of Mitchell, Vanderveer, and Fearing, can not be doubted. The two former did not give an inch of ground to the enemy, though thrown into single lines, cut off from support, surrounded, and compelled to fight in front and rear. The action of Fearing's brigade was not less important, as it disturbed and defeated General Johnston's combination to utilize for complete success his first advantage. General Fearing fought in complete isolation for some time, without defenses, and when his right flank was struck by the enemy with such force as to shatter it, he changed front upon his left, rallied his shattered troops, and held the ground essential to the stability of the new line. The later dispositions and resistance by the whole command gave a symmetry and brilliancy to the conflict which have seldom found expression in such urgent improvision.

To the enemy the issue must have been dispiriting in the extreme. Sadly and hopelessly must the Confederate chieftain have witnessed the failure of his initiative, in destroying General Sherman's corps consecutively, in their isolation. He had constructed his fortifications, which were strong and elaborate, to accomplish this object. His intrenchments crossed the main Goldsboro' road at right angles, then extended to the west one mile, and then curved more than two miles to the west-northwest, nearly parallel to the road, but concealed by distance and forests. He then resisted strongly on the Bentonville road to conceal his fortifications at that point, that he might throw his whole army around the Fourteenth Corps

and interpose between it and the Twentieth, which, at the
first, was nearly ten miles in the rear, and restrained from
swift motion by exceedingly boggy roads, made almost impassable by the wagons and artillery of the Fourteenth Corps.
The failure of the initiative of this elaborate plan, was therefore entirely unexpected to General Johnston, and was doubtless as much a surprise to himself as was the presence of his
army at Bentonville to General Sherman, who scattered his
columns the morning before the battle, believing that the Confederate army was far to the north, having abandoned the
purpose of offering further resistance to his advance to Goldsboro.

In the evening the remainder of the Twentieth Corps
reached the field, and was placed on the left of the line of battle, with Kilpatrick's troopers covering that flank.

When General Sherman was informed by General Slocum,
through a messenger late in the day, that General Johnston's
army had been developed, he directed him to call up his
two divisions guarding the wagon trains, and also General
Hazen's division of the Fifteenth Corps, then in the rear of
the right wing, but several miles distant, and to act defensively
until he could direct the remaining divisions of the right wing
to the enemy's left and rear, from the direction of Cox's bridge
over the Neuse river.   At the time, General Howard's advance
was near this bridge, about ten miles from Goldsboro.   General Sherman did not give full credit to General Slocum's reports of General Johnston's concentration at Bentonville, as
he did not believe that he would accept or invite battle with
the Neuse river in his rear.

On the morning of the 20th, Generals Baird and Geary,
each with two brigades, and General Hazen, with his entire
division, arrived on the field.   General Hazen, by direction of
General Slocum, formed his command on the right of General
Morgan, and General Baird moved out in front of the line of
battle of the preceding day.   These three generals received
orders to press the enemy, and General Morgan gained a portion of his line on the right.

At 2 A. M., on the 20th, General Sherman informed General

Slocum that he would go to his support with his whole army. He turned back the right wing from the Neuse river, ordered General Schofield to push for Goldsboro and then move toward Smithfield, and instructed General Terry to move on Cox's bridge and establish a crossing. By daylight, General Howard's columns were in motion toward Bentonville. Cavalry was encountered earlier, but the first infantry was found behind barricades near Bentonville, three miles east of the battle-field. General Logan, in moving forward, ascertained that General Johnston's left was refused behind a parapet, connecting with the intrenchments before General Slocum, with a salient on the main Goldsboro road between the two wings. His flanks rested on Mill creek, covering the road to Smithfield, which crosses the stream on a bridge. General Sherman directed General Howard to approach cautiously, who connected his left flank with General Slocum's right at 4 P. M., and then a strong line was presented to the enemy.

On the 21st, General Sherman gave orders to press the enemy with skirmishers, use artillery freely, but not give battle unless at an advantage. The same day, General Schofield reached Goldsboro, and General Terry laid a pontoon bridge at Cox's bridge, and then the three armies, in the aggregate nearly one hundred thousand men, were virtually united.

During the day, General Mower's division of the Seventeenth Corps worked round the enemy's left flank, and nearly reached the bridge so essential to General Johnston. This movement and the approach of Generals Schofield and Terry induced General Johnston to abandon his position the following night. General Johnston, in this case as in all others during the war, made a safe retreat. He sacrificed his pickets and left his wounded in hospitals, but lost nothing of value besides.

General Slocum lost nine officers and one hundred and forty-five men killed, fifty-one officers and eight hundred and sixteen men wounded, and two hundred and twenty-three captured. The aggregate loss was twelve hundred and forty-seven. He buried on the field one hundred and sixty-seven of the enemy, and captured three hundred and thirty prisoners.

General Howard's total loss was three hundred and ninety-nine, and he captured twelve hundred and eighty-seven.*

General Johnston was pursued at dawn the next morning, but the troops were soon recalled, when General Sherman renewed his orders for the concentration at Goldsboro.

After the armies had been placed in encampments, General Sherman visited General Grant to confer with regard to the final operations of the war on the Atlantic coast. He returned with the impression that General Lee would unite with General Johnston after abandoning Richmond. But whatever the specific action of the two Confederate generals might be, he was to co-operate with General Grant by advancing against General Johnston and then moving north.

At Goldsboro, General Sherman proposed a new organization for his combined armies, giving General Schofield the command of the "center," and thus designating his forces, retaining for the right wing its old designation, Army of the Tennessee, and styling the two corps of the Army of the Cumberland, the Fourteenth and Twentieth, the "Army of Georgia." The left wing had informally borne this name during the march through Georgia and the Carolinas, but these corps were only really detached from the Army of the Cumberland after they had fought their last battle.

This fact gives the Fourth, Fourteenth, and Twentieth Corps a community of fame and glory achieved at Nashville and Bentonville. General Sherman had assigned them separate fields of operation, but had not formally separated them until it was too late to give them new historic relations. The fame of "Bentonville," quite as much as that of "Franklin" and "Nashville," belongs to the Army of the Cumberland. At Bentonville, the Fourteenth Corps, long under the personal command of General Thomas, and the Twentieth, of more recent connection with the Army of the Cumberland, but of friendly alliance, achieved a great victory. Indeed, all the achievements of these three corps, in union or separation, are portions of the history of the same army, as by hearty consent each has an interest in the aggregate glory. They have an

---

* General Sherman's statement in official report.

undivided tenure in the fame of the army, achieved in all the battles from Lookout Mountain to Jonesboro; not less do they hold in common the glory of the fields so widely separated. The shouts of the Fourteenth and Twentieth Corps at Savannah for victory at Nashville, in which the Fourth and their own representatives had a share, and their beloved commander the chief glory, was answered in glad response from every camp in Tennessee and Alabama for the repulse of General Johnston in his attempt to bring defeat and disgrace to the oldest corps of the unequaled Army of the Cumberland.

On the 9th of April, General Lee surrendered himself and his army to General Grant, and on the following morning, General Sherman's armies moved from the vicinity of Goldsboro toward Smithfield and Raleigh, against the only remaining Confederate army east of the Mississippi river. General Johnston knew well that he could not resist the hundred thousand men moving against him, but to make the most of his slender possibilities, he retreated through Raleigh as General Sherman advanced, and fell back to Greensboro. His objects were to avoid the crime of waging a hopeless warfare, to get the best possible terms in a surrender which would terminate it, and disband his troops on such conditions as would prevent their plundering their friends as they sought their homes. The last campaigns had inflicted upon the South losses of a magnitude transcending approximate estimation and a desolated country, wasted resources and the traditions of a lost cause (but a cause which, during the bloody trial of its existence and supremacy, had commanded the persistent efforts and strongest aspirations of millions) were now the sad inheritance of a proud people. And General Johnston sought to save what material resources remained, and to return his soldiers to their homes with as little demoralization as possible.

At Smithfield, General Sherman heard of the surrender of General Lee, and pressed forward with the conviction that he would soon give the final blow. At Raleigh, he dropped his trains, and directed General Howard to follow the line of retreat, and General Slocum to take a route to the south through Pittsville and Ashboro, in expectation that General Johnston would follow the railroad to Salisbury. On the 14th, he received a note which opened negotiations and resulted in a convention embracing conditions of peace as well as the surrender of the remaining Confederate forces and armies, and declaring a truce until after notice should be given of its discontinuance, on account of the disapproval of the government of the terms agreed upon. The government did disapprove, and the stipulated notice of forty-eight hours, as the limit of the truce, was given on the 24th. Two days later, there was a second conference at General Johnston's request, which resulted in the surrender of all the forces of the Confederacy east of the Chattahoochee river. The next day General Sherman announced in orders the cessation of hostilities, and made provision for the relief of the people. He then directed Generals Howard and Slocum to move their armies through Richmond to Washington.

CHAPTER XXXIX.

GENERAL GEORGE STONEMAN'S CAVALRY OPERATIONS IN TENNES-
SEE AND NORTH CAROLINA.

IN terminating the pursuit of General Hood's army, General Thomas' first thought was to put his forces in winter cantonments to rest after their severe service since early spring,
and to prepare for such operations as the future movements
of the enemy might render necessary, or such as might promise
the entire supremacy of the national government within the
limits of the Military Division of the Mississippi or throughout
the Southern States; but General Grant ordered otherwise,
and on the 31st of December the troops of the military division
were disposed with a view to immediate active operations. General A. J. Smith's corps, and four divisions of cavalry under
General Wilson, were ordered to Eastport, Mississippi, and the
Fourth Corps to take post at Huntsville, Alabama, according to
previous arrangement, for a different purpose, and the Twenty-
third Corps was left at Columbia, instead of taking position at
Dalton, Georgia.

General Sherman was desirous that General Thomas should
conduct a campaign in Northern Alabama and Georgia, and
expressed this wish to General Grant; but the latter had
formed other plans before this wish had been expressed, and
had ordered General Schofield's corps, and the detachments
from the corps with General Sherman, to North Carolina, to
co-operate with him. Subsequently, he directed General
Thomas to send General A. J. Smith's forces and five thousand
cavalry, by river, to report to Major-General Canby, at New
Orleans, to take part in the operations against Mobile. Accordingly, General Smith's troops started from Eastport on the

6th of February, and General Knipe's division of cavalry from Eastport and Nashville on the 12th. These transfers of forces reduced the troops under General Thomas to the Fourth Corps, the infantry and artillery garrisons of the military division, the cavalry divisions under General Wilson, and the one under General Stoneman in East Tennessee.

Early in February, General Thomas ascertained from various sources that a remnant of General Hood's army, under Generals Cheatham and S. D. Lee, were on their way from Mississippi to South Carolina, moving through Selma and Montgomery, Alabama, to reinforce the army opposing General Sherman, and that other fragments of the Confederate Army of the Tennessee—a skeleton corps—under General Richard Taylor, and seven thousand cavalry, under General Forrest, remained in Mississippi, with headquarters at Meridian.

February 6th, General Grant directed that General Stoneman should be sent on an expedition to penetrate North Carolina and well down toward Columbia, South Carolina, to destroy the enemy's railroads and military resources which were out of the reach of General Sherman; and on the 13th, General Grant directed General Thomas to prepare a cavalry expedition to penetrate Northern Alabama and co-operate with General Canby in his movement against Mobile. Preparations for both expeditions were completed about the same time, and on the 22d of March Generals Stoneman and Wilson moved as respectively directed.

The cavalry division in East Tennessee, commanded by Brigadier-General A. C. Gillem, comprised three brigades, under the respective command of Colonel Palmer, Brigadier-General Brown, and Colonel Miller. It was concentrated at Mossy creek on the 22d of March, in readiness for movement into North Carolina under the personal direction of General Stoneman. It was known at this time that General Sherman had captured Columbia, South Carolina, and was moving into North Carolina. Rumors were current that General Lee's army would evacuate Richmond and Petersburg, and might force a passage through Lynchburg to Knoxville. To guard against such a contingency, General Stoneman was directed to move toward Lynchburg, to destroy the railroad and resources of that region, and then sweep through Western North Carolina with the same destructive intent; and the Fourth Corps was ordered by General Thomas to advance from Huntsville as far into East Tennessee as it could supply itself, to repair the railroad as it advanced, and form at last with General Tillson's division of infantry, a strong support to General Stoneman, should he meet the enemy in such force as to drive him back.

On the 24th, General Stoneman moved to Morristown, and there detached the Third brigade, Colonel Miller commanding, to make a detour from Bull's Gap, to reach the railroad between Jonesboro and Carter's Station, in the rear of a force reported to be in the vicinity of the former place. The other two brigades advanced directly forward, and encamped on the night of the 25th ten miles west of Jonesboro. Here all incumbrances were left, save one ambulance, one wagon, and four guns with their caissons.

At noon on the 26th, the division was reunited at Jonesboro. Colonel Miller had complied with his instructions, but the Confederate general, Jackson, had fled in haste the night previous. General Stoneman then moved forward, and reached the Watauga river on the 27th, and the town of Boone, North Carolina, on the 28th. At the latter place, Major Keogh, of General Stoneman's staff, with a detachment of the Twelfth Kentucky, routed a company of home guards, capturing sixty. Here the brigades again separated—General Stoneman, with Palmer's brigade, moving on Wilkesboro, by Deep Gap, and General Gillem, with the other two brigades and the artillery, to the same point, by the Flat Gap road. From Wilkesboro, the whole command moved through Mount Airy, and over the Blue Ridge, to Hillsville, Virginia, with no incidents, save the capture of a small forage train. At Hillsville, Colonel Miller, with five hundred picked men, moved on Wytheville, destroyed a depot of supplies there, and a bridge over Reedy creek, and another at Max Meadows. The command then advanced to Jacksonville, where Major Wagner, of the Fifteenth Tennessee, with two hundred and fifty select men, dashed on to Salem, Virginia, and destroyed bridges and the railroad track extensively. On the 6th of April, two brigades were at Christianburg, and had possession of ninety miles of the Virginia and Tennessee railroad, from Wytheville to Salem. From Christianburg, after destroying twenty miles of railroad, and several bridges over Roanoke river, and disabling the bridge over New river, Colonel Palmer moved to Martinsville, and General Brown to Taylorsville, and at 10 A. M. on the 8th, Palmer and Brown united at that place, and then the whole command converged upon Danbury, North Carolina, arriving there on the 9th. At Germantown, beyond, Colonel Palmer was detached, and ordered to Salem, North Carolina, to destroy the large factories, which were supplying the Confederate armies with clothing, and then to send parties to destroy the railroad south of Greensboro, and between that place and Danville, the main column turned south from Germantown toward Salisbury, bivouacking at night on the 11th, twelve miles north of Salisbury. A little after midnight, the South Yadkin river was crossed, without opposition, as had not been expected. From the river, the main force advanced on a new road on the left, while a battalion of the Twelfth Kentucky was sent on the road to the right, to demonstrate strongly at the crossing of Grant creek, and, if successful in passing that stream, to attack in rear the forces defending the upper bridge. At daylight, the head of the main column met the enemy's pickets, who were driven back to the bridge over Grant creek, and his artillery and musketry opened from the other side. A reconnoissance developed the fact that a portion of the floor of the bridge had been taken up from two spans of the bridge, and trains could be heard leaving the town on the South Carolina and Morgantown railroads. General Gillem now ordered Colonel Miller and General Brown to close up their brigades, and a section of Reagan's battery to move forward. At this juncture, General Stoneman directed that a detachment should cross the creek two and a half miles above, cut the railroad, and, if practicable, capture the train, and then get in the rear of the town, and annoy the enemy as much as possible. Lieutenant-Colonel Slater, of the Eleventh Kentucky, was designated with his regiment for this service, and Captain Morrow, of General Stoneman's staff, joined the detachment. At the same time, Major Donnelly, of the Thirteenth Tennessee, with one hundred men, and Lieutenant-Colonel Smith, with a party of dismounted men, were ordered to cross at lower points. As soon as these parties engaged the enemy across the stream, and the rattling fire of the Spencer rifles of the Eleventh Kentucky announced that the enemy's left had been turned, Colonel Miller's brigade was ordered to advance on the main road. A detachment of the Eighth and Thirteenth Tennessee regiments restored the floor of the bridge, and Miller charged across. By this time the enemy was falling back along his entire line. Brown was thrown forward to support Miller, who continued to press the enemy back. The retreat soon terminated in rout. Major Keogh, who had led the charge of the Eleventh Kentucky on the right, having been joined by Major Sawyer's battalion of the Eighth Tennessee, charged the enemy again at the intersection of the Statesville road with the one upon which Colonel Miller was advancing, and captured all the artillery which had been used on the enemy's left flank. The pursuit was continued until the enemy's troops lost even the semblance of organization, and all who escaped capture, hid themselves in the woods. Three thousand men, under command of Major-General W. M. Gardener, with eighteen pieces of artillery, in charge of Colonel J. C. Pemberton, recently a lieutenant-general, were thus routed. Nearly thirteen hundred prisoners were captured, eighteen pieces of artillery, and public property of immense value, most of which was destroyed. At 2 P. M. Major Barnes, to whom the destruction of public property had been committed, reported having destroyed ten thousand stand of small arms, one million pounds of (small) ammunition, ten thousand pounds of artillery ammunition, six thousand pounds of powder, three magazines, six depots, ten thousand bushels of corn, seventy-five thousand suits of uniform clothing, two hundred and fifty thousand blankets (English manufacture), twenty thousand pounds of leather, six thousand pounds of bacon, one hundred thousand pounds of salt, twenty-seven thousand pounds of rice, ten thousand pounds of saltpetre, fifty thousand bushels of wheat, eighty barrels of turpentine, fifteen million of Confederate money, and medical stores worth over one hundred thousand dollars in gold. Besides the detachments which had been sent to Virginia, destroyed the railroad nearly to Lynchburg, seven thousand bales of cotton and two large factories, and captured four hundred prisoners. The railroad south of Salisbury having been destroyed for some distance, and it having been determined to send the prisoners, and captured artillery, not destroyed, to East Tennessee, the forces withdrew on the 13th, and reached Lenoir on the 15th.

Here General Stoneman turned over the command to General Gillem, with instructions as to the disposition and service of the troops. Colonel Palmer was to take post at Lincolnton, and scout down the Catawba; General Brown, at Morgantown, to connect with Colonel Palmer on the Catawba, and Colonel Miller, at Asheville, to open communications through to Greenville, Tennessee. The objects in leaving the cavalry on this side of the mountains, were to obstruct, intercept, or disperse any troops moving south, and to capture trains.

When General Gillem, with Brown's and Miller's brigades, reached the Catawba, two and a half miles from Morgantown, he found the bridge torn up, the ford blockaded, and his passage of the stream disputed by Major-General McCown, with about three hundred men and one piece of artillery. He then sent Major Kenner, of the Eighth Tennessee, to cross up the river and reach the enemy's rear, and threw forward another battalion of the same regiment as directly toward the bridge as shelter could be found. Opening with his artillery, he disabled the enemy's gun and drove him from his defenses, and the dismounted men charging over the sleepers of the bridge, drove him from the ford, and captured his gun and fifty men.

On the 19th, General Gillem moved toward Asheville, by way of Swananoa Gap. He found the gap the nex day, to be held by about five hundred men, with four pieces of artillery. Leaving Colonel Miller to make feints, he moved rapidly to Rutherford forty miles distant, and at sundown on the 22d, he passed the Blue Ridge, at Hammond's Gap, and was in the rear of the enemy, who retreated through Andersonville, pursued by Slater, who, in a charge, captured the four guns and seventy men At this time he learned that Colonel Palmer had not moved as he had been ordered, in consequence of information through

General Echols, that a truce had been proclaimed. Deeming it essential to the safety of his command that he should hold one of the gaps of the Blue Ridge, General Gillem ordered Palmer to move as previously directed, and advanced with his own column to attack Asheville. At 3 P. M. on the 23d, he received a flag of truce from Asheville, covering a communication from General Martin, which stated that he had received official notification of a truce. Later, General Martin proposed a meeting for the next day. That night at 11 o'clock, the fact of the existence of a truce was established by an official announcement, coming from General Sherman, and at 11 P. M. he received an order from him, directed to General Stoneman, requiring the command to move to Durham Station or Hillsboro. Being convinced that this order had been issued by General Sherman, under the conviction that this cavalry division was at or near Salisbury, he decided to draw back to his base at Greenville, Tennessee, rather than advance two hundred miles to Durham's Station. At the meeting with General Martin, he announced this decision, and requested three days' rations for his men, to save the people on his route from supplying his wants by constraint. General Martin furnished supplies, but demanded the rendition of the artillery which had been captured the day before; but General Gillem positively refused to do this, as the capture had been made prior to his reception of any authentic announcement of a truce.

This expedition was ably conducted and eminently successful. General Stoneman's strategy put the enemy under positive disadvantage, at each objective, in receiving the intended blow. When the Blue Ridge was first passed, the enemy supposed that Salisbury was menaced. This supposition placed the Tennessee and Virginia railroad at General Stoneman's mercy, and the advance for its destruction was a surprise, and cost the enemy three trains, and the loss of more than two hundred wagons, and twenty-one pieces of artillery, spiked and abandoned, while the troops that were separated from the main body by this movement, returned to Kentucky. Again, when the column turned south, Colonel Palmer's divergence toward Danville and Greensboro, by Martinsville, caused the enemy to withdraw troops from Salisbury, which fell more easily in consequence when it was attacked, as the paramount object of the advance southward. The enemy discovered his mistake, and made effort to reinforce Salisbury when the danger was apparent, but the railroad being cut in five places south of Danville, the effort miscarried, as the reinforcing division of infantry and brigade of cavalry did not reach the vicinity of the town until after the destruction of the depots, magazines, and stores. And at last a brigade held the enemy at Swananoa Gap, until another passed to the rear and surprised and captured a large portion of his force. The captures were twenty-five guns taken in action, twenty-one abandoned in Southwest Virginia, and over six thousand prisoners and seventeen battle-flags.

CHAPTER XL.

GENERAL J. H. WILSON'S CAVALRY OPERATIONS IN ALABAMA AND GEORGIA.

GENERAL WILSON's column of cavalry, comprising Generals McCook's, Long's, and Upton's divisions, having crossed the Tennessee river on the 18th of March, was put in motion southward on the 23d. General Hatch's division not having a full remount, was deprived of all horses for the other divisions, and left at Eastport, to join the column subsequently, should horses be obtained in time. General Wilson's wagon and pontoon trains, including about two hundred and fifty teams, were put under the direction of Captain Brown, protected by fifteen hundred dismounted men, under Major Archer. The destitution of forage, in the region immediately south of the Tennessee river, imposed the necessity of starting the troops in detachments to glean over a broad belt of country, what little produce might be left, where war had so long and so heavily laid its hand. This diffusion, however, involved no hazard, as General Forrest's command was at West Point, Mississippi, one hundred and fifty miles south of Eastport, and General Roddy's forces were holding Montevallo, on the Alabama and Tennessee railroad, as remote, to the southeast. There was, besides, an important advantage in this divergence in the beginning of the enterprise, as thereby the enemy was put in doubt as to the first objectives, and was compelled to watch equally the roads to Selma, Tuscaloosa, and Columbus.

General Grant's orders required the movement of a force of five or six thousand men, to demonstrate against Tuscaloosa and Selma, to co-operate with General Canby. General

Wilson expressed the conviction that he could capture these places and conduct other decisive operations, and General Thomas gave him permission to take with him all his available force, giving him such freedom of action as the nature and proposed objects of the expedition, positive and contingent, demanded.   Thus, by General Grant's instructions, the license given by General Thomas, and the conditions of his enterprise, General Wilson became an independent commander, at least as far as all special combinations and minor objectives were concerned.   He was subject still to General Thomas, as actual commander of all the forces within the geographical limits of the military division; but he had discretion within exceedingly extended limits.

General Upton's division, followed by his train, moved rapidly on the most easterly route, passing Barton's Station, Throgmorton's Mills, Russellville, Mount Hope, and Jasper, to Sanders' Ferry, on the west fork of the Black Warrior river.   General Long's division marched through Cherokee Station, Frankfort, and Russellville, and then followed the Tuscaloosa road to the Black Water creek, twenty-five miles from Jasper.   General McCook's division followed Long's to the Upper Bear creek, then moved on the Tuscaloosa road to Eldridge, afterward turning east to Jasper.   The crossing of the Black Warrior river was beset with difficulties, but the knowledge that General Chalmers was moving to Tuscaloosa, and the danger of a full river, permitted no delay, and the corps was hurried across, with the loss of a few horses, and then, with pack-mules bearing supplies, wagons and artillery being far in the rear, the command moved rapidly through Elyton to Montevallo.   At Elyton, General Croxton was detached with his brigade to advance to Tuscaloosa, to burn the public stores, military school, bridges, foundries, and factories at that place, and then join the main column at Selma, if practicable.   The direction of Croxton's movement somewhat covered the trains and artillery in the rear, and was intended to develop any movement of the enemy in that quarter.   On the march, General Upton destroyed the Red Mountain, Central, Bibb, and Columbiana iron-works, Cahawba rolling-mills, and much valuable property.   The other divisions followed, and when General Wilson reached Montevallo, on the 31st of March, General Upton was ready to move forward. And for this there was need, as the enemy had appeared on the Selma road, and General Upton, with General Alexander's brigade leading, was sent against him. Alexander soon provoked a sharp conflict, which he terminated by a charge, driving the enemy, a portion of Roddy's division and Crossland's Kentucky brigade, in confusion toward Randolph. General Roddy attempted to make a stand five miles south of Montevallo, when General Upton threw Winslow's brigade to the front, and opened Rodney's battery, Fourth United States Artillery, causing the retreat of the enemy and loss of fifty prisoners in the pursuit by Winslow. This action gave the type of the campaign.

At night, General Upton bivouacked fourteen miles from Montevallo, and the next day advanced to Randolph. Here he turned to the east by Maplesville to the old Selma road, while General Long pushed forward on the new road. A message from General Croxton to the effect that he was in the rear of General Jackson's division, near Trion, and dispatches captured from the enemy revealing his plans and the dispositions of his forces, called for new combinations and their prompt execution. General Forrest, with a portion of his command, was in the front of the main column; Jackson's division was involved with Croxton.

General Chalmers was under orders to cross from Union, to join Forrest, either in Wilson's front or in the works at Selma, and the enemy's dismounted men were holding an important bridge over the Cahawba, at Centreville. To secure this bridge and prevent the junction of Jackson's division with Forrest, General Wilson directed General McCook to strengthen the battalion en route to Centreville, by a regiment, and to follow with La Grange's brigade with all speed, leaving even his pack trains, to seize the bridge, and then hasten to support Croxton against Jackson. Having provided for his right flank, he next looked to the protection of his rear, against the traditional strategy of Forrest, by ordering Upton and Long to push him without rest toward Selma. These officers moved forward rapidly, without changing roads, and brushing back small parties, developed Forrest in position for battle, on the north bank of Bigler's creek, his right resting on Mulberry creek, and left on a high wooded ridge, covered by a battery of artillery. A portion of his front was covered by slashed timber and rail barricades. His force comprised Crossland's brigade, Armstrong's brigade of Chalmers' division, Roddy's division, and a battalion just arrived from Selma, in all about five thousand men. Perceiving the enemy in strength in his immediate front, General Long reinforced his vanguard by a battalion of the Seventy-second Indiana Mounted Infantry, with the remainder of the regiment dismounted, and formed on the left of the road. This regiment drove back the enemy in broken ranks. At this juncture General Long ordered forward four companies of the Seventeenth Indiana, Lieutenant-Colonel Frank White commanding, with drawn sabers. These companies drove the enemy to his works, dashed against his main line, broke through it, rode over his guns, and finally turning to the left cut their way out, but leaving one officer and sixteen men with the enemy. In this charge Captain Taylor lost his life, having led his men into the midst of the enemy, and engaged in a running fight for two hundred yards with General Forrest himself.

Hearing the noise of this preliminary fighting, Alexander's brigade of Upton's division hurried up on the trot, and formed on the left of General Long, and as soon as everything was in readiness, the brigade advanced, dismounted. In less than an hour, although Forrest resisted stubbornly, his forces were completely routed. Alexander captured two guns and about two hundred prisoners. Long's division took one gun. Winslow's brigade pressed forward in pursuit, but could not bring the enemy to a stand. At sundown the corps bivouacked near Plantersville, in sharp conflict with the enemy, who had been driven twenty-four miles during the day.

At daylight the next day, the columns were in motion toward Selma. General Long advanced to the town and crossed to the Summerville road. General Upton moved on the Range Line road, sending a squadron on the Burnsville road. Lieutenant Rundlebrook, with a battalion of the Fourth United States Cavalry, followed the railroad, burning stations and bridges to Burnsville. By 4 P. M. the troops were in position and ready to assault. General Wilson had previously obtained a complete description of the defenses, and having corroborated its correctness by observation and formal reconnoissance, he gave orders for the assault. General Long was instructed to move across the road,. upon which his troops were posted, and General Upton was permitted, as he had requested, with three hundred picked men, to penetrate a swamp on his left, and break the line covering it, thus to turn Forrest's right, while the remainder of his division should conform to his movements.

A single gun from Rodney's battery was to be the signal for a general advance, and this was to be given as soon as Upton's success was revealed. Before this signal gun could be fired, General Long was informed that a heavy force of cavalry was skirmishing with his rear-guard, and threatening an attack from that quarter. He left six companies well posted at the creek, in anticipation of the movement which General Chalmers was now making in obedience to orders from General Forrest. This force was known to have been the day before at Marion, and fearing that its appearance on the road, as had been expected, might compromise the assault upon the town, General Long determined not to wait for the development of General Upton's turning movement. He simply strengthened his rear with a regiment, and then dismounting four regiments from the brigades of Miller and Minty, he, with these officers, led them in charging over an open space for six hundred yards, over a stockade, a deep ditch, and the parapet, and drove the enemy in confusion to the city. At the moment of victory, General Wilson reached that part of the field, and directed Colonel Minty, who had assumed command of the division in consequence of a severe wound to General Long, to advance toward the town. He ordered Colonel Vail to place his own regiment, the Seventeenth Indiana, and the Fourth Ohio, in line inside the works, and the Fourth United States Cavalry and the Board of Trade battery to participate in the attack. When the division again advanced, the enemy was occupying unfinished defenses near the town. The Fourth Cavalry, Lieutenant O'Connell commanding, was repulsed, but formed again on the left. In the meantime, General Upton had succeeded in his movement, and was now advancing on the left of Minty. A charge was again made by the Fourth Ohio, Seventeenth Indiana, and Fourth Cavalry dismounted, and the whole line participating with wildest enthusiasm, the enemy was hurled from position, and the city was penetrated in all directions.

The charge of General Long, his brigade commanders leading with him, and fifteen hundred and fifty men following, was brilliant in the extreme. A single line without support advanced in utmost exposure for five or six hundred yards, leaped a stockade five feet high, a ditch five feet deep and fifteen wide, and a parapet six to eight feet high, and drove Armstrong's brigade, the best of Forrest's command, over fifteen hundred strong, in rout from works of great strength and advantages of wonderful superiority, and this was done while sixteen field-guns were playing upon them. In the charge, Colonel Dobbs, of the Fourth Ohio, was killed. General Long, and Colonels Miller, McCormick, and Biggs were wounded. The general loss of the division was forty killed, two hundred and sixty wounded, and seven missing.

The fruits of the victory were in correspondence with the gallantry of the troops that won it. Thirty-one field-guns and one thirty-pounder Parrott, two thousand seven hundred prisoners, including one hundred and fifty officers, and public property of great value. Lieutenant-General Taylor sought safety in flight early in the afternoon, and under cover of the darkness, Generals Forrest, Roddy, Armstrong, and Adams escaped with a number of men. A portion of Upton's division pursued on the Burnsville road till late in the night, capturing four guns and many prisoners. The enemy destroyed twenty-five thousand bales of cotton, but left the foundries, machine-shops, arsenals, and warehouses of this immense depot of war material, for the torch.

General Wilson placed Brevet Brigadier-General Winslow in command of the city, and instructed Lieutenant Haywood, engineer officer, to press the construction of pontoons for a bridge over the Alabama river. The next day at daylight, General Upton marched to draw General Chalmers to the west side of the Cahawba river and open communications with General McCook, who was expected with the train from Centerville. This movement looked to an advance of the whole command toward Montgomery as soon as it could be gathered together and other conditions were favorable. The capture of Selma and so large a portion of Forrest's force gave General Wilson the assurance of successful movements whatever objectives he might choose.

Generals McCook and Upton arrived at Selma, April 5th, with the train. The former had been successful against Centreville, but on reaching Scottsboro had found General Jackson so strongly posted that he did not attack him, but burning the cotton factories and the bridge, turned toward Selma. General Croxton had not been found nor even heard from; but his protracted separation from the corps did not cause uneasiness, as it was confidently believed that he had taken care of himself and gone in a new direction.

On the 6th, General Forrest requested a conference with General Wilson, with reference to an exchange of prisoners. His arrogance and manifest hope that he could recapture his men made the interview brief, but through it, General Wilson learned that General Croxton had had an engagement two days before with General Adams at Bridgeville, forty miles southwest of Tuscaloosa. His safety being assured, as also General Canby's ability to take Mobile without support, there was no barrier to the movement to Montgomery but the Alabama river, whose deep, swift current gave an unsteady resting to a pontoon bridge eight hundred and seventy feet long. Three times the bridge was broken, but Major Hubbard, aided by Generals Upton and Alexander and the staff of General Wilson, succeeded in connecting the banks by the floating bridge, and the command passed safely over by daylight on the 10th of April Selma had been so far destroyed as to be of no use to the enemy for military purposes; and Forrest's force had been so greatly diminished and so thoroughly demoralized that General Wilson moved fearlessly forward toward Montgomery, intending to destroy railroads and army supplies and material, and then sweep on to the theater of operations in North Carolina. His mounted force was now stronger than at starting, as he had captured horses for all his dismounted men, and he now disincumbered himself of all wagons and pontoons which could be spared, to give him facility for quick movement. The able-bodied negroes who had joined his column were organized into regiments under efficient officers. These men, in the first flush of freedom, became soldiers, keeping pace with the troopers, gathering supplies from the country, and marching thirty-five miles per day.

The march from Selma to Montgomery was retarded by bad roads and bridgeless streams; but at 7 A. M. on the 12th, Colonel La Grange, whose brigade was in advance, received the surrender of the capital of the State of Alabama, and the first capital of the Southern Confederacy. But how great had been the changes of four years of civil war! On the 4th of March, 1861, the insurgent Congress had asserted, with the pomp and circumstance befitting a nation's birth, the independence of seven slaveholding states. The national government was boldly defied, and blindly ignoring the contingencies of their venture, the members of this Congress boldly assumed the independence of the South as an actuality, and talked of war as if its invocation involved no guilt, and its progress compassed naught but victories and speedy triumph. The outlying crowds of men drawn to Montgomery by the culmination of Southern frenzy in the assumption of a new nationality, echoed the bold utterances of the provisional President and Congress in jubilant ecstasy through the streets. The illuminated city was a blazing type of the fire that was burning in the Southern heart, and all the assumptions of prospective empire, in the frenzy of the moment, were removed beyond the sphere of doubt. Now, the mayor of the city—the dispirited representative of a conquered people—comes meekly forth from the provisional capital of the war-broken Confederacy and tenders its surrender to a commander of brigade. How different the beginning and end of Montgomery in the "great conflict!" The burning of ninety thousand bales of cotton, the ideal king of commerce, is now the illumination which betokens the loss of his crown and the loyalty of his subjects, for it is they who, in their desperation, set fire to this immense mass of royalty. The quiet streets and silent halls, the fleeing troopers and hiding citizens, are in striking antithesis to the pomp, the boast, and the maddened multitude of a former day.

Having destroyed five steamboats, several locomotives, one armory, and several foundries, General Wilson resumed motion on the 14th. General Upton moved through Mount Meigs and Tuskegee, toward Columbus, Georgia, and Colonel La Grange followed the railroad through Opelika, to West Point. Two days later, General Upton, with three hundred dismounted men, assaulted and carried the breastworks at Columbus, saving by the impetuosity of his attack the bridges over the Chattahoochee, and capturing fifty-two guns in position, and twelve hundred prisoners. The ram Jackson, nearly ready for the sea, and carrying six seven-inch guns, was destroyed; also the navy-yard, foundries, arsenal, armory, sword and pistol factory, accouterment-shops, paper-mills, four cotton factories, fifteen locomotives, two hundred cars, and one hundred and fifteen thousand bales of cotton. The assault was made at night, by men from the Third Iowa, Colonel Noble commanding, the Fourth Iowa and Tenth Missouri being held in support. Generals Upton and Winslow directed the movement in person. The enemy opened a heavy artillery and musketry fire as the troops advanced, but their Spencer rifles gave response as they rushed through the abatis and over the parapet. When this had been accomplished, General Upton sent Captain Glassen, with two companies of the Tenth Missouri, to get possession of the bridge over the Chattahoochee. The captain passed through the inner line of defenses, under cover of the darkness, and seized the bridge before the enemy was aware of his movement. Then General Upton made a general charge, swept away all opposition, seized the bridges, and stationed his troops thoughout the city. .The fortifications were held by three thousand men, and yet three hundred penetrated the main line, and this primal success was followed by overwhelming victory, with a loss in all of twenty men killed and wounded.

Colonel La Grange had spirited skirmishing on the way to

West Point, but reached the vicinity with his advance at 10
A. M., April 16th. Beck's Indiana battery and the Second
and Fourth Indiana held the attention of the enemy until the
arrival of the remainder of the brigade. Then after a reconnoissance, preparations were made for an assault. Detachments from the First Wisconsin, Second Indiana, and Seventh
Kentucky regiments were dismounted to make the charge.
At 1 P. M. the signal was given, and these troops moved forward, drove into the fort the skirmishers, and reached the
ditch, which was too wide to leap and too deep to pass.
Sharpshooters kept the enemy down until materials for
bridges were gathered, when the charge was sounded again,
and the detachments rushed over the parapets, on three sides
of the square fort and captured the entire garrison of two hundred and sixty-five men, General Tyler commanding, and
eighteen officers and men were killed and twenty-eight
wounded. Colonel La Grange lost seven killed and twenty-
nine wounded. He captured three guns and five hundred
stand of small arms. Simultaneously with the storming of the
fort, the Fourth Indiana dashed through the town, scattered
a superior cavalry force which had just arrived, and burned
five locomotives and trains; also securing the bridges over
the Chattahoochee. Colonel La Grange here destroyed two
bridges, nineteen locomotives, and two hundred and forty-five
cars loaded with quartermaster, commissary, and ordnance
stores. Before departure, he established a hospital for the
wounded of both sides, and left for them ample supplies with
the mayor. He then moved toward Macon, through La
Grange, Griffin, and Forsyth, breaking the railroad at these
points.

April 17th, General Wilson commenced his movement on
Macon, giving Minty's division the advance, and instructing
that commander to send forward a detachment to seize the
double bridges over Flint river. Captain Hudson, of the Fourth
Michigan, was put upon this service, and, at 7 A. M. the next
day, gained the bridges, scattering the guards, and capturing
forty prisoners. The whole command followed the detachment on the 18th. Two days later, Colonel White, of the
Seventeenth Indiana in the advance, encountered two hundred

cavalrymen, and driving them rapidly toward Macon, saved the Echconnee and Tobesofke bridges. When within thirteen miles of Macon, he met a flag of truce in charge of General Robinson, bearing a written communication addressed to the commanding officer United States forces. Colonel White halted and sent the communication to Colonel Minty, his division commander, who, having read it, sent it to General Wilson, but instructed Colonel White to resume his advance, and so informed General Robinson. The communication was from General Cobb, inclosing a dispatch from General Beauregard, advising that a truce was existing, which was applicable to all the forces under Generals Sherman and Joseph E. Johnston, and declaring that he was ready to comply with the terms of the armistice, and proposing a meeting with the commander of the United States forces, to make arrangements for a more perfect enforcement of the armistice.

Without giving entire credence to the communication, General Wilson rode rapidly forward to halt his troops at the defenses of Macon, and by seeing General Cobb to convince himself with regard to the questions at issue, before acknowledging the armistice. But Colonel White had been too quick, and had dashed into the city and received its surrender before General Wilson overtook him. The garrison made a show of resistance, but promptly laid down their arms at the demand of Colonel White. When, however, General Wilson arrived, General Cobb protested against what he termed a violation of the armistice, overlooking the fact that he could not claim to be an authoritative channel of communication for a message of such importance, and demanded that he should withdraw his forces to the point where General Robinson had met his advance. General Wilson had no reason to doubt the existence of the truce, but he was unwilling to give it recognition, until he had received notice and instructions from proper authority authentically transmitted, especially as his subordinate officers had captured the city before he could respond to the message which had been sent under the flag of truce. His force, though known as the cavalry corps of the Military Division of the Mississippi, and organized under General Sherman's order, had not yet served under his personal command, but had, by his direction, reported to General Thomas, as commander of all the forces of the military division not present with the commanding general, and all his orders subsequently had either originated with General Thomas or had been transmitted by him from General Grant. Without authentic instructions from either General Grant, General Sherman, or General Thomas, he hesitated to recognize the application of the armistice to his command. He therefore determined to hold Generals Cobb, Smith, Mackall, Robinson, and Mercer, and the garrison of Macon, as prisoners of war, until his conduct was disapproved by competent authority, after full investigation. However, to relieve himself from suspense, at the earliest possible moment, he sent a dispatch in cipher to General Sherman, the evening of the 20th of April, and the next day received an official notification from him of the existence of the armistice. Upon receiving it, he suspended all operations until he should receive orders to renew them, or until circumstances should justify independent action.

On the 1st of May, General Croxton, who during his separation from the main column, had made a tortuous ride of six hundred and fifty miles, arrived at Macon. He skirmished with General Jackson near Trion, on the 2d of April, and finding that his force was double his own, he declined battle and moved rapidly in simulated flight to the Black Warrior river, crossed to the west side, and reached Northport, April 4th. Fearing that his presence might be known, he moved at midnight, surprised the force at the bridge, crossed into Tuscaloosa, captured three guns and one hundred and fifty prisoners, scattered the state militia and cadets, and destroyed the military school edifice, and the public works and stores. Here he tried to communicate with General McCook, but failed. He then abandoned Tuscaloosa, and moved to the southeast to avoid Jackson and Chalmers. When near Eutaw, he heard of the arrival of Adams' division, and fearing to risk an engagement with a force of cavalry more than double his own strength, supported by militia, he countermarched toward Tuscaloosa; then diverging to the left, moved through Jasper, crossed the Coosa, and marched to Talladega. Near this place he defeated General Hill, capturing one gun and one hundred and fifty prisoners, and then marched through Carrollton, Newnan, and Forsyth, to Macon. During the period of his isolation, he had no knowledge of the movements of the main column, but having faith in the success of the general plan, he sought General Wilson at Macon.

CHAPTER XLI.

CAPTURE OF THE CONFEDERATE PRESIDENT.

THE two cavalry columns were arrested about the same time, by the armistice established by Generals Sherman and Johnston, under circumstances of embarrassment to the generals commanding them, though fortunately there were no conditions of great hazard, in suspending their operations, as each had swept through the enemy's country in ceaseless success and triumph. Their orders were so positive as to allow no discretion, even had the suspension of their operations given advantage to the enemy, through whom the knowledge of the truce was communicated. Neither did the embarrassments produced by the truce stop with the commanders in the field, but reached General Thomas, who was charged with the management of the affairs of the Military Division of the Mississippi, and who had organized these expeditions under orders from Lieutenant-General Grant. For, although telegraphic communications did not reach either General Wilson or General Stoneman, General Thomas heard of the armistice through each of these generals before he received official information of its existence from the lieutenant-general. Referring to the time of receiving information from his subordinates, he thus, in his official report, mentioned his own embarrassments in relation to the armistice and the manner of its announcement: "Up to that period I had not been officially notified of the existence of any armistice between the forces of Generals Sherman and Johnston, and the information only reached me through my sub-commanders, Generals Wilson and Stoneman, from Macon, Georgia, and Greenville, East Tennessee, almost simultaneously. The question naturally arose in my mind, whether the troops acting under my direction, by virtue of General Sherman's Special Field Order No. 105, series of 1864, directing me to assume control of all the forces of the Military Division of the Mississippi, 'not absolutely in the presence of the general-in-chief,' were to be bound by an armistice or agreement made at a distance of several hundred miles from where those troops were operating and of which they were advised through an enemy, then in such straitened circumstances that any ruse, honorable at least in war, was likely to be practiced by him to relieve himself from his difficult position. Then, again, General Sherman was operating with a movable column, beyond the limits of his territorial command, viz., the Military Division of the Mississippi, and far away from all direct communication with it; whereas 'the troops not absolutely in the presence of the general-in-chief,' were operating under special instructions and not even in co-operation with General Sherman against Johnston, but, on the contrary, General Stoneman was dismantling the country to obstruct Lee's retreat and General Wilson was moving independently in Georgia or co-operating with General Canby. Before I could come to any conclusion how I should act under the circumstances, and without disrespect to my superior officer, General Sherman, Secretary Stanton telegraphed to me from Washington, on the 27th of April, and through me to my sub-commanders, to disregard all orders except those coming from General Grant or myself, and to resume hostilities at once, sparing no pains to press the enemy firmly, at the same time notifying me that General Sherman's negotiations with Johnston had been disapproved."

Having now full authority for independent action, and having learned that President Davis with a party had started south from Charlotte, North Carolina, on the cessation of the armistice, General Thomas at once made dispositions to capture the fugitive President, and those who still clung to him and his fortunes. He directed General Stoneman to send the brigades of Miller, Brown, and Palmer, to concentrate at Anderson, South Carolina, and scout down the Savannah river to Augusta, Georgia, in search of the fugitives. General Gillem was absent from the command at the time, and Colonel

W. F. Palmer, of the Fifteenth Pennsylvania Cavalry, assumed direction of the expedition. By rapid marching, he reached and crossed the Savannah river in advance of Mr. Davis, and so disposed his troops as to change the direction of the flight, from the west toward the Mississippi river, to the Atlantic coast. General Thomas also notified General Wilson, at Macon, Georgia, of the issue of the negotiations in North Carolina, and ordered him to resume hostilities at once, with special reference to the capture of Mr. Davis.

These orders had scarcely been issued before the surrender of the Confederate forces east of the Chattahoochee river, to General Sherman, by General Johnston, was officially announced to both General Thomas and General Wilson, and the latter at once adopted measures looking to the surrender of the enemy's military establishments at Atlanta, Georgia, and Tallahassee, Florida, and to throw a cordon of cavalry across the State of Georgia to intercept and capture Mr. Davis and his party. He sent General Upton to Augusta; General Winslow, with the Fourth division, to march to Atlanta "for the purpose of carrying into effect the terms of the convention, as well as to make such a disposition of his forces, covering the country northward, from Forsyth to Marietta, so as to secure the arrest of Jefferson Davis and party;" General McCook, with five hundred men of his division, to move to Tallahassee, Florida, "to receive the surrender of the enemy in that state;" Colonel Minty, "to extend his troops along the line of the Ocmulgee and Altamaha rivers, as far as Jacksonville; and General Croxton, commanding a division (the First), "to distribute it along the line of the Ocmulgee," connecting with Winslow, and reaching to Macon. Besides, General Wilson directed that detachments should watch the crossings of Flint river, and the stations on the railroad from Atlanta to Eufala, as well as Columbus, West Point, and Talladega. These general and special dispositions, with thorough scouting, promised the interception of all large parties and the arrest of prominent persons.

Evading the terms of General Johnston's surrender, Mr. Davis moved south from Charlotte, North Carolina, through Yorkville, toward Unionville and Abbeville, South Carolina, with evident purpose of passing through to the trans-Mississippi Department, with a vague hope that he could there continue the war. He was, at first, accompanied by his staff and cabinet, under escort of cavalry, from the commands of Ferguson, Duke, Harris, and Butler. Finding, upon reaching the Savannah river from Abbeville, where his last council of war was held, which expressed the utter despair of all but himself, that he was enveloped by the national cavalry, Mr. Davis dismissed his retinue, and with a few friends pushed on to Washington, reaching that place on the morning of the 3d of May. In dismissing his escort, he abandoned the idea of fighting his way to the west, and attempted to accomplish the passage by the most secret means. During the day, he left Washington, by rail, for Atlanta, but abandoned his car at Union Point, and started southwest on horseback. Colonel Palmer having ascertained this fact, scattered his forces to intercept him, and at the same time gather up the fragments of the Confederate forces roaming over the country. But, notwithstanding great vigilance and activity, Mr. Davis slipped through Palmer's detachments, to be caught by Wilson's troopers, farther west and south. On the 7th of May, Colonel Harnden, of the First Wisconsin, with one hundred and fifty men, having advanced from Macon, ascertained that Mr. Davis had crossed the Oconee at Dublin, fifty-five miles southeast of Macon, and had fled on the Jacksonville road. He pursued rapidly, marching forty miles on the 8th on the footsteps of the fugitive. On the 9th he crossed the Ocmulgee, at Brown's ferry, and at Abbeville learned that Mr. Davis had left that point at 1 A. M. on the road to Irwinsville. Hastening forward, he reached the vicinity of Irwinsville at nightfall, and awaited daylight to make the capture.

Having learned at Abbeville of the approach of Colonel Pritchard of the Fourth Michigan, Colonel Harnden went, after halting, to meet him and inform him of his success in tracing the steps of Mr. Davis. The former stated that he had been sent to Abbeville to watch for Mr. Davis, but that he would go no farther that night. However, after making this stipulation, he moved into Irwinsville during the night, and at dawn captured Mr. Davis in disguise, and the small party with him.

Soon after this accomplishment, Colonel Harnden approached, and having been hailed by Colonel Pritchard's detachment, answered "friends," and fell back. In the mutual uncertainty as to the identity of the two commands, several shots were fired, killing several men—a sad issue of a misunderstanding that should not have existed. The pursuit had been conducted with great vigor by all the parties from the two general commands. A reward had been offered of which they were ignorant, from a conjecture that Mr. Davis was remotely connected with the assassination of Mr. Lincoln, President of the United States.

Mr. Davis would have made a better appearance in history, had he met the final issue with General Johnston in preference to seeking, by stealthy flight, the preservation of the life which he had often declared should not survive the fall of his country. This termination of his vaunted presidency, and the disgrace of his flight, were foreign to his grand promises and lofty aspirations. His humiliation and helplessness were, however, the fitting symbols of the cause and the government, of which in the days of his glory and power he was the most prominent representative. His descent from power was as sudden and as marked as the oft-repeated transfer of kings and emperors from thrones to dungeons, but history furnishes no parallel to such emphatic loss of a cause which commanded the real and nominal allegiance of so many millions of men. And the philosophical historian must ask the question, could it have collapsed so suddenly, had its foundation been laid at the beginning in the hearts of the Southern people?

The overthrow of the rebellion was doubtless due to a variety of causes, which were strictly subjective. The maladministration of the Confederate government was a prominent cause, but could not have been the most potential one. It has been claimed, however, by Southern historians, that it had this rank, as it demoralized the people and divorced them from the cause which they at first so earnestly espoused.

The palpable immediate cause of the collapse of the rebellion was the lack of soldiers to fight for it, not of supplies or strict war material. And this need of soldiers did not result from the failure of the conscription more than from the desertion of both volunteers and conscripts; for, at the last, nearly a moiety of those who had borne arms were deserters. The first armies had been formed from volunteers, but soon mere enlistment was abandoned, and then soldiers and supplies could only be secured by despotic constraint. And it has been assumed that the final despotic measures of the government produced a fatal disaffection, which did not originally exist. But it should be considered, in estimating the force and exact influence of the severe measures of the government— the conscription which enrolled for military service all able-bodied male persons between the ages of eighteen and fifty-five years, and the sweeping impressment of supplies—that there was need of these expedients, or the government would never have adopted them, and that consequently the potential cause of failure produced the state of things from which originated the objectionable demands of the government. Mr. Davis and the Confederate Congress would never have ignored the rights of the states, for the maintenance of which they invoked the war, had it been possible to maintain the conflict without trenching upon the sovereignty of the individual states composing the Confederacy. It was a pleasant doctrine for days of harmony and peace, but unsuited to those of war. The despotism of the government, then, was only a secondary cause of the failure of the rebellion.

The ruling cause was that the war on the part of the South was the expression of an insurrection and not a true revolution; and the inherent vices of a false revolution may be traced from the very beginning of the despotic measures of the government. All true revolutions of popular expression have their foundation and force in the sentiments of the masses engaged in them, and will be maintained to the direst extremity. No insurrection that is impressed upon a people by a few leaders or by an influential or powerful minority, can command the perpetual support of the masses. The people may be deceived for a time by false issues and delusive hopes, and the enthusiasm which may thus be called forth may take on the appearance of genuine revolutionary sentiment, but it will not survive the revelation of the real issues or the disappointments that follow groundless hopes. To say that the Southern people were deprived of their moral force and patriotism by their government, through mere errors in the conduct of the war or absolute despotism, is to attribute to them character too weak to warrant any movement which would involve a protracted war of immense proportions; and the only supposition that gives room for the existence of manhood and strong character in the Southern people is, that the masses were beguiled into insurrection against a good government by a few men of great influence, and that they abandoned it when they discovered the deception.

The original opposition to secession by a party of great numerical strength, but of feeble and incomplete organization, may be cited as evidence that the movement toward disunion was not supported by the people generally with such heartiness and spontaneous purpose as indicated a true revolution. A fallacy, glaring in absurdity when strictly analyzed, yet subtle, imposing, and of momentous force, when accepted, swept a multitude of originally sincere Union men into the rebellion, inducing their allegiance to the several seceding states and to the Confederate government formed by them. The fallacy was that a formal act of secession, though unconstitutionally enacted and pronounced, bound all citizens of a state to serve the state in the extreme consequences of the act. Its force prevented all organization in opposition to the resulting war in any stage of its progress, and long enforced its support; but it did not and could not create the foundations of a true revolution, and when the awakening to the grand mistake did occur, the seeming revolution failed in default of the general support of the Southern people.

The want of sympathy between the leaders and the masses was never so apparent as during the later campaigns of the war, especially during the last operations of the national cavalry, when perhaps hundreds of millions of property might have been saved from destruction if the leaders of the rebellion had recognized the fact that the majority of the Southern people had abandoned it.

CHAPTER XLII.

THE surrender of the remaining Confederate armies and forces east and west of the Mississippi river soon followed the capitulation of General Johnston and the capture of Mr. Davis. Preparations were then promptly made to disband the national armies, with the retention of such forces only as were necessary to prevent political and social chaos in the Southern States.

The formal unity of the Army of the Cumberland was restored before its dissolution by the return of the Fourteenth and Twentieth Corps within the territorial limits of the Department of the Cumberland. This reunion of the grand units under their revered commander was eminently appropriate as well as historically imperative. Their dismemberment at Goldsboro, North Carolina, occurring after their last battle had been fought, did not really impair the historical unity of this great army. Still, there would have been a painful lack of complete roundness in its mere organic unity, had two corps been disbanded outside the territorial limits of the department.

During the summer of 1865, the Fourth Corps was also temporarily detached, and sent upon a mission to Texas under General Sheridan. But it, too, was soon remanded to the Department of the Cumberland, to be disbanded, as were the Fourteenth and Twentieth, by General Thomas.

From the 1st of June, 1865, to February 1, 1866, there were mustered out of the service of the United States, from the Army of the Cumberland, five thousand and eighty-three commissioned officers and one hundred and thirty-seven thousand five hundred and thirty-three enlisted men, exclusive of sixteen regiments of cavalry, whose strength was not definitely reported. About twenty thousand volunteer troops were retained within the Military Division of the Tennessee, under the command of Major-General George H. Thomas, until a later period. From the data given, the strength of the Army of the Cumberland, at the close of the war, may be placed, with approximate correctness, at one hundred and seventy-five thousand men. And when these heroic citizen soldiers were remanded to the duties of civil life, the Army of the Cumberland passed from organic existence to live in history as an army unsurpassed, if equaled, by any of the great armies which participated in our gigantic civil war—as one of the grandest that ever battled for country or freedom.

This army fought, unaided, the battles of " Mill Springs," " Perryville," " Stone River," " Chickamauga," " Wauhatchee," and " Bentonville ;" gave essential aid to the Army of the Tennessee, at " Fort Donelson " and " Pittsburg Landing ;" in combination with that army, but in twofold strength, gained the decisive victories on Lookout Mountain and Missionary Ridge ; furnished more than half the forces for the Atlanta campaign, placing upon its banners the historic fields of " Buzzard's Roost," " Resaca," " Rome," " New Hope Church," " Kenesaw Mountain," " Peachtree Creek," " Atlanta," and " Jonesboro ;" at Jonesboro, represented by the Fourteenth Corps, made the only successful assault, in force, during the Atlanta campaign, carrying intrenchments held by Hardee's corps; formed the left wing of the army which marched from Atlanta to Savannah, and then swept through the Carolinas to Richmond and Washington; divided the glory of " Franklin " with the Army of the Ohio, and that of " Nashville " with the Armies of the Tennessee and Ohio ; and, represented by the troopers of Generals Wilson and Stoneman, rushed through Alabama, Georgia, Tennessee, and North Carolina, in swift and brilliant sequence to the great central battles of the war. This army, in its unity, never gave but one field to the enemy. But when it yielded the bloody ground of Chickamauga, it had revealed, under conditions of battle greatly unequal, its invincibility within fair terms of conflict. But even here it gained the fruits of victory, under the semblance of defeat, as it held Chattanooga, the objective of the campaign.

———

CHAPTER XLIII.

THE DEAD AND THEIR DISPOSITION.

THE history of the Army of the Cumberland would not be complete was the disposition of its heroic dead omitted; for never, in the history of war, have the slain of any other army been so honored in burial.

The first permanent National Cemetery for soldiers established by military order, was the one founded by General George H. Thomas, near Chattanooga, Tennessee. The circumstances under which this site was selected, have historic interest far transcending the mere fact of priority of establishment.

During the battle, which resulted in the dislodgment of General Bragg's army from Missionary Ridge, a reserve force, in line over a hill near the field position of General Thomas, revealed its beautiful contour and suggested its use as a National Cemetery. This hill, conical in general outline, but fruitful in lateral hillocks and varied in expression from every point of view, is located equidistant from Cameron hill, which rises abruptly from the Tennessee river, where it turns toward Lookout Mountain and Missionary Ridge on the east, and is central between General Hooker's point of attack on Lookout Mountain, and General Sherman's, on the northern summit of Missionary Ridge. Thus it is the center of this complex battle-field.

Soon after the battle, General Thomas issued the following order:

[GENERAL ORDERS, NO. 296.]

CHATTANOOGA, TENN., *December* 25, 1863.

It is ordered that a National Cemetery be founded at this place, in commemoration of the battles at Chattanooga, fought November 23d, 24th,

25th, 26th, and 27th, and to provide a proper resting-place for the remains of the brave men who fell upon the fields fought over upon those days, and for the remains of such as may hereafter give up their lives in this region in defending their country against treason and rebellion.

The ground selected for the cemetery is the hill lying beyond the Western and Atlantic railroad, in a southeasterly direction from the town.

It is proposed to erect a monument upon the summit of the hill, of such materials as are to be obtained in this vicinity, which, like all the work upon the cemetery, shall be exclusively done by the troops of the Army of the Cumberland.

Plans for the monument are invited to be sent in to these headquarters. When the ground is prepared, notice will be given, and all interments of soldiers will thereafter be made in the cemetery, and all now buried in and around the town removed to that place.

By command of Major-General George H. Thomas.
    (Signed,)   WM. D. WHIPPLE,
                                      Assistant Adjutant-General.

The exigencies of war prevented the execution of all the work upon this cemetery by the troops of the Army of the Cumberland, and the monument contemplated has never been erected. Neither was it subsequently practicable to obtain a brief history of the many thousands interred in this classic ground, as at first contemplated. However, while the war lasted, troops from the Army of the Cumberland continued the work of burial and embellishment. When the volunteers were mustered out of the service, employes of the quartermaster's department completed the enterprise as far as practicable.

The establishment of the Chattanooga National Cemetery was followed, first, by one upon the battle-field of Stone River, and later, by one at Nashville, Tennessee, and another at Marietta, Georgia. Chaplain William Earnshaw was charged with the burial of the dead and the ornamentation of the grounds at Stone River and Nashville, and another chaplain sustained a similar relation to the cemeteries at Chattanooga and Marietta. In these four cemeteries were finally interred the remains of more than forty thousand soldiers. Many smaller cemeteries were established within the limits of the Department of the Cumberland, within the States of Kentucky, Tennessee, Mississippi, Alabama, and Georgia, and more than one hundred thousand soldiers were interred in cemeteries commemorative, often, of great battles, and always of the nation's gratitude to those who gave their lives to maintain the nation's life.

In expression of the value of each citizen who fell in the war, the body of each was placed in a separate grave. And so thorough was the search for the dead upon every battlefield and over the whole country, that their friends may be assured that, whether identified or not, all rest in grounds consecrated for their abode forever.